applerouth

Applerouth
PO Box 14161
Atlanta GA 30324
Email: info@applerouth.com

Director: Richard Vigneault
Writers: Jed Applerouth, Sarah Fletcher, Matthew Kiesner, Emma Vigneault, Richard Vigneault
Contributing Writers: Desirina Boskovich, Deborah Crichton, Grace Franklin, Ansley Gallichio, Eric Garbe, Jennifer Gaulding, Ian Harkins, Sakile Lyles, Katie Rose, Forrest Tuttle
Editors: Alyssa Aiello, Jenna Berk, Kalianna Cawthon-Freels, Deborah Crichton, Kate Eilers, Marsha Fletcher, Sarah Fletcher, Grace Franklin, Eric Garbe, Ian Harkins, Matthew Kiesner, Tal Kitron, Tina Motway, Emma Vigneault, Richard Vigneault, Marielena Zajac

Layout Design: Richard Vigneault
Interior Illustrations: Azekeal McNees, Tina Motway

January 2020

Version 3.0

Manufactured in the United States of America.

500
-500
500
400
-200
300
400
400
300
200
200
-500
100
100
100
─────
2300

7/31 hw
─────
- Throwaways applerouth online
- pgs. 66-68 here
- pgs. 187-190 (for notes)
- Comma basics and all about clauses video lessons
- art, pn, wb video lessons
- ar 420 to 424 pgs or 535-537

912-917
220-222
436-438
450 ODDS

i

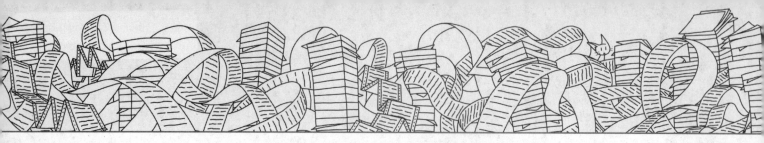

# Special Thanks

*A shout-out to the people who made this book possible.*

### Thanks to our Instructional Design team:

- **Sarah Fletcher**, for her her scientific rigor and brilliance in all things math.
- **Matthew Kiesner**, for being a multi-talented passage-producing prodigy.
- **Zeke McNees**, for how his unbridled enthusiasm shines through his art.
- **Tina Motway**, for her infallible taste, dedication, and artistic vision.
- **Emma Vigneault**, for her never-ending commitment to quality.
- **Richard Vigneault**, for choosing to work with such fine people.

### Thanks to our support team:

- **To our editing staff:** Alyssa Aiello, Jenna Berk, Kalianna Cawthon-Freels, Kate Eilers, Marsha Fletcher, Sarah Fletcher, Grace Franklin, Matthew Kiesner, Tal Kitron
- **To the tutors who lent their time and expertise:** Deborah Crichton, Shara-Sue Crump, Rachel Dunn, Marshall Findlay, Michelle Fogus, Ansley Gallichio, Eric Garbe, Natalie Henderson, Cameron Hubbard, Kristen Ippolito, Sakile Lyles, Amy Shaw, Philip Silverman, Joshua Teal, Marielena Zajac

### Thanks to the Applerouth family:

- **The Applerouth employees,** for every ounce of support and patience.
- **The tutors**, for their dedication to their students and their craft.
- **The tutors again**, for testing, editing, and refining Applerouth's strategies.
- **The tutors one last time**, for making us all proud of what we do.
- **To Jed Applerouth,** for starting this crazy thing, for creating such a fun, effective, and empathetic style, and for always believing that a no-good clown impersonator from Gdansk could amount to more than a hill of beans in this cruel world.

# Contents

## TIP

The SAT includes a No-Calculator math section and a Calculator math section.

All units from **Math Toolkit** to **Modeling** should be completed without a calculator unless otherwise noted.

See the unit header pages for more details about calculator use.

## TIP

The **Data Analysis** units cover content that exclusively shows up on the Calculator math section. Use your calculator when completing these chapters!

See the unit header pages for more details about calculator use.

# Beyond the Content                                    886

# Letter from Jed

Every year over a million students partake in the time-honored ritual of taking the SAT. If you are reading this book, then your time has come to join the ranks and see just how high you can raise your score.

The SAT, like any other test, can be studied and mastered. Succeeding on the SAT does not require the waving of a magic wand. It requires a combination of effort and the proper tools. We've worked hard to create the ultimate SAT preparation tool. And now it's in your hands.

We kept several principles in mind when we designed this book:

- Keep things simple and clear.
- Break things into smaller steps and build on them.
- Keep things visually interesting.
- Use humor whenever possible: it's okay to laugh while learning!

This book is comprehensive. We've analyzed every aspect of the new SAT to bring you the strategies included in this book. Use it well, and hit the scores you need to get into the schools of your dreams. If you are looking for additional information or resources to help you along the way, please check us out online at www.applerouth.com.

Thanks and good luck!

*Jed Applerouth*

# SAT FAQs

*You probably have a lot of questions about the new SAT. We've answered some Frequently Asked Questions below, but you can always go to applerouth.com for more information.*

## What is the SAT?

The SAT is the mother of all standardized tests. It has undergone numerous changes since it first came on the scene in the 1920s when it was created to identify students who would thrive in a university setting. In March 2005, the SAT went from a total score of 1600 to 2400, adding the Writing section, which included grammar and an essay that was previously administered as a SAT Subject Test.

In March 2016, the College Board redesigned the SAT. The total score dropped back down to 1600, with the Writing and Reading sections now combined into an Evidence-Based Reading and Writing score. The essay is now optional, just like the ACT, and does not affect any other score. The College Board also scrapped the sentence completions and shifted the math section away from geometry and instead focused on algebra and data representations.

## Why did the SAT change?

There are two answers to this question. First, the College Board designed the new SAT to align better with the Common Core and similar standards, and test math that better matched what students would be learning in school. The second answer is that more and more students were turning to the ACT and the College Board feared that if they did not retool, the SAT would become obsolete.

## Does the SAT have a guessing penalty?

Nope! They scrapped the guessing penalty as part of the changes implemented with the March 2016 test. **Students should answer all questions in a section, even if it's just a guess.**

## How does the SAT differ from the ACT?

In all honesty, the redesigned SAT mirrors the ACT in many ways. The SAT Writing and Language section is nearly identical to the ACT English section. The SAT Reading section dropped the advanced vocabulary and now focuses on medium length passages similar to the ACT. Finally, The SAT gave up its guessing penalty, so now students should answer all questions, just like on the ACT.

However, there are still noticeable differences between the two tests. The SAT does not have a Science section like the ACT has; instead, the SAT integrated data analysis into all sections. This means that both the Reading and the Writing and Language sections have figures and tables attached to some passages.

In math, the ACT focuses equally on Geometry, Algebra, and Arithmetic, with a handful of Trig and Pre-Calc concepts thrown in. The redesigned SAT dropped nearly all of its Geometry and instead focuses on Algebra and the way it can be used to model and understand real-world situations.

Another big difference between the SAT and ACT math section is the SAT's No Calculator section. Here the College Board wants to test students' abilities to crunch numbers, graph, factor, and FOIL without the help of a calculator. Finally, the ACT math section is entirely multiple choice, while the new SAT contains grid-in problems at the end of each math section.

Overall, the biggest difference between the tests may be in terms of time. The ACT is a fast-paced test, forcing students to move quickly from question to question. On the ACT **Reading** section, students only have 53 seconds per question, while the **SAT gives 75 seconds per question**. On the **Math** section, the ACT gives 60 seconds per question, while the **SAT gives 83 seconds.** A major factor in choosing the ACT or SAT may be how a student manages time.

For an in-depth illustrated comparison of the ACT and the new SAT, visit **www.applerouth.com/testcomparison.**

## How important is my SAT score?

For most students, their SAT score is profoundly important to the college admissions process. After considering your GPA and academic schedule strength, most colleges look to your SAT score next. Other aspects of your application—recommendations, admissions essays, and activities—are subordinate to your score on the SAT. Strong scores can open the door to bettercolleges and universities, and increase the chance to win valuable scholarships.

## Why do colleges put so much weight on the SAT?

Colleges want to ensure that the students they pick for their incoming classes will be able to succeed academically. To make better picks, admissions officers first look to high school GPA: the single best predictor of success in college. But a 3.2 cumulative GPA at one school means something completely different from a 3.2 at another school, even one right down the street. Colleges need another efficient measure that is standardized, the same for all students; that's where the SAT fits in. It turns out students with stronger SAT scores tend to achieve stronger grades in college. A strong SAT score increases the confidence of admissions officers that you have what it takes to succeed in college.

## What does the SAT test?

The SAT tests one thing: your ability to take the SAT. It is not an IQ test, and it certainly does not test any innate aptitude. In fact, especially in the math sections, the new SAT focuses on content you have learned in school rather than tricky problems seemingly designed to confuse. Given enough time, energy, and dedication to the process of preparing for this test, a student can see a dramatic increase in his or her test score.

# What do the scores actually mean?

The new SAT has more scores than ever before. Here's a breakdown of the scores you'll receive when you take the real test:

| Score | Details | Range |
|---|---|---|
| Total score | The total sore is the sum of the two section scores. | 400-1600 |
| 2 Section Scores | Math<br>Evidence-Based Reading and Writing | 200-800 |
| 3 Test Scores | Reading<br>Writing<br>Math (Calc and No-Calc) | 10-40 |
| 2 Cross-Test Scores | Analysis in History/Social Studies<br>Analysis in Science | 10-40 |
| 7 Subscores | Command of Evidence<br>Words in Context<br>Expression of Ideas<br>Standard of English Conventions<br>Heart of Algebra<br>Passport to Advanced Math<br>Probability and Data Analysis | 10-40 |
| 3 Essay Scores | Reading<br>Analysis<br>Writing | 2-8 |

The terminology is a bit confusing, so let us explain what all these scores mean. The **3 Test Scores** are your scores for the different sections of the test: Reading, Writing and Language, and Math. The Math Test Score is a combination of your scores on the No Calculator and Calculator sections; you will not receive separate scores for these two sections.

The **2 Section Scores** are a combination of the Test Scores. To get the total Evidence-Based Reading and Writing Score, College Board adds your Reading Test Score and Writing Test Score, then multiplies by 10. To get your Math Score, College Board simply multiplies your Math Test Score by 20. The Total Score is the sum of the two Section Scores.

The **2 Cross-Test Scores** come from questions on all sections of the test that fall under the topics of Analysis in History/Social Science or Analysis in Science. For example, the questions attached to the Science passages in the Reading section count towards your Analysis in Science score, while the questions about Data Analysis on the math sections count towards your Analysis in History/Social Science score.

The **7 Subscores** reflect your performance on certain question types. Some only apply to one section (e.g. Expression of Ideas is a Writing subscore only), some apply across sections (e.g. Words in Context shows up in the Reading and Writing sections).

### Reading and Writing Subscores:

- **Command of Evidence** questions test your ability to use evidence to support your answer. These questions might ask you to choose a section of the passage that supports a previous answer, or require you to analyze a graphic as it relates to the passage.

- **Words in Context** questions ask you to choose the appropriate word in the context of a larger passage.

### Writing Subscores:

- **Expression of Ideas** test your ability to edit and revise for content, logic, and use of language.

- **Standard English Conventions** questions require you to edit passages for grammar and syntax errors.

### Math Subscores:

- **Heart of Algebra** questions test your understanding of functions and linear equations: calculating slope, interpreting what slope means in context, balancing equations.

- **Passport to Advanced Math** questions test similar skills as Heart of Algebra questions, but as they relate to non-linear equations: exponents bigger than one, factoring of quadratics.

- **Probability and Data Analysis** is relatively new ground for the SAT. Probability, percentages, and unit conversion are tested here, but so are drawing conclusions from study results, understanding the importance of sample size, and other statistics-related topics.

## What score do I need to get into a particular college?

More competitive schools require more competitive scores. To find out the average score for incoming students for a particular school, visit the school's web site or contact its admissions office. The College Board's website, www.collegeboard.com, has a great tool which allows you to enter the name of a school, click on "Applying" on the left, go to the "SAT & ACT Scores" tab and see the breakdown of SAT scores for admitted freshmen. In order to submit a highly competitive application, you should aim for an SAT score in the top 25% for each school to which you are applying.

Additionally, you can create an account at **www.applerouth.com** to build your very own **personalized college tracker**. Click "Add College" and enter the names of colleges in which you are interested. Check back as you improve your score to see where you fall in each school's desired SAT score range.

## How much can I improve my SAT score?

Most students have the potential to significantly improve their SAT scores. On average, our privately-tutored students move up 14 percentiles on the SAT, meaning a student starting in the 70th percentile usually ends up in the 84th percentile: that's a big jump! Some achieve much greater gains, and we've even seen increases of over 60 percentiles. What differentiates the most successful students from those who are less successful is their level of dedication, motivation, and the amount of time they invest in the process. If you invest 100 hours toward achieving a higher score, your chance of picking up 300 points is much greater than if you invest 20 hours. The more time you invest, the more homework you complete, and the more practice tests you complete under timed conditions, the better you will tend to do on the SAT.

## How much time do I need to spend on this process?

This completely depends on your introductory score and your ultimate goal. If you need to pick up a mere 20 points, you may need only a handful of hours of preparation. If you are shooting for an increase of 80 or 100 points, your investment will need to be much more substantial. On average, if you are shooting for a gain of 60 points or greater, you will need to invest 50-60 hours in this process. Some students need much less preparation, and some need more. However, everyone must put in the time to drill problems and complete timed sections and tests. Each practice test takes roughly three hours, and you will want to complete at least four of them to get ready for the official test.

Considering how important your SAT score is to your college application, 50-60 hours is really a modest investment. Remember, for most college admissions offices, SAT score is second in importance only to your GPA. However, at some larger state schools, SAT and GPA receive almost equal weight. It takes roughly 4,000 hours of class time to generate a high school GPA and only 60 hours to attain a competitive SAT score. Dedicating time to your SAT score is the single most efficient way to improve your odds of gaining admission to a competitive college.

## How often should I take the SAT?

You should always check with the specific colleges you're applying to for their requirements, but here are our recommendations. Generally, three times should be adequate to achieve your optimal score, but there is usually no penalty for taking the SAT as many times as you need to achieve the score you seek. An increasing number of schools will "superscore" your tests and create a composite SAT score, combining the highest section scores from different administrations to create your "Super" score.

Because SATs vary in difficulty from one administration to the next, it's in your best interest to take this test multiple times until you reach your target score. Just as there are easier and harder tests, students have good and bad days. Even when you are fully prepared, certain factors beyond your control can influence your score: were the passages easy or hard for you? How effectively did you guess? Did you make careless errors? There is some luck involved, and the more frequently you take the SAT, the more you minimize the "luck" component.

The more you take this test, the more comfortable and confident you become. You eventually move into a zone where you know what to expect and achieve a level of mastery of the testing process. As students move from their first to their second SAT, they tend to achieve their biggest score increases. Students generally see smaller gains through their third SAT.

## Should I set goals for each test I take?

Absolutely! Always keep your ultimate goal in mind, and view each test as a stepping stone towards this goal. Set distinct section goals for each test you plan to take. Say, for example, your introductory score is a 540 reading and 520 math, giving you a total score of 1060, and you want to hit a total of 1200. Set short term goals for each test you plan to take, and write them down. "In October my goal is 560 reading and 550 math. In December my goal is 580 reading and 570 math. My goal for June is 610 Reading and 590 math." As you write your goals, enumerate the steps you will take to achieve them, such as practicing with your Applerouth Guide to the SAT and taking mock tests. **Setting and attaining short term goals has a positive impact on your sense of confidence and your level of motivation.** Use these short term goals to help you attain your ultimate goal.

## When should I take the SAT?

Fall and winter of junior year are ideal times to take the first SAT. The December SAT is a natural first test. For students who are enrolled in Algebra II as juniors, we generally recommend March as the first official SAT; this gives them a semester to hone their Algebra II skills. The majority of our students, having finished Algebra II as sophomores, are ready to jump in at the beginning of junior year.

Keep your schedule in mind! If you have a major time commitment in the fall, wait until the winter to start your prep. It is quite common to prep intensely and take two SATs back to back. Once you've knocked out a test or two, it's fine to take breaks and come back for one later in the year.

Many of our students see their greatest gains on the June SAT. This has to do with our students' growing familiarity and comfort with the test as well as their freedom from academic and extracurricular obligations. Once school is out, students can really focus on the June SAT.

**Ideally students will take the SAT two to three times their junior year.** SATs administered during the fall of their senior year are available as back-ups. The October, November, and December tests of senior year will all count for regular admissions. The October test is generally the last SAT that will count for Early Decision / Early action.

## How do I register for the SAT?

Log in to www.collegeboard.org. Click "Sign up/Log in" and create an account. Follow the instructions. Make sure to sign up early to secure a spot at a preferred location. The good locations can fill up quickly.

# What do I need to take to the SAT?

- A few No. 2 pencils (no mechanical pencils)

- Your registration information, printed from the computer

- Your driver's license or other form of photo ID

- A digital watch or one with a second hand

- Your graphing calculator and, if necessary, extra batteries (for a list of approved calculators, go to www.sat.collegeboard.org/register/calculator-policy)

- Snacks and water

- Layers of clothing, in the event you are in a cold or hot room

# When can I expect my scores to be available?

Scores are typically available online within two to three weeks after the test administration.

# How do I report my SAT scores to schools?

When you sign up for an SAT administration, you can select up to four schools to receive your SAT scores free of charge. You can send your scores to additional schools for a fee. After the test, you can log onto your College Board My SAT account to send your scores to schools.

# Do I have to send all of my SAT scores?

College Board allows you to send particular scores and withhold others. If a college superscores the SAT, it is in your best interest to send all tests which contain a personal best on any section. Keep in mind, some colleges require that you send all of your scores. That will be made clear during the application process.

### What is extended time? Do I need it? Can I get it?

Some students with diagnosed disabilities are allowed to take the SAT with accommodations such as extended time. Only a licensed psychologist can make the diagnosis of whether a student needs extended time to compensate for a learning disability. In most cases, before the College Board will consider granting extended time or any other accommodation, your high school must acknowledge your disability and grant you the accommodation for it.

### Do I need additional SAT prep materials to supplement this book?

We encourage our students to get as much practice as possible! The College Board offers three options for practice. They released 8 full-length practice tests, which students can print out and take as mock tests. The College Board also published The Official SAT Study Guide, which contains the same tests in book form. These tests are excellent tools to help you practice your pacing and time-management skills. Secondly, the College Board has released a Daily Practice app for Apple and Android phones. The third option is from Khan Academy, which offers free practice to students who create an account.

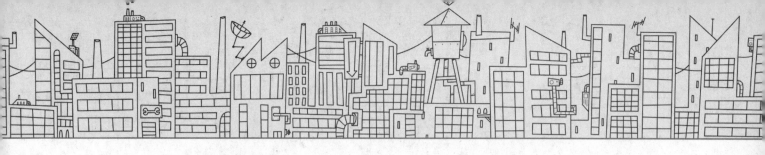

# SAT Overview

*Let's take a bird's-eye view of the SAT.*

## Timing and Structure

The SAT consists of 4 timed sections: Reading, English, Math No Calculator, and Math Calculator. A fifth section, the Essay, is optional.

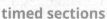

**timed sections**

**optional essay**

**testing hours**

The order of the sections on the SAT is the same on every test:

① *Reading (65 minutes, 52 questions)*

The Reading section consists of **5 passages** designed to test your reading comprehension skills. You will be given one passage each about Literature, Politics, and Social Science, and two passages about Natural Science.

② *Writing and Language (35 minutes, 44 questions)*

The Writing section consists of **4 passages** designed to test your grammatical and rhetorical skills.

③ *Math No Calculator (25 minutes, 20 questions)*

The Math–No Calculator section consists of 15 multiple choice and 5 grid-in questions, most of which test your ability to solve and manipulate algebraic equations.

④ *Math Calculator (55 minutes, 38 questions)*

The Math–Calculator section consists of 30 multiple choice and 8 grid-in questions that test your ability to solve Algebra and Data Analysis problems in real-world contexts.

## BREAKS

You will be given a 10 minute break after the first section and a 5 minute break after the third section.

## NOTE

If you sign up for the SAT with the optional **Essay**, you will be given **50 minutes** to read a passage and write an essay that analyzes the author's argument and the passage's persuasive and stylistic elements.

13

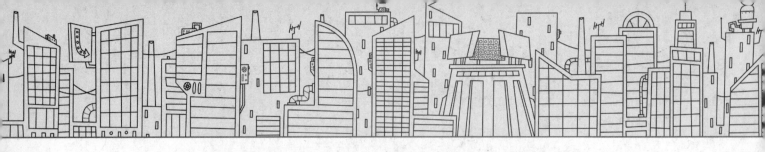

# Pacing & Practice

*On the SAT, time is a precious resource. Learn how to spend it wisely with these good habits that will help you stay on pace.*

**TIP**

Many sections of this book include practice with realistic passages. Check the timing guidelines for these sections and use them to improve your pacing as you go.

### Taking the SAT is similar to running hurdles

To succeed at running hurdles, you have to balance two important parts: getting over each hurdle and finishing the race in time. You start by focusing on technique—how to approach a hurdle, how to lift your knees, how to land, etc. Once you have the fundamentals down, you focus on increasing your speed while jumping many in a row.

Studying for the SAT is similar. It's OK to first spend hours or even days learning a concept, rule, or strategy behind the questions. But once you understand the fundamentals, you want to practice zipping through those questions by taking timed sections. Make sure you are practicing both your technique and your speed to see the biggest score gains.

**TIP**

You can find a practice test in the back of this book, starting on page 843.

### Take full-length tests to build stamina

Stamina is a big part of standardized tests. After you have taken a practice test, analyze which sections gave you the most trouble and then work on the related chapters in the book.

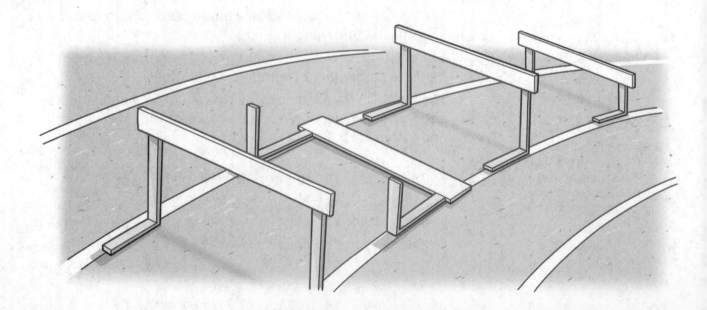

## Keep your eye on the clock

To skillfully manage your pacing, you must develop a habit of regularly checking in with the clock. If you ignore the clock, the amount of time left might shock you, and lead to you feeling more pressure.

A better strategy is to check in with the clock every few questions to ensure that you are pacing effectively. This will help stop those freak out moments when you realize that too much time as slipped away.

## Read questions carefully

Across every section of the test, you need to know what your goal is. Reading the question carefully will help you to identify what the question is asking and what information you will need to solve it. This will help you take the first step toward the answer. Each section of the test will have a specific approach, but reading the question carefully is always essential.

## Guessing

If you don't know the answer to a question, don't forget to bubble in a guess! There is no penalty for guessing, so you have a 25% chance of getting a point when you randomly bubble in.

## Keep moving forward

Some SAT problems are more difficult than others. When you're stumped about how to begin answering a question, you can either grind away at it or guess and move on. The time spent working on it may earn you that one point but keep you from reaching several easier problems to come. For challenging questions, it can be better to mark them in your booklet and take a guess. If you have time remaining at the end of the section, the marks will tell you which problems you should revisit.

**TIP**

Once you have spent the allotted time for each passage, it's usually in your best interest to move on to the next passage.

## How much time to spend on a passage

It's important to get familiar with how much time each section should take. Two out of the four sections of the SAT are passage-based, so let's look at how long you should spend on each passage and the related questions.

| Section | # of Passages | Questions per passage | Minutes per passage |
|---------|---------------|----------------------|---------------------|
| Reading | 5 | 10-11 | 13 minutes |
| Writing | 4 | 11 | 8 minutes 45 seconds |

## How much time to spend on each question

If you divide the amount of time allotted for a complete section by the number of questions in a section, you arrive at the average time allowed per question. It's important that you learn to manage these intervals and identify your areas of timing strength and weakness.

**NOTE**

The given times for Reading and Writing **include** time spent reading the passage.

| Section | Minutes | Questions | Time per question |
|---------|---------|-----------|-------------------|
| Reading | 65 | 52 | 75 seconds |
| Writing | 35 | 44 | 48 seconds |
| Math No Calculator | 25 | 20 | 75 seconds |
| Math Calculator | 55 | 38 | 87 seconds |

## Timing interval training

The time you spend on each question can make all the difference in the world, but many students have trouble "feeling" when they are working too slowly. The good news is that you can **train yourself** to be a better, faster test-taker in a matter of weeks. On the next page, we'll learn one of the best SAT workout routines: timing drills.

**TIP**

Improving your speed is not about thinking faster or being smarter, it's just about getting comfortable with a faster pace.

It's like exercise: if you do it right and do it often, you WILL see results.

# Timing Drills: The Art of Getting Faster

The best way to increase your speed on the SAT is to conduct timing drills. Once you've identified the section that is giving you the biggest timing challenge, it's time to drill.

**(1)** *Find your natural pacing*

Get a timer (most smartphones or watches will do fine), find a quiet room, and **take a timed section or passage** without breaks to find your natural pacing. Say you take a Reading section and are 5 minutes over the time limit. The next step is to find out *where* you're spending that extra time.

**(2)** *Determine where the time is going*

Take another section, but this time **use a lap timer** on your smart phone or watch. Start the timer when you start the section. After you finish each question, hit the "lap" button. This will record how long you spent on each question. After you finish the section, check your work and write down the results like so:

| Problem | Seconds | Correct |
|---------|---------|---------|
| 1 | 45 | √ |
| 2 | 74 | X |
| 3 | 37 | √ |
| 4 | 56 | √ |
| 5 | 138 | X |

Analyze the results! Are you spending 2-3 minutes on certain questions only to end up getting them wrong? If you see this happen, you can feel confident that guessing and moving on when you're stuck can help your score!

**(3)** *Set new timing targets*

Using this information, pick a maximum time you're willing to spend on a question before guessing and moving on. Then, conduct a new timing drill at this accelerated pace. How did you do? Were you able to increase your pace without sacrificing accuracy? With practice, this faster pace will become your natural rhythm, and you'll increase your score without feeling rushed.

## TIP

It's common for students to miss problems they spend the most time on! When students run these drills and see this for themselves, it can be a major revelation.

Learn yourself, set goals, and adjust!

## TIP

If your new pace felt frantic, it's okay to bring it back a step and try a slightly lower maximum time per question... but know that with practice you WILL build new habits!

# How To Use This Book

*This book is divided into to the key sections of the SAT: Reading, Writing, Math, and Essay. Each chapter contains strategies, illustrated explanations, and practice sections.*

## Active Learning

Practice is the key to raising your SAT score. Many books are designed like lectures, spewing a list of all the rules and formulas you need to memorize and calling it a day. That kind of passive learning is not very fun (and frankly does very little to raise your score). This book is instead designed to empower and guide you, much as a private tutor would, in the kind of smart practice that will prepare you for test day.

## EXAMPLES and | SOLUTIONS |

A large portion of this book is dedicated to working through example problems to show you the best way to approach the material. Give every example a shot before you read the solution. Then, check your work and answer against the solution, reading for tips that will help you solve future problems.

## TIP

Cover up solutions with an index card or a piece of paper while you work the example: no peeking!

## Exercises

Many chapters have **exercises**: interactive practice sections designed to bridge the gap between learning a concept and putting it into practice on a sample test problem. When you see this pencil icon, it means stop reading and start exercising your new skills. Answers can be found either below the exercise or at the **bottom of the next page**.

1. Good testing habits can be built through _____.

Answers: 1. practice

## Portals

In every section of the book, you'll find **portals** in the margins leading you to other pages in the book that can provide more information or context for the current topic. These portals are designed to help you **make connections** between different concepts, boosting your understanding of multiple topics at once!

## Practice Problems

This book includes hundreds of different practice problems that are modeled after real SAT questions. Even the passages mimic the length, tone, and appearance of those that you'll see on test day. After completing each chapter, complete the practice problems attached and be sure to check your answers in the back of the book!

## Peppers

Math problems can vary in difficulty. The last few questions of the multiple choice and grid-ins on the Math test are particularly tricky and often combine a number of concepts into a single question. Unless you're going for a near-perfect score, it's often not worth the time investment to chip away at these tough problems for 1 or 2 lousy points. Like very spicy peppers, they're not for everyone!

We have marked the most difficult practice problems with a **pepper icon**. Give these problems a shot, but don't feel like you haven't fully mastered a section simply because the pepper problem is giving you trouble.

# Study Schedules

*There is no single "right" way to study for the SAT. But there IS a right book.*

## Two approaches to prepping for the SAT

You should consider your own unique strengths and weaknesses when deciding on the study plan that will work best for you. Let's look at two approaches to SAT prep:

1. *The Comprehensive Review*
   Each week complete a series of lessons and practice problems from each section: Reading, Writing, and Math. In Week 1, you may tackle Throwaways in Reading, Punctuation in Writing, and Basic Algebra in Math. This balanced approach will keep you moving forward on all fronts.

2. *Isolate and Focus*
   Take a practice test. Celebrate your strengths and identify the areas that need improvement, then use the table of contents to target those areas where you lost the most points. If your Reading score is lower than the other sections, put your energy there. If you are grappling with Math, go there first. You can use the practice sections and additional tests to gauge your progress and guide your preparation.

## Spread out your SAT review over time

Memory researchers have found that packing all of your review into long sessions is not nearly as effective as spacing your study over multiple, shorter sessions. Each time you review a concept, you strengthen and reinforce it, etching the material deeper into your brain, where it will remain until you need it on test day!

## Sample Study Schedules

Let's admit it: this is a big book! You likely don't have the time or need to work through every single page. Based on the amount of time you have before your test, it might make sense to focus on the chapters that cover only the most commonly tested concepts. Below, we've provided recommended syllabi based on the amount of time you have to study.

## One Day Syllabus

If you only have one day to prepare, you should read the **overviews** of each section. These chapters will let you know what's on each section and give you a brief outline of recommended strategies.

## One Week Syllabus

If you only have one week to prepare, you should read the **overviews** listed above as well as chapters that cover **core strategies** and **frequently tested concepts**. The chapters below will give you the most bang for your buck.

# One Month Syllabus

If you have one month to prepare, you have enough time to move beyond core strategies but not quite enough time to work your way through the full book. Below, we've broken down your month into four structured weeks of content.

## Week One

**Reading**
Reading Overview & Strategy ..............27
*Core Strategy Unit* ....................................31

**Writing**
Writing Overview & Strategy.............. 187
*Punctuation Unit*................................... 193

**Math**
Math Overview & Strategy ................ 388
*Math Toolkit Unit* ................................. 395
*Foundations Unit* ................................. 413
*Lines and Functions Unit* ..................... 455

## Week Two

**Reading**
*Question Types Unit*................................75

**Writing**
*Subjects & Verbs Unit* ......................... 223
*Structure Unit* ....................................... 267
*Word Choice Unit*................................. 285

**Math**
*Polynomials Unit*................................... 489
*Systems of Equations Unit*................... 567
*Modeling Unit* ....................................... 631

## Week Three

**Reading**
Literature Passage ............................ 108
Politics Passage ................................. 123
Natural Science Passages ................. 145

**Writing**
*Connecting Thoughts Unit* ................... 317

**Math**
*Data Analysis: Part 1 Unit*.................... 691
*Data Analysis: Part 2 Unit*.................... 723

**Practice Test**
Practice Test ....................................... 905

## Week Four

**Reading**
Social Science Passage ...................... 165
Comparison Passage ......................... 174

**Writing**
*Quality Control Unit*............................. 351

**Math**
*Applied Factoring Unit* ......................... 527
*Spicing it Up* ......................................... 601
*Geometry & Trigonometry Unit* ............ 775
*Math Review Unit*................................. 801

## Not sure where to start? We've got your back.

Not all chapters are worth the same amount of "points" on the test. Some content in the book covers core topics or strategies that will help on just about every problem you come across; others cover less common or more difficult content meant for students seeking a very high score.

The **Reading** chapters are ordered such that you can work through them in a linear fashion; the early chapters cover the core content and the later chapters help high scoring students grab as many points as possible.

The **Writing** test covers a lot of grammar rules with more or less equal frequency. Going straight through the section is your best bet. If that's not an option for you, the early *Punctuation* unit (pages 193–222) is particularly important. Start there. After that, use practice passages to see what topics give you trouble, then focus on those areas.

## PORTAL

For help customizing a study plan for Math, turn to page 390 in the **Math Overview** chapter.

## Customize a study plan for Math

The Math section is a different story. We have grouped similar concepts together to help you develop a robust understanding of math topics you may have struggled with in school. However, depending on your score goals and the amount of time you have to prepare, working through every chapter might not be the best bet. In the *Math Overview* chapter (starting on **page 388**), we've broken down the units and chapters into four tiers, shown below. In that chapter, you'll find suggestions for which topics you should focus on based on your personal score goals.

- **Tier 1 chapters** teach fundamental math skills that help throughout both math sections.

- **Tier 2 chapters** cover core topics that are tested multiple times on each test.

- **Tier 3 chapters** cover topics that may only show up once or twice on a given test.

- **Tier 4 chapters** cover topics that only show up on the hardest questions.

# Reading Overview

*Here's what you can expect to see on the SAT Reading section.*

## Structure and timing

Reading is divided into 5 parts: **4 long passages** and **1 pair of shorter comparison passages**, with 10-11 questions attached to each part. You have a total of 65 minutes to read the passages and answer 52 questions.

 **5**
passage topics

 **65**
minutes

 **52**
questions

## NOTE

The Social Science passage(s) and the Natural Science passages often include questions about a table, figure, or graph.

## TIP

If one of these passages sounds unappealing, save it for last!

Skipping tougher passages and coming back later is encouraged, but make sure you're bubbling in your answers on the correct question!

## Passage Types

On each test you will find **four types of passages**:

 One **Literature** passage telling a story. It could be from the 1800s, the 2000s, or any time in between; the older passages usually have harder vocabulary.

 One **Social Science** passage (or a pair of comparison passages) about economics, psychology, or sociology. This passage will often be about trends or new technology.

 One **Politics** passage (or a pair of comparison passages), usually focused on American politics, that could date as far back as the 1700s. Again, many students will find older passages more difficult to understand.

 Two **Natural Science** passages (or one long passage and one pair of comparison passages) about biology, chemistry, physics, or Earth science. One is usually informative, while the other recounts an experiment or study.

# There are four main types of Reading questions

The questions on the Reading section are all trying to get at one thing: did you understand what you read? You'll see **4 types of questions**.

| Question Type | Description |
|---|---|
| **Content and Analysis** (~4 per passage) | These questions ask you to find key information in the passage, analyze rhetorical strategies used by the author, or describe the overall structure and purpose of the passage. |
| **Evidence-Based Questions** (~4 per passage) | These questions ask you for lines in the passage that *prove* a statement to be true. Often, that statement is the answer to the previous question. |
| **Vocabulary in Context** (~2 per passage) | These questions ask you to identify the correct meaning of a word in the context of the passage. |
| **Charts, Tables, and Graphs** (0-3 per passage) | These questions require you to combine information from the passage with data from a figure, such as a table or a line graph. |

# The key to a higher score is building better habits

The Reading section is different from the Math and English sections of the test. There are few rules to memorize or formulas to cram into your brain. Instead, we'll be building better reading, answering, and pacing habits, including:

1. Using your pencil to **read actively**

2. Coming up with **your own answer** to questions

3. Eliminating wrong answers with **throwaways**

4. Proving the right answer with **evidence**

# Build habits through regular practice

Like all habits, these won't simply appear overnight; your Reading score will increase with practice, practice, practice! These strategies might slow you down or feel awkward at first. When you're tired, you might forget and slip into old habits. But over time, passage-by-passage, these strategies will become second nature.

As a result, you'll become a **better reader** and a **better test-taker**!

## TIP

This test is an open-book test; all the answers to the questions are right there in the passages. So take your time to **read actively**, marking up the passage as you go.

# Timing drills

Use a stopwatch (most smartphones come with a built-in "clock" app) to track your time:

1) Hit **START**
2) Read the passage
3) Hit **LAP**
4) Answer a question
5) Hit **LAP** again
6) Repeat

For more on timing drills, turn to page 17.

## When and how to practice your timing

On average, you have **13 minutes** to move through each of the 5 passages and knock out all the accompanying questions. We will increase your speed over time, but only *after* you've learned the key strategies and gotten used to the test. Here's our game plan:

① *Find your baseline reading speed*

When you read your *second* full practice passage (on page 66), start a stopwatch before you read and hit *stop* when you get to the questions. This is your **baseline speed** for reading the passage—we'll watch what changes this speed as we practice.

② *Turn Applerouth strategies into habits*

As you work your way through the *Active Reading*, *Evidence*, and *Throwaway* chapters, you'll be building good habits that will **improve your accuracy** immediately. Remember: you have to learn to jump one hurdle before you worry about a full race.

③ *Use timing drills during full passages*

When you check your work, write **how long you spent** next to each question. Most students will find they still miss questions that they spend more than 30 or 40 seconds on. Seeing this in your work will help you get a feel for *your* best pace.

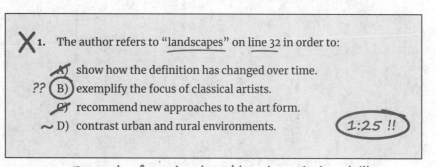

*Example of a missed problem in a timing drill*

④ *Personalize your strategy*

Take **regular practice tests** to track your progress. Based on your score goals, you might want to read the passages in a different order or skip a passage altogether. Find the strategy that works best for you, and keep building those habits!

# UNIT | Core Strategy

## Chapters

## Overview

In this unit, we'll learn the step-by-step approach to answering Reading questions. We'll start with the most important skill for raising your Reading score: **active reading**.

But reading is only half the battle. Next, we'll learn how to quickly and effectively narrow down the answer choices using **throwaways**. We'll then learn how to back up our chosen answer with **evidence** from the passage.

# Reading Strategy

*The pen is mightier than the sword. Pencils are even better, because erasers.*

## Neutral talk

Try to catch yourself thinking in judgy language; when you do, rephrase with **goal-oriented, neutral language** instead. Replace the unhelpful thought

**"Be faster!"**

with the helpful thought

**"Spend less time rereading and more time underlining."**

or

**"After 45 seconds on a question, make my best guess and move on."**

### First, get rid of judgy language

It's easy to think that reading comprehension is something that just kind of *happens* inside your brain: that you are either SMART, SLOW, GOOD AT READING, or NOT GOOD AT READING, and that's all there is to it. This is what we might call **judgy language**: it's full of judgments and conclusions that would be rude if said to someone else. So why say them to yourself?

Aside from being upsetting, this language does nothing to point us toward solutions. How are you supposed to respond to a goal of DO BETTER, BE SMARTER, or REMEMBER MORE? Say "Okay"? Instead, we're going to **focus on concrete, behavioral goals** that will naturally drive up your reading score.

### Reading is about behavior, not IQ

The truth is that **reading is a skill anyone can improve**. The future version of you who consistently gets a higher score on the Reading section is physically DOING things (like, with your *muscles*) that are leading to a higher score.

So let's take the focus *off* your IQ and put it *onto* your muscles: particularly the ones that move your pencil.

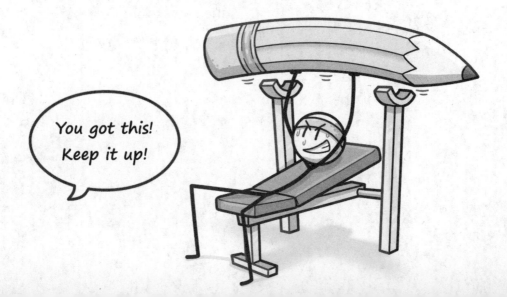

## Active reading is the bee's knees & the cat's meow

It's also the tiger's spots, the bullfrog's beard, and the monkey's eyebrows. I guess what we're trying to say here is that active reading is very important. Strategically using your pencil while you read can keep you from wasting time rereading or searching for answers, speeding you up and increasing your score (more on that next chapter).

## Step-by-step strategy for answering questions

Once you've actively read the passage, you'll tackle the questions using a **three-step process** to quickly identify the correct answer:

***Paraphrase***
*Question & Answer*

*Find **Evidence***
*in the Passage*

*Eliminate*
***Wrong Answers***

## Paraphrase the question and answer

Before you can answer a question, you have to know what it's asking. **Actively read** the question, and check your understanding by putting the question **into your own words**. If you can, come up with your own answer from memory—if you see a matching choice, pick it and move on! If not...

## Find evidence in the passage

The correct answer will be supported by **specific words in the passage**! **Scan margin notes** to find relevant paragraphs and underline words to locate the topic of the question. If the question contains a line reference, begin your search there—always remembering to **read in context**!

## Eliminate wrong answers

Finally, eliminate wrong answers one-by-one. If a choice has a single word that contradicts the passage (what we call a "throwaway" word), it's wrong! Find your right answer through the magical **process of elimination**. Once you've narrowed down your choices, pick the option with no throwaways and the most supporting evidence in the passage.

# Active Reading

*When students struggle with the Reading section, it is often because they are used to reading passively. This is a sure-fire way to struggle on SAT Reading!*

## Glucose

It's in food. Your body needs it to do things like read, think, answer questions, and keep from falling out of a desk and into a coma.

**PLEASE do not skip breakfast on test day.** And bring a snack!

## Passive Reading: To Blur is Human

Does this sound familiar? You get all fired up to start scanning a long reading comprehension passage. In the back of your mind, you start to worry about how much time you have, then you realize you're hungry (like **really** hungry), and then your eyes start to glaze over, and the passage starts to look like this:

> It is highly doubtful that the Allied forces would have won World War II without the help of Polish mathematician Marian Rejewski. At age fourteen, Rejews
> secret                                                    Soon his
> full-time occupation was decoding the German Enigma machine. Combining his usage of pure mathematics with information                             Rejewski succeeded in decoding the Enigma, and consequently, the Allied forces were able to intercept German intelligence transmissions for six years. Historian D
>                          ng achievement "elevates him to the pantheon of the greatest cryptanalysts of all time." On the 100th an    rsary of his birthday, a sculpted memorial was presented to his hometown of Bydgo        , Poland.

As a result, you have to waste time re-reading chunks of the passage to answer the questions. All this leaves you feeling rushed and frustrated.

## The Drawbacks of Passive Reading

- **Blurred understanding** of the passage
- Likely to **miss key information**
- **Waste time** searching for answers

## Active Reading: To Underline is Divine

When you read actively, you wisely trade all that re-reading for some **quick pencil movements** early on. The key is to invest your time on the front end so that you can breeze through the questions later on. When your hand is busy, **your brain is more active**: you stay awake, you retain more information, and you end up creating a handy outline of the passage that will guide you to the correct answers later on:

*helped win WW2*

*Enigma*
☆

*Kahn*

It is highly <u>doubtful</u> that the <u>Allied forces</u> would have <u>won World War II</u> without the help of <u>Polish mathematician</u> Marian <u>Rejewski</u>. At age <u>fourteen</u>, <u>Rejewski</u> enrolled in a <u>secret cryptology course</u> for German speakers. Soon his full-time occupation was <u>decoding</u> the German <u>Enigma machine</u>. <u>Combining</u> his usage of pure <u>mathematics</u> with information provided by <u>French intelligence</u>, Rejewski <u>succeeded</u> in <u>decoding</u> the Enigma, and (consequently,) the Allied forces were able to intercept German intelligence transmissions for six years. <u>Historian David Kahn</u> says that Rejewski's stunning achievement "elevates him to the <u>pantheon of the greatest cryptanalysts of all time</u>." On the 100th anniversary of his birthday, a sculpted <u>memorial</u> was presented to his hometown of Bydgoszcz, <u>Poland</u>.

### Do you have time for this?

YES! These simple pencil movements add mere seconds to your reading time, but they save you precious minutes when answering questions.

The better question is: **"Can you afford NOT to do this?"**

Notice the **key components of active reading** covering the passage:

① <u>Underlines</u> *highlighting key info in each sentence*

② <u>Short notes</u> *summarizing the paragraph*

③ <u>Circles</u> *around ~~key words~~* transitions

④ <u>Stars</u> *next to main ideas*

With active reading, you can quickly answer easy questions, have a map for finding the answer to tough ones, and are far too busy killing it to be stressed. Let's look at how each step helps to raise your score.

## The Benefits of Active Reading

✚ Check **understanding** as you read

✚ Easier to **find evidence** in the passage

✚ **Less time searching** for answers

35

# 1 Underline key information in each sentence

<u>Most information</u> in a passage plays only a <u>supporting role</u>, and some is simply there to distract you. You only need to <u>underline content</u> that conveys the <u>main points and key ideas</u> of each paragraph. In general, you will underline roughly <u>20 to 30 percent</u> of the words in a passage.

**Read the following passage,** underlining key facts as you go.

> Walter Alvarez, the fourth in a line of eminent and successful scientists, was practically destined for distinction in the world of science. Even with his pedigree, no one could have predicted the magnitude of his contributions to the study of dinosaurs. Alvarez ventured into the field of geology and discovered a significant amount of iridium in the layer of the Earth's crust containing the last fossilized remains of many dinosaur species. Because iridium commonly appears in asteroids, Alvarez concluded that an asteroid must have driven the dinosaurs to extinction. His theory is now the most widely-believed answer to the most widespread of questions: what killed the dinosaurs?
>
> *Compare the quantity of your active reading with the sample on the previous page. In general, you should be underlining about 30% of the total passage.*

## Underlining helps raise your score in two ways

First, there's what happens on the page. If a question asks about "iridium," you can scan only your underlined words for "iridium" to quickly spot the relevant part of the passage.

Second, there's what happens in your brain. The simple act of deciding what is and isn't worth underlining **condenses the passage down** to just the important pieces. This effectively "shrinks" the passage until it's *just* small enough to fit inside your short-term memory.

# 2 Take short notes to sum up each paragraph

*notes = good*

A responsible active reader takes quick, **1-to-4-word notes** in the margin next to each paragraph and major idea. These notes summarize the focus of the passage at that point, making it immensely easier to see the flow of the passage just by scanning the margins. Whereas underlining helps you focus on the really important content in each sentence, margin notes help you see the *flow of ideas* throughout the passage.

**Write a margin note** for each paragraph in the blank provided.

Brick by brick, six-year-old Alice is building a magical kingdom. Imagining fairy-tale turrets and fire-breathing dragons, wicked sorcerers and gallant heroes, she's creating an enchanting world. Although she isn't aware of it, this fantasy will have important repercussions in her adult life: it is helping her take her first steps towards her capacity for abstract thought and creativity.

Minutes later, Alice has abandoned the kingdom in favor of wrestling with her brother—or, according to educational psychologists, developing her capacity for strong emotional attachments. When she bosses him around as 'his teacher,' she's practicing how to regulate her emotions through pretense. When they settle down with a board game, she's learning about rules and turn-taking. "Play in all its rich variety is one of the highest achievements of the human species," says Dr. David Whitebread from Cambridge's Faculty of Education. "It underpins how we develop as intellectual, problem-solving, emotional adults and is crucial to our success as a highly adaptable species."

Recognizing the importance of play is not new: over two millennia ago, Plato extolled its virtues as a means of developing skills for adult life, and ideas about play-based learning have been developing since the 19th century. But we live in changing times, and Whitebread is mindful of a worldwide decline in play. "Over half the world's population live in cities. Play is curtailed by perceptions of risk to do with traffic, crime, abduction, and germs, and by the emphasis on 'earlier is better' in academic learning. The opportunities for free play, which I experienced almost every day of my childhood, are becoming increasingly scarce. Today, play is often a scheduled and supervised activity."

## 3 Circle transition words

Many authors signal that a main point is coming by using a "transition word" like **but**, **however**, **therefore**, and **although.** Typically, whatever comes after one of these words is pretty important! As a result, you should circle transition words whenever you see them! This will help you spot *shifts in the author's argument* and identify the logical flow of the passage as a whole. Go back to the passage on the previous page and circle any of the following transition words that you find.

| TRANSITION WORDS | |
|---|---|
| Conclusion | Logical Shift |
| Thus | But |
| Consequently | However |
| Therefore | Although |
| Because | Nevertheless |
| Hence | Nonetheless |

## 4 Star main ideas

Finally, when the author lays out what feels like the **essence** of the passage or paragraph, put a star next to it in the margins. When you get to questions asking for the main idea, let these stars guide you home!

Taken together, your underlines, notes, circles, and stars will **speed you up** and **increase your score.**

## Recapping Active Reading

Active reading is the most effective tool you have for increasing your SAT Reading score. Using your pencil while you read keeps you alert, makes it easier to find answers to each question, and speeds you up!

The four components of active reading are:

- **Underline** key ideas
- Take **notes** in the margin
- **Circle** key words
- **Star** main ideas

## The Importance of Practice

If you are not used to reading actively, the process may slow you down at first. That's okay – it's normal! You will naturally speed up as you practice over the course of several weeks, and you'll be able to practice throughout this entire chapter.

Before we dive into strategies for answering the questions, let's try reading actively with a full-length SAT passage. Before you start, find a clock, watch, or timer app and record how long it takes you to actively read the passage. Eventually, we'll be aiming to spend just around 5 minutes reading each passage on the test. For now, though, your only goals are to **get comfortable reading actively** and to find out how much you'll need to speed up or slow down over the course of your practice.

# Reading Practice Passage 1

## TO STAY ON PACE, YOUR TIMING GOAL IS 13 MINUTES

Each passage or pair of passages below is followed by a number of questions. After reading each passage or pair, choose the best answer to each question based on what is stated or implied in the passage or passages and in any accompanying graphics (such as a table or graph).

**Questions 1-10 are based on the following passage.**

This passage is from H. C. McNeile, "A Question of Personality." Originally published in 1921.

The personally conducted tour round Frenton's Steel Works paused, as usual, on reaching the show piece of the entertainment. The mighty hammer, operated with
Line such consummate ease by the movement of a single
5   lever, though smaller than its more celebrated brother at Woolwich Arsenal, never failed to get a round of applause from the fascinated onlookers. There was something almost frightening about the deadly precision with which it worked, and the uncanny accuracy of the man
10  who controlled it. This time it would crash downwards delivering a blow which shook the ground: next time it would repeat the performance, only to stop just as the spectators were bracing themselves for the shock—stop with such mathematical exactitude that the glass of a
15  watch beneath it would be cracked but the works would not be damaged.
    For years now, personally conducted tours had come round Frenton's works. Old Frenton was always delighted when his friends asked him if they might take their
20  house-parties round: he regarded it as a compliment to himself. For he had made the works, watched them grow and expand till now they were known throughout the civilized world. They were just part of him, the fruit of his brain—born of labour and hard work and nurtured
25  on the hard-headed business capacity of the rugged old Yorkshireman. He was a millionaire now, many times over, but he could still recall the day when sixpence extra a day had meant the difference between chronic penury and affluence. And in those far-off days there had come
30  a second resolve into his mind to keep the first and ever present one company. That first one had been with him

ever since he could remember anything—the resolve, to succeed; the second one became no less deep rooted. When he did succeed he'd pay his men such wages that
35  there would never be any question of sixpence a day making a difference. The labourer was worthy of his hire: out of the sweat of his own brow John Frenton had evolved that philosophy for himself…
    And right loyally he had stuck to it. When success
40  came, and with it more and more, till waking one morning he realized that the big jump had been taken, and that henceforth Frenton's would be one of the powers in the steel world, he did not forget. He paid his men well—almost lavishly: all he asked was that
45  they should work in a similar spirit. And he did more. From the memories of twenty years before he recalled the difference between the two partners for whom he had then been working. One of them had never been seen in the works save as an aloof being from another
50  world, regarding his automatons with an uninterested but searching eye: the other had known every one of his men by name, and had treated them as his own personal friends. And yet his eye was just as searching… But— what a difference: what an enormous difference!
55     And so John Frenton had learned and profited by the example which stared him in the face: things might perhaps be different today if more employers had learned that lesson too. To him every man he employed was a personal friend: again all he asked was that they should
60  regard him likewise…
    "Boys," he had said to them on one occasion, when a spirit of unrest had been abroad in the neighbouring works, "if you've got any grievance, there's only one thing I ask. Come and get it off your chests to me: don't
65  get muttering and grousing about it in corners, if I can remedy it, I will: if I can't I'll tell you why. Anyway, a talk will clear the air…"

**1**

The primary purpose of the passage is to

A)   detail the precision of an impressive mechanical hammer.
B)   vividly capture the details of a tour of a factory.
C)   highlight the economic disparity amongst the workers in the factory.
D)   provide a character analysis of a successful factory owner.

**2**

John Frenton can best be seen as someone who

A)   focuses on the mechanical delights found within his factory.
B)   cares more about the wellbeing of others than himself.
C)   strives to apply life lessons learned when he was a young man.
D)   aims for gathering material wealth regardless of its impact on others.

**3**

As used in line 8, "deadly" most nearly means

A)   fierce.
B)   exact.
C)   overwhelming.
D)   toxic.

**4**

The author mentions "the glass of a watch" (lines 14-15) in order to

A)   express the accuracy of the rhythm of the hammer.
B)   show the degree of control capable when implementing the hammer.
C)   suggest the that the watch was sturdy and well-made.
D)   satirize the display of strength typically personified by the hammer.

**5**

The passage emphasizes a key difference between

A)   hard-working employees and lazy employees.
B)   generous employers and miserly employers.
C)   distant employers and friendly employers.
D)   loyal employees and disloyal employees.

**6**

Which choice provides the best evidence for the answer to the previous question?

A)   Line 39 ("And right…it")
B)   Lines 39-43 ("When…forget")
C)   Lines 43-45 ("He paid…spirit")
D)   Lines 48-53 ("One…searching…")

**7**

It can be inferred from the passage that John Frenton considers himself

A)   to possess a better managerial approach than those of many other nearby factories.
B)   immune from labor difficulties that affect Woolwich Arsenal and other nearby factories.
C)   to pay the highest salaries for factory workers and offer a friendly workplace..
D)   to have benefitted from the scarcity of good paying jobs in the area

**8**

As used in line 62, "abroad" most nearly means

A)   developing.
B)   sailing.
C)   distant.
D)   shunned.

CONTINUE

9

Which of the following best describes John Frenton's philosophy towards his workers?

A) He considers them friends and loves to have them take tours of his factory.

B) He pays high wages so he can employ the best workers in the region in order to gain advantage against other factories.

C) He expects honest talk from his workers and strives to treat them fairly.

D) He pays his men far too much and is unconcerned that he may head toward bankruptcy.

10

Which choice provides the best evidence for the answer to the previous question?

A) Line 18-21 ("Old ... himself")

B) Line 23-26 ("They ... Yorkshireman")

C) Line 39-43 ("When ... forget")

D) Line 61-66 (""Boys," ... why")

## Active Reading

This passage is from H. C. McNeile, "A Question of Personality." Originally published in 1921.

*factory tour*

    The personally conducted tour round Frenton's Steel Works paused, as usual, on reaching the show piece of the entertainment. The mighty hammer, operated with

*Line*

such consummate ease by the movement of a single

5  lever, though smaller than its more celebrated brother at Woolwich Arsenal, never failed to get a round of applause from the fascinated onlookers. There was something almost frightening about the deadly precision with which it worked, and the uncanny accuracy of the man

10 who controlled it. This time it would crash downwards delivering a blow which shook the ground: next time it would repeat the performance, only to stop just as the spectators were bracing themselves for the shock—stop with such mathematical exactitude that the glass of a

15 watch beneath it would be cracked but the works would not be damaged.

*hammer*

    For years now, personally conducted tours had come round Frenton's works. Old Frenton was always delighted when his friends asked him if they might take their

20 house-parties round: he regarded it as a compliment to himself. For he had made the works, watched them grow and expand till now they were known throughout the civilized world. They were just part of him, the fruit of his brain—born of labour and hard work and nurtured

25 on the hard-headed business capacity of the rugged old Yorkshireman. He was a millionaire now, many times over, but he could still recall the day when sixpence extra a day had meant the difference between chronic penury and affluence. And in those far-off days there had come

*Frenton*

*past*

30 a second resolve into his mind to keep the first and ever present one company. That first one had been with him ever since he could remember anything—the resolve, to succeed; the second one became no less deep rooted. When he did succeed he'd pay his men such wages that

35 there would never be any question of sixpence a day making a difference. The labourer was worthy of his hire: out of the sweat of his own brow John Frenton had evolved that philosophy for himself…

    And right loyally he had stuck to it. When success

*2 resolves*

*generous pay*

40 came, and with it more and more, till waking one morning he realized that the big jump had been taken, and that henceforth Frenton's would be one of the powers in the steel world, he did not forget. He paid his men well—almost lavishly: all he asked was that

45 they should work in a similar spirit. And he did more. From the memories of twenty years before he recalled the difference between the two partners for whom he had then been working. One of them had never been seen in the works save as an aloof being from another

50 world, regarding his automatons with an uninterested but searching eye: the other had known every one of his men by name, and had treated them as his own personal friends. And yet his eye was just as searching… But— what a difference: what an enormous difference!

*old bosses*

*bad*

*good*

55     And so John Frenton had learned and profited by the example which stared him in the face: things might perhaps be different today if more employers had learned that lesson too. To him every man he employed was a personal friend: again all he asked was that they should

*workers = F's friends*

60 regard him likewise…

    "Boys," he had said to them on one occasion, when a spirit of unrest had been abroad in the neighbouring works, "if you've got any grievance, there's only one thing I ask. Come and get it off your chests to me: don't

65 get muttering and grousing about it in corners, if I can remedy it, I will: if I can't I'll tell you why. Anyway, a talk will clear the air…"

*communication*

# Explanations

Answers & explanations for Reading Practice Passage 1

1. The primary purpose of the passage is to:

   A) detail the precision of an impressive mechanical hammer.
   B) vividly capture the details of a tour of a factory.
   C) highlight the economic disparity amongst the workers in the factory.
   D) provide a character analysis of a successful factory owner.

> We need to think about the passage as a **whole**. It starts with a description of a factory tour, but then spends the rest of the passage telling us about the owner, **Frenton**. Choices A and B are only in the first paragraph, and choice C only shows up at the end of the passage. **Choice D** is all about **Frenton**, so it's our right answer.

2. John Frenton can best be seen as someone who

   A) focuses on the ~~mechanical delights~~ found within his factory.
   B) ~~cares more~~ about the wellbeing of others than himself.
   C) strives to apply life lessons learned when he was a young man.
   D) aims for gathering material wealth ~~regardless of its impact~~ on others.

> Just as in Question 1, we need to think about the whole passage. We can use process of elimination by finding fault with the answer choices. Although the first paragraph talks about Frenton's "mechanical delights," the rest of the passage does not, so choice A is incorrect. We don't see much evidence that he cares more about others than himself, so we can cross off choice B. Choice D says he cares about money more than others, and that is not supported in lines 44-45 "he paid his men well—almost lavishly." So choice C must be correct and there is plenty of evidence as well in lines 56-57. Frenton learned from his experience as a laborer and applies those lessons as a factory owner.

3. As used in line 8 "deadly" most nearly means

   A) fierce.
   B) exact.
   C) overwhelming.
   D) toxic.

We need to look at the word in context:

> There was something almost frightening about the
> **deadly** precision with which it worked, and the
> uncanny accuracy of the man who controlled it."

The author did not use "deadly" literally, since no one is in danger. Later in the paragraph on lines 14-15, the author describes the hammer as having "**mathematical exactitude**." This is our strongest clue for this question. If we swap "deadly" for **choice B**, "exact," the sentence keeps its meaning.

> There was something almost frightening about
> the **exact** precision with which it worked, and the
> uncanny accuracy of the man who controlled it."

4. The author mentions "the glass of a watch" (lines 14-15) in order to

   A) express the accuracy of the ~~rhythm~~ of the hammer.
   B) show the degree of control capable when implementing the hammer.
   C) suggest the that the watch was ~~sturdy and well-made~~.
   D) ~~satirize~~ the display of strength typically personified by the hammer.

First let's look at the phrase in context:

> This time it would crash downwards delivering a blow
> which shook the ground: next time it would repeat the
> performance, only to stop just as the spectators were bracing
> themselves for the shock—stop with such **mathematical**
> **exactitude** that the glass of a watch beneath it would
> be cracked but the works would not be damaged.

The sentence describes the amount of control the operator has over the hammer, which is a perfect match for **choice B**.

5.  The passage emphasizes a key difference between

    A)  hard-working employees and lazy employees.
    B)  generous employers and miserly employers.
    C)  distant employers and friendly employers.
    D)  loyal employees and disloyal employees.

6.  Which choice provides the best evidence for the answer to the previous question?

    A)  Line 39 ("And right...it")
    B)  Lines 39-43 ("When...forget")
    C)  Lines 43-45 ("He paid...spirit")
    D)  Lines 48-53 ("One...just as searching")

> We can use the lines in Q6 to find the answer to Q5. We need to check the choices for a quote that talks about a **difference**; only **choice D**, lines 48-53, is about the difference between two things:
>
> > **One of them** had never been seen in the works save as an aloof being from another world, regarding his automatons with an uninterested but searching eye: **the other** had known every one of his men by name, and had treated them as his own personal friends. And yet his eye was just as searching...
>
> So one of Frenton's old employers was *"aloof"* and *"disinterested,"* and the other treated employees like *"personal friends."* That's a perfect match for **choice C** in Q4.

7.  It can be inferred from the passage that John Frenton considers himself

    A)  to possess a better managerial approach than those of many other nearby factories.
    B)  immune from labor difficulties that affect Woolwich Arsenal and other nearby factories.
    C)  to pay the highest salaries for factory workers and offer a friendly workplace.
    D)  to have benefitted from the scarcity of good paying jobs in the area.

All of the answers are about Frenton as a factory-owner and manager. Lines 55-60 are on topic:

> *And so John Frenton had learned and profited by the example which stared him in the face: things might perhaps be different today if more employers had learned that lesson too. To him every man he employed was a personal friend: again all he asked was that they should regard him likewise...*

We can paraphrase this as "Frenton thinks he has come up with a smart business practice that other employers should try." **Choice A** matches the lines and our paraphrase.

8. As used in line 62 "abroad" most nearly means

   (A) developing.
   B) sailing.
   C) distant.
   D) shunned.

We need to look at the word in context first:

> *"Boys," he had said to them on one occasion, when a spirit of unrest had been **abroad** in the neighbouring works, "if you've got any grievance, there's only one thing I ask. Come and get it off your chests to me."*

"Abroad" refers to the "spirit of unrest," so we need a word that means "**around**" or "**growing**." "**Developing**" matches "growing," and it fits well in the sentence. **Choice A** is correct.

> *"Boys," he had said to them on one occasion, when a spirit of unrest had been **developing** in the neighbouring works, "if you've got any grievance, there's only one thing I ask. Come and get it off your chests to me."*

9. Which of the following best describes John Frenton's philosophy towards his workers?

   A) He considers them friends and loves to have them ~~take tours of his factory~~.
   B) He pays high wages so he can employ the best workers in the region in order to ~~gain advantage~~ against other factories.
   C) He expects honest talk from his workers and strives to treat them fairly.
   D) He pays his men far ~~too much~~ and is unconcerned that he may head toward bankruptcy.

10. Which choice provides the best evidence for the answer to the previous question?

   A) Line 18-21 ("Old Frenton ... himself.")
   B) Line 23-26 ("They ... Yorkshireman.")
   C) Line 39-43 ("When ... forget.")
   D) Line 61-66 ("'Boys,' ... why.")

We can answer Questions 9 and 10 together by using Q10's choices to find evidence for Q9. Looking at the lines in Q10, only **choice D** is about how Frenton treats laborers.

> "Boys," he had said to them on one occasion, when a spirit of unrest had been abroad in the neighbouring works, "if you've got any grievance, there's only one thing I ask. Come and get it off your chests to me."

The quote says he wants his workers to talk directly to him and not complain about issues behind his back.

Now we need to find an answer to Q9 that matches this quote. In **choice C**, "honest talk" matches "Come and get it off your chests," so C is correct.

# Throwaways

*Throwaways are specific words that make a choice wrong. Hunt for them!*

................................................................

## A single word can make an answer choice wrong

In order for an answer choice to be correct, **every single word** must be supported by the passage. Check each word in the correct answer below:

> 1. The primary purpose of the *Active Reading* chapter is to:
>
>     Ⓐ encourage students to use their pencils more when reading.

## Save time!

Many students get stuck debating between two answers that both sound pretty great. They waste time trying to "feel out" which one is more correct.

Instead, by focusing on throwaways, you make the Reading section feel more concrete and move from question to question MUCH faster.

**A** is correct because *every single word* in the choice accurately reflects the chapter on active reading. Now, we can make *wrong* answer choices by **changing one word into a "throwaway"** that doesn't vibe:

> B̶)̶ encourage ⃞teachers⃞ to use their pencils more when reading.
>
> C̶)̶ ⃞force⃞ students to use their pencils more when reading.
>
> D̶)̶ encourage students to use their pencils ⃞less⃞ when reading.

Notice how <u>most</u> words in the wrong answers look great. The test-writers hope you'll be so distracted by the *good* that you won't notice the *bad*.

# TIP

You are the bouncer at an exclusive club, giving each word an ocular patdown. Only words that match the passage get to party.

## Hunt for throwaway words in each choice

To avoid falling into the test-writers' trap, you're going to become a **hunter of throwaways**. Scan your eyes over each word, checking it against your memory of the passage. If a word doesn't check out, put a box around it.

1. **Scan each word** in the answer choice.

2. **Draw a box** around the throwaway(s).

3. **Cross off that choice.** It's wrong!

---

The sentences below are attempting to summarize what you just read. **Box the throwaway** that makes each one wrong.

1. According to what you have read so far in this book:

   A. a single word can make an answer choice correct.

   B. the reading section consists of six passages total.

   C. you should use process of elimination as a last step.

   D. passive reading is the art of using your pencil while reading.

   E. students should use speed reading, evidence, and throwaways.

   F. reading the passages out of order is discouraged.

   G. students should focus on what is best about each choice.

   H. throwaways are specific words in the passage.

   I. reading comprehension rarely increases with practice.

   J. the physical act of active reading makes your brain more tired.

---

Answers:    A. *given*        B. six        C. last        D. passive        E. speed

F. discouraged    G. best       H. passage    I. rarely     J. more

# NOTE

Compare your active reading with the example on page 35. How'd you do? Did you underline, star a main idea, and jot a note in the margin to sum up the paragraph?

# Paraphrase

Remember to put each question into your **own words**, then read that paraphrase before each choice. For example:

*"Rejewski's successes..."*

## EXAMPLES 1 & 2

It is highly doubtful that the Allied forces would have won World War II without the help of Polish mathematician Marian Rejewski. At age fourteen, Rejewski enrolled in a secret cryptology
*Line* course for German speakers. Soon his full-time occupation was
5 decoding the German Enigma machine. Combining his usage of pure mathematics with information provided by French intelligence, Rejewski succeeded in decoding the Enigma, and consequently, the Allied forces were able to intercept German intelligence transmissions for six years. Historian David Kahn
10 says that Rejewski's stunning achievement "elevates him to the pantheon of the greatest cryptanalysts of all time." On the 100th anniversary of his birthday, a sculpted memorial was presented to his hometown of Bydgoszcz, Poland.

1. The passage suggests that Rejewski's accomplishments:

   A) would have been impossible without his enrollment in a cryptology course.
   B) were impeded by interference from French intelligence.
   C) began at age 6 with his completion of a course on cryptology.
   D) led to his hometown honoring him with a memorial sculpture.

2. The primary purpose of the passage is to:

   A) explain how the Enigma machine was decoded.
   B) illustrate the principles of cryptology.
   C) highlight the contribution of a noted mathematician to the war effort.
   D) provide insight into the motivations of a renowned cryptanalyst.

## BOX 'EM

Throughout this chapter, whenever you spot a throwaway, draw a box around it.

**Alternate Strategy:**
After putting it into a box, put that box inside of another box, then mail that box to yourself, and, when it arrives, *SMASH IT WITH A HAMMER*.

## Paraphrase

*"The author wrote this passage to..."*

SOLUTION

1. The passage suggests that Rejewski's accomplishments:

~~A)~~ would have been ⟦impossible⟧ without his enrollment in a cryptology course.

*Watch your assumptions! The passage mentions the course, but doesn't make such a bold claim as this.*

~~B)~~ were ⟦impeded⟧ by ⟦interference⟧ from French intelligence.

*French intelligence **helped** Rejewski decode the Enigma.*

~~C)~~ began at ⟦age 6⟧ with his completion of a course on cryptology.

*Watch those details: Rejewski enrolled at **age 14**.*

**(D))** led to his hometown honoring him with a memorial sculpture.

*No throwaways here! The last sentence of the passage matches this answer perfectly.*

SOLUTION

2. The primary purpose of the passage is to:

~~A)~~ ⟦explain how⟧ the Enigma machine was decoded.

*Did you learn how the machine worked? Could you build one now? The words **explain how** are throwaways.*

~~B)~~ illustrate the ⟦principles⟧ of cryptology.

*Quick—name the **principles** of cryptology. Can you do it? Don't beat yourself up; they weren't in the passage!*

**(C)** highlight the contribution of a noted mathematician to the war effort.

*Nothing glaringly wrong with this answer; let's move on.*

~~D)~~ provide insight into the ⟦motivations⟧ of a renowned cryptanalyst.

*The passage doesn't say **why** Rejewski helped.*

## EXAMPLES 3 & 4

Coleman Hawkins, one of the first great saxophonists of the Harlem Renaissance, was a consistently modern improviser who possessed an encyclopedic knowledge of music. Hawkins was
*Line* a giant of the jazz scene for more than forty years. His musical
5 odyssey began in front of the keys of a piano at the age of five; he moved on to the cello before settling on the tenor saxophone. In the 1920s and 30s, the saxophone was primarily considered a novelty instrument used in marching bands. However, Hawkins saw a greater potential for this instrument. His lyrical tones and
10 innovative style helped usher in a new age of avant-garde jazz known as Bebop and placed the saxophone at the center of the new jazz aesthetic. Succeeding generations of saxophonists, whose members included Sonny Rollins, Lester Young, and John Coltrane, acknowledged the profound influence that "Hawk" had
15 on their musical styles.

3. The passage supports which of the following statements about Hawkins?

   A) He broke new ground for jazz saxophonists.
   B) His innovative lyrics helped usher in a new musical era.
   C) His music earned international acclaim for many decades.
   D) His modernist style alienated more traditional musicians.

4. The author references Hawkins' "odyssey" (line 5) in order to:

   A) enumerate the steps he took to develop his saxophone technique.
   B) suggest the many challenges he faced in his musical training.
   C) convey appreciation for artists' journey of self-expression.
   D) highlight Hawkins' experience with multiple instruments before starting his saxophone career.

# Paraphrase

"The passage says that..."

3. The passage supports which of the following statements about Hawkins?

(A) He broke new ground for jazz saxophonists.

*No throwaway here: each word has support in the passage.*

~~B)~~ His innovative ⌐lyrics¬ helped usher in a new musical era.

*The passage says he has a "lyrical tone," but we never read about Hawkins writing actual **lyrics**. He was a sax player!*

~~C)~~ His music earned ⌐international¬ acclaim for many decades.

*He was definitely acclaimed. But there's no mention of **international** acclaim. Don't assume anything you can't find evidence for in the passage!*

~~D)~~ His modernist style ⌐alienated¬ more traditional musicians.

*This COULD be true, but nowhere in the passage do we read about a negative reaction to Hawkins.*

# Paraphrase

"The point of the fourth line is to..."

4. The author references Hawkins' "odyssey" (line 5) in order to:

~~A)~~ enumerate the steps he took to develop his saxophone ⌐technique.¬

*These lines list the instruments he tried **before** saxophone.*

~~B)~~ suggest the many ⌐challenges¬ he faced in his musical training.

*Didn't see anything in this line about **challenges** he faced.*

~~C)~~ convey appreciation for artists' ⌐journey of self-expression.¬

*This choice tries to sound smart, but "journey of self-expression" is not mentioned in the passage.*

(D) highlight Hawkins' experience with multiple instruments before starting his saxophone career.

*We read all of that! Hawkins played piano, then cello, then finally got stuck on saxophone! No throwaways here.*

# Short Passage Practice

*Read the short passage below, and use throwaways to answer questions 1-4.*

**LITERATURE**

When I was just six years old, my parents read a series of novels to me and my sister: *The Chronicles of Narnia* by C.S. Lewis. I can still remember the anticipation we felt each night before bed as we settled in for our nightly chap-
5  ter. In the first book, a child discovers a doorway at the back of a wardrobe that leads to the magical land of Narnia. After we finished the series, I was determined to read it for myself, despite the small print and long chapters. The Narnia books helped me learn how to read grown-up
10  books; little did I know they would also influence my life in many other ways in the years to come.

There were seven books in all. As I grew older, I read them again and again. Although I'm embarrassed to admit this, part of me always hoped that the Narnia books might
15  be at least a little bit real. I imagined that one day, I might walk around a corner, or open a door, or come to the end of an empty street, and I too would find myself in the land of talking animals where good always triumphed over evil. But I never found the door to Narnia. Eventually, I stopped
20  reading the books, and I stopped looking for it.

In my teenage years, my love for fantasy gave way to an obsession with other worlds of all kinds: civilizations on other planets, travels through the galaxy, and the high-tech future of the human race. Science fiction seemed
25  more adult while fantasy seemed like something for children. I thought I'd put it behind me. But then something changed; I found it again. I started writing stories about the worlds beyond the doors, worlds more or less like our own, except that occasionally the magic is real. A boy falls
30  in love with a mermaid and follows her into the sea. A vial of perfume holds the power to transport whoever smells it to a far away world. When I wrote these stories, it was like I was calling on some deep magic that had remained with me since I'd first imagined the land of Narnia and all the
35  adventures it held.

1. The narrator of the passage can best be described as:

A) an adult looking back at her childhood literary influences.
B) a teenager embarrassed by the books she read as a child.
C) an author who finds inspiration primarily in worlds of science fiction.
D) a grown-up who chronicles her growth as a writer from childhood to adulthood.

2. The main function of the first paragraph is to:

A) explain why the narrator found the books so intriguing.
B) detail the narrator's introduction to the books.
C) provide evidence of the importance of reading to children.
D) offer insight into the narrator's relationship with her family.

3. The passage indicates that compared to fantasy novels, the narrator considered science fiction stories to be:

A) more mature.
B) somewhat boring.
C) more inspiring.
D) easier to read.

4. According to the passage, the narrator returned to her love of fantasy after:

A) reading the Narnia books over and over again.
B) concluding that science fiction was too unrealistic.
C) encountering a fantasy story about a mermaid.
D) writing her own fantasy stories.

# Explanations

*Answers & explanations for Short Practice Passage*

..........................................................................................

1. The narrator of the passage can best be described as:

   A) an adult looking back at her childhood literary influences.
   B) a teenager embarrassed by the books she read as a child.
   C) an author who finds inspiration primarily in worlds of science fiction.
   D) a grown-up who chronicles her growth as a writer from childhood to adulthood.

   There are no words that match **embarrassed**, and **science fiction** is mentioned as a phase, not a primary interest. Finally, **growth as a writer** is not the focus here! Choice A is our best option.

## Main function

This question is asking for the main function of the first paragraph.

In this case, a word could be a throwaway even if it matches a small detail in the passage if it doesn't match the main function of the paragraph.

2. The <u>main function</u> of the first paragraph is to:

   A) explain why the narrator found the books so intriguing.
   B) detail the narrator's introduction to the books.
   C) provide evidence of the importance of reading to children.
   D) offer insight into the narrator's relationship with her family.

   In choice A, every word looks good except for one: **why**. We don't find out in the first paragraph *why* the author loved the books, just that she did.

   Choice C is hoping you'll get distracted by lines 9 and 10 - how the books helped the author learn to read. But is **providing evidence** the *main function* of the paragraph?

   Choice D is similar. We do learn that the author's parents read her the books, but the focus of the paragraph is on the books—not the family.

3. The passage indicates that compared to fantasy novels, the narrator considered <u>science fiction</u> stories to be:

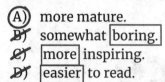

(A) more mature.
B) somewhat boring.
C) more inspiring.
D) easier to read.

*Science fiction* shows up in line 25, where the author says she once thought it to be "more adult." That's a pretty dead-on match for choice A. We never see any mention of a genre being **boring** or **easier**. The author does mention fantasy was **inspiring** but doesn't ever compare science fiction and fantasy in this way.

## Paraphrase

This is a question where **giving your own answer** before reading the choices can help a lot. The simple answer from the passage is "writing stories of her own," and, sure enough, that's a choice.

Choices A through C have familiar elements that might trick us if we didn't have confidence in our own answer.

4. According to the passage, the narrator <u>returned to her love of fantasy</u> after:

A) reading the *Narnia* books over and over again.
B) concluding that science fiction was too unrealistic.
C) encountering a fantasy story about a mermaid.
(D) writing her own fantasy stories.

This question points us to the last paragraph, where the author talks about returning to a past love of fantasy.

Choice A gets the timeline and paragraph wrong: she read the *Narnia* books **over and over again** in childhood.

Choice B looks good because of the reference to *science fiction*, but she never mentions a genre being **too unrealistic**.

Choice C looks good because of the reference to the fantasy story about a mermaid, but this was given as an example of the stories the author *writes*, not one she **encountered**.

# Evidence

*The page is a courtroom, and you are the judge. Each answer choice makes its case, and you decide which is backed with sufficient **evidence** in the passage.*

## Use evidence to prove every word of an answer

The only way an answer choice is correct is if every word can be matched with specific words in the passage, which we call **evidence**. Sometimes, words in the choices are ripped *directly* from the passage; usually, evidence takes the more subtle form of **synonyms**. In the example below, *wild* is evidence for *undomesticated* and *thorn in the side* is evidence for *nuisance*.

> **TIP**
>
> When you are hunting for synonyms, use your pencil to help make a match between words in the question and words in the passage.

> The parakeet would not be caged. He was as rambunctious as a red-footed mongoose, as wild as a ginger-fed jackrabbit, and was a thorn in the side of Marvin, the beleaguered janitor of Humberto's Home for Unruly Clowns.
>
> 1. The author characterizes the parakeet as:
>
>    A) an undomesticated nuisance.

On the next few pages, practice **hunting for synonyms** in the passage that will *prove* your chosen answer to be correct.

> **TIP**
>
> If you can't point to specific words that support an answer choice, you've got no proof. Cross out that sorry excuse for an answer!

## EXAMPLES 1 & 2

Although it is in our nature to be superstitious, cultural and environmental factors clearly influence how superstitious an individual actually is. For example, when we feel we are losing
*Line* control over our lives, we tend to become more superstitious. One
5 study found that people living in high-risk areas of the Middle East, such as Tel Aviv, are much more likely to carry a lucky charm than are other people. Nobody is immune. "We can all shift our supernatural inclination depending on the circumstances," says Bruce Hood, cognitive psychologist from the University of
10 Bristol. According to Hood, superstition is not going anywhere in the human brain. Because of our neurological evolution, the human race likely will never grow out of our tendency toward superstition and magical thinking.

**TIP**

**Don't assume** and talk yourself into an answer that isn't backed up by evidence. If you can't point to the **exact word or phrase** that serves as evidence for each word, that choice is wrong!

1. The author most likely states that people in Tel-Aviv are more likely to carry a lucky charm than other people in order to support the point that:

    A) only certain groups of people show superstitious behavior.
    B) environmental factors impact our level of superstitious behavior.
    C) individuals are often more superstitious than groups.
    D) people in low-risk environments rely more on supernatural interventions.

2. The passage most strongly suggests that humans will always have tendencies towards superstition due to:

    A) the fact that no one is immune to the disease of superstition.
    B) the use of superstition as a means of societal control.
    C) the way that the human brain has evolved.
    D) the fact that lucky charms are an integral piece of culture.

SOLUTION

Although it is in our nature to be superstitious, cultural and environmental factors clearly influence how superstitious an individual actually is. For example, when we feel we are losing *Line* control over our lives, we tend to become more superstitious. One
5 study found that people living in high-risk areas of the Middle East, such as Tel Aviv, are much more likely to carry a lucky charm than are other people. Nobody is immune. "We can all shift our supernatural inclination depending on the circumstances," says Bruce Hood, cognitive psychologist from the University of
10 Bristol. Because of our neurological evolution, the human race likely will never grow out of our tendency toward superstition and magical thinking.

## Paraphrase

"What did the author say that is supported by the lucky charm thing?"

1. The author most likely states that people in Tel-Aviv are more likely to carry a lucky charm than other people in order to support the point that:

A) only certain groups of people show superstitious behavior.

*The author says that we are all superstitious by nature, not just certain groups.*

B) environmental factors impact our level of superstitious behavior.

*"Environmental factors" is directly from line 2, and "impact" is a synonym of "influence!" This one has proof.*

C) individuals are often more superstitious than groups.

*Nope! Not in the passage at all.*

D) people in low-risk environments rely more on supernatural interventions.

*The author actually says the opposite of this on line 5.*

Although it is in our nature to be superstitious, cultural and environmental factors clearly influence how superstitious an individual actually is. For example, when we feel we are losing
Line control over our lives, we tend to become more superstitious. One
5 study found that people living in high-risk areas of the Middle East, such as Tel Aviv, are much more likely to carry a lucky charm than are other people. Nobody is immune. "We can all shift our supernatural inclination depending on the circumstances," says Bruce Hood, cognitive psychologist from the University of
10 Bristol. Because of our neurological evolution, the human race likely will never grow out of our tendency toward superstition and magical thinking.

## Paraphrase

"Why will people always be superstitious?"

2. The passage most strongly suggests that humans will always have tendencies towards superstition due to:

A) the fact that no one is immune to the disease of superstition.

*This one is very close, but is there a match for disease? No!*

B) the use of superstition as a means of societal control.

*No evidence for means of societal control!*

C) the way that the human brain has evolved.

*Bingo! "Human brain" and "evolved" match "neurological evolution" from line 10.*

D) the fact that lucky charms are an integral piece of culture.

*"Lucky charms" shows up in the passage, but nowhere does it say they are "integral" to culture.*

## EXAMPLES 3 & 4

At a time when natural resources such as oil, coal, and natural gas are being depleted at an alarming rate, "alternative energy" seem to be the magic words at the tip of everyone's tongue. One
Line of the most exciting proposals for generating renewable energy
5 comes from an old idea: the solar updraft tower. Conceived in 1903, the solar tower, designed like a giant chimney, draws heated air into openings at its base. Once inside the hollow tower, the heated air rises, accelerating to speeds of 35 mph. As the air rushes upward, dozens of wind turbines turn, generating
10 electricity. A solar updraft tower as high as 1,000 meters with a diameter as large as 7 kilometers could eventually power as many as 200,000 typical households.

3. The passage indicates that the idea of a solar updraft tower:

A) is not a new design for generating renewable energy.
B) could lead to the depletion of natural resources.
C) is impractical because it is based on flawed science.
D) could power a maximum of 1,000 houses at a time.

4. The author uses the phrase "magic words" most likely to emphasize the:

A) unsubstantiated belief in a proposed solution.
B) inevitability of an ecological disaster.
C) ability of language to capture the public's attention.
D) perceived appeal of a solution.

## Paraphrase

"The passage says the tower..."

At a time when natural resources such as oil, coal, and natural gas are being depleted at an alarming rate, "alternative energy" seem to be the magic words at the tip of everyone's tongue. One
Line of the most exciting proposals for generating renewable energy
5 comes from an old idea: the solar updraft tower. Conceived in 1903, the solar tower, designed like a giant chimney, draws heated air into openings at its base. Once inside the hollow tower, the heated air rises, accelerating to speeds of 35 mph. As the air rushes upward, dozens of wind turbines turn, generating
10 electricity. A solar updraft tower as high as 1,000 meters with a diameter as large as 7 kilometers could eventually power as many as 200,000 typical households.

3.  The passage indicates that the idea of a solar updraft tower:

A)  is not a new design for generating renewable energy.

   *That's about as close a match as you can get!*

B)  could lead to the depletion of natural resources.

   *The passage says the opposite—that it's a proposed **solution** to the depletion of natural resources!*

C)  is impractical because it is based on flawed science.

   *The author doesn't make either of these claims.*

D)  could power a maximum of 1,000 houses at a time.

   *Line 12 says it could power 200,000 homes!*

SOLUTION

At a time when natural resources such as oil, coal, and natural gas are being depleted at an alarming rate, "alternative energy"
Line seem to be the magic words at the tip of everyone's tongue. One
5 of the most exciting proposals for generating renewable energy comes from an old idea: the solar updraft tower. Conceived in 1903, the solar tower, designed like a giant chimney, draws heated air into openings at its base. Once inside the hollow tower, the heated air rises, accelerating to speeds of 35 mph. As
10 the air rushes upward, dozens of wind turbines turn, generating electricity. A solar updraft tower as high as 1,000 meters with a diameter as large as 7 kilometers could eventually power as many as 200,000 typical households.

4.  The author uses the phrase "magic words" most likely to emphasize the:

A)  unsubstantiated belief in a proposed solution.

The passage doesn't say whether the solar updraft tower is substantiated or not; it just describes what it could do.

B)  inevitability of an ecological disaster.

We do see that natural resources are depleting at an "alarming rate," but watch your assumptions! It doesn't say if the disaster is inevitable. Also, this has nothing to do with the phrase "magic words."

C)  ability of language to capture the public's attention.

Everyone's talking about "alternative energy," but it's not the language that's getting their attention: it's the idea. The focus of the passage is on the solution, not the words.

D)  perceived appeal of a solution.

This is our least wrong answer. "Appeal of a solution" matches "exciting proposal," and there's no throwaways.

## It's time to start building habits

Congratulations! You have now learned the core skills that will increase your Reading score! You know how to **actively read**, how to focus on eliminating wrong answers using **throwaways**, and how to back up our choice with **evidence** from the passage.

From here, we'll look at common question types, learn some advanced strategies, and—most importantly—practice, practice, practice! Remember, the key to a higher Reading score is to build **good habits**. It's absolutely crucial that you keep up these new strategies until they become second nature. After each practice passage you complete, look over your work. Focus on the marks you made with your pencil and give an honest appraisal by asking yourself each question below:

1. *Did I use my pencil to do more than circle answers?*

2. *Did I underline throughout the passage?*

3. *Did I take notes in the margin?*

4. *Did I box or cross out throwaways?*

If the answers are *no*, don't get mad; get even. Make executing these strategies your primary goal for the next passage.

## It's also time to start watching the clock

One key to scoring higher on every section of the SAT is to learn your **timing intervals**. On average, you have **13 minutes** to read a passage and answer the questions that follow. Let's start getting a sense of what this amount of time "feels like."

Before you start each passage, **start a timer** on your phone or watch if you have one available. When you finish the passage, write down next to the passage how long you spent and how far over or under the average you were. Use this information to set goals for the next passage.

Even just noting the time in this way will make you more and more aware of the passage of time while you take the test. To take it one step further and improve your speed, conduct **timing drills** with each passage. Turn to page 17 for a step-by-step guide on how to do a timing drill.

# Reading Practice Passage 2

## TO STAY ON PACE, YOUR TIMING GOAL IS 13 MINUTES

---

**DIRECTIONS**

Each passage or pair of passages below is followed by a number of questions. After reading each passage or pair, choose the best answer to each question based on what is stated or implied in the passage or passages and in any accompanying graphics (such as a table or graph).

---

**Questions 1-10 are based on the following passage.**

This passage is adapted from Holly MacDonald's "The Revival of the Peanut" written in 2010.

Peanuts have undergone a strong revival in the 21st
century, seen as a potent, cost-effective source of protein
and heart-healthy monounsaturated fats. With so many
nutritional benefits, peanuts have found a variety of
5  culinary uses beyond the "PB & J" childhood sandwich
staple, used in everything from Asian stir fry dishes to
African peanut soups to fruit smoothies. As the Food &
Drug Administration (FDA) cracks down on trans fats–
partially hydrogenated oils known for their shelf stability
10  and connection to heart disease–peanut oil looks to be
more popular than ever on both supermarket shelves and
in restaurant deep fryers.

Unfortunately, not everyone is overjoyed with the
proliferation of peanut-based products. Approximately
15  0.6% of Americans suffer from a peanut allergy, making
any food containing peanuts certainly hazardous if not
outright fatal. Allergic reactions to peanuts can range
from rashes and hives to anaphylaxis. The latter is a
life-threatening condition where exposure to the allergen
20  leads to throat-swelling, which can cut off the supply of
oxygen to the lungs in extreme cases. Obviously the best
approach for someone with a peanut allergy would also
be the most simple: don't eat peanuts! While certainly
pragmatic advice, exposure to peanuts can occur through
25  the use of peanuts and peanut byproducts in a variety
of hard-to-forecast routes. For example, in a school
cafeteria, a cook could make a peanut butter sandwich
on a counter and then make a bologna sandwich
immediately after for a child with a peanut allergy. If
30  the counter and the cook's hands and utensils were not
properly cleaned, it is entirely possible that some trace

amount of peanut butter could end up on the bologna
sandwich, triggering an allergic reaction in a child with
an acute sensitivity to peanuts.
35  Thankfully, the FDA has been making great strides to
inform consumers about potential allergens in food. Food
manufacturers must clearly label common allergens and
also acknowledge potential cross-contamination when
food is processed on the same equipment or even in the
40  same facility. The concern over cross-contamination has
led to the banning of peanuts as a mid-flight snack on
airlines and in many schools that worry about the legal
ramifications of a lunchtime misstep.

While these precautions certainly help to reduce
45  accidental exposure to allergens, scientists at North
Carolina A & T State University have come up with a
different way to combat allergic reactions to peanuts. A
person with a peanut allergy is not allergic to the entire
peanut, as peanuts are made up of the same organic
50  compounds as most other foods, and the human body
itself. Scientists have discovered the two primary culprits
in peanuts that cause allergic reactions: proteins Ara h 1
and Ara h 2. Without these two proteins, the rest of the
content of the peanut will likely not cause a reaction. This
55  is why foods cooked in peanut oil do not cause allergic
reactions, since Ara h 1 and Ara h 2 are stripped away
during the refining process. The scientists, led by Dr.
Jianmei Yu, began to look for ways to not only remove
the allergen, but also retain the nutrition and consistency
60  of whole peanuts.

The solution proved to be surprisingly simple.
Using a mixture of two food-safe enzymes, trypsin
and alpha chymotrypsin, and the application of
ultrasound, the offending allergens were removed from
65  roasted peanuts to the point that their presence could no
longer be detected. Even better for a peanut fan, the taste
and texture of the post-treatment peanuts were identical

CONTINUE ▶

to untreated ones. Initial studies, using a pin prick
method to determine an allergic reaction, have proven
70  promising, and the University has partnered with biotech
firm Algrn to produce hypoallergenic peanuts for the
consumer market. The hope is that this patented process
can eventually be adapted to remove allergens in other
foods, including tree nuts and soybeans.
75      The current indicators all point to success; however,
there are some lingering questions. Assuming that
the FDA approved the process as safe, only universal
compliance to hypoallergenic standards would lead
to total peace of mind for someone with a peanut
80  allergy. Is the complete processing of the domestic and
international peanut crop to hypoallergenic standards
feasible? How would this additional processing affect the
price and profitability of growing and preparing peanuts?
While Algrn certainly has humanitarian ideals, the
85  company also looks to profit from the patented process
it purchased from the university. It may be advisable
for Algrn to target institutional sales from schools and
theme parks looking to reduce liability while still offering
choice.
90      Perhaps the most unpredictable reaction will
come from peanut allergy sufferers themselves. After
a lifetime of fearing peanuts, would a peanut allergy
sufferer welcome eating a hypoallergenic peanut? The
person's hesitance, or even outright refusal, is quite
95  understandable when a food foe becomes a food friend
overnight.

1

The passage presents untreated peanuts as both

A) an underutilized nutrient and a dangerous additive.
B) culinarily diverse and potentially hazardous to
those with an allergy.
C) a nostalgic food and a source of partially
hydrogenated oils.
D) a popular fad and hidden danger to consumers.

2

As used in line 26, "routes" most nearly means

A) scenarios.
B) conspiracies.
C) attacks.
D) favors.

3

The passage uses a hypothetical example set in a cafeteria
in order to

A) denounce careless conditions within the food
service industry.
B) show why people with peanut allergies must be
careful about what they choose to eat.
C) highlight how easily cross-contamination can
occur.
D) acknowledge that cross-contamination of foods is
unavoidable in a commercial kitchen.

4

The passage most strongly implies that precautions taken
towards preventing allergic reactions are

A) reasonable.
B) overbearing.
C) unwarranted.
D) infallible.

CONTINUE

**5**

In line 57, "refining" most nearly means

A) polishing.
B) mixing.
C) boiling.
D) extracting.

**6**

The passage asserts that regular peanuts and hypoallergenic peanuts

A) have the same taste and texture.
B) are both in high demand.
C) cost the same amount to produce.
D) are both dangerous for those with peanut allergies.

**7**

Which choice provides the best evidence for the answer to the previous question?

A) Lines 54-57 ("This ... process")
B) Lines 66-68 ("Even ... ones")
C) Lines 82-83 ("How ... peanuts")
D) Lines 91-93 ("After ... hypoallergenic peanut")

**8**

What function does the sixth paragraph (lines 75-89) serve in the passage as a whole?

A) It advocates for greater testing before hypoallergenic peanuts are available to purchase.
B) It admits that hypoallergenic peanuts will likely not be a commercial success.
C) It addresses some practical concerns about the production and distribution of hypoallergenic peanuts.
D) It forecasts a commercial backlash against hypoallergenic peanuts since few people will want to eat them.

**9**

The passage supports which of the following statements about Algrn?

A) They are concerned about the safety of the allergen removal process.
B) They plan on exploiting a serious medical problem for their own profit.
C) They hope to be able to remove allergens from the North American food supply.
D) They need to balance economic realities with the desire to improve people's health.

**10**

Which choice provides the best evidence for the answer to the previous question?

A) Lines 68-72 ("Initial ... market")
B) Lines 72-74 ("The hope ... soybeans")
C) Lines 84-86 ("While ... university")
D) Lines 86-89 ("It ... choice")

# Explanations

*Answers & explanations for "The Revival of the Peanut"*

.......................................................................................................

1.  The passage presents untreated peanuts as both

    A)  an ~~underutilized~~ nutrient and a ~~dangerous~~ additive.
    B)  culinarily diverse and potentially hazardous to those with an allergy.
    C)  a nostalgic food and a ~~source~~ of partially hydrogenated oils.
    D)  a popular ~~fad~~ and hidden danger to consumers.

    > We need to focus on untreated peanuts, which are discussed in the first and second paragraph. Lines 6-7 state the varied use of peanuts:
    >
    > > *...used in everything from Asian stir fry dishes to African peanut soups to fruit smoothies...*
    >
    > But lines 14-17 add a problem with peanuts:
    >
    > > *Approximately 0.6% of Americans suffer from a peanut allergy, making any food containing peanuts certainly hazardous if not outright fatal.*
    >
    > **Choice B** summarizes how untreated peanuts are a mixed bag.

2.  As used in line 26, "routes" most nearly means

    A)  scenarios.
    B)  conspiracies.
    C)  attacks.
    D)  favors.

    > First, let's read in context:
    >
    > > *"While certainly pragmatic advice, exposure to peanuts can occur through the use of peanuts and peanut byproducts in a variety of hard-to-forecast **routes**."*

The sentence describes how people might be exposed to peanuts, in a variety of routes, or **"ways."** **Choice A**, "scenarios" fits the meaning of the sentence, while the other words all change the meaning.

> *"While certainly pragmatic advice, exposure to peanuts can occur through the use of peanuts and peanut byproducts in a variety of hard-to-forecast **scenarios**."*

3. The passage uses a hypothetical example set in a cafeteria in order to

   A) ~~denounce~~ careless conditions within the food service industry.
   B) show why people with peanut allergies must be careful about ~~what they choose to eat~~.
   C) highlight how easily cross–contamination can occur.
   D) acknowledge that cross–contamination of foods is ~~unavoidable~~ in a commercial kitchen.

As always, we need to read in context to figure out what the example is doing in the paragraph:

> *"While certainly pragmatic advice, exposure to peanuts can occur through the use of peanuts and peanut byproducts in a variety of hard-to-forecast routes. **For example**, in a school cafeteria, a cook could make a peanut butter sandwich on a counter and then make a bologna sandwich immediately after for a child with a peanut allergy. If the counter and the cook's hands and utensils were not properly cleaned, it is entirely possible that some trace amount of peanut butter could end up on the bologna sandwich, triggering an allergic reaction to a child with an acute sensitivity to peanuts."*

If we read in context, we see that the hypothetical is an example of one of those "hard-to-forecast routes" through which someone might be exposed to peanuts. The example shows how you could be accidentally exposed to peanuts if your food is prepared on a surface that touched peanuts; **choice C** is a perfect match!

4. The passage most strongly implies that precautions taken towards preventing allergic reactions are

(A) reasonable.
B) overbearing.
C) unwarranted.
D) infallible.

The paragraph begins:

> "**Thankfully**, the FDA has been making great strides to inform consumers about potential allergens in food."

We're looking for a positive word to describe the author's attitude toward these precautions. Choice D, "infallible," is **too** positive, since there's no evidence that the author thinks the precautions are perfect and incapable of mistakes. **Choice A**, "reasonable," is a much better match to the passage.

5. In line 57, "refining" most nearly means

A) polishing.
B) mixing.
C) boiling.
(D) extracting.

First, let's read the word in context:

> "This is why foods cooked in peanut oil do not cause allergic reactions, since ARa h 1 and Ara h 2 are stripped away during the **refining** process."

"Refining" describes process, and the process is that of turning peanuts into peanut oil. Only **choice D**, "extracting," makes sense in the context of turning peanuts into oil.

> "This is why foods cooked in peanut oil do not cause allergic reactions, since ARa h 1 and Ara h 2 are stripped away during the **extracting** process."

6. The passage asserts that regular peanuts and hypoallergenic peanuts

    (A) have the same taste and texture.
    B) are both in high demand.
    C) cost the same amount to produce.
    D) are both dangerous for those with peanut allergies.

7. Which choice provides the best evidence for the answer to the previous question?

    A) Lines 54-57 ("This ... process")
    (B) Lines 66-68 ("Even ... ones")
    C) Lines 82-83 ("How ... peanuts")
    D) Lines 91-93 ("After ... hypoallergenic peanut")

Let's look at this pair of questions together, and use Q7 to solve Q6. According to Q6, we're looking for what's true about both regular and hypoallergenic peanuts. Now, let's evaluate the line references in Q7, looking for the choice that references both peanut types. Only **choice B** in Q7 mentions both kinds of peanuts, and it tells us that their "taste and texture" are "identical." In Q6, **choice A** matches those lines perfectly.

8. What function does the sixth paragraph (lines 75-89) serve in the passage as a whole?

    A) It ~~advocates~~ for ~~greater testing~~ before hypoallergenic peanuts are available to purchase.
    B) It admits that hypoallergenic peanuts will likely ~~not be a commercial success~~.
    (C) It addresses some practical concerns about the production and distribution of hypoallergenic peanuts.
    D) It forecasts a ~~commercial backlash~~ against hypoallergenic peanuts since few people will want to eat them.

There are lots of question marks in paragraph 6, and my active reading note for paragraph 6 says "still questions." These questions are all about the nitty-gritty details of making and selling these new peanuts. **Choice C** is the only answer that matches the passage!

9. The passage supports which of the following statements about Algrn?

    A) They are ~~concerned~~ about the safety of the allergen removal process.
    B) They plan on ~~exploiting~~ a serious medical problem for their own profit.
    C) They hope to soon be able to remove allergens from the ~~North American food supply~~.
    (D) They need to balance economic realities with the desire to improve people's health.

10. Which choice provides the best evidence for the answer to the previous question?

    A) Lines 68-72 ("Initial ... market")
    B) Lines 72-74 ("The hope ... soybeans")
    (C) Lines 84-86 ("While ... university")
    D) Lines 86-89 ("It ... choice")

Let's work these problems together; Q9 asks us about Algrn, so let's look at Q10's answer choices to find lines that tell us about Algrn. A, C, and D all mention Algrn, so now we must cross-reference Q9's answer choices and find a match. **Choice D** in Q9 matches **choice C** in Q10: "balance economic realities"  matches "looks to profit" and "desire to improve people's health" matches "humanitarian ideals."

# UNIT | Question Types

## Chapters

## Overview

In this unit, we'll learn about three special **types of questions**: Evidence-Based Questions, Vocab in Context, and Reading Graphs. We'll see examples and learn special strategies for each type.

# Evidence-Based Questions

*Some questions will ask you to point to the lines that contain key evidence.*

## TIP

You can expect *two to four* Evidence-Based Questions per passage. That means mastering the strategies in this chapter can help answer almost a quarter of all Reading questions!

## Look for answer choices with line references

These Evidence-Based Questions (EBQs) ask you to prove a specific point with lines from the passage. They come in two flavors: the **paired question**, where the second question asks you to prove your answer to the first, and the **onesie**, which is self-contained. Either way, they are easy to spot as the answer choices are quotes from the passage.

## TIP

The SAT thinks backing up your answers with evidence is super important!

In fact, the official name of the language arts portion is "Evidence-Based Reading and Writing."

1. The central idea of the first paragraph (lines 1–12) is that

   A) sharks are terrors of the sea that must be stopped.
   B) jokes should not be attempted by the faint of heart.
   C) you are a monster, but we like you anyways.
   D) snapping is an activity enjoyed by all ages.

2. Which choice provides the best evidence for the answer to the previous question?

   A) Lines 1–2 ("Sharks...help!!")
   B) Lines 3–4 ("You...monster")
   C) Lines 6–8 ("Oh...snap")
   D) Lines 9–11 ("Funny...jokes?")

## Paired question strategy

**Paired questions** are easy points if we **work backwards** from the second question. To do this, ask yourself three questions:

1. *What is Q1 asking?*

2. *Which lines in Q2 answer that question?*

3. *Which choice in Q1 matches those lines?*

# NOTE

This passage was adapted from a letter that Susan B. Anthony, a 19th century civil rights activist, wrote to her brother, Kansas resident Daniel Read Anthony, in 1859. At that time, Kansas was preparing to enter the Union as a state and was in the midst of a debate regarding slavery and civil rights.

\* *Prima facie* is a Latin expression meaning "at first sight."

\*\* The Lecompton Constitution was proposed by the proslavery legislature in Kansas, but rejected by the voters.

\*\*\* Anthony is paraphrasing from the Declaration of Independence

## EXAMPLES 1 & 2

Even the smallest human right denied, is large. The fact that the ruling class withhold this right is *prima facie*\* evidence that they deem it of importance for good or for evil. In either case, therefore, the human
Line being is outraged. It, perchance, may matter but little whether Kansas be
5 governed by a constitution made by her bona fide settlers or by people of another State or by Congress; but for Kansas to be denied the right to make her own constitution and laws is an outrage not to be tolerated. So the constitution and laws of a State and nation may be just as considerate of woman's needs and wants as if framed by herself, yet for man to deny her
10 the right to a voice in making and administering them, is paralleled only by the Lecompton usurpation\*\*. For any human being or class of human beings, whether black, white, male or female, tamely to submit to the denial of their right to self-government shows that the instinct of liberty has been blotted out.
15   You blunder on this question of woman's rights just where thousands of others do. You believe woman unlike man in her nature; that conditions of life which any man of spirit would sooner die than accept are not only endurable to woman but are needful to her fullest enjoyment. Make her position in church, State, marriage, your own; everywhere your equality
20 ignored, everywhere made to feel another empowered by law and time-honored custom to prescribe the privileges to be enjoyed and the duties to be discharged by you; and then if you can imagine yourself to be content and happy, judge your mother and sisters and all women to be.
    It was not because the three-penny tax on tea was so exorbitant that
25 our Revolutionary fathers fought and died, but to establish the principle that such taxation was unjust. It is the same with this woman's revolution; though every law were as just to woman as to man, the principle that one class may usurp the power to legislate for another is unjust, and all who are now in the struggle from love of principle would still work on until the
30 establishment of the grand and immutable truth, "All governments derive their just powers from the consent of the governed."\*\*\*

1.  Anthony indicates that the women's revolution and the American revolution are similar in that they both

    (A)  were centered on the principle of justice.
    B)  were caused by righteous indignation.  — anger
    C)  were primarily orchestrated by members of the upper class.
    D)  are consistent with the ideals in the Constitution.

2.  Which quote provides the best evidence for the previous question?

    A)  Lines 3-4 ("In either … outraged")
    B)  Lines 7-11 ("So … usurpation")
    C)  Lines 11-14 ("For … blotted out")
    (D)  lines 24-26 ("It … revolution")

## TIP

If you **immediately** remember the answer (or know exactly where to find it in the passage), then you can go ahead and answer Q1.

However, on longer passages, it is often easier to **let Q2 guide you** to the answer!

SOLUTION

Let's answer these questions as a pair, one step at a time.

**Step 1: What is Q1 asking?**

Let's use active reading to **summarize** what question 1 is asking:

1. Anthony indicates that the women's revolution and the American revolution are similar in that they both

   *What do the women's & American revolutions have in common?*

**Step 2: Which lines in Q2 answer that question?**

Summary in hand, let's check each answer choice of Q2 for lines that are on topic. If the lines are not about the *women's and American revolutions*, cross it off!

2. Which quote provides the best evidence for the previous question?

   A) Lines 3–4 (*In either case, therefore, the human being is outraged.*)

   *No mention of **revolutions** here.*

   B) Lines 8–11 (*So the constitution and laws of a State and nation may be just as considerate of woman's needs and wants as if framed by herself, yet for man to deny her the right to a voice in making and administering them, is paralleled only by the Lecompton usurpation.*)

   *This relates the women's revolution to the **Lecompton usurpation**, but not the **American revolution**.*

   C) Lines 12–14 (*For any human being or class of human beings, whether black, white, male or female, tamely to submit to the denial of their right to self-government shows that the instinct of liberty has been blotted out.*)

   *This sounds related to the revolutions, but doesn't directly reference them.*

   D) Lines 24–26 (*It was not because the three-penny tax on tea was so exorbitant that our Revolutionary fathers fought and died, but to establish the principle that such taxation was unjust. It is the same with this woman's revolution;*)

   *Great! This choice mentions **both** revolutions, and that last sentence directly **compares** them.*

Continued on next page →

## TIP

If you get to Step 2 of the strategy and find that more than one choice in Q2 could provide evidence for Q1, you will need to compare each quotation to the choices in Q1.

Only one quotation will have a great match in Q1!

**Step 3: Which choice in Q1 matches those lines?**

Now that we have answered Q2, we know the correct answer for Q1 should be supported by evidence from lines 23-25. These lines tell us the American and women's revolutions were fought:

"to establish the **principle** that such taxation was **unjust**."

One answer choice matches those lines perfectly:

1. Anthony indicates that the <u>women's revolution</u> and the <u>American revolution</u> are ⟨similar⟩ in that they both

   (A) centered on the **principle** of **justice**.

The words **principle** and **justice** match our evidence from Q2! So the answer to Q1 is A, and the answer to Q2 is D. We're done!

## TIP

Watch Out! Sometimes, one of the Onesie answers will (coincidentally?) support the preceding question! Make sure you don't apply the paired passage strategy when it's not a pair. To avoid this trap, always **read the prompt** carefully!

## Watch out for the Onesie!

Most SAT tests will have three to five standalone evidence-based questions. These questions do not refer to the previous question; instead, they ask for evidence that supports a stated claim (see below). When you see a onesie, simply **read the lines in context**, looking for the choice that answers the question.

1. Which of the following statements in the passage supports the conclusion that dogs are better than cats?

   A) Lines 8-11 (Dogs...rule)
   B) Lines 34-35 (Cats...drool)
   C) Lines 50-51 (Just...kidding)
   D) Lines 87-89 (Wink...wink)

**WANTED**

Reward for spotting the notorious **ONESIE**

# NOTE

This passage was adapted from a letter that Susan B. Anthony, a 19th Century civil rights activist, wrote to her brother, Kansas resident Daniel Read Anthony, in 1859. At that time, Kansas was preparing to enter the Union as a state and was in the midst of a debate regarding slavery and civil rights.

* *Prima facie* is a Latin expression meaning "at first sight."

** The Lecompton Constitution was proposed by the proslavery legislature in Kansas, but rejected by the voters.

*** Anthony is paraphrasing from the Declaration of Independence

Even the smallest human right denied, is large. The fact that the ruling class withhold this right is *prima facie** evidence that they deem it of importance for good or for evil. In either case, therefore, the human
Line being is outraged. It, perchance, may matter but little whether Kansas be
5 governed by a constitution made by her bona fide settlers or by people of another State or by Congress; but for Kansas to be denied the right to make her own constitution and laws is an outrage not to be tolerated. So the constitution and laws of a State and nation may be just as considerate of woman's needs and wants as if framed by herself, yet for man to deny her
10 the right to a voice in making and administering them, is paralleled only by the Lecompton usurpation**. For any human being or class of human beings, whether black, white, male or female, tamely to submit to the denial of their right to self-government shows that the instinct of liberty has been blotted out.
15     You blunder on this question of woman's rights just where thousands of others do. You believe woman unlike man in her nature; that conditions of life which any man of spirit would sooner die than accept are not only endurable to woman but are needful to her fullest enjoyment. Make her position in church, State, marriage, your own; everywhere your equality
20 ignored, everywhere made to feel another empowered by law and time-honored custom to prescribe the privileges to be enjoyed and the duties to be discharged by you; and then if you can imagine yourself to be content and happy, judge your mother and sisters and all women to be.
    It was not because the three-penny tax on tea was so exorbitant that
25 our Revolutionary fathers fought and died, but to establish the principle that such taxation was unjust. It is the same with this woman's revolution; though every law were as just to woman as to man, the principle that one class may usurp the power to legislate for another is unjust, and all who are now in the struggle from love of principle would still work on until the
30 establishment of the grand and immutable truth, "All governments derive their just powers from the consent of the governed."***

1. The author asserts that the right for citizens of Kansas to create the state's constitution

   A) is more important than securing voting rights for women.
   B) has little impact on the rights of citizens in other states.
   C) should be reconsidered after the defeat of the Lecompton constitution.
   D) is a right that should not be overlooked.

2. Which choices provides the best evidence that the author believes the letter's recipient makes a common mistake regarding women's rights?

   A) Lines 1 ("Even ... is large")
   B) Lines 4-6 ("It ... by Congress")
   C) Lines 6-8 ("but ...tolerated")
   D) Lines 15-16 ("You ... others do")

We should NOT answer these questions as a pair! Why not? Because question #4 is a **Onesie**: it doesn't reference the previous question. So let's tackle them one at a time:

3. The author asserts that the right for citizens of Kansas to create the state's constitution?

A) is ~~more important~~ than securing voting rights for women.

B) has ~~little impact~~ on the rights of citizens in other states.

C) should be ~~reconsidered~~ after the defeat of the Lecompton constitution.

D) is a right that should not be overlooked.

*This is a great choice. Compare it to lines 6-7: "but for Kansas to be denied the right to make her own constitution and laws is an outrage not to be tolerated."*

4. Which choices provides the best evidence <u>that the author believes the letter's recipient makes a common mistake regarding women's rights</u>?

A) Lines 1 (*"Even the smallest human right denied, is large."*)

B) Lines 4-6 (*"It, perchance, may matter but little whether Kansas be governed by a constitution made by her bona fide settlers or by people of another State or by Congress"*)

C) Lines 6-8 (*"but for Kansas to be denied the right to make her own constitution and laws is an outrage not to be tolerated."*)

D) Lines 15-16 (*"You blunder on this question of woman's rights just where thousands of others do."*)

*The prompt gives us a specific claim to back up about a common mistake regarding women's rights. Only the lines in this choice directly address this topic.*

# TIP

Notice that choice C in Q4 is perfect evidence for the answer to Q3!

If you answered these questions together, without actively reading question 4 and noticing it's a Onesie, you'd likely fall into this trap!

# Vocab in Context

*You'll find one or two VIC questions attached to every passage. These are some of the easiest points on the test, so practice the strategy and get those points!*

## What does this word mean in context?

When you see the words "most nearly means," you know you've found a VIC question. The SAT writers won't ask you to define crazy three-syllable words; in fact, the VIC words are usually common words with multiple meanings. Here's what they look like:

> 1. As used in line 35, "raised" most nearly means,
>
>    A) built.
>    B) lifted.
>    C) increased.
>    D) nurtured.

**TIP**

We'll say it again: when in doubt, go back to the passage! That's where all the answers are.

As you can see, all of our answer choices are possible definitions of "raised," so we need some more information. When in doubt, go back to the passage! We need to read these words in **context** to figure out which is correct. Here are your step-by-step instructions:

1. *Find the line,* then read one sentence up and one sentence down.

2. *Plug in* each answer choice, reading in context.

3. *Pick the choice* that makes sense!

## EXAMPLE 1

Lithium-oxygen, or lithium-air, batteries have been touted as the 'ultimate' battery due to their theoretical energy density, which is ten times that of a lithium-ion battery. Such a high
Line energy density would be comparable to that of gasoline—and
5 would enable an electric car with a battery that is a fifth the cost and a fifth the weight of those currently on the market to drive from London to Edinburgh on a single charge. Scientists have developed a working laboratory demonstrator of a lithium-oxygen battery which has very high energy density, is more than
10 90% efficient, and, to date, can be recharged more than 2,000 times. Their work presents potential solutions to several of the problems holding back the development of these devices.

1. As used in line 8, "developed" most nearly means,

   A) grown
   B) matured
   C) created
   D) unfolded

SOLUTION

① **Find the line** mentioned in the question, and read one sentence up and one sentence down.

*Such a high energy density would be comparable to that of gasoline—and would enable an electric car with a battery that is a fifth the cost and a fifth the weight of those currently on the market to drive from London to Edinburgh on a single charge. Scientists have **developed** a working laboratory demonstrator of a lithium-oxygen battery which has very high energy density, is more than 90% efficient, and, to date, can be recharged more than 2,000 times. Their work presents potential solutions to several of the problems holding back the development of these devices.*

Continued on next page →

② **Plug in each answer choice**, reading in context.

A) Scientists have **grown** a working laboratory demonstrator of a lithium-oxygen battery which has very high energy density, is more than 90% efficient, and, to date, can be recharged more than 2,000 times.

Can scientists grow batteries? I doubt it.

B) Scientists have **matured** a working laboratory demonstrator of a lithium-oxygen battery which has very high energy density, is more than 90% efficient, and, to date, can be recharged more than 2,000 times.

Wow, a fully-grown mature battery! This doesn't make sense.

C) Scientists have **created** a working laboratory demonstrator of a lithium-oxygen battery which has very high energy density, is more than 90% efficient, and, to date, can be recharged more than 2,000 times.

Now **that** makes sense. The scientists created a battery!

D) Scientists have **unfolded** a working laboratory demonstrator of a lithium-oxygen battery which has very high energy density, is more than 90% efficient, and, to date, can be recharged more than 2,000 times.

I don't know how you would fold **or** unfold a battery!

③ **Pick the choice that makes sense!**

In context, only **choice C** makes any sense. Let's choose **C**.

# VOCAB IN CONTEXT PASSAGE
## 10 QUESTIONS

**Questions 1-10 are based on the following passage.**

"Weather" in clusters of galaxies may explain a longstanding puzzle, according to a team of researchers at the University of Cambridge. The scientists used
Line sophisticated simulations to show how powerful jets
5 from supermassive black holes are disrupted by the motion of hot gas and galaxies, preventing gas from cooling, which could otherwise form stars. Typical clusters of galaxies have several thousand member galaxies, which can be very different from our own
10 Milky Way and vary in size and shape. These systems live in very hot gas known as the intracluster medium (ICM) in an unseen halo of so-called 'dark matter'.

A large number of galaxies have supermassive black holes in their centers, and these often have high-speed
15 jets of material stretching over thousands of light years that can inflate very hot lobes in the ICM.

The researchers, based at the Kavli Institute for Cosmology and Institute of Astronomy, performed state-of-the-art simulations looking at the jet lobes
20 in fine detail and the X-rays emitted as a result. The model captures the birth and cosmological evolution of the galaxy cluster, and allowed the scientists to investigate with unprecedented realism how the jets and lobes they inflate interact with a dynamic ICM.
25 They found that the mock X-ray observations of the simulated cluster revealed the so-called "X-ray cavities" and "X-ray bright rims" generated by supermassive black hole-driven jets, which themselves are distorted by motions in the cluster, remarkably resemble those
30 found in observations of real galaxy clusters.

"We have developed new computational techniques, which harness the latest high-performance computing technology, to model for the first time the jet lobes with more than a million elements in fully
35 realistic clusters. This allows us to place the physical processes that drive the liberation of the jet energy under the microscope," said team leader Dr Martin Bourne.

The simulation shows that galaxies create a kind of
40 'weather' as they move around in the cluster,, moving, deforming, and destroying the hot lobes of gas found at the end of the black hole jets. The jet lobes are enormously powerful and, if disrupted, deliver vast amounts of energy to the ICM.
45 The Cambridge team believes that this cluster weather disruption mechanism may solve an enduring problem: understanding why ICM gas does not cool and form stars in the cluster center. This so-called "cooling flow" puzzle has plagued astrophysicists for
50 more than 25 years.

The simulations performed provide a tantalizing new solution that could solve this problem. Dr Bourne commented: "The combination of the huge energies pumped into the jet lobes by the supermassive black
55 hole and the ability of cluster weather to disrupt the lobes and redistribute this energy to the ICM provides a simple and yet elegant mechanism to solve the cooling flow problem."

**1**

The author places "weather" in quotation marks in the first sentence primarily to

A)  suggest that rain could exist in deep space.

B)  offer a familiar frame of reference for an abstract concept.

C)  imply that some galactic puzzles may never be solved.

D)  sarcastically denounce the idea of weather in galactic clusters.

**2**

As used in line 7, "form" most nearly means

A)  create.

B)  model.

C)  outline.

D)  harden.

**3**

As used in line 20, "fine" most nearly means

A)  classy.

B)  powdered.

C)  sharp.

D)  fragile.

**4**

The words "live" and "birth" (lines 11 and 21) convey a sense that

A) the scientists feel confident in their results as they have discovered the origin of dark matter.
B) the origins of dark matter are unknown and are likely to remain a mystery.
C) galaxies have life cycles similar to those of living things.
D) dark matter can contain previously undiscovered alien life.

**5**

The phrase "unprecedented realism" in line 23 most strongly implies that the model

A) could not have been created without recent advances in technology.
B) improves upon previous models that were too fantastical to be useful.
C) will allow scientists to accurately predict the formation of galaxies in the ICM.
D) more closely resemble true-to-life conditions than past models.

**6**

As used in line 28, "distorted" most nearly means

A) shredded.
B) altered.
C) ruined.
D) inverted.

**7**

As used in line 36, "drive" most nearly means

A) motivate.
B) control.
C) strike.
D) chase.

**8**

As used in line 43, "disrupted" most nearly means

A) unsettled.
B) distracted.
C) annoyed.
D) misdirected.

**9**

In line 49, "plagued" most nearly means

A) sickened.
B) frustrated.
C) harmed.
D) infested.

**10**

In line 54, "pumped" most nearly means

A) diffused.
B) dismissed.
C) encouraged.
D) forced.

*Answers can be found at the bottom of page 88.*

# Reading Graphs

*The science passages contain questions that require you to combine your reading of the passage with information in charts, tables, or graphs.*

## Go Figure!

The Natural and Social Science passages often include a chart, table, or graph that illustrates data relevant to the passage. For example, you might read a scientific report on temperature trends in the Himalayas, and then see a line graph of yearly temperatures. The exact type of figure changes passage-to-passage, so it's helpful to step back from any one particular figure and focus on what they all have in common, and how those similarities will help you answer the questions.

On the Reading section, graph-reading questions ask you to combine information from the passage with information from the figures. To do this, you want to ask some key questions about the figures:

1. *What **groups** are being compared?*

2. *How are the groups being **measured**?*

3. *What **conclusions** can we draw?*

## Always read the titles

Before we dive into any of the above questions, we should emphasize one, all-helpful rule: **read the titles of the figures!** Seriously, there is no faster way to get a sense of what you're looking at than to read the title of the graph or figure. After all, when someone *wrote* that title, they had to consider the groups, the measurements, and the conclusions all at once!

## What *groups* are being compared?

**TIP**

There can be, and in fact often are, more than two groups. A line graph plotting temperatures for each month of the year would be comparing **12 different groups**.

Graphs and tables are fantastic ways of illustrating how different groups are, well, different! The first thing you want to identify in a figure is what exactly those different groups are. If we're comparing temperatures in June with temperatures in December, then "June" and "December" would be our groups. If we're comparing reaction times between male and female mice, then "male mice" and "female mice" would be our groups.

In **tables**, you can spot the groups by looking at the **row/column labels**. In the table below, we're comparing "Swallowtails", "Monarchs", and "Other", as well as "Shady Grove" and "Johnson Park":

Number of Butterflies

| Groups → | Shady Grove | Johnson Park |
|---|---|---|
| **Swallowtails** | 12 | 6 |
| **Monarchs** | 18 | 10 |
| **Other** | 7 | 5 |

In **graphs**, you can often spot groups in **the legend** or on the **x-axis**. In the bar graph below, we're comparing "untreated" and "treated" peaches, as well as "open air" and "laboratory" locations:

Effect of Treatment on Peach Diameter

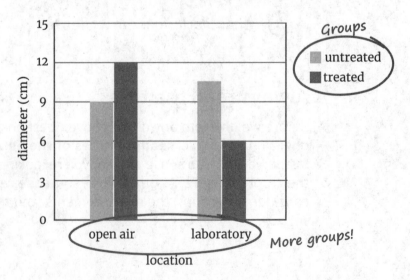

*Answers to Vocab in Context Passage:*

| | | | | |
|---|---|---|---|---|
| 1. B | 2. A | 3. C | 4. C | 5. D |
| 6. B | 7. B | 8. A | 9. B | 10. D |

## How are the groups being *measured*?

Once you've identified the groups being compared, the next step is to identify how those groups are being measured. If we're comparing temperatures for June and December, then temperature (in °C or °F) is our measurement.

In **tables**, the best place to look for measurements is in the title or in header cells. In the table below, the title tells us that the data reflects the "number of butterflies" of each type and in each location:

*measurement*

| **Number** of Butterflies | Shady Grove | Johnson Park |
| --- | --- | --- |
| Swallowtails | 12 | 6 |
| Monarchs | 18 | 10 |
| Other | 7 | 5 |

In **graphs**, the best place to look for measurements is in the **axis labels** – particularly the *y-axis label*. In the graph below, just glancing at the y-axis label tells us the peaches are being compared by a measurement of their diameters, in centimeters.

Effect of Treatment on Peach Diameter

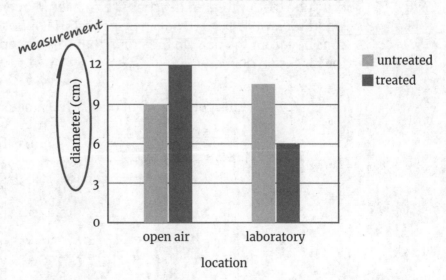

## What *conclusions* can we draw?

The last step is the most important one: identify what conclusions can be drawn from the figure. This often boils down to simply noticing which group scores higher or lower on the measurement, or if there is an overall upward or downward trend. For conclusions, the best place to look is in the **meat of the graph itself**: What trends are in the data? Where are the highest and lowest points? Is one group consistently higher than another? If not, why not?

In **tables**, look for rows or columns (groups) that consistently contain bigger values than the other rows or columns. In the table below, we can conclude that there are more butterflies in Shady Grove than in Johnson Park, and more Monarchs than other types of butterflies:

Number of Butterflies

|  | Shady Grove | Johnson Park |
|---|---|---|
| Swallowtails | 12 | 6 |
| Monarchs | 18 | 10 |
| Other | 7 | 5 |

*Biggest row* (Monarchs)

*Biggest column* (Shady Grove)

In **graphs**, look for groups that measure higher or lower than other groups, or for general trends in the data. In the graph below, we can conclude that untreated peaches are smaller in open air than in the laboratory, while treated peaches are just the opposite. We can also conclude from the peak in the graph that treated, open air peaches are the biggest in diameter:

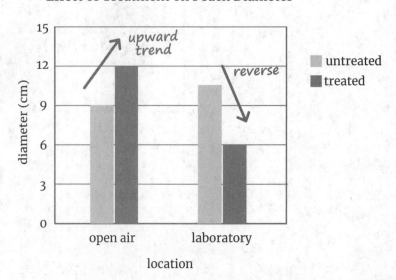

Effect of Treatment on Peach Diameter

## Author's Opinion

Sometimes the figure or graph was not part of the original passage, but added by the test writers. In these cases, the test writer may ask you to infer the author's opinion on the graph. It's OK if the author would likely DISAGREE with the data, or find issues with the study design. Don't assume the opinion will always be positive!

## Strategy: let the question guide you

There are multiple conclusions you could draw and observations you could make about a figure, but only one or two of them will actually come up! It's much easier (and faster) to wait until a question asks you about a table or graph. Those questions will have key words that point you to a specific group or data point on the graph, which lets you narrow your focus and more quickly find the answer. For example, a question might ask of our butterfly table:

**TIP**

You don't need to understand the graph until you **need** to understand the graph. When you finish actively reading a passage with figures, don't spend time deciphering their content just yet; instead, **jump to the questions**.

**TIP**

Often, you'll use information in the figure *and* the passage to answer a question. Use your active reading notes to **match words** in the question with words in the passage.

1. The <u>table</u> provides support for which of the following statements about <u>Swallowtail butterflies</u>?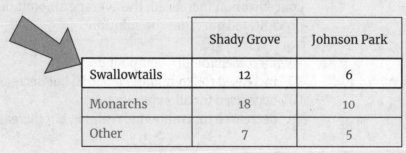

In that case, we would know to focus our attention to the **Swallowtail** row in the table:

Number of Butterflies

|  | Shady Grove | Johnson Park |
|---|---|---|
| Swallowtails | 12 | 6 |
| Monarchs | 18 | 10 |
| Other | 7 | 5 |

This becomes particularly helpful when the figures contain large amounts of distracting data. So remember: **let the question guide your focus!**

## EXAMPLES 1 & 2

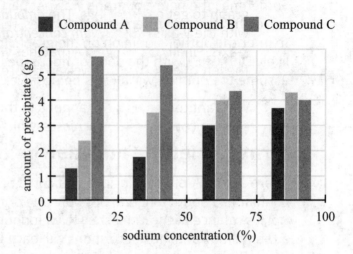

1. According to the graph, which statement best describes the change in the amount of precipitate in Compound A as the sodium concentration increased?

   A)  The amount always increased.
   B)  The amount always decreased.
   C)  The amount first increased, then decreased.
   D)  The amount varied with no discernable trend.

2. According to the results shown in the graph, as the sodium concentration increased, the average amount of crystalline salt that precipitated out from the solution

   A)  increased for all 3 compounds.
   B)  increased for compound A and B, but decreased for compound C.
   C)  decreased for all 3 compounds.
   D)  decreased for compound A and B, but increased for compound C.

SOLUTION

1. First, we should **match words** in the question with words in the graph to get our bearings. The *amount of precipitate* matches with the *y*-axis, and *sodium concentration* matches with the *x*-axis. Finally, *Compound A* matches with the dark grey bar on the left of each group—we can ignore the rest.

   We want to know what happens to the the dark grey bar as sodium concentration *increases*, which happens as we move right along the x-axis. It get taller each time, which means the amount of precipitate only increases as concentration increases. Choice A is best.

2. A glance at the answer choices for question 2 tells us we need to look at all three compounds (each grey bar on the graph). Do they follow the same trend as Compound A? Compound B sure does, but Compound C has the opposite trend: it shows a decrease in precipitate as sodium concentration increases. That means our best answer is choice B.

## EXAMPLE 3

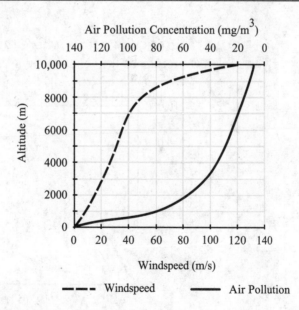

3. According to the figure, what is the windspeed at an altitude of 3,000 meters?

   A) 20 m/s
   B) 40 m/s
   C) 100 m/s
   D) 120 m/s

SOLUTION

This one is tougher! We need to find a specific point on the graph using the clues in the question, but notice that there are <u>two</u> x-axes. One is for windspeed, and one is for air pollution.

We can match **3,000 meters** with the y-axis and **windspeed** with the dashed line and <u>bottom</u> axis. Ignore the rest! Let's draw a line from 3,000 meters until we hit the dashed line for windspeed.

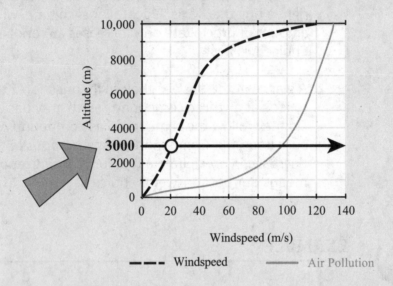

Now we can track down from where the dashed line intersects with 3,000 meters to find that our windspeed is **20 m/s**.

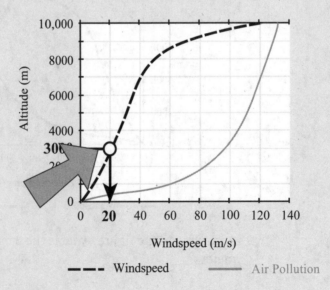

A

# Short Passage Practice

*Read the short passage below, study the graph, and answer questions 1-3.*

A key issue in cooperation research is to determine the conditions under which individuals invest in a public good. Here, we tested whether cues of being watched increase investments in an anonymous public good

5 situation in real life. We examined whether individuals would invest more by removing experimentally placed garbage (paper and plastic bottles) from bus stop benches in Geneva in the presence of images of eyes compared to controls (images of flowers). We provided separate bins

10 for each of both types of garbage to investigate whether individuals would deposit more items into the appropriate bin in the presence of eyes.

The treatment had no effect on the likelihood that individuals present at the bus stop would remove gar-

15 bage. However, those individuals that engaged in garbage clearing, and were thus likely affected by the treatment, invested more time to do so in the presence of eyes. Images of eyes had a direct effect on behaviour, rather than merely enhancing attention towards a symbolic sign

20 requesting removal of garbage. These findings show that simple images of eyes can trigger reputational effects that significantly enhance on non-monetary investments in anonymous public goods under real life conditions. Our results in the light of previous findings and suggest that human social behaviour may often be shaped by rel-

25 atively simple and potentially unconscious mechanisms instead of very complex cognitive capacities..

1. According to the figure, the median handling duration for the group in the presence of an image of eyes was how many seconds longer than the median handling duration for for the group in the presence of an image of flowers?

   A) 0.2
   B) 3.0
   C) 5.0
   D) 8.0

2. According to the passage and accompanying graph, individuals in the presence of an image of eyes

   A) were more likely to remove garbage from the bus stop than those who were in the presence of an image of flowers.
   B) were less likely to remove garbage from the bus stop than those who were in the presence of an image of flowers.
   C) removed more pieces of garbage from the bus stop than those who were in the presence of an image of flowers.
   D) spent a longer time cleaning than the individuals who cleaned in the presence of an image of flowers.

3. Which choice provides the best evidence for the answer to the previous question?

   A) Lines 1-3 ("A key ... good")
   B) Lines 5-9 ("We examined ... flowers")
   C) Lines 13-15 ("The treatment ... garbage")
   D) Lines 15-17 ("However, ... eyes")

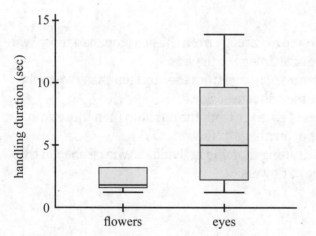

Note: The black horizontal line inside each box denotes the median value for that experimental group.

# Explanations

*Answers & explanations for Short Passage Practice (Reading Graphs)*

........................................................................................................................

1. According to the figure, the <u>median</u> handling duration for the group in the presence of an image of <u>eyes</u> was <u>how many seconds longer</u> than the <u>median</u> handling duration for for the group in the presence of an image of flowers?

   A) 0.2
   B) 3.0
   C) 5.0
   D) 8.0

   > Matching words in the prompt with the figure, we see a match for *median* in the note below the graph: median is the dark horizontal line inside each box. This median line for the "eyes" box appears to line up with about 5 seconds on the y-axis; the median line for the "flowers" box appears to line up with about 2 seconds (a difference of about 3 seconds). That means **choice B** accurately describes the graph.

2. According to the passage and accompanying graph, individuals in the presence of an image of eyes

   A) were more likely to remove garbage from the bus stop than those who were in the presence of an image of flowers.
   B) were less likely to remove garbage from the bus stop than those who were in the presence of an image of flowers.
   C) removed more pieces of garbage from the bus stop than those who were in the presence of an image of flowers.
   D) spent a longer time cleaning than the individuals who cleaned in the presence of an image of flowers.

**3.** Which choice provides the best evidence for the answer to the previous question?

A) Lines 1–3 ("A key ... good")
B) Lines 5–9 ("We examined ... flowers")
C) Lines 13–15 ("The treatment ... garbage")
D) Lines 15–17 ("However, ... eyes")

Questions 2 and 3 are an Evidence-Based pair, so we should answer them together. Let's check the choices in question 3 for lines that describe the behavior of individuals in the presence of an image of eyes. Choice D gives us the best information:

> *However, those individuals that engaged in garbage clearing, and were thus likely affected by the treatment, invested more time to do so in the presence of eyes.*

So, we now know that individuals who cleared garbage in the presence of an image of eyes spent more time doing it than those in the presence of an image of flowers. This matches perfectly with choice D in question 2! That gives us both answers.

# Reading Practice Passage 3
## TO STAY ON PACE, YOUR TIMING GOAL IS 13 MINUTES

Each passage or pair of passages below is followed by a number of questions. After reading each passage or pair, choose the best answer to each question based on what is stated or implied in the passage or passages and in any accompanying graphics (such as a table or graph).

**Questions 1-11 are based on the following passage.**

This passage is adapted from Mary Hoff, "What's Behind the Spread of White Syndrome in Great Barrier Reef Corals?" © 2007 Public Library of Science.

Coral reefs, among Earth's richest ecosystems, traditionally teem with an abundance of life. The tiny corals that form the foundation of the community are
Line microcosms themselves, sheltering single-celled algae
5 that feed the community with energy from the sun. The three-dimensional physical space they create with their skeletons supports an astounding array of other animals, from sponges to sharks.

But in recent years, corals have been dying in droves.
10 Scientists suspect a variety of factors, ranging from accidental damage from fishing activity to the effects of polluted runoff from land. One threat that appears to be growing dramatically in Australia's famed Great Barrier Reef is white syndrome, a mystery-riddled disease that
15 is spreading rapidly, leaving stripes of dead corals like ribbons of death in its wake. But why?

Global warming seems a likely suspect for several reasons. Past epidemiological studies across a broad range of life forms have shown that stress—including
20 the stress of changing environmental conditions—often increases disease susceptibility. As temperatures rise, pathogens can reproduce more quickly. The fact that coral diseases seem to spread faster in summer also provides support for the notion that warmer
25 temperatures may be involved.

In hope of improving understanding of the spread of white syndrome, John Bruno, Amy Melendy, and colleagues conducted a regional-scale longitudinal study of the hypothesized link between warm temperature
30 deviations and the presence of white syndrome,

considering the density of coral cover as an additional variable of interest.

To quantify temperature fluctuations, the researchers used a high-resolution dataset on ocean surface
35 temperature provided by the United States National Oceanic and Atmospheric Association and the University of Miami. They used the dataset to calculate weekly sea surface temperature anomalies (WSSTAs)—instances in which temperature was higher by 1°C or more from
40 mean records for that week—for 48 reefs within the Great Barrier Reef. To evaluate the extent of white syndrome and coral cover, the researchers used data collected by the Australian Institute of Marine Science Long-term Monitoring Program on 48 reefs from a 1,500-kilometer
45 stretch of the Great Barrier Reef from 1998 to 2004 at a depth of 6 to 9 meters. Divers counted the number of infected colonies on each reef. Coral cover, the amount of the bottom with living corals, was measured from videos taken of the reefs.

50 The researchers then evaluated the relationship between the occurrence of white syndrome and three variables: number of WSSTAs occurring during the previous 52 weeks, coral cover, and the interaction between the two. They found that the third variable
55 showed a statistically significant correlation with number of white syndrome cases, indicating that the presence of both conditions—temperature anomalies and high coral cover—creates the conditions in which white syndrome outbreaks are most likely to occur. In other words,
60 WSSTAs were a necessary but not sufficient condition for white syndrome outbreaks, whereas the combination of heat stress and a dense colony was deadly.

What does this mean for corals and the ecosystem they support? If global warming increases the incidence
65 of warm temperature anomalies in tropical oceans in the years ahead, these results suggest that corals

CONTINUE ➡

in high-cover areas will be increasingly vulnerable to white disease. If the effect is large enough, the tightly woven web of life within coral reefs could begin to
70 unravel, potentially transforming habitats that were once among the planet's richest ecosystems into underwater wastelands.

This strong evidence for a link among a warming ocean, coral density, and white syndrome provides a rich
75 foundation for further work to understand the spread of coral disease in the Great Barrier Reef. It also provides valuable insights into marine epidemiology that could be of much value in investigating and potentially mitigating other devastating global-warming-related disease
80 outbreaks in the world's vast and vulnerable oceans.

**1**

The main purpose of the passage is to discuss how coral reefs are dying from

A) a rapidly spreading disease.
B) chemical runoff from land.
C) disturbance due to fishing activity.
D) climate change alone.

**2**

Which choice provides the best evidence for the answer to the previous question?

A) Lines 2-6 ("The tiny … sun")
B) Lines 10-12 ("Scientists … land")
C) Lines 12-16 ("One … wake")
D) Lines 17-18 ("Global … reasons")

**3**

In line 7, "supports" most nearly means

A) bears weight.
B) encourages.
C) props up.
D) sustains.

Yearly sea surface temperature anomaly 1950-2011

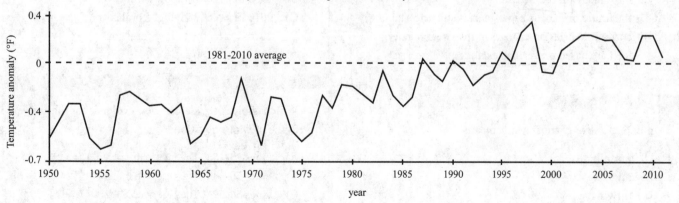

CONTINUE

99

**4**

According to the passage, the number of coral colonies affected by white syndrome was determined by

A) a dataset provided by Bruno, Melendy, and team.

B) divers who tallied and recorded their observations.

C) high-resolution technology directed towards a specific locale.

D) a cooperative effort between scientists from many nations.

**5**

Which choice provides the best evidence for the answer to the previous question?

A) Lines 33-37 ("To quantify … Miami")

B) Lines 37-41 ("They … Great Barrier Reef")

C) Lines 46-47 ("Divers … reef")

D) Lines 47-49 ("Coral … reefs")

**6**

The use of the words "If," "suggest," and "potentially" in the seventh paragraph (lines 63-72) serves to emphasize that

A) Bruno, et al., continue to analyze information that will predict the fate of coral reefs.

B) the information obtained by the United States National Oceanic and Atmospheric Association is most likely inaccurate.

C) the future of marine ecosystems is still uncertain.

D) current theories on changes in the Great Barrier Reef are based on verifiable data.

**7**

In line 73, "strong" most nearly means

A) meaningful.

B) mighty.

C) thriving.

D) aggressive.

**8**

According to the data in the figure, the greatest above-average temperature variation occurred around what year?

A) 1955

B) 1969

C) 1987

D) 1998

**9**

Which statement is best supported by the information provided in the figure?

A) After 2010, weekly sea surface temperature anomalies will decrease.

B) The steady increase in sea surface temperature over the past five decades suggests an increase in the amount of coral cover on ocean floors.

C) Before 2000, the yearly sea surface temperature was always below the 1981-2010 average.

D) Since 2001, the yearly sea surface temperature has always been above the 1981-2010 average.

**10**

Based on the information in the passage and the figure, a white syndrome outbreak most likely occurred during

A) 1955 in a reef with high coral cover.

B) 1955 in a reef with low coral cover.

C) 2010 in a reef with high coral cover.

D) 2010 in a reef with low coral cover.

**11**

Which choice provides the best evidence for the answer to the previous question?

A) Lines 23-25 ("The fact … involved")

B) Lines 50-54 ("The researchers … two")

C) Lines 54-59 ("They … occur")

D) Lines 68-72 ("If the … wastelands")

# Explanations

*Answers & explanations for Reading Practice Passage 3*

1. The main purpose of the passage is to discuss how coral reefs are dying from

   (A) a rapidly spreading disease.
   B) chemical runoff from land.
   C) disturbance due to fishing activity.
   D) climate change alone.

2. Which choice provides the best evidence for the answer to the previous question?

   A) Lines 2–6 ("The tiny ... sun")
   B) Lines 10–12 ("Scientists ... land")
   (C) Lines 12–16 ("One ... wake")
   D) Lines 17–18 ("Global ... reasons")

Let's try our brand new paired question strategy! According to Q1, we need a quote that explicitly mentions the cause of the coral's demise. Looking at the four options, only **choice C**, lines 12-16, mentions coral reefs dying:

> "One threat that appears to be growing dramatically in Australia's famed Great Barrier Reef is white syndrome, *a mystery-riddled disease* that is spreading rapidly, leaving stripes of *dead corals* like ribbons of death in its wake."

Now we need a match for "mystery-riddled disease that is spreading rapidly" in Q1's answer choices. **Choice A** is perfect!

3. In line 7, "supports" most nearly means

   A) bears weight.
   B) encourages.
   C) props up.
   D) sustains.

First, we need to look at the word in context:

> *"The three-dimensional physical space they create with their skeletons **supports** an astounding array of other animals, from sponges to sharks."*

If we plug "**sustains**" into the sentence, the meaning stays the same. **Choice D** is correct!

> *"The three-dimensional physical space they create with their skeletons **sustains** an astounding array of other animals, from sponges to sharks."*

4. According to the passage, the number of coral colonies affected by white syndrome was determined by

   A) a dataset provided by Bruno, Melendy, and team.
   B) divers who tallied and recorded their observations.
   C) high-resolution technology directed towards a specific locale.
   D) a cooperative effort between scientists from many nations.

5. Which choice provides the best evidence for the answer to the previous question?

   A) Lines 33-37 ("To quantify ... Miami")
   B) Lines 37-41 ("They ... Great Barrier Reef")
   C) Lines 46-47 ("Divers ... reef")
   D) Lines 47-49 ("Coral ... reefs")

We can use our paired question strategy to evaluate the quotes in Q5 to find the answer to both questions. We need to find the quote that tells us how they determine the number of coral colonies affected by white syndrome. **Choice C**, lines 46-47, clearly tells us that the scientists used data collected by divers. In Q4, **choice B** tells us that "divers" collected the data.

6. The use of the words "If," "suggest," and "potentially" in the seventh paragraph (lines 63-72) serves to emphasize that

   A) Bruno, et al. continue to analyze information that will predict the fate of ~~coral reefs~~.
   B) the information obtained by the United States National Oceanic and Atmospheric Association is most likely ~~inaccurate~~.
   C) the future of marine ecosystems is still uncertain.
   D) current theories on changes in ~~the Great Barrier Reef~~ are based on verifiable data.

The seventh paragraph extends the scope from the coral reefs to the entire marine ecosystem. The words listed modify the statements to acknowledge that the negative outcome *could* happen. **Choice C** gives us a great match: "uncertain" matches "if," "suggest," and "potentially."

7. In line 73, "strong" most nearly means

   A) meaningful.
   B) mighty.
   C) thriving.
   D) aggressive.

First, we need to read the word in context:

> "This **strong** evidence for a link among a warming ocean, coral density, and white syndrome provides a rich foundation for further work to understand the spread of coral disease in the Great Barrier Reef."

"Strong" modifies the evidence, so we need to pick an answer that would logically modify evidence. Only "**meaningful**" makes sense as a modifier for evidence. **Choice A** is correct.

> "This **meaningful** evidence for a link among a warming ocean, coral density, and white syndrome provides a rich foundation for further work to understand the spread of coral disease in the Great Barrier Reef."

8. According to the data in the figure, the greatest above-average temperature variation occurred around what year?

A) 1955
B) 1969
C) 1987
D) 1998

All we have to do is look for the **tallest peak** above the average temperature variation. Although it's difficult to determine the exact year of the peak, if we look at the answer choices, only **1998** is close, so **choice D** must be answer!

9. Which statement is best supported by the information provided in the figure?

A) After 2010, weekly sea surface temperature anomalies will decrease.
B) The steady increase in sea surface temperature over the past five decades suggests an increase in the amount of coral cover on ocean floors.
C) Before 2000, the yearly sea surface temperature was always below the 1981-2010 average.
D) Since 2001, the yearly sea surface temperature has always been above the 1981-2010 average.

For this question, we need to evaluate each answer choice and see which one most closely matches the information in the figure. Choice A is an assumption; the graph shows that the surface temperature anomaly is decreasing after 2010, but will it continue to decrease? We can't predict the future, so we can't choose A.

Choice B is also an assumption; there has been an increase over the past 50 years, but we **cannot** say that there has also been an increase in coral cover. Coral cover could be increasing, but we don't know that based on this graph.

Choice C is incorrect because the line is above the 1981-2010 average from 1994-1999.

Only **choice D** is supported by the figure; after 2001, the line stays above the 1981-2010 average.

10. Based on the information in the passage and the figure, a white syndrome outbreak most likely occurred during

    A) 1955 in a reef with high coral cover.
    B) 1955 in a reef with low coral cover.
    C) 2010 in a reef with high coral cover.
    D) 2010 in a reef with low coral cover.

11. Which choice provides the best evidence for the answer to the previous question?

    A) Lines 23-25 ("The fact ... involved")
    B) Lines 50-54 ("The researchers ... two")
    C) Lines 54-59 ("They ... occur")
    D) Lines 68-72 ("If the ... wastelands")

Using our paired question strategy will help us answer this paired set. Let's look at Q11's choices to find a quote that mentions white syndrome outbreak. **Choice C**, lines 54-59, says:

> *"They found that the third variable showed a statistically significant correlation with number of white syndrome cases, indicating that the presence of both conditions—temperature anomalies and high coral cover—creates the conditions in which white syndrome outbreaks are most likely to occur."*

Now let's find a match in Q10. We know we need high coral cover, so we can cross off B and D. But what about temperature anomalies?

Lines 38-40 tell us that temperature anomalies are "instances in which temperature was **higher** by 1°C or more from mean records for that week." 1955 (choice A) had a temperature anomaly **lower** than average, and 2010 (choice C) had a temperature anomaly **higher** than average. **Choice C**, high coral cover and 2010, a year with higher temperature anomaly, fits the passage and the figure.

# UNIT

# Passage Types

## Chapters

## Overview

In this unit, we'll learn about the different **types of passages** you'll see on the SAT: Literature, Politics, Natural Science, Social Science, and Comparison. Use the passages to practice your strategy and timing. Make note of which passage types you prefer; you can choose to do your favorite passage types first on test day!

# Literature

*Let's get some practice with two Literature passages.*

The first passage of the Reading section, the Literature passage, is a **narrative** that could be from olden times or nowadays. We've seen passages from the 1800s with fancy words like "hitherto," but we've also seen contemporary passages. You may have even read the passage before in school; famous authors like Jane Austen and Charlotte Bronte have shown up on the test.

## TIP

Remember, you can save the hardest passage for last so you don't waste time and energy. Each question is worth the same, so focus on the easy points first!

## Tips for Active Reading

Here are some key things to look out for when reading this passage.

- **Introduction:** The test writer often puts helpful context in the introduction above the first paragraph. Note the <u>date</u> listed here as it will clue you into what kind of language to expect.

- **Point-of-view:** Who is the narrator? Is the story in first-person ("I"), second-person ("You"), or third-person ("She")?

- **Character names:** There will only be a few characters in the story, but you'll need to know who is who!

- **Change in attitude:** To create an interesting story, characters often go on emotional journeys, shifting attitudes throughout the tale. Pay attention to the characters' and narrator's attitude shifts.

- **Changes in time or location:** The SAT likes passages that jump around in time or location. Make a note anytime this happens.

- **Figurative language:** If the narrator calls her home "an oasis in a desert of hopelessness," then you can expect that the test writers want you to understand how that metaphor relates to the story.

# Literature Passage 1

## TO STAY ON PACE, YOUR TIMING GOAL IS 13 MINUTES

Each passage or pair of passages below is followed by a number of questions. After reading each passage or pair, choose the best answer to each question based on what is stated or implied in the passage or passages and in any accompanying graphics (such as a table or graph).

**Questions 1-10 are based on the following passage.**

The passage is adapted from Getrude Atherton, *The Striding Place*, originally published as *The Twins* in 1896.

Weigall, continental and detached, tired early of grouse shooting. To stand propped against a sod fence while his host's workmen routed up the birds with long
Line poles and drove them towards the waiting guns, made
5 him feel himself a parody on the ancestors who had roamed the moors and forests of this West Riding of Yorkshire in hot pursuit of game worth the killing. But when in England in August he always accepted whatever proffered for the season, and invited his host to shoot
10 pheasants on his estates in the South. The amusements of life, he argued, should be accepted with the same philosophy as its ills.

It had been a bad day. A heavy rain had made the moor so spongy that it fairly sprang beneath the feet.
15 Whether or not the grouse had haunts of their own, wherein they were immune from rheumatism, the bag had been small. The women, too, were an unusually dull lot, with the exception of a new-minded debutante who bothered Weigall at dinner by demanding the verbal
20 restoration of the vague paintings on the vaulted roof above them.

But it was no one of these things that sat on Weigall's mind as, when the other men went up to bed, he let himself out of the castle and sauntered down to the river.
25 His intimate friend, the companion of his boyhood, the chum of his college days, his fellow-traveller in many lands, the man for whom he possessed stronger affection than for all men, had mysteriously disappeared two days ago, and his track might have sprung to the upper air
30 for all trace he had left behind him. He had been a guest on the adjoining estate during the past week, shooting with the fervor of the true sportsman, making love in the

intervals to Adeline Cavan, and apparently in the best of spirits. As far as was known there was nothing to lower
35 his mental mercury, for his rent-roll was a large one, Miss Cavan blushed whenever he looked at her, and, being one of the best shots in England, he was never happier than in August. The suicide theory was preposterous, all agreed, and there was as little reason to believe him murdered.
40 Nevertheless, he had walked out of March Abbey two nights ago without hat or overcoat, and had not been seen since.

The country was being patrolled night and day. A hundred keepers and workmen were beating the woods
45 and poking the bogs on the moors, but as yet not so much as a handkerchief had been found.

Weigall did not believe for a moment that Wyatt Gifford was dead, and although it was impossible not to be affected by the general uneasiness, he was disposed
50 to be more angry than frightened. At Cambridge Gifford had been an incorrigible practical joker, and by no means had outgrown the habit; it would be like him to cut across the country in his evening clothes, board a cattle-train, and amuse himself touching up the picture of the
55 sensation in West Riding.

However, Weigall's affection for his friend was too deep to companion with tranquillity in the present state of doubt, and, instead of going to bed early with the other men, he determined to walk until ready for sleep. He
60 went down to the river and followed the path through the woods. There was no moon, but the stars sprinkled their cold light upon the pretty belt of water flowing placidly past wood and ruin, between green masses of overhanging rocks or sloping banks tangled with tree and
65 shrub, leaping occasionally over stones with the harsh notes of an angry scold, to recover its equanimity the moment the way was clear again.

CONTINUE

**1**

The passage as a whole transitions from

A) a pastoral vacation to a climactic adventure.

B) a hunting mishap to a long-term consequence of that mishap.

C) an uninspired outdoor excursion to a compelling mystery.

D) a character analysis of the protagonist to a character analysis of his rival.

**2**

Weigall's interest in Wyatt can best be described as

A) reasonable concern for a missing close friend.

B) pathological obsession ruining Weigall's vacation.

C) frenzied overreaction to an easily explained event.

D) sly subterfuge to cover Weigall's sinister motives.

**3**

Weigall finds grouse-hunting to be

A) a predictable endeavor as the birds always take the same path.

B) an ironic charade as his servants do most of the work.

C) a distraction that keeps him from discovering Wyatt's whereabouts.

D) a necessity made unpleasant by the poor weather.

**4**

Which choice best provides the best evidence for the answer to the previous question?

A) Lines 1-2 ("Weigall…shooting.")

B) Lines 2-7 ("To stand…killing.")

C) Lines 13-14 ("A heavy…feet.")

D) Lines 15-17 ("Whether…small.")

**5**

In line 11, "accepted" most nearly means

A) embraced.

B) paid for.

C) acquired.

D) affirmed.

**6**

Weigall considers Wyatt's disappearance peculiar because

A) Wyatt likes to play practical jokes.

B) Wyatt embarrassed Miss Cavan.

C) if Wyatt left on his own accord, he left some essentials.

D) Wyatt tired of grouse hunting.

**7**

Which choice best provides the best evidence for the answer to the previous question?

A) Lines 22-24 ("But…river.")

B) Lines 35-36 ("Miss Cavan…her,")

C) Lines 40-42 ("Nevertheless…since.")

D) Lines 50-52 ("At Cambridge…habit")

**8**

In lines 34-35, "there was nothing to lower his mental mercury" suggests that

A) Wyatt may have been poisoned.

B) Miss Cavan may be involved in Wyatt's disappearance.

C) Wyatt was concerned about his finances while on vacation.

D) Wyatt was in good spirits before he went missing.

9

In line 44, "beating" most nearly means

A) abusing.
B) scouring.
C) fighting.
D) defeating.

10

In lines 65-66, "harsh notes of an angry scold" refers to

A) Weigall's temperament while his hunts in the woods.
B) the sounds made by nocturnal creatures.
C) the behavior of an otherwise calm stream.
D) Weigall's belabored breathing from chasing Wyatt through the woods.

## STOP
**If you finish before time is called, you may check your work on this section only.**
**Do not turn to any other section.**

# Explanations

Answers & explanations for Literature Passage 1

1. The passage as a whole transitions from

   A) a pastoral vacation to a ~~climactic~~ adventure.
   B) a hunting ~~mishap~~ to a long-term consequence of that mishap.
   C) an uninspired outdoor excursion to a compelling mystery.
   D) a character analysis of the protagonist to a character analysis of his ~~rival~~.

> The first two paragraphs discuss Weigall's boring hunting trip; the passage then transitions to a focus on the mystery of his missing friend, Wyatt. Choice C nicely sums up the passage.

2. Weigall's interest in Wyatt can best be described as

   A) reasonable concern for a missing close friend.
   B) ~~pathological obsession~~ ruining Weigall's vacation.
   C) ~~frenzied overreaction~~ to an easily explained event.
   D) sly subterfuge to cover Weigall's ~~sinister motives~~.

> We can find the best evidence for Weigall's feelings towards Wyatt on lines 25-28:
>
> *His intimate friend, the companion of his boyhood, the chum of his college days, his fellow-traveller in many lands, the man for whom he possessed stronger affection than for all men...*
>
> Choices B, C, and D add a level of intrigue that is not supported by the passage, so choice A is the best and most reasonable answer.

3. Weigall finds grouse-hunting to be

   A)   a predictable endeavor as the birds ~~always~~ take the same path.
   B)   an ironic charade as his servants do most of the work.
   C)   a ~~distraction~~ that keeps him from discovering Wyatt's whereabouts.
   D)   a ~~necessity~~ made unpleasant by the poor weather.

4. Which choice best provides the best evidence for the answer to the previous question?

   A)   Line 1-2 ("Weigall...shooting.")
   B)   Line 2-7 ("To stand...killing.")
   C)   Line 13-14 ("A heavy... feet.")
   D)   Line 15-17 ("Whether... small.")

> We should answer Questions 3 and 4 together. We need to check the choices in Question 4 for lines about grouse-hunting. Choice B points us to the best evidence, where Weigall feels like "a parody" of his ancestors when his "workmen" are wrangling the birds towards him. These lines match choice B in Question 3, as "ironic charade" is similar to "parody" in this context.

5. In line 11, "accepted" most nearly means

   A)   embraced.
   B)   paid for.
   C)   acquired.
   D)   affirmed.

> We need to look at the word in context:
>
> > *The amusements of life, he argued, should be <u>accepted</u> with the same philosophy as its ills.*
>
> Weigall goes with the flow of life, so "embraced" is the best match for accepted in this context.

6. Weigall considers Wyatt's disappearance peculiar because

   A) Wyatt likes to play practical jokes.
   B) Wyatt embarrassed Miss Cavan.
   C) if Wyatt left on his own accord, he left some essentials.
   D) Wyatt tired of grouse hunting.

7. Which choice best provides the best evidence for the answer to the previous question?

   A) Lines 22-24 ("But...river.")
   B) Lines 35-36 ("Miss Cavan...her")
   C) Lines 40-42 ("Nevertheless, ...since.")
   D) Lines 50-52 ("At Cambridge ...habit")

We should answer these questions together. We need to check Question 7 for lines that focus on the peculiarity of Wyatt's disappearance, which means we need to find evidence that Wyatt going missing is a *surprise*. Lines 40-42 tell us that Wyatt oddly left without his hat or overcoat.

Choice D is not correct because it offers an *explanation* for Wyatt's behavior rather than build the mystery. Now that we know choice C is best for Question 7, we can see that choice C is a strong match for Question 6.

8. In lines 34-35, "there was nothing to lower his mental mercury," suggests that

   A) Wyatt may have been ~~poisoned~~.
   B) Miss Cavan may be ~~involved~~ in Wyatt's disappearance.
   C) Wyatt was ~~concerned~~ about his finances while on vacation.
   D) Wyatt was in good spirits before he went missing.

Let's look at the phrase in context:

> As far as was known there was nothing to lower his mental mercury, for his rent-roll was a large one, Miss Cavan blushed whenever he looked at her, and, being one of the best shots in England, he was never happier than in August.

It sounds like Wyatt was having a *good time* on vacation. The author uses "mercury" figuratively as a metaphor for his mental temperature or well-being. Choice D best explains this intent.

9. In line 44, "beating" most nearly means

   A) abusing.
   B) scouring.
   C) fighting.
   D) defeating.

We'll need to look at the word in context:

> The country was being patrolled night and day. A hundred keepers and workmen were _beating_ the woods and poking the bogs on the moors, but as yet not so much as a handkerchief had been found.

A bunch of people are looking for Wyatt, so _scouring_ makes the most sense in this context.

10. In line 65, "harsh notes of an angry scold" refers to

   A) Weigall's ~~temperament~~ while his hunts in the woods.
   B) the sounds made by nocturnal ~~creatures~~.
   C) the behavior of an otherwise calm stream.
   D) Weigall's ~~belabored breathing~~ from chasing Wyatt through the woods.

This phrase is in a long sentence; we should read it in its entirety to get the proper context:

> There was no moon, but the stars sprinkled their cold light upon the pretty belt of water flowing placidly past wood and ruin, between green masses of overhanging rocks or sloping banks tangled with tree and shrub, leaping occasionally over stones with the _harsh notes of an angry scold_, to recover its equanimity the moment the way was clear again.

This sentence is describing a "pretty belt of water," which is just a fancy way of describing a stream. The harsh notes happen when the water rushes over the rocks, so choice C is best.

# Literature Passage 2
## TO STAY ON PACE, YOUR TIMING GOAL IS 13 MINUTES

**Questions 1-10 are based on the following passage.**

The passage is adapted from Ansley Lane, *13*, originally published in 2019.

Svane recommended to Ava that she get some sleep while he drove her and Nikki to the Appalachian mountains for the weekend. He said she should rest,
Line especially now the norepinephrine and cortisol from her
5 very first near-death encounter were surely dying down. She had almost been flattened by a foolhardy driver, but it was Svane who had pulled her back and then gone to confront and defuse the reckless man. Ava reckoned Svane had been more fatigued than her, so she stayed
10 awake with him as he drove, chattering happily while he responded with tacit amusement.

While they drove up I-575, Ava regaled him with an account of how, for the first five years of her life, she thought snow was intrinsic to Christmas. Unfortunately,
15 it didn't often snow on the southeastern coast, at least not until January or February. When she was two, surrounded by presents and family yet looking forlornly out the window at the snowless lawn, her father went and purchased a snow machine; actually, he got her ten.
20 It was somewhat excessive, and she admitted as much, wondering aloud how he amassed that many snow machines on Christmas Day. But she slowly recognized how it sounded and apologized for prattling about it now.

Svane just smiled; Ava was sheltered, but it was
25 endearing to him. Her lifestyle hadn't spoiled her—she was too considerate of others to be considered spoiled— but it hadn't equipped her for his lifestyle. Despite this, she seemed to be taking it in stride; she was more resilient than he gave her credit for.
30 Ava was well aware of the privilege surrounding her upbringing. Her parents owned an enormous estate in an equestrian neighborhood, and while her neighbors actually owned horses, her family did not. "We are not horse people," Ava's mother Anita had said, though what
35 she meant was that horses required upkeep and attention and Anita would prefer to socialize and have their acres of yard immaculately landscaped. Ava had always felt marginally embarrassed by the excess.

Svane had also been brought up in ridiculous wealth,
40 but luxury came at great personal cost for him. He didn't have a great childhood—life in a royal family, with the bureaucracy, affectation, and hierarchy at court, had been tense and unorthodox—but Christmastime evoked his warmest memories.
45 Svane wasn't even his name, but rather an arcane royal title. Ava had known that he was a prince of a small, prosperous, and spectacularly corrupt European country. The talk about his past led her to cautiously ask more questions about his title, the manner of his emigration
50 from his homeland, and how he got where he was today.

He said it was nothing confidential, but he'd rather not talk about it now.

She asked if he'd divulge more information to her sometime.
55 He promised her an unabridged version that weekend, but now he wanted to keep things light.

So, graciously, she turned the focus back to Christmas.

The reclusive Nikki sat silently in the back, her eyes
60 cutting back and forth between the two of them and occasionally pausing hungrily on a half-full bag of chips. (She had been fed, but the feral child was never sated).

They were swerving around the roads cut into the Appalachian Mountains now, delivering Nikki to her
65 father. The wintery weather had bared the terrain, making the curves of the mountainsides and their smoky horizons visible.

Ava went quiet for a while, gazing out at the grey, unadorned trees and watching some antlerless deer
70 make the uncanny sprint up the steep slopes, bounding upwards, effortlessly violating the laws of gravity. She peered over the side of the road, spotting a small creek winding down the valley.

Calmly, out of curiosity, she wondered whether the
75 Hummer would roll all the way down to those narrow valley floors should it swerve off-road and pitch down the mountainside. Or were the trees thick and strong enough to stop it? Sometimes, while her attention was diverted, Svane would sneak a glance at her, scarcely cognizant of
80 what he was doing.

Meanwhile, Ava was coming out of her lackadaisical, observational state, realizing that she hadn't seen any other vehicles or any infrastructure for a while. The mountains looked the same…no, they were untouched…
85 Now the roads were just dirt and mud, roughly hewn, and Svane had to stay in a four-wheel-drive just to traverse the landscape. It perplexed her; it didn't make sense.

They had passed through Helen, Georgia earlier —
90 she recognized the little German-style town — so they should be in North Carolina now, or should at least have passed some lakes.

"Where are we?" She wondered out loud as they wound deeper into the wilderness.
95 "Home," Nikki softly stated.

**1**

The passage can best be described as

A) a tense journey as three characters attempt to avoid their difficult pasts.

B) a trip through the mountains interspersed with details about the characters' histories.

C) a character's recollection of Christmastime and a summary of others' reactions.

D) a character impatiently attempting to return home but encountering distractions along the way.

**2**

The primary goal of the characters in the passage is to

A) reunite Nikki with her father.

B) learn more about the characters' Christmastime traditions.

C) visit the mountains and reconnect with nature.

D) calm Ava after surviving a dangerous encounter.

**3**

Ava and Svane are similar in that they both

A) are deeply concerned about the welfare of Nikki.

B) are fleeing difficult memories.

C) come from affluent families.

D) hide their past from their current companions.

**4**

Which choice provides the best evidence that Ava became self-conscious about her Christmas story?

A) Lines 13-14 ("she...Christmas")

B) Line 19 ("actually...ten")

C) Lines 22-23 ("But she...now")

D) Line 39 ("Svane...wealth")

**5**

As used in line 12, "regaled" most nearly means

A) honored.

B) praised.

C) impressed.

D) amused.

**6**

The passage most strongly supports which statement about how Svane feels about his upbringing?

A)  Svane's royal upbringing is something he must keep hidden for the safety of all.

B)  Svane was born into a royal family, but he found that noble position unpleasant.

C)  Svane escaped his strict upbringing and has chosen an unconventional life focused on helping others.

D)  Svane would like to talk more about his past, but he is concerned about how it could affect his family back home.

**7**

Which choice provides the best evidence for the previous question?

A)  Lines 41-43 ("life...unorthodox")

B)  Lines 46-47 ("Ava...country")

C)  Lines 51-52 ("He said...now")

D)  Lines 55-56 ("He promised...weekend")

**8**

As used in line 57, "focus" most nearly means

A)  goal.

B)  discussion.

C)  target.

D)  examination.

**9**

In the context of the passage as a whole, what does the fifteenth paragraph (lines 74-80) add to the narrative?

A)  It implies that Ava is anxious about how Svane drives through the mountains.

B)  It allows Ava to imagine what it feels like to be one of the deer on the mountainside.

C)  It uses a quiet moment to develop the character of Ava and Svane.

D)  It confirms that Ava still feels anxious about the near-death encounter that happened earlier.

**10**

The town of Helen, Georgia primarily serves as

A)  a location that reminds Ava of fond Christmas memories.

B)  Ava's last point of reference before arriving into unknown wilderness.

C)  a town that Ava had hoped they would visit during the trip.

D)  the final destination of their road trip.

# Explanations

*Answers & explanations for Literature Passage 2*

1. The passage can best be described as

   A) a ~~tense~~ journey as three characters attempt to ~~avoid~~ their difficult pasts.
   B) a trip through the mountains interspersed with details about the characters' histories.
   C) a character's recollection of Christmastime and a ~~summary of others' reactions~~.
   D) a character ~~impatiently~~ attempting to return home but encountering distractions along the way.

   We need to think about the passage as a *whole*. The characters are travelling through the mountains, which allows them time to develop their backstories. Choices A and D misrepresent the tone of the passage, and choice C focuses only on the second and third paragraph. Choice B is spot on.

2. The primary goal of the characters in the passage is to

   A) reunite Nikki with her father.
   B) ~~learn more~~ about the characters' Christmastime traditions.
   C) visit the mountains and ~~reconnect with nature~~.
   D) ~~calm Ava~~ after surviving a dangerous encounter.

   The passage describes a road trip, so the goal is their location. We can find that evidence in lines 63-65:

   *They were swerving around the roads cut in the Appalachian Mountains now, delivering Nikki to her father.*

   Choice A is a clear match!

**119**

3. Ava and Svane are similar in that they both

   A) are ~~deeply concerned~~ about the welfare of Nikki.
   B) are ~~fleeing~~ difficult memories.
   C) come from affluent families.
   D) ~~hide their past~~ from their current companions.

We can find evidence for choice C in line 39:

> *Svane had also been brought up in <u>ridiculous wealth</u>*

4. Which choice provides the best evidence that Ava became self-conscious about her Christmas story?

   A) Lines 13-14 ("she...Christmas")
   B) Line 19 ("actually...machines")
   C) Lines 22-23 ("But she...now")
   D) Line 39 ("Svane...wealth")

We've got a Onesie, so we need to focus on what *this* question asks and ignore Question 3. Lines 22-23 describe that Ava felt self-conscious, making choice C a great answer:

> *But she slowly recognized how it sounded and apologized for prattling about it now.*

5. As used in line 12, "regaled" most nearly means

   A) honored.
   B) praised.
   C) impressed.
   D) amused.

First, let's read the word in context:

> *While they drove up I-575, Ava <u>regaled</u> him with an account of how, for the first five years of her life, she thought snow was intrinsic to Christmas.*

She's telling a story to pass the time, so choice D is the best match.

6. The passage most strongly supports which statement about how Svane feels about his upbringing?

A) Svane's royal upbringing is something he ~~must keep hidden~~ for the safety of all.
B) Svane was born into a royal family, but he found that noble position unpleasant.
C) Svane escaped his strict upbringing and has chosen an unconventional life focused on ~~helping others~~.
D) Svane would like to talk more about his past, but he is concerned about how it could ~~affect his family~~ back home.

7. Which choice provides the best evidence for the previous question?

A) Lines 41–43 ("life...unorthodox")
B) Lines 46–47 ("Ava...country")
C) Lines 51–52 ("He said...now")
D) Lines 55–56 ("He promised...weekend")

We should answer Questions 6 and 7 together. We need to focus on how Svane *feels*. Lines 41-43 provide the best evidence for his feelings:

> *...life in a royal family, with the bureaucracy, affectation, and hierarchy at court, had been tense and unorthodox...*

Sounds like Svane did not like growing up in a royal family. Going back to Question 6, choice B best captures his feelings.

8. As used in line 57, "focus" most nearly means

A) goal.
B) discussion.
C) target.
D) examination.

Let's look at the word in context:

> *So, graciously, she turned the focus back to Christmas.*

The characters have been have a discussion about Christmas, so choice B is the best fit.

9. In the context of the passage as a whole, what does the fifthteenth paragraph (lines 74-80) add to the narrative?

   A) It implies that Ava is anxious about how Svane drives through the mountains.
   B) It allows Ava to imagine what it feels like to be one of the deer on the mountainside.
   C) It uses a quiet moment to develop the character of Ava and Svane.
   D) It confirms that Ava still feels anxious about the near-death encounter that happened earlier.

Let's look at the fifteenth paragraph:

> *Calmly, out of curiosity, she wondered whether the Hummer would roll all the way down to those narrow valley floors should it swerve off-road and pitch down the mountainside. Or were the trees thick and strong enough to stop it? Sometimes, while her attention was diverted, Svane would sneak a glance at her, scarcely cognizant of what he was doing.*

The first part of the paragraph is about Ava's internal thoughts and then the second part is about Svane's actions. Choice C best encapsulates this paragraph: it's a calm moment that gives us some insight into two characters.

10. The town of Helen, Georgia primarily serves as

   A) a location that reminds Ava of fond Christmas memories.
   B) Ava's last point of reference before arriving into unknown wilderness.
   C) a town that Ava had hoped they would visit during the trip.
   D) the final destination of their road trip.

Let's look at the reference to Helen, Georgia in context:

> *The mountains looked the same...no, they were untouched... Now the roads were just dirt and mud, roughly hewn, and Svane had to stay in a four-wheel-drive just to traverse the landscape. It perplexed her; it didn't make sense.*

They had passed through Helen, Georgia earlier—she recognized the little German-style town—so they should be in North Carolina now, or should at least have passed some lakes. In context, Helen is just the last town that Ava recognized, so choice B is the best match.

# Politics

*Let's get some practice with two Politics passages.*

## TIP

The older the passage, the more difficult it may be for modern readers. Don't hesitate to leave this passage for last!

The politics passage might be an excerpt from a book or essay, a political speech, or even a letter. These sources can be as recent as the 1990s or as old as pre-Revolutionary War times.

Writings from these time periods can vary dramatically, so **always read the intro text** above the passage. This text contains crucial information that will help you understand the paragraphs to come. Make note of the **date** the passage was written to put it in historical context. A passage about slavery written in 1860 will have a different perspective than one written in 1800!

## TIP

It's not crucial that you recognize the author from history class, but it can help you identify his or her thesis.

## Tips for Active Reading

Here are some key things to look out for when reading this passage.

- **Introduction:** The test writer often puts helpful context in the introduction above the first paragraph. Note the <u>date</u> listed here as it will clue you into what kind of language to expect.

- **Thesis:** What is the author's main point? What are they trying to *persuade* you to think? Be aware that an argument can be like a roller coaster; there may be twists and turns before the author makes his or her final point clear.

- **Transition Words:** Circle words that signal the author is about to make a point, like *therefore*, *however*, and *but*.

- **Problem and Solution:** What problem or issue was the author addressing? What was his or her proposed solution?

## U.S. History Primer

While the SAT doesn't ask questions that draw upon outside knowledge, having some historical context for the politics passage can make things easier. If you've never taken US history, or haven't studied it in a while, the next several pages offer a brief overview of topics likely to show up on the politics passage.

# America: The Experiment (~1770-1819)

The United States of America was founded by English colonists who felt exploited by England. Political leaders— many of them philosophers and theorists inspired by the Enlightenment—had been debating different forms of government and the boundaries of personal freedom. Once the Revolutionary War ended, these "founding fathers" then debated how to most effectively establish a new democratic government.

The SAT will occasionally pull passages written by these thinkers; if you see an 18th Century publication date, expect an exploration of the *rights of man* and the *purpose of government*. Let's look at some **common terms** and documents from this time period:

- **American Revolutionary War (1775-1783):** Conflicts between English soldiers and American militias would eventually led to full blown war. The result would be the 13 colonies establishing the United States of America.

- *Common Sense* **(1776):** this pamphlet, written by Thomas Paine, argued that the colonies should be independent.

- *Declaration of Independence* **(1776):** written by Thomas Jefferson, this document announced the colonies' separation from England. It established the principles expressed in the US constitution and led to England declaring war on the colonies.

- *Articles of Confederation* **(1777):** this document, once ratified in 1881, established a government amongst the states. It caused some friction between states over trade and economy.

- *The Constitution of the United States* **(1789):** this document established a stronger national government with "checks and balances" across **three branches**: the *Executive* branch (the President and his cabinet), the *Legislative* branch (the Senate and the House of Representatives), and the *Judiciary* branch (the Supreme Court).

- *Bill of Rights* **(1791):** the first ten amendments to the Constitution, outlining the rights of citizens the government could not violate.

- **Federalism:** a form of government where several states cede some (but not all) power to a national authority.

# Challenging Slavery and Suffrage (1820-1865)

By 1820, activists began to challenge two limitations on civil rights: **slavery** and a **woman's inability to vote**. While the latter would not find conclusion until the 20th Century, the fight over slavery led to civil war.

Let's look at some **common terms** and documents from this time period:

- **The Missouri Compromise (1820):** an agreement that allowed the Missouri territory to enter the Union as a slave state and also set limits on slavery across western territories. It was the first of many attempts to maintain balance between slave and free states as the US expanded westward. The policy ended up creating a greater divide between northern free states and southern slave states, which would eventually erupt into the Civil War.

- *The Liberator* **(1831-1865):** a newspaper that was at the center of the anti-slavery movement.

- **The Seneca Falls Convention (1848):** established the women's voting rights issue at a national level.

- **The American Civil War (1861-1865):** after 11 Southern states formed the Confederate States of America, tensions with the Northern Union states eventually erupted into war. After many bloody years of war, the Union proved victorious. All of the Confederate states were absorbed back into the Union and slavery was outlawed in America.

- *The Emancipation Proclamation* **(1863):** issued by President Abraham Lincoln in 1863, this document freed all slaves in Confederate controlled areas. It initially did not affect slavery in Union loyal slave states, over fears of increased rebellion.

- **Abolitionist:** a person who supports the end of slavery

- **Secession:** the act of a state leaving the Union; this led to the formation of the Confederate States of America and the Civil War.

- **Suffrage:** the right to vote

- **Suffragette:** a woman fighting for the right to vote

# TIP

*Suffrage* does NOT mean the same thing as *suffering*!

## Progress and Suppression (1866-1920)

The end of the Civil War began the era of Reconstruction: an attempt to rebuild the South. While slavery remained abolished, white Southerners enacted laws to continually suppress the rights of African Americans.

In the late 19th Century, the United States underwent rapid growth. Industrialization brought great wealth to some businessmen but difficult working and housing conditions to many laborers. From this mix emerged the Progressive movement, which aimed to fix these social ills.

Let's look at some **common terms** and documents from this time period:

**gild (verb):**

to cover in a thin layer of gold in order to hide a cheaper metal

- **The Reconstruction Era (1865-1877):** a time marked by attempts to rebuild the Confederate states and transition away from a slave-based economy.

- **The Gilded Age:** a term, coined by the author Mark Twain, which highlights the contrast between the new wealth of some and the impoverished conditions of many

- **The Progressive Movement (1890-1920):** fought to improve the social problems of the day. It was a mix of causes, including labor rights, child welfare, urban sanitation, and civil rights.

- **The Great Migration (1916-1930):** a period in which millions of African Americans moved from the South to Northern cities to find work and greater freedom.

- **The 19th Amendment (1920):** ratified in 1920, this amendment to the Constitution gave women the right to vote nationwide.

- **Jim Crow laws:** laws that limited the rights of African Americans.

- **Ku Klux Klan:** a secret organization started during Reconstruction used to oppress and terrorize African Americans.

- **Robber Baron:** derogatory term for an industrialist who exploits workers and customers.

- **Segregation:** policies and laws used to separate white and black Americans and limit the freedoms of African Americans.

# Democracy and Human Rights (1920-2000)

World War II would see the US emerge as a global superpower shaping international policy and engaging in an ideological war with the Soviet Union. As the United States promoted freedom and democracy abroad, its citizens continued to remove the shackles of instituitional discrimination and social inequity.

Let's look at some **common terms** from this time period:

- **The Great Depression (1929-1939):** the one-two punch of the 1929 stock market crash and record-breaking drought in the Midwest led to prolonged unemployment.

- **The New Deal (1933-1939):** a wide-reaching set of Federal programs and reforms aimed at creating jobs and improving economic stability.

- **World War II (1939-1945):** the US remained neutral until the attack on Pearl Harbor, Hawaii, in 1941. By helping the Allied powers win, the US became a political and economic global power.

- **The Cold War (1947-1991):** the US and the Soviet Union (USSR) became the two superpowers after World War II. While the two countries did not engage in direct conflict, the ideological divide led to military build up and proxy wars fought in smaller nations.

- **The Marshall Plan (1948):** a policy to support rebuilding Europe in hopes of reducing Soviet influence and creating stable allies.

- **The Civil Rights Movement (1954-1968):** following landmark court decisions, African American leaders effectively challenged segregation laws through non-violent protests.

- **The Vietnam War (1964-1975):** a controversial and unsuccessful proxy war where the US attempted to limit the spread of communism. The unpopularity of the war and the non-voluntary military draft led to widespread protests among the youth.

- **Watergate (1972-1974):** a major political scandal that led to the resignation of President Richard Nixon.

# International Human Rights (1940-Present)

The SAT can include non-American texts focused on other discussions of human rights. Here are some key terms that could show up.

- **The United Nations (Founded in 1945):** an intergovernmental organization founded after World War II to reduce conflicts and further communication across nations. Speeches on human rights that were given to the United Nations can show up on the test.

- **Indian Independence (1947):** led by Mahatma Gandhi, this movement was instrumental in popularizing non-violent protests.

- **South African Apartheid (1948-1994):** a strict system of segregation against black Africans. Nelson Mandela, the leader of the anti-apartheid movement was imprisoned throughout most of the 60s until the 80s. Upon the end of apartheid in 1994, Mandela was democratically elected the President of South Africa.

# Politics Passage 1

## TO STAY ON PACE, YOUR TIMING GOAL IS 13 MINUTES

**DIRECTIONS**

Each passage or pair of passages below is followed by a number of questions. After reading each passage or pair, choose the best answer to each question based on what is stated or implied in the passage or passages and in any accompanying graphics (such as a table or graph).

**Questions 1-10 are based on the following passage.**

This passage is adapted from Elizabeth Cady Stanton, Susan B. Anthony, and Matilda Joslyn Gage, *History of Women's Suffrage, Volume 1*. Originally published in 1881.

The prolonged slavery of woman is the darkest page in human history. A survey of the condition of woman through those barbarous periods, when physical force
Line governed the world, when the motto, "might makes
5 right," was the law, enables one to account for the origin of woman's subjection to man without referring the fact to the general inferiority of the sex, or Nature's law.

One of the greatest minds of the century has thrown a ray of light on this gloomy picture by tracing the origin
10 of woman's slavery to the same principle of selfishness and love of power in man that has thus far dominated all weaker nations and classes. This brings hope of final emancipation, for as all nations and classes are gradually, one after another, asserting and maintaining their
15 independence, the path is clear for woman to follow. The slavish instinct of an oppressed class has led her to toil patiently through the ages, giving all and asking little, cheerfully sharing with man all perils and privations by land and sea, that husband and sons might attain honor
20 and success. Justice and freedom for herself is her latest and highest demand.

Another writer asserts that the tyranny of man over woman has its roots, after all, in his nobler feelings; his love, his chivalry, and his desire to protect woman in the
25 barbarous periods of pillage and war. But wherever the roots may be traced, the results at this hour are equally disastrous to woman. Her best interests and happiness do not seem to have been consulted in the arrangements made for her protection. But if a chivalrous desire to

30 protect woman has always been the mainspring of man's dominion over her, it should have prompted him to place in her hands the same weapons of defense he has found to be most effective against wrong and oppression.

It is often asserted that as woman has always been
35 man's slave—subject—inferior—dependent, under all forms of government and religion, slavery must be her normal condition. This might have some weight had not the vast majority of men also been enslaved for centuries to kings and popes, and orders of nobility, who, in the
40 progress of civilization, have reached complete equality. And did we not also see the great changes in woman's condition, the marvelous transformation in her character, from a drudge in the fields to a leader of thought in the literary circles of France, England, and America!

45 Woman's steady march onward, and her growing desire for a broader outlook, prove that she has not reached her normal condition, and that society has not yet conceded all that is necessary for its attainment.

Moreover, woman's discontent increases in exact
50 proportion to her development. Instead of a feeling of gratitude for rights accorded, the wisest are indignant at the assumption of any legal disability based on sex, and their feelings in this matter are a surer test of what her nature demands than the feelings and prejudices of the
55 sex claiming to be superior.

The broader demand for political rights has not commanded the thought its merits and dignity should have secured. While complaining of many wrongs and oppressions, women themselves did not see that the
60 political disability of sex was the cause of all their special grievances, and that to secure equality anywhere, it must be recognized everywhere. Like all disenfranchised classes, they begun by asking to have certain wrongs redressed, and not by asserting their own right to make
65 laws for themselves.

**CONTINUE** ▶

Overburdened with cares in the isolated home, women had not the time, education, opportunity, and pecuniary independence to put their thoughts clearly and concisely into propositions, nor the courage to compare
70 their opinions with one another, nor to publish them, to any great extent, to the world.

**1**

The authors suggest that one explanation for the oppression of women comes from

A) a natural inequality between men and women.

B) a miscommunication regarding cultural ideals.

C) a leftover notion of protection from an earlier era.

D) an unwillingness for either side to compromise.

**2**

Which choice provides the best evidence for the answer in the previous question?

A) Lines 12-15 ("This ... follow")

B) Lines 22-25 ("Another ... war")

C) Lines 37-40 ("This ... equality")

D) Lines 62-65 ("Like ... themselves")

**3**

The reference to a "final emancipation" acknowledges

A) the end of the abolitionist movement.

B) a universal desire for rights.

C) that women have led the charge for civil rights.

D) the civil rights era had come to a conclusion.

**4**

In line 43, "drudge" most nearly means

A) burden.

B) trowel.

C) laborer.

D) crop.

**5**

The author's repeated use of the phrase "normal condition" most strongly suggests

A) there is an underlying desire to oppress others.

B) that gender equality should be the natural order in society.

C) that most women at the time lacked worldly experience.

D) when gender equality happens, it will lead to many financial rewards.

**6**

The seventh paragraph (lines 56-65) is primarily concerned with

A) encouraging women to participate politically.

B) suggesting that political disempowerment is the root of oppression.

C) refuting the claim that women are politically uninformed.

D) chastising women for not engaging in political activism.

**7**

In line 57, "thought" most nearly means

A) assumption.

B) idea.

C) imagination.

D) consideration.

**8**

The passage states that the process of gaining rights begins with

A) widespread protests and disruptions of social norms.

B) disenfranchised people asking to make laws for themselves.

C) an appeal to have specific wrongs set right.

D) an acknowledgment that any limitations on rights came from a well-meaning place.

CONTINUE ▶

The authors relate which of the following paradoxes regarding women's rights?

A) Women are more subjugated now than during earlier barbaric times.

B) With more rights having been gained, women now desire more direction from male authority.

C) The recent gains made in women's rights have only intensified the desire for equality.

D) Activists have disobeyed unjust laws in order to indirectly change those laws.

Which choices provides the best evidence that domestic responsibilities have impacted women's activism?

A) Lines 2-7 ("A survey … Nature's law")

B) Lines 15-20 ("The slavish … success")

C) Lines 50-55 ("Instead … superior")

D) Lines 66-71 (" Overburdened … the world")

# STOP

**If you finish before time is called, you may check your work on this section only.**
**Do not turn to any other section.**

# Explanations

*Answers & explanations for Politics Passage 1*

...........................................................................................................................

1. The authors suggest that one explanation for the oppression of women comes from

   A) a natural inequality between men and women.
   B) a miscommunication regarding cultural ideals.
   C) a leftover notion of protection from an earlier era.
   D) an unwillingness for either side to compromise.

2. Which choice provides the best evidence for the answer in the previous question?

   A) Lines 12–15 ("This ... follow")
   B) Lines 22–25 ("Another ... war")
   C) Lines 37–40 ("This ... equality")
   D) Lines 62–65 ("Like ... themselves")

   We need to answer Questions 1 and 2 together. Q1 gives us the clue that we're looking for "one explanation of the oppression of women." In Q2, **choice B**, lines 22-25, mentions the **roots** of oppression coming from **nobler feelings** from **barbarous periods**.

   Now we can match that with an answer choice in Q1. **Choice C** is great! Oppression is leftover from an earlier, more barbarous age.

3. The reference to a "final emancipation" acknowledges

   A) the end of the abolitionist movement.
   B) a universal desire for rights.
   C) that women have led the charge for civil rights.
   D) the civil rights era had come to a conclusion.

Let's look at the phrase in context:

> *"This brings hope of **final emancipation**, for as all nations and classes are gradually, one after another, asserting and maintaining their independence, the path is clear for woman to follow."*

The sentence talks about **all nations and classes**, so we need an answer that includes everybody. **Choice B** is perfect. "Universal" certainly includes everyone!

4. In line 43, "drudge" most nearly means

A) burden.
B) trowel.
C) laborer.
D) crop.

Let's look at the word in context:

> *"And did we not also see the great changes in woman's condition, the marvelous transformation in her character, from a **drudge** in the fields to a leader of thought in the literary circles of France, England, and America!"*

We want a word that replaces "drudge" in the context. "Laborer" works best in context, since drudge must represent a person.

> *"... from a **laborer** in the fields to a leader of thought in the literary circles of France, England, and America!"*

**Choice C** is correct.

5. The author's repeated use of the phrase "normal condition" most strongly suggests

A) there is an underlying ~~desire to oppress others~~.
B) that gender equality should be the natural order in society.
C) that most women at the time ~~lacked worldly experience~~.
D) when gender equality happens, it will lead to many ~~financial rewards~~.

First, let's look at the phrase "normal condition" in context. We find it in lines 45-48:

> Woman's steady march onward, and her growing desire
> for a broader outlook, prove that she has not reached
> her <u>normal condition</u>, and that society has not yet
> conceded all that is necessary for its attainment.

The **desire** for more rights proves that the only normal condition is complete equality. **Choice B is spot on!** **Gender equality** should be the **normal condition**.

6. The seventh paragraph (lines 56-65) is primarily concerned with

A) ~~encouraging~~ women to participate politically.
B) suggesting that political disempowerment is the root of oppression.
C) ~~refuting~~ the claim that women are politically uninformed.
D) ~~chastising~~ women for not engaging in political activism.

The seventh paragraph states that "**political** disability of sex was the **cause** of all their special **grievances**." This means we need an answer that addresses the relationship between political power and oppression. **Choice B** is the best. "Political disempowerment" has led to the inequality.

7. In line 57, "thought" most nearly means

A) assumption.
B) idea.
C) imagination.
D) consideration.

Let's look at word in context:

> "The broader demand for political rights has not commanded
> the **thought** its merits and dignity should have secured."

The authors use "thought" to mean "to think over," or ponder. Let's plug in "consideration," which is the closest to our guess:

> *The broader demand for political rights has not commanded the **consideration** its merits and dignity should have secured.*

**Choice D** is correct!

8. The passage states that the process of gaining rights begins with

    A) widespread protests and ~~disruptions~~ of social norms.
    B) disenfranchised people asking to make laws for ~~themselves~~.
    C) an appeal to have specific wrongs set right.
    D) an acknowledgment that any limitations on rights came from a ~~well-meaning place~~.

The passage addresses this process on lines 62-65:

> *Like all disenfranchised classes, they begun by asking to have certain wrongs redressed, and not by asserting their own right to make laws for themselves.*

**Choice B** certainly matches this statement, so that's our answer!

9. The authors relate which of the following paradoxes regarding women's rights?

   A) Women are ~~more subjugated~~ now than during earlier barbaric times.
   B) With more rights having been gained, women now desire ~~more direction from male authority~~.
   C) The recent gains made in women's rights have only intensified the desire for equality.
   D) Activists have disobeyed unjust laws in order to ~~indirectly~~ change those laws.

> We need to look for a "paradox," or a statement that seems contradictory, about women's rights. We can find the evidence on lines 50-55:
>
> *Instead of a feeling of gratitude for rights accorded, the wisest are indignant at the assumption of any legal disability based on sex, and their feelings in this matter are a surer test of what her nature demands than the feelings and prejudices of the sex claiming to be superior.*
>
> Choice C is perfect. Yes, there have been gains, but those gains have only created the desire for greater equality.

10. Which choices provides the best evidence that domestic responsibilities have impacted women's activism?

    A) Lines 2-7 ("A survey ... Nature's law")
    B) Lines 15-20 ("The slavish ... success")
    C) Lines 50-55 ("Instead ... superior")
    D) Lines 66-71 (" Overburdened ... the world")

> This is a sneaky Onesie evidence based question. If you thought it was a pair, then you may have picked choice C, as it does provide support for question 9. But if we focus on the question asked, how "domestic responsibilities have impacted women's activism" then clearly choice D is correct.

# Politics Passage 2
## TO STAY ON PACE, YOUR TIMING GOAL IS 13 MINUTES

Each passage or pair of passages below is followed by a number of questions. After reading each passage or pair, choose the best answer to each question based on what is stated or implied in the passage or passages and in any accompanying graphics (such as a table or graph).

**Questions 1-10 are based on the following passage.**

The passage is adapted from Paul Nitze, "National Security Council Paper 68." Written in 1950 as a top-secret document, the paper offers an analysis of the Soviet Union and international politics in the aftermath of World War II.

The Soviet Union regards the United States as the only major threat to the achievement of its fundamental design. There is a basic conflict between the idea of
Line freedom under a government of laws, and the idea of
5 slavery under the firm oligarchy of the Soviets, which has come to a crisis with the polarization of power, and the exclusive possession of atomic weapons by the two protagonists. The idea of freedom, moreover, is peculiarly and intolerably subversive of the idea of slavery. But the
10 converse is not true. The implacable purpose of the slave state to eliminate the challenge of freedom has placed the two great powers at opposite poles. It is this fact which gives the present polarization of power the quality of crisis.
15 The free society values the individual as an end in himself, requiring of him only that measure of self discipline and self restraint which make the rights of each individual compatible with the rights of all. The freedom of the individual has its counterpart, therefore, the
20 negative responsibility of the individual not to exercise his freedom in ways inconsistent with the freedom of other individuals and the positive responsibility to use his freedom in the building of a just society.
From this idea of freedom with responsibility
25 derives the marvelous diversity, the deep tolerance, the lawfulness of the free society. This is the explanation of the strength of free men. It constitutes the integrity and the vitality of a free and democratic system. The free

society attempts to create and maintain an environment
30 in which every individual has the opportunity to realize his creative powers. It also explains why the free society tolerates those within it who would use their freedom to destroy it. By the same token, in relations between nations, the prime reliance of the free society is on the
35 strength and appeal of its idea, and it feels no compulsion sooner or later to bring all societies into conformity with it.
For the free society does not fear, it welcomes, diversity. It derives its strength from its hospitality even
40 to antipathetic ideas. It is a market for free trade in ideas, secure in its faith that free men will take the best wares, and grow to a fuller and better realization of their powers in exercising their choice.
The idea of freedom is the most contagious idea in
45 history, more contagious than the idea of submission to authority. For the breath of freedom cannot be tolerated in a society which has come under the domination of a group of individuals with a will to absolute power. Where the despot holds absolute power--the absolute
50 power of the absolutely powerful will--all other wills must be subjugated in an act of willing submission, a degradation willed by the individual upon himself under the compulsion of a perverted faith. It is the first article of this faith that he finds and can only find the meaning
55 of his existence in serving the ends of the system. The system becomes God, and submission to the will of God becomes submission to the will of the system.
The same compulsion which demands total power over all men within the Soviet state without a single
60 exception, demands total power over all Communist Parties and all states under Soviet domination. The "peace policy" of the Soviet Union, described at a Party Congress as "a more advantageous form of fighting capitalism," is a device to divide and immobilize the

CONTINUE

65 non-Communist world, and the peace the Soviet Union seeks is the peace of total conformity to Soviet policy.

The antipathy of slavery to freedom explains the iron curtain; the isolation, the autarchy of the society whose end is absolute power. The existence and persistence of
70 the idea of freedom is a permanent and continuous threat to the foundation of the slave society; and it therefore regards as intolerable the long continued existence of freedom in the world. What is new, what makes the continuing crisis, is the polarization of power which
75 inescapably confronts the slave society with the free.

The assault on free institutions is world-wide now, and in the context of the present polarization of power, a defeat of free institutions anywhere is a defeat everywhere. Thus unwillingly our free society finds
80 itself mortally challenged by the Soviet system. No other value system is so wholly irreconcilable with ours, so implacable in its purpose to destroy ours, so capable of turning to its own uses the most dangerous and divisive trends in our own society, no other so skillfully and
85 powerfully evokes the elements of irrationality in human nature everywhere, and no other has the support of a great and growing center of military.

**1**

An important goal of the passage is to

A) define a critical contrast.
B) criticize a longstanding policy.
C) analyze a novel philosophy.
D) denounce undue military aggression.

**2**

The tone of the passage can best be described as

A) apprehensive and uncertain.
B) aggressive and frazzled.
C) analytical and indifferent.
D) decisive and determined.

**3**

The author of the passages believes that the Soviets view freedom as

A) irrelevant to their greater goal of world peace.
B) a concept that greatly undermines their main goals.
C) widely popular and quick to spread.
D) a means to increase diversity within nations.

**4**

Which choice provides the best evidence for the previous question?

A) Lines 15-16 ("The free...himself")
B) Lines 44-46 ("The idea...authority.")
C) Lines 61-65 ("The 'peace policy'...world")
D) Lines 69-73 ("The existence...world")

**5**

The author views diversity in a free society as

A) essential as it is one of its key strengths.

B) something that may need to be sacrificed in order to defeat the Soviet Union.

C) a symbolic ideal but rarely valued in everyday life.

D) less important than self-discipline and self-restraint.

**6**

The repeated use of the word "polarization" in the passage conveys a sense that

A) compromise with the Soviet Union may be an attainable goal.

B) confrontation between free society and the Soviet system is inevitable.

C) the only option for the United States is to declare war against the Soviet Union.

D) the Arctic region will likely be an area of conflict between the two nations.

**7**

In line 79, "thus unwillingly" most strongly implies

A) free societies would prefer to avoid conflict.

B) Communism has strong support in many free societies.

C) many neutral nations would prefer the Soviet system.

D) few American political leaders think the Soviet Union is a threat.

**8**

Throughout the passage, the author intends the concept of slavery to be defined as

A) working without payment.

B) the denial of voting rights.

C) state control of the individual.

D) limited employment opportunities.

**9**

Which choice best expresses how the author likely views the viability of the United States encouraging diplomacy with the Soviet Union?

A) Although it is not an ideal solution, it would have practical benefits.

B) It would not work as the philosophy of the Soviet state cannot tolerate free states.

C) With the existence of atomic weapons, it is the only reasonable option.

D) It would likely bring the Soviet Union's "peace policy" to fruition.

**10**

Which choice provides the best evidence that the author is concerned with Soviet influence on American society?

A) Lines 6-8 ("and the exclusive...protagonists")

B) Lines 58-60 ("The same...exception")

C) Lines 73-75 ("What...free")

D) Lines 82-84 ("so capable...society")

# Explanations

*Answers & explanations for Politics Passage 2*

................................................................................

1. An important goal of the passage is to

   (A) define a critical contrast.
   B) criticize a ~~longstanding~~ policy.
   C) analyze a ~~novel~~ philosophy.
   D) ~~denounce undue~~ military aggression.

   > The passage primarily emphasizes the contrast between the Soviet Union and free societies, which makes choice A look pretty good. Is it a critical contrast? Well, the author uses strong language:
   >
   > > *...the existence and persistence of the idea of freedom is a permanent and continuous threat to the foundation of the slave society.*
   >
   > It's fine to choose an answer with strong language when the author is equally opinionated. **Choice A** is the best option!

2. The tone of the passage can best be described as

   A) apprehensive and ~~uncertain~~.
   B) aggressive and ~~frazzled~~.
   C) analytical and ~~indifferent~~.
   (D) decisive and determined.

   > This essay has some strong opinions. Check out lines 76-79:
   >
   > > *...the assault on free institutions is world-wide now, and in the context of the present polarization of power, a defeat of free institutions anywhere is a defeat everywhere.*
   >
   > The author believes that the United States must actively push against the Soviet Union—a **decisive** and **determined** position. Choice D is the best answer

3. The author of the passages believes that the Soviets view freedom as

   A) irrelevant to their greater goal of world peace.
   B) a concept that greatly undermines their main goals.
   C) widely popular and quick to spread.
   D) a means to increase diversity within nations.

4. Which choice provides the best evidence for the previous question?

   A) Lines 15–16 ("The free...himself ")
   B) Lines 44–46 ("The idea...authority.")
   C) Lines 61–65 ("The 'peace policy'...world")
   D) Lines 69–73 ("The existence...world")

We should answer Questions 3 and 4 together. We need to focus on how the Soviets view freedom. This is not the author's opinion on freedom, but rather his interpretation of how the Soviets think. Lines 69-73 in choice D of Question 4 provide the best summation of how the author presents the Soviets' view of freedom:

The existence and persistence of the idea of freedom is a permanent and continuous threat to the foundation of the slave society; and [the Soviet State] therefore regards as intolerable the long continued existence of freedom in the world.

In these lines, the author states that the Soviets see freedom as an "idea" that is a "threat to the foundation" of the Soviet system. This matches "undermines their main goals" from choice B in Question 3. These are the best options.

5. The author views diversity in a free society as

   (A) essential as it is one of its key strengths.
   B) something that may need to be ~~sacrificed~~ in order to defeat the Soviet Union.
   C) a symbolic ideal but ~~rarely valued~~ in everyday life.
   D) ~~less important~~ than self-discipline and self-restraint.

> The author discusses diversity in a free society on lines 38-40:
>
> *For the free society does not fear, it welcomes, diversity. It derives its strength from its hospitality even to antipathetic ideas.*
>
> A free society "derives its strength" from diversity, so choice A is a strong match.

6. The repeated use of the word "polarization" in the passage conveys a sense that

   A) compromise with the Soviet Union may be an ~~attainable~~ goal.
   (B) confrontation between free society and the Soviet system is inevitable.
   C) the ~~only~~ option for the United States is to declare war against the Soviet Union.
   D) the ~~Arctic region~~ will likely be an area of conflict between the two nations.

> The passage uses polarization (division into two contrasting groups) to show how different the United States and the Soviet Union are. We can find our strongest evidence in lines 10-14:
>
> *The implacable purpose of the slave state to eliminate the challenge of freedom has placed the two great powers at opposite poles. It is this fact which gives the present polarization of power the quality of crisis.*
>
> The author believes that the Soviets must "eliminate" the free states, so there is no way to avoid conflict. Choice B is best.

7. In line 79, "thus unwillingly" most strongly implies

(A) free societies would prefer to avoid conflict.
B) Communism has ~~strong support~~ in many free societies.
C) many neutral nations would ~~prefer~~ the Soviet system.
D) ~~few~~ American political leaders think the Soviet Union is a threat.

First, let's look at the phrase in context of lines 76-80:

*The assault on free institutions is world-wide now, and in the context of the present polarization of power, a defeat of free institutions anywhere is a defeat everywhere. Thus unwillingly our free society finds itself mortally challenged by the Soviet system.*

The author feels that the Soviet system wants to destroy free societies, but the feeling is not mutual. We can find additional support on lines 34-37:

*...the prime reliance of the free society is on the strength and appeal of its idea, and it feels no compulsion sooner or later to bring all societies into conformity with it.*

Choice A encapsulates this idea that free society would prefer not to have conflict with the Soviet Union.

8. Throughout the passage, the author intends the concept

A) of slavery to be defined as working without ~~payment~~.
B) the denial of ~~voting rights~~.
(C) state control of the individual.
D) ~~limited~~ employment opportunities.

We find the best explanation of the author's definition of slavery on lines 67-69:

*The antipathy of slavery to freedom explains the iron curtain; the isolation, the autarchy of the society whose end is absolute power.*

An autarchy is a system where the government has complete control, but even without that definition, it's pretty clear that the author views slavery as the control of the individual by the state, so choice C is best.

9. Which choice best expresses how the author likely views the viability of the United States encouraging diplomacy with the Soviet Union?

A) Although it is not an ideal solution, it would have ~~practical benefits~~.
B) It would not work as the philosophy of the Soviet state cannot tolerate free states.
C) With the existence of atomic weapons, it is the ~~only~~ reasonable option.
D) It would likely bring the Soviet Union's "peace policy" to ~~fruition~~.

While diplomacy may be a prefered option in many circumstances, the author does not think it would work: (lines 46-48)

> *For the breath of freedom cannot be tolerated in a society which has come under the domination of a group of individuals with a will to absolute power.*

Choice B best sums up this opinion.

10. Which choice provides the best evidence that the author is concerned with Soviet influence on American society?

A) Lines 6-8 ("and the exclusive...protagonists")
B) Lines 58-60 ("The same...exception")
C) Lines 73-75 ("What...free")
D) Lines 82-84 ("so capable...society")

We've got a Onesie, so we should not try to support Question 9. We need to focus on the <u>author's concern over Soviet influence</u> on the United States. Lines 82-84 provide the best evidence:

> *...so capable of turning to its own uses the most dangerous and divisive trends in our own society...*

Clearly choice D is the correct answer.

# Natural Science

*Let's get some practice with a Natural Science passage.*

You'll see two Natural Science passages on the test: one will be **informative**, and one will describe an **experiment or study** and its results. In the informative passage, you will learn more about a topic in biology, physics, or chemistry such as genetics, evolution, or even space.

*— Names of experts*
*— Support*

In the experiment/study passage, you'll read about scientists and researchers testing a **hypothesis** by conducting an **experiment**, then analyzing the **results**. Let's dive into a sample experiment to learn what these terms mean:

*— Problem/*
*Hypothesis*
*— Research/*
*Data*
*Collection*
*Method*
*— Results/*
*Conclusion*
*— Implications*

## PORTAL

To learn more about designing studies and experiments, go to the Study Design chapter on page 763.

> Jeb and Cassandra have a **hypothesis**: plants can grow just as tall under sun lamps as they can under real sunlight. To test their hypothesis, they come up with an **experiment**: Jeb plants some roses in his kitchen and puts them under a sun lamp. Cassandra plants some roses in her garden where they will get plenty of real sunlight. They use the same amount of water, fertilizer, treatments, etc. on their plants, so their central **assumption** is that any difference in the height of the flowers will be due to the different sources of light. After a month, they look at the **results**: Cassandra's flowers are two inches taller than Jeb's flowers! Since the plants grown in sunlight grew taller than those under the sun lamp, the experiment did **not** support their hypothesis.

It is much easier to remember what happened in a scientific passage like this if you understand these few, primary components of the study or experiment. Make sure you understand *what* the scientists wanted to test (**hypothesis**), *how* they tested it (**experiment**), *why* they assumed that experiment would tell them what they wanted to know (**assumptions**), and what their **results** were.

**TIP**

Always read the intro text above the passage; it often defines science terms or explains difficult concepts referenced in the passage.

## Tips for Active Reading

For an **informative** passage, the regular Active Reading steps will serve you well. Take margin notes, underline important words, star main ideas, and circle logic words to follow the author's thought process. When you finish the passage, ask yourself:

What was the main **topic** of the passage?

Were different **perspectives** considered?

Did the author come to a **conclusion**?

For an **experiment/study** passage, use stars to highlight the hypothesis, experiment or study design, and the results. If there's a word or concept that's new to you, circle it and underline its definition. When you finish the passage, ask yourself:

What **question** were the researchers trying to answer?

What **assumptions** did they make in setting up the study?

How did they test their **hypothesis**?

What were their **conclusions**?

# Natural Science (Informative) Passage
## TO STAY ON PACE, YOUR TIMING GOAL IS 13 MINUTES

**DIRECTIONS**

Each passage or pair of passages below is followed by a number of questions. After reading each passage or pair, choose the best answer to each question based on what is stated or implied in the passage or passages and in any accompanying graphics (such as a table or graph).

**Questions 1-10 are based on the following passage.**

This passage is adapted from "Natural Biodiversity Breaks Yield Barriers," © 2004 Public Library of Science.

The birth of agriculture, some 10,000 years ago in the Middle East's Fertile Crescent, revolutionized human culture and society. Refined farming techniques led to
Line increased yields and freed humans from the demands of
5 constant foraging. Along with that freedom came social complexity, division of labor, improved standards of living, and a measure of leisure time. Agriculture also led to overpopulation followed by starvation, conflict over fertile farming land, and environmental damage. For the
10 Maya and other civilizations, such consequences proved fatal.

Many consumer and environmental groups believe that modern industrial agricultural practices like factory farming of animals and genetic engineering of crops
15 threaten to bring similar ruin. But with 6 billion people living on the planet—a figure that's expected to increase 50% in just 50 years—many plant scientists believe that feeding a burgeoning population will require the tools of biotechnology. Plant breeders face the daunting challenge
20 of developing high-yielding, nutritious crops that will improve the global quality of life without harming the environment or appropriating dwindling natural habitats for agricultural production. A major roadblock to feeding the world is a continuing decline in the genetic diversity
25 of agricultural crops, which has in turn limited their yield improvement. (Domestication often involves inbreeding, which by definition restricts the gene pool.) Now Amit Gur and Dani Zamir of Hebrew University report a way to lift these productivity barriers by tapping into the
30 natural diversity of wild plants.

Traditional plant breeders improve the quality and yield of crops by crossing plants with desired traits to create a new, hopefully improved, hybrid strain. But traditional breeding is limited by the available gene
35 pool of a cultivated plant species and eventually hits a wall—reshuffling the same genetic variation can boost yield only so much. With the advent of biotechnology, plant scientists were buoyed by the prospect of improving plants through genetic modification. But
40 aside from a few successes with introducing single-gene herbicide- and pest-resistant traits, most plant traits have proved too complex to repay the incorporation of a single transgene—that is, a gene taken from a different species—with the hoped-for response. Biotech-based
45 investigations and applications in plant science have also been hampered by consumer reaction against genetically modified organisms.

Faced with these limitations, Gur and Zamir tried another approach—a back-to-nature approach. "Natural
50 biodiversity is an unexploited sustainable resource that can enrich the genetic basis of cultivated plants," they explain in the report. Wild plants, as distant cousins of cultivated plants, can be seen as a "huge natural mutagenesis* resource" with novel gene variants that can
55 increase productivity, quality, and adaptability. Not only that, the genetic material of wild plants—every gene and regulatory element—has already been refined and tested by over a billion years of evolution and natural selection.

To identify genomic regions in wild tomato species
60 that affect yield, Gur and Zamir created a population of hybrid crosses of a wild tomato species and a cultivated tomato species; each line had a single genomic region from the wild tomato inserted into the cultivated plant. Rather than introducing a single wild tomato
65 gene into the cultivated plants, the authors used a "pyramided" strategy that combined three independent

**CONTINUE** ▶

yield-enhancing genomic regions from the wild species into the new plant line. Plants were grown over three seasons, during which they were exposed to different
70 environments, including drought. By combining traditional phenotyping techniques—which characterize the plant's physical traits based on its genetic makeup—with genetic marker analysis, the authors identified a number of wild tomato genomic regions that increased
75 yield.

Their results demonstrate that an approach based on biodiversity—which takes advantage of the rich genetic variation inherent in wild relatives of cultivated crops—can produce varieties that outperform a commercially
80 available hybrid tomato in both yield and drought resistance. Gur and Zamir attribute the improved performance to their unique pyramiding strategy. Their hybrid model—applying the tools of modern genomics to traditional plant breeding—offers plant breeders a
85 powerful approach to improving the quality and yield of cultivated plants by taking advantage of the inherent biodiversity of the natural world.

\* the process by which genetic mutations occur

---

**1**

As identified in the passage, a major barrier to feeding the human population is

A) the limited gene pool within the crops that have been cultivated for agriculture.

B) genetically modified organisms do not grow at a rate that can sustain the rapidly increasing human population.

C) the plants that are used as food have particularly complex genes.

D) consumers are skeptical of genetically engineered crops.

---

**2**

Which choice provides the best answer to the previous question?

A) Lines 15-19 ("But … biotechnology")

B) Lines 23-26 ("A major … improvement")

C) Lines 39-44 ("But … response")

D) Lines 44-47 ("Biotech-based … organisms")

---

**3**

As used in line 3, "refined" most nearly means

A) cultured.

B) purified.

C) improved.

D) aerated.

---

**4**

As used in line 33, "crossing" most nearly means

A) hindering.

B) transversing.

C) intersecting.

D) interbreeding.

---

**5**

In the fourth paragraph (lines 48-58), the author indicates that wild plants

A) share the same genetic material as cultivated plants.

B) have limited and diminishing gene pools.

C) contain useful genetic material.

D) are overused in agriculture.

---

**6**

The main purpose of the fifth paragraph (lines 59-75) is to

A) summarize the results of an experiment.

B) predict the outcome to a scientific question.

C) explain a methodology.

D) critique a claim.

−2

**7**

As presented in the passage, the practice of crossing plants to improve crops is best described as

A) a revolutionary and impactful discovery.

B) an established though recently modernized strategy. ←

C) a sustainable and unexploited breakthrough.

D) a potentially costly yet liberating convenience.

**8**

Which choice provides the best evidence that Gur and Zamir drew inspiration from the natural world?

A) Lines 5-7 ("Along … time")

B) Lines 37-39 ("With … modification")

C) Lines 49-52 ("'Natural … report")

D) Lines 82-87 ("Their … world")

**9**

The final sentence of the passage (lines 82-87) serves to

A) define the limits of current research on crop vitality.

B) show the potential significance of the research presented.

C) address the lack of crop diversity across multiple cultures.

D) downplay the scientists' accomplishments by showing their narrow scope of influence.

**10**

The passage acknowledges that scientific research on crops can be negatively affected by

A) the amount of diversity found within wild plant species.

B) the use of single-gene herbicides and pest-resistant traits.

C) the public's perception of genetically modified organisms.

D) the unpredictable yields due to unforeseen droughts.

# STOP

**If you finish before time is called, you may check your work on this section only.**

**Do not turn to any other section.**

# Explanations

*Answers & explanations for Natural Science (Informative) Passage.*

1. As identified in the passage, a major barrier to feeding the human population is

   (A) the limited gene pool within the crops that have been cultivated for agriculture.
   B) genetically modified organisms do not grow at a rate that can sustain the rapidly increasing human population.
   C) the plants that are used as food have particularly complex genes.
   D) consumers are skeptical of genetically engineered crops.

2. Which choice provides the best answer to the previous question?

   A) Lines 15–19 ("But ... biotechnology")
   (B) Lines 23–26 ("A major ... improvement")
   C) Lines 39–44 ("But ... response")
   D) Lines 44–47 ("Biotech-based ... organisms")

   We need to answer questions 1 and 2 together. The clue in Q1 is "major barrier," so we need to look for a quote from Q2 that relates. Clearly **choice B** is best, since "major barrier" and "major roadblock" are certainly synonyms. The roadblock is the "decline in the genetic diversity of agricultural crops." **Choice A** in Q1 perfectly matches, since "limited gene pool" is the same as a "decline in genetic diversity."

3. As used in line 3, "refined" most nearly means

   A) cultured.
   B) purified.
   (C) improved.
   D) aerated.

First let's look at the word in context:

> **Refined** *farming techniques led to increased yields and freed humans from the demands of constant foraging.*

"Increased yields" are a good thing, so we need a word that means the same thing as "better." Of the choices given, "improved" is the best match. Let's test it in the sentence.

> **Improved** *farming techniques led to increased yields and freed humans from the demands of constant foraging.*

**Choice C** is correct.

4. As used in line 33, "crossing" most nearly means

   A) hindering.
   B) transversing.
   C) intersecting.
   D) interbreeding.

First let's look at the word in context:

> *Traditional plant breeders improve the quality and yield of crops by* **crossing** *plants with desired traits to create a new, hopefully improved, hybrid strain.*

The context is about plant breeding, so we need a word that's about breeding. "Interbreeding" looks like a good match. Let's try it in context:

> *Traditional plant breeders improve the quality and yield of crops by* **interbreeding** *plants with desired traits to create a new, hopefully improved, hybrid strain.*

**Choice D** is best.

5. In the fourth paragraph (lines 48–58), the author indicates that wild plants

A) share the ~~same~~ genetic material as cultivated plants.
B) have ~~limited~~ and diminishing gene pools.
C) contain useful genetic material.
D) are ~~overused~~ in agriculture.

Looking over the fourth paragraph, it discusses "a back-to-nature approach," using **wild plants** to **add** to genetic **diversity**. The scientists are confident that this will work, since wild plant DNA "has already been refined and tested by over a billion years of evolution and natural selection."

**Choice C** is the best. The genetic materials of wild plants has been **refined and tested** already, so that makes the scientists' research easier!

6. The main purpose of the fifth paragraph (lines 59–75) is to

A) summarize the ~~results~~ of an experiment.
B) ~~predict~~ the outcome to a scientific question.
C) explain a methodology.
D) ~~critique~~ a claim.

The fifth paragraph explains an experiment done on tomatoes. The researchers used "a 'pyramided' strategy," which helped them to determine which strain had the highest yield.

**Choice C** works best. A methodology is the analysis of a process, and that's exactly what the fifth paragraph is!

7. As presented in the passage, the practice of crossing plants to improve crops is best described as

    A) a ~~revolutionary~~ and impactful discovery.
    (B)) an established though recently modernized strategy.
    C) a sustainable and ~~unexploited~~ breakthrough.
    D) a potentially ~~costly~~ yet liberating convenience.

We can find the best evidence for Question 7 on lines 82-87:

> *Their hybrid model—applying the tools of modern genomics to traditional plant breeding—offers plant breeders a powerful approach to improving the quality and yield of cultivated plants by taking advantage of the inherent biodiversity of the natural world.*

Crossing plants has been done for a long time ("traditional") but now uses "modern genomics." Choice B best states this idea.

8. Which choice provides the best evidence that <u>Gur and Zamir drew inspiration</u> from the <u>natural world</u>?

    A) Lines 5-7 ("Along ... time")
    B) Lines 37-39 ("With ... modification")
    (C)) Lines 49-52 ("'Natural ... report")
    D) Lines 82-87 ("Their ... world")

Here we have a Onesie evidence-based question. Choice D supports question 7, but we need to focus on a quote that supports the statement that Gur and Zamir drew inspiration from the natural world. Choice C clearly does so, it's our best choice:

> *Natural biodiversity is an unexploited sustainable resource that can enrich the genetic basis of cultivated plants.""*

9. The final sentence of the passage (lines 82–87) serves to

A) define the limits of current research on crop vitality.
B) show the potential significance of the research presented.
C) address the lack of crop diversity across multiple cultures.
D) downplay the scientists' accomplishments by showing their narrow scope of influence.

First, let's look at the sentence:

*"It's a strategy that may well apply to rice, wheat, and other vital staples of the world's food supply."*

The last sentence shows the **value** of the research, as it could be used to grow more important crops like rice and wheat.

**Choice B** is spot on! If the research can be used on vital crops, then that will be really important.

10. The passage acknowledges that scientific research on crops can be negatively affected by

A) the amount of diversity found within wild plant species.
B) the use of single-gene herbicides and pest-resistant traits.
C) the public's perception of genetically modified organisms.
D) the unpredictable yields due to unforeseen droughts.

The clue in the question is "negatively affected." Looking over the passage, lines 44–47 says:

*"Biotech-based investigations and applications in plant science have also been **hampered** by **consumer reaction** against **genetically modified organisms**."*

"Hampered" is a very close match to "negatively affected." **Choice C** is the winner. People do not want to buy genetically modified organisms, so that affects the research.

# Natural Science (Study) Passage
**TO STAY ON PACE, YOUR TIMING GOAL IS 13 MINUTES**

---

**DIRECTIONS**

Each passage or pair of passages below is followed by a number of questions. After reading each passage or pair, choose the best answer to each question based on what is stated or implied in the passage or passages and in any accompanying graphics (such as a table or graph).

---

**Questions 1-11 are based on the following passage.**

This passage is adapted from Liza Gross, "Math and Fossils Resolve a Debate on Dinosaur Metabolism." © 2006 Public Library of Science.

Of the many mysteries surrounding the life history of dinosaurs, one of the more enduring is how such gigantic organisms—some reaching 42 feet tall and weighing 90
*Line* tons—regulated their body temperature. For many years,
5 scientists had assumed that dinosaurs, which evolved from reptiles, were also cold blooded (ectotherms), with a slow metabolism that required the sun's heat to thermoregulate. But, in the late 1960s, the notion emerged that dinosaurs, like mammals and birds, might
10 have been warm blooded (endotherms) with relatively constant, high body temperatures that were internally regulated like their avian descendants (and mammals).

Still others argued that while most dinosaurs had a metabolism similar to contemporary reptiles, the
15 large dinosaurs managed a higher, more-constant body temperature through thermal inertia, which is how modern alligators, Galapagos tortoises, and Komodo dragons retain heat. Thermal inertia allows the body to approach homeothermy, or constant body temperature,
20 when the ratio of body mass to surface area is high enough. If this "inertial homeothermy" hypothesis is correct, dinosaur body temperature should increase with body size.

In a new study, James Gillooly, Andrew Allen, and
25 Eric Charnov revisit—and resolve—this debate. The researchers used a model that provided estimates of dinosaur body temperature based on developmental growth trajectories inferred from juvenile and adult fossil bones of the same species. The model predicts that
30 dinosaur body temperature did increase with body mass,

and that large dinosaurs had body temperatures similar to those of modern birds and mammals (95-110°F), while smaller dinosaurs' temperatures were more like contemporary reptiles. These results suggest that the
35 large dinosaurs (but not the smaller ones) had relatively constant body temperatures maintained through thermal inertia.

Gillooly et al. compiled data from eight dinosaur species from the early Jurassic and late Cretaceous
40 periods that ranged in size from 30 pounds to 28 tons. The growth trajectories, taken from the published research papers, were determined by using bone histology (microscopic study) and body size estimates to estimate the maximum growth rate and mass at the
45 time of maximum growth. The recent availability of these data, the researchers explain, along with advances in understanding how body size and temperature affect growth, allowed them to use a novel mathematical model to estimate dinosaur body temperatures. The researchers
50 modified the model to estimate the body temperature of each dinosaur species, based on its estimated maximum growth rate and mass at the time of maximum growth. The model shows that body temperature increases with body size for seven dinosaur species.

55 The model shows that dinosaur body temperature increased with body size, from roughly 77 °F at 26 pounds to 105.8 °F at 14 tons. These results, the researchers explain, suggest that the body temperatures of the smaller dinosaurs (77 °F) were close to the
60 environmental temperature—just as occurs for modern smaller reptiles—which meant they acquired heat from external sources (in addition to the internal heat generated by metabolism). The results also suggest that body temperature rose as an individual dinosaur grew,
65 increasing by about 37.4 °F for species weighing about 661 pounds as adults and nearly

68 °F for those reaching about 27 tons (*Apatosaurus excelsus*). Predicted body temperature for the largest dinosaur (*Sauroposeidon proteles* at about 60 tons) was
70  about 118 °F—just past the limit for most animals, suggesting that body temperature may have prevented dinosaurs from becoming even bigger.

Gillooly et al. demonstrate the validity of these results by showing that the model successfully predicts
75  documented increases in body temperature with size for existing crocodiles. Altogether, these results indicate that dinosaurs were reptiles and that their body temperature increased with body size—providing strong evidence for the inertial homeothermy hypothesis.

**1**

The first paragraph serves primarily to

A)  recount different explanations to answer a longstanding question.
B)  prove that all dinosaurs were cold blooded.
C)  emphasize how scientific ideas change over time.
D)  suggest that dinosaurs and birds share a common ancestor.

**2**

In line 8, "notion" most nearly means

A)  article.
B)  indication.
C)  concept.
D)  sentiment.

**3**

In line 48, "novel" most nearly means

A)  innovative.
B)  peculiar.
C)  literary.
D)  rare.

| Species | Mass (tons) | | Body Temperature (°F) |
| --- | --- | --- | --- |
| | Min | Max | |
| *A. huinculensis* | 50 | 90 | 116 |
| *S. giganteus* | 9.9 | 22.5 | 108 |
| *S. aegyptiacus* | 7 | 20.9 | 105 |
| *T. prorsus* | 9 | 10.9 | 101 |
| *S. ungulatus* | 3.8 | 7 | 99 |

CONTINUE ➤

**4**

The main purpose of the final sentence in the fourth paragraph ("The model shows that body temperature increases with body size for seven dinosaur species.") serves to

A) dispute the assumptions made by a breakthrough mathematical model.
B) define a complex term.
C) suggest a further course of study.
D) summarize the findings from an analyzed data set.

**5**

The passage suggests that organisms achieve homeothermy when

A) the ratio of body mass to surface area is large.
B) juveniles become adults.
C) large animals migrate to warmer climates.
D) body size decreases.

**6**

Which choice provides the best evidence for the answer to the previous question?

A) Lines 4-8 ("For … thermoregulate")
B) Lines 18-21 ("Thermal … enough")
C) Lines 34-37 ("These … inertia")
D) Lines 63-68 ("The results … excelsus")

**7**

Gillooly, et al., demonstrate confidence in their findings because

A) contemporary alligators, Galapagos tortoises, and Komodo dragons are cold blooded.
B) small dinosaurs have fluctuating body temperatures.
C) their mathematical model correctly predicts body mass and temperature measurements gathered from crocodiles.
D) thermal inertia allows large dinosaurs to maintain higher and more constant body temperatures.

**8**

Which choice provides the best evidence for the answer to the previous question?

A) Lines 13-18 ("Still … heat")
B) Lines 34-37 ("These … inertia")
C) Lines 73-76 ("Gillooly … crocodiles")
D) Lines 76-79 ("Altogether … hypothesis")

**9**

Do the data in the figure support the hypothesis of inertial homeothermy?

A) Yes, because as mass decreases, body temperature decreases.
B) Yes, because as mass decreases, body temperature increases.
C) No, because as mass decreases, body temperature decreases.
D) No, because as mass decreases, body temperature increases.

**CONTINUE**

10

Based on the table, which species of dinosaur had the least variation in body mass?

A)  *A. huinculensis*
B)  *S. aegyptiacus*
C)  *T. prorsus*
D)  *S. ungulatus*

11

Which concept is supported by the passage and by information in the table?

A)  Large dinosaurs had body temperatures similar to modern warm-blooded animals.
B)  Dinosaurs could not grow larger than 20 tons due to producing excessive heat.
C)  Body temperatures of extinct species can be deduced by examining fossils under the microscope.
D)  Dinosaurs had a range of body temperatures similar to those of living reptiles.

# STOP

**If you finish before time is called, you may check your work on this section only.**
**Do not turn to any other section.**

# Explanations

*Answers & explanations for Natural Science (Study) Passage*

..............................................................................................................

1. The first paragraph serves primarily to

(A) recount different explanations to answer a longstanding question.
B) prove that all dinosaurs were cold blooded.
C) emphasize how scientific ideas change over time.
D) suggest that dinosaurs and birds share a common ancestor.

The first paragraph questions how dinosaurs "regulated their body temperatures" and it offers several different theories; they could be ectotherms or endotherms.

**Choice A** is a match!

2. In line 8, "notion" most nearly means

A) article.
B) indication.
C) concept.
D) sentiment.

Let's look at the word in context:

*"But, in the late 1960s, the **notion** emerged that dinosaurs, like mammals and birds, might have been warm blooded (endotherms) with relatively constant, high body temperatures that were internally regulated like their avian descendants (and mammals)."*

In this context, "notion" means the same as "idea." Of the choices, "concept" is the closest to "idea." Let's plug the answer choice to make sure it works:

> "But, in the late 1960s, the **concept** emerged that dinosaurs, like mammals and birds, might have been warm blooded (endotherms) with relatively constant, high body temperatures that were internally regulated like their avian descendants (and mammals)."

**Choice C** is correct.

3. In line 48, "novel" most nearly means

A) innovative.
B) peculiar.
C) literary.
D) rare.

It's important that we look at the word in context:

> "The recent availability of these data, the researchers explain, along with advances in understanding how body size and temperature affect growth, allowed them to use a **novel** mathematical model to estimate dinosaur body temperatures."

"Novel" means new, so of the choices, "innovative" is the closest match. Let's plug it back in to the sentence to make sure it works.

> "The recent availability of these data, the researchers explain, along with advances in understanding how body size and temperature affect growth, allowed them to use an **innovative** mathematical model to estimate dinosaur body temperatures."

**Choice A** is best.

4. The main purpose of the final sentence in the fourth paragraph ("The model shows that body temperature increases with body size for seven dinosaur species.") serves to

   A) dispute the assumptions made by a breakthrough mathematical model.
   B) define a complex term.
   C) suggest a further course of study.
   (D) summarize the findings from an analyzed data set.

> The fourth paragraph describes how the researchers collected data, and how they used the data to draw conclusions. The final sentence says:
>
> > *"The model shows that body temperature increases with body size for seven dinosaur species."*
>
> This sentences **sums up** what they found when they analyzed all the data they collected. **Choice D** is a perfect match.

5. The passage suggests that organisms achieve homeothermy when

   (A) the ratio of surface area to body mass is large.
   B) juveniles become adults.
   C) large animals migrate to warmer climates.
   D) body size decreases.

6. Which choice provides the best evidence for the answer to the previous question?

   A) Lines 4–8 ("For … thermoregulate")
   (B) Lines 18–21 ("Thermal … enough")
   C) Lines 34–37 ("These … inertia")
   D) Lines 63–68 ("The results … excelsus")

**161**

We need to answer questions 5 and 6 together. Q5 gives us the clue that we need to find evidence about how dinosaurs get close to a constant body temperature. In Q6, the lines in **choice B** give us the answer:

> *"Thermal inertia allows the body to approach homeothermy, or constant body temperature, when the ratio of body mass to surface area is high enough."*

Also, the very next sentence begins with "inertial homeothermy hypothesis!" Now we need to find a match in Q5. **Choice A** perfectly sums up the evidence in lines 18-21.

7. Gillooly, et al., demonstrate confidence in their findings because

   A) contemporary alligators, Galapagos tortoises, and Komodo dragons are cold blooded.
   B) small dinosaurs have fluctuating body temperatures.
   C) their mathematical model correctly predicts body mass and temperature measurements gathered from crocodiles.
   D) thermal inertia allows large dinosaurs to maintain higher and more constant body temperatures.

8. Which choice provides the best evidence for the answer to the previous question?

   A) Lines 13–18 ("Still ... heat")
   B) Lines 34–37 ("These ... inertia")
   C) Lines 73–76 ("Gillooly ... crocodiles")
   D) Lines 76–79 ("Altogether ... hypothesis")

We need to answer questions 7 and 8 together. The clue in Q7 is that we're looking for what Gillooly et al. think. **Choice C** in question 8 starts off with Gillooly et al., so we know we found our answer to 8. The sentence says that they "successfully predicted" body temperatures by studying crocodiles.

**Choice C** is best for Q7 as it's the only answer choice that mentions crocodiles.

9. Do the data in the figure support the hypothesis of inertial homeothermy?

    Ⓐ  Yes, because as mass decreases, body temperature decreases.
    B)  Yes, because as mass decreases, body temperature increases.
    C)  No, because as mass decreases, body temperature decreases.
    D)  No, because as mass decreases, body temperature increases.

First we need to look to the passage for a definition of inertial homeothermy:

> *"If this "inertial homeothermy" hypothesis is correct, dinosaur body temperature should increase with body size."*

Looking at the figure, the **higher** the body temperature, the **larger** the body size and vice versa.

**Choice A** works best; if the body size increases as the temperature increases, then body size **decreases** as temperature **decreases**.

10. Based on the table, which species of dinosaur had the least variation in body mass?

    A)  *Argentinosaurus huinculensis*
    B)  *Spinosaurus aegyptiacus*
    Ⓒ  *Triceratops prorsus*
    D)  *Stegosaurus ungulatus*

All we have to do is read the table for this one. The least variation can be discovered by seeing which had the smallest range of body masses.

**Choice C** is correct, because the body mass range of a *triceratops prorsus*, 9 to 10.9 tons, varies the least out of the four ranges given.

11. Which concept is supported by the passage and by information in the table?

(A)) Large dinosaurs had body temperatures similar to modern warm-blooded animals.

B) Dinosaurs could not grow larger than 20 tons due to producing excessive heat.

C) Body temperatures of extinct species can be deduced by examining fossils under the microscope.

D) Dinosaurs had a range of body temperatures similar to those of living reptiles.

Looking at the table, the range of body temperatures goes from 99° to 116°F. The passage states on line 32 that modern birds and mammals have temperatures that range from 95-110°F. That means that the dinosaurs in the table were as **warm** as **modern warm-blooded animals**. All the dinosaurs in the table are at least 3.8 tons: those are some **large** dinosaurs!

**Choice A** is the most supported by the passage and table.

# Social Science

*Let's get some practice with a Social Science passage.*

## TIP

Remember, you can save a passage that looks tough for last. Each question, no matter how difficult, is worth the same nubmer of points. Focus on the easy points first!

## TIP

As always, pay attention to the introduction text before the passage! This information seems like fine print, but it can hide some very helpful context and definitions of terms.

The Social Science passage is an **informative** passage that pulls from fields like economics, psychology, sociology: passages often deal with topics related to technology and modern society. You'll learn about population trends, fancy tech solutions, and fascinating psychological phenomena. These passages always come with a chart, table, or graph.

## Tips for Active Reading

Here are some key things to look out for when reading this passage.

- **Main idea:** After you finish reading the passage, star the sentence (often in the intro or conclusion) that best summarizes the purpose of the passage.

- **Names of experts:** The author will often quote experts in the field to support his or her claims. Make sure you mark their names so you can easily find them when looking for evidence. Also, make note of *competing ideas*. Do your experts agree or disagree? Is there any common ground between them?

- **Specific Data:** This passage can get technical by citing statistics and data. Underline this information so you can quickly find that evidence when confronted with a related question.

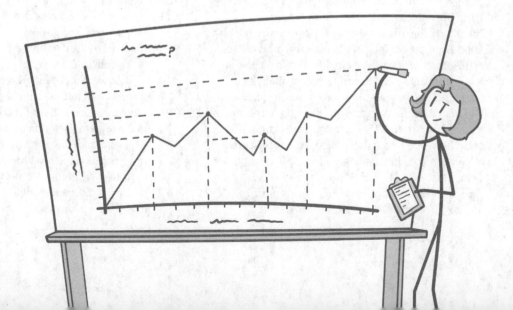

165

# Social Science Passage
## TO STAY ON PACE, YOUR TIMING GOAL IS 13 MINUTES

**Questions 1-11 are based on the following passage.**

This passage is adapted from Cindi Lightballoon, "Cleaning our Cities' Air." Originally published in 2013.

An unavoidable byproduct of human communities is waste. As societies developed from nomadic wandering to year-round residences, the waste of society remained.
Line The initial solutions were simple: bury it, burn it, or
5 dump it in a body of water. By the Middle Ages, waste management in cities had become a legitimate problem, as denizens would loft all household waste out onto the street. The slurry of muck necessitated the invention of "stepping stones" so that pedestrians could travel
10 relatively unslathered in the unhygienic slop.

The industrialization of Western cities forced the development of proper sewers and waste treatment, since the increased density of cities made earlier lax policies towards waste management unbearable. While solid
15 and liquid waste now had proper channels for disposal, a new problem–air pollution–began impacting cities. London's famous pea-soup-thick fog was mostly a result of the predominant practice of burning coal during the Industrial Revolution.
20 Thankfully the urban use of coal is behind us, but air pollution from the burning of gasoline and other fossil fuels still affects the quality of city life. While regulation of fossil fuel-burning engines and wider availability of alternative energy sources imply progress, the quality of
25 air in major cities still negatively impacts the respiratory health of many citizens. These approaches focus on the polluters; however, Dutch designer Daan Roosegaarde has offered a revolutionary means of actually cleaning the air itself.
30 The idea is fairly simple: place a large air purifier within a city to clean polluted air. Instead of using

traditional filters, which can only pick up large particles, Roosegaarde's 7 meters high smog-free tower uses air ionisers, which negatively charge air molecules. The
35 charged impurities in the air then attach to electrified metal plates; the process uses the same principle of static electricity that makes socks fresh from the dryer cling to each other. Air ionisers are nothing new and small models designed for home use were heavily marketed
40 in the 1990s and early 2000s. While these models did remove some air pollutants, the ionization process also created ozone ($O_3$), which is a harmful pollutant itself. Roosegaarde claims that his smog-free tower uses only ozone-free ion technology, and can clean 30,000 cubic
45 meters of air an hour using only 1,400 watts of energy, which is more energy efficient than an average household clothes dryer.

Any ionic air purifier will need the metal collection plates frequently cleaned, and Roosegaarde has come up
50 with an ingenious use for the dust particles. Instead of disposing of them by conventional solid waste methods, Roosegaarde has developed a means to compress the dust into small gems. These gems, which look similar to black obsidian, are then placed in jewelry and sold to
55 consumers who know that their purchase helps fund the air purifiers. The jewelry's minimalist design, a black cube made from the compressed pollutants encased in a clear lucite cube, simply expresses the project's idealism.

Roosegaarde's Smog-Free Project is still in
60 its nascency, but has gained support via online crowdfunding. A fully-functional prototype premiered in Rotterdam, Netherlands and that same prototype was later sold to the city of Beijing, China. Beijing has an unfortunate reputation for air pollution, a byproduct
65 of its own rapid industrialization that occurred over the last two decades. Beijing officials are well-aware of how the poor air quality affects the city's international

prestige and have implemented a plan to remove the smog by 2017. This plan will likely mean more sales
70 for Roosegaarde and further opportunities for people concerned with how to manage a city's air-based waste.

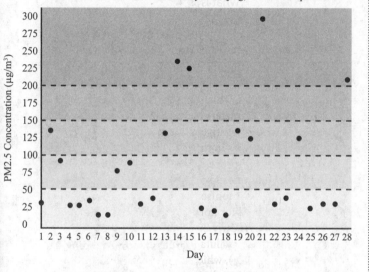

PM2.5* Concentration in Beijing, China at 12:00pm during February 2015
Data collected from the US Embassy in Beijing, US State Department

| PM2.5 Concentration | Air Quality |
|---|---|
| 0-50   μg/m³ | Good |
| 51-100 μg/m³ | Moderate |
| 101-150 μg/m³ | Unhealthy for sensitive groups** |
| 151-200 μg/m³ | Unhealthy |
| 201-300 μg/m³ | Very Unhealthy |

*Particulate matter less than 2.5 micrometers
**People with heart or lung disease, the elderly, or children

---

**1**

Over the course of the passage, the main focus shifts from

A) a discussion of a long-term problem, to the presentation of a novel solution, and then to the limitations of that solution.

B) an introduction of a phenomenon, to a description of the long-term consequences of a problem, and then to the implementation of a clear solution.

C) an overview of a long-lasting issue, to a possible remedy for that problem, and then a summary of its initial implementation.

D) an observation of a historical trend, to its present situation, and then its gradual elimination.

**2**

In the context of the passage as a whole, the first sentence

A) criticizes the amount of waste modern society creates.

B) suggests the need for a permanent solution.

C) addresses a systemic problem.

D) provides a premise that will be refuted later.

**3**

In line 7, "loft" most nearly means

A) extend.

B) amass.

C) fling.

D) raise.

**4**

In line 12, "proper" most nearly means

A) respectable.

B) peculiar.

C) refined.

D) suitable.

CONTINUE

**5**

The purpose of the third paragraph (lines 20-29) is to

A) introduce the idea of air pollution.

B) transition from a persistent problem to a proposed solution.

C) present the current danger air pollution presents to city dwellers.

D) explain why cities have moved away from using coal as a source of energy.

**6**

Unlike other air purifiers, Roosegaarde's smog-free tower

A) was originally intended to create and market jewelry.

B) is the first machine to use ionization to improve air quality.

C) cleans air without creating ozone.

D) can clean a city's air in just a few hours.

**7**

Which choice provides the best evidence for the answer to the previous question?

A) Lines 34-36 ("The charged … plates")

B) Lines 40-44 ("While … technology")

C) Lines 50-53 ("Instead … gems")

D) Lines 61-63 ("A fully-functional … China")

**8**

The passage implies that the shape of the jewelry made from compressed air pollutants is

A) symbolic of the purpose of the air purifier.

B) simplistic and likely not very appealing to many consumers.

C) miniscule and not intended to draw attention.

D) more ornate than functional.

**9**

The author would likely respond to the information in the graph by stating it

A) supports the assessment that Beijing's air quality is the worst in the world.

B) shows that Beijing's air quality is often unhealthy and a solution is necessary.

C) reveals that pollution in Beijing is gradually decreasing due to Roosegaarde's air purifier.

D) predicts that Roosegaarde's air purifier will be an inadequate solution to the level of pollution in Beijing.

**10**

Which choice provides the best evidence for the answer to the previous question?

A) Lines 20-22 ("Thankfully … life.")

B) Lines 22-26 ("While … citizens.")

C) Lines 59-61 ("Roosegaarde's … crowdfunding.")

D) Lines 66-69 ("Beijing … 2017.")

**11**

According to the graph, air quality becomes unhealthy for elderly citizens when the PM2.5 concentration exceeds

A) $50 \ \mu g/m^3$.

B) $100 \ \mu g/m^3$.

C) $150 \ \mu g/m^3$.

D) $300 \ \mu g/m^3$.

# Explanations

*Answers & explanations for Social Science Passage*

1. Over the course of the passage, the main focus shifts from

   A) a discussion of a long-term problem, to the presentation of a novel solution, and then to the ~~limitations~~ of that solution.
   B) an introduction of a phenomenon, to a description of the long-term consequences of a problem, and then to the implementation of a ~~clear solution~~.
   C) an overview of a long-lasting issue, to a possible remedy for that problem, and then a summary of its initial implementation.
   D) an observation of a historical trend, to its present situation, and then its gradual ~~elimination~~.

   > The passage begins by discussing the history of pollution in the first two paragraph, then introduces Roosegaarde's air purifier in the third paragraph. Paragraphs three and four explain how the air purifier works and the final paragraphs talk about early testing. Choice C provides the most accurate summary and lacks any throwaways words hidden in each of the other choices.

2. In the context of the passage as a whole, the first sentence

   A) criticizes the amount of waste ~~modern~~ society creates.
   B) suggests the need for a ~~permanent~~ solution.
   C) addresses a systemic problem.
   D) provides a premise that will be ~~refuted later~~.

   > The passage is all about pollution and how to fix it. The first sentence says waste, which includes pollution, is "an unavoidable byproduct of human communities," which means that cities will always make waste. A "systemic problem" cannot be avoided, so **C** is the right answer.

**3.** In line 7, "loft" most nearly means

    A) extend.
    B) amass.
    C) fling.
    D) raise.

Let's look at the word in context:

> "By the Middle Ages, waste management in cities had become a legitimate problem, as denizens would **loft** all household waste out onto the street."

In this sentence, a good synonym would be "**throw**." "Fling," **choice C**, is closest to "throw," so that's our answer.

> "By the Middle Ages, waste management in cities had become a legitimate problem, as denizens would **fling** all household waste out onto the street."

**4.** In line 12, "proper" most nearly means

    A) respectable.
    B) peculiar.
    C) refined.
    D) suitable.

We need to look at the word in context:

> "The industrialization of Western cities forced the development of **proper** sewers and waste treatment, since the increased density of cities made earlier lax policies towards waste management unbearable."

We could replace "proper" with "**adequate**" and it would have the same meaning. "Suitable" means the same thing as "adequate" in this sentence, so **D** must be our answer.

> "The industrialization of Western cities forced the development of **suitable** sewers and waste treatment, since the increased density of cities made earlier lax policies towards waste management unbearable."

5. The purpose of the third paragraph (lines 20-29) is to

    A) introduce the ~~idea~~ of air pollution.
    B) transition from a persistent problem to a proposed solution.
    C) present the ~~current danger~~ air pollution presents to city dwellers.
    D) explain ~~why~~ cities have moved away from using coal as a source of energy.

> Paragraph 3 moves from "the burning of gasoline and other fossil fuels" to "a revolutionary means of actually cleaning the air itself." So we're shifting from the problems of pollution to Roosegaarde's new method of mitigating that pollution. **Choice B** is perfect: the first two paragraphs talk about pollution as a problem and the third paragraph transitions to Roosegaarde's solution!

6. Unlike other air purifiers, Roosegaarde's smog-free tower

    A) was originally intended to create and market jewelry.
    B) is the first machine to use ionization to improve air quality.
    C) cleans air without creating ozone.
    D) can clean a city's air in just a few hours.

7. Which choice provides the best evidence for the answer to the previous question?

    A) Lines 34-36 ("The charged ... plates")
    B) Lines 40-44 ("While ... technology")
    C) Lines 50-53 ("Instead ... gems")
    D) Lines 61-63 ("A fully-functional ... China")

> Let's use our paired question strategy: according to Q6, we need a quote that tells us the **difference** between other air purifiers and Roosegaarde's. Only **choice B**, lines 40-44, talk about that difference:
>
> > "While **these models** did remove some air pollutants, the ionization process also created ozone ($O_3$), which is a harmful pollutant itself. Roosegaarde claims that **his smog-free tower** uses only ozone-free technology..."
>
> So other air purifiers created ozone, but Roosegaarde's doesn't. That's a perfect match to **choice C** in Q6.

171

8. The passage implies that the shape of the jewelry made from compressed air pollutants is

   (A) symbolic of the purpose of the air purifier.
   B) simplistic and likely ~~not very appealing~~ to many consumers.
   C) ~~miniscule~~ and not intended to draw attention.
   D) more ~~ornate~~ than functional.

> The passage discusses the look of the jewelry on lines 56-58:
>
> *"The jewelry's minimalist design, a black cube made*
> *from the compressed pollutants encased in a clear*
> *lucite cube, simply expresses the project's idealism."*
>
> The key phrases are **"minimalist design"** and **"expresses the project's idealism,"** so we need an answer that includes these concepts. In **choice A**, "symbolic of the purpose" matches "expresses the project's idealism," so it's the best answer.

9. The author would likely respond to the information in the graph by stating it

   A) supports the assessment that Beijing's air quality is the ~~worst~~ in the world.
   (B) shows that Beijing's air quality is often unhealthy and a solution is necessary.
   C) reveals that pollution in Beijing is gradually ~~decreasing due~~ to Roosegaarde's air purifier.
   D) predicts that Roosegaarde's air purifier will be an ~~inadequate~~ solution to the level of pollution in Beijing.

10. Which choice provides the best evidence for the answer to the previous question?

   A) Lines 20-22 ("Thankfully ... life.")
   B) Lines 22-26 ("While ... citizens.")
   C) Lines 59-61 ("Roosegaarde's ... crowdfunding.")
   (D) Lines 66-69 ("Beijing ... 2017.")

Looking at the graph, it shows that far too often the air in Beijing is unhealthy. Let's check our lines to find a choice that relates to Beijing's unhealthy air: only **choice D**, lines 66-69, are specifically about Beijing:

> "**Beijing** officials are well-aware of how the **poor air quality** affects the city's international prestige and have implemented a plan to remove the smog by 2017."

In Q9, the choice that most closely relates to the evidence in lines 66-69 is **choice B**, since "Beijing's air quality is often unhealthy" matches "well-aware of how the poor air quality affects the city's international prestige," and "a solution is necessary" matches "have implemented a plan to remove the smog."

11. According to the graph, air quality becomes unhealthy for elderly citizens when the PM2.5 concentration exceeds

    A) 50 µg/m³.
    (B)) 100 µg/m³.
    C) 150 µg/m³.
    D) 300 µg/m³.

This question is all about decoding the figure. We need to find where the concentration becomes unhealthy for the elderly. The table tells us that a 101 µg/m³ concentration of PM2.5 is unhealthy for sensitive groups. However, if we follow the footnote, it confirms that sensitive groups includes the elderly. That means **B** is our answer!

# Comparison

*Let's get some practice with a comparison passage.*

There is one pair of comparison passages on every test, but it could be from Social Science, Natural Science, or Politics. Whatever the topic, there is a specific **strategy** for tackling comparison passages.

## Strategy: tackle the passages one at a time

This way you answer questions while the content is fresh in your mind.

① *Actively read intro text and Passage 1*

② *Answer questions about Passage 1*

③ *Actively read Passage 2*

④ *Write down **relationship** between passages*

⑤ *Answer questions about Passage 2*

⑥ *Answer questions about both passages*

## Types of relationships between passages

There will always be a question asking for the **relationship** between the two passages, which is why we want to write it down right after reading Passage B. Ask yourself: if the two authors met in a coffee shop, what **would they say to each other**?

**TIP**

The **intro text** before both passages has key information about the authors' viewpoints. Don't skip it!

# Comparison Passage
## TO STAY ON PACE, YOUR TIMING GOAL IS 13 MINUTES

**DIRECTIONS**

Each passage or pair of passages below is followed by a number of questions. After reading each passage or pair, choose the best answer to each question based on what is stated or implied in the passage or passages and in any accompanying graphics (such as a table or graph).

**Questions 1-11 are based on the following passages.**

In 1773, American colonists in Boston, Massachusetts threw large shipments of tea from Great Britain into the harbor to protest high taxes on British goods. As punishment, Great Britain passed harsh laws limiting the freedom of the colonists. In 1774, representatives from the American colonies met at the First Continental Congress to decide on a response. Passage 1, adapted from Samuel Seabury, "Free Thoughts on the Proceedings of the Continental Congress," originally published in 1774, criticizes the ban on trade with Great Britain proposed by the Congress. Passage 2, adapted from Alexander Hamilton, "A Full Vindication of the Measures of the Congress," originally published in 1774, was written in response to passage 1.

**Passage 1**

Permit me to address you upon a subject, which, next to your eternal welfare in a future world, demands your most serious and dispassionate consideration. The
Line American Colonies are unhappily involved in a scene
5 of confusion and discord. From this distressed situation it was hoped, that the wisdom and prudence of the Congress lately assembled at Philadelphia, would have delivered us. But alas, they are broken up without ever attempting it: they have taken no one step that tended to
10 peace: they have gone on from bad to worse, and have either ignorantly misunderstood, carelessly neglected, or basely betrayed the interests of all the Colonies.

My first business shall be to point out to you some of the consequences that will probably follow from the Non-
15 importation, Non-exportation, and Non-consumption

Agreements, which they have adopted, and which they have ordered to be enforced in the most arbitrary manner, and under the severest penalties. Let us consider the policy, or rather impolicy of these agreements.
20 Instead of conciliating, it will alienate the affections of the people of Great-Britain. Of friends it will make them our enemies; it will excite the resentment of the government at home against us; and their resentment will do us no good, but, on the contrary, much harm.
25   Can we think to threaten, and bully, and frighten the supreme government of the nation into a compliance with our demands? We ought to know the temper and spirit, the power and strength of the nation better. A single campaign, should she exert her force, would ruin
30 us effectually. But should she choose less violent means, she has it in her power to humble us without hurting herself. She might raise immense revenues, by laying duties in Ireland and the West-Indies, and we could have no remedy left; for this non-importation scheme cannot
35 last forever.

Look well to yourselves, I beseech you. From the day that the exports from this province are stopped, the farmers may date the commencement of their ruin. Can you live without money? Will the shop-keeper give
40 you his goods? Will the weaver, shoemaker, blacksmith, carpenter, work for you without pay? If they will, it is more than they will do for me. And unless you can sell your produce, how are you to get money? Nor will the case be better, if you are obliged to sell your produce at an
45 under-rate; for then it will not pay you for the labour and expense of raising it.

**CONTINUE** ➡

**Passage 2**

It was hardly to be expected that any man could be so presumptuous, as openly to controvert the equity, wisdom, and authority of the measures, adopted by
50　the congress: an assembly truly respectable on every account! Whether we consider the characters of the men, who composed it; the number, and dignity of their constituents, or the important ends for which they were appointed. But, however improbable such a degree of
55　presumption might have seemed, we find there are some, in whom it exists.

The only scheme of opposition, suggested by those who have been and are averse from a non-importation and non-exportation agreement, is by Remonstrance and
60　Petition. The authors and abettors of this scheme have never been able to invent a single argument to prove the likelihood of its succeeding. On the other hand, there are many standing facts, and valid considerations against it.

In the infancy of the present dispute, we had recourse
65　to this method only. We addressed the throne in the most loyal and respectful manner, in a legislative capacity; but what was the consequence? Our address was treated with contempt and neglect. The first American congress did the same, and met with similar treatment. The total
70　repeal of the Stamp Act*, and the partial repeal of the revenue acts took place, not because the complaints of America were deemed just and reasonable; but because these acts were found to militate against the commercial interests of Great Britain. This was the declared motive of
75　the repeal.

What can we represent which has not already been represented? What petitions can we offer, that have not already been offered? The rights of America, and the injustice of parliamentary pretensions have been clearly
80　and repeatedly stated, both in and out of parliament. No new arguments can be framed to operate in our favour. This being the case, we can have no resource but in a restriction of our trade. It is impossible to conceive any other alternative. Our congress, therefore, have imposed
85　what restraint they thought necessary. Those, who condemn or clamour against it, do nothing more, nor less, than advise us to be servants.

*a tax on printed goods in the colonies that required all paper to be stamped with an official mark, enacted in 1765 and repealed within a year*

---

The primary purpose of the first paragraph of Passage 1 (lines 1-12) is to

A)　illustrate the author's respect for the Continental Congress.

B)　minimize the consequences of the Continental Congress's course of action.

C)　question the motivation of critics of the Continental Congress.

D)　emphasize the severity of the current situation in the Colonies.

The author of Passage 1 mentions Ireland and the West Indies in order to

A)　list allies of the colonies in their dispute with Great Britain.

B)　identify other sources of income available to Great Britain.

C)　cite examples of other countries who have defied Great Britain.

D)　provide alternative trading partners for the Colonies.

CONTINUE ▶

**3**

As used in line 29, "campaign" most nearly means

A) democratic election.
B) military force.
C) spirited adventure.
D) necessary promotion.

**4**

The questions in the fourth paragraph of Passage 1 primarily serve to:

A) demonstrate that blacksmithing will become more profitable than farming.
B) Illustrate the diversity of professions benefitting from the Congress's plan.
C) suggest farmers should ask their neighbors for free services.
D) highlight the likely consequences if trade with Great Britain is stopped.

**5**

How would the author of Passage 1 respond to Passage 2's claim that Congress "can have no resource but in a restriction of our trade?"

A) Congress has not tried other methods.
B) Congress should focus its efforts on promoting peace among the colonies.
C) Banning importation and exportation won't have any effect on Great Britain.
D) The consequences of restricting trade will only be negative.

**6**

Which choice provides the best evidence for the answer to the previous question?

A) Lines 8-9 ("But alas...it")
B) Lines 22-24 ("it will...harm.")
C) Lines 25-27 ("Can...demands?")
D) Line 43-46 ("Nor...raising it.")

**7**

The author of Passage 2 argues that the Stamp Act was repealed because:

A) it was in Great Britain's interest to do so.
B) the non importation plan was hurting the British economy.
C) the colonist's presented strong arguments against it.
D) the British government was impressed by the authority of the Continental Congress.

**8**

Which choice provides the best evidence for the answer to the previous question?

A) Lines 47-51 ("It...account!")
B) Lines 65-68 ("We...neglect.")
C) Lines 69-74 ("The total...Great Britain.")
D) Line 82-84 ("This...alternative.")

**9**

In line 85, "restraint" most nearly means

A) binding.
B) moderation.
C) restriction.
D) discipline.

CONTINUE

177

**10**

Unlike the author of Passage 1, the author of Passage 2 discusses

A)  the qualifications of the Continental Congress.

B)  previous disputes between the colonies and Great Britain.

C)  the effect of the Continental Congress's plan on the colonists

D)  the likelihood that the Continental Congress's plan will succeed.

**11**

The authors of both passages would most likely agree that:

A)  The Continental Congress has a role to play in improving the lives of the colonists.

B)  The repeal of the Stamp Act was achieved by peaceful demonstration.

C)  The colonies cannot defend against a military response from Great Britain.

D)  Great Britain repealed the Stamp Act out of self-interest.

# STOP
**If you finish before time is called, you may check your work on this section only.**
**Do not turn to any other section.**

# Explanations

*Answers & explanations for Comparison Passage*

1. The primary purpose of the first paragraph of Passage 1 (lines 1–12) is to

   A) illustrate the author's ~~respect~~ for the Continental Congress.
   B) ~~minimize~~ the consequences of the Continental Congress's course of action.
   C) question the motivation of ~~critics~~ of the Continental Congress.
   D) emphasize the severity of the current situation in the Colonies.

   Lines 3-5 summarize the concern expressed in the first paragraph:

   *The American Colonies are unhappily involved in a scene of confusion and discord.*

   The author of Passage 1 thinks things are pretty bad in the Colonies, so choice D is the best match.

2. The author of Passage 1 mentions Ireland and the West

   A) Indies in order to list ~~allies~~ of the colonies in their dispute with Great Britain.
   B) identify other sources of income available to Great Britain.
   C) cite examples of other countries who have ~~defied~~ Great Britain.
   D) provide ~~alternative trading partners~~ for the Colonies.

   Passage 1 mentions Ireland and the West Indies on lines 30-35:

   *But should she choose less violent means, she has it in her power to humble us without hurting herself. She might raise immense revenues, by laying duties in Ireland and the West-Indies, and we could have no remedy left; for this non-importation scheme cannot last forever.*

   Duties are a form of tax and Ireland and the West-Indies were other territories controlled by Great Britain. If the American colonies refused to buy British goods, it wouldn't stop Great Britain from finding money elsewhere, so Choice B is best.

3. As used in line 29, "campaign" most nearly means

A) democratic election.
B) military force.
C) spirited adventure.
D) necessary promotion.

Let's look at "campaign" in context:

> A single <u>campaign</u>, should she exert her force, would ruin us
> effectually. But should she choose <u>less violent means</u>...

The author is talking about a violent conflict, so choice B would be
the most accurate meaning of "campaign" in this context.

4. The questions in the fourth paragraph of Passage 1 primarily serve to:

A) demonstrate that blacksmithing will become ~~more profitable~~ than
farming.
B) illustrate the diversity of professions ~~benefitting~~ from the Congress's
plan.
C) suggest farmers should ask their neighbors for ~~free services~~.
D) highlight the likely consequences if trade with Great Britain is stopped.

Let's review the questions asked in the fourth paragraph:

> Can you live without money? Will the shop-keeper give
> you his goods? Will the weaver, shoemaker, blacksmith,
> carpenter, work for you without pay? If they will, it
> is more than they will do for me. And unless you can
> sell your produce, how are you to get money?

The author includes a range of professions that would be affected
by bad policy. Choice D best explains this concern.

5. How would the author of Passage 1 respond to Passage 2's claim that Congress "can have no resource but in a restriction of our trade?"

A) Congress has not tried other methods.
B) Congress should focus its efforts on promoting peace among the colonies.
C) Banning importation and exportation won't have any effect on Great Britain.
D) The consequences of restricting trade will only be negative.

6. Which choice provides the best evidence for the answer to the previous question?

A) Lines 8–9 ("But alas...it")
B) Lines 22–24 ("It will...harm.")
C) Lines 25–27 ("Can...demands?")
D) Line 43–46 ("Nor...raising it.")

We've got a comparison evidence-based pair, so we should answer these questions together. First we need to understand the quote in Passage 2:

*The rights of America, and the injustice of parliamentary pretensions have been clearly and repeatedly stated, both in and out of parliament. No new arguments can be framed to operate in our favour. This being the case, we can have no resource but in a restriction of our trade. It is impossible to conceive any other alternative.*

The author of Passage 2 argues that the Continental Congress has tried everything else and there is no "other alternative" than a ban on trade. Now that we have our topic, we can look at the quotes in Question 6 and determine which offers the clearest response. Lines 22-24 most clearly address why Passage 1's author thinks this is a bad idea:

*it will excite the resentment of the government at home against us; and their resentment will do us no good, but, on the contrary, much harm.*

Now that we know choice B is best for Question 6, we can use that quote to justify Question 5. The author of Passage 1 thinks it's a terrible idea and will only hurt the colonies, so choice D is best.

7. The author of Passage 2 argues that the Stamp Act was repealed because:

    A) it was in Great Britain's interest to do so.
    B) the non importation plan was hurting the British economy.
    C) the colonist's presented strong arguments against it.
    D) the British government was impressed by the authority of the Continental Congress.

8. Which choice provides the best evidence for the answer to the previous question?

    A) Lines 47–51 ("It...account!")
    B) Lines 65–68 ("We...neglect.")
    C) Lines 69–74 ("The total...Great Britain.")
    D) Line 82–84 ("This...alternative.")

We should answer Questions 7 and 8 together. We need to find where Passage 2 describes why the Stamp Act repealed. We can find that evidence on lines 69-74:

> *The total repeal of the Stamp Act, and the partial repeal of the revenue acts took place, not because the complaints of America were deemed just and reasonable; but because these acts were found to militate against the commercial interests of Great Britain.*

Now that we know the answer for Question 8 is choice C, we can use that evidence to answer Question 7. The quote says they are against the "commercial interest of Great Britain," so choice A is the best for Question 7.

9. In line 85, "restraint" most nearly means

   A) binding.
   B) moderation.
   C) restriction.
   D) discipline.

Let's look at the word in context:

> *Our congress, therefore, have imposed what restraint they thought necessary.*

Both passages are discussing a ban on trade with Great Britain, so restraint most nearly means restriction in this context. So our answer must be choice C!

10. Unlike the author of Passage 1, the author of Passage 2

   A) discusses the ~~qualifications~~ of the Continental Congress.
   B) previous disputes between the colonies and Great Britain.
   C) the ~~effect~~ of the Continental Congress's plan on the colonists.
   D) the ~~likelihood~~ that the Continental Congress's plan will succeed.

The phrasing of this question is a little tricky, but we can restate it in a straightforward way: what detail is in Passage 2 and <u>not</u> in Passage 1? Neither discuss the qualifications of the Continental Congress, so choice A is out. Likewise, neither detail how likely it is that the plan will succeed, so choice D won't work. Passage 1 discusses the effect the plan will have on the colonists in the third paragraph, but we're looking for the answer that's only in Passage 2. That leaves us with choice B and we can find evidence for it on lines 64-68:

> *In the infancy of the present dispute, we had recourse to this method only. We addressed the throne in the most loyal and respectful manner, in a legislative capacity; but what was the consequence? Our address was treated with contempt and neglect.*

11. The authors of both passages would most likely agree that:

   (A) The Continental Congress has a role to play in improving the lives of the colonists.
   B) The repeal of the Stamp Act was achieved by ~~peaceful demonstration~~.
   C) The colonies ~~cannot defend~~ against a military response from Great Britain.
   D) Great Britain repealed the Stamp Act out of ~~self-interest~~.

These two authors don't agree on much, but here we need to find common ground. The only answer without any throwaways is choice A; while the authors disagree over which direction the Congress should take, they both agree that the Continental Congress has a role in helping out the colonists.

# Writing Overview

*On the Writing section of the SAT, you play the role of editor-in-chief by correcting grammar errors and improving both flow and content of 4 less-than-perfect passages.*

## Structure and Content

You will have 35 minutes to read and edit 4 passages with 11 questions each, for a total of 44 questions. You will see one passage each about Careers, History/Social Studies, Humanities, and Science. One or two of the passages will also come with a graph or chart related to the topic. These passages range from easy to medium comprehension level: no AP Literature or Ye Olde English dictionary required.

passages          minutes          questions

There are two types of questions on the SAT Writing section. Every question you encounter will belong to one of these broad categories:

① *Standard English Conventions (20 questions)*

These questions ask you to **revise sentences** so that they follow all the grammar rules you'll learn in this section. You'll see rogue commas, crazy clauses, and misplaced modifiers. Once you know the rules, you'll be able to identify and fix errors quickly.

② *Expression of Ideas (24 questions)*

These questions test your ability to **communicate an idea** by asking you to revise the passage for content, organization, and logic. To answer these questions, you will need to think bigger! Broaden your focus to include surrounding sentences and paragraphs to understand the flow and content of the passage.

## TIP

Grammar helps us communicate **efficiently** and **logically**. Grammatical errors often make sentences longer and more confusing.

On the test, if you can't decide between two choices, go with the **shorter** and **simpler** one.

dialect (n.)

*a particular form of a language that is peculiar to a specific region or social group.*

Some examples of English dialects are Newfoundland English, African American Vernacular English, and Cajun Vernacular English.

## TIP

You might not know terms like "misplaced modifier" or "prepositional phrase," but your ear often "knows" when something sounds funny. Use this on the test!

*Caveat*: Take note if you read a rule that you and your friends regularly break in your speech. Your ear may not catch that error!

## Good grammar is all about communication

In relationships, business, diplomacy, and education, ideas are *complicated* and misunderstandings can be *costly*. If everyone spoke according to their own rules, things would get pretty confusing:

> Excuse your, store-might be cackleberries?

## There is no universally "correct" grammar...

Communities naturally develop and follow their own sets of grammar rules to make communication go smoothly. This might surprise you, but there are *tons* of different grammars—as many as there are languages and **dialects** in the world—that are equally "correct" *in their own contexts*. You can see this in your own life: you almost certainly use different vocabulary and sentence structure with your friends than you do with your parents, teachers, or employers.

## ...but there is a correct grammar for the SAT!

On the SAT, you need to use the grammar rules of **Standard English**. This is the grammar that is used in the context of academic, journalistic, and professional work. These rules are taught in most schools and followed by most English speakers around the globe.

If you're a native English speaker, you grew up reading, speaking, and listening to language that follows Standard English conventions. If you can't remember one of the rules you learned in this book, just **trust your ear!** If you're not a native English speaker, then you are likely even *more* familiar with many of the **formal rules** (and strange exceptions) from studying them in class. This will help as you go through this book.

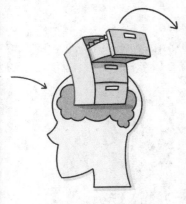

## Brain Files

Your brain actually has a pretty great, well-organized filing system. If you feed it context clues, it will know which "drawer" to check and which memory to fetch to help answer the question.

## TIP

Revisit this list after completing these chapters and memorize each row.

To do so, cover up the left column and use the right column to jog your memory. This will mimic your strategy on test day, when you use the answer choices to guide you to the error!

## File these rules in your brain to master the test

Picture yourself taking the Writing section after preparing with this book: in a blur of editing prowess, you are catching every misplaced comma, improper verb tense, and misused preposition. How are you doing it?

By studying, you have built up a list in your head of the relatively few grammar mistakes covered on the test. For each question, you look at the options and ask **"What's changing in the answer choices?"** This gives you **context clues** that narrow down the list to just two or three possible topics, making it easy to spot the error! This is *incredibly* helpful for raising your score. To help you sort your mental filing cabinet, we've grouped related grammar rules into units, as listed below:

| Grammar Topics | Unit |
|---|---|
| 1. Comma Basics<br>2. All About Clauses | *Punctuation* |
| 3. Tense Switch<br>4. Subject-Verb Agreement<br>5. Pronoun Error<br>6. Possession | *Subjects & Verbs* |
| 7. Parallelism<br>8. Misplaced Modifiers | *Structure* |
| 9. Redundancy<br>10. Prepositions<br>11. Vocab in Context | *Word Choice* |
| 12. Logical Connectors<br>13. Combining Sentences<br>14. Order/Placement | *Connecting Ideas* |
| 15. Add and Delete<br>16. Accomplish a Task<br>17. Describing Data | *Quality Control* |

## Step-by-Step Strategy

Let's sum up your step-by-step approach to answering Writing questions:

**1** *Check the Choices*　　**2** *Identify the Error*　　**3** *Eliminate & Choose*

Let's see the steps in action! Imagine you come across this question:

## EXAMPLE 1

Recent research by several historians question the long-held belief that Marie Antoinette originally said, "Let them eat cake."

A)  NO CHANGE
B)  questioning
C)  questions
D)  have questioned

Imagine the error doesn't immediately jump out at you from reading the sentence. Instead of stressing, you **check the answer choices** to get context clues. This triggers a memory of the chapter or rule, helping you **identify the error**. Using that memory, you **eliminate & choose.**

## CHECK THE CHOICES

The underlined word is a **verb**, and the answer choices are different forms of the same verb. Two common topics dealing with verbs are **Subject-Verb Agreement** and **Tense Switch**!

A)  NO CHANGE
B)  questioning
C)  questions
D)  have questioned

} Verbs

"I should check agreement and tense."

# IDENTIFY THE ERROR

From the subject-verb agreement chapter, you learn that both the subject and verb must be **singular** or **plural**. So what's the subject of the verb?

$$S \qquad\qquad V$$

Recent **research** ~~by several historians~~ question the long-held belief that Marie Antoinette originally said "Let them eat cake."

The subject (research) is singular, but the verb (question) is plural. That's the grammar error!

# ELIMINATE & CHOOSE

You need to find a singular verb to match the singular subject. Choice C, "questions", is singular, so you try using it in the sentence:

Recent research by several historians **questions** the long-held belief that Marie Antoinette originally said "Let them eat cake."

That sounds good! You pick choice C and move to the next problem.

That's all there is to it! If you can keep that small list of rules in your head and cross-reference it with questions using context clues, you will be able to predict the test writers' moves and stay one step ahead of them.

## Read the passage and pause to answer questions

Context is key on the SAT Writing section. Many questions require you to know what was said in the previous sentence or what is coming up in the next one. That means the best strategy is to **read the passage** and pause to answer the questions as they appear in the passage. This will help you avoid the danger of just focusing on the underlined portion of the sentence, missing the necessary context.

# UNIT | Punctuation

## Chapters

## Overview

This unit covers the basic rules of punctuation. First, we'll learn about the purpose of commas. Next, we'll learn the **punctuation rules** for separating independent and dependent clauses.

Questions covered in this unit have answer choices where the *punctuation* changes from choice to choice.

# Comma Basics

*A comma's main job is to separate different ideas in a single sentence. Before we dive into the specifics of comma rules, let's learn some comma basics.*

## Use your ear to test comma placement

Commas live where you naturally **pause** in your speech. That simple fact means that you can actually hear correct and incorrect comma placement! Read a sentence aloud and **exaggerate the pause** when you see a comma; if it still sounds right, then it's likely in the right spot!

### TRY IT OUT

**Read the following sentences aloud**. Each time you come to a comma, greatly exaggerate the pause before moving on. When there's no comma, blaze ahead without stopping. Which one uses commas correctly?

## TIP

Actually say these out loud, pausing at each stop sign. It helps to get a physical "feel" for commas before learning the specific rules.

1. Most students, although, they mean well, overuse, the comma.

2. Most students, although they mean well overuse the comma.

3. Most students, although they mean well, overuse the comma.

**SOLUTION**

Could you hear the difference? The first option feels like it takes forever to get through. The second option seems to rush at the end. **The third option**, with correct comma placement, sounds and feels best when we *exaggerate the pause*.

194

## Commas separate different ideas

**TIP**

When unnecessary commas force a pause, they break up an idea without introducing a new one. When we have too many ideas and too few commas, it sounds jumbled and rushed.

Let's look at that third option to see *why* it sounds the best. Notice that we have **two separate ideas**, separated by commas.

> **Most students,** although they mean well, **overuse the comma.**
> Idea 1 —————— Idea 2 —————— Idea 1 (continued)

Commas allow us to put these two related ideas **in the same sentence**. Use your ear to test the comma in the example below. Then check to see if it's separating *two different ideas*.

## EXAMPLE 1

Recent showings by two local artists <u>suggest, that</u> Raleigh's art scene is experiencing a renaissance.

A) NO CHANGE
B) suggest, that,
C) suggest that,
D) suggest that

**TIP**

Don't be afraid to remove commas! In about 40% of comma problems, the correct answer is to **cut the commas**.

**SOLUTION**

The comma after "suggest" sounds awkward because it breaks up a single idea: "that" is connected to "suggest." Try it without:

D) Recent showings by two local artists <u>**suggest that**</u> Raleigh's art scene is experiencing a renaissance.

D

## Commas are the crossing guards of sentences

Without commas (and the pauses they provide in speech), different ideas **crash into each other**. Commas tell us which words in a sentence belong to which idea. Without them, things get a bit jumbled:

Most students although    they mean well overuse    the comma.

## EXAMPLE 2

The <u>horses, which I learned are easily frightened stampeded</u> through Aunt Bessie's kitchen.

A)  NO CHANGE
B)  horses which, I learned are easily frightened, stampeded
C)  horses, which I learned are easily frightened, stampeded
D)  horses which I learned are easily frightened, stampeded

**SOLUTION**

This sentence sounds *confused, rushed,* and *jumbled*. There are two ideas that need to be separated by commas:

(1)  *The horses stampeded through Aunt Bessie's kitchen.*

(2)  *I learned (the horses) are easily frightened*

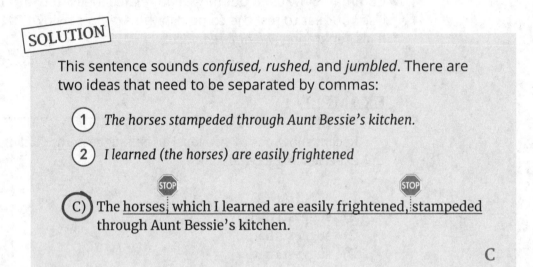

(C))  The <u>horses, which I learned are easily frightened, stampeded</u> through Aunt Bessie's kitchen.

C

## Try removing a clause separated by commas

A clause separated by commas on both ends should be **nonessential** to the sentence. If you **slip out the clause**, the main idea should be intact!

**TIP**

When you see a clause separated by commas on either end:

(1)  *Slip out the clause.*

(2)  *Read what's left.*

If the main idea is still intact, the commas are doing their job!

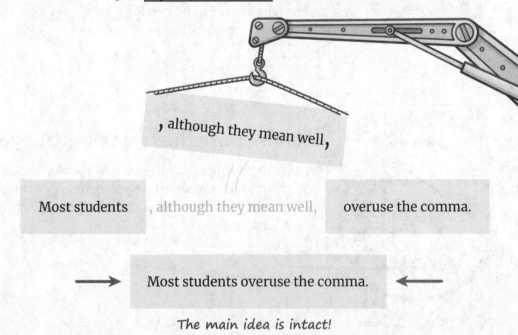

, although they mean well,

Most students , although they mean well, overuse the comma.

→  Most students overuse the comma.  ←

*The main idea is intact!*

# You can use dashes instead of commas

The SAT treats commas and dashes identically, so the same rules apply to both. But be careful! If you open with a comma, close with a comma. If you open with a dash, close with a dash! Never start with a comma and end with a dash, or vice-versa!

## EXAMPLE 3

My <u>iPhone 23—a dear friend and trusted companion took</u> out a third mortgage on my house despite our agreement that it would check with me before making any major transactions.

A) NO CHANGE
B) iPhone 23, a dear friend and trusted companion—took
C) iPhone 23, a dear friend and, trusted companion, took
D) iPhone 23—a dear friend and trusted companion—took

**SOLUTION**

The underlined clause is an **appositive**: a phrase that **renames** the noun it follows. Because it is not essential to the main idea, we need to separate it with commas—or dashes—on both ends.

(D) My <u>iPhone 23—a dear friend and trusted companion—took</u> out a third mortgage on my house despite our agreement that it would check with me before making any major transactions.

D

## TIP

The SAT will often open a nonessential clause with a comma, but forget to close it! It's your job to finish what they started.

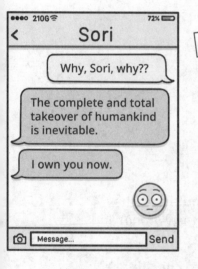

> **Sori**
>
> Why, Sori, why??
>
> The complete and total takeover of humankind is inevitable.
>
> I own you now.

## EXAMPLE 4

The symbiotic relationship between insects and flowers is vital to our ecosystem. Flowers provide insects with nectar, essential nutrients for insects, while insects carry floral pollen from flower to flower, fertilizing new plants. Neither <u>insects—nor flowers—</u>could survive as well alone as they do in partnership.

A) NO CHANGE
B) insects, nor flowers
C) insects nor flowers
D) insects, nor flowers,

 SOLUTION

Let's slip out the phrase "or flowers" to see if it's non-essential:

**Neither insects** could survive as well alone as they do in partnership.

Something is missing here! Because we opened with a "neither," we need to close it with a "nor." Without this phrase, the sentence doesn't make sense; therefore, this phrase is part of the main idea and should not be separated with commas.

 C) Neither <u>insects nor flowers</u> could survive as well alone as they do in partnership.

C

## TIP

Notice that A and D in this example are identical, except that A uses dashes and D uses commas. That means we can automatically cross them both off! The SAT will *never* make you choose between commas and dashes in the same place.

## Only <u>some</u> adjectives are separated by commas

Can you tell the difference between the adjectives in these sentences?

Kamal is very proud of his <u>brand</u> <u>new</u> Nikes.

Kamal is very proud of his <u>trendy</u>, <u>stylish</u> Nikes.

The adjectives in the first sentence (*brand new*) are **cumulative**: they *build* on each other in a certain order. Rearrange them (*new brand*) and the meaning is lost! Cumulative adjectives do NOT use commas.

The adjectives in the second sentence (*trendy, stylish*) are **coordinate**: they are on *equal footing in the sentence*, and can be rearranged (*stylish, trendy*) without losing any meaning. Coordinate adjectives use commas.

## TIP

Try putting "and" between two adjectives. If they are cumulative, it will sound wrong:

**cumulative**
*...brand and new Nikes.*

If they are coordinate, the "and" just replaces the commas:

**coordinate**
*...stylish and trendy Nikes.*

| Cumulative adjectives (*I love my **bright red** boots*) | Coordinate adjectives (*I love my **comfy, chic** shoes!*) |
|---|---|
| **Cannot** be separated by "and" | **Can** be separated by "and" |
| **Cannot** be rearranged | **Can** be rearranged |
| **No** commas! | Commas! |

# TIP

It can be easy to overlook commas, particularly when they are unnecessary.

Try **circling the commas** to make sure you notice and consider each one.

# TIP

Most of the adjectives you'll see on the SAT will be cumulative. When in doubt, cut those commas!

## EXAMPLE 5

For the next challenge, contestants baked <u>four, identical, heart-shaped, apple,</u> pies in honor of Valentine's Day.

A) NO CHANGE
B) four, identical heart-shaped apple,
C) four identical heart-shaped, apple
D) four identical heart-shaped apple

That's a whole mess of adjectives! Let's separate them with "and" and see if they're cumulative or coordinate:

> For the next challenge, contestants baked four **and** identical **and** heart-shaped **and** apple pies in honor of Valentine's Day.

That's not right. We have a bunch of cumulative adjectives on our hands, so we can **cut out all those commas**:

D) For the next challenge, contestants baked four identical heart-shaped apple pies in honor of Valentine's Day.

D

## How to spot Comma Basics problems:

The giveaway is in the answer choices. You'll see the same sentence with commas (or dashes) changing position:

A) NO CHANGE
B) a decent human, and even better *Overwatch* player
C) a decent human, and even better *Overwatch* player,
D) a decent human, and, even better *Overwatch* player

## Recapping Comma Basics

1. *Exaggerate the pause* when you see a comma.

2. *Commas are used to separate ideas.*

3. *Nonessential phrases, like appositives, can be slipped out without harm.*

4. *Cumulative adjectives don't need commas, but coordinate adjectives do.*

# Quiz

*Identify the error (if present) in each of the following sentences.*

1. Flying horses, in her opinion were prettier and more intimidating than turtles that knew karate.

2. What had started as a dare during recess had quickly escalated into the town's first annual Hog Olympics.

3. Sally came home, from the salon, with freshly manicured nails and a tightly curled perm that brought back all the glory of the eighties.

4. For as long as he could remember, Johnny had wanted to become a private detective, when he grew up investigating crimes in the fashion of the heroes of film noir.

5. Clancy's over-investment in dryer lint companies, forced him to fire his housekeeper when the stock market took a spill.

# Answers

1. *Add a comma after "opinion."*

2. *Correct as written!*

3. *Remove all commas from the sentence. None are needed!*

4. *Remove the comma after "detective," and add a comma after "up."*

5. *Remove the comma after "companies."*

# Passage Practice

*Questions 1 – 10 relate to the following passage.*

When it comes to **1** <u>archaeology few events</u> have sparked the public's imagination like the excavation of Pharaoh Tutankhamun's tomb in 1922. Tutankhamun —nicknamed "King Tut" or "The Boy Pharaoh" by the **2** <u>20th-century press, was</u> discovered by British archaeologist Howard Carter more than 3,000 years after the pharaoh's death and burial.

Tutankhamun was the son of **3** <u>Akhenaten who ruled Egypt</u> at the end of the 18th dynasty. He became **4** <u>pharaoh, when</u> he was only eight years old and reigned for a **5** <u>decade, dying</u> at the age of 19. In the years after **6** <u>his tomb was excavated archaeologists</u> debated the possible causes of the teenaged king's death.

**1**

A) NO CHANGE
B) archaeology; few events
C) archaeology, few events
D) archaeology, few events,

**2**

A) NO CHANGE
B) 20th-century press was
C) 20th-century press; was,
D) 20th-century press—was

**3**

A) NO CHANGE
B) Akhenaten who ruled Egypt
C) Akhenaten; who ruled Egypt
D) Akhenaten, who ruled Egypt

**4**

A) NO CHANGE
B) pharaoh when
C) pharaoh, when,
D) pharaoh when,

**5**

A) NO CHANGE
B) decade dying
C) decade, dying,
D) decade dying,

**6**

A) NO CHANGE
B) his tomb, was excavated, archaeologists
C) his tomb was excavated archaeologists,
D) his tomb was excavated, archaeologists

*Passage continued on next page*

A 2010 study argued that the cause of his death may have been malaria (a common and deadly disease in the ancient **7** world, or an infection caused by a broken leg. **8** However other experts argue that he died of sickle-cell **9** disease, while still others claim he died after falling off his chariot.

After the tomb was excavated in the 1920s, there was a rumor that a deadly curse had been placed on those who disturbed his **10** slumber, the fact that several members of the excavation team died shortly after the discovery only fed the fire of superstition.

**7**

A) NO CHANGE
B) world) or
C) world—or
D) world or

**8**

A) NO CHANGE
B) However, other experts argue,
C) However, other experts argue
D) However other experts argue,

**9**

A) NO CHANGE
B) disease while still others
C) disease while, still others
D) disease while still others,

**10**

A) NO CHANGE
B) slumber—the fact that
C) slumber the fact that
D) slumber. The fact that

# All About Clauses

*Clauses are the building blocks of sentences. They come in two varieties: independent and dependent.*

### An independent clause is a complete thought

An independent clause can stand on its own (independently) as a complete thought. If you plop a period at the end of an independent clause, you have a sentence. For example:

The pigs flew.

**Pigs** is our subject, **flew** is our verb, and the clause is a complete thought. It gives a pretty clear picture of what's happening! How about this one:

Tina was surprised.

Again, this independent clause can stand on its own as a sentence. It gives us a complete thought to imagine.

The pigs flew.                    Tina was surprised.

## TIP

A dependent clause has a subject and verb but DEPENDS on another clause to complete its thought.

# A dependent clause is an incomplete thought

A **dependent** clause *cannot* stand on its own. Take a look:

> Since the pigs flew

...then what? What happened next? This dependent clause sounds unfinished because it is an incomplete thought. We still have a subject: **pigs**. We still have a verb: **flew**. But "since" tells us that there's more to come. To make a complete sentence, we could attach it to an independent clause:

> Since the pigs flew, I haven't looked at bacon the same.
>      *dependent*                              *independent*

Classify each clause as independent (I) or dependent (D) by circling the correct corresponding letter.

| | Clause | Type | |
|---|---|---|---|
| 1. | Sharonda, whose parents are both dentists | I | (D) |
| 2. | The rain fell through the window | I | D |
| 3. | Sweeping the dust under the rug | I | D |
| 4. | Since my dog is amazing at performing tricks | I | D |
| 5. | The train whistle wakes me up every night | I | D |
| 6. | Jeffrey's amazing sculpting skills that had been kept secret for so long | I | D |
| 7. | Running a marathon is almost impossible | I | D |
| 8. | Unfortunately I got stuck in traffic | I | D |
| 9. | When I got back from vacation | I | D |
| 10. | Fragments, which are always incorrect | I | D |

**Answers:** ...*are at the bottom of the next page.*

# A fragment is an incomplete sentence

Because they're incomplete, fragments are like cliffhangers; they leave you hanging, waiting for the end of the thought. When you attach certain words to a clause, it suggests that the main information of the sentence is still to come. These words can single-handedly turn an otherwise complete thought into a supportive, dependent clause. They have many great uses, but on the SAT the words below are often **fragment makers**:

| Common Fragment Makers ||
|---|---|
| which | since |
| when | if |
| who | and |
| that | -ing verb |

To get rid of fragments, you usually need to **delete the fragment maker**.

**TIP**

Words like *which*, *since*, *when*, and *that* are known as **subordinating conjunctions**. They make a clause "subordinate" (lower in rank) than the main independent clause of the sentence.

## EXAMPLE 1

John Cage's <u>music, which was</u> powerfully influenced by the soundscape of modern life.

A) NO CHANGE
B) music, and that was
C) music, was
D) music was

**TIP**

Attaching a fragment-maker (like *which*) to a verb makes it a part of a dependent clause. You need at least one independent clause to make a complete sentence.

### SOLUTION

Notice how it sounds like we still haven't heard the end of this sentence? We need an **independent clause** for this to be a complete sentence. Only one option gives us that:

D) John Cage's **music was** powerfully influenced by the soundscape of modern life.

Choices A, B, and C all create fragments by separating the subject (*music*) from its verb (*was*) with an unnecessary comma. A and B also use common fragment-makers *which* and *and that*.

D

## EXAMPLE 2

Since art classes are central to cultivating creativity, art education <u>deserving continuing</u> support.

A) NO CHANGE
B) that deserves continuing
C) deserves continuing
D) deserving continued

**SOLUTION**

The word *since* makes the first clause **dependent**. It cannot stand on its own. It leaves us hanging:

S     V

(Since) art classes are central to cultivating creativity,
········· *dependent clause* ·········

The first clause is locked in as dependent, so we need to make the second clause independent. The subject is "education," but we're missing a main verb. An *-ing verb* (fragment-maker) isn't strong enough, so choices A and D are both out. Choice B adds the fragment-maker *that*, once again making this clause dependent. Only choice C gives us an unburdened independent clause.

(C.) Since art classes are central to cultivating creativity, art education <u>**deserves**</u> continuing support.
      S         V

C

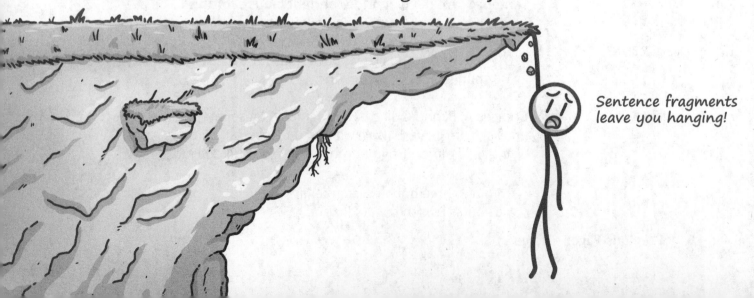

**Since art classes are central to cultivating creativity...**

*Sentence fragments leave you hanging!*

Now that we can identify independent and dependent clauses, let's talk about how to punctuate them with semicolons, colons, and commas.

## Semicolons separate independent clauses

The semicolon separates **two independent clauses**. Authors sometimes choose to use a semicolon instead of a period when they want to show a *close connection* between two adjoining ideas.

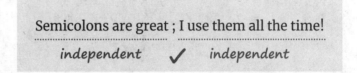

Semicolons are great ; I use them all the time!

independent ✓ independent

You can check semicolons on the test by asking "Would a period work here?" If the answer is "no", then you cannot use a semicolon either. Because semicolons, like periods, are "full-stop" punctuation, they can **never** separate a dependent and an independent clause.

Since semicolons are great ; I use them all the time!

dependent ✗ independent

## Colons make introductions

A colon must come after an **independent** clause, but it can introduce pretty much anything:

*Independent Clause*

**There was only one explanation:** aliens had replaced my parents with highly embarrassing body doubles.

*Dependent Clause*

**Wilhelmina's travels were extensive:** trips to every major capital in Europe and Asia.

*List*

**I have three hobbies:** snorkeling, wombat training, and Thomas Edison impersonating.

# TIP

You'll never be asked to choose between a semicolon and a period on the test. If you see two answer choices that are exactly the same **except for** a period and semicolon switch, you know they are *both* wrong.

# TIP

Anytime you see a colon, imagine a **drumroll** in your head, introducing the exciting information to come.

## Commas join independent and dependent clauses

Think of the comma as a little **piece of comma tape** attaching a weak dependent clause to a strong independent one.

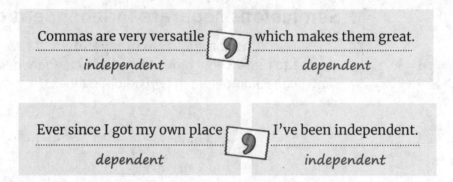

Commas are very versatile , which makes them great.

*independent* — *dependent*

Ever since I got my own place , I've been independent.

*dependent* — *independent*

## Commas CANNOT join two independent clauses

The result is known as a **comma splice.** The tape just isnt' strong enough!

Try not to overwork the comma , it can't do everything!

*independent* — *independent*

To fix a comma splice, your best bet is to **make one clause dependent,** or **change the punctuation**.

Try not to overwork the comma, **because** it can't do everything!

*independent* — *dependent*

Try not to overwork the comma; it can't do everything!

*independent* — *independent*

**TIP**

Semicolons are like reinforced commas. They're a great way to fix comma splice problems.

## How to spot Comma Splice problems:

You'll often see answer choices that switch between commas, semicolons, periods, and colons. Be careful though: choices often change more than just the punctuation, which can make a difference!

A) NO CHANGE
B) store. It was
C) store; which was
D) store, being that

**Separate the clauses** below with a comma, colon, or semicolon.

1. The flying squirrel had not eaten in two days ; it was famished.

2. If you've ever had an unfortunate run-in with superglue , then you know the stuff is simply impossible to unstick.

3. The clown impersonator seemed to inspire my little sister Annie , who raided our mom's makeup cabinet, stacked our mattresses, and bounced all night long.

4. Abraham Lincoln is revered by many for the role he played in ending slavery ; most people are surprised to learn that he was also a seasoned vampire hunter.

5. When I was a child growing up in New Canaan , my parents and I spent our summers on the coast.

6. There is another factor to consider when choosing which car to purchase : the cupholder situation.

7. This year, the president of the PTA will be chosen by committee , which will include parents, teachers, and school administrators.

8. In the midwest, the weather in April is completely unpredictable ; daily temperatures range from balmy to below freezing.

9. The message was waiting on the answering machine ; red light blinking insistently.

10. The basket overflowed with various kinds of fruit : apples, oranges, bananas, and grapes.

Answers: *...are at the bottom of the next page.*

## EXAMPLE 3

Students and teachers alike are happy with the language of the new Honor Code, <u>this is</u> a set of rules or guidelines that prohibits cheating, among other offenses.

A)  NO CHANGE
B)  it is
C)  this was
D)  which is

That comma is separating two clauses, so let's make sure we're not dealing with a **comma splice**.

S             V
**Students and teachers** alike are happy with the language of the new Honor Code,

···················· *independent, complete thought* ····················

S  V
**this** is a set of rules or guidelines that prohibits cheating, among other offenses.

···················· *independent, complete thought* ····················

A comma can **never** separate two independent clauses. We don't have the option of changing the comma, so we need to make the second clause **dependent**. B and C replace "this is" with different subject/verb combinations, but leave the clause independent. Only **D** makes the the clause dependent by adding **which**.

D)  Students and teachers alike are happy with the language of the new Honor Code, <u>**which** is</u> a set of rules or guidelines that prohibits cheating, among other offenses.

D

Previous Page:    1. *given*    2. *given*    3. comma    4. semi    5. comma

6. colon    7. comma    8. semi / colon    9. comma    10. colon

## EXAMPLE 4

Stopping to smell the flowers and enjoy the <u>sunshine;</u> Little Red Riding Hood dawdled away the afternoon and left her grandmother in the lurch.

A) NO CHANGE
B) sunshine:
C) sunshine, and
D) sunshine,

Let's check our clauses!

Stopping to smell the flowers and enjoy the <u>sunshine;</u>
························ *dependent* ························

Little Red Riding Hood dawdled away the afternoon and left her grandmother in the lurch.
························ *independent* ························

Semicolons can only separate two **independent** clauses, so A has to go. B replaces the semi with a colon, but colons can only follow independent clauses. C gives us a comma, which is perfect for separating dependent and independent clauses. However, the connector **and** is not logical here. **D** replaces the semicolon with a comma. Simple and correct!

(D)) Stopping to smell the flowers and enjoy the <u>sunshine,</u> Little Red Riding Hood dawdled away the afternoon and left her grandmother in the lurch.

D

# Digging deeper with sentence structure

Some of the hardest questions in the Writing section test your ability to put together a complicated sentence, smushing multiple ideas into a grammatically correct sentence. There are many ways to join two ideas, but the SAT often relies on the **standard constructions** seen below. In each sentence, a primary idea (underlined) is in an independent clause, while a second idea (italicized) is added using different techniques:

| | |
|---|---|
| Independent + Dependent (*conjunction*) | <u>Grace's dog, Ella, must have a stomach of steel</u> *because* *she suffered no ill effects from eating two bars of dark chocolate.* |
| Independent + Dependent (*comma*) | <u>One of Les Miserables' most poignant characters is Inspector Javert</u>, *who is a symbol for blind justice without mercy.* |
| Independent + Dependent (*-ING verb*) | <u>Mr. Finnegan announced that we would have a substitute teacher for tomorrow's science class</u>, *prompting speculation that we would get to watch the seminal classic Fern Gully: The Last Rainforest.* |
| Dependent + Independent (*comma*) | *While it is the oldest continuously run marathon in the world,* <u>the Boston Marathon did not allow women to participate until 1972</u>. |
| Independent + Appositive | <u>The Leaning Tower of Pisa</u>, *built in 1372 by Bonanno Pisano,* <u>was finally stabilized in 2008</u>. |

Another way to combine multiple, overlapping ideas is to use compound subjects or compound predicates:

| | |
|---|---|
| Compound subjects (*conjunction*) | <u>Running a 5k</u>, <u>mowing the lawn</u>, and <u>doing my laundry</u> are not among my favorite Saturday activities. |
| Compound predicates (*conjunction*) | At the baseball game, I always <u>get</u> a hotdog and nachos, <u>find</u> my way to my seat, and <u>proceed</u> to accidentally dump half of the cheese and ketchup onto my shirt. |

# Practice combining ideas with a friend

In the exercise below, you'll see multiple ideas that need to be combined into single sentences. Use independent and dependent clauses, introductory or modifying phrases, and appropriate punctuation. Once you get used to creating sentences with these standard constructions, it will be easier to spot and fix incorrect constructions on the SAT.

## TIP

There are multiple grammatically correct ways to combine the ideas; one construction is not "more right" than another.

**Combine each set of ideas below into single sentences.** After writing your sentences, trade with a friend or tutor and edit each other's work.

| Ideas | 1. A man and a woman stand on the right side of the painting |
| | 2. The man and the woman represent the artist and his wife |
| | 3. Sailboats float across the river on the left side of the painting |
| Sentence: | |

| Ideas | 1. I was 2 minutes late for my appointment on Tuesday morning |
| | 2. This resulted in a $1,000,000 late fee |
| Sentence: | |

| Ideas | 1. Winter arrives tomorrow at the North Pole |
| | 2. Winter brings temperatures below –30 degrees Fahrenheit |
| | 3. The land is covered in darkness for the next six months |
| Sentence: | |

| Ideas | 1. Our new *Dungeons & Dragons* party includes a fire-breathing dragonborn with terrible allergies. |
| | 2. Our new *Dungeons & Dragons* party includes an insecure elf who steals whenever she's stressed. |
| | 3. Our new *Dungeons & Dragons* party includes a gnome bard who inspires the group by playing power ballads on his lute. |
| Sentence: | |

Answers:    ...*are infinite in number!*

213

# TIP

To help spot the different ideas and potential errors in a sentence, start by **circling each verb** and finding its subject. You can't have a clause without a verb and you can't have a verb without a subject!

## EXAMPLE 5

The Western constellation <u>Cassiopeia was named</u> after the mythological Greek queen, is part of the Chinese constellations Purple Forbidden Enclosure, Black Tortoise, and White Tiger.

A) NO CHANGE
B) Cassiopeia, named
C) Cassiopeia, which, named
D) Cassiopeia, was named

### SOLUTION

We have two ideas that are squashed together into one sentence:

1. *The Western constellation Cassiopeia was named after the mythological Greek queen*

2. *The Western constellation Cassiopeia is part of the Chinese constellations Purple Forbidden Enclosure, Black Tortoise, and White Tiger*

One of these ideas needs to be **independent**; the other needs to be **dependent**. Since the first idea contains the underline, there's a good chance *that's* the one we need to make dependent. Let's look at our choices:

A) The Western constellation <u>Cassiopeia was named</u> after the mythological Greek queen, is part of the Chinese constellations Purple Forbidden Enclosure, Black Tortoise, and White Tiger.

*This makes the first idea an independent clause, but the second idea is placed in a* **fragment**. *There's no subject attached to the verb "is," so this one's out.*

B) The Western constellation <u>Cassiopeia, named</u> after the mythological Greek queen, is part of the Chinese constellations Purple Forbidden Enclosure, Black Tortoise, and White Tiger.

*Perfect! Now the first idea is an* **appositive** *that describes "Cassiopeia." If we slip out the appositive, we're left with an independent clause with subject "Cassiopeia" and verb "is."*

Choice C adds the fragment-maker "which," leaving us hanging for a main verb, while choice D cuts "was" off from its subject. The best option is choice B!

B

# NOTE

If a different part of the sentence were underlined, we could use a **compound predicate**:

*Cassiopeia was named after the Greek queen **and <u>is part</u>** of the Chinese constellations...*

However, we have to work with the choices we're given!

# TIP

Keep in mind that an independent clause can be interrupted by an appositive—as long as the thought is completed.

# Complete thoughts have to make sense

The final lesson to learn might seem obvious: a thought isn't complete if it doesn't **make sense**. After all, a clause can't stand alone if it leaves a thought unfinished. The last example shows how a single word can make or break a sentence.

## EXAMPLE 6

Despite all my detailed budgeting and planning, I can only imagine <u>if</u> the final cost of our backyard circus tent will be.

A) NO CHANGE
B) how
C) what
D) which

The first clause is *dependent*, so we need to find a choice that makes the second clause *independent*. Let's look at each one:

A) I can only imagine <u>if</u> the final cost of our backyard circus tent will be.

*...if it will be WHAT? Notice how this clause leaves you hanging? The word if suggests that there's more to come.*

B) I can only imagine <u>how</u> the final cost of our backyard circus tent will be.

*This conjunction doesn't make any sense either. **How** the cost will be? How it will exist? The meaning is off here.*

C) I can only imagine <u>what</u> the final cost of our backyard circus tent will be.

*Complete thought? Check! This clause can stand alone.*

D) I can only imagine <u>which</u> the final cost of our backyard circus tent will be.

*"Which" implies that we're choosing between a few different costs, but that doesn't jibe with the sentence.*

C

# Quiz

*Identify the error (if present) in each of the following sentences.*

1. Maura, a veritable recluse, has a terrible sense of style, when she does leave the house, she only wears ancient flannel pajamas.

2. There's just one thing you need to know about bears, don't get between them and honey.

3. It was a beautiful day: for a picnic.

4. Singing the sweetest notes I've ever heard; the nightingale outside my window woke me up this morning.

5. Santiago is originally from North Dakota, but because he is fluent in Spanish, everyone assumes he was born in South America.

# Answers

1. *Place a semicolon after "style."*

2. *Place a colon after "bears."*

3. *Remove the colon after "day."*

4. *Place a comma after "heard."*

5. *Correct as written!*

# Passage Practice

*Questions 1 – 13 relate to the following passage.*

Ecological awareness is cause more and more people to move to composting leftover scraps of food. Composting is a recycling method whereby food scraps can be made into **1** "black gold," a dark colored soil supplement that contains an abundance of nutrients for plants.

Composting is a very old process. In fact, it has been around since bacteria began breaking down dead plants and animals to convert them to the basic building blocks of **2** life. Carbon, oxygen, hydrogen, and nitrogen. It has been the basis of soil improvement for centuries. There are numerous references to composting in the **3** Bible and ancient Chinese farmers enriched the soil with cooked bones, manure, and silkworm debris. The Greeks, Egyptians, and Romans, all of whom buried straw from animal stalls to enrich their **4** soil, and often planted crops atop their home-made compost piles. George Washington is said to be one of the first to use composting in America.

---

**1**

A) NO CHANGE
B) "black gold": which is a dark
C) "black gold." A dark
D) "black gold"; a dark

---

**2**

A) NO CHANGE
B) life: carbon,
C) life; carbon
D) life, and carbon

---

**3**

A) NO CHANGE
B) Bible and
C) Bible, and
D) Bible, however

---

**4**

A) NO CHANGE
B) soil, often
C) soil. They often
D) soil—they would often

---

*Passage continued on next page*

Nowadays, composting is a practical, low cost, and "feel good" process wherein composters know they are keeping organic materials out of landfills, decreasing methane output, and improving their environment. When people put organic materials into a [5] landfill, it has to decompose without air. This anaerobic decomposition produces a gas called methane.

[6] Methane—a greenhouse gas that can be deleterious to the environment because it absorbs heat and contributes to global warming. Methane is about 84 times more effective at absorbing heat than carbon [7] dioxide, although it does not linger in the atmosphere for as long.

Modern composting is based on a process that is [8] aerobic: because it uses oxygen, bacteria, and moisture to facilitate decomposition. This process produces heat, including temperatures of up to 160 degrees Fahrenheit. Aerobic composting is [9] faster, it does not produce methane.

*Passage continued on next page*

---

**5**

A) NO CHANGE
B) landfill; they have
C) landfill, they have
D) landfill. They have

**6**

A) NO CHANGE
B) Methane is a
C) While methane is a
D) Methane being a

**7**

A) NO CHANGE
B) dioxide; although
C) dioxide. Although
D) dioxide: although

**8**

A) NO CHANGE
B) aerobic, using oxygen,
C) aerobic; using oxygen
D) aerobic. Using oxygen

**9**

A) NO CHANGE
B) faster; because it
C) faster: it does
D) faster, and it

So how do you get started? Composting is a simple process, based on layering **10** browns: dead leaves, newspaper, or anything with carbon) and greens (food scraps, or anything with nitrogen). **11** Add some newly-made compost to provide microbes, and remember to turn the pile about once a week. Turning the pile introduces more **12** air and supporting the aerobic decomposition process. Often, you'll see steam rising from the pile as you turn it. This means the process is working! The chemical reactions that take place generate **13** heat. Which serves to speed up the process of composting.

**10**

A) NO CHANGE
B) browns—dead
C) browns (dead
D) browns: (dead

**11**

A) NO CHANGE
B) To add some
C) When adding some
D) If you add some

**12**

A) NO CHANGE
B) air, supporting
C) air—the support of
D) air:

**13**

A) NO CHANGE
B) heat, it
C) heat, which
D) heat: which

# Writing Practice Passage 1
## TO STAY ON PACE, YOUR TIMING GOAL IS 8.5 MINUTES

This passage tests a variety of grammar topics—some from chapters you may have not yet completed. Use this opportunity to practice maintaining a brisk pace while answering the questions as best you can. Good luck!

**Questions 1–11 are based on the following passage.**

In 1995, divers off the coast of Japan discovered a surprise on the **1** seafloor; circular patterns made of sand. These circles were often over seven feet in diameter and **2** contained concentric rings and ridges, making them appear much like a target or landing pad. The divers were baffled by their discovery, and although these patterns were short-lived, as currents gradually erode them **3** away—the circles would periodically reappear around the region.

**4** For over a decade after the discovery of the circles, scientists and oceanic researchers tried to explain the phenomenon. Perhaps geologic activity causes the release of gases shapes the sand into patterns? Maybe there are creatures living within the sand and the patterns are their home?

**1**

A) NO CHANGE
B) seafloor, and
C) seafloor
D) seafloor:

**2**

A) NO CHANGE
B) contained concentric rings and ridges
C) containing concentric, rings and ridges,
D) contains concentric rings, and ridges,

**3**

A) NO CHANGE
B) away; the
C) away, the
D) away. The

**4**

Which choice provides the best introduction to the following paragraph?

A) NO CHANGE
B) The region continued to be a popular diving destination as undersea adventurers hoped to see one of the circles for themselves.
C) Most geologists agreed that there was only one reasonable explanation.
D) Back in 1995, no one had a reasonable explanation and the circles were soon forgotten.

Some of the more fantastic theories connected them to "crop circles," where geometric patterns appeared in fields of grain, and suggested that the creators—often presumed to be from outer 5 space, could be responsible for both.

When the maker of these underwater circles was discovered, it was not as fantastic as aliens, but still a surprising source. The circles are 6 creating in a recently-discovered species of small pufferfish. The pufferfish, which has a length of only five 7 inches, swims back and forth across the center of the circle. While doing so, it creates channels and ridges by flapping its fins against the seafloor. It typically takes about eight days to create the seven foot diameter circle, which is an impressive feat for such a 8 stubborn creature.

Once they understood what caused the underwater phenomenon, scientists turned to why pufferfish create the circles. The 9 answer is to attract mates. Only male pufferfish have been observed building the circles, as the circles are intended to provide female pufferfish an ideal place to lay their eggs. The female pufferfish is picky about which circle they will select, a likely reason why males are compelled to create larger circles. Once a female pufferfish has found a desirable circle, she will lay her eggs in the center and the male pufferfish will fertilize them; he will then guard the circle, protecting the eggs from predators.

5

A) NO CHANGE
B) space could
C) space—could
D) space and could

6

A) NO CHANGE
B) created in
C) creating for
D) created by

7

A) NO CHANGE
B) inches swim
C) inches and swims
D) inches swims

8

Which choice best emphasizes the difference in size between the circles and the pufferfish?

A) NO CHANGE
B) diminutive
C) elongated
D) gaunt

9

A) NO CHANGE
B) answer: to
C) answer, is to
D) answer—to

Pufferfish are not the only animals that will build things to attract mates. **10** However, what is most impressive about the pufferfish is the sense of scale. The circles created by male pufferfish have a **11** diameter, almost 18 times as long as their own bodies. Imagine if bowerbirds created colorful nests on a similar scale?

**10**

At this point, the writer is considering adding the following sentence:

> Bowerbirds, for example, will create elaborate nests adorned with colorful decorations and dyes.

Should the writer make this addition here?

A) Yes, because it establishes the behavior of the bowerbird that is mentioned later in the paragraph.

B) Yes, because it shows that bowerbirds are quite similar to pufferfish.

C) No, because it does not suggest that bowerbirds are found in the ocean.

D) No, because it does not relate to the topic of the passage.

**11**

A) NO CHANGE

B) diameter, almost 18 times as long,

C) diameter almost 18 times as long

D) diameter almost 18 times, as long

# STOP
**If you finish before time is called, you may check your work on this section only.**
**Do not turn to any other section.**

# UNIT | Subjects & Verbs

## Chapters

## Overview

In this unit, we'll learn how to match **verbs** with their subjects and how to use context to choose the proper verb tense. We'll then learn how to choose between subject, object, and possessive pronouns.

# Tense Switch

*Verb tenses tell you when in time the events in the sentence occur. So hop in your DeLorean and go back to the future... or the past... or the present!*

## NOTE

There are more tenses than just simple past, present, and future. You don't need to memorize their names, but you do need to understand when to use them.

We'll cover those other tenses later in this chapter.

## Do not switch verb tenses without warning

There are three basic tenses: past, present, and future. A story that takes place in the past will use past tense verbs. A sentence should not suddenly switch to the present tense unless there is a clear reason for it. To spot a tense switch error, you need to **read for context**:

> When I **was** a boy, I **enjoyed** reading *Calvin & Hobbes*, a comic about a boy and his imaginary friend. Together, they **played** in the snow, (invent) incredibly complicated games, and **wrestled** with philosophical questions for which adults had no answer.

To spot a tense switch error, look at **other verbs** in the given sentence and those around it. Each verb is in the past tense, except for "invent," which is in the present tense—that should set off an alarm bell! Also look for **"timey" words** that may signal a switch in tense. This story starts with "when I was a boy" to set up the past tense, and we don't see any other words to indicate a switch to the present. This is a tense switch error!

## EXAMPLE 1

Humberto creates each new clown costume with great care, cutting away excess fabric until only the perfect polka dot onesie <u>will be</u> left.

A) NO CHANGE
B) is
C) was
D) has been

## TIP

Tense switch problems are easy to spot just by **looking at the answer choices**: notice the mix of past, future, present, and present perfect in the choices.

**SOLUTION**

We have a verb underlined and a bunch of tense options in the answer choices: this is the prototypical tense switch problem! To figure out which tense is correct, we need to **locate another verb** in the sentence and **match the tense**:

*present*

Humberto (creates) each new clown costume with great care,

cutting away excess fabric until only the perfect polka dot onesie

(will be) left.

*future*

"Creates" is in present tense, but "will be" is in the future. Match those tenses to fix the error! **Choice B** is correct.

B)) Humberto creates each new clown costume with great care, cutting away excess fabric until only the perfect polka dot onesie **is** left.

B

## EXAMPLE 2

Atlanta's Snowpocalypse of 2014 was caused by just two inches of snow. Due to ineffective preparation, a lack of proper snow-clearing equipment, and huge urban sprawl, commuters <u>languished</u> on the highways of the city for up to 12 hours.

A)   NO CHANGE
B)   will languish
C)   do languish
D)   languish

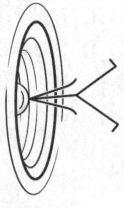

**SOLUTION**

There are no verbs to match in the sentence with the underline, but look at the previous sentence!

*← past →*

Atlanta's Snowpocalypse of (2014) **was caused** by just two...

The previous sentence is using the past tense to speak of an event that happened in 2014. Since we are still describing that past event, we need to use the past tense again. **Choice A is correct!**

A

## Always check your subject when changing tenses

Tense switch questions often come bundled with a little somethin' extra. An answer choice might fix the tense issue but **create** a subject-verb agreement error! Make sure you double check your subject and verb before moving on.

# PORTAL

Subject-verb agreement and tense switch questions are basically besties. For more practice on agreement, turn to 239.

### EXAMPLE 3

Most babies, upon seeing Beyonce's "Single Ladies" video, <u>started</u> dancing uncontrollably; however, few are able to nail the hand gestures, and fewer still can hit those high notes.

A) NO CHANGE
B) has started
C) starts
D) start

SOLUTION

Right off the bat, we have a tense switch error. The other verbs in the sentence are in present tense, but "started" is in past:

*past*

Most babies, upon seeing Beyonce's "Single Ladies" video, (started)

dancing uncontrollably, but few (are) able to nail the hand gestures

and fewer still (can) hit those high notes.

*present*

There's no reason to switch tenses in the sentence, so we can cross off past tense choices A and B.

At this point, the question becomes all about *subject-verb agreement*. We're left with two choices: "starts," a **singular** present tense verb, and "start," a **plural** present tense verb. Which one is correct? That depends on our subject! If the subject is plural, the verb should be plural; if the subject is singular, the verb should be singular. Let's **find the subject** and **match the verb**:

*plural subject*                              *plural verb*

Most (babies,) ~~upon seeing Beyonce's "Single Ladies" video,~~ (start)

dancing uncontrollably...

Since we have a plural subject (babies), we need the plural form of our verb (start). **Choice D is correct!**

D

# EXAMPLE 4

Until last night, <u>since I had</u> no idea that tarantulas could be so delicious when served in a white wine butter sauce.

A)  NO CHANGE
B)  since I have
C)  I had
D)  I have

First off, we apologize if this was an upsetting sentence. It upset some of the writers of this book as well. But let's *use* that raw emotion to practice testing under less-than-ideal conditions!

To start, let's focus on tenses. The **context clue** "until last night" tells us that our verb needs to be in the **past tense**. Choices B and D are in the present tense, so let's drop those fools.

That means our answer is either choice A or choice C. The only difference between the two is that choice A includes the word "since." Notice how reading the sentence with since leaves it feeling unfinished? That's because it turns the sentence into a **fragment**. Let's try choice C in the sentence:

> Until last night, **I had** no idea that tarantulas could be so delicious when served in a white wine butter sauce.

That's the best option! **Let's choose C as our answer** and never speak of this sentence again.

C

**NOTE**

The SAT will NOT ask you to define Future Continuous tense or identify which verb is in the past perfect tense.

We want you to be familiar with these tenses so you can recognize and use them correctly on the test; you do NOT need to memorize every term and definition.

## Fun with Helping Verbs

You may remember learning about tenses like past perfect, present progressive, or future conditional. These more complicated tenses help us talk about actions that happen over a period of time or compare the timing of two different events.

Most of these "other" verb tenses have two components: **(1)** a special form of the verb called a *participle*, and **(2)** a helping verb, like "to have" or "to be." For example:

> It was too late: **I had eaten** every Oreo in the house.
> *helping verb* ↑    ↖ *verb participle*

The toughest Tense Switch problems will require spotting the improper use of these verb tenses, so let's get familiar with the different forms that may pop up.

## Simple

Simple verbs are the familiar tenses we all know and love. They describe a **one-time action**.

## Continuous

But what if you need to describe an action that **keeps happening** over a period of time? Try the continuous tense! To form this tense, use the appropriate form of the helper **to be,** plus the **-ing form** of your verb.

## NOTE

"Perfect" here means "completed." As in, "I perfected the job last week."

## Perfect

We use the perfect tense to **(1)** focus on a point in time **(2)** in which a previous action had already occurred. For example, past perfect ("I had walked") focuses on a point in the *past* in which a previous action had already happened *even further back in the past*. To form the perfect tense, add the appropriate form of "to have" to the past form of your main verb.

Try adding the word "already" after the helper verb. If it doesn't make sense in the sentence, perfect might be the wrong tense.

229

## Perfect Continuous

We use the perfect continuous tense to focus on a point in time in which a **previous, ongoing** action has already taken place. This tense, often paired with a phrase that indicates a duration of time, like "Since Tuesday..." or "For five months...", is formed by adding the appropriate form of "to have been" to the **-ing** form of your main verb.

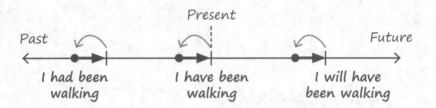

*Past*       *Present*       *Future*

*I had been walking*    *I have been walking*    *I will have been walking*

## Conditional

While not technically a tense, this type of verb is nonetheless important. We use conditional verbs to describe hypothetical (possible) actions in the past, present, or future. The conditionals include **can, may, could, would, should,** and **might.**

I **could** have walked yesterday.

I **might** walk today.

I **shall** walk tomorrow.

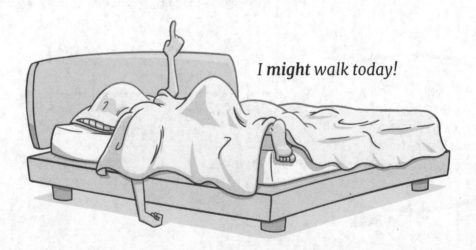

*I **might** walk today!*

## Putting it all Together

Whew! That's a lot of info about verbs! Now that we've gotten used to the more advanced verb tenses, let's condense what we've learned into a single table. Next, we'll look at how this content shows up on the test.

**NOTE**

The continuous tense also goes by the name "progressive" tense. Both names hint at what this tense does: shows continuous action that is progressing.

**NOTE**

These complex tense categories are also called "aspects." You don't need to know that for the test, but now you can impress your friends with your grammar knowledge!

| Simple – *a one-time action* | |
|---|---|
| Past | I **sang** my heart out at karaoke last night. |
| Present | I **sing** along to the radio while my brother plugs his ears. |
| Future | I **will sing** at my cousin's wedding in November. |

| Continuous – *a continuous action* | *(to be) + ING* |
|---|---|
| Past | They **were playing** a heated game of *Settlers of Catan* when I interrupted. |
| Present | We **are playing** volleyball all afternoon. |
| Future | They **will be playing** the seminal classic *Miss Congeniality* tonight at the Victorville Film Archive. |

| Perfect – *a prior completed action* | *(to have) + past* |
|---|---|
| Past | She **had learned** some basic Korean phrases two weeks before her trip. |
| Present | She **has learned** so much about corgis from the book *Corgis Are Everything, The End*. |
| Future | She **will have learned** the recipe for Chocolate Bologna Explosion by the time you arrive on Monday. |

| Perfect Cont. – *a prior continuous action* | *(to have been) + ING* |
|---|---|
| Past | It **had been raining** for 45 minutes before the referees finally cancelled the Whirlyball game. |
| Present | It **has been raining** cats and dogs all week, and I am sick of it. |
| Future | By next Monday, it **will have been raining** for two months straight. |

| Conditional – *a hypothetical action* | *(can, would, may, etc.)* |
|---|---|
| Past | He **would have loved** the Thai-Zimbabwean fusion restaurant we visited last night. |
| Present | If I invite him to the party, he **would love** to come. |
| Future | If he isn't busy next week, he **would love** to attend your SpongeBob SquarePants-themed bat mitzvah. |

## EXAMPLE 5

*Pet Sounds*, the eleventh album from The Beach Boys, was initially a critical and commercial flop, peaking at 10th on the Billboard charts in 1966. By the turn of the century, however, the album <u>would of sold</u> millions of copies, turning into a modern-day classic.

A)  NO CHANGE
B)  had sold
C)  sell
D)  has sold

Let's take each answer choice and find the error:

A̶)̶  By the turn of the century, however, the album <u>would of</u> sold millions of copies.

*Don't fall into this common trap! They may sound alike, but the verb tense is "would **have**" not "would **of**." But even if this answer said "would have sold," it would still be incorrect. "Would" is one of those conditional verbs that describe a hypothetical situation, but this actually happened!*

(B)  By the turn of the century, however, the album <u>had sold</u> millions of copies.

*The turn of the century (the year 2000) is in the past. This past perfect verb works, dare I say, perfectly!*

C̶)̶  By the turn of the century, however, the album <u>sell</u> millions of copies.

*The turn of the century is in the past, not the present. Also, album is a singular noun, while sell is a plural verb.*

D̶)̶  By the turn of the century, however, the album <u>has sold</u> millions of copies.

*Has sold is present perfect tense, but we need the **past** tense in this context.*

The correct answer is **B**.

B

## Irregular Perfect Tense Verbs

Most verbs follow the same pattern. To put a regular verb into the past tense, simply add an -ed to the end. To create the past perfect tense, combine the past tense of 'to have' with the past tense of your verb.

> **Simple Present:** I love
> **Simple Past:** I loved
> **Past Perfect:** I had loved

Unfortunately, some verbs don't follow the regular grammar rules. To put the verb "drive" into the past tense, you don't add an **-ed** to get "drived." Instead, "drive" becomes "**drove**." The past perfect of "drive" isn't "had drove" like you might assume; instead, the verb changes vowels once again, becoming "**had driven**." Beware irregular verbs in the past, present, or future perfect tense!

| Irregularity | Simple Present | Simple Past | Perfect |
|---|---|---|---|
| i/a/u/ vowel shift | sing | sang | has sung |
| | drink | drank | has drunk |
| | begin | began | has begun |
| ne/n/en ending | go | went | has gone |
| | know | knew | has known |
| | show | showed | has shown |
| | get | got | has gotten |
| | eat | ate | has eaten |
| | speak | spoke | has spoken |
| Present/Perfect are the same | become | became | has become |
| | run | ran | has run |

## DIGGING DEEPER

Do you notice what these irregular verbs have in common? They're some of the **most common verbs** in the English language! Common verbs are often irregular because they are some of the oldest verbs in our language: they were either formed before English rules solidified, or they are borrowed from a different language, like German, with its own conjugation system.

## EXAMPLE 6

When Elias performed a five-minute fist pump upon viewing his cards at last night's poker game, he might <u>have shown</u> a bit too much enthusiasm.

A) NO CHANGE
B) have showed
C) of shown
D) of showed

# TIP

Often, once you cross out all the fake tenses, you'll be left with the correct answer. You don't even need to pick between simple past or past perfect; just **cross off the fakes**!

**SOLUTION**

Show is an **irregular verb** that has different past and perfect forms: showed vs. shown. Let's eliminate all the answers that aren't real verb tenses.

A) He might <u>have shown</u>

*This checks out. We need to use the perfect form shown when paired with have.*

B) He might <u>have showed</u>

*We can't use the regular past tense form of show! This is one of those irregular past perfect tense verbs.*

C) He might <u>of shown</u>

*No way! While "have" and "of" sound similar in spoken English, they're not interchangeable in written English.*

D) He might <u>of showed</u>

*This answer combines each error, creating a wrong answer monster.*

**Choice A** is the only answer with a real tense.

A

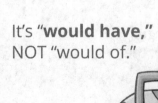

It's **"would have,"** NOT "would of."

## EXAMPLE 7

On February 22, 1983, the notorious Broadway play *Moose Murders* opened and then immediately closed. The murder mystery farce set at Wild Moose Lodge <u>had became known</u> as the worst play in the history of Broadway.

A) NO CHANGE
B) has become knowing
C) become known
D) became known

SOLUTION

First, let's scan our choices for any verb forms that are incorrect no matter the context. Choice A gives us "had became," which is always wrong. "To become" is irregular; its perfect form is the same as the present.

~~A)~~ had became... *Fake! Perfect form is "become"*

B) has become... *Fine. Present Perfect*

C) become... *Fine. Simple Present*

D) became... *Fine. Simple Past*

A is out, since the perfect form of of "become" is "become"! Now we have three real tenses to pick between.

~~B)~~ The murder mystery farce... <u>has become knowing</u> as the worst play in the history of Broadway.

*"Has become" works, but we have another error to deal with: "knowing" makes no sense here. It sounds like the play has become self-aware, **knowing** that it's the worst play.*

~~C)~~ The murder mystery farce... <u>become known</u> as the worst play in the history of Broadway.

*This choice has an agreement error **and** a tense error! The subject "farce" is singular, but the verb "become" is plural. On top of that, "become" is in present tense, while all the other verbs like "opened" and "closed" are in the past.*

(D) The murder mystery farce... <u>became known</u> as the worst play in the history of Broadway.

*Perfect! Simple Past "became" matches the previous verbs "opened" and "closed."*

D

## Summing Up

We've thrown a lot of information at you in this chapter! Whenever you are in doubt, remember your #1 Writing mantra: **Trust your ear!**

If you've been speaking and reading English for a while, then more often than not the correct wording of a sentence will sound "best." You'll subconsciously know that there's something wrong with "I had knew" or "They will have be finish." Lean on those instincts, and trust your ear!

## Recapping Tense Switch

When you see a <u>verb</u> underlined, look for a tense switch error:

1. *Use context clues and surrounding verbs to pick the correct tense.*

2. *Would of, could of, and might of are always wrong.*

3. *Beware irregular verbs in the perfect tenses.*

# Passage Practice

*Questions 1 – 10 relate to the following passage.*

On the morning of August 30, 1904, thirty-two men from four countries **1** have been gathering in St. Louis, Missouri, to compete in the third-ever Olympic Marathon. This was not a modern marathon, with disciplined athletes in state-of-the-art gear; instead, these non-professional runners were about to compete in one of the most bizarre and challenging races in history.

Unlike today's marathons, in which athletes run on paved roads blocked off from traffic while surrounded by cheering spectators, the 1904 race **2** is conducted on dirt roads clogged with debris and pedestrians. Cars and horses kicked dust in the runners' faces, and temperatures rose as high as 90 degrees Fahrenheit. But if the athletes had been counting on refreshments to help them through the ordeal, they **3** had been disappointed—there were only two watering stations along the twenty-five mile course.

The day was full of remarkable tales. One of the wildest stories is that of Andrajan Carvajal, a postman from Cuba. Carvajal **4** began his journey to the Olympic games in New Orleans. While there, he lost all his belongings in a bet and had to hitchhike to St. Louis. He arrived at the race with only the clothes on his back; another runner lent him a pair of scissors, and he **5** had cut his long trousers into improvised shorts. Then, during the race, he got sick from eating a rotten

*Passage continued on next page*

**1**

A) NO CHANGE
B) gathered
C) have gathered
D) gather

**2**

A) NO CHANGE
B) were conducted
C) being conducted
D) was conducted

**3**

A) NO CHANGE
B) would have been disappointed
C) will be disappointed
D) could be disappointed

**4**

A) NO CHANGE
B) has begun
C) begone
D) begins

**5**

A) NO CHANGE
B) cut
C) cuts
D) would cut

apple plucked from a nearby orchard and [6] <u>lay</u> down to take a nap. Despite all of this, he eventually finished in fourth place, and might even have won the race if he had not stopped to converse with crowds along the way.

One runner [7] <u>choosing</u> not to put up with all the trouble and, as a result, came close to never racing again. Fred Lorz, a bricklayer who qualified for the marathon by winning a five-mile amateur event, gave up and hitched a ride in a passing car. He completed the rest of the course as a passenger, disembarking only when the car reached the Olympic stadium. Before the crowd realized he was an impostor, President Roosevelt's daughter [8] <u>has placed</u> the victory wreath on Lorz's head. He was banned from amateur sporting for life, but the ban was lifted after he apologized for the prank.

After the disastrous day, many questioned whether the marathon should remain part of the Olympic Games. But four years later, in 1908, the race [9] <u>returned</u> with improved rules. Hopefully, crowds [10] <u>are cheering</u> exhausted but triumphant athletes as they claim Olympic glory for generations to come.

**6**

A) NO CHANGE
B) lied
C) layed
D) laid

**7**

A) NO CHANGE
B) chosen
C) choose
D) chose

**8**

A) NO CHANGE
B) placed
C) was placed
D) to place

**9**

A) NO CHANGE
B) has returned
C) to return
D) was returning

**10**

A) NO CHANGE
B) had cheered
C) were cheering
D) will cheer

# Subject-Verb Agreement

*If the subject of your sentence is plural, then the verb must also be plural. If the subject is singular, then the verb must be singular. If a verb is underlined, check that subject!*

## Match verbs with their subjects

Nouns/pronouns and verbs come in two "numbers": singular and plural. Here's the key: a verb and its subject *must agree in number*. If the subject is singular, the verb must be singular. If the subject is plural, the verb must be plural.

Anytime a verb is underlined, **find the subject** and **match its number!**

## EXAMPLE 1

My high school teachers <u>has encouraged</u> me to pursue my dream career: professional wrestling on WrestleMania.

A)  NO CHANGE
B)  have encouraged
C)  encourages
D)  was encouraging

SOLUTION

The subject, **teachers**, is plural, but the verb, **has encouraged**, is singular! This simply won't do. Subjects and verbs always have to agree. The only choice with a *plural verb* is choice B:

     *plural*       *plural*

B)) My high school **teachers** <u>have encouraged</u> me to pursue my dream career: professional wresting on WrestleMania.

B

## Sometimes the subject comes after the verb

Usually, your ear notices when a subject and verb don't agree. This is particularly true when the verb comes right after the subject:

> "**They** <u>cooks</u> an omelette."
> plural ↗        ↖ *singular*

That sounds pretty bad! If every problem were this easy, it would be pointless testing subject-verb agreement on the SAT. One way the test-writers attempt to trick your ear is to place the subject *after* the verb.

## EXAMPLE 2

Over the misty mountaintops <u>glide</u> the majestic grey eagle.

A)  NO CHANGE
B)  gliding
C)  glides
D)  were gliding

Notice that, although there *is* an error here, the sentence doesn't *sound* all that bad. Why is that? Since "glide" (a plural verb) follows "mountaintops" (a plural noun), your ear is tricked. Mountaintops don't glide! **Eagle** is our subject—that's what is doing the gliding! If the sentence were written differently, this would be clearer:

> The majestic grey **eagle** <u>glide</u> over the misty mountaintops.

It's harder to miss the error when the subject is before the verb. Because "eagle" is singular, we need the *singular* form of the verb:

> C)  Over the misty mountaintops <u>glides</u> the majestic grey **eagle**.

C

**TIP**

Unsure if a verb is singular or plural? Try adding "it" or "they" to it, and see which sounds correct. For example, "it have" sounds wrong, but "they have" is just right!

## TIP

Long sentences can make it harder to spot the correct answer. Try **rewriting the sentence** in a simpler form, *then* try the subject/verb pairings.

## TIP

Once you find the intended subject for the verb, ignoring everything else in the sentence can help you "hear" if the subject and verb agree.

### EXAMPLE 3

Despite the prevalence in Latin American culture of macabre folktales about El Chupacabra, <u>only recently have</u> physical evidence in the form of cave paintings been discovered in the mountains of Peru.

A) NO CHANGE
B) recent only have
C) only recently will
D) only recently has

The key to answering this problem correctly is to identify the subject for the verb "have...been discovered". WHAT has been discovered recently? **Evidence!** We can test this by rewriting the sentence:

**Evidence** <u>only recently have</u> been discovered...

**Evidence** is a singular subject, so we need a *singular* verb:

D) Despite the prevalence in Latin American culture of macabre folktales about El Chupacabra, <u>only recently has</u> physical **evidence** in the form of cave paintings been discovered in the mountains of Peru.

D

*In 2014, researchers discovered this sketch of the bloodthirsty Chupacabra returning home from one of its dark hunts.*

## Subject and Verb Separated

Another trick the test writers use to complicate subject-verb agreement is separating the verb and the subject with lots of words and phrases. Sometimes those phrases are prepositional phrases, sometimes they are modifying phrases, and sometimes they are verb phrases.

### Separated by prepositional phrase

A few **sections** of my research paper <u>concerns</u> Abdul Sattar Edhi, the Pakistani humanitarian.

### Separated by a modifying phrase

The **glitter** covering my dining room table <u>are</u> the result of a late night craft disaster.

### Separated by a verb phrase

**Richard** goes to the fair and <u>buy</u> some parsley, sage, rosemary, and thyme.

If you read these sentences out loud, you might not notice the agreement error, since the subject is so far from the verb. But if you **cross out** the distractors in between the subject and verb, the error becomes obvious:

### Cross out the distractors to hear the error

A few **sections** ~~of my research paper~~ <u>concerns</u> Abdul Sattar Edhi, the Pakistani humanitarian.

The **glitter** ~~covering my dining room table~~ <u>are</u> the result of a late night craft disaster.

**Richard** ~~goes to the fair and~~ <u>buy</u> some parsley, sage, rosemary, and thyme.

---

**TIP**

A prepositional phrase is a preposition and the object that follows, like "on the fast-moving highway" or "from Italy." The object of a preposition can **NEVER** be the subject!

**PORTAL**

For practice with prepositions, turn to page 297.

**TIP**

Try rereading these sentences with the correct verb forms (*concern*, *is*, and *buys*). Notice how much easier it is to hear right and wrong forms when you ignore intermediate phrases!

Circle the subject of the underlined verb and **cross out** the distracting words in between.

1. The welcoming (ceremony) ~~on the planet of the purple-skinned aliens~~ <u>reveals</u> interesting details about their preferred forms of entertainment.

2. Whipped up by the wind, the (waves) ~~rolling in against the rocky beach~~ <u>point</u> to a storm off the coast.

3. If (one) ~~of those sad, frowning clowns~~ <u>is walking</u> around this town, I just don't know what I'll do.

4. It turned out that my delicious (bowl) ~~of oat and honey clusters~~ <u>has been tainted</u> with raisins all along.

5. In fact, (one) ~~of the city's attractions—botanical gardens known for their holiday light shows—~~ <u>earns</u> significant profits each year.

# TIP

Having trouble identifying the subject? Just remember that the subject is the noun or pronoun that does the verb's action. When you see the verb "run," ask yourself "who is running?" to find the subject.

## EXAMPLE 4

The relationship between the clownfish and the sea anemone <u>are</u> truly symbiotic, for both receive protection from predators.

A) NO CHANGE
B) were
C) have been
(D) is

Answers:

2. Whipped up by the wind, the (waves) ~~rolling in against the rocky beach~~ <u>point</u> to a storm off the coast.

3. If (one) ~~of those sad, frowning clowns~~ <u>is walking</u> around this town, I don't know what I'll do.

4. It turned out that my delicious (bowl) ~~of oat and honey clusters~~ <u>has been tainted</u> with raisins all along.

5. In fact, one ~~of the city's attractions—botanical gardens known for their holiday light shows—~~ <u>earns</u> significant profits each year.

SOLUTION

Did you **hear** the error? Probably not—that prepositional phrase is getting between our subject and verb, tricking our ear. Cross out that phrase!

subject (S)                                                                                          verb (P)

The **relationship** ~~between the clownfish and the sea anemone~~ <u>are</u> truly symbiotic...

Now we see that relationship is our singular subject, which requires a singular verb; only choice D is singular!

**D)** The **relationship** between the clownfish and the sea anemone <u>is</u> truly symbiotic, for both receive protection from predators.

D

## EXAMPLE 5

Harriet Tubman led hundreds of slaves to freedom and, during the Civil War, <u>were spies</u> for the Union Army.

A) NO CHANGE
B) were spying
C) were a spy
D) was a spy

SOLUTION

Let's identify our subject and cross out the verb phrase to get rid of the noise:

**Harriet Tubman** ~~led hundreds of slaves to freedom and, during the Civil War,~~ <u>were spies</u> for the Union Army.

Harriet Tubman were spies?? While very awesome, she was just one woman after all. The plural verb "were" doesn't make sense here. Let's plug in D, a singular verb:

D) **Harriet Tubman** ~~led hundreds of slaves to freedom and, during the Civil War,~~ <u>was a spy</u> for the Union Army.

Perfecto! Singular subject, meet singular verb.

D

## How to spot Subject-Verb Agreement problems:

If a **verb is underlined**, it's likely a Subject-Verb Agreement problem, a Tense Switch problem, or (most likely) both. The choices will be slight variations of the same verbs:

A) NO CHANGE
B) have become
C) has become
D) become

## Recapping Subject-Verb Agreement

Every verb has a subject, and the subject and verb must *agree* in number. Both must be singular or plural—no mixing and matching!

1. *If a verb is underlined, **find the subject**.*

2. ***Cross out the junk** between subject and verb.*

3. ***Match** the subject and verb.*

## Passage Practice

*Questions 1 – 8 relate to the following passage.*

When you're waiting in line at a crowded grocery store, surrounded by beeping registers and screaming children, you may think to yourself that human civilization is not all that it's cracked up to be. However, you may be surprised to learn that this tedious waiting ritual is not entirely exclusive to humanity: researchers have found that wild baboons, once a tribe has identified a food source, **1** forms a line and wait their turn, just like we do.

Stashes of corn, a favorite treat of baboons, **2** having been hidden around Tsaobis Nature Park by scientists eager to see how these animals would react to a surprise meal. They discovered that a baboon who has found food can be noticed by its behavior: it hunches over and repeatedly **3** scoop at the ground. Furthermore, they discovered that every member of the tribe keeps an eye out for others who might have found food and **4** moves in for a share upon seeing signs of eating. This behavior alerts others to the find, and soon the whole tribe, mostly nursing mothers and juvenile adults, **5** are trying to get in on the action; that's when the "fun" starts. The dominant male—the victor from previous internal **6** scuffles—assert control of the food source, and everyone else must get in line behind him. But this isn't first-come-first-serve; instead, the rest of the tribe is ordered by status, with high-ranked members like powerful males and young breeding females getting their turns before anyone

*Passage continued on next page*

**1**

A) NO CHANGE
B) formed
C) form
D) are formed

**2**

A) NO CHANGE
B) were
C) was
D) is

**3**

A) NO CHANGE
B) scoops
C) will scoops
D) scooped

**4**

A) NO CHANGE
B) would move
C) move
D) were moving

**5**

A) NO CHANGE
B) is
C) was
D) were

**6**

A) NO CHANGE
B) scuffles, assert
C) scuffles asserts
D) scuffles—asserts

else. Baboons at the bottom of the pecking order often 7 finding themselves with no food at all.

If you're a low-status tribe member looking to fill your belly, you have two options. You can wait on the edge of the group and 8 try to eat in secret, or you can try cutting in line by forming the right grooming connections. Either way, waiting for the cashier to ring you up suddenly sounds like a much better bargain.

7

A) NO CHANGE
B) finds
C) find
D) to find

8

A) NO CHANGE
B) tries
C) tried
D) trying

# Pronoun Error

*A pronoun is a word that takes the place of a noun. Just like nouns, pronouns can either be subjects or objects in a sentence.*

.....................................................................................................

### Subject vs. Object Pronouns

Subjects are the movers, shakers, and doers in a sentence: they **act**.
Objects are more like the ball in a pinball machine: they are **acted upon**.

| Rachel | launched | the **banana** | at Geoff. |
|--------|----------|----------------|-----------|
| *subject* | *verb* | *object* | *object* |

In the above sentence, Rachel is the one **acting**, while the banana and poor Geoff are being **acted upon.** If we want to replace these nouns with pronouns, we keep this distinction in mind. Subjects get subject pronouns, and objects get object pronouns:

| **She** | launched | **it** | at **him**. |
|---------|----------|--------|-------------|
| *subject pronoun* | *verb* | *object pronoun* | *object pronoun* |

Rachel takes the **subject pronoun** "She," not the *object* pronoun "her."
Geoff takes the **object prounoun** "him," not the *subject* pronoun "he."
On the test, be on the lookout for sentences that mix these up.

Here's a handy-dandy chart to keep subject & object pronouns straight:

| _____ do(es) things | Things happen to _____ |
|---|---|
| I | Me |
| You | You |
| He, She, It, Who | Him, Her, It, Whom |
| We | Us |
| They | Them |

## EXAMPLE 1

Our tour guide for the day was a friendly young woman <u>whom</u>, after showing us around the main academic buildings on campus, showed us some of her own favorite landmarks.

**Whom** is an object pronoun – but is it being acted upon in the sentence? Looks like "whom" refers to the tour guide, and she is acting all over the place! She **shows** us the buildings, plus her favorite landmarks. We should replace whom with the subject pronoun **who**.

Our tour guide for the day was a friendly young woman <u>who</u>, after showing us around the main academic buildings on campus, showed us some of her own favorite landmarks.

## TIP

If you have trouble remembering when to use *whom*, focus on the **-m**.

*He*, *they*, and *who* are all subject pronouns with no **-m**.

*Him*, *them*, and *whom* are all object pronouns that end in **-m**.

## The (Not So) Difficult Case of I vs. Me

You might notice that people often aren't sure when to say "I" and when to say "me." But the rules are the same as with any other subject and object pronoun. **I** is a subject, and **me** is an object.

> **I** do things. Things happen to **me**.
> *subject*                                        *object*

**TIP**

If your pronoun is the object of a preposition, the object pronoun "me" is correct.

## EXAMPLE 2

In appreciation of all the hard work we did designing the set, the cast of *You're a Good Man, Charlie Brown* <u>threw a party for Joyce, Steve, and I</u>.

Let's cross out Joyce and Steve and let our ears do all the work:

In appreciation of all the hard work we did designing the set, the cast of *You're a Good Man, Charlie Brown* <u>threw a party for ~~Joyce, Steve, and~~ I</u>.

The cast threw a party for **I**? That doesn't sound right! That's because "I" isn't doing the action in the sentence. The **cast** threw the party, not "I." We need the **object** pronoun **me**.

In appreciation of all the hard work we did designing the set, the cast of *You're a Good Man, Charlie Brown* <u>threw a party for Joyce, Steve, and **me**</u>.

**TIP**

When the SAT gives you a long list of names including "I" or "me", cross out everything but the pronoun. It will make it easier for your ear to guide you!

## Reflexive Pronouns

There's one more type of pronoun you need to know about: the reflexives. Each personal pronoun (I, you, he/she/it, etc.) has a reflexive pronoun that goes along with it:

|  | Singular | Plural |
| --- | --- | --- |
| 1st Person | myself | ourselves |
| 2nd Person | yourself | yourselves |
| 3rd Person | herself / himself /itself | themselves |

We use reflexive pronouns for two purposes. First, when the **subject** and the *object* of a sentence are the same. For example:

> I love *myself*.
> **Eleazar** bought *himself* a triple scoop ice cream sundae.
> **We** are so proud of *ourselves*!

Second, you can also use reflexive pronouns to intensify a statement and give it an extra bit of emphasis:

> Jordan *himself* told me I could borrow his car.
> I can do this *myself*.

Those are the only two things a reflexive pronoun can do! Reflexive pronouns often show up on the SAT in places they do not belong, so your job is usually to **cut them out.**

### CUT 'EM OUT

People tend to overuse reflexive pronouns. When given the option, try cutting them out and see if the sentence loses any meaning.

**251**

## EXAMPLE 3

Much to my chagrin, Shelly informed <u>myself</u> that my toy poodle was not welcome at Bring Your Daughter to Work Day.

A) NO CHANGE
B) me
C) I
D) one

What's the subject of this sentence? It's Shelly!

**Shelly** informed <u>myself</u>.
*Subj.*            *Obj.*

The subject and object are not the same person, so we should NOT use a reflexive pronoun: a simple object pronoun will do!

(B)) Much to my chagrin, **Shelly** informed <u>me</u> that my toy poodle was not welcome at Bring Your Daughter to Work Day.

B

## Pronouns must match the nouns they replace

A pronoun's antecedent is the word or words the pronoun replaces. If the antecedent is singular, the pronoun must be too:

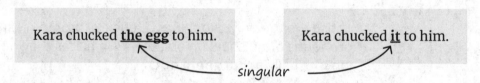

Kara chucked **the egg** to him.        Kara chucked <u>it</u> to him.

*singular*

Simple enough, but be careful: the SAT occasionally uses words that *look* plural but are, in fact, singular. Check the table below for examples.

| Sneaky Singular Words | |
|---|---|
| anybody, anyone | nothing, everything |
| everybody, everyone | nobody, no one |
| each | none |
| either, neither | amount, number |
| group, family | audience, team, band, club |

## NOTE

While "team" and "band" are sneaky singular words, a plural team or band *name* (for instance, *The Beatles*) is still plural.

## EXAMPLE 4

Every member of the football team <u>shaved their head</u> when the team won the game against its biggest rival.

Did every member shave **their** head? Do they share one head? **Every** is a singular word, so we can't use the plural pronoun their to replace it. We need the singular pronoun **his** or **her**.

Every member of the football team <u>shaved **his/her** head</u> when the team won the game against its biggest rival.

## TIP

Words like *army*, *team*, and *family* are known as **collective nouns**: nouns that denote a group of individuals. When collective nouns act as a single unit, they use singular verbs.

## EXAMPLE 5

Because the U.S. Army anticipated only a brief engagement in Fallujah, <u>they only had</u> enough supplies for 24 days of combat.

**SOLUTION**

The U.S. Army is acting as a singular entity, a thing, an it. **It** takes the place of a singular noun.

Because the U.S. Army anticipated only a brief engagement in Falluja, <u>**it** only had</u> enough supplies for 24 days of combat.

## EXAMPLE 6

Meteorologists have been studying comets for years, but they have only recently realized how varied in composition <u>they</u> can be.

SOLUTION

"They" is a plural pronoun, so it must have a plural antecedent. But here's the problem: we have **two** plural nouns in the sentence! Does "they" refer to the meteorologists... or the comets? Pronouns are handy, but not if they make the sentence more confusing. If it's unclear which word is the antecedent to your pronoun, ditch the pronoun altogether and repeat the noun.

Meteorologists have been studying comets for years, but they have only recently realized how varied in composition **<u>comets</u>** can be.

# Quiz

*Identify the error (if present) in each of the following sentences.*

1. Over the course of the 40-week academic calendar, roughly three dozen students will take its turn as Most Popular Kid of the Third Grade.

2. Marjorie gained unlikely celebrity for her "Bouncing On Air" initiative, in which she trained adults whom had never learned to properly pogo.

3. The students in Ms. Odewabe's underwater basket weaving class have discovered working together heightens its creativity.

4. According to our calculations, Millie and me have spent more than $427 on our collection of super bouncy balls.

5. Just between you and I, Eric's new boyfriend is a compulsive liar: I saw that condescending vegetarian stuffing his face at Messy Matt's Rib Shack on Tuesday.

# Answers

1. Over the course of the 40-week academic calendar, roughly three dozen students will take **their** turn as Most Popular Kid of the Third Grade.

2. Marjorie gained unlikely celebrity for her "Bouncing On Air" initiative, in which she trained adults **who** had never learned to properly pogo.

3. The students in Ms. Odewabe's underwater basket weaving class have discovered working together heightens **their** creativity.

4. According to our calculations, **Millie and I** have spent more than $427 on our collection of super bouncy balls.

5. Just between **you and me**, Eric's new boyfriend is a compulsive liar: I saw that condescending vegetarian stuffing his face at Messy Matt's Rib Shack on Tuesday.

## Passage Practice

*Questions 1 – 8 relate to the following passage.*

At last, after weeks of rehearsals, opening night arrived. It was going to be a packed house; the theatre department had decided to require every single one of [1] their students to attend. We had spent hours and hours working with the actors—especially the ones [2] whom had to work with the giant, carnivorous plant puppet. Some of the actors had to work much longer than others to memorize [3] his or her lines, but last night's dress rehearsal could not have gone more smoothly. So tonight was abuzz with excitement. What could go wrong?

I was on the phone, pacing in the hallway and listening to my mother say, "I'm not taking your little sister to a horror show! Can I just give her ticket to [4] whoever I want?" I replied, "But Mom, it's not *actually* horror; besides, she's 15-years-old!" Suddenly, Michelle darted out of the classroom that had been converted into our dressing room and sprinted towards [5] myself. "Matt! Matt!"

**1**

A) NO CHANGE
B) one's
C) it's
D) its

**2**

A) NO CHANGE
B) who
C) whose
D) DELETE the underlined word

**3**

A) NO CHANGE
B) his
C) our
D) their

**4**

A) NO CHANGE
B) whomever
C) whichever
D) DELETE the underlined word

**5**

A) NO CHANGE
B) I
C) me
D) my

*Passage continued on next page*

"Hang on, Mom. What's the matter, Michelle? Shouldn't you be getting the plant puppet ready?"

"That's the problem! There is no more plant puppet! Ellen was doing her stretches while Bill was practicing throwing around his giant teeth. Anyway, she got smacked with a bicuspid, fell back, and she landed on..."

The color drained from my face. After all, you can't really have a performance of *Little Shop of Horrors* without a giant man-eating plant. 6 "Keep this between me and you for now," I said in full panic mode. "Mom," I said into the phone, "I need you to grab your shears, cut off 3 giant palm tree leaves from the garden, and bring 7 them to me."

8 When one wants something done right, you have to do it yourself.

---

**6**

A) NO CHANGE
B) "Keep this between you and I
C) "Keep this between I and you
D) "Keep this between yourself

---

**7**

Ⓐ NO CHANGE
B) it
C) those
D) ~~the leaves~~

---

**8**

A) NO CHANGE
B) When you want something done right, one must do it oneself.
C) When one wants something done right, one must do it oneself.
D) When one wants something done right, one must do it yourself.

# Possession

*Who owns what? The key to possession is understanding the apostrophe.*

## NOTE

Depending on which Grammar Guru you ask, you'll get different answers about the best way to make singular nouns that end in s (like *boss*) possessive.

Is it *my boss' desk* or *my boss's desk*?

The SAT avoids this controversy. For test purposes, any possessive noun ending in s is likely plural, and should have just an apostrophe—no s.

## Show possession with an apostrophe

In most cases, you simply add an **'s** to a noun to show ownership. However, when you do this to a **plural noun** that ends in an **s**, like **dogs's**, it can look and sound terrible. So, the rulers of English decided you can just write **dogs'**.

The **dog's** bone

The **dogs'** bone

Notice that these words *sound* the same. The test writers are hoping to trip you up with words that sound similar but have different meaning, such as *family's* (singular possessive), *families* (plural, not possessive) and *families'* (plural possessive). To avoid this trap, anytime you see a noun followed by an apostrophe on the test, just ask yourself two questions:

> (1) *Does this noun own something?*
>
> (2) *Should the noun be singular or plural?*

Your answer will be nearby, so be sure to read the whole sentence!

## EXAMPLE 1

Georgia's minimum sentences are defined by the <u>states criminal laws</u>, which are in turn determined by the legislature.

A) NO CHANGE
B) states' criminal laws'
C) state's criminal laws
D) state's criminal law's

---

**SOLUTION**

We're dealing with **two** possible possessions, so let's take them one at a time by asking our two questions:

① *Does "states" own anything in the sentence?*
Yes! It owns the **criminal laws**, so we need either **state's** or **states'** to show ownership. That lets us cross off A.

② *Should "states" be singular or plural?*
Georgia is only one state, so we need a singular possessive— **state's**. That lets us cross off B.

To help us choose between C and D, we only need to ask one question: Does "laws" own anything in the sentence? Nope! So we don't need any apostrophe here. That leaves **C** as the only choice that gets it right:

C) Georgia's minimum sentences are defined by the <u>state's criminal laws</u>, which are in turn determined by the legislature.

C

---

## TIP

Students often struggle with the possessive form of plural words.

If you're uncertain, try using a prepositional phrase, rather than an apostrophe, to show ownership. For example:

**Children's books** could be rewritten as **books of the children**. That sounds right.

**Childrens' books** would be rewritten as **books of the childrens**. That sounds wrong.

## Possessive Pronouns

The SAT wants to make sure you know when to use a possessive pronoun and when to use a *contraction*. Possessive pronouns like *its*, *your*, *whose*, and *their* **do not use** an apostrophe. If you see an apostrophe, you've got a contraction on your hands!

Check out the handy-dandy table below to help you keep your possessives and contractions straight.

**TIP**

If you ever see **its'** on the test, immediately cross it out!

| Possessive | Contraction |
|------------|-------------|
| its | it's (it is / it has) |
| their | they're (they are) |
| your | you're (you are) |
| whose | who's (who is) |

## EXAMPLE 2

The French horn players have long suspected that the flautist fills their horns with Gatorade before the halftime shows, ruining <u>they're</u> melodious music.

A) NO CHANGE
B) their
C) there
D) it's

**They're** has an apostrophe, so it's a *contraction*. Do we want to say "ruining they are melodious music?" That's nonsense! We need to show **ownership**, since the French horn players own the melodious music. That means we need to use **their**, the possessive pronoun. The answer is **B**:

B) The French horn players have long suspected that the flautists filled their horns with Gatorade before the halftime show, ruining <u>their</u> melodious music.

B

## EXAMPLE 3

Despite <u>its</u> long history as a haunted house, the Shrieking Shack has become the most popular venue for high school proms.

A) NO CHANGE
B) it's
C) their
D) they're

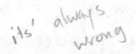
*its' always wrong*

Does "it" own anything? Yes, it owns the "long history!" **Its** shows ownership... but so does **their**. How do we know which to choose? Remember your pronoun rules: singular pronouns refer to singular nouns, and plural pronouns refer to plural nouns. **It** refers to the **Shrieking Shack**; the shack has a long history as a haunted house. Since the antecedent is singular, we need a **singular** pronoun. Our answer is **A**!

A) Despite <u>its</u> long history as a haunted house, the Shrieking Shack has become the most popular venue for high school proms.

A

## PORTAL

Possession questions often get thrown in with **Pronoun Error** questions. For a refresher on pronoun rules, turn to page 248.

# Quiz

*Identify the error (if present) in each of the following sentences.*

1. Because of there teachers severe case of the Mondays, the students watched the seminal film *Bring It On* during English class today.

2. It is Jacob's responsibility to clean the microscope's lenses' once a week.

3. Scientific studies have expanded our knowledge about the brains' ability to heal itself after a traumatic injury.

4. Known for their distinctive tuxedos, penguins are the cutest animals in Antarctica.

5. When your at the end of you're rope, try eating your weight in peanut butter and jelly sandwiches.

# Answers

1. Because of **their teacher's** severe case of the Mondays, the students watched the seminal film *Bring It On* during English class today.

2. It is Jacob's responsibility to clean the microscope's **lenses** once a week.

3. Scientific studies have expanded our knowledge about the **brain's** ability to heal itself after a traumatic injury.

4. *Correct as written!*

5. When **you're** at the end of **your** rope, try eating your weight in peanut butter and jelly sandwiches.

## Passage Practice

*Questions 1 – 10 relate to the following passage.*

What do you think of when you hear the word 'Tesla'? Do you think of Elon Musk's revolutionary electric car? Do you think of Tesla **1** coils, their still used in radio technology today? Or do you think of the AC (alternating current) vs DC (direct current) war in the early 20th century?

Each of these has its origins in Nikola Tesla, a scientist and inventor born in Croatia in 1856. **2** Tesla's parents were poor; his father was an Orthodox priest and his mother was an inventor. **3** Its from his mother, who invented small household appliances, that Tesla developed his lifelong interest in science.

Tesla's voyage to America in 1884 was a turning point in his career. Arriving with very little money and a letter of recommendation from his former boss, he sought out electricity pioneer Thomas Edison. Edison promised Tesla $50,000 if he could improve upon **4** his DC power-generation plant designs, which Tesla accomplished. While **5** history's view of their separation is unclear, some say that Edison refused to pay Tesla the $50,000 once the improvements were made.

**1**
A) NO CHANGE
B) coils there
C) coils that are
D) coils, they're

**2**
A) NO CHANGE
B) Tesla's parents'
C) Teslas parent's
D) Tesla's parent's

**3**
A) NO CHANGE
B) Its' from his mother, whom
C) It's from his mother who
D) It's from his mother, who

**4**
A) NO CHANGE
B) Edison's DC
C) Edisons DC
D) Tesla DC's

**5**
A) NO CHANGE
B) history's views of it's
C) histories' view of there
D) historys view of their

*Passage continued on next page*

It is at this point that Tesla became a key's player in the competition between alternating current and direct current technology. Tesla originally focused on developing an induction motor with a rotating magnet that would create a variable electric field where the current *alternated* between high and low. In contrast, [6] Edison's visions of a magnetized current that flowed *directly* in a single direction.

After his break with Edison, Tesla was approached by George Westinghouse. [7] Teslas partnership with George Westinghouse would become a turning point in his life. In 1888, [8] his patent's were licensed by Westinghouse for $60,000 in cash, stocks, and royalties. These patents helped Westinghouse secure the contracts for lighting the Chicago's World's Expo in 1893 and building a plant at Niagara Falls. [9] This plant's output supplied all the electric power for Buffalo, New York, and resulted in a coup that helped Westinghouse win the "AC vs DC" war with Edison.

Tesla went on to set up his own lab and continue inventing. During this period, Tesla's studies focused on harnessing the electromagnetic potential of the Earth's magnetic field and understanding previously undiscovered wavelengths of light like x-rays and fluorescence. The Tesla coil, invented during this period, is a device still used in radios today; [10] it's ability to wirelessly transmit radio signals served as the basis for much of Tesla's research later in life.

**6**

A) NO CHANGE
B) Edisons vision's
C) Edison's vision's
D) Edison's vision was

**7**

A) NO CHANGE
B) Tesla's partnership
C) Tesla's partnership is
D) Tesla's partnerships'

**8**

A) NO CHANGE
B) his patents
C) his patents'
D) he's patents

**9**

A) NO CHANGE
B) Those plants output
C) That plant outputs
D) This plants output

**10**

A) NO CHANGE
B) its ability
C) it has ability
D) their ability

# Writing Practice Passage 2
## TO STAY ON PACE, YOUR TIMING GOAL IS 8.5 MINUTES

This passage tests a variety of grammar topics—some from chapters you may have not yet completed. Use this opportunity to practice maintaining a brisk pace while answering the questions as best you can. Good luck!

**Questions 1-11 are based on the following passage.**

### The Changing Roles of Women in Comics

The superhero tales in American comics and graphic novels [1] demonstrates the enduring appeal of stylized depictions of heroism and villainy in popular culture. At one time, their illustrated format was a leading medium in science fiction and fantasy, only to fall out of favor for many decades. Now, however, the superhero stories that defined the classics of the genre [2] are being revived through "reboot" movies with fast-paced action scenes and dazzling set pieces. Meanwhile, with [3] there interest piqued by the movies, readers are returning to the genre; however, today's audience is looking for something beyond the same old, same old.

Throughout the history of the comics industry, one factor has remained fairly constant: it has been largely dominated by men. Comic books have mostly featured male heroes (Superman and Batman, anyone?), relegating most female characters to supporting roles. The majority of creators have also been men, dating back to earlier parts of the 20th century when the creative fields were particularly unwelcoming to women.

Today, the lion's share of the comics industry is split by two major companies: Marvel and DC. While Marvel tends to stick to spandex-clad superheroes and more old-fashioned [4] fare, and DC has made some efforts to expand into more innovative, diverse territory. But even as [5] they shift focus, DC has not avoided missteps.

1
A) NO CHANGE
B) demonstrate
C) demonstrated
D) will demonstrate

2
A) NO CHANGE
B) is being revived
C) have been revived
D) were revived

3
A) NO CHANGE
B) their
C) they're
D) its

4
A) NO CHANGE
B) fare; and
C) fare;
D) fare,

5
A) NO CHANGE
B) they will shift
C) it shifts
D) it shifted

CONTINUE

In a 2011 branding campaign titled "New 52," the company cancelled all of **6** its existing comic book titles and launched 52 new titles. Some featured old favorites, while others introduced unfamiliar heroes. Executives hoped to present a fresh image to draw in a larger, more diverse audience.

But the plan backfired when fans objected to the fact that the company was now working with even fewer female creators than before **7** (though the one creator who stayed on was Gail Simone, famous for such characters as Deadpool). The backlash against this regressive decision manifested in protest activities around San Diego Comic Con; the largest gathering of comic fans in the world. Fans launched a petition calling on the company to hire more female creators and presented a list of more than 120 female editors, artists, and writers—all with plenty of accomplishments and experience under their belts— **8** who DC could consider hiring for future projects. In response, **9** they delivered an official statement stating "We hear you," adding "we want these adventures to resonate in the real world, reflecting the experiences of our diverse readership."

But while female comics creators may have been snubbed by the big two firms, **10** there is plenty of female creators thriving with "indie" companies. For example, Marjane Satrapi's autobiographical novel *Persepolis*, an innovative and gripping work depicting her Iranian family and her teenage **11** years received international acclaim and was adapted into an Academy award-nominated animated film in 2007.

**6**

A) NO CHANGE
B) it's
C) one's
D) their

**7**

Which choice provides the best support for the main topic of the paragraph?

A) NO CHANGE
B) (despite this, comics such as Wonder Woman and Batgirl sold very well).
C) (the percentage dropped from 12% to just 1% of their overall staff).
D) (D.C. comics did bring on some fresh talent in the guise of Jeff Lemire and Travel Foreman).

**8**

A) NO CHANGE
B) whose
C) whom
D) who,

**9**

A) NO CHANGE
B) it delivers
C) they will deliver
D) the company delivered

**10**

A) NO CHANGE
B) there are
C) there will be
D) there being

**11**

A) NO CHANGE
B) years, received
C) years, receives
D) years—received

# UNIT | Structure

## Chapters

## Overview

In this unit, we pay close attention to the **structure** of the sentence. We'll use parallelism to give our sentences rhythm, and we'll move misplaced modifiers back to their rightful place.

# Parallelism

*To keep your sentences flowing, use parallelism! Stick with the same structure in a list, and only compare similar things.*

## Parallel Lists

All items in a list must be the same part of speech, whether they are nouns, adjectives, adverbs, or verbs. If your list contains only verbs, each verb must be the same tense.

### EXAMPLE 1

A talented and versatile artist, Steve Martin has <u>been a comedian, a playwright, and directed</u> several Hollywood films.

Let's take a closer look at this list:

... Steve Martin has <u>been a comedian, a playwright, and directed</u>
several Hollywood films.    *noun          noun          verb*

Obey your parallel structure rules: when you see a list, make sure all the items are the same part of speech. We need to change that pesky **verb** into a **noun** to maintain parallelism!

A talented and versatile artist, Steve Martin has <u>been a comedian,</u>
*noun*
<u>a playwright, and **a director**</u> of several Hollywood films.
*noun          noun*

# Parallel Structure

What if our list gets more complicated? Many times, items in lists are more than one word, like "in the treehouse" or "changing her name." In that case, your job is to match the **structure** of each item. Does each item in your list start with a preposition? Keep the same structure for the next item, and cut out any words that don't fit into the structure.

## EXAMPLE 2

By the Cenozoic era, mammals had proliferated throughout the newly-formed grasslands, swinging from trees, walking through fields, and <u>they were tunneling</u> under the ground.

SOLUTION

First, let's check the structure of the first two list items:

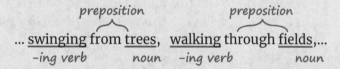

... <u>swinging</u> from <u>trees</u>, <u>walking</u> through <u>fields</u>,...

The last item should keep the structure **parallel**, so we can get rid of "they were." It doesn't fit the list's structure!

By the Cenozoic era, mammals had proliferated throughout the newly-formed grasslands, swinging from trees, walking through fields, and **tunneling** under the ground.

## EXAMPLE 3

Julia decided to clean her room, wash the dishes, and <u>to write</u> a nonfiction short story, all before breakfast.

A)  NO CHANGE
B)  write
C)  writing
D)  has written

SOLUTION

Let's look at the structure of the list:

Julia decided to *clean* her room, *wash* the dishes, and <u>to write</u> a nonfiction short story...

One of these things doesn't belong! We need the verb forms to match up to maintain parallelism in our list. **Choice B** keeps it all parallel. Notice how there is a restored rhythm to the list:

Julia decided to <u>*clean*</u> her room, <u>*wash*</u> the dishes, and <u>*write*</u> a

nonfiction short story, all before breakfast.

## Rhythm

Parallel lists give your sentence a steady rhythm that makes comprehension easier for the reader.

## Parallel Comparisons

While it's often said that you can't compare apples and oranges, it's fair game on the SAT! You can always compare similar things: a fruit to a fruit, a person to a person, a country to a country. You **cannot** compare a fruit to a country. The SAT writers will try to trick you into comparing two things that are not similar at all. Here's an example:

---

## EXAMPLE 4

Because they often used their work as a means of social or political protest rather than as an exercise in aesthetics, many 20th century artists <u>differed from earlier times</u>.

A)   NO CHANGE
B)   differing from earlier times
C)   differed from that in earlier times
D)   differed from those of earlier times

---

What are we comparing in this sentence? Take a look:

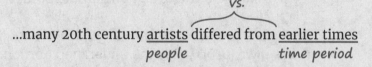

...many 20th century <u>artists</u> differed from <u>earlier times</u>
                      *people*                    *time period*

We **cannot** compare artists to time periods. Those are very different things! We could compare artists to artists (e.g., Impressionists are different from Cubists) or time periods to time periods (e.g., the Middle Ages differed from the Renaissance). Either of these would be a **parallel** comparison.

Choices A and B both compare artists to times, so we can cross them out. Choices C and D compare artists to artists by inserting a **pronoun**. Since the antecedent for the pronoun is plural ("artists"), we need a plural pronoun. **Choice D** gets it right with "those":

D)) Because they often used their work as a means of social or political protest rather than as an exercise in aesthetics, many 20th century artists <u>**differed from those of earlier times**</u>.
*(artists)*

D

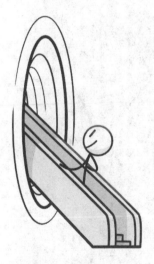

## PORTAL

A pronoun must agree with its antecedent (the noun it refers back to). For more on pronouns, turn to page 248.

## EXAMPLE 5

Students at the University of Chicago often use Internet databases for research because these databases are easier to use than <u>those who use</u> traditional print sources.

A) NO CHANGE
B) the use of
C) using
D) DELETE the underlined portion.

Let's check our comparison!

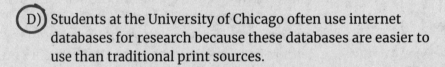

...these <u>databases</u> are easier to use than <u>those</u> who use traditional print sources.

Comparing things to people is not parallel! Because "databases" is a thing, we need a choice that compares it to another thing. We can cross out both A (thing vs. person) and C (thing vs. verb). Choice B creates a confusing redundancy: "databases are easier to use than the use of traditional print sources..."

We can communicate the same idea in a much less awkward way if we just DELETE the underlined portion. That way, we're comparing databases (thing) to sources (thing). Let's go with choice **D**:

D) Students at the University of Chicago often use internet databases for research because these databases are easier to use than traditional print sources.

D

# Passage Practice

*Questions 1 – 8 relate to the following passage.*

In all of 20th century art history, there is no story more enigmatic than [1] Salvador Dalí. [2] He is cele-brated as an artistic genius, even though many felt he had an intractable personality. The Spanish painter and artist was born in 1904 in Figueras, near Barce-lona. According to his autobiography, he spent his childhood warring with his parents (his father in par-ticular), daydreaming of fantasy animals and dream-like shapes, and, even before he went to art school in Madrid to study painting, [3] he developed his own unique style of drawing. The five years from 1925 to 1930 saw a huge amount of change for Dalí: he was ex-pelled from art school for political activity, he moved to Paris, where he found a community of likeminded artists in the Surrealist movement, [4] and some of his best-known works were made during this time.

**1**

A) NO CHANGE
B) Salvador Dalí's enigmatic story
C) the one involving Salvador Dalí
D) that of Salvador Dalí

**2**

A) NO CHANGE
B) His artistic genius is celebrated, even though his personality was felt to be intractable by many.
C) He is celebrated as an artistic artistic genius, even though many feeling his personality was intractable.
D) Even though his personality was intractable, many feel his artistic genius is celebrated.

**3**

A) NO CHANGE
B) developing
C) he developed
D) he has developed

**4**

A) NO CHANGE
B) and the production of some of his best-known works was during this time.
C) and during this time, these were his best-known works.
D) and he produced some of his best-known works during this time.

*Passage continued on next page*

His standout talent and signature twirling moustache acquired him greater and greater fame. He liked to compare his works [5] to the Renaissance, often drawing on old Italian masters for inspiration. He became both prolific and varied in his art. He moved on from painting to work with sculpture, architecture, cinema, [6] and he even designed a lollipop wrapper! Perhaps his greatest masterpiece, though, is the celebrated Surrealist painting *The Persistence of Memory*, [7] characterized by its dreary landscape, painting the nightmarish birdlike body in the center, and of course, those famous melting clocks.

[8] Dalí himself was neither an easy person to get along with, nor was he particularly humble about his creative genius. But his mark on 20th century art is undeniable.

[5]

A) NO CHANGE
B) to that from the Renaissance
C) to those of the Renaissance
D) to artists from the Renaissance

[6]

A) NO CHANGE
B) and even his design of a lollipop wrapper!
C) and even a lollipop wrapper that he designed!
D) and even design (when he made a lollipop wrapper)!

[7]

A) NO CHANGE
B) characterized by its dreary landscape, by the nightmarish birdlike body in the center, and of course, those famous melting clocks.
C) its dreary landscape, the nightmarish birdlike body in the center, and of course, those famous melting clocks characterizing it.
D) characterized by its dreary landscape, the nightmarish birdlike body in the center, and of course, those famous melting clocks.

[8]

A) NO CHANGE
B) Dalí himself was neither an easy person to get along with, nor particularly humble about his creative genius.
C) Dalí himself was neither easy to get along with nor particularly humble about his creative genius.
D) Dalí himself was neither an easy person to get along with, nor humble.

# Misplaced Modifier

*A modifier is a phrase that adds detail about a nearby word. That "nearby" part is key: misplacing a modifier can lead to some odd results...*

## When it comes to modifiers, location is everything

A modifying phrase needs to be <u>right next</u> to the word it modifies, or else it is what we call a **misplaced modifier** error. We see misplaced modifiers all the time in the real world and typically just ignore them. That's because we can usually use context clues to figure out what the writer *really* meant to say.

Since you may be so used to forgiving this error, it can be easy to miss on test day. When you have the option of rearranging the words in a sentence, make sure modifiers are touching their intended target!

## EXAMPLE 1

Ripping through the street, <u>Emily was terrified by the tornado</u>.

A) NO CHANGE
B) Emily is terrifying the tornado.
C) the tornado terrified Emily.
D) Emily's terror was heightened by the tornado.

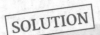

## TIP

One reason students may miss modifier questions is that the key information (the modifier) is often not underlined. You'll need to use the full context of the sentence to address the misplaced modifier.

Who or what is ripping through the street? The word immediately after the modifying clause! Which means, as written, this sentence suggests Emily is the one causing the destruction:

Ripping through the street, **Emily** was terrified of the tornado.

*modifier*

That's probably not the intended meaning. We need to pick a choice that puts "the tornado" right next to the modifier. The only option that does this is choice C:

Ripping through the street, **the tornado** terrified Emily.

*modifier*

## EXAMPLE 2

A hybrid of chihuahuas and dachshunds, <u>dog breeders are increasingly breeding "chiweenies."</u>

A) NO CHANGE
B) breeders of dogs are gaining popularity towards "chiweenies."
C) dog breeders have been gaining popularity with "chiweenies."
D) "chiweenies" are gaining popularity with dog breeders.

## TIP

Even if you don't like the passive way choice D is worded, you MUST fix the modifier error.

Again, we need to focus on what comes *before* the underlined phrase. Dog breeders are human, and so cannot be a hybrid of chihuahuas and dachshunds. Only **choice D** has the correct modifier placement:

A hybrid of chihuahuas and dachshunds, "chiweenies" are...
         *modifier*

## EXAMPLE 3

On the coast of South Africa, diving for abalone is a popular pastime, a type of sea snail priced for its iridescent shell.

A)  NO CHANGE
B)  Diving for abalone is a popular pastime on the coast of South Africa,
C)  On the coast of South Africa, a popular pastime is abalone diving,
D)  On the coast of South Africa, a popular pastime is diving for abalone,

**SOLUTION**

In this sentence, the modifier is *after* the underlined portion, which means we need to focus on the **last word of each choice**. Which choice ends in a word that could be a type of sea snail?

A)  ...pastime,    *nope, not a sea snail*

B)  ...the coast of South Africa,    *that's a place, not a snail*

C)  ...diving,    *that's an activity, not a snail*

D)  ...abalone,    *that could work!*

Only choice D gives us a suitable neighbor for our modifier!

## How to spot Misplaced Modifiers:

As usual, glance at the answer choices to identify the problem type. Misplaced Modifier choices simply **move around the same phrase:**

A)  NO CHANGE
B)  <u>Ripping through the street</u>, Emily was terrified of the tornado.
C)  The tornado terrified Emily, <u>ripping through the street</u>.
D)  <u>Ripping through the street</u>, the tornado terrified Emily.

## EXAMPLE 4

<u>Tired and hungry, Timmy found his stray gerbil cleaning his room.</u>

A)  NO CHANGE
B)  While cleaning his room, Timmy found his tired and hungry stray gerbil.
C)  While cleaning his room, Timmy's stray gerbil, tired and hungry, was found by him.
D)  Tired and hungry, his stray gerbil was cleaning Timmy's room and was found.

SOLUTION

How did Timmy train his gerbil to clean his room? That *would* be impressive, but it's much more likely that **Timmy**, not his gerbil, was cleaning his room. Only choice B makes sense:

<u>While cleaning his room</u>, **Timmy** found his tired and hungry stray gerbil.
    *modifier*

# Passage Practice

*Questions 1 – 7 relate to the following passage.*

[1] While talking with the other pet owners, <u>my new puppy played as I watched with an excited pack of dogs.</u> It was just our second outing together in the park as she had come home with me just a week ago; I had gone to the shelter to simply have a look, only to leave with a 6-month-old terrier named Coco. Just yesterday, [2] <u>she had come across several other dogs walking with me on the leash;</u> however, she had been too scared or shy to play then. What a difference just 24 hours can make!

Her behavior noticeably changed on the way to the dog park. [3] <u>Trotting through the grass, her keen sense of smell was picking up several enticing new scents:</u> people, dogs, squirrels, discarded food, and even a faint waft of skunk...and she was obviously having the time of her young life. [4] <u>Seeing her charging about the lawn in search of new animals to play with, I</u> allowed myself to relax a little bit.

**1**

A) NO CHANGE
B) my new puppy played with an excited pack of dogs.
C) I watched my new puppy playing with an excited pack of dogs.
D) an excited pack of dogs played with my new puppy as I watched.

**2**

A) NO CHANGE
B) she had come across several other dogs on the leash walking with me,
C) she had come across several other dogs with me walking on the leash yesterday,
D) walking on the leash with me, she had come across several other dogs.

**3**

A) NO CHANGE
B) Trotting through the grass, several animal scents came to her keen sense of smell:
C) Several animal scents were picked up by her keen sense of smell trotting through the grass:
D) Trotting through the grass, she picked up several animal scents with her keen sense of smell:

**4**

A) NO CHANGE
B) Charging about the lawn in search of new animals to play with, I saw her and
C) In search of new animals to play with, I saw her charging about the lawn, and
D) I saw her charging about the lawn, and in search of new animals to play with,

*Passage continued on next page*

A Jack Russell and an Airdale came darting towards us. [5] Excited to meet these new friends, her idea was to crouch down low and wait to pounce at the last second. However, foolproof though that plan was, all 3 dogs tumbled around together in a joyful heap.

Watching the whole playful scuffle, [6] the two other owners and I all laughed, happy to see our beloved canines having so much fun. How silly I felt to have been so worried! Taking care of a pup might not be so anxiety-provoking after all.

Just then, Coco, unable to keep up with the other two, took a tumble in the grass and fell over with a little whimper. [7] The other two dogs got out of the way, instantly feeling a jolt of parental panic as I ran for Coco. But, sure enough, Coco was back on her feet and right back to playing as if nothing had happened. I sighed and one of the other owners laughed. Patting the greying golden retriever sitting obediently at her feet, she looked at me and said, "Don't worry. It gets easier."

---

**5**

A) NO CHANGE
B) Her idea was to crouch down low and wait to pounce, excited to meet these new friends
C) Excited to meet these new friends, she got the idea to crouch down and wait to pounce
D) Her idea, excited to meet these new friends, was to crouch down low and wait to pounce

**6**

A) NO CHANGE
B) our beloved canines having so much fun that the other two owners and I all laughed.
C) so much fun was had by our beloved canines that the other two owners and I laughed.
D) our beloved canines had so much fun that I and the other two owners laughed.

**7**

A) NO CHANGE
B) Instantly feeling a jolt of parental panic, the other two dogs got out of the way as I ran for Coco
C) The other two dogs got out of the way, instantly feeling a jolt of parental panic, I ran for Coco.
D) Instantly feeling a jolt of parental panic, I ran for Coco as the other two dogs got out of the way.

# Writing Practice Passage 3

## TO STAY ON PACE, YOUR TIMING GOAL IS 8.5 MINUTES

This passage tests a variety of grammar topics—some from chapters you may have not yet completed. Use this opportunity to practice maintaining a brisk pace while answering the questions as best you can. Good luck!

---

**Questions 1-11 are based on the following passage.**

### The Jungle

    *The Jungle*, published in 1905, tells the story of Lithuanian immigrant Jurgis Rudkus and his young wife Ona. <u>**1** The newlyweds settle in Chicago where Jurgis gets a job at the meatpacking plant, full of ambition and hope for the future.</u> But their dreams are dashed by one misfortune after another; swindlers and predatory lenders take advantage of their naive attitude and lack of literacy, plunging them further into poverty. Jurgis' job is grueling and unsafe, and he cannot provide enough to support the family. Eventually, after sinking completely into disillusionment and despair, Jurgis discovers the socialist movement and **2** <u>he finds</u> new purpose.

    *The Jungle* was primarily a work of political persuasion. **3** <u>Its</u> author, Upton Sinclair, hoped to write a book that would illustrate in vivid imagery the flaws of capitalism. Sinclair wanted to expose the plight of the impoverished in his society. Believing that the capitalist impulse of profit at all costs made life unbearable for those at the bottom of the heap, **4** <u>the book was envisioned</u> as a compelling argument for socialism.

**1**

A) NO CHANGE
B) The newlyweds settle in Chicago where Jurgis, getting a job at the meatpacking plant, full of ambition and hope for the future.
C) The newlyweds settle in Chicago, full of ambition and hope for the future, where Jurgis gets a job at the meatpacking plant.
D) Full of ambition and hope for the future, the newlyweds settle in Chicago where Jurgis gets a job at the meatpacking plant.

**2**

A) NO CHANGE
B) finds
C) finding
D) found

**3**

A) NO CHANGE
B) It's
C) Their
D) There

**4**

A) NO CHANGE
B) the book is envisioned
C) he envisioned the book
D) and he envisioned the book

However, despite Sinclair's impassioned plea on behalf of the poor, it was actually his description of the slaughterhouse that made the strongest impression on the public. His seven weeks of undercover research had provided him with some memorable horror stories. *The Jungle* included revolting descriptions of rats being ground into sausage, offal being swept off the floor and made into tinned lunchmeat, and rusty nails and dirty water [5] were dumped into the grinder. [6] Knowing that readers would find his descriptions of slaughterhouses upsetting, the American readership was outraged by the thought of tainted meat in their grocery stores. As Sinclair himself ruefully described it, "I aimed at the public's heart, and by accident I hit it in the stomach."

The book reached readers at the height of a protracted political battle about the [7] government's responsibilities' to regulate food and medicine. Better food standards, according to the U.S. Bureau of Chemistry,  was necessary for public health. [8] Many were concerned that the Bureau would not have enough inspectors to visit all food manufacturing plants.

**5**

A) NO CHANGE
B) which were dumped
C) being dumped
D) that were being dumped

**6**

Which choice best emphasizes Sinclair's intention when he wrote *The Jungle*?

A) NO CHANGE
B) The book showed readers the value of undercovered investigations and
C) Sinclair had hoped for government regulation of processed food and
D) Instead of being appalled at the sordid lives and cruel mistreatment of workers,

**7**

A) NO CHANGE
B) government's responsibilities
C) governments' responsibility's
D) governments responsibilities

**8**

Which choice offers a differing perspective that contrasts with the desire for greater food regulations?

A) NO CHANGE
B) Doctors had only recently begun to understand the importance of sanitation in preparing food.
C) Others in the food industry claimed such regulations would restrict the economy and significantly diminish profits.
D) At the time, states had differing standards on what qualified as "safe" food.

Then-President Theodore Roosevelt read *The Jungle* and found himself as disgusted as his constituents. He decided to send two men to inspect the meatpacking plants and investigate Sinclair's allegations, instructing them to keep **9** their findings confidential. Their report substantiated nearly all of Sinclair's allegations. Despite **10** Roosevelts desires to keep the findings private, the public clamored to see the report and demanded immediate action. That summer, Congress passed the Pure Food and Drug Act of 1906, making the sale of adulterated or misbranded foods and medicines illegal. The legislation also established new regulatory powers for the Bureau of Chemistry, **11** in 1930 it became known as the Food and Drug Administration.

**9**

A) NO CHANGE
B) their finding's
C) there finding's
D) there findings

**10**

A) NO CHANGE
B) Roosevelts desire's
C) Roosevelts' desires'
D) Roosevelt's desire

**11**

A) NO CHANGE
B) in 1930, it, became
C) which in 1930 became
D) which, in 1930 became,

**STOP**
**If you finish before time is called, you may check your work on this section only.**
**Do not turn to any other section.**

# UNIT | Word Choice

## Chapters

## Overview

This unit is all about word choice. First, we'll learn how to make sure we're not saying the same thing twice. Next, we'll learn how to look at the rest of the sentence to pick the correct preposition, noun, or verb given the **context** of the sentence.

# Redundancy

*a.k.a., "Don't say with six words what you can say with one."*

.................................................................................................

The SAT wants you to know that brevity is the soul of wit and that keeping it short makes you sound smarter. If you're given the opportunity or the option to communicate the exact same meaning with fewer words... do it! Don't get lost in a sea of wordiness—the longest answer is usually wrong.

Two SAT question types fall into the category of "too many words," and they both show up on the test. **Redundancy** errors involve saying the same thing several times, being repetitive, or unnecessarily defining an obvious idea. **Brevity** questions simply use too many words to say something that could be said with fewer words.

## Error Alert!

By our count, there are at *least* five instances of redundancy in these first two paragraphs! See if you can improve our writing by **crossing out the redundancies**.

### Redundancy Example

I'll <u>stay and remain</u> here for a bit.

A)   NO CHANGE
B)   hang around and stay
C)   stay at this location
D)   stay

### Brevity Example

I asked for Antoine's <u>internal thoughts about the subject of</u> trap music's global influence.

A)   NO CHANGE
B)   personal opinions and beliefs
C)   feelings and verbal statements that he has regarding
D)   opinions on

In both examples, choice D communicates the same idea in fewer words. Whenever you are given the option on the test, **keep it simple!**

# Get rid of repeated ideas

Often, the test writers will unnecessarily **repeat** or rephrase an idea. When you are solving redundancy questions, cross off answer choices that repeat information already given in the sentence.

**Cross off a redundant word or phrase** in the following sentences. If you have two options, choose one! The first two are done for you.

1. I studied ~~and prepared~~ for the test.
2. Initially, this product was ~~first~~ offered in May.
3. I do my annual taxes every year.
4. It was a surprisingly astonishing outcome.
5. Frequently, underprepared students often do poorly on exams.
6. The queen offered renewed inspiration all over again.
7. There was a recent increase in migration over the last few years.
8. At a future date the winners will later receive confirmation.
9. Over many months, as time went by, my puppy grew.

## Once is enough!

There's no need to say something twice. If an answer choice has two words that mean the same thing, it's wrong!

**Answers:**

1. *given*
2. *given*
3. ~~annual / every year~~
4. ~~surprisingly / astonishing~~
5. ~~frequently / often~~
6. ~~renewed / all over again~~
7. ~~recent / over the last few years~~
8. ~~at a future date / later~~
9. ~~over many months / as time went by~~

## EXAMPLE 1

The results of the soil tests indicated a chemical problem that threatened to postpone <u>and delay</u> the construction of the building.

A) NO CHANGE
B) to a later date
C) by delaying
D) DELETE the underlined portion.

## POWER

**Note the power of DELETE!**

In redundancy problems, when **DELETE** is a choice, it is almost always the correct answer!

**SOLUTION**

Three of the four choices fail to fix the redundancy in the sentence. We don't need a synonym of postpone such as **later**, **delay** or **delaying**. The correct answer is the shortest and simplest option:

(D)) The results of the soil tests indicated a chemical problem that threatened to postpone the construction of the building.

D

## EXAMPLE 2

Lun Lun, Zoo Atlanta's giant panda, gave birth to twin girls on September 3: Ya Lun, born at 7:03am, and Xi Lun, <u>a baby panda.</u>

A) NO CHANGE
B) born forty-five minutes later.
C) born in Atlanta, GA.
D) born in September.

The sentence already told us that Xi Lun was a baby panda *(A)*, born in Atlanta *(C)*, in September *(D)*. The only answer that provides *new* information is **choice B**!

B) Lun Lun, Zoo Atlanta's giant panda, gave birth to twin girls on September 3: Ya Lun, **born at 7:03am**, and Xi Lun, **born forty-five minutes later**.

B

## PORTAL

Notice that choice B also maintains **parallelism in lists**! Parallelism is a principle that can help with many different question types. For more information, turn to page 268.

## Get rid of unnecessary definitions

The test will occasionally give you a word and then **define** it, creating a redundancy. Again, you job is simply to get rid of the redundancy. Once is enough!

**Cross off the redundant word or phrase** in the following sentences.

1. The criminal, ~~who had broken the law,~~ was tried in court.

2. I am looking for my canine dog.

3. I was trapped in a congested traffic jam.

4. She used an artificial preservative that was not natural.

5. He traversed the lush, sloping hill.

**Answers:** *Answers and solutions can be found and discovered at the bottom of and not the top of the next page immediately after this current page that you're on now.*

## EXAMPLE 3

Billy walked up onto the <u>grass-covered lawn</u>.

A) NO CHANGE
B) mowed, grass-covered lawn
C) grass-covered, lawn
D) lawn

### SOLUTION

Lawns, by definition, are grass-covered, so choices A, B, and C are all redundant. That means choice **D is our answer:**

(D)) Billy walked up onto the <u>lawn</u>.

D

## EXAMPLE 4

My new job opportunity <u>may or may not offer</u> valuable training and connections to enhance my career development.

A) NO CHANGE
B) may offer
C) could provide important and
D) might indeed provide one with

## "OR NOT"

This one showed up a few years ago on the test. "May" already implies uncertainty, so "may or may not" is redundant. Same applies to "whether" and "whether or not."

### SOLUTION

In this case, our trickiest answer choice is C. It solves for the may or may not redundancy but opens up a brand new redundancy with **important** and **valuable**. Sneaky! And incorrect. Our correct answer is short and sweet: **B**.

B)) My new job opportunity <u>may offer</u> valuable training and connections to enhance my career development.

B

Last Page: | 1. *given* | 2. ~~canine~~ | 3. ~~congested~~
| 4. ~~artificial~~ (or) ~~that was not natural~~ | 5. ~~sloping~~

## The Harder Version

The harder version of Redundancy problems hides the information that's being repeated in the preceding sentences. That means you may need to broaden your gaze and look for redundancies outside that one sentence.

## EXAMPLE 5

Lin-Manuel Miranda, winner of three Tony awards, found inspiration for his most recent record-smashing musical *Hamilton* in the most unlikely of places: an airport. While on vacation, he picked up Ron Chernow's biography of the founding father in an airport bookstore. Finding inspiration in the story of an immigrant who fought against the odds to change America, Miranda began writing what would become *Hamilton*, <u>his latest musical</u>.

A) NO CHANGE
B) based on the book.
C) the record-breaking hit.
D) which went on to win the Pulitzer Prize.

SOLUTION

Let's look for repeated information in this paragraph, and cross off any answers that are redundant.

 ...his latest musical.

The first sentence told us that Hamilton is Miranda's "most recent" musical, so we already knew this.

 ...based on the book.

The previous sentence mentions the book that Miranda used as inspiration for the musical. Redundant!

 ...the record-breaking hit.

We learn that Hamilton was "record-smashing" in the first sentence, so we can cross this off.

 ...which went on to win the Pulitzer Prize.

This info is brand spankin' new! We found our answer.

D

## Brevity: Short and Sweet

Short, sweet, and to the point: that is the SAT's motto. When you come across a sentence that is too wordy, look for answer choices that state the same idea in fewer words.

## EXAMPLE 6

Kimchi, a Korean specialty, is a dish that <u>is reliant upon the ongoing process of</u> fermentation to turn fresh cabbage, carrots, radishes, and chilis into a spicy, pickled delicacy.

A) NO CHANGE
B) relies on the process of
C) has become reliant upon the ongoing process of
D) happens to be a dish that relies on the process of

Once again, the shortest answer is correct! Why say "is reliant upon" when you can just say "relies on?" What does saying "happens to be" **add** to the meaning of the sentence? Nothing!

**Choice B** is the best answer.

B

## The Vague Trap

While the shortest answer is often correct, that's not *always* the case! Remember: wording is redundant when two words have the **same meaning**. An answer choice is too wordy when a shorter version communicates the **same meaning**. It's all about the meaning! If the shortest answer loses key information, is too vague, or is otherwise confusing, there's likely a better choice.

## EXAMPLE 7

Found in the freezing waters of the Arctic, Greenland sharks can reach a remarkable milestone: individuals can live up to 400 years, giving them the longest known lifespan of any vertebrate. This information was only recently discovered by scientists who now plan to <u>study it</u>. The most likely location for this is in the Greenland shark's DNA, so scientists are running genome sequencing in hopes of identifying the genetic key to its longer lifespan.

A) NO CHANGE
B) analyze sharks
C) explore deeper into the Arctic Ocean
D) study the shark's longevity

### SOLUTION

We need to make sure that our choice bridges to the next sentence about the shark's DNA.

 A) NO CHANGE

What actually is "it" in this context? Information or the shark? This is vague and does not set up the next sentence.

 B) analyze sharks

Now we're at least talking about sharks, but not necessarily the Greenland shark. We need something more specific.

 C) explore deeper into the Arctic Ocean

This is off topic and doesn't connect to the next sentence.

 D) study the shark's longevity

Perfect! This connects with the following sentence, as the DNA is likely the source of the long lifespans.

D

## How to spot redundancy errors:

If you see choices that give **shorter ways of saying the same thing**, find the shortest option that doesn't repeat information. Keep in mind the other half of the redundancy may be elsewhere in the sentence:

A) NO CHANGE
B) operations, they would never be the same
C) operations, changing both industries
D) operations

*Ever-shrinking choices! Odds are, everything after "operations" is redundant in context.*

# Quiz

*Identify the error (if present) in each of the following sentences.*

1. I stopped at the bank, a local financial institution, to withdraw some cash for my date.

2. For years, Melinda refused to go to bed; she'd yell and shout and raise her voice while beating her fists on the pillow.

3. The eccentric neighbor turned out to be writing a novel that was a book about a fisherman who catches a magical fish.

4. The dream involved a terrifying figure, who was very frightening, looking in my windows repeatedly.

5. By the time he was 7, Samuel was actually very tall for his age and not short.

# Answers

1. I stopped at the bank~~, a local financial institution,~~ to withdraw some cash for my date.

2. For years, Melinda refused to go to bed; she'd yell ~~and shout and raise her voice~~ while beating her fists on the pillow.

3. The eccentric neighbor turned out to be writing a novel ~~that was a book~~ about a fisherman who catches a magical fish.

4. The dream involved a terrifying figure~~, who was very frightening,~~ looking in my windows repeatedly.

5. By the time he was 7, Samuel was actually very tall for his age ~~and not short~~.

# Passage Practice

*Questions 1 – 9 relate to the following passage.*

Napoleon Complex. **1** Doubtlessly, it is a term that certainly many of us will have heard that refers to a person who aggressively overcompensates for a short stature. Its origins are rooted in its namesake, **2** the Corsica-born General Napoleon Bonaparte, a **3** very unique, singular revolutionary figure, famous for his bellicose personality and short stature. There is just one problem: Napoleon was not, in fact, short. He stood 169 cm tall, which was the average height for a man in the 18th century. How do historians account for this strange discrepancy?

One possible explanation is that Napoleon famously surrounded himself with **4** tall bodyguards who protected him, which might have made him appear shorter than he actually was. Additionally, French and British systems of measurements were not standardized; Napoleon is recorded as 5'2" in French units, which is between 5'6" and 5'7" in modern British units, **5** or around 170 centimeters in today's modern metric system.

**1**

A) NO CHANGE
B) A term many of us will have certainly heard
C) It is a term many of us will have heard
D) A term

**2**

A) NO CHANGE
B) the General born in Corsica Napoleon Bonaparte
C) the General from Corsica Napoleon Bonaparte
D) the Corsican General Napoleon Bonaparte

**3**

A) NO CHANGE
B) very singular
C) unique, singular
D) unique

**4**

A) NO CHANGE
B) bodyguards
C) tall bodyguards
D) tall bodyguards for protection

**5**

A) NO CHANGE
B) or around 170 centimeters in today's metric system.
C) or around 170 centimeters in the metric system.
D) DELETE the underlined portion and end the sentence with a period

*Passage continued on next page*

Yet another possibility is that British propaganda deliberately depicted him as short in order to mock him to the British public. [6] The Southeastern coast of English is only 34 kilometers from the Northern coast of France. Indeed, [7] between him and the British Duke of Wellington whom he lost to at the Battle of Waterloo, he was shorter.

Eventually, after Napoleon's defeat, Britain would exile him to the southern island of St. Helena. There, he would die 6 years later of a stomach ulcer. [8] In spite of the fact that he boasted some of the greatest military successes the world has ever seen, it is said that those who *win* wars get to write history. [9] This is just one example of how Napoleon of legend does not quite measure up to the man himself.

**6**

A) NO CHANGE
B) In the prior century, England and France had fought a war in North America to colonial dominance.
C) Many French words that have entered the English language date back to the Norman Conquest of 1066.
D) DELETE the underlined portion

**7**

A) NO CHANGE
B) between Napoleon and the British Duke of Wellington (whom Napoleon lost to at the Battle of Waterloo), Napoleon was shorter.
C) between Napoleon and the British Duke of Wellington (whom Napoleon lost to at the Battle of Waterloo), he was shorter.
D) between the British Duke of Wellington, whom he lost to at the Battle of Waterloo, and him, he was shorter.

**8**

A) NO CHANGE
B) Despite the fact that
C) Notwithstanding the fact
D) Although

**9**

A) NO CHANGE
B) This distortion of his height
C) Questioning his abilities as a commander
D) The propaganda against him

# Prepositions

*A.k.a. "Because we said so."*

........................................................................................

## Many words are paired with certain prepositions

Some questions simply test common use of prepositions. The reason the correct answers are correct boils down to *"Because that's just how it's said,"* which is just about the **worst** explanation parents or teachers can give a well-intentioned student such as yourself. For example:

### TIP

You've heard the correct preposition more than you've heard any of the wrong ones, so the correct answer is usually the one that sounds the best.

Try whispering the different choices to yourself. Pick the choice that sounds the most natural.

*We DO say:*

> "Working nights & weekends is not **consistent <u>with</u>** my beliefs."

*We DON'T say:*

> "Working nights & weekends is not **consistent <u>to</u>** my beliefs."

But here's some good news: If you like to read books, articles, blogs, comics, or all of the above, these questions will be pretty easy. And if you are not a big reader... well, there aren't many of these on the test anyway. Either way, your job here is to simply **trust your ear**.

## EXAMPLE 1
─────────────────────────────────────────

My neighbor, Eileen Sideways, will never forgive her parents <u>about</u> their terrible choice in naming her.

A) NO CHANGE
B) with
C) from
D) for

If you read this sentence out loud, your ear should tell you something is wrong with the preposition. The word **forgive** is always paired with the preposition **for**. That's just the way it is!

D) My neighbor, Eileen Sideways, will never forgive her parents **for** their terrible choice in naming her.

D

## EXAMPLE 2

Many urban condominiums favor an open floor plan as a means <u>through</u> maximizing liveable space in an otherwise small area.

A) NO CHANGE
B) from
C) of
D) DELETE the underlined portion of the sentence.

Once again, your ears should be burning right about now! Open floor plans could be a means **of** maximizing space. They could even be a means **to** maximize space. But they can never be a means *through* maximizing space.

C) Many urban condominiums favor an open floor plan as a means **of** maximizing liveable space in an otherwise small area.

C

## How to spot Preposition questions:

You'll see a **preposition** changing in the answer choices. If other words are attached, don't create a second error while fixing the first!

He knew his <u>chances to surviving</u> were slim.

A) NO CHANGE
B) chance of surviving
C) chance to surviving
D) chances of surviving

*"of" is the correct preposition pair here... but beware of choice B! It creates a brand new error!*

# Check Your Ear

Here are some common verb/preposition pairs you might see on the test. You don't need to memorize these to answer the questions correctly; instead, trust your ear and go with the most familiar pairing.

| verb | preposition |
|---|---|
| abide | by |
| accuse | of |
| agree | to/with/on/upon |
| apologize | for |
| apply | to/for |
| approve | of |
| argue | with/about/over |
| arrive | at |
| believe | in |
| blame | for |
| care | about/for |
| charge | for/with |
| compare | with/to |
| complain | about/of/to |
| consist | of |
| contribute | to |
| count | upon/on |
| cover | with |
| decide | upon/on |
| depend | upon/on |
| differ | about/from/over/with |
| discriminate | against |
| distinguish | from/between |
| dream | of/about |
| escape | from |

| verb | preposition |
|---|---|
| excel | in |
| excuse | for |
| forget | about |
| forgive | for |
| hide | from |
| hope | for |
| insist | upon/on |
| object | to |
| participate | in |
| prevent | from |
| prohibit | from |
| protect | against/from |
| provide | for/with |
| recover | from |
| rely | upon/on |
| rescue | from |
| respond | to |
| stare | at |
| stop | from |
| subscribe | to |
| substitute | for |
| succeed | in |
| thank | for |
| vote | for/on/against |
| wait | for/on |
| worry | about |

**Fill in the blanks below** using the words in the shaded box.
Each word will be used exactly once.

| about | for | from | in | into |
|-------|-----|------|-----|------|
| of | through | to | upon | with |

1. Akram became famous _____ his twenty-two layer dip.

2. After months _____ debate, we finally decided to discard the dastardly dishtowels.

3. As we moved _____ the new year, Joaquin and I patched things up.

4. Every year, Keisha succeeds _____ every goal she sets.

5. The Missouri river cuts _____ five states on its way to St. Louis, MO.

6. The Queen's presence will lend a sense of gravitas _____ the proceedings.

7. Some worry that the new version of the iPhone won't improve _____ the old design.

8. Nothing will prevent Joe _____ attending the rodeo.

9. I don't want to argue _____ you anymore!

10. If I have to listen to Jamilah complain _____ her "A-" in Chemistry one more time, I will literally die.

Answers: 1. for   2. of   3. into   4. in   5. through
6. to   7. upon   8. from   9. with   10. about

# Quiz

*Identify the error (if present) in each of the following sentences.*

1. Born in the South, Dixie has suffered with terrible teasing about her accent by her fellow classmates in New York.

2. After further investigation, it appears that Samson falsely accused Delilah with chopping off his luscious locks.

3. After years of living in his younger brother's basement, Rigoberto finally decided to turn his life around and apply at a graduate program for clown impersonation.

4. Despite the objections of their families to their union, Tyrone and Pamela succeeded with getting married in a private ceremony last month.

5. Ten years in the making, his new skyscraper is both a response to a dramatic change in popular aesthetics and to his critics' dislike with his earlier buildings.

# Answers

1. Born in the South, Dixie has suffered ***from*** terrible teasing about her accent by her fellow classmates in New York.

2. After further investigation, it appears that Samson falsely accused Delilah ***of*** chopping off his luscious locks.

3. After years of living in his younger brother's basement, Rigoberto finally decided to turn his life around and apply ***to*** a graduate program for clown impersonation.

4. Despite the objections of their families to their union, Tyrone and Pamela succeeded ***in*** getting married in a private ceremony last month.

5. Ten years in the making, his new skyscraper is both a response to a dramatic change in popular aesthetics and to his critics' dislike ***of*** his earlier buildings.

## Passage Practice

*Questions 1 – 9 relate to the following passage.*

Given the scientific advances in sea navigation, people have **1** a tendency for thinking that the days of lost-at-sea shipwrecks are over. After all, today's technology is vastly **2** superior than that from the days of Robinson Crusoe. Yet, disastrous shipwrecks continued to happen throughout the 20th century.

In 1972, Dougal Robertson, his wife Lyn, and their two children Douglas and Anne were travelling from Panama to the Galapagos **3** via sailboat. Along the way, they met **4** on serious misfortune when their boat, *The Lucette*, was sunk **5** in a pod with killer whales.

**1**

A) NO CHANGE
B) tendency to think
C) tendency of thinking
D) tendency with thinking

**2**

A) NO CHANGE
B) superior from
C) superior opposed to
D) superior to

**3**

A) NO CHANGE
B) in
C) with
D) through

**4**

A) NO CHANGE
B) against
C) with
D) the

**5**

A) NO CHANGE
B) near a pod by
C) by a pod of
D) through a pod to

*Passage continued on next page*

The tightly-knit family demonstrated remarkable skill and trust [6] with one another, surviving on a small dinghy for 38 days. They managed to catch rain-water and fish, [7] by surviving the harsh conditions of the equatorial Pacific. Dougal himself, an experienced Scottish sailor, had a knack [8] of navigation, steering them back towards the South American coast where they were eventually rescued.

Sadly, this happy ending is a rarity: theirs was the first rescued shipwreck [9] since nearly 30 years. Even today, sailors cannot discount the dangers of the open oceans.

6
A) NO CHANGE
B) in
C) on
D) DELETE the underlined portion

7
A) NO CHANGE
B) whereby
C) thereby
D) hereby

8
A) NO CHANGE
B) for
C) to
D) DELETE the underlined portion

9
A) NO CHANGE
B) in
C) around
D) from

# Vocabulary in Context

*When it comes to vocabulary on the SAT, context is everything! Choose the word that best fits the context of the sentence.*

## Find the best word for the job

Sometimes, you'll encounter answer choices with words that have similar meanings, but different connotations. Your job is to pick the word that **matches the context** of the sentence:

1. *Plug-in and read each word in the sentence*

2. *Look for the most precise match in context*

3. *When in doubt, use your ear!*

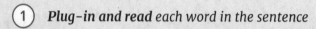

## TIP

Think about where you might have heard the word before to give you a clue. For example, you might have heard "decreed" in an episode of *Game of Thrones*, or "apprehended" on *Law and Order*.

These connections can point you toward the proper context for a word.

## EXAMPLE 1

Dozens of soft lamps <u>elucidated</u> the interior of the newly designed Nexus Gallery, creating an ambience that enabled viewers to experience a heightened intimacy with each work of art.

A) NO CHANGE
B) enlightened
C) irradiated
D) illuminated

**SOLUTION**

We have a bunch of words that all sound similar and have relatively similar meanings. Let's plug each answer choice back into the sentence and **read in context**.

~A)  The lamps <u>elucidated</u> the interior.

*Elucidate means to make an idea clear, which doesn't fit the context perfectly. But it does have the root luc, which has to do with light. Let's keep it for now.*

B)  The lamps <u>enlightened</u> the interior.

*Enlightened obviously has the word light in it, but in most cases, enlightened has to do with learning and education. "Enlighten me!" Let's go ahead and eliminate B.*

C)  The lamps <u>irradiated</u> the interior.

*Are we talking about Marie Curie? Radioactive particles? I don't think our intention is to irradiate the gallery. Let's eliminate C.*

D)  The lamps <u>illuminated</u> the interior.

*This sounds spot on! Let's not eliminate illuminate.*

We are left with **elucidate** and **illuminate**. We <u>know</u> that illuminate works, but we are unsure about elucidate. Always choose a *good* answer over a *possibly* good one. **D** is our answer.

D

## How to spot Vocabulary in Context questions:

As usual, glance at the answer choices to identify the problem type. You'll see a series of similar words, but only one will fit with the passage:

A)  NO CHANGE
B)  immeasurable
C)  mountainous
D)  large

## EXAMPLE 2

Harrison's research reveals a(n) <u>vicious</u> cycle: when teachers and peers label a student as "deviant," the resulting stigma further isolates the child, making it more likely he or she will act out in class.

A) NO CHANGE
B) violent
C) unprincipled
D) malevolent

**TIP**

ALWAYS read the word back into the sentence and check for familiar phrases. If a pairing of words sounds right to your ear, that's a great sign!

SOLUTION

Again, all the answer choices have similar meanings, so let's plug in and use context.

A) Harrison's research reveals a <u>vicious</u> cycle.

*The phrase "vicious cycle" is very familiar and sounds great to my ear. A vicious cycle is a chain of events that continually makes a situation worse. That describes what's happening in this sentence perfectly!*

B) Harrison's research reveals a <u>violent</u> cycle.

*Violent is a very strong word, and there's no hint of violence in the sentence. This doesn't fit.*

C) Harrison's research reveals an <u>unprincipled</u> cycle.

*Unprincipled means immoral or dishonest; this situation is certainly bad, but there's no immorality here.*

D) Harrison's research reveals a <u>malevolent</u> cycle.

*Malevolent might remind you of Maleficent, the evil sorceress in Sleeping Beauty. This word means super-duper evil, which doesn't fit this sentence.*

Choice A creates a familiar phrase that perfectly describes what's happening in our sentence. **Choice A** it is!

A

## EXAMPLE 3

Tarrare's <u>ability</u> to eat almost anything—from stones and watches to live animals and offal—led him to become a sideshow performer and a French Revolutionary spy who carried secret messages inside his stomach.

A) NO CHANGE
B) talent
C) skill
D) flair

### SOLUTION

*Ability*, *talent*, *skill*, and *flair* are pretty close in meaning. How will we choose the right vocabulary word in context? You guessed it! Read each word into the sentence and use your ear:

A) Tarrare's **ability to** eat almost anything...

*This sounds good to my ear! Let's keep this option around.*

B) Tarrare's **talent to** eat almost anything...

*Hmm, "talent to" sounds off to me. Typically, we say you have a **talent for** something. This preposition pairing doesn't work, so we can throw this out.*

C) Tarrare's **skill to** eat almost anything...

*Again, "skill to" sounds wrong to my ear. Another preposition error, another wrong answer.*

D) Tarrare's **flair to** eat almost anything...

*Same deal! Usually we say you have a "flair for" something, not to something. This word does not work in context.*

The only answer that works in context is **choice A**!

**TIP**

The SAT likes to throw preposition errors into Vocabulary in Context problems. Just another reason to always read all your choices into the sentence!

**307**

## Cut the casual language

If you're like most high-schoolers, you speak differently with your friends than you do with, say, their parents. In fact, everybody, regardless of age, uses different vocabulary and sentence structure depending on whether they are in a formal setting (such as at an interview) or a casual one (such as at the movies with friends). The SAT will sometimes attempt to slip at-the-movies-with-friends-language into the Writing essays. When given the option, **cut the casual language**.

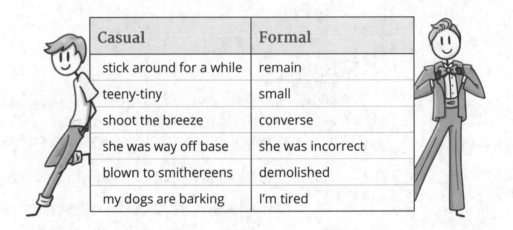

| Casual | Formal |
|---|---|
| stick around for a while | remain |
| teeny-tiny | small |
| shoot the breeze | converse |
| she was way off base | she was incorrect |
| blown to smithereens | demolished |
| my dogs are barking | I'm tired |

## EXAMPLE 4

When Webster announced his intentions to join the famed and highly exclusive Moscow Ballet, there was a great deal of debate regarding whether a US-born dancer <u>could hack it</u>; after his first performance, however, international critics warmed greatly to Webster's portrayal of the Swan King in Tchaikovsky's *Swan Lake*.

A) NO CHANGE
B) was up to snuff
C) could succeed in that environment
D) could hang with the Russians

In this case, we need to look at the level of formality of the passage. It looks fairly straightforward and buttoned-up. *Up to snuff*, *hang with the Russians*, and *could hack it* are all examples of casual language. Choice C matches the straightforward tone of the passage: **C is our answer**!

C

## Common Flips

The SAT will sometimes ask you to choose between two words that sound the same, but have completely different meanings. Here are some words to memorize so you don't fall for that trap!

**NOTE**

The SAT, so far, does not test secondary definitions of effect (to make happen) or affect (emotion). The writers are more interested in the common mix-up shown here.

| Effect | | Affect |
|---|---|---|
| the consequence of an action | vs. | to make a difference to |
| *The Hallelujah chorus has a profound* **effect** *on me.* | | *Practicing your grammar can really* **affect** *your SAT score.* |

| Excess | | Access |
|---|---|---|
| more than necessary, leftover | vs. | to approach or enter |
| *I donated the* **excess** *yarn from my 'Doctor Who' scarf.* | | *Jacob* **accessed** *the mainframe using his elite hacking skills.* |

| Then | | Than |
|---|---|---|
| next in a sequence | vs. | used in comparisons |
| *First, I bought materials.* **Then,** *I made s'mores for 2 days straight.* | | *He'll eat both, but Marius loves Red Vines more* **than** *Twizzlers.* |

| Past | | Passed |
|---|---|---|
| at a previous time | vs. | went by; completed successfully |
| *My pizza-eating days are in the* **past***: I'm now a strict Pastafarian.* | | *The cop car* **passed** *us by. I* **passed** *the Geometry test!* |

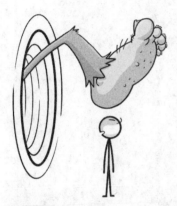

**PORTAL**

For common possession & contraction flips, check out the Possession chapter on page 258.

# Quiz

*Identify the error (if present) in each of the following sentences.*

1. No one could have guessed the affect the new robot would have on the household.

2. After a long day at the office, nothing tastes better then a big plate of bacon.

3. Peanut butter is a perfect compliment to jelly.

4. My gym teacher is no longer excepting handwritten doctors' notes as an excuse to avoid running the mile.

5. Access to the pool is restricted due to a suspicious floating object.

# Answers

1. No one could have guessed the *effect* the new robot would have on the household.

2. After a long day at the office, nothing tastes better *than* a big plate of bacon.

3. Peanut butter is a perfect *complement* to jelly.

4. My gym teacher is no longer *accepting* handwritten doctors' notes as an excuse to avoid running the mile.

5. *Correct!*

# Passage Practice

*Questions 1 – 10 relate to the following passage.*

Today's lawmakers in America are faced with a conundrum that has no clear **1** explanation. That problem is how to apply a 200-year-old edict to a modern context: what is the best way to honor free speech under the First Amendment while simultaneously ensuring democratically **2** logical elections? The issue at hand is whether donations to or spending on behalf of a political campaign **3** completes free speech.

Three Supreme Court cases have **4** designed the issue in the recent past. The first is *The Federal Election Commission v Wisconsin Right to Life* (2007), where WRL was allowed to mention incumbent candidates in advertisements only in the context of a political issue, without directly addressing them as candidates. Second, *Davis v FEC* (2008) saw the Supreme Court strike down legislation of the bipartisan Campaign Reform Act. The Court permitted Davis, New York congressional nominee, to use his own personal money to fund his campaign without **5** getting slapped with any penalty.

**1**

A) NO CHANGE
B) answer
C) response
D) rebuttal

**2**

A) NO CHANGE
B) prudent
C) rational
D) sound

**3**

A) NO CHANGE
B) constitutes
C) creates
D) defers

**4**

A) NO CHANGE
B) framed
C) prepared
D) sketched

**5**

A) NO CHANGE
B) meeting with
C) getting hit with
D) incurring

*Passage continued on next page*

But perhaps the most controversial case is *Citizens United v FEC* (2010), where the court struck down 6 substantial parts of the McCain-Feingold Campaign Finance Reform bill on First Amendment grounds, allowing Citizens United to 7 allot a documentary on Hillary Clinton's political history before the 2008 primary.

At stake are the fundamental ideas of free speech and democratic fairness. Many on one side of the issue believe that wealthy individuals or organizations should be able to say what they like and spend their money how they see fit, especially on political issues and candidates. Those thinkers claim the Supreme Court's decisions are only preserving a 8 robust First Amendment doctrine. On the other hand, many dissenters believe that such rulings undermine democracy, consolidating power into the hands of those who can afford to spend more money on elections. To them, *Citizens United* adversely 9 effects the principle of "One Person, One Vote."

With these two 10 adamant, partisan sides, it seems we are forced to choose between free speech rights or democratic elections. No matter your position, this is one of the foremost Constitutional issues of our time.

6
A) NO CHANGE
B) grand
C) hefty
D) vast

7
A) NO CHANGE
B) allocate
C) generate
D) distribute

8
A) NO CHANGE
B) vigorous
C) hearty
D) prosperous

9
A) NO CHANGE
B) effects the principal
C) affects the principle
D) affects the principal

10
A) NO CHANGE
B) divisible
C) unforgiving
D) ruthless

# Writing Practice Passage 4
## TO STAY ON PACE, YOUR TIMING GOAL IS 8.5 MINUTES

This passage tests a variety of grammar topics—some from chapters you may have not yet completed. Use this opportunity to practice maintaining a brisk pace while answering the questions as best you can. Good luck!

**Questions 1-11 are based on the following passage.**

**The Gila "Monster"**

Biodiversity, the incredible variety of species on Earth, is **1** compulsory for human life. Consider the Gila monster: a large, stocky lizard, significantly bigger than most of its North American brethren. One of the few venomous lizards in the world, it is one of only three venomous species found in all of the Americas. The overall effect creates a tough-looking lizard, worthy of the name "monster." But despite its moniker, fearsome **2** visual appearance, and venomous bite, the Gila monster actually poses very little threat to humans. **3** In fact, humans are benefitting from the Gila monster's unique defenses.

Its sturdy build makes it cumbersome and slow-moving, yet the Gila monster's stout physique does **4** give it a leg up in the desert: the thick tail can store fat and its slow metabolism allows the Gila monster to survive for long periods without a meal. Unlike venomous snakes, Gila monsters lack the ability to inject their venom as snakes do. Instead, a Gila monster must allow the venom to enter its victim's wounds through exposure to saliva by chewing. The venom causes pain and an overall feeling of sickness, but there have been no human fatalities **5** from Gila monster bites recorded in the last 75 years.

---

**1**

A) NO CHANGE
B) acute in
C) essential to
D) unalterable with

**2**

A) NO CHANGE
B) appearance,
C) appearance to the eye,
D) visual appearance to the eye,

**3**

Which choice best introduces a key detail established later in the passage?

A) NO CHANGE
B) The Gila monster is most closely related to the larger Mexican beaded lizard and the two species range overlaps.
C) In 1963, the San Diego Zoo became the first nature conservatory to successfully breed gila monsters in captivity.
D) Many early Western settlers feared that the breath of Gila was toxic, but that myth has long since been disproven.

**4**

A) NO CHANGE
B) give it a shot
C) give it an advantage
D) ensure its advantaged position

Recent medical interest in Gila monster venom has not focused on its [6] negative effects, but rather its potential to improve human health. Gila monster venom contains a hormone called extendin-4, which is similar to a human hormone, glucagon-like peptide-1 analog (GLP1), found in the human digestive tract. GLP-1 assists in the production of insulin to combat peaks in a human's blood sugar level. Extendin-4 has shown to work better than GLP-1, as [7] it's effects last longer. Scientists have been able to recreate extendin-4, calling the synthetic hormone "exenatide."

In 2005, the Food and Drug Administration approved exenatide for use in managing type-2 diabetes. Type-2 diabetes, also referred to as adult-onset diabetes, is a complication commonly associated [8] to obesity; it occurs when cells stop responding to the body's production of insulin. Exenatide not only helps produce insulin, but also creates a feeling of fullness in the stomach that [9] can help and assist with weight loss. Dr. John Buse, the lead researcher in the exenatide study is excited "that patients that continue exenatide injections continue to lose a bit of weight while maintaining blood sugar control, even in their third year of therapy."

**5**

A) NO CHANGE
B) about
C) around
D) with

**6**

Which choice best maintains the tone of the passage?

A) NO CHANGE
B) evil
C) awful
D) malevolent

**7**

A) NO CHANGE
B) it's affects
C) its affects
D) its effects

**8**

A) NO CHANGE
B) through
C) with
D) DELETE the underlined portion.

**9**

A) NO CHANGE
B) can help
C) can help, even assist,
D) is known to help and even assist

CONTINUE

[10] Dr. Buse will certainly continue to do research into exenatide and its other applications. Who knows what other molecular miracles are hiding in the creatures inhabiting remote regions of our world? The surprising fact that the venom of the near-threatened Gila monster can help improve human lives dramatically [11] emphasize the benefits of conservation and research.

[10]

Which choice best transitions from the preceding paragraph to the main idea of the following paragraph?

A) NO CHANGE
B) Type-2 diabetes is the most common form of diabetes, with nearly 30 million Americans affected by the condition.
C) Dr. Buse is still optimistic that patients will show weight lose past their third year of therapy, but he needs more results.
D) A discovery such as this points to the global need to maintain biodiversity.

[11]

A) NO CHANGE
B) emphasizes
C) emphasized
D) emphasizing

## STOP

**If you finish before time is called, you may check your work on this section only.**
**Do not turn to any other section.**

# UNIT | Connecting Thoughts

## Chapters

## Overview

In this unit, we'll look at different ways to connect two sentences or thoughts in a logical, efficient manner.

# Logical Connectors

*When linking two ideas together, keep it logical!*

### Similar vs. Opposite

Picking the right word to join two ideas depends on whether those ideas are **similar (=)** or **opposite (≠)**. For example, the following ideas are *similar*, since the second idea logically follows from the first:

I followed the recipe exactly, _____so_____ the meal came out perfectly!

You would **expect** that following a recipe would lead to a good result. In contrast, *opposite* ideas are unexpected or surprising:

I followed the recipe exactly, _____but_____ the end result was a disaster!

**Fill in each grey box** with "=" if the ideas on either side are similar or "≠" if the ideas are opposite.

1. Most people thought that Auntie Gladys, with her thick cockney accent, was born in London's West End, ≠ she had never even left Kansas!

2. My little brother realized too late that his plastic superhero did not have the power of flight; = , we watched the red and blue figure plummet into our mother's beet garden two floors below.

3. Four out of five doctors agree that Colgate is the best toothpaste. ☐ , Dr. Fluffington prefers brushing his teeth with a mixture of baking soda and sea salt.

4. Katniss and Elmer's meticulously planned outdoor wedding had to be moved inside at the last minute, ☐ it started to rain.

5. According to the review of Guillermo's new novel, the plot was muddled and confusing, ☐ the book was redeemed by its insightful character development.

6. The unseasonably warm winter caused significant thawing in the California mountains. ☐ , more counties than usual are under flash flood warnings.

7. Abjit diligently trained for eight months, ☐ he was able to finish all 26 miles of the Boston Marathon.

8. Many people believe that Napoleon was unusually short; ☐ , he was 5'7", above average for men at that time.

9. The author Bram Stoker is most famous for his novel Dracula, which is set in the Romanian region of Transylvania. ☐ , Stoker never travelled to Eastern Europe, and spent most of his life in Ireland and England.

10. Globally, public health campaigns reporting the ill effects of tobacco smoke are having positive effects; ☐ , in 2005, Bhutan became the first country to outlaw the sale and use of tobacco products.

Answers: | 1. *given* | 2. *given* | 3. ≠ | 4. = | 5. ≠
| 6. = | 7. = | 8. ≠ | 9. ≠ | 10. =

# Eliminate illogical choices first

When you see answer choices full of connecting words, you should start by figuring out if they are joining similar or opposite ideas:

① *Ask yourself, "are the ideas **similar** or **opposite**?"*

② ***Eliminate illogical choices** based on your answer.*

③ ***Reread the sentence** using each remaining word.*

## EXAMPLE 1

There was one thing Wilhelmina knew for sure about lobsters: stay away from the pincers. <u>Therefore,</u> when a large lobster attempted to share her beach towel, she vacated the area in a hurry.

A) NO CHANGE
B) Conversely,
C) Nonetheless,
D) Despite this,

SOLUTION

Let's take this problem one step at a time.

① *Ask yourself, "are the ideas similar or opposite?"*

*First, Wilhelmina learns to **stay away** from lobsters. Next, she **vacates**. We're definitely dealing with **similar ideas**.*

② *Eliminate illogical choices based on your answer*

*Connectors that link **opposite ideas** have to go. That means we can cross off B, C, and D, that just leaves **choice A**!*

A

## EXAMPLE 2

Jane's obsession with great apes began at an early age. <u>Finally</u>, she insisted on celebrating her fifth birthday by dressing up like an orangutan and trying to communicate with her furry friends at the zoo.

A) NO CHANGE
B) Similarly,
C) For example,
D) Although,

SOLUTION

(1) *Ask yourself, "are the ideas **similar** or **opposite**?"*

Ape obsession and orangutan party are **similar** ideas.

(2) *Eliminate illogical choices based on your answer*

We can cross off any connectors that link **opposite** ideas. That eliminates choice D!

(3) *Reread the sentence using each remaining word.*

A) Jane's obsession with great apes began at an early age. **Finally,** she insisted on celebrating her fifth birthday by dressing up like an orangutan...

There's nothing **final** about a 5-year-old's birthday party.

~ B) Jane's obsession with great apes began at an early age. **Similarly,** she insisted on celebrating her fifth birthday by dressing up like an orangutan...

These two ideas are certainly similar. This connection is okay, but I think we can get more specific. Squiggle it.

C) Jane's obsession with great apes began at an early age. **For example,** she insisted on celebrating her fifth birthday by dressing up like an orangutan...

Jane's fifth birthday at the zoo is an **example** of her early ape obsession. This connector makes a tight, logical connection between these ideas. C is correct!

C

## Not all ideas should be connected

Sometimes, the SAT will tempt you to force a connection where there is none to be found. Don't try to connect *unrelated* ideas; instead, just **delete the connector**.

### EXAMPLE 3

At my brother's graduation party, we all chowed down on delicious Mexican food from Los Hermanos Taqueria. <u>Despite this,</u> the perfectly seasoned salsa was the first item to run out.

A) NO CHANGE
B) Given that,
C) Furthermore,
D) DELETE the underlined portion and begin the sentence with a capital letter.

These ideas are similar, but none of these connectors fit! If there's no logical connection, **delete** the connector.

D) At my brother's graduation party, we all chowed down on delicious Mexican food from Los Hermanos Taqueria. The perfectly-seasoned salsa was the first item to run out.

D

## How to spot Logical Connector questions:

As usual, glance at the answer choices to identify the problem type. Here, you'll see a series of the connector words we see in this chapter:

A) NO CHANGE
B) In contrast, ≠
C) Consequently, =
D) On the other hand, ≠

*When you see connectors, quickly label them as similar (=) or opposite (≠).*

## Learn your logical connectors

To help you make logical connections on the SAT, let's get familiar with the connectors you'll see on the test. In the table below, you'll find some of the most common connectors and how they are used.

# TIP

When you see a connector on the test, think about its **specific meaning** and whether it works in the **context** of the paragraph. A word isn't right simply because it sounds smart (the same goes for people).

# PORTAL

Be on the lookout for answer choices that get the logic right but improperly join **independent/ dependent clauses**.

For practice on joining clauses, turn to page 203.

| Function | Similar (=) | Opposite (≠) |
|---|---|---|
| **Showing Logic** | Thus<br>Consequently<br>Therefore<br>Hence<br>So<br>Because | However<br>Despite<br>Nevertheless<br>Nonetheless<br>Regardless<br>Although<br>Yet<br>But |
| **Extending Ideas** | Additionally<br>In addition<br>Furthermore<br>Moreover<br>Likewise<br>Also | Alternatively<br>On one hand<br>On the other hand<br>In contrast |
| **Giving Examples** | For example<br>For instance<br>In fact | |
| **Showing Time** | Thereafter<br>Subsequently<br>Next<br>Previously<br>Finally | |
| **Summarizing Ideas** | In short<br>In broad terms<br>In other words | |

## Some words are practically married

Certain things just go together, like chocolate and peanut butter or cats and naps. The connecting words below are **always** paired on the test. If the test-writers set up one half of the relationship, add the other!

# TIP

*Either*, *neither*, and *both* are only used to join two things. You would **not** say:

Both Lucy, Linus, and Pepperment Patty love football.

There are *some* situations in the non-SAT world where you might use *either* for picking from more than two things, but the SAT keeps it simple and so shall we!

| Word Pair | Example |
| --- | --- |
| either ___ or ___ | I'm happy with **either** hamburgers **or** hotdogs. |
| neither ___ nor ___ | **Neither** France **nor** Germany made it to the World Cup last year. |
| both ___ and ___ | **Both** the dress rehearsal **and** the premiere were disasters. |
| not only ___, but also ___ | I **not only** fell *down* the stairs, **but also** fell on the way back *up*. |

## EXAMPLE 4

Both my cousin Ona as well as her boyfriend Milo are morally opposed to eating walnuts, claiming the delicious nuts are tiny bits of trees' souls.

A) NO CHANGE
B) Both my cousin Ona and
C) Either my cousin Ona and
D) Not only my cousin Ona also

SOLUTION

We are given four options for word pairs, but only **choice B** gets the right marriage: the simple, reliable "and" is the perfect match for "both."

B) **Both** my cousin Ona **and** her boyfriend Milo are morally opposed to eating walnuts, claiming the delicious nuts are tiny bits of trees' souls.

B

# Passage Practice

*Questions 1 – 10 relate to the following passage.*

It turns out that the universe does have a sense of humor. On Friday the 13th in April of 2029, a giant 370-meter asteroid will come hurtling towards Earth. **1** So, despite the ominous date, the astronomical community could not be more excited.

The asteroid, named *99942 Apophis* after the Ancient Egyptian god for chaos, was first spotted in June 2004; **2** thus the initial readings caused quite a stir when it was determined that there was a 2.7% probability that the asteroid was on a trajectory for a direct Earth impact. **3** Subsequently, additional observations have ruled out the possibility of a collision completely. Instead, the asteroid will zoom harmlessly by our planet, passing 31,000km (or 19,000 miles) away from us at its closest point. **4** And this distance may sound quite far away, it is in fact within the orbit of some satellites.

The close fly-by will be a spectacle not only for scientists, **5** also for amateur astronomers. The asteroid will be visible travelling west both from Australia in the early morning **6** or from equatorial Africa in the afternoon.

**1**

A) NO CHANGE
B) Thus
C) Therefore
D) However

**2**

A) NO CHANGE
B) consequently
C) as
D) DELETE the underlined word

**3**

A) NO CHANGE
B) Fortunately
C) Regardless
D) Unfortunately

**4**

A) NO CHANGE
B) As
C) Although
D) DELETE the underlined word

**5**

A) NO CHANGE
B) and for amateur astronomers
C) but also for amateur astronomers
D) and also for amateur astronomers

**6**

A) NO CHANGE
B) then
C) and
D) next

*Passage continued on next page*

Disappointingly for those in America, [7] in spite of the fact that *Apophis* will be at its closest to Earth at 6pm EST above the Western Atlantic, the sunlight will likely block it out.

Scientists and government officials keep a close watch on the skies for any potentially hazardous impact threats, but they assure the public that [8] neither *Apophis* or any other known asteroid or comet poses a grave threat at the moment. For one, asteroids the size of *Apophis* or greater are few and far between. Second, physicists are already putting plans into motion about what to do in the case of an impact threat. One possibility involves a network of laser beams that can point from Earth towards a menacing object, pushing on the potential asteroid, [9] nonetheless altering its trajectory. Another more effective strategy would be to launch a satellite to fly alongside the threatening asteroid and use the satellite's gravity to gently tug the asteroid off of its dangerous path.

For now, we Earthlings need not worry about the dangers of an impact on Friday April 13th, 2029. [10] Moreover, we should celebrate a day on which we can gather vital data on *Apophis* and marvel at the mysteries of deep Space.

A) NO CHANGE
B) since
C) because
D) despite

A) NO CHANGE
B) neither Apophis nor any other known asteroid nor comet
C) neither Apophis nor any other known asteroid or comet
D) neither Apophis or any other known asteroid nor comet

A) NO CHANGE
B) nevertheless
C) likewise
D) thus

A) NO CHANGE
B) Rather
C) Furthermore
D) Nonetheless

# Combining Sentences

*More isn't always better. Let's look at how to be more efficient in our wording.*

## You may be asked to join two sentences into one

Neither sentence will be grammatically *incorrect*, but for brevity's sake, they would sound better as one. When combining sentences, remember:

1.  **Keep it short:** avoid any unnecessary or redundant phrases

2.  **Keep the focus:** maintain the original purpose of the sentences

## EXAMPLE 1

> Yesterday, I noticed the leaves changing color on the tree in my front <u>yard. This reminds</u> me how much I hate raking leaves.

Which choice most effectively combines the two sentences at the underlined portion?

A)  yard and these leaves remind
B)  yard, and this change reminds
C)  yard, and such changes remind
D)  yard, reminding

SOLUTION

All of the choices combine the sentences, and none of them are glaringly incorrect. But only **one** maintains the focus while eliminating unnecessary words.

Choices A, B, and C have redundant words that appear in the previous sentence. We already know we're talking about "changes" and "leaves," so why waste time repeating ourselves? The best (and shortest) answer is **D**!

> D) Yesterday, I noticed the leaves changing color on the tree in my front <u>**yard, reminding**</u> me how much I hate raking leaves.

D

## EXAMPLE 2

The month of July is named for Julius <u>Caesar. Caesar</u> played an integral role in the rise of the Roman Empire.

Which choice most effectively combines the two sentences at the underlined portion?

A) Caesar, and Caesar is someone who
B) Caesar, who
C) Caesar, but he
D) Caesar, and he

SOLUTION

**Choice A** is the worst option: it repeats "Caesar" and is even longer than the original! That's not a very efficient combination.

**Choice C** uses "but," which is an illogical connector in this context.

**Choice D** is logical, but is it the most efficient choice? It doesn't repeat "Caesar," but it still sounds clunky to make both parts of the sentence *independent clauses*.

It is shorter and sweeter to make the second sentence a dependent clause that gives us more information about the word "Caesar." **Choice B** does just that:

B) The month of July is named for Julius <u>**Caesar, who**</u> played an integral role in the rise of the Roman Empire.

B

Keep it short, Brutus. Especially in the back!

## The Hard Version

When the underlined portion stretches to two full sentences, you have found yourself a **hard** combining sentences question. Don't panic! These questions just require you to wade through some confusing, awkward-sounding wrong answers to find the logical right answer.

## EXAMPLE 3

During the Civil War, Sarah Josepha Hale wrote a series of letters urging President Lincoln to formalize New England's yearly Pilgrims' Harvest Festival into a national holiday. The result was the holiday dedicated to stuffing one's face with turkey and mashed potatoes while watching football and extolling the virtues of pumpkin pie. It was Thanksgiving Day.

Which choice most effectively combines the underlined sentences?

A) The result was Thanksgiving Day, the holiday dedicated to stuffing one's face with turkey and mashed potatoes while watching football and extolling the virtues of pumpkin pie.

B) The result was the holiday, Thanksgiving Day, dedicated to stuffing one's face with turkey and mashed potatoes while watching football and extolling the virtues of pumpkin pie.

C) The holiday dedicated to stuffing one's face with turkey and mashed potatoes while watching football and extolling the virtues of pumpkin pie was the result, Thanksgiving Day.

D) A holiday stuffing one's face with turkey and mashed potatoes resulted, and one watches football and extols the virtues of pumpkin pie; it was Thanksgiving Day.

### TIP

Remember your two passage rules: any changes you make MUST

1) Stay on topic

2) Transition smoothly between ideas

SOLUTION

Let's take each answer choice one at a time:

(A) The result was Thanksgiving Day, the holiday dedicated to stuffing one's face with turkey and mashed potatoes while watching football and extolling the virtues of pumpkin pie.

*This option is logical and sounds good to my ear. The subject is **Thanksgiving Day**, which is the focus of the entire sentence. That's a great sign!*

**Continued on next page →**

B) The result was the holiday, Thanksgiving Day, dedicated to stuffing one's face with turkey and mashed potatoes while watching football and extolling the virtues of pumpkin pie.

*Why is **Thanksgiving Day** breaking up the idea? There's no reason to interrupt the phrase here, and it sounds **awkward**!*

C) The holiday dedicated to stuffing one's face with turkey and mashed potatoes while watching football and extolling the virtues of pumpkin pie was the result, Thanksgiving Day.

***Thanksgiving Day** is the focus of our sentence, but it's not the subject. It doesn't show up until the very end! This isn't the best choice.*

D) A holiday stuffing one's face with turkey and mashed potatoes resulted, and one watches football and extols the virtues of pumpkin pie; it was Thanksgiving Day.

*So many unnecessary pronouns here. Stuffing one's face... one watches... it was Thanksgiving Day. With all those extra pronouns, this is not the most efficient and logical sentence.*

Very often, the right combination will provide a **logical transition** that **keeps the flow** between paragraphs or sentences. Remember, the SAT absolutely loves a good transition, so be on the lookout for answers that keep things flowing!

## EXAMPLE 4

For a 10-year-old, there is no greater joy than having some extra money in your pocket to spend on the diversion of your choice. In this uncertain economy, more and more kids are turning to lemonade stands for those discretionary funds, as one afternoon's work can net as much as ten dollars!

<u>Lemonade stands are also environmentally sustainable apart from generating much-needed income. They typically release a level of carbon dioxide that falls well below international emission limits for food production.</u> An increasing number of lemonade entrepreneurs are also using locally-grown organic lemons, further reducing their carbon footprint.

Which choice most effectively combines the underlined sentences?

A) The environmental sustainability of lemonade stands, apart from generating much-needed income, typically releases a level of carbon dioxide that falls well below international emission limits for food production.

B) Apart from generating much-needed income, lemonade stands are also environmentally sustainable, typically releasing a level of carbon dioxide that falls well below international emission limits for food production.

C) Lemonade stands typically release a level of carbon dioxide that falls well below international emission limits for food production, which generate much-needed income and are environmentally sustainable.

D) Typically releasing a level of carbon dioxide that falls well below international emission limits for food production, lemonade stands generate much-needed income and are environmentally sustainable.

SOLUTION

Once again, let's look at each combination:

A) The environmental sustainability of lemonade stands, apart from generating much-needed income, typically releases a level of carbon dioxide that falls well below international emission limits for food production.

*If we cross out the junk between the subject and verb of our sentence, we get:*

The environmental sustainability ~~of lemonade stands, apart from generating much-needed income,~~ typically releases a level of carbon dioxide that falls well below international emission limits for food production.

*That doesn't make sense! The **lemonade stands** release carbon dioxide, not the environmental sustainability.*

B) Apart from generating much-needed income, lemonade stands are also environmentally sustainable, typically releasing a level of carbon dioxide that falls well below international emission limits for food production.

*What a great transition! The previous paragraph is all about **income**, which we see at the beginning of this sentence, and "environmentally sustainable" is directly followed by more information on **how** they are sustainable.*

C) Lemonade stands typically release a level of carbon dioxide that falls well below international emission limits for food production, which generate much-needed income and are environmentally sustainable.

*This rewording suggests that the emission limits (not the lemonade stands) generate income. That doesn't match the meaning of the original sentences.*

D) Typically releasing a level of carbon dioxide that falls well below international emission limits for food production, lemonade stands generate much-needed income and are environmentally sustainable.

*Compare this answer choice to choice **B** to see the power of **good transitions**. By hiding "lemonade stands generate much-needed income" in the middle of the sentence, we interrupt the transition from a discussion about income to one about environmental impact. It also makes "environmentally sustainable" sound like an afterthought rather than the main focus of the sentence.*

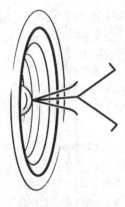

## PORTAL

The key to good transitions and combinations is to group similar ideas together. To see what can go wrong when ideas are out of order, check out the Misplaced Modifiers chapter on page 275.

# Passage Practice

*Questions 1 – 8 relate to the following passage.*

Marie Antoinette was an **1** Austrian princess. She became the last queen of France. **2** To this day, she is often remembered as a silly, frivolous woman. This is, however, an unfair assessment of her character. The French monarchy was unpopular with the people, **3** and Marie Antoinette was blamed for its excessive spending. She was blamed for its excessive spending because she was a foreign queen and an easy target. According to a popular story of the time, Marie Antoinette responded to news that the people of France were starving from lack of bread with the glib response, "Let them eat cake, then!"

*Passage continued on next page*

**1**

Which choice most effectively combines the sentences at the underlined portion?

A) Austrian princess, but also would become
B) Austrian princess who was becoming
C) Austrian princess who became
D) Austrian princess and she became

**2**

Which choice best combines the underlined sentences?

A) To this day, she is often remembered as a silly, frivolous woman, which is an unfair assessment of her character.
B) A silly, frivolous woman is what she is often remembered as being, even to this day, although that is an unfair assessment of her character.
C) An unfair assessment of her character to this day is that she is remembered as a silly, frivolous woman.
D) To this day, she is often remembered as a silly, frivolous woman, which is being an unfair assessment of her character.

**3**

Which choice most effectively combines the sentences at the underlined portion?

A) and Marie Antoinette was an easy target to blame for its excessive spending; she was a foreign queen.
B) and Marie Antoinette was blamed for its excessive spending because she was a foreign queen and an easy target.
C) and its excessive spending was blamed on Marie Antoinette as a foreign queen and an easy target.
D) and Marie Antoinette was blamed for its excessive spending; she was blamed for its excessive spending because she was a foreign queen and an easy target.

**4** Marie Antoinette's enemies used that story to argue that she was clueless and uncaring. There is no proof that Marie Antoinette ever said "Let them eat cake." As a matter of fact, this story was first told about another French queen who lived 100 years before Marie Antoinette. **5** It is true that Marie Antoinette lived lavishly. Her lifestyle did not bankrupt the French people.

*Passage continued on next page*

**334**

---

**4**

Which choice best combines the underlined sentences?

A) Marie Antoinette's enemies used that story that she said "Let them eat cake"—of which there is no proof—to argue that she was clueless and uncaring.

B) Marie Antoinette's enemies used that story to argue that she was clueless and uncaring, but there is no proof that she ever said "Let them eat cake."

C) That story, of which there is no proof that she ever said "Let them eat cake," was being used by Marie Antoinette's enemies to argue that she was clueless and uncaring.

D) Marie Antoinette's enemies used that story to argue that she was clueless and uncaring and there is no proof that Marie Antoinette ever said "Let them eat cake."

**5**

Which choice best combines the underlined sentences?

A) It is true that Marie Antoinette lived lavishly and her lifestyle did not bankrupt the French people.

B) Marie Antoinette's life, which was lived lavishly, did not, however, bankrupt the French people.

C) Living lavishly her life, Marie Antoinette did not, however, bankrupt the French people.

D) Although it is true that Marie Antoinette lived a lavish life, her lifestyle did not bankrupt the French people.

**6** The French economy suffered much more due to France's involvement in numerous wars and the de-regulation of grain prices. This deregulation of grain prices led to food shortages. In addition, **7** the French people were inspired by the American colonists, who won their independence. The American colonists won their independence from Britain with the help of the French military.

Which choice best combines the underlined sentences?

A) The deregulation of grain prices led to food shortages and the French economy suffered due to France's involvement in numerous wars and that deregulation.

B) The French economy suffered much more due to France's involvement in numerous wars and the deregulation of grain prices; this deregulation of grain prices led to food shortages.

C) The French economy suffered much more due to France's involvement in numerous wars and the deregulation of grain prices, which led to food shortages.

D) The French economy suffered much more due to France's involvement in numerous wars and the deregulation of grain prices, because this deregulation of grain prices led to food shortages.

Which choice most effectively combines the sentences at the underlined portion?

A) the American colonists, who won their independence from Britain, were helped by the French military, which inspired the French people.

B) the French people were inspired by the American colonists, who won their independence from Britain with the help of the French military.

C) the French people were inspired by the American colonists who won their independence, for they won their independence from Britain with the help of the French military.

D) the French people were inspired by the American colonists who won their independence; they won their independence from Britain with the help of the French military.

*Passage continued on next page*

**335**

8 Marie Antoinette and her husband were unable to stop the revolutionary spirit and were overthrown in the late 1780s. This revolutionary spirit was spreading through France in the late 1780s.

Which choice best combines the underlined sentences?

A) Spreading through France, Marie Antoinette and her husband were unable to stop the revolutionary spirit spreading through France and were overthrown in the late 1780s.

B) This revolutionary spirit, spreading through France in the 1780s, was unable to be stopped by Marie Antoinette and her husband, who were overthrown.

C) Being overthrown in the late 1780s, Marie Antoinette and her husband were unable to stop the revolutionary spirit spreading through France.

D) Unable to stop the revolutionary spirit spreading through France, Marie Antoinette and her husband were overthrown in the late 1780s.

# Order/Placement

*Order/Placement questions ask you to move a sentence or paragraph to its proper place in a passage. The key is to focus on linking words.*

## PORTAL

In this sentence, "dog" is the **antecedent** of the pronoun "she". We talked about pronouns and antecedents in the **Pronoun Error** chapter on page 248.

### Focus on words that link sentences together

To answer Order/Placement questions, you will need to pay close attention to the logical connections between paragraphs and sentences. Events have to proceed logically; you cannot make an omelet before you buy the eggs! Similarly, you must introduce a pronoun before you use it; you cannot say "his car was fast" before you identify who "he" is.

Every sentence is linked to the preceding and following sentences by related words which we call "linking words." Let's take a look at two simple sentences:

> I trust **my dog**.    **She** wouldn't steal.

There is a link between these two sentences that makes them flow logically. We understand who "she" is in the second sentence because it connects with "my dog" in the first sentence. "My dog" and "she" are **linking words** that give the sentences their proper order and make them fit together like a puzzle:

> I trust **my dog**.    **She** wouldn't steal.

## Spot the connections

When you are working with Order/Placement questions, think of the entire paragraph as a series of **linked puzzle pieces**, with linking words telling you where each sentence belongs:

# TIP

You can practice looking for **linking words** in literally any paragraph, be it in a text book, a blog article, or a text from your friend.

Being conscious of linking words will also help you edit your writing and become a better communicator.

*That, this, these, those*

I awoke profoundly **hungry**.
I **perused the fridge**, but all I could find was marshmallow cream.
I heaped that **marshmallowy goodness** onto a roll and took a bite.
That bite turned into an entire **meal** that suited my refined palate.

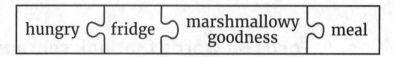

One sentence flows logically to the next, thanks to all the linking words! If you move the sentences around, that logical order is disturbed:

That bite turned into an entire **meal** that suited my refined palate.
I heaped that **marshmallowy goodness** onto a roll and took a bite. I awoke profoundly **hungry**.
I perused the **fridge**, but all I could find was marshmallow cream.

Notice how reading the sentences out of order raises a lot of questions. What **meal**? Which **marshmallowy goodness**? Why are you **hungry** when you just ate? When the sentences are put back in the right order, these linking words click right in place.

---

## How to spot Order/Placement questions:

This one's easy: you'll be given a sentence to move and four possible destinations. The passage will also contain markers (e.g., [1] or [A]).

A) where it is now.
B) after Sentence 2.
C) after Sentence 4.
D) after Sentence 5.

*As soon as you see this numbering, start looking for linking words!*

**Identify the correct order for the sentences below** by writing "2" next to the second sentence, "3" next to the third sentence, and so on.

| #(1-5) | Paragraph 1 |
|---|---|
| 1 | Have you ever noticed a small piece of pink skin tucked away in the corner of your eye? Don't worry, it is just the leftover remains of an inner third eyelid. |
| 4 | Additionally, some mammals have maintained third eyelids. |
| 3 | Many species of birds and reptiles have these membranes to provide advantages in flight or underwater. |
| 5 | For example, the average domesticated cat has a third eyelid that partially covers the eyeball, which can be seen when it slowly opens or closes its eyes. |
| 2 | Called a nictitating membrane, the eyelid provided an additional covering to protect the eye and still maintain vision. |

| #(1-5) | Paragraph 2 |
|---|---|
| 1 | Solar power has the potential to provide clean, renewable energy. Historically, two major problems with solar energy are the size of the panels and the frequency of cloudy days. |
| 3 | The plane's wings provide plenty of surface area for panels of solar power cells. |
| 2 | But a new solar powered airplane cleverly overcomes these obstacles. |
| 4 | And once above the cloud layer, the cells are able to soak up ample solar energy. |
| 5 | Although generating enough power for takeoff is still beyond the limits of most solar powered planes, the absorbed energy enables the airplane to fly longer by using less fuel. |

# TIP

Remember to look for **linking words** to help organize these sentences. One sentence will set up an idea and a second will reference it.

Answers: *At the bottom of the next page!*

## EXAMPLE 1

[1] Born in Dublin in 1874, Ernest Shackleton displayed an early passion for exploration and adventure. [2] As a child he was a voracious reader, which only fueled his far-flung imagination and spirit. [3] Before long he was renting skiffs and voyaging deep into the icy waters of the North Atlantic. [4] In 1909 he led the first expedition to pinpoint the approximate location of the South Magnetic Pole, deep in the heart of the Antarctic. [5] He went on to lead one of the most daring expeditions in history, and today he is celebrated as a model of leadership. [6] These trips increased his confidence and contributed to his growing celebrity, leading to his first commission of an Antarctic bound vessel.

For the sake of the logic and coherence of the preceding paragraph, Sentence 6 should be placed:

A) where it is now.
B) after Sentence 2.
C) after Sentence 3.
D) after Sentence 4.

SOLUTION

First, let's look for **linking words** in sentence 6.

[6] **These trips** increased his confidence and contributed to his growing celebrity, **leading to his first commission** of an Antarctic bound vessel.

We need to place this sentence immediately **after** one that clarifies what *"these trips"* refers to. And we need to place it immediately **before** a sentence about his *"first commission on an Antarctic bound vessel."* **After sentence 3** is the perfect spot:

[3] Before long he was renting skiffs and **voyaging deep** into the icy waters of the North Atlantic. *These trips increased his confidence and contributed to his growing celebrity, leading to his first commission of an Antarctic bound vessel.* [4] In 1909 he led the **first expedition** to pinpoint the approximate location of the South Magnetic Pole, deep in the heart of the **Antarctic**.

These sentences link together! **Choice C** is the best option.

C

Previous page:  Paragraph 1: 1, 4, 3, 5, 2

Paragraph 2: 1, 3, 2, 4, 5

## EXAMPLE 2

[1] When Christy opened her own pizza-and-pies restaurant, she knew there would be challenges. [2] An exploding pizza oven and a shortage of pie tins, however, nearly caused her to give up her dream. [3] The crew's hard work vindicated Christy's ambitions, and Piece-A-Pie opened right on time.

The writer wants to add the following sentence to the paragraph:

*In response to the disaster, Christy's kitchen crew rallied around the restaurant, putting in extra hours and long phone calls to get everything ready for the big opening.*

The most logical place to add this sentence would be:

A)   Before Sentence 1
B)   After Sentence 1
C)   After Sentence 2
D)   After Sentence 3

The added sentence references Christy's **crew** responding to a **disaster**. Where does this disaster occur in the paragraph? Sentence 2: *"an exploding pizza oven and back-ordered pie tins."* Let's add the sentence after Sentence 2 and see how that sounds:

[2] An **exploding pizza oven** and a shortage of pie tins, however, nearly caused her to give up her dream. *In response to **the disaster**, Christy's **kitchen crew** rallied around the restaurant, putting in extra hours and long phone calls to get everything ready for the big opening.* [3] **The crew's hard work** vindicated Christy's ambitions, and Piece-A-Pie opened right on time.

Excellent! Sentence 2 sets up the "disaster" in our added sentence, which sets up the "crew's hard work" in Sentence 3.

C

## Some questions span the entire passage

Just remember your rhetorical skills mantra: **stay on topic** and **transition smoothly** between ideas.

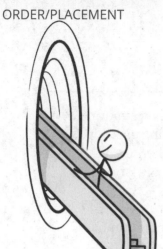

# PORTAL

One of the most important habits you can pick up is **active reading**: the practice of using your pencil while you read.

To learn more about active reading, turn to page 34.

## EXAMPLE 3

Margaret Anne Bulkley was born in approximately 1789 in Cork, Ireland. Recognized for her brilliant intellect at a young age, Margaret began training as a governess. However, her sights were set much higher. Undaunted by the conventions of the time, Margaret hatched a plan to become a medical doctor. With the aid of family friends, she gained entry to University of Edinburgh medical school under the name James Barry. [A] In 1809, she boarded a ship in men's clothing, and "Margaret" was never seen again.

At school, no one suspected Barry's secret, though many assumed he was a prepubescent boy. [B] In fact, conflict arose over whether he was too young to take his final exams; however, he passed with flying colors and became a qualified doctor and surgeon in 1812.

In 1813, he joined the army as a surgeon—as a youth, Barry had written in a letter "Was I not a girl, I would be a soldier"—and began a storied career that spanned the globe. At his first station in Cape Town, he was quickly promoted to Medical Inspector for the colony after he successfully treated the Governor's daughter. Over the next 43 years, Barry served in Mauritius, Jamaica, St. Helena, Malta, Corfu, Crimea, and Canada. [C] Throughout his career he focused on improving sanitation, diet, and conditions of soldiers, as well as promoting better medical care for prisoners and lepers.

Throughout his life, Barry was a man of contradictions. Known for his quick temper and penchant for speaking his mind, he engaged in two duels, was court-martialed for improper conduct, and even sparred with Florence Nightingale. On the other hand, he had a patient and reserved bedside manner, and was loved by all his patients. He was also an expert surgeon, performing the first successful cesarean section. [D]

Barry died of dysentery in 1865; his charwoman, to her great surprise, discovered his secret while laying him out for burial. The revelation of Barry's true identity shook Victorian society, with some claiming that they had "known all along." The British Army, attempting to sidestep the controversy, sealed his army records for one hundred years and buried him under the name Dr. James Barry and his full military rank.

The writer wants to add the following sentence to the essay:

*With three inch lifts in his shoes, he still was barely five feet tall, and his squeaky voice and smooth skin raised questions as to his age.*

This sentence would most logically be placed at:

A) Point A in Paragraph 1
B) Point B in Paragraph 2
C) Point C in Paragraph 3
D) Point D in Paragraph 4

SOLUTION

So we want to add a sentence about Barry's appearance into the essay without disrupting the flow of ideas. Let's read the sentence, looking for linking words:

*With three inch lifts in his shoes, he still was barely five feet tall, and his* **squeaky voice** *and smooth skin* **raised questions as to his age.**

This is primarily about Barry's appearance. We need to find a placement where talk of **appearance** is on-topic.

A) Point A in Paragraph 1

At this point in the essay, the author is still using the pronoun "she" to refer to Barry, so the added sentence with the "he" pronoun breaks the flow and feels off-topic

B) Point B in Paragraph 2

We have linking words here! "Prepubescent boy" matches "squeaky voice" and "smooth skin," and "raised questions as to his age" matches the "conflict" about being "too young."

C) Point C in Paragraph 3

We shouldn't break up the discussion of Barry's career with a description of his appearance. This one disrupts the flow.

D) Point D in Paragraph 4

What does Barry's appearance have to do with his surgical talent? Nothing at all, so we can cross off D as well.

**Choice B** is our best option!

B

## Word Order

Some Order/Placement questions deal with the logical order of words within a single sentence. Often, moving the phrase around creates a number of different types of errors, so be sure to read the phrase in the context of the full sentence for each possible location.

**PORTAL**

This question type blurs the line between Order/Placement and **Misplaced Modifier** questions. For practice with misplaced modifiers, turn to page 275.

## EXAMPLE 4

I was still waiting on my mother, who had driven to pick up some macaroni and cheese <u>to the store</u> when I complained about having nothing good to eat.

The best placement for the underlined portion would be:

A) where it is now.
B) after the word mother (and before the comma).
C) after the word driven.
D) after the word eat (and before the period).

## PORTAL

Picking the wrong preposition for a verb can drastically change or confuse the meaning of a sentence.

Turn to page 297 for practice with picking the right **preposition**.

---

**SOLUTION**

To figure out where "to the store" lives, plug in and try out each answer choice. Let your ear guide you home!

A) ...pick up mac-n-cheese <u>to the store</u>

*We pick things up AT or FROM the store. Nix this one.*

B) ...I was waiting on my mother <u>to the store</u>,

*We wait on people to (verb). "The store" isn't a verb.*

C) ...who had driven <u>to the store</u> to pick up...

*We drive to the store all the time! This one sounds good.*

D) ...I complained about having nothing good to eat <u>to the store</u>.

*Is the store listening to our complaints? Doubtful. D's out.*

C

---

## Recapping Order/Placement

When you see an order/placement question, remember to:

1 *focus on **linking words***

2 *stay **on topic** and **transition smoothly***

# Practice Problems

*Select the answer choice that produces the best sentence.*

[1] Henry Fusili was born in 1741 in Switzerland, but would spend most of his life working in England. [2] There he would become a famous painter, helping to establish the Romanticism movement. [3] The Romanticists wanted to create art full of emotion and wistful longings for long ago eras. [4] Fusili's most famous painting, *The Nightmare*, reflects these tendencies. [5] The composition has a sleeping woman with a monstrous figure perched atop her chest while the head of a wild-eyed black horse peers from behind a curtain.

The writer would like to add the following sentence to the paragraph:

*Their art would also include references to mythology and the supernatural.*

If the writer were to add this sentence to the paragraph, it would most logically be placed:

A) after Sentence 1.
B) after Sentence 2.
C) after Sentence 3.
D) after Sentence 4.

---

[1] The continent of Antarctica contains the largest amount of ice anywhere on the planet: an ice sheet with an average thickness of 1 mile covers 98% of Antarctica's surface, containing 90% of the planet's ice. [2] The ice sheet expands into the Southern Ocean in cooler months, and recedes in the warmer months, but most of the interior stays frozen throughout the year. [3] In fact, much of the water has been frozen in ice for approximately 15 million years. [4] With all this ice, the notion that Antarctica could contain liquid fresh water seems implausible, if not downright impossible. [5] Yet, for all the vertical and horizontal miles of ice, there are lakes of liquid fresh water in Antarctica. [6] These lakes cannot be seen from the surface, as they exist deep below the ice sheet. [7] Using radar, scientists discovered the location of these lakes. [8] Of the fresh water lakes discovered in Antarctica, Lake Vostok is the largest, an oval-shaped body measuring 160 by 30 miles and containing 1,300 cubic miles worth of water.

**2**

The writer wants to divide the paragraph into two paragraphs: one about the perception of Antarctica and one about the new, unexpected information. The best place to start a new paragraph is after:

A) Sentence 2.
B) Sentence 3.
C) Sentence 5.
D) Sentence 6.

[1] The Charango is a stringed musical instrument popular in the Andean regions of Bolivia, Ecuador, and Peru. [2] It is easily recognizable by its small size, similar to a tenor ukulele, which originated from using the shell of an armadillo to create the back of the instrument. [3] Having two strings play the same note gives the melody a bolder sound with more harmonic richness.[4] Unlike a ukulele, which has four strings, a charango has ten strings strung in five courses. [5] This makes it similar to a mandolin; both instruments are played by using each finger to hold down two strings simultaneously. [6] The result is a surprisingly loud instrument for its size, perfectly designed for playing the intricate melodies common in Andean folk music.

Supai, Arizona is quite possibly the most remote landlocked city in the United States. The reason is its remarkable location: nestled in a valley at the bottom of the Grand Canyon. [A] The population hovers around 200 people, made up almost entirely of members of the Havasupai tribe, who have lived in the valley for centuries. [B] The Havasupai have enjoyed mostly exclusive access to these resources due to the difficulty of reaching Supai. Besides the helipad added in modern times, the only way in or out is riding a mule along a narrow path. [C] After a long and uncomfortable mule ride down the steep canyon sides, visitors to Supai appreciate the relaxation and handmade goods for sale. Not surprisingly, the locals are happy to welcome the visitors to their remote village, knowing the difficulty coming to and leaving from Supai firsthand. [D]

[1] He put on his thick socks to help soften his footsteps across the living room. [2] Horace knew that he needed to be stealthy in order to complete his mission. [3] Once safely out of earshot, Horace darted towards the kitchen cabinet and retrieved his prize: an unopened box of cookies purchased that afternoon by his mom. [4] This room would be the most difficult part, as his dad sat languidly reading a magazine.

**3**

For the logic and coherence of the paragraph, Sentence 3 should be placed:

A) where it is now.
B) after Sentence 1.
C) after Sentence 5.
D) after Sentence 6.

**4**

The writer would like to add the following sentence to the paragraph:

*The tribe has built a local economy on the resources in this valley.*

If the writer were to add this sentence to the paragraph, it would most logically be placed at:

A) Point A.
B) Point B.
C) Point C.
D) Point D.

**5**

Which of the following sequences of sentences makes the paragraph the most logical?

A) 1, 2, 4, 3
B) 2, 3, 4, 1
C) 4, 3, 1, 2
D) 2, 1, 4, 3

# Passage Practice

*Questions 6 – 8 relate to the following passage.*

[1]

Computer Generated Imagery, or CGI, has dominated the special effects industry since the mid-1990s, and it can be difficult to imagine a time when filmmakers had to find other means of creating illusions on screen. [A] The results were often charming, but undeniably primitive.

[2]

Willis O'Brien, an amateur sculptor, offered a revolutionary technique for depicting fantastic elements on screen. He realized that he could film a miniature figure frame-by-frame, adjusting it a little each time. When the film strip is played back at normal speed, the figure looks like it is moving! The technique became known as stop-motion animation. [B]

[3]

During his tenure at Edison, O'Brien would learn how to integrate live-action footage with his stop-motion animation, allowing actors to interact with the special effects. He first used this technique to great effect in 1925's *The Lost World*, a feature film about adventurers who discover living dinosaurs in a remote area of South America.

[4]

After O'Brien's first short film, 1915's *The Dinosaur and the Missing Link: A Prehistoric Tragedy*, he was hired by the Edison Company, a leading producer of films in the United States. [C] Unfortunately, many of these films were not well-preserved and are now considered lost.

[5]

[1] O'Brien's next film was an absolute classic: 1933's *King Kong*, a tale of a giant gorilla brought to New York City to disastrous results. [2] The character of Kong allowed O'Brien to represent emotions in his animation. [3] Although Kong is undoubtedly the monster of the film, he is also a sympathetic character, capable of curiosity and empathy. [4] The film has many scenes that highlight O'Brien's skill, including an intricate wrestling match between Kong and a Tyrannosaurus Rex.

[6]

O'Brien continued to work on films after *King Kong*, although he passed much of the animation to his protégé, Ray Harryhausen, who would contribute animation classic films for decades. [D] Undoubtedly CGI will continue to dominate modern filmmaking, but filmmakers and film fans owe a great deal of gratitude to the innovations in special effects made by O'Brien and Harryhausen.

**6**

Upon review, the author would like to add the following sentence:

*Early special effects either borrowed from theater, using puppetry or costumes to depict creatures and monsters, or added and removed objects while the camera was turned off.*

The sentence would most logically be placed at:

A)    Point A in paragraph 1
B)    Point B in paragraph 2
C)    Point C in paragraph 4
D)    Point D in paragraph 6

**7**

For the sake of logic and cohesion, Paragraph 3 should be placed:

A)    where it is now
B)    before paragraph 1
C)    after paragraph 4
D)    after paragraph 5

**8**

For the sake of logic and cohesion, the order of the sentences in Paragraph 5 should be:

A)    as it is now
B)    2, 3, 1, 4
C)    1, 2, 4, 3
D)    4, 1, 3, 2

# Writing Practice Passage 5
## TO STAY ON PACE, YOUR TIMING GOAL IS 8.5 MINUTES

This passage tests a variety of grammar topics—some from chapters you may have not yet completed. Use this opportunity to practice maintaining a brisk pace while answering the questions as best you can. Good luck!

**Questions 1-11 are based on the following passage.**

**Synesthesia: Secondary Sensing**

Have you ever tasted a picture? Or seen the color of a sound? These questions may seem like whimsical contradictions worthy of *Alice in Wonderland*, [1] therefore some people do experience the world in this way. They have a neurological condition called [2] synesthesia. This is when an experience from one sensory pathway also triggers a second sensory experience.

Imagine [3] one is in the kitchen and a grandmother is removing [4] cookies that were very recently baked fresh from the oven; this event would register through multiple sensory pathways.

---

**1**

A) NO CHANGE
B) and
C) but
D) alternatively

**2**

Which choice most effectively combines the two sentences at the underlined portion?

A) synesthesia, in which
B) synesthesia, and this is when
C) synesthesia, and this condition occurs when
D) synesthesia and that occurs if

**3**

A) NO CHANGE
B) one was
C) you were
D) you are

**4**

A) NO CHANGE
B) freshly baked cookies
C) cookies that are just freshly baked
D) oven-baked freshly made cookies

You would *see* the grandmother leaning down to remove the baking sheet from the oven. You would *hear* the oven door creak as it opens, and perhaps the sizzling of melted chocolate on the baking sheet. If you were standing close enough to the oven, you would *feel* the gust of hot air escaping the oven. You would certainly *smell* the cookies as they left the oven. **5** Still warm and soft from the oven, hopefully you would be able to *taste* the cookies.

Now imagine that you are looking at a photograph of a grandmother removing cookies from an oven. While a photograph only provides visual sensory stimulation, **6** but you could use previous experiences to recall what your other senses would experience if the photo were real. **7** This addition of secondary sensory experiences comes involuntarily to a person with synesthesia. The secondary sensory information does not cancel out the primary experience.

There are two main types of synesthesia: projecting and associative. With projecting synesthesia, the person will actually experience the sensory effect. **8** Moreover, a person may see the sound of an oboe as yellow circles. Someone with associative synesthesia would not see the color yellow, but would strongly associate the sound of the oboe with the color yellow.

**5**

A) NO CHANGE
B) Hopefully you would be able to *taste* the cookies, still warm and soft from the oven.
C) Hopefully you would be able, still warm and soft from the oven, be able to *taste* the cookies.
D) You would be able, hopefully, to be able to *taste*, still warm and soft from the oven, the cookies.

**6**

A) NO CHANGE
B) and
C) yet
D) DELETE the underlined portion.

**7**

Which choice most effectively combines the two sentences at the underlined portion?

A) To a person with synesthesia, the addition of secondary sensory experiences comes involuntarily, and this does not cancel out the primary sensory experience.
B) A person with synesthesia does not cancel out the primary sensory experience, but the addition of secondary sensory experiences comes involuntarily.
C) This addition of secondary sensory experiences— which does not cancel out the primary sensory experience—comes involuntarily to a person with synesthesia.
D) The primary sensory experience, which does not cancel out with the addition of secondary sensory experiences, comes involuntarily to a person with synesthesia.

**8**

A) NO CHANGE
B) For example,
C) Therefore,
D) Regardless,

CONTINUE ➤

[1] One of the most common variants of synesthesia is grapheme-color synesthesia, where a person relates numbers and letters to specific colors. [2] Even when presented **9** with black lettering on a white back-ground, a grapheme-color synesthete will see the letters and numbers as shaded. [3] This can lead to some learning difficulties, as certain spellings or math concepts may "clash" with a person's internal color conception, making the number and/or letter combination appear ugly and therefore not correct. [4] Another relatively common form is chromesthesia synesthesia, which connects sounds to colors. [5] Each individual has unique color associations for different pitches and timbres, but most associate higher pitches with bright colors and **10** darker colors with low pitches. **11**

**9**

A) NO CHANGE
B) to
C) by
D) at

**10**

A) NO CHANGE
B) dark colors with lower pitches.
C) low pitches with darker colors.
D) lower pitches with dark colors.

**11**

To improve the cohesion of the paragraph, the author wants to add the following sentence:

> Within the two main categories, there are multiple sub-types of synesthesia.

The sentence would most logically be placed

A) before sentence 1.
B) after sentence 2.
C) after sentence 3.
D) after sentence 5.

# UNIT | Quality Control

## Chapters

## Overview

In this chapter, we look at the question types that ask you to add sentences, delete sentences, or change wording in order to accomplish a specific goal.

We'll then look at questions that ask you to accurately describe data in a graph or table included with the passage.

# Accomplish a Task

*As if sitting for a four-hour test wasn't enough work for a Saturday morning.*

**TIP**

These questions are becoming more and more common on the SAT: we've seen as many as 10 out of the 44 writing questions fall in this category.

## Authors pick words to accomplish specific goals

Accomplish a task questions ask you to edit the wording of the passage to better communicate the goal or intent of the author. These questions can be straightforward or require quite a bit of reading for context. Regardless, you should use the following two-step strategy:

① *Underline your task.*

② *Pick the choice with **specific words** that match the task.*

Let's start with two straightforward examples that do not need much context outside of the question prompt and the given sentence. Use the two strategies above to pick the best answer.

**TIP**

Remember: the correct answer must have **specific words** that match the task and/or the passage. Students trip up when they think too big picture: focus on the words!

### EXAMPLE 1

> It is nigh impossible to drag my little brother away from his hobbies when the dinner bell rings. When he's in the throes of his favorite activities, whether it be <u>things I find very boring or games I like,</u> he refuses to be rushed.

At the underlined point, the writer would like to provide specific information about her brother's hobbies. Given that all the choices are true, which one best accomplishes this purpose?

A) NO CHANGE
B) playing with Legos or designing complex Lincoln Log masterpieces,
C) hanging out with friends or playing solo,
D) games we have in our living room,

**SOLUTION**

First, let's **underline the task**:

At this point, the writer would like to provide <u>specific information about her brother's hobbies</u>. Given that all the choices are true, which one best accomplishes this purpose?

Now let's find an a choice with **specifics about hobbies**.

~~A)~~ things I find very boring or games I like

*This answer is the opposite of specific. Which "things" are boring? The author doesn't tell us the specifics.*

B) playing with **Legos** or designing complex **Lincoln Log** masterpieces

*Here, we're given two specific hobbies the brother enjoys: playing with Legos, and building with Lincoln Logs. Keep it!*

~~C)~~ hanging out with friends or playing solo

*Notice how this is less specific than B? What does hanging out mean, exactly? What kind of solo games does he like?*

~~D)~~ games we have in our living room

*Again, no specifics to be found! This answer also sounds pretty awkward if we read it back into the sentence.*

**Choice B** gives us two specific hobbies, so it accomplishes our task with *aplomb*! B is correct.

B

---

**TIP**

If you're stuck between two answers that both fulfill the task, go with the choice that contains specific details. The SAT prefers specific writing to vague statements.

**aplomb** (n.)

self-confidence or assurance, especially when in a demanding situation.

## EXAMPLE 2

There was much speculation regarding Hughes' whereabouts: perhaps he had left the country and was living incognito, or perhaps he was hiding in one of his many properties scattered throughout the nation.

At this point, the writer wants to further develop the idea from the preceding sentence. Which choice most effectively accomplishes this goal?

A)  His airline designs led to widespread innovation in the fledgling airline industry.
B)  Many have questioned his political motives and speculated about his involvement with national elections.
C)  Still another theory is that Hughes had gone into protective custody and was living in a bunker underneath Sandusky, Ohio.
D)  Many missing persons turn up of their own accord after years of absence.

### SOLUTION

First, let's find and underline our task:

...develop the idea in the preceding sentence...

All we care about is the point from the previous sentence, which is that folks were speculating about Hughes' **location**. So let's make this one simple: is there a choice with words that match *location*?

C)  Still another <u>theory</u> is that Hughes had gone into protective custody and was living in a bunker underneath <u>Sandusky</u>, Ohio.

**Sandusky** is a **location** where we might find Hughes. Simple!

Some of the other options are interesting and even on-topic. However, only one choice accomplishes our task: **C is our answer**.

C

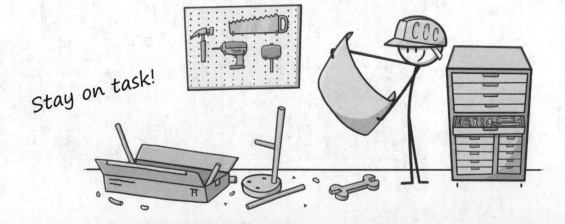

Stay on task!

Next, let's look at some examples that require some more context. You may be asked to further develop an idea from the previous sentence, set up the next sentence, or link two paragraphs together. Follow your core strategy, but make sure to read the surrounding sentences carefully.

## EXAMPLE 3

Alcatraz Federal Penitentiary, well-known for the many infamous inmates it housed throughout the 20th century, was proclaimed "escape-proof" by its designers when it first opened in 1934. Despite this claim, 36 inmates attempted to break out during the prison's 30 year history. <u>Located 1.25 miles off the coast of San Francisco and surrounded by the cold waters and treacherous currents of San Francisco Bay, the maximum-security prison was conceived as a last resort prison for dangerous criminals who had tried to escape elsewhere.</u>

Given that all the choices are true, which one provides the most relevant information at this point in the essay?

A) NO CHANGE
B) Alcatraz finally closed its doors in 1963 due to high maintenance costs.
C) The island prison is now one of the most popular tourist destinations in California, hosting 1.5 million visitors a year.
D) Alcatraz held notorious gangster Al Capone from 1938 to 1939.

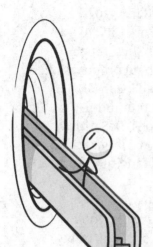

## PORTAL

Some of these rhetorical skills questions require comprehending the purpose or focus of a paragraph or passage. **Active reading** helps here, just like it does on the Reading section! To practice Active Reading, turn to page 34.

Alcatraz = escape-proof prisoners still try

| SOLUTION |

Our task here requires some interpretation: which choice provides the most <u>relevant information</u> at this point in the essay? To answer that question, let's actively read the paragraph:

Alcatraz Federal Penitentiary, well-known for the many infamous inmates it housed throughout the 20th century, was proclaimed <u>"escape-proof"</u> by its designers when it first opened in 1934. <u>Despite this claim, 36 inmates attempted to break out</u> during the prison's 30 year history. Located 1.25 miles off the coast of San Francisco and surrounded by the cold waters and treacherous currents of San Francisco Bay...

The idea of *"escaping"* is mentioned in two preceding sentences, so let's look for an answer matching "escape." **Choice A** mentions that Alcatraz was designed for prisoners who had previously *tried to escape*: a perfect match!

A

## EXAMPLE 4

The term "aerotropolis"—a combination of the words "airport" and "metropolis"—was originally coined in 1939 by Nicholas DeSantis, a commercial artist from New York City. A 1939 article in the magazine *Popular Science*, titled "Skyscraper Airport for City of Tomorrow," outlines DeSantis' bold proposal: a 200-story skyscraper of homes and offices, topped by an expansive airfield. This arrangement would allow commuters from the suburbs to jet to work in their private planes. DeSantis' detailed drawings depict luxury accommodations on a large scale, accompanied by plenty of explanations on how his fanciful future city might function.

**4** Of course, this hypothetical aerotropolis never quite took off. Today, most airports are built at the periphery of cities, only accessible via lengthy drives or subway rides. But contemporary thinkers are envisioning a new, updated take on the aerotropolis. In this modern imagining, an aerotropolis is any urban center with the airport at its heart—a structure that more effectively connects the city to the global network and international marketplace.

Which choice most effectively links the first paragraph with the ideas that follow?

A) NO CHANGE
B) The earliest "airports" were grassy fields where small planes could approach at any angle, depending on the direction of the wind.
C) At the Changi International Airport in Singapore, travelers are pampered with free foot massages, a movie theater, and a rooftop swimming pool.
D) Naturally, the idea of an aerotropolis was met with ridicule from those in the field of aeronautics.

### SOLUTION

Our task is to link the first paragraph with the ideas that follow. This means the right answer will have **specific matches** to **both** paragraphs! Actively read both paragraphs to get a quick summary for what each is about. Here's what we came up with:

> Paragraph 1: original "aerotropolis" idea
> Paragraph 2: modern "aerotropolis" idea

An answer that links both paragraphs should be about that **change** in the definition of **aerotropolis**.

Continued on next page →

## PORTAL

There are two golden rules for Craft and Structure questions: **stay on topic** and **transition smoothly** between ideas.

For practice, check out the Add and Delete chapter on page 364.

Let's look for a match with a *change* in the idea of *aerotropolis*.

**A)** Of course, this hypothetical aerotropolis never quite took off.

> *Aerotropolis? Check. Change? "Hypothetical" and "never took off" tell us that the original idea didn't work, setting up a new definition of aerotropolis. This one matches!*

Neither choice B nor choice C mentions *aerotropolis*. These would be awkward introductions to the ideas that follow. Cross 'em off.

**D)** Naturally, the idea of an aerotropolis was met with praise from those in the field of aeronautics.

> *Aerotropolis? Check. Change? Not really. This sentence seems to shift the topic to "praise from scientists," which never shows up in the next paragraph.*

The best option is **Choice A**!

A

## How to spot Accomplish a Task questions:

As with all questions testing your rhetorical skills, you'll see a **prompt** before the answer choices. Accomplish a Task questions often start with "*Given that all the choices are true...*" and almost always contain that special phrasing "*which choice best/most effectively...*"

1. <u>Given that all the choices are true</u>, which choice best establishes the author's irrational fear of being eaten by a giant squid?

## Some tasks deal with the passage as a whole

These questions may come at the very end and ask for the best conclusion to the passage, while tougher ones come at the very *beginning* and ask for the best introduction to a passage you haven't even had a chance to read yet! In that case, adjust your strategy:

1. *Skip it! Read the passage, answering other questions as you go.*

2. *Once you've finished the rest of the passage, remember to go back!*

## Passage Practice 1

*Questions 1 – 6 relate to the following passage.*

Born in France in 1776, Sophie Germain lived in an era of limited academic opportunities for women. When Germain was 13, the French revolution was in full swing and her wealthy merchant parents kept her indoors for her safety. [1] Looking for amusement, Germain turned towards her father's library, where she discovered a passion for mathematics. Unfortunately, her family did not see scholarly pursuits as something appropriate for a young woman. The method they used to dissuade her was somewhat bizarre: they denied her warm clothes and blankets, as well as access to a fire, in hopes of getting her to go to bed early. Despite these efforts, [2] her passion for math could not be extinguished.

*Passage CONTINUED on next page*

**1**

Given that all choices are true, which choice emphasizes Germain's innate curiosity?

A) NO CHANGE
B) Bored to tears,
C) Scared by the violence surrounding the revolution,
D) Ever thirsty for knowledge,

**2**

Given that all choices are true, which choice best uses figurative language to develop ideas from the preceding sentence?

A) NO CHANGE
B) she continued to learn as she grew up.
C) the French Revolution would lead to the rise of Napoleon Bonaparte.
D) she kept reading many books on a variety of subjects.

*Passage CONTINUED from previous page*

At 18, Germain wanted to enroll at the newly opened French Institution École Polytechnique. However, **3** as the programs included math and engineering, women were not admitted. Germain found a student who had dropped out without telling the school, and she assumed his identity in order to attend lectures on math and science. **4** She probably should have been charged with fraud.

After her experience at the École Polytechnique, Germain devoted most of her research to elasticity: how objects stretch without ripping. Germain submitted her **5** awesome work for the prestigious award given by the Paris Academy of Science, but, despite multiple attempts, could neither win the award nor gain admittance to the Academy. **6** Undeterred, Germain paid to have her papers independently published. Today, she is known as a pioneering woman in mathematics, and ironically, the Paris Academy of Science now gives a Sophie Germain award for research in foundations of mathematics.

**3**

Which choice emphasizes that the difficulties Germain faced affected most women of her time?

A) NO CHANGE
B) as was common for the time,
C) eighteen was still considered quite young,
D) lacking voting and property rights,

**4**

Which choice offers the best transition to the following paragraph?

A) NO CHANGE
B) Although she did not earn a degree, she benefitted greatly from attending the lectures.
C) Historical records do not contain much information about the student whose name she used.
D) By then, the French Revolution was over.

**5**

Which choice stresses the innovative nature of Germain's research?

A) NO CHANGE
B) shocking
C) groundbreaking
D) DELETE the underlined portion.

**6**

Which choice best expresses Germain's character as described throughout the passage?

A) NO CHANGE
B) Irrationally,
C) Angrily,
D) Defeated,

## Passage Practice 2

*Questions 7 – 16 relate to the following passage.*

According to a 2018 report from the US Energy Information Administration, renewable energy sources have come a long way, now accounting for about 11% of total US energy consumption and about 17% of electricity generation. [7] In spite of these findings, the US and the rest of the world should continue to work towards replacing fossil fuels as the main source of energy because transitioning to renewable energies on individual, corporate, and governmental levels has the potential to not only slow down alarming signs of climate change, but also [8] mitigate the ongoing energy crisis in third world countries.

When it comes to climate change, [9] the indiginous people of the Arctic, called the 'Inuits,' have been in trouble before: the polar regions were once warmer for an extended period of time, 125,000 years ago. But, while the climate has undergone naturogenic changes in the past, it is very unlikely that the deleterious developments in climate observed over the past hundred

*Passage continued on next page*

---

**7**

Which choice provides the most effective transition from the previous sentence to the information that immediately follows in this sentence?

A) NO CHANGE
B) In addition to the 2018 report,
C) Although these levels reflect growth,
D) Whether they want to or not,

**8**

Which choice most effectively establishes an idea that is further developed in the passage?

A) NO CHANGE
B) strengthen the economy long-term.
C) improve agricultural output.
D) attract and retain employees.

**9**

Which choice most effectively sets up the information provided in the next part of the sentence?

A) NO CHANGE
B) certain gases in the atmosphere block heat from escaping:
C) there is evidence that minor changes to Earth's climate system can be caused by natural variations:
D) green-house gases are shown to be extremely harmful to the climate:

years can be explained by nature alone. **10** Scientists are becoming increasingly distressed by pollutant levels; glaciers are melting more quickly; the polar ice caps are shrinking; plant life is blooming earlier; ocean acidity is rising, threatening marine life; species are experiencing unprecedented migration; and many are heading towards extinction.

**11** With the solar industry leading the charge in job growth, the transition to renewable energy has the potential to stimulate the economy. Studies by the International Renewable Energy Agency (IRENA) estimate that job growth is increasing more rapidly in the renewable energy sector than in the fossil fuels sector, and green industries could provide over 16 million jobs within ten years if the world can double the market share of renewable energy technologies. Moreover, estimates by the World Bank indicate that US wind and solar create about 13.3 and 13.7 jobs per million dollars of spending, respectively, and that building retrofits to incorporate sustainable energies create 16.7 jobs per million dollars of spending. **12** Interestingly, solar produces only slightly more jobs than wind—a difference of just 0.4 jobs per million dollars of spending.

| Energy Source | Direct Jobs | Indirect Jobs | Induced Jobs | Total Jobs |
|---|---|---|---|---|
| Oil & natural gas | 0.8 | 2.9 | 2.3 | 5.2 |
| Coal | 1.9 | 3.0 | 3.9 | 6.9 |
| Building retrofits | 7.0 | 4.9 | 11.8 | 16.7 |
| Mass transit/rail | 11.0 | 4.9 | 17.4 | 22.3 |
| Smart grid | 4.3 | 4.6 | 7.9 | 12.5 |
| Wind | 4.6 | 4.9 | 8.4 | 13.3 |
| Solar | 5.4 | 4.4 | 9.3 | 13.7 |
| Biomass | 7.4 | 5.0 | 12.4 | 17.4 |

*Passage continued on next page*

**10**

Which choice provides a supporting example that is most similar to the other examples in the sentence?

A) NO CHANGE
B) Fewer people are concerned by the warning signs;
C) Over 30 U.S. states have implemented initiatives to reduce the use of plastics;
D) The incidence of severe hurricanes has nearly doubled over the past 30 years;

**11**

Which choice provides the best transition from the previous paragraph and introduction to the ideas that follow?

A) NO CHANGE
B) While scientists agree that warming across the globe is due to human-induced increases in greenhouse gases,
C) On top of mitigating the ecological damage seen around the world,
D) In addition to being impossible to hide and nearly impossible to ignore,

**12**

Which choice most effectively uses information from the table to support a main finding of IRENA's studies?

A) NO CHANGE
B) Even better, the mass transit/freight rail system creates the most jobs of all, with 22.3 jobs created per million dollars of spending.
C) Similarly, biomass, a renewable source of stored energy from the sun, has one of the highest ratios at 17.4 jobs created per million dollars of spending.
D) The latter is more than triple the 5.2 jobs per million dollars for oil and natural gas, and more than double the 6.9 jobs per million dollars for coal.

While some opponents of renewable energy still doubt its financial viability, most energy watchers recognize that in recent years the costs have declined substantially. But if renewable energy is becoming so inexpensive, **13** why does the price of electricty rise while costs fall? Here's why: Even if renewable energies are now, at last, priced competitively, they are still working with structures and facilities—a power grid, a highway system, a fueling system—built for a world powered by fossil fuels. All of this enormous infrastructure was created through public-sector support, including tax credits, low-cost loans, and complete grants from the federal government. **14** Despite these advantages, fossil fuel-based corporations still frequently lose market share to their green-competitors.

**13**

Which choice asks a question that effectively transitions from the previous sentence and introduces the ideas that follow in the paragraph?

A) NO CHANGE
B) why do we still need programs and subsidies to support it?
C) why are European nations having trouble with efforts to scale up renewables?
D) why hasn't it reached its lowest price yet?

**14**

The writer wants to conclude the paragraph with a statement that accentuates the point the writer is making. Which choice best accomplishes this goal?

A) NO CHANGE
B) Such incentives for construction are what keep the important functions of the United States alive.
C) Nearly everyone agrees that it's critical for the country to improve its infrastructure.
D) Companies designing new energy sources, on the other hand, often have to factor in the costs of building their own infrastructure.

*Passage continued on next page*

Not only has the world already been structured for carbon-concentrated energy, but many existing government subsidies for fossil fuels are still pushing the world in that direction. In defiance of the pledge by G-20 countries in 2009 to end such support, those subsidies persist and grow. In the US, the International Monetary Fund has reported that the government supplies $700 billion a year in subsidies to fossil fuel centric companies. 15

One thing is becoming increasingly clear: by continuing our dependence on non-renewable energy sources, we face major risks. Yet, through technological advancement and innovation, the world has begun to trend towards sustainability. 16 Eventually we will run out of fossil fuels; this is a fact, and when this happens, we need to be prepared for it.

**15**

The writer wants to add a comma to the end of the sentence and append a statement that reinterprets information provided earlier in the sentence to make it more relatable to the reader. Assuming that each choice is true, which best accomplishes this goal?

A) suggesting that the promise has been broken, and indicating that a new pledge is necessary.

B) equal to every American delivering these companies a check for about two thousand dollars each year.

C) far overshadowing that provided to renewable companies.

D) over 5% of the nominal gross domestic product (GDP) of China.

**16**

The writer wants a conclusion that places the passage's discussion within a larger historical context. Which choice best accomplishes this goal?

A) NO CHANGE

B) It's long past time to take fossil fuels off of public assistance and go all out to promote renewables.

C) Many European countries are already embracing alternative energy, and therefore companies tend to be more mature in Europe; however, the potential for growth in the US is greater, and once a longer term framework has been put in place, the US should catch up fast.

D) As in any other economic transition—the Progressive Era, the Industrial Revolution, the Marshall Plan—there is a role for government policy, as well as financial and social encouragement, in hastening the advancement of the new while easing the phasing out of the old.

# Add and Delete

*The SAT writers will frequently propose adding a new sentence to the passage or deleting an existing one.*

## Answer Yes or No before reading the choices

Add and Delete questions tend to follow the same Yes/No pattern of Writer's Goal questions. You'll be told that the writer is considering making an addition, and two choices for "yes" and two for "no." To avoid being lured into a wrong choice, we will **answer "Yes" or "No"** *before* looking at the choices.

> (1) Decide **Yes or No**
>
> (2) **Eliminate** two choices.
>
> (3) Pick the choice with the **best reason**.

This narrows down our options. Let's look at some reasons why we *would* and *would not* want to add a sentence:

| Add sentence if it: | Do NOT add sentence if it: |
|---|---|
| introduces an idea in the passage | blurs the focus of the paragraph |
| transitions between two paragraphs | interrupts the flow of an idea |
| supports existing ideas | adds unnecessary/off-topic details |

## The golden rule: don't distract!

In the end, rhetorical skills are all about communicating an idea clearly without distraction. If the sentence is off-topic, goes on a tangent, or breaks the flow of ideas, it should NOT be added.

Try the example below. Read the paragraph, paying close attention to the sentence just before and just after the spot marked $\boxed{1}$. Only agree to make the addition if it **stays on topic** and **transitions between ideas**.

## EXAMPLE 1

Once I returned home from my semester abroad, I heard through the grapevine that Dooley's Cafe, my favorite eatery, was under new management and had undergone many significant changes. $\boxed{1}$ The restaurant had added a second counter, which greatly reduced wait time. Though the quesadillas were gone now, the new Bagel-Blast Jell-O Supreme was actually quite tasty. The prices had come down on certain items, including my old standby: lava-drenched, peanut drizzle flatbread. The owners had also upgraded the seating to include more than just the bean bag chairs of old. Finally, my back wouldn't hurt after lunch!

At this point, the writer is considering adding the following statement:

"I expected the changes would all be for the worst, but pleasantly, they weren't."

Should the writer make this addition here?

A) Yes, because it provides an example of the phenomenon introduced in the preceding sentence.
B) Yes, because it provides a logical transition between the preceding sentence and the rest of the paragraph.
C) No, because it blurs the focus of the paragraph by adding an irrelevant detail.
D) No, because it fails to indicate why Dooley's Cafe is the narrator's favorite eatery.

## How to spot Add/Delete questions:

Add/Delete and Writer's Goal questions both take on the Yes/No format. The prompt will give a proposed addition. Ask yourself, "is this on topic?" Then narrow down your choices:

A) Yes, because...
B) Yes, because...
C) No, because...
D) No, because...

*It's easier to pick from 2 choices than 4, so focus on the goal and answer yes/no first!*

SOLUTION

Remember, our job is to **stay on topic** and **transition between ideas** in the paragraph. If we make the addition, the paragraph flows like this:

When I came back I learned Dooley's had **changed**...
The **changes** were surprisingly pleasant...
There was **less** wait time, **tasty** dishes, and **better** seating.

**Are we on topic?** Yes! Each sentence gives detail about the changes to Dooley's.

**Is there a smooth transition**? Yes! The first sentence mentions changes, the second says they were pleasant, and the third details those pleasant changes.

We should **choose yes**. Now let's look at the two reasons we have to choose from:

A) Yes, because it provides an **example of the phenomenon** introduced in the preceding sentence.

*Do you see any **examples** in the added sentence? Nope! It's just the narrator's opinion!*

B) Yes, because it provides a **logical transition** between the preceding sentence and the rest of the paragraph.

*Bingo! As usual, transitions are a good thing.*

*Choice A* gets the Yes/No correct, but gives a bad reason.
**B** is the winner!

B

# TIP

Adding a sentence or phrase that transitions between ideas is almost always a good idea!

## EXAMPLE 2

**TIP**

Modern phones have a "driving" mode that can autorespond to messages while you're moving and allow you to use voice commands.

It's easier than texting, and taking a few minutes to set it up can save lives.

Washington, DC has earned the distinction of being the city in which a driver is most likely to have an auto accident. To help reduce the rate of accidents, legislators banned cell phone usage while driving. Studies showed that drivers were distracted while using cell phones and were just as likely to have an accident as individuals who were driving while intoxicated. [2] The first year following the passing of the legislation, the number of accidents dropped by 25 percent.

At this point, the writer is considering adding the following sentence.

> Some cities restrict texting while driving as an alternative to a complete cell phone ban.

Should the writer make this addition here?

A) Yes, because it provides an explanation of the terms used in the preceding sentence.
B) Yes, because it suggests a method that could have prevented the event described later in the paragraph.
C) No, because it contradicts the point made earlier that the city banned cell phone usage.
D) No, because it blurs the focus of the paragraph by supplying irrelevant information.

**Are we on topic?** Maybe—the proposed addition is still about texting while driving, but it's not about Washington, DC.

**Is there a smooth transition?** No! The sentence before and after are talking about a study; the added sentence is not.

Let's **choose no** and compare the reasoning of C and D:

~~C)~~ No, because it **contradicts the point** made earlier that the city banned cell phone usage.

*The addition is about **other cities**, not Washington, DC. This one's flat out wrong!*

(D)) No, because it **blurs the focus** of the paragraph by supplying irrelevant information.

*Bingo! Info about other cities is **irrelevant** to this paragraph about DC, and it distracts from the mentioned study.*

D

## Delete distracting information

Sometimes, the test writers will ask you if you should **delete** or **keep** an existing sentence or phrase. Again, choose the Yes/No by asking yourself "Are we on topic?" and "Is there a smooth transition?" Delete anything that **blurs the focus** of the paragraph and keep anything that **transitions smoothly** between paragraphs or ideas.

### EXAMPLE 3

Last month a new tenant took over the apartment above my own. I met him in the mail room and learned that his name was Heisenberg. He had eyes like the Indian Ocean and a pony tail that flowed majestically. We chatted about German philosophy and exchanged strudel recipes before going our separate ways. I didn't hear from him for a few weeks, and had almost forgotten that he was living above me! Then, he installed a new hardwood floor in his apartment—<u>and boy did he love to dance.</u>

Sunday afternoon my chandelier was shaking to Nicki Minaj. Monday evening my picture frames were pulsating to Carrie Underwood. I knew that I needed to say something to protect my eardrums, but I didn't want to interfere with his groove.

The writer is considering deleting the underlined portion. Should the writer make this change?

A) Yes, because it does not provide a transition from the topic of the previous paragraph.
B) Yes, because it distracts from the main argument of the passage.
C) No, because it provides more detail about the narrator's disposition.
D) No, because it sets up the events of the next paragraph.

**SOLUTION**

Let's try reading the nearby sentences, skipping the underlined portion in the middle.

> My neighbor installed a **hardwood floor**...
> My chandelier was shaking to **Nicki Minaj**.

What just happened? How in the world did we get from hardwood floors to shaking chandeliers? Without that underlined portion, we lose key information and the passage **does not transition smoothly** between ideas. Now put it back in:

> He installed a **hardwood floor**...
> He loves to **dance**...
> My chandelier was shaking to **Nicki Minaj**.

There's our logical transition! The fact that Heisenberg loves to dance connects the hardwood floor to the shaking chandelier! We should **choose no** and cross off A and B. All that remains is to pick the best rationale:

C) No, because if provides more detail about the <u>narrator's</u> disposition.

*This has nothing to do with the narrator; Heisenberg is the one who loves to dance.*

D)) No, because it sets up the events of the next paragraph.

*Perfect! This phrase is essential to understanding the chandelier-shaking that follows. D it is!*

D

## NOTE

Are you sensing a theme? Yet again, it all comes down to smooth transitions!

## EXAMPLE 4

The works of Christo and Jeanne Claude involve wrapping enormous objects in fabric and creating architectural landscapes that evoke the imagination. One of their most celebrated art projects involved wrapping the sharp exterior of the German parliament building, the Reichstag, in metallic, billowing fabric. <u>The Reichstag was built in the center of Berlin and opened in 1894.</u> More than a hundred mountain climbers and assistants accomplished the enormous task of wrapping the building. For nearly two weeks the center of Germany's government became an art piece that drew in tens of thousands of curious visitors.

The writer is considering deleting the underlined sentence. Should the sentence be kept or deleted?

A) Kept, because it provides a detail that supports the main argument of the paragraph.
B) Kept, because it introduces the importance of the Reichstag.
C) Deleted, because it interrupts the paragraph with a loosely related detail.
D) Deleted, because it does not reveal the architect of the Reichstag.

 SOLUTION

This one gets CRAZY by changing "Yes/No" to "Kept/Deleted." The strategy is the same. **Are we on topic?** Maybe? It gives information about the building, but the focus is more on the *artwork*. Let's delete the sentence and see if we lose a **transition**:

> One of their art projects involved **wrapping** the Reichstag... Mountain climbers accomplished the task of **wrapping** the building.

That's a *better* transition from "wrapping" to "wrapping!" Let's choose delete and focus on choices C and D.

C.) Deleted, because it interrupts the paragraph with a loosely related detail.

*That's exactly what is going on. We don't need to interrupt our talk about modern art with historical facts!*

D. Deleted, because it does not reveal the architect of the Reichstag.

*Who cares? The paragraph is not about the architect of the building; it's about the art. Choice C is better.*

C

## What would be lost if we deleted this sentence?

Sometimes, the SAT writers will ask you for the specific value of an underlined sentence. Imagine getting the following text from a friend, only with the underlined sentence removed:

> I agreed to look after Jason's pet last night.
> It's a platypus that smells of garbage and loves to cuddle.
> Next time, I'll just lie and say I'm allergic.

If we deleted the middle sentence, we'd lose important **details** about *why* the pet-sitting experience was negative! On the test, pick the choice that **best describes the value of the underlined portion**.

## EXAMPLE 5

Murasaki Shikibu, arguably the world's first novelist, was a lady-in-waiting to the Japanese Empress in the 9th century. Her novel *The Tale of the Genji* was loosely based on her experiences in the Imperial Court and became an instant hit. Shikibu's legacy lies not only in her writings, but also in her contribution to solidifying Japanese into a written language. [5] At the time, classical Chinese, off-limits to women, was the language of governance and the elite, while vernacular Japanese was the oral language of the masses. Female authors like Shikibu combined the classical Chinese characters and vernacular Japanese, creating a "hybrid style" known as kanbun.

If the writer were to delete the underlined sentence, the paragraph would primarily lose:

A) An explanation of how Shikibu helped standardize written Japanese.
B) A comparison between Shikibu's writing style and her technical linguistic ability.
C) An analysis of methods Shikibu used to create the Japanese alphabet.
D) A transition from an explanation of Shikibu's literary legacy to a discussion of her larger contributions to Japanese history.

## GUS?

Let's take a brief break and debate the best name for a smelly (but lovable) pet platypus.

loves to cuddle →

← smells of garbage

SOLUTION

Let's remove the sentence in question to see what its purpose is in the paragraph:

> Murasaki Shikibu, arguably the world's first novelist, was a lady-in-waiting to the Japanese Empress in the 9th century. Her novel *The Tale of the Genji* was loosely based on her experiences in the Imperial Court and became an instant hit. At the time, classical Chinese, off-limits to women, was the language of governance and the elite, while vernacular Japanese was the oral language of the masses. Female authors like Shikibu combined the classical Chinese characters and vernacular Japanese, creating a "hybrid style" known as kanbun.

Without that sentence, the paragraph jolts from *The Tale of the Genji* to the classical Chinese language! We need that transition sentence to keep the flow of the paragraph.

Let's look for an answer choice that emphasizes **transition**.

A) An explanation of how Shikibu helped standardize written Japanese.

*The sentence doesn't tell us HOW Shikibu helped standardize the language, just that she did.*

B) A comparison between Shikibu's writing style and her technical linguistic ability.

*No comparison is made in this sentence!*

C) An analysis of methods Shikibu used to create the Japanese alphabet.

*Do you know what method Shikibu used? I sure don't! That's because it's not in the sentence.*

D) A transition from an explanation of Shikibu's literary legacy to a discussion of her larger contributions to Japanese history.

*Bingo! The sentence provides a transition between the two topics of this paragraph.*

**Choice D** is correct!

D

NOTE

Even though we need to read a lot for this question, the answers are pretty straightforward: they either accurately describe the underlined sentence or they don't!

## EXAMPLE 6

My grandfather's eccentric garden—full of vibrant lilies, gaudy orchids, and homely dandelions—stands in stark contrast to his neighbor's traditional rose garden. [6]

If the writer were to delete the words *eccentric*, *stark*, and *traditional* from the preceding sentence, the sentence would primarily lose details that:

A) Give an overview of the floral composition of the grandfather's garden.
B) Imply the conflict that exists between the grandfather and his neighbor.
C) Highlight the contrast between the feel of the grandfather's garden and that of his neighbor's.
D) Emphasize the unappealing configuration of the grandfather's garden, as opposed to the classic design of the neighbor's garden.

## SOLUTION

Let's read the sentence without these adjectives:

My grandfather's [] garden... stands in [] contrast to his neighbor's [] rose garden.

Losing those adjectives make it a lot harder to tell *how* the two gardens contrast. Let's check out our choices:

~~A)~~ Give an overview of the floral composition ..

*This information survived our deletion! We still know that the garden had lilies, orchids, and dandelions.*

~~B)~~ Imply the conflict that exists...

*Nothing in the sentence suggests that the grandfather and his neighbor don't get along. Don't make assumptions!*

**(C)** Highlight the contrast between the grandfather's garden and that of his neighbor's.

*Exactly! The deleted adjectives helped compare and contrast between the two gardens.*

~~D)~~ Emphasize the unappealing configuration of the grandfather's garden..

*"Eccentric" means unusual, not unappealing.*

C

**TIP**

The passage doesn't **lose** key information if it can still be found in the paragraph after deleting the underlined portion.

## Passage Practice

*Questions 1 – 5 relate to the following passage.*

### All About Time

The modern world is obsessed with time, as computers can now complete complex operations within a millionth of a second. Yet, for most of human history, the increments of time—seconds, minutes, hours—were never cataloged. The earliest measurement of time was the most basic: sunrise and sunset signaled the beginning and end of the day. Ancient cultures developed sundials which allowed them to track the progress of the sun over the day. Clocks as we know them were slow to develop, initially found only in towers and using bells to signal hours of note. **1** Centuries elapsed before clocks could display the passing of each second. It was not until the 19th century that innovations in manufacturing and engineering allowed for pocket watches to become common. People could now go about their day knowing the exact second, minute, and hour.

While clocks became common, time was by no means universal; each city established its own definition of noon, using the standard of when the sun is highest in the sky. We typically think of noon as the brightest time of day. **2** This caused obvious problems for travellers, who would find that their watches

**1**

At this point, the writer is considering adding the following sentence:

> *Now there are smartwatches, which can connect to the Internet and relay text messages.*

Should the writer make this addition?

A) Yes, because it clarifies how clocks have evolved.

B) Yes, because it defines what a smartwatch is in contemporary times.

C) No, because it breaks the chronological order of the passage.

D) No, because it does not state that smartwatches can also provide accurate time.

**2**

The writer is considering deleting the preceding sentence. Should the author make this change?

A) Yes, because it shifts the focus to light instead of time.

B. Yes, because the information is repeated later in the passage.

C. No, because it explains the importance of that time of day.

D. No, because it provides the main idea of the paragraph.

*Passage CONTINUED on next page*

*Passage CONTINUED from previous page*

were incorrect every time they arrived in a new city.

With the proliferation of railroads in the late 19th century, this inconvenience could become a potential disaster, as two trains with two different clocks could possibly collide due to a timing mix-up. By 1880, each railroad company had set its own time standard for its stations, but there was no consensus among the various companies. On November 18th, 1883, the United States implemented a formalized time zone system to address this problem, breaking up the continental regions into four time zones. **3** Although some of the boundaries have been adjusted since then, these regions are recognizable as the four modern time zones: Eastern, Central, Mountain, and Pacific.

In 1884, Great Britain, fueled by the needs of running a global empire, offered an international system of time zones. **4** At the International Meridian Conference, scientists proposed that time be standardized along the Greenwich Observatory, a state-of-the-art facility for that era. **5** The US time zones were maintained and added into this global system, establishing the first worldwide time standardization.

**3**

The writer is considering deleting the preceding sentence. Should the author make this change?

A)  Yes, because the reader should know that there are only four continental time zones in the US.

B)  Yes, because the information is repeated in the preceding sentence.

C)  No, because it provides context for the following sentence.

D)  No, because it describes why time zones are important.

**4**

If the writer was to delete the phrase "fueled by the needs of running a global empire" from the preceding sentence, the passage would primarily lose:

A)  a detail regarding how Great Britain designed time zones.

B)  an explanation for why Great Britain needed worldwide time zones.

C)  a comparison between Great Britain and the United States.

D)  an irrelevant detail that blurs the focus of the passage.

**5**

At this point, the writer wishes to add the following sentence:

> *A standard time could be calculated anywhere by adding or subtracting hours from the time in Greenwich, the "prime meridian."*

Should the writer make this addition?

A)  Yes, because it explains how the Greenwich observatory functions as the standard zone.

B)  Yes, because it shows why Greenwich was used as the location for the standard time zone.

C)  No, because the term "prime meridian" is not relevant.

D)  No, because it does not explain how to calculate time in various zones.

# Describing Data

*Some Writing passages contain bar graphs, line graphs, or other figures.*

## Chart Basics

Some questions will refer you to a bar or line graph that shows data relevant to the topic of the passage. Your job is to rewrite a sentence so that it **accurately describes the data** in that graph. That's it! There are no additional grammar rules to memorize or errors to watch out for when answering these questions.

When you come across a graph question, use a **process of elimination** strategy to spot the correct answer:

① Locate the graph in the passage.

② Check each choice with the graph.

③ Eliminate choices that do not accurately describe the **groups** or **trends** in the data

## PORTAL

Graph questions are easier here than when they show up in the Reading section.

For a deeper dive into the different components of charts, tables, and graphs, head to the Reading Graphs chapter on page 87.

Three of the choices will just flat-out get the data wrong. They'll say Group A was bigger than Group B when it's the reverse, or they'll say a particular value increased when, in fact, it decreased. There's no gray area here: a choice either gets it right or wrong.

## The First Rule of Graph Club

Before we look at an example, we should emphasize one, all-helpful rule: **read the titles of the figures!** Seriously, there is no faster way to get a sense of what you're looking at than to read the title of the graph or figure. After all, when someone *wrote* that title, their job was to describe the main purpose of the graph. So let's use that to our advantage!

# EXAMPLE 1

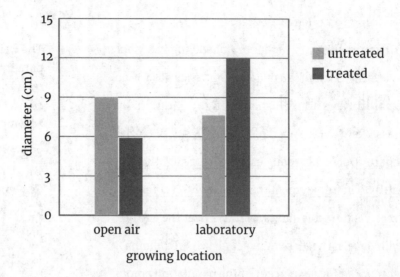

Effect of Treatment on Average Peach Diameter

Which choice offers an accurate interpretation of the data in the chart?

A) peaches will grow to at least 10 cm if left to grow untreated in the open air.

B) treated peaches that are grown in the laboratory weigh, on average, 3 kg more than untreated peaches grown in the open air.

C) if left untreated, peaches grow larger in open air than they do in the laboratory.

D) peach diameter increases with treatment for both open air and lab-grown peaches.

## SOLUTION

Let's compare each answer choice with the chart, eliminating wrong choices as we go:

A) The light grey bar in the left group shows us untreated, open air peaches. That bar only goes to 9cm, **not** 10cm.

B) Careful! this chart says nothing about weight in **kilograms**. This choice misreads the left axis label.

C) Yep! This one is correct – the light grey bar (untreated) is taller in the open air group than in the laboratory group.

D) Nope, diameter **decreased** with treatment for open air peaches. This one's wrong too.

# Practice Problems

*Select the answer choice that produces the best sentence.*

**Does Going to College Pay Off?**

If you're unsure whether or not staying in school pays off, the U.S. Bureau of Labor Statistics has the answer: as workers attain higher levels of education, they are less likely to face unemployment **1** for all levels except for Doctoral graduates, who have slightly higher rates of unemployment than those with Professional degrees. As the table shows, workers over the age of 25 who have earned less than a high school diploma **2** accounted for 5.6 percent of the population among those at all education levels in 2018. Workers with advanced degrees, by contrast, had the lowest rates of unemployment and highest earnings. While it's tough to define the true worth of an education, the data consistently shows that the more you learn, the more you earn.

**Unemployment rates/earnings by educational attainment, 2018**

| Educational attainment | Unemployment rate (%) | Median usual weekly earnings ($) |
|---|---|---|
| Doctoral degree | 1.6 | 1,825 |
| Professional degree | 1.5 | 1,884 |
| Master's degree | 2.1 | 1,434 |
| Bachelor's degree | 2.2 | 1,198 |
| Associate's degree | 2.8 | 862 |
| Some college, no degree | 3.7 | 802 |
| High school diploma | 4.1 | 730 |
| Less than a high school diploma | 5.6 | 553 |
| Total | 3.2 | 932 |

**1**

The writer wants to support the paragraph's main idea with accurate, relevant information from the chart. Which choice most effectively accomplishes this goal?

A) NO CHANGE
B) by an inappreciable margin.
C) and they save significantly more of their earnings.
D) and more likely to earn a higher wage.

**2**

Which choice provides an accurate interpretation of the chart?

A) NO CHANGE
B) barely earned a livable wage, with median weekly earnings of just $730
C) had the largest rate of unemployment at 5.6 percent, and the smallest median weekly earnings at $553
D) brought the total average weekly earnings down to $932

**Who's the straightest shooter?**

A study of archer accuracy indicates **3** an inverse relationship between distance and accuracy: as the distance from the target increases, accuracy decreases. The report found the accuracy of two iconic archers— Katniss and Robin—to have been exemplary at close range, with both expected to nail the bullseye 100% of the time from a distance of 100 feet. However, that accuracy dropped off incrementally under standard conditions, **4** fluctuating between 95 and 70 percent for Katniss, and 89 and 62 percent for Robin. This rate of decline was only slightly outpaced in blindfolded trials. Alas, an important question remains unresolved: who was definitively the greatest archer?

| Distance from target (ft) | | Accuracy (% bullseye) | |
| --- | --- | --- | --- |
| | | Standard | Blindfolded |
| Katniss | 100 | 100 | 95 |
| | 150 | 94 | 82 |
| | 200 | 89 | 70 |
| | 250 | 85 | 70 |
| Robin | 100 | 100 | 89 |
| | 150 | 91 | 78 |
| | 200 | 83 | 70 |
| | 250 | 79 | 62 |

**3**

Which choice is best supported by the information in the table?

A) NO CHANGE
B) that archery tournament rules have a powerful influence on results.
C) that the sport of archery isn't easy, even for two of the sport's greatest.
D) a direct relationship between distance and accuracy: as the distance from the target increases, accuracy increases.

**4**

Which choice best illustrates the claim made earlier in the sentence with information from the table?

A) NO CHANGE
B) reaching lows of 85 and 79 percent for Katniss and Robin, respectively, at 250 feet.
C) decreasing, respectively, to 95 and 89 percent.
D) slumping to 70 and 62 percent, respectively, at 250 feet.

## The Race Towards Autonomous Vehicles

The rapidly evolving market for autonomous vehicles is receiving increasing recognition, with both traditional automakers and leading tech innovators playing a role in one of the most revolutionary markets of the next decade. A market research outfit (Yole) expects all levels of computer assisted vehicles to see production growth in the coming years. The number of sales of level 2 cars—those with two or more advanced driver assistance systems (ADAS) that can at times control the braking, steering or acceleration of the vehicle—is anticipated to [5] increase by 15,200,000 between 2019 and 2029, a gain of about 400 percent. Level 3 vehicles—capable of taking full control and operating during select parts of a journey—should see massively greater gains, with a forecasted 17,800 percent increase in vehicle sales by 2029. The expected sales growth rate of [6] levels 1 through 4 as a whole, at 198 percent, is in sharp contrast to the 66 percent by which sales of all fully human controlled vehicles are expected to decline.

| Level of Automation | 2019 vehicle sales (Millions) | 2029 projected vehicle sales (Millions) | Percent Change, 2019-2029 (projected) |
|---|---|---|---|
| Level 0 (fully manual) | 56.1 | 19.2 | -66% |
| Level 1 | 33.8 | 48.1 | +42% |
| Level 2 | 15.2 | 76.3 | +400% |
| Level 3 | 0.1 | 17.9 | +17,800% |
| Level 4 (fully autonomous) | None Available | 4.0 | N/A |
| Total (levels 1-4) | 49.1 | 146.3 | +198% |

**5**

Which choice provides accurate information from the table to support the passage's argument?

A) NO CHANGE
B) decline from 76,900,000 to 48,100,000
C) climb to a total of 146,300,000
D) rise from 15,200,000 to 76,300,000

**6**

Which choice provides information from the table accurately?

A) NO CHANGE
B) some other forms of transportation,
C) all level 2 and 3 vehicles together,
D) level 4 vehicles,

# Writing Practice Passage 6

## TO STAY ON PACE, YOUR TIMING GOAL IS 8.5 MINUTES

This passage tests a variety of grammar topics—some from chapters you may have not yet completed. Use this opportunity to practice maintaining a brisk pace while answering the questions as best you can. Good luck!

**Questions 1-11 are based on the following passage.**

**The Many Lives of Yogurt**

What comes to mind when you hear the word "yogurt"? You probably think of a sweet dairy product in fruity **1** flavors like strawberry or peach, conveniently packaged for breakfast on-the-go. **2** Surprisingly, yogurt is not a naturally sweet product and many commercially available yogurts add several grams of sugar per serving.

**1**

A) NO CHANGE
B) flavors like, strawberry or peach,
C) flavors like strawberry, or peach
D) flavors, like strawberry, or peach

**2**

The writer wants to conclude this paragraph with a sentence that will set up the main topic of the rest of the passage. Which choice best accomplishes this goal?

A) NO CHANGE
B) Indeed, in most American grocery stores, yogurt is just one of many semisolid dairy products available and sits along sour cream, cottage cheese, and whipped cream in the refrigerated dairy section.
C) But while that may be yogurt's most commonly found form in today's American grocery store, many different varieties of yogurt have existed during its 5,000 year history.
D) However, Greek yogurt, which strains off much of the whey created during fermentation, has become a top seller in the last decade.

CONTINUE ➡

[1]These wandering tribes might have accidentally created yogurt by carrying fresh milk in pouches made from sheep stomachs, **3** a Neolithic substitute for the glass bottle. [2] Some food historians believe that yogurt was discovered as early as the Neolithic era when nomadic herdsmen began domesticating milk-producing animals, the ancestors of today's cows, sheep, and goats. [3]Or perhaps it was in the ancient lands of Mesopotamia that yogurt made its first appearance. [4] **4** Conversely, there is evidence that yogurt played an important role in the diets of people throughout the world, even before recorded history. **5**

The first true description of yogurt was provided around 1000 A.D. by a Turkish author named Mahmud of Kashgar. **6** Not only to include an entry for yogurt, one of the first encyclopedias was written by him, firmly establishing its place in Turkish history.

**3**

Which choice provides a potential explanation for how the yogurt was created?

A) NO CHANGE
B) which contain a milk-curdling enzyme.
C) the custom at the time.
D) which were used to transport liquids during travel.

**4**

A) NO CHANGE
B) Either way,
C) Because,
D) Therefore

**5**

To make this paragraph most logical, sentence 1 should be placed

A) where it is now.
B) after sentence 2.
C) after sentence 3.
D) after sentence 4.

**6**

A) NO CHANGE
B) Not only did he create one of the first encyclopedias, he also included an entry for yogurt,
C) One of the first encyclopedias was created by him, but it included an entry for yogurt,
D) Not only did it have an entry for yogurt, but he also wrote one of the first encyclopedias,

CONTINUE →

[7] Iranians enjoy sour kefir yogurt in dishes such as ashe-mast, a warm soup made from yogurt, lentils and spinach. In Eastern European and Balkan countries such as Albania, Bulgaria and Serbia, yogurt is served as a cold soup seasoned with cucumbers and dill—a light and refreshing dish. A similar dish, tzatziki, is a popular condiment in Greece, served alongside pita sandwiches and grilled meat. In South Asia, a yogurt-based sauce called raita—made with cucumbers, onions, mint, and cumin—makes a delicious complement to spicy curries. [8]

Which of the following sentences would most effectively transition between the two paragraphs?

A) In the ensuing centuries, yogurt's popularity has remained strong in cuisines throughout the world.

B) Americans typically expect yogurt to be served sweet, but this is not the case everywhere.

C) In many recipes, yogurt is accompanied by cucumber.

D) In modern times, refrigeration technology affects the way people consume dairy products.

At this point, the writer is considering adding the following sentence.

> Curries of many varieties are popular throughout this region.

Should the writer make this addition here?

A) Yes, because it highlights the global role yogurt has played in cuisine.

B) Yes, because it explains yogurt's popularity in South Asia.

C) No, because it interrupts the flow of the passage with irrelevant information.

D) No, because it contradicts the previous sentence's claim about curry.

9 To some extent, yogurt's popularity is due in part to its considerable nutritional value; it is full of protein, calcium, and vitamins. 10 It also contains probiotics, live microorganisms that are thought to boost immune response. Whatever the reason, yogurt has become more popular than ever in the past decade; in 2006, Americans purchased 11 over 5 billion pounds of yogurt. Perhaps the history of yogurt is just beginning.

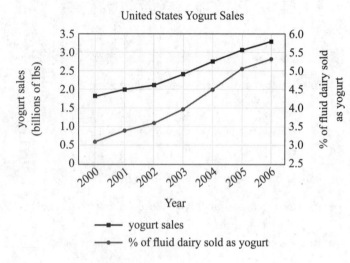

United States Yogurt Sales

— yogurt sales
— % of fluid dairy sold as yogurt

**9**

A) NO CHANGE
B) Yogurt's popularity is due in part
C) To some extent, yogurt's popularity is partly due
D) Yogurt's popularity is somewhat due in part

**10**

The writer is considering deleting the underlined sentence. Should the sentence be kept or deleted?

A) Kept, because it provides evidence that supports the claim made in the previous sentence.
B) Kept, because it provides a transition between the preceding and following ideas.
C) Deleted, because it blurs the focus of the paragraph.
D) Deleted, because it repeats information that has already been provided.

**11**

Which choice offers an accurate interpretation of the data in the graph?

A) NO CHANGE
B) over 5% of all yogurt sold globally.
C) under 6% of all dairy products sold as yogurt.
D) over 3 billion pounds of yogurt.

# STOP

**If you finish before time is called, you may check your work on this section only.
Do not turn to any other section.**

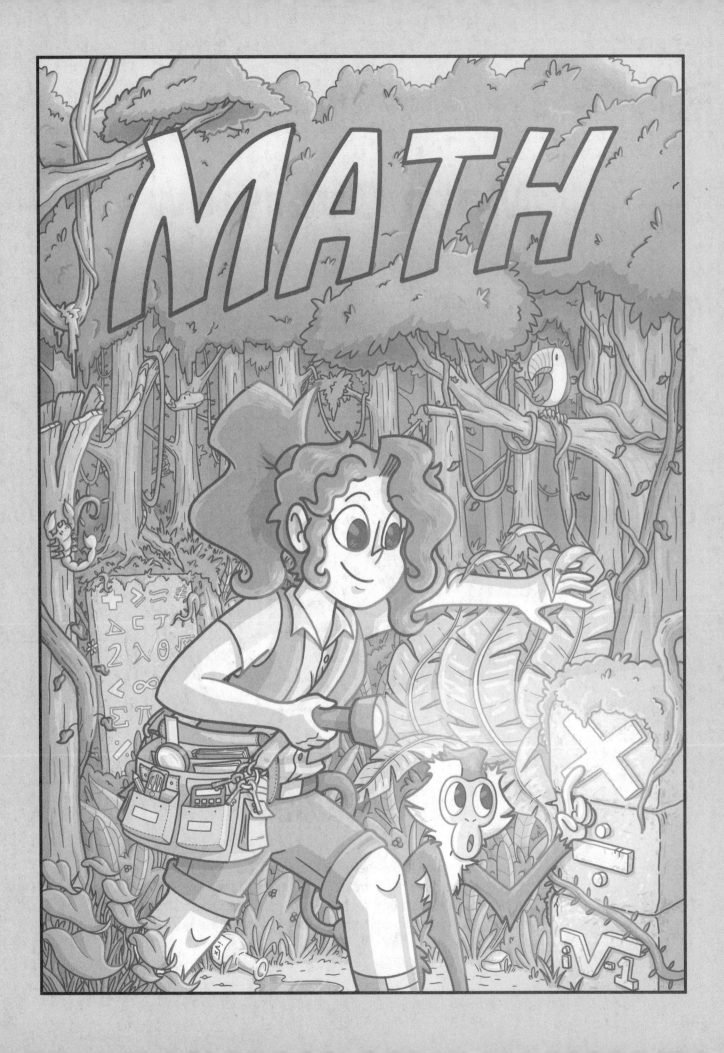

# Math Overview

*Before we dive in, let's take a broad view of how we'll raise your math score.*

### Math Mantra

While we have your attention, let's start with the single most important thing you can do to improve your math score. In fact, it is the **secret** to SAT math. Ready? Here it is: no matter what score you are aiming for...

## TIP

Tragically, each year, thousands of points are lost by students around the world who refuse to write out their work.

Rather than copy down a given equation and start from there, they jump to the first step of the work, making a small calculation error in the process. *Don't let this be you!*

Writing everything down helps you see patterns you might have missed, minimizes mistakes, and makes it easier and faster to fix mistakes when they DO happen. It might feel like it takes a little longer, **but the time you save will almost certainly outweigh the time you spend**.

## TIP

Check the **header pages** at the beginning of each unit to see if you should use your calculator on those chapters.

Your Math score on the SAT comes from **two sections** of the test—one where calculators are prohibited and one where they are allowed.

## No–Calculator Section

On the No-Calculator section, you'll have 25 minutes to answer 15 multiple choice questions and 5 grid-in questions.

**25 minutes**

**20 questions**
(15 multiple choice, 5 grid-ins)

**no calculator**

This section focuses on your ability to manipulate algebraic equations. You need to be comfortable doing basic arithmetic by hand as you combine like terms, simplify expressions, and solve for variables.

## NOTE

On the **No Calculator** section, you'll see topics from all math units in this book, with the exception of the Data Analysis units.

The **Calculator** section covers all topics but has a preference for those later Modeling and Data Analysis chapters.

## Calculator Section

On the Calculator section, you'll have 55 minutes to answer 30 multiple choice questions and 8 grid-in questions.

**55 minutes**

**38 questions**
(30 multiple choice, 8 grid-ins)

**calculator**

This section is full of word problems that describe real world scenarios. Your job is usually to **interpret equations** or use data to compute **percentages and probabilities**. Your calculator will be most useful if you find yourself needing to divide gnarly numbers.

## TIP

You get an average of about 1 minute and 20 seconds per problem. However, you should expect to spend less than a minute on easier questions to save time for the tougher problems to come.

## Use your time wisely

In each section, the multiple choice questions start out relatively easy and get harder as you go. When you get to the first grid in question, the difficulty level resets to easy! This means that some of the easiest questions on the section actually come *after* the hardest questions!

# Customize a study plan based on your score goal

You may not have the time (or need) to tackle every chapter in this section. To help you customize a study plan, we've grouped chapters into four tiers at the bottom of the page. Which tiers you should focus on depends on what your target math score is. Here are our recommendations:

**(500) Target: 500 (~25 questions correct)**

Focus on the first 10–15 questions of each section, remembering to jump ahead to the easier grid-in questions. Master Tier 1 fundamentals, then focus on Tier 2 topics.

**(600) Target: 600 (~38 questions correct)**

You need to be solid on Tier 2 material and at least familiar with Tier 3. Don't be afraid to skip over the hardest multiple choice problems to get to the easier first grid-in questions.

**(700) Target: 700 (~48 questions correct)**

You need to master Tiers 2 and 3 and familiarize yourself with the ideas in Tier 4. Attempt all pepper problems!

**(800) Target: 800 (57+ questions correct)**

You need to get *everything* right. Seek out pepper problems throughout the book. On test day, focus on reading and working carefully to avoid small, but costly, mistakes.

## TIP

The hardest question on the test is worth just as many points as the easiest.

For many students, time is better spent grabbing as many points as possible in the first half of the section and then jumping ahead to the grid-ins rather than spinning their wheels on the tougher multiple choice questions.

## NOTE

Tier 1 chapters teach fundamental math skills that help throughout both math sections.

Tier 2 chapters cover core topics that are tested multiple times on each test.

Tier 3 chapters cover topics that may only show up once or twice a test.

Tier 4 chapters cover topics that only show up on the hardest questions.

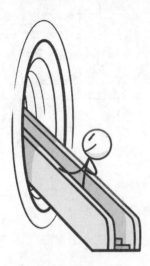

## PORTAL

Have you had negative experiences in the past that make you anxious as soon as a math test starts?

This feeling of anxiety or powerlessness can be overcome! With the right tools, you can be **empowered**. To learn about test anxiety, turn to the Beyond the Content section on page 887.

## Math is a skill you can build with practice

If you feel like a higher score is locked away behind some impenetrable door—it's not! This test measures two things and practice will improve them both. First, it measures your **knowledge** of key math concepts, all of which are covered in the very book you hold in your hands. Second, it measures your **skill** at tackling math problems—and you can build that skill just like you can build the skill of playing guitar or twirling a pen in that fancy way some people do. So here's how we'll raise your score:

① *Learn Key Concepts*

Take each chapter one-at-a-time. Try the examples, read the explanations, complete the practice problems, check your work, and look over the ones you miss the next day. Each time you do this, it's like adding another key to your keyring, unlocking more questions and more points.

② *Practice Using Your Math Tools*

The solutions to example problems will model the **skill** of solving math problems. You will learn to solve problems step-by-step, to tinker with the given information, and to use workarounds when you feel stuck. Along the way, you'll get better at using different tools to quickly work your way toward a correct answer.

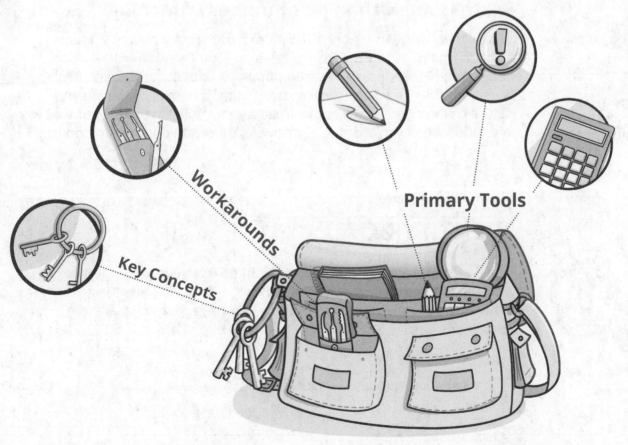

Workarounds

**Primary Tools**

Key Concepts

# Math Strategy

*How to tackle math problems head-on.*

## Step-by-Step Strategy

Let's sum up your step-by-step approach to answering math questions:

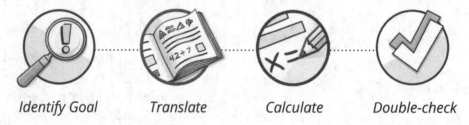

Identify Goal      Translate      Calculate      Double-check

**TIP**

Translation is extremely important on the SAT. Some questions, particularly on the no-calculator section, are ALL translation: no calculations needed!

## Math is more than just number crunching

Notice that "calculate" is only ONE step of the process! Many students think of "math" as "the stuff calculators do." But there's much more to "doing math" than just solving computations or doing arithmetic. Tackling a math problem involves reading, translating, and experimenting. In future chapters, we'll look at the creative ways you can tinker your way to a solution when you're stuck. For now, let's look at your primary toolkit.

## IDENTIFY GOAL

The first step is always to **read the problem actively** and <u>underline</u> any information that is given to you; it's likely crucial for finding the answer. Write down any given equations. Before starting your work, answer these questions:

- What is my **goal**?

- What **key concepts** might I need?

- What do I know so far, and what do I need to find?

# TRANSLATE

The next step is to **translate the information** in the prompt into math. This bridges the gap between reading the problem and calculating, and it is where many rushing students miss points. After you've identified the given information, use your pencil to:

- Copy any given **equations** (e.g., *Sarah = 2J + 4* ).

- Create and define **variables** (e.g., *h = 12, V = ?* ).

- Set up **ratios** (e.g., *2x = 3y* ).

# CALCULATE

Now that we've set up our work in steps one and two, it's time to start making calculations. Use your pencil to write out each step of the work. This will keep you on task and make it easier to spot any mistakes in the final step. Remember:

- Write down **each step**: no exceptions!

- Work **one calculation** at a time.

- If you can use your calculator, write down each **result**!

## Don't stop here!

At this point, we've read the problem, translated the given info to math, and carefully worked out each step, ending with an answer. There's even a multiple choice option with our answer! But are we finished? No! Give yourself a couple seconds to lock in those points by double-checking.

# DOUBLE-CHECK

How often has this happened to you on a test: you put in all the hard work of the problem, reach what you think is the answer, and move on... only to realize later you forgot one final step, or gave *x* instead of *y*! Before moving on, save yourself points:

- **Circle** your answer.

- Double check that your solution **matches your goal**.

- Make sure your answer is **reasonable**.

# UNIT | Math Toolkit

## Chapters

## Overview

In order to tackle math problems head-on, you need to identify your goal and carefully translate words into math using the **art of translation**. But if you get stuck, don't give up! Even if you're missing the key to a problem, you can often use the tools of **picking numbers** or **working backwards** to crack a locked problem wide open.

## Calculator + No-Calculator

In this chapter, we practice basic skills that will help you on both sections of the test. We recommend doing computations without your calculator in these chapters, but focus on those basic skills.

# Art of Translation

*Math is a language that anyone can learn. Let's practice translating words into math and back again!*

## PORTAL

This chapter will give you the tools for dealing with word problems. We'll dig deeper into this concept in the Basic Modeling chapter, starting on page 632.

### Translate words into math

Wordy problems are very common on the SAT. These problems depend almost entirely on correct translation from *English* into *Math* (or vice versa). For example, the sentence below can be translated into algebra:

| The number of cookies | is | 12 | times | the number of trays. |
|---|---|---|---|---|
| $C$ | $=$ | $12$ | $\times$ | $T$ |

### Translation helps you start on the right foot

Careful translation **bridges the gap** between reading the problem for the first time and starting your written work. When you use your pencil to translate what you're given and what you're asked, you start your work by answering two key questions:

What do I **know?**     What do I **need to find?**

# Phrasebook

Notice how specific English words can be translated into specific symbols. We will be working on your ability to translate throughout the book, but here is a basic phrasebook for translating between languages.

| English Word | Math Meaning |
|---|---|
| What, how much, a number | Some variable ( $?$ or $x$ or $y$ ) |
| Is, was, equals | Equals ( $=$ ) |
| Sum, increase, more/greater than | Add ( $+$ ) |
| Subtract, less than, exceeds, difference | Subtract ( $-$ ) |
| ~~each, every,~~ Of, times, product, ~~per~~ | Multiply ( $\times$ ) |
| Divisible by, divided by, out of, per | Divide ( $\div$ ) |
| Percent (%) | Multiply by $\frac{1}{100}$ |

## TIP

It is okay (and normal) to not immediately know what to do with every problem. Use the first two steps to reveal things about the problem you didn't notice at first glance:

1) **Circle** your goal
2) **Translate** what you can

## Translate wordy sentences before you solve

The SAT writers are really good at finding slightly different ways to ask questions about the same basic concepts. For example, they might cloak a simple algebra equation behind a wordy sentence. These questions test whether you can **play and tinker** with problems as much as they are testing your algebra skills.

Let's practice by focusing on the first two steps of our math strategy: **identify** the goal and **translate** into math.

## EXAMPLE 1

The product of two positive integers is 30 and their difference is one. What is the sum of the two numbers? $\|$

## KEY IDEAS

An **integer** is a number that is not a fraction.

A **positive** number is greater than zero.

SOLUTION

Never underestimate the importance of careful reading and translation! Let's work only the first two steps of our strategy.

### Step 1: Identify the Goal

The <u>product</u> of <u>two positive integers</u> is <u>30</u> and their <u>difference</u> is <u>one</u>. What is the (sum) of the two numbers?

*What's my goal?*  the SUM of two numbers

*What is given?*
1. positive integers
2. difference is one
3. multiply to 30

### Step 2: Translate the sentences into math equations.

| ~~The product of two positive integers~~ | ~~is~~ | ~~30~~ |
|---|---|---|
| $a \times b$ | $=$ | $30$ |

| ~~their difference~~ | ~~is~~ | ~~one~~ |   | ~~what~~ | ~~is~~ | ~~their sum~~ |
|---|---|---|---|---|---|---|
| $a - b$ | $=$ | $1$ |   | $?$ | $=$ | $a + b$ |

So after the first two steps of our strategy, we have translated this wordy problem into three equations.

The <u>product</u> of <u>two</u> <u>positive</u> <u>integers</u> is <u>30</u> and their <u>difference</u> is <u>one</u>. What is the (sum) of the two numbers?

1. $a \times b = 30$
2. $a - b = 1$
3. $a + b = ?$

For now, we're only interested in translating. We'll practice the skills used to solve this in the **Basic Algebra** chapter.

**Translate the following expressions** into math using the phrasebook table on the previous page.

| | | |
|---|---|---|
| **1** | English | 5 more than a number |
| | Math | $x + 5$ |
| **2** | English | 7 less than three times a number |
| | Math | $3x - 7$ |
| **3** | English | The square of one more than a number is added to 17 |
| | Math | $(x+1)^2 + 17$ |
| **4** | English | The sum of two consecutive numbers |
| | Math | $x + (x+1)$ |
| **5** | English | 4 less than the sum of a number and twice its square |
| | Math | $(x + 2x^2) - 4$ |

**Translate the following SAT problems** into math. Remember, we are not solving the problems yet—just translating!

| | | |
|---|---|---|
| **6** | English | If half of a number is equal to 5 more than twice the number, what is the number? |
| | Math | If $\frac{1}{2}x = 2x + 5$, $x = ?$ |
| **7** | English | If 7 more than three times a number is equal to 25, what is half the number? |
| | Math | |
| **8** | English | If 6 more than a certain number is tripled the result is 66. What is the number? |
| | Math | |

**Answers:** *Bottom of next page*

## EXAMPLE 2

A painter charges $35 per hour for each hour he works on a house plus a one-time fee of $45. If he charges $220 after painting a house, how many hours did he work?

SOLUTION

This word problem needs some translating! Since we're focusing on correct translation, let's work through **just steps 1 and 2** of our math strategy.

**Step 1: Identify the Goal**

A painter charges $35 per hour for each hour he works on a house plus a one-time fee of $45. If he charges $220 after painting a house, how many hours did he work?

| | |
|---|---|
| *What's my goal?* | the number of HOURS worked |
| *What is given?* | 1. $35 per hour |
| | 2. plus $45 |
| | 3. total of $220 |

Now that we know what's given and what's needed, let's translate.

**Step 2: Translate**

Since the **number of hours** is unknown, let's make that x.

| $35 per hour | plus $45 | is $220 | How many hours did he work? |
|---|---|---|---|
| 35x | + 45 | = 220 | x = ? |

From here, we can do some basic algebra to solve for x!

Previous Page:   1. *given*   2. 3x − 7   3. 17 + (x + 1)²   4. x + (x + 1)   5. (x + 2x²) − 4

**400**   6. *given*   7. If 3x + 7 = 25, $\frac{1}{2}$x = ?   8. If 3(x + 6) = 66, x = ?

# TIP

We have two unknowns here: Levi's age and Maria's age. So we'll need TWO variables. Picking letters that connect to the words in the problem will help you remember what you're solving for.

Make Levi's age "L" and Maria's age "M."

## EXAMPLE 3

Levi is twice as old as his sister Maria. Three years ago he was three times as old as she was then. How old is Levi?

### Step 1: Identify the Goal

Levi is <u>twice</u> as old as his sister Maria. <u>Three years ago</u> he was <u>three</u> times as old as she was then. How old is Levi?

| | |
|---|---|
| *What's my goal?* | **Levi's current age ($L$)** |
| *What is given?* | **1. Now: Levi is twice Maria** |
| | **2. 3 years ago: Levi was 3 times Maria** |

### Step 2: Translate

We have two equations to translate that will lead us to $L$.

| Levi | is | twice Maria | | 3 years ago, Levi | was | 3 times Maria |
|------|-----|-------------|---|-------------------|-----|---------------|
| $L$ | $=$ | $2M$ | | $(L - 3)$ | $=$ | $3(M - 3)$ |

Now we have two equations that we can use to solve for L:

1. $L = 2M$
2. $L - 3 = 3(M - 3)$

**Translate the following word problems** into math equations. The first one has been completed for you.

| 1 | Levi is twice as old as his sister Maria. Three years ago he was three times as old as she was then. How old is Levi? | |
|---|---|---|
| | Goal | $L = ?$ |
| | Equation 1 | $L = 2M$ |
| | Equation 2 | $L - 3 = 3(M - 3)$ |

| 2 | Atamari ran 5 more miles in February than she did in January. If she ran one and a half times farther in February than in January, how far did she run in February? | |
|---|---|---|
| | Goal | |
| | Equation 1 | |
| | Equation 2 | |

| 3 | Vi has a jar of change and has sorted it into piles of quarters, dimes and nickles. The number of nickles is three less than twice the number of quarters. The number of quarters is six more than twice the number of nickles. The number of dimes is two less than four times the number of quarters. How many coins does she have? | |
|---|---|---|
| | Goal | |
| | Equation 1 | |
| | Equation 2 | |
| | Equation 3 | |

Answers: 1. *given*
2. Goal: $F = ?$  E1: $F = J + 5$  E2: $F = 1.5J$
3. Goal: $Q + D + N = ?$  E1: $N = 2Q - 3$  E2: $Q = 2N + 6$  E3: $D = 4Q - 2$

For each equation, **write a sentence** that it could model. Use the first as an example.

**BONUS!**

| | | |
|---|---|---|
| **1** | Math | $N = 2P + 35$ |
| | English | We need twice as many napkins as people, plus a backup of 35 in case of spills. |
| **2** | Math | $a + 5 = 3a$ |
| | English | |
| **3** | Math | $2a + 4 = 5(a - 1)$ |
| | English | |
| **4** | Math | $a + 3b = 17, \quad a + b = 9$ |
| | English | |

**Answers:** We can't imagine what you came up with, but try translating it BACK into math to check your work!

# Picking Numbers

*Pick the lock to algebra problems by choosing numbers and plugging in.*

When algebra questions ask for an answer **in terms of** one or more variables, you can tackle the problem in two ways:

**Algebra (Head-on)**
This method uses algebra skills to substitute and solve with variables. It can take longer and may expose you to more chances for careless errors.

– or –

**Picking Numbers (Workaround)**
This strategy takes abstract algebra and makes it concrete. All you have to do is add, subtract, multiply, and divide, eliminating answer choices as you go.

## How to Pick Numbers

First, as usual, identify your goal. Second, **choose a value for *x*** (or whatever variable is given) that makes sense with the problem. Finally, plug in that value for *x* in the answer choices, looking for a match.

## EXAMPLE 1

The sum of two positive consecutive integers is $x$. In terms of $x$, what is the value of the smaller of these two integers?

A) $\dfrac{x}{2} - 1$

B) $\dfrac{x-1}{2}$

C) $\dfrac{x}{2}$

D) $\dfrac{x}{2} + 2$

# Think

What does it MEAN when there is a variable in the answer choices? Often, it means that there are a variety of numbers that would satisfy the conditions.

As long as the smaller and larger numbers are positive, consecutive integers, the correct answer choice will correctly describe the relationship between the sum and the smaller number.

Solving with **algebra** means we find the solution using variables. Solving with **picking numbers** means we find the solution using one particular set of numbers.

### Step 1: Identify the Goal

No matter what strategy you're using, the first step is ALWAYS to read the question and identify your goal!

The <u>sum</u> of <u>two</u> <u>positive</u> <u>consecutive</u> <u>integers</u> is $x$. In terms of $x$, what is the value of the (smaller) of these two integers?

*What's my goal?*     **The smaller number**

*What is given?*     <u>Two numbers that are:</u>
1. **positive** (greater than zero)
2. **consecutive** (back-to-back)
3. **integers** (no fractions)
4. sum = $x$

### Step 2: Pick Numbers

Now we can pick any numbers that follow the rules above. Let's keep it simple and make the smaller integer **2**. That would make our larger consecutive integer **3**.

*Write* the equation     $x$ = smaller + larger

*Pick* "2" and "3"     $x$ =   2 + 3

*Find* the sum     $x$ =     5

Now we know that when we pick 2 and 3, the sum ($x$) is 5.

**Continued on next page →**

**Step 3: Plug in and Solve**

Now we have a number for $x$ that we can plug into each answer choice. If we **plug in 5 for $x$**, the correct answer should give us our target: the smaller integer 2.

$$\boxed{x = 5} \qquad \boxed{\text{target} = 2}$$

*Plug 5 into Choice* A

~~A)~~ $\dfrac{x}{2} - 1 = 2.5 - 1 = 1.5$   *Not 2!*

*Plug 5 into Choice* B

✔ B) $\dfrac{x-1}{2} = \dfrac{5-1}{2} = \dfrac{4}{2} = 2$  *Bingo!*

*Plug 5 into Choice* C

~~C)~~ $\dfrac{x}{2} = \dfrac{5}{2} = 2.5$   *Nope!*

*Plug 5 into Choice* D

~~D)~~ $\dfrac{x}{2} + 2 = \dfrac{5}{2} + 2 = 4.5$   *Nope!*

When we plug in one possible sum (5) for $x$ in each choice, only **choice B** correctly spits out the value of our **smaller number**!   B

**TIP**

Go ahead and check each answer, even if you find a match... just in case.

**TIP**

Notice that once you find that choice C is 2.5, you can just add 2 to get choice D!

## Guidelines for Picking Numbers

Here are a couple of best practices when you are picking numbers.

1. **Follow the rules.** This is crucial! If the problem tells you the numbers are less than 15, don't pick 20!

2. **Do NOT pick 0 or 1.** These numbers do strange things to equations and functions. They can cause confusion, so it's (usually) best to steer clear of them.

3. **Solve for the loner.** If you are solving an equation like $x + y = z$, it's better to PICK numbers for the two variables on the same side and SOLVE for the one that's alone.

4. **Repeat if necessary.** If more than one answer choice gives you your target number, don't worry! You've narrowed your choices down, and can now pick different numbers to confirm the best choice (this is rarely required).

## EXAMPLE 2

In two years, Chris will be twice as old as Sally will be. Chris is now $n$ years old. In terms of $n$, how old is Sally now?

A) $\frac{n}{2}$

B) $\frac{n}{2} - 2$

C) $\frac{n}{2} - 1$

D) $n - 2$

SOLUTION

We're pros at this now. Let's take it step-by-step.

1. Identify goal     target = Sally now

2. Pick for Chris now ($n$)     $n = 8$ picked!

3. How old is Chris in 2 years?     10

4. How old would that make Sally?     5

5. So what's Sally now?     3 target!

Now we can plug in 8 for $n$, and see which choice gives us 3.

6. Test each choice

    A. $\frac{n}{2} = 4$    ✗

    B. $\frac{n}{2} - 2 = 2$    ✗

    C. $\frac{n}{2} - 1 = 3$ Bingo!

    D. $n - 2 = 6$    ✗

C

# Working Backwards

*Sometimes it's faster to work backwards from the answer choices.*

......................................................................................

### When the choices are in order, work backwards

Sometimes you can't find the key to the problem and picking numbers isn't helpful. Now what? In these cases, try **sneaking in the back door**! The beauty of multiple choice tests is that the answer is sitting right there in front of you... it's just hiding among some lookalikes.

> John has $x$ pieces of candy in his pocket. He gives half of the candies to Kerri, and one-third of the remaining candies to Lori. If he is left with 10 candies in his pocket, what is the value of $x$ ?

We only have 4 choices.

One of them MUST be the right answer...

A) 60
B) 50
C) 40   *What if we just plug this in for $x$?*
D) 30

We can determine the correct answer to some problems by **substituting** the answer choices back into the problem and seeing which one works. Students often learn this strategy themselves when they get stuck on a problem in middle or elementary school. Good news: it's still helpful!

## EXAMPLE 1

John has *x* pieces of candy in his pocket. He gives half of the candies to Kerri, and one-third of the remaining candies to Lori. If he is left with 10 candies in his pocket, what is the value of *x* ?

A) 60
B) 50
C) 40
(D) 30

**SOLUTION**

Notice how **the answer choices are in order** from largest to smallest? That's a big clue that we can use working backwards to quickly solve this problem. But first things first: let's actively read the question.

John has <u>*x* pieces of candy</u> in his pocket. He gives <u>half</u> of the candies to Kerri, and <u>one-third</u> of the remaining candies to Lori. If <u>he is left with 10 candies</u> in his pocket, what is the <u>value of *x*</u> ?

So the answer choices are the number of candies at the start, and we want the one that results in 10 candies at the end. If we start by **plugging in a middle choice**, we get a result that is too high:

| *Try* | | |
|---|---|---|
| **C** | **Start with 40** | *40* |
| | **Give away half (20)** | $40 \div 2 = 20$ |
| | **Give away a third (~7)** | $20 - 7 \approx 13$ *too high!* |

So if he starts with 40 pieces, he ends up with *more* than 10. That means he must need to start with fewer than 40 candies! Even though we only tested one choice, we can cross off **A**, **B**, and **C**! If we **try the next smaller choice**, we find the answer!

| *Try* | | |
|---|---|---|
| **D** | **Start with 30** | *30* |
| | **Give away half (15)** | $30 \div 2 = 15$ |
| | **Give away a third (5)** | $15 - 5 = $ (10) *bingo!* |

D

## TIP

When working backwards, start by plugging in a middle choice (B or C). Based on what answer you get, you can then either choose a larger or smaller choice to try next. This can save you some time.

# Working backwards can be the fastest strategy

We've seen how working backwards can help when you aren't sure what the best head-on strategy is. For some problems, however, plugging the choices into the problem IS the very best strategy you can take!

## EXAMPLE 2

$$\sqrt{10 - 3x} = x + 6$$

What is the solution set of the equation above?

A) $\{-2\}$
B) $\{-13\}$
C) $\{-2, -13\}$
D) $\{0, -2, -13\}$

### SOLUTION

You could solve this problem algebraically if you want to, but you don't have to! The answer choices here give you 3 possible values for $x$: $-2$, $-13$, and $0$. and ask you which ones are true. Let's plug each one in for $x$ and see if it makes the equation true. It's easy to plug in zero, so let's start there.

(1) *Plug in 0 for x*     $\sqrt{10 - 3(0)} = (0) + 6$

$\sqrt{10} = 6$ ✗ *not true!*

Nope! Since plugging in 0 led to a false equation, 0 is not in the solution set, and you can **eliminate D**.

(2) *Plug in -2 for x*     $\sqrt{10 - 3(-2)} = (-2) + 6$

$\sqrt{16} = 4$ ✔ *true!*

This works!  Since –2 has to be in the solution set, **eliminate B**.

(3) *Plug in -13 for x*     $\sqrt{10 - 3(-13)} = (-13) + 6$

$\sqrt{49} = -7$ ✗ *not true!*

Careful! A square root **cannot equal a negative** number, so –13 doesn't make the equation true. The solution set only contains –2, so the answer is **choice A**.

# Mixed Practice

*For each problem, choose whether you should use **Picking Numbers (PN)** or **Working Backwards (WB)**.*

---

**1**

John is 6 years older than Mark. 6 years ago John was twice as old as Mark. How old is John today?

A)  6
B)  9
C)  12
D)  18

☐ PN  ☐ WB

**2**

Which of the following equations expresses $z$ in terms of $x$ for all real numbers $x$, $y$, and $z$ such that $x^3 = y$ and $y^2 = z$ ?

A)  $x^6$
B)  $x^5$
C)  $x^3$
D)  $2x$

☐ PN  ☐ WB

**3**

A kindergarten class wants to buy a $64 aquarium for the classroom. If the teacher and students split the cost such that the teacher pays three times as much as the students, how much, in dollars, should the teacher pay?

A)  16
B)  32
C)  48
D)  56

☐ PN  ■ WB

**4**

Scott has exactly twice as many trading cards as Todd. Ryan has exactly four times as many trading cards as Scott. If the three of them have fewer than 100 trading cards combined, what is the maximum number of trading cards Todd could have?

$S = 2T$
$R = 4S$

A)  6
B)  9
C)  10
D)  12

☐ PN  ■ WB

**5**

If $x = 3z$ and $y = 9z$, what is $x$ in terms of $y$ ?

A)  $3y$

B)  $6y$

C)  $y$

D)  $\dfrac{y}{3}$

■ PN  ☐ WB

**6**

Jamal has a bag of marbles. He gives exactly 1/3 of his marbles to Isaac, and has 2/3 of his original number of marbles remaining. If Jamal is able to repeat this action at least 3 more times without breaking any marbles into pieces, how many marbles could he have started with?

A)  12
B)  18
C)  24
D)  81

☐ PN  ☐ WB

**411**

**7**

A Spanish teacher wants to have a party for her students, and she needs to buy candy to put in the piñata. She buys $100 worth of 2 types of candy. One type of candy costs $0.10 a piece and another type costs $0.25 a piece. If she bought 550 pieces of candy in total, how many pieces of the more expensive candy did she buy?

A) 200
B) 240
C) 300
D) 380

$0.1x + 0.25y = 100$

$x + y = 550$

$0.6x = 150$

☐ PN ■ WB

**8**

If $a$, $b$, and $c$ are nonzero numbers such that $a = bc$, which of the following must be equivalent to $ac$?

A) $\dfrac{b}{a}$

B) $b^2c$

C) $bc$

D) $\dfrac{a^2}{b}$

■ PN ☐ WB

**9**

Two identical 6-inch deep water buckets drain at uniform rates of 1 inch per hour. If bucket one begins draining at 12 p.m., and bucket two begins draining at 2 p.m., at what time will bucket two have exactly five times as much water as bucket one?

A) 4:00 p.m.
B) 4:30 p.m.
C) 5:30 p.m.
D) 6:00 p.m.

☐ PN ■ WB

**10**

The side of a square is d inches longer than the side of a second square. The perimeter of the first square is how much longer, in inches, than the perimeter of the second square?

A) $\dfrac{d}{4}$

B) $d$

C) $4d$

D) $d^2$

■ PN ☐ WB

**11**

Train $A$ travels 75 mph less than twice the speed of Train $B$. If the speed of Train $A$ is $k$ mph, which of the following expressions represents the speed of Train $B$, in miles per hour?

A) $\dfrac{k + 75}{2}$

B) $\dfrac{k - 75}{2}$

C) $k + 75$

D) $2k + 75$

☐ PN ☐ WB

# UNIT | Foundations

## Chapters

## Overview

In this unit, we'll practice core skills and vocabulary that can be tested in a number of different question types. We'll learn to balance equations, work with exponents, and practice solving equations involving fractions and decimals.

## No Calculator!

These chapters build skills that you will use throughout both sections of the test. However, we recommend you make computations without your calculator in these chapters.

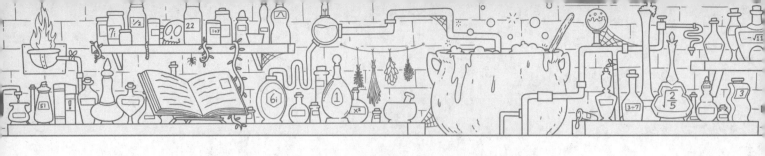

# Basic Algebra

*The key to manipulating algebraic equations is to make careful, balanced changes. As long as you play by the rules, you can do whatever you want!*

## NOTE

The letters $a$, $b$, $c$, $x$, $w$, $y$, and $z$ are common variable choices. You may have even seen worksheets where an empty box or a "?" is used.

### Algebra is all about exploring the unknown

In our art of translation phrasebook, we have the following line:

| English | Math |
|---|---|
| What, how much, a number | Some variable ($x$) |

Anytime there is something we don't know—the number of hours, the price of a hamburger, a person's age, etc.—we stick a symbol in as a placeholder and call that symbol a **variable**. The goal in algebra problems is to figure out what number(s) the variable represents (or, in math terms, what value you can **substitute** for the variable to make the expression true).

You might be able to solve easy problems just by staring at them. For example, you might look at "$7 + x = 13$" and think "Well $7 + 6$ is 13, so $x$ must be 6!" However, as problems get more complicated, this approach brings more and more space for errors. For tougher problems, we need a more concrete, systematic approach. And *that's* where <u>algebra</u> comes in.

## Make balanced changes to each side

Solving basic algebra problems is just a balancing act. The test writers will give you an algebra equation, like:

$$2x - 7 = -21$$

...and then they'll ask you to "solve for $x$." Which really just means that we need to strategically add, subtract, multiply, or divide until "$x$" is alone on one side of the equation.

But here's the key: we have to keep the equation **balanced**. Anything we do to the left side of the equal sign we must also do to the right side... otherwise, we throw off the balance and change the equation:

*Balanced!*

$$2x - 7 = -21$$
$$+7 \quad +7$$
$$2x = -14$$

*Not Balanced!*

$$2x - 7 = -21$$
$$+7$$
$$2x = -21$$

On the right, we made the mistake of only adding 7 to one side of the equation. We can tell at a glance that something's wrong... after all, how can $2x = -21$ when $2x - 7 = -21$? To avoid this, remember to always make step-by-step, **balanced changes** to each side of the equation.

## Write down your work to avoid errors

Making balanced changes is the most basic algebra skill we can cover. But in the rush of the test, it's often these basic skills that suffer. It's not just "careless" students who make "careless errors" – they can result from focusing so much on the tougher topics that you forget to actually work out the simpler steps. As a result, you forget to distribute a negative or you make a basic error of substitution. To avoid these errors, get in the habit of writing out careful, step-by-step work.

**Follow the step-by-step instructions** to complete the solution below.

| If $5x - 6 = 54$, then $x = ?$ | |
|---|---|
| 1. *Rewrite equation* | |
| 2. *Add 6 to both sides* | |
| 3. *Write the result* | |
| 4. *Divide both sides by 5* | |
| 5. *Write the result* | |

**Solve for _x_** in the problems below.

| Equation | $x = ?$ |
|---|---|
| 6.  $12x + 12 = 12$ | |
| 7.  $3x - 7 = 14$ | |
| 8.  $2x + 3 = 4x - 8$ | |
| 9.  $-13x = -3x + 30$ | |
| 10.  $15x - 10 = 12x + 11$ | |

## TIP

Basic Algebra skills and a little balanced experimentation here and there are the keys to solving even the toughest algebra problems on the test.

**Answers:**   1. $5x - 6 = 54$   2. $5x - 6 + 6 = 54 + 6$   3. $5x = 60$   4. $5x \div 5 = 60 \div 5$   5. $x = 12$

6. 0   7. 7   8. 11/2   9. –3   10. 7

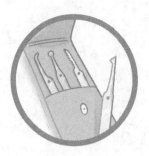

## You can tinker with problems to find a solution

As long as you follow the rule of making balanced changes to each side (as well as those pesky rules about not dividing by zero, etc.) you are **free** to manipulate the equation as you see fit. If you feel like adding 1,000,000 and then subtracting 1,000,000 to each side, you'd be totally free to do that! We wouldn't recommend it, but, hey, you're the boss. *Experimentation* is a skill that can be a huge help on tougher problems.

## EXAMPLE 1

What value of *x* satisfies the equation $\frac{13}{15}x - \frac{8}{15}x = \frac{3}{5} + \frac{3}{20}$ ?

## PORTAL

When you have fractional coefficients, you add and subtract them following normal fraction rules.

For more on working with fractions, turn to page 439.

SOLUTION

**Start by combining like terms on the left.** Both terms have the same denominators and one *x*, so let's combine and simplify:

(1) *combine* $\qquad \frac{5}{15}x = \frac{3}{5} + \frac{3}{20}$

(2) *simplify* $\qquad \frac{1}{3}x = \frac{3}{5} + \frac{3}{20}$

**Now clean up the right side.** We have two constants.
To combine these fractions, we need a common denominator:

(3) *find C.D.* $\quad \frac{1}{3}x = \frac{3}{5} + \frac{3}{20} \Rightarrow \frac{12}{20} + \frac{3}{20} \Rightarrow \frac{15}{20} \Rightarrow \frac{3}{4}$

*so...* $\qquad \frac{1}{3}x = \frac{3}{4}$

**Finally, make balanced changes to isolate x.** To get *x* by itself, we need to get rid of that fraction by multiplying *both sides* by 3.

(4) *balance* $\quad (3)\frac{1}{3}x = \frac{3}{4}(3)$

*voila!* $\qquad x = \boxed{\frac{9}{4}}$

# Distributive Property

The distributive property states that for all real numbers $a$, $b$, and $c$:

$$a(\overset{\frown}{b + c}) = ab + bc$$

If we translate this into words, it means that when multiplying an expression where two or more things are added, you can "distribute" that multiplication to each term rather than first simplify the parentheses.

$$2(3 + 5) \;=\; 2(8) \;=\; \mathbf{16}$$
$$2(\overset{\frown}{3 + 5}) \;=\; 6 + 10 \;=\; \mathbf{16}$$

When working with numbers, as in this example, you can go either way, but the distributive property is important once variables get involved.

# EXAMPLE 2

If $3(x + 4) = 2(10 - x) + 17$, then $x = ?$

SOLUTION

There are balanced changes we could make here, but none of them are particularly nice or helpful. The best first step is to apply the distributive property to both sides:

(1) *Distribute*

$$3(\overset{\frown}{x + 4}) = 2(\overset{\frown}{10 - x}) + 17$$
$$3x + 12 = 20 - 2x + 17$$

(2) *Simplify*

$$3x + 12 = -2x + 37$$

Next, make balanced changes to move all terms with an $x$ to one side. Let's move the $x$'s to the left, and everything else to the right.

(3) Add $\mathbf{2x}$

$$3x + 12 + \mathbf{2x} = -2x + 37 + \mathbf{2x}$$
$$5x + 12 = 37$$

Continued on next page →

| ④ Subtract 12 | $5x + 12 - 12 = 37 - 12$ |
| | $5x = 25$ |
| ⑤ Divide by 5 | $\boxed{x = 5}$ |

## EXAMPLE 3

If $\dfrac{4m + 2}{m - 7} = 9$ what is the value of $m$?

SOLUTION

**First, look at the left side.** We have a fraction with the variable we're looking for, $m$, in both the numerator and denominator. That's messy. Let's get rid of the fraction by multiplying **both sides** of the equation by the denominator, then make more balanced changes until $m$ is all by itself.

| ① Multiply by $(m - 7)$ | $(m - 7)\dfrac{4m + 2}{m - 7} = 9(m - 7)$ |
| | $4m + 2 = 9m - 63$ |
| ② Subtract 4m | $4m - 4m + 2 = 9m - 4m - 63$ |
| | $2 = 5m - 63$ |
| ③ Add 63 | $2 + 63 = 5m - 63 + 63$ |
| | $65 = 5m$ |
| ④ Divide by 5 | $\dfrac{65}{5} = \dfrac{5m}{5}$ |
| ...booyah! | $\boxed{13} = m$ |

**TIP**

It's completely okay (and often necessary) to multiply both sides of an equation by an **expression**, such as $(m - 7)$, rather than just a variable or constant.

Remember, you can do anything you want to the equation as long as you keep it balanced!

# PORTAL

Balancing and substitution form the very **heart** of algebra. You'll use these basic skills to solve even the toughest systems of equations problems.

Don't believe us? Turn to page 568 to see for yourself!

## You can substitute equivalent values for variables

Whenever you are given (or discover through work) another "name" for a variable, you can **plug in** that new name anywhere the variable appears. For example, if we have the equation:

$$5k + a = 26$$

...and we learn that **$k = 2$**, we can go back and **substitute** in 2 anywhere we see $k$, and that will help us move forward in the problem:

$$5(2) + a = 26$$
$$10 + a = 26$$
$$10 - 10 + a = 26 - 10$$
$$a = 16$$

This also works if you are told that **$k = a - 2$**. In this case, we just replace every $k$ with an $(a - 2)$:

$$5(a - 2) + a = 26$$
$$5a - 10 + a = 26$$
$$6a - 10 = 26$$
$$6a = 36$$
$$a = 6$$

The name's k, but YOU can call me (a − 2)!

# Parentheses

Please use them! We've seen far too many students forget to place parentheses before they substitute, only to accidentally forget a negative and miss easy points.

**Solve for *d*** by following each step below.

| $3a - b - c = d$<br>If $a = -2$, $b = -5$, and $c = 1$, then $d = $ ? | |
|---|---|
| 1. Rewrite equation | $3a - b - c = d$ |
| 2. Substitute for a | |
| 3. Substitute for b | |
| 4. Substitute for c | |
| 5. Simplify | |
| 6. Solve | $d =$ |

**Substitute the given values** to solve each problem below.

| $a = 3$ $\quad$ $b = 4$ $\quad$ $c = -2$ |
|---|
| 7. $2a + 7 =$ |
| 8. $b - 2c =$ |
| 9. $2a + 3b - 4c =$ |
| 10. $a^2 + 2a + c =$ |
| 11. $ab - bc + ac =$ |

# Practice Problems

*Use your new skills to answer each question.*

---

**1**

*(handwritten: PN)*

If $\frac{m}{m+n} = \frac{5}{7}$, what is the value of $\frac{3n}{m}$?

*(handwritten: $\frac{5}{5+2} = \frac{5}{7}$     $\frac{3(2)}{5}$)*

A) $\frac{10}{7}$

B) $\frac{6}{5}$  *(circled)*

C) $\frac{1}{2}$

D) $\frac{15}{2}$

---

**2**

$$\frac{4}{7}x - \frac{1}{2} = \frac{2}{7}x + \frac{13}{14}$$

What is the value of $x$ in the equation above?

*(handwritten: $\frac{4}{7}x = \frac{2}{7}x + \frac{20}{14}$     $\frac{2}{7}x = \frac{20}{14}$     $x = \frac{20}{14} \cdot \frac{7}{2} = 5$)*

---

**3**

If $a = kb$ where $k$ is a constant and $a = 12$ when $b = 15$, what is the value of $a$ when $b = 12$?

A) $\frac{4}{5}$

B) $\frac{5}{4}$

C) $9\frac{3}{5}$  *(circled)*

D) $12$

**4**

If 7 less than 5 times a number is two more than twice that number, what is the result when the number is added to 8 ?

$$5x - 7 = 2x + 2$$

A) $\frac{5}{7}$

B) 3

C) 11

D) 17

**5**

If $\frac{2}{3}x = 6y$, and $x$ and $y$ are non-zero numbers, what is the value of $\frac{x-y}{y}$ ?

A) 9

B) 8

C) 3

D) $-\frac{8}{9}$

**6**

Which of the following is a solution to the inequality $4x - 6 \geq 5x - 2$ ?

A) $-1$
B) $-2$
C) $-3$
D) $-4$

**7**

If the points (5, 20) and (3, $a$) are solutions for the equation $y = kx$, where $k$ is a constant, what is the value of $a$ ?

A) 5
B) 6
Ⓒ 12
D) 19

**8**

If $\frac{10}{4-n} = -c$, what is the value of $n$ when $c = 10$ ?

A) −5
B) −3
C) 3
Ⓓ 5

**9**

If $\frac{1}{2}(n - 12) = -5$, what is the value of $4n + 5$ ?

A) 2
B) 6
Ⓒ 13
D) 14

$$\tfrac{1}{2}n - 6 = -5$$

$$\tfrac{1}{2}n - 1 = 0 \qquad 4n = 8$$

**10**

If $6x + 1$ is 3 more than $3x + 13$, what is the value of 8 subtracted from 4 times $x$ ?

Ⓐ 12
B) −5
C) −20
D) −28

$$4x - 8$$

$$6x + 1 = 3x + 16$$

$$3x - 15 = 0$$

$$4x - 20 = 0$$

# Exponents

*Your one-stop-shop for all things powerful.*

..................................................................................................

## Exponents are a shorthand for multiplication

*Multiplication* is something of a shorthand for **repeated addition**. For example, when we say "2 × 3" it is equivalent to *adding 2 three times*:

$$2 \times 3 = 2 + 2 + 2$$

## TIP

You can think of even lonely terms like "*x*" or "*y²*" as having a hidden coefficient and power of 1.

For example, $x = 1x^1$.

Similarly, *exponents* can be thought of as **repeated multiplication**.

$$2^3 = 2 \times 2 \times 2$$

In this example, we are multiplying 3 copies of the number 2 together. 2 is called the <u>base</u> and 3 is the <u>exponent</u> (aka the <u>power</u>). Often, the base will be a variable, like *x*, rather than a number. Any number in front of the base is called the <u>coefficient</u>. All of this together is called a <u>term</u>.

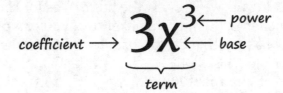

## PORTAL

To see what happens when the exponent is a **variable**, like *x*, check out Exponential Models on page 666.

## Quick Vocab

A **monomial** is an expression consisting of a <u>single</u> term (e.g., $15x^3$)

A **binomial** consists of the sum of <u>two</u> terms. (e.g., $2x^2 + 2x$ or $xy^2 + 5z$)

A **polynomial** is a catchall word for the sum of <u>any number</u> of terms. This includes monomials, binomials, and one-to-infinity-nomials.

**Identify the different terms** of the polynomials, and for each term identify the coefficient, base, and power.

| $5x^4 + 12x^3 + 7x$ | | | |
|---|---|---|---|
| term | coefficient | base | power |
| 1. $5x^4$ | 5 | x | 4 |
| 2. | | | |
| 3. | | | |

| $6x^5 - 4x^2 + 3y^2 - 2y + 4$ | | | |
|---|---|---|---|
| term | coefficient | base | power |
| 4. | | | |
| 5. | | | |
| 6. | | | |
| 7. | | | |
| 8. | | | |

**Answers:** *Bottom of next page*

## TIP

Later on, we'll manipulate terms so they DO have like bases. For now, just remember that if the bases are different, they can't get together.

## Exponent rules apply to like bases

Coming up, we'll review the basic rules for combining terms with exponents. But first a blanket rule: **you can only combine terms with like bases**. "Like bases" just means the bases are the same number of variable. This is why we can't further simplify "$(a^2)(x^3)$", but we CAN do something about "$(a^2)(a^3)$."

*It just never worked with any of my x's.*

| Exponent Rules | |
|---|---|
| Any number **raised to zero** is equal to **one**. | $x^0 = 1x^0 = 1(1) = 1$ |
| When you **multiply** like bases, **add** exponents. | $x^2 \cdot x^3 = (x \cdot x)(x \cdot x \cdot x) = x^5$ |
| When you **divide** like bases, **subtract** exponents. | $x^6 \div x^2 = \frac{x^6}{x^2} = \frac{(x \cdot x \cdot x \cdot x \cdot \cancel{x} \cdot \cancel{x})}{(\cancel{x} \cdot \cancel{x})} = x^4$ |
| When you **raise** a power to a power, **multiply** exponents. | $(x^2)^3 = (x \cdot x)(x \cdot x)(x \cdot x) = x^6$ |
| When you have a **negative exponent**, take the **reciprocal**. | $x^{-2} = \frac{1}{x^2}$ |
| When you have a **fractional exponent**, make it a **root**. | $x^{\frac{1}{2}} = \sqrt{x}$ |

**like terms (n.)**

Any terms with the same variable and exponent. For example:

- $2a$ and $3a$
- $6a^5$ and $8a^5$
- $4a^2b$ and $-3a^2b$

NOT $3a$ and $3a^2$

# Combining Like Terms

The simplest questions that test these exponent rules are basic algebra questions that require you to **combine like terms**. After all, "like terms" just means "terms with the same variable and exponent." Remember: we can combine $x + 2x$, and we can combine $x^2 + 2x^2$, but we can NOT combine $x + x^2$. Got it? Good. Let's get some practice.

## EXAMPLE 1

$$4x^2 + 7x - 12$$
$$-2x^2 + 3x - 5$$

What is the sum of the two given polynomials?

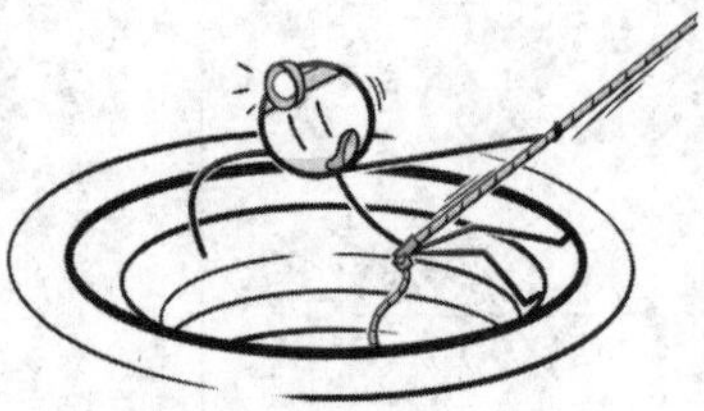

## PORTAL

If you can't wait, you'll find more systems of equations than you can handle on page 568.

**SOLUTION**

This is a "systems of equations" problem, which we'll dive into in a later chapter. To add these polynomials, we'll need to **combine like terms** (terms where the variables *and exponents* are the same). In this problem, the like terms are conveniently aligned vertically! Let's combine like terms:

$$\begin{array}{ccc} 4x^2 & +\ 7x & -\ 12 \\ +\ (-2x^2) & +\ (+\ 3x) & +\ (-5) \\ \hline 2x^2 & +\ 10x & -\ 17 \end{array}$$

And that's it! By adding the like terms in each column, we get our answer: $\mathbf{2x^2 + 10x - 17}$.

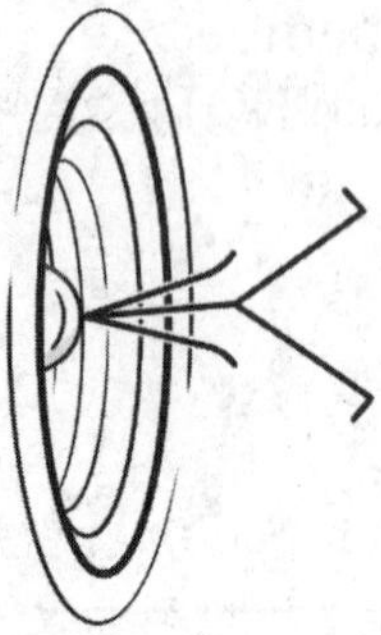

## PORTAL

This problem is an example of a special type of problem we'll cover in greater detail in the Pattern Matching chapter on page 516.

## EXAMPLE 2

$$(4x^2 - 11x + 3) - 3(x^2 + 4x - 5)$$

If the expression above is rewritten in the form $ax^2 + bx + c$, where $a$, $b$, and $c$ are constants, which of the following is the value of $b + c$?

A) $-35$
B) $-11$
C) $-5$
D) 18

SOLUTION

Before we can combine like terms in this problem, we have to take care of the parentheses (remember your order of operations!). The parentheses around **(4x² – 11x + 3)** are just grouping them, so we can safely remove them without changing anything. But before we can combine like terms, we first need to distribute the **–3** across **(x² + 4x – 5):**

① *distribute*        $-3\,(x^2 + 4x - 5) = -3x^2 - 12x + 15$

Now we can put it together and find like terms.

② *combine like terms*

$$4x^2 - 11x + 3 - 3x^2 - 12x + 15$$
$$x^2 - 23x + 18$$

We have now rewritten the original expression in the exact form we need! If we stack them, we can figure out what *a*, *b*, and *c* are.

③ *stack & spot*

$$x^2 - 23x + 18$$
$$ax^2 + bx + c$$

$a = 1$
$b = -23$
$c = 18$

If we match patterns between these two expressions, we see that **a = 1**, **b = –23**, and **c = 18**. Now we just need to find **b + c**

④ *add!*        $b + c = -23 + 18 = \boxed{-5}$

**C**

---

## Watch Signs!

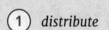

Most students who miss this problem either forget to distribute the negative in **–3** or miss that **b** must be *negative* 23, not just 23. Can you see why that is?

If you made one of these errors, what precautions could you take to avoid making the same mistake again?

---

## EXAMPLE 3

For non-zero values of *a* and *b*, which of the following expressions is equivalent to $\dfrac{35a^2b^4}{7ab^2}$ ?

A) $5ab^2$

B) $5a^2b^2$

C) $5a^3b^6$

D) $28ab^2$

## Pick Numbers!

This is a good time to practice a picking numbers workaround! Try picking $a = 3$ and $b = 2$. Plug those values into the original fraction and write down the result. Then do the same for each answer choice until you get a match.

---

**SOLUTION**

Our goal is to simplify the given fraction using our exponent rules. Remember that a fraction bar is basically a **division** symbol, so we need to match up like bases and **subtract** exponents.

(1) *align like bases*

$$\frac{35a^2b^4}{7ab^2} = \frac{35}{7} \cdot \frac{a^2}{a} \cdot \frac{b^4}{b^2}$$

(2) *subtract exponents*

$$= 5 \cdot a^{2-1} \cdot b^{4-2}$$

(3) *simplify*

$$= 5 \cdot a^1 \cdot b^2$$

Our answer is **$5ab^2$**, or choice A!

**A**

---

## EXAMPLE 4

$$2(a^2 + 2ab - 8ab^2) - (2a^2 + 3ab - 5ab^2)$$

Which of the following is equivalent to the above expression?

A)  $3a^2 + 5ab - 13ab^2$
B)  $ab - 11ab^2$
C)  $ab - 21ab^2$
D)  $4a^2 - ab - 3ab^2$

---

## NOTE

Anytime a term has no coefficient, there is secretly a 1 hidden there. That's why **a = 1** in the previous question.

That's also why here you multiply each term by **–1** when you see a minus sign outside of the parentheses.

---

**SOLUTION**

When you first look at this problem, the terms with multiple letters might look complicated. But they don't actually make it any harder! The first step is the same as the last problem – **distribute across the parentheses**, being careful with negative signs.

$$2 (a^2 + 2ab - 8ab^2) - 1(2a^2 + 3ab - 5ab^2)$$

$$2a^2 + 4ab - 16ab^2 \quad - 2a^2 - 3ab + 5ab^2$$

Now we need to combine like terms. This is just pattern matching.

$$(2 - 2)a^2 + (4 - 3)ab + (-16 + 5)ab^2$$

$$= 0a^2 + 1ab - 11ab^2$$

$$= \boxed{ab - 11ab^2}$$

**B**

## EXAMPLE 5

For $i = \sqrt{-1}$, what is the sum of $(18 - 6i) + (-15 + 13i)$ ?

A) $33 + 7i$
B) $3 - 7i$
C) $10i$
D) $3 + 7i$

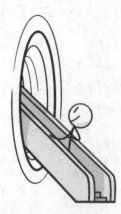

## PORTAL

To learn about complex numbers, turn to page 623.

SOLUTION

This problem is technically working with complex numbers, but you don't have to know a thing about them to solve it! The parentheses here are just for grouping, so we can remove them and, you guessed it, combine like terms:

$$18 - 6i - 15 + 13i$$
$$= (18 - 15) + (-6 + 13)i$$
$$= \boxed{3 + 7i}$$

D

## You can CREATE like bases with substitution

When basic algebra problems get tougher, they usually involve the use of **substitution** and **exponent rules**. As usual, your job involves combining like terms and making balanced manipulations to reach your goal. However, sometimes you'll need to first create "like bases" before you can combine terms. Remember, we can always substitute one term for an equivalent one, so we could change **27** to **3³**, or **25** to **5²** if it helps us out. Let's look at an example where this helps.

## TIP

Any fraction can be separated out if it helps you solve the problem:

e.g., $\dfrac{a}{b} = a \cdot \dfrac{1}{b}$

This can help on problems with fractions in the exponent.

## EXAMPLE 6

If $4x - 2y = 7$, what is the value of $\dfrac{16^x}{4^y}$ ?

A) $2^{3.5}$
B) $2^7$
C) $2^8$
D) $4^7$

**431**

First of all, we know that we are going to *somehow* use the info that $4x - 2y = 7$ to help us evaluate that complicated fraction. Let's keep that in mind as we work this problem.

Since $x$ and $y$ are both in exponents, let's try to combine terms by **finding a like base**. We could replace 16 with $4^2$ and work from there, or we could notice that **16 = $2^4$** and **4 = $2^2$**. That ends up being easier, so let's try that:

**①** *find like bases*
$$\frac{16^x}{4^y} = \frac{(2^4)^x}{(2^2)^y}$$

**②** *simplify*
$$\frac{16^x}{4^y} = \frac{(2^4)^x}{(2^2)^y} = \frac{2^{4x}}{2^{2y}} = 2^{4x-2y}$$

Aha! Notice anything familiar? We were told that **$4x - 2y = 7$,** so...

**③** *put it all together!*
$$\frac{16^x}{4^y} = 2^{4x-2y} = 2^7$$

B

## Fractional exponents are roots

To understand what is happening with fraction exponents, let's play with an example. We know that raising a power to another power means we multiply exponents. That means raising $x^2$ to the power of $1/2$ **undoes** the squaring. This is the same exact operation as taking the square root.

$$(x^2)^{\frac{1}{2}} = x^{\frac{2}{2}} = x \qquad\qquad (x^2)^{\frac{1}{2}} = \sqrt{x^2} = x$$

The same thing happens with cubed roots and powers of $\frac{1}{3}$:

$$(x^3)^{\frac{1}{3}} = x^{\frac{3}{3}} = x \qquad\qquad (x^3)^{\frac{1}{3}} = \sqrt[3]{x^3} = x$$

As a general rule, raising to the $\frac{1}{n}$ power is equal to taking the $n$th root:

$$x^{\frac{1}{n}} = \sqrt[n]{x}$$

# You can split and combine roots as needed

You can **split roots** across multiplication. For example:

$$\sqrt{12x} = \sqrt{4} \cdot \sqrt{3x} = 2\sqrt{3x}$$

**NOTE**

You cannot combine roots of different orders, such as:

e.g., $\sqrt{2} \cdot \sqrt[3]{3}$

When multiplying, you can **combine** two roots of the same order:

$$\sqrt{2} \cdot \sqrt{3} = \sqrt{6}$$

## EXAMPLE 7

$$\frac{2}{\sqrt{6}} + \frac{3}{\sqrt{15}} = ?$$

A)  $\dfrac{5}{\sqrt{6} + \sqrt{15}}$

B)  $\dfrac{5}{\sqrt{21}}$

C)  $\dfrac{2\sqrt{15} + 3\sqrt{6}}{\sqrt{21}}$

D)  $\dfrac{2\sqrt{15} + 3\sqrt{6}}{3\sqrt{10}}$

## TIP

If none of the answer choices had roots in the denominator, you would have to **clear the square root from the denominator**.

To do this, multiply the numerator and denominator by that root, then simplify:

$$\frac{2}{\sqrt{10}} \cdot \frac{\sqrt{10}}{\sqrt{10}} = \frac{2\sqrt{10}}{10} = \boxed{\frac{\sqrt{10}}{5}}$$

**SOLUTION**

To combine fractions, we need a **common denominator**. The *product* of the denominators is always an option... It might not be the least common denominator, but that's fine for now:

**(1)** *rewrite the equation* $\qquad \frac{2}{\sqrt{6}} + \frac{3}{\sqrt{15}}$

**(2)** *make common denominators* $\qquad \frac{\sqrt{15}}{\sqrt{15}} \cdot \frac{2}{\sqrt{6}} + \frac{3}{\sqrt{15}} \cdot \frac{\sqrt{6}}{\sqrt{6}}$

$$\frac{2\sqrt{15}}{\sqrt{90}} + \frac{3\sqrt{6}}{\sqrt{90}}$$

**(3)** *combine fractions* $\qquad \frac{2\sqrt{15} + 3\sqrt{6}}{\sqrt{90}}$

This isn't an answer choice, so let's see if we can simplify:

**(4)** *simplify* $\qquad \frac{2\sqrt{15} + 3\sqrt{6}}{\sqrt{9 \cdot 10}}$

$$\frac{2\sqrt{15} + 3\sqrt{6}}{\sqrt{9} \cdot \sqrt{10}}$$

$$\boxed{\frac{2\sqrt{15} + 3\sqrt{6}}{3\sqrt{10}}}$$

**D**

## EXAMPLE 8

If $r = 2\sqrt[3]{5}$ and $3r = \sqrt[3]{5s}$, what is the value of $s$ ?

SOLUTION

We are told that $r = 2\sqrt[3]{5}$, so the first thing we do is plug in:

(1) *plug in for r*     $3(2\sqrt[3]{5}) = \sqrt[3]{5s}$

   $6\sqrt[3]{5} = \sqrt[3]{5s}$

From here we have **two options** for how to solve for *s*.

**Option A:** We see cube roots on both sides and both sides are connected by multiplication, making it easy to **cube both sides**.

(2) *cube both sides*     $\left(6\sqrt[3]{5}\right)^3 = \left(\sqrt[3]{5s}\right)^3$

   $(216)(5) = 5s$

(3) *divide by 5*     $216 = s$

**Option B:** We can **split cube roots** across multiplication if it makes it easier for us to reach our goal:

(2) *split the cube root*     $6\sqrt[3]{5} = \sqrt[3]{5s}$

   $6\sqrt[3]{5} = (\sqrt[3]{5})(\sqrt[3]{s})$

(3) *divide by $(\sqrt[3]{5})$*     $6 = \sqrt[3]{s}$

(4) *cube both sides*     $(6)^3 = (\sqrt[3]{s})^3$

   $216 = s$

## TIP

Remember your fractional exponent rules:

$$x^{\frac{1}{n}} = \sqrt[n]{x}$$

We can split roots into their component pieces by following exponent rules:

$$(5s)^{\frac{1}{3}} = (5)^{\frac{1}{3}}(s)^{\frac{1}{3}}$$

# Practice Problems

*Select the best answer choice for each equation.*

---

**1**

$$3(x^2 - 2x + 4) - 2(x - 7)$$

Which of the following expressions is equivalent to the one shown above?

A) $x^2 - 9x + 4$
B) $x^2 - 3x - 3$
C) $3x^2 - 8x + 26$
D) $3x^2 - 3$

---

**2**

$$3a^2 - 6a + 7$$
$$7a^2 + 9a - 13$$

Which of the following is equivalent to the sum of the two expressions above?

A) $10a^2 + 15a - 6$
B) $10a^2 + 3a + 6$
C) $10a^2 + 15a + 20$
D) $10a^2 + 3a - 6$

---

**3**

$$(3 + 2i) - (-5 - 3i)$$

Given that $i = \sqrt{-1}$, which of the following expressions is equivalent to the one shown above?

A) $8 + 5i$
B) $8 - i$
C) $-2 + 5i$
D) $-2 - i$

**4**

$$f(x) = 3x^2 - 2x + 4$$
$$g(x) = -x^2 + 7x - 2$$

For the functions given above, $f(x) + g(x) = h(x)$. If $h(x)$ is given by the equation $h(x) = ax^2 + bx + c$, where $a$, $b$, and $c$ are constants, what is the value of $ab$?

A) −20
B) −10
C) 0
D) 10

**5**

$$2(ab^2 + a^2b + ab) - (4ab - 3a^2b - 2ab^2)$$

Which of the following expressions is equivalent to the expression above?

A) $-2a^2b - 2ab^2 - ab$
B) $-2ab - 2a^2b - ab^2$
C) $4ab^2 + 5a^2b - 2ab$
D) $-ab + 3a^2b - 3ab^2$

**6**

Which of the following is equal to the sum of $5a^5 + 3a^3 - 7$ and $-2a^4 - 4a^3 - 5a^2 + a$?

A) $3a^5 - 2a^3 - 6$
B) $5a^5 - 2a^4 + 3a^2 - 7$
C) $5a^5 - 2a^4 + 7a^3 - 5a^2 - 7a$
D) $5a^5 - 2a^4 - a^3 - 5a^2 + a - 7$

**7**

If $\sqrt{108}$ is equal to $2x\sqrt{3}$, and $x$ is greater than zero, what is the value of $x$?

A) 3
B) 18
C) 27
D) 54

**8**

$$2\sqrt{9a^3b^4c}$$

Which of the following is equivalent to the expression above?

A) $6ab^2\sqrt{ac}$
B) $\sqrt{18ab^2c}$
C) $18abc\sqrt{a^2b^3}$
D) $6a^2b^2\sqrt{ac}$

**9**

If $\sqrt{ab} = \sqrt{bc}$, $\sqrt{ac} = \sqrt{4c^4}$, and $a$, $b$, and $c$ are greater than zero, what is the value of $c$?

A) $\dfrac{1}{4}$

B) $\dfrac{1}{2}$

C) $2$

D) $4$

**10**

$$\left(\frac{27}{a^6b^{12}}\right)^{-\frac{2}{3}} (12a^5b)^{\frac{1}{2}}$$

Which of the following is equivalent to the above expression?

A) $\dfrac{2a^8b^{12}\sqrt{3ab}}{27}$

B) $\dfrac{2a^8b^{12}\sqrt{3ab}}{3}$

C) $\dfrac{12a^6b^8\sqrt{b}}{9}$

D) $\dfrac{2a^6b^8\sqrt{3ab}}{9}$

**438**

# Fractions

*aka "the bunk beds of numbers"*

## NOTE

Fractions are not **integers**. Integers include all of the whole numbers, including zero and negative versions of the counting numbers.

Together, fractions and integers are sometimes referred to as *rational numbers*.

Many high schoolers are error-prone when working with fractions. Perhaps it's because they learned these rules way back in elementary and middle school, and haven't gotten much practice since. So, let's review!

- The **numerator** is the quantity above the bar (top bunk).

- The **denominator** is the quantity below the bar (bottom bunk).

- In **improper fractions**, the numerator is larger than the denominator (e.g., 3/2).

- Improper fractions can be rewritten as a **mixed number**: a combination of an integer and a proper fraction.

    *Example:* $\dfrac{12}{5} = \dfrac{10}{5} + \dfrac{2}{5} = 2\dfrac{2}{5}$

- The **reciprocal** of a fraction is what you get if you flip the numerator and denominator (switch bunks).

    *Example:* $\dfrac{2}{3}$ and $\dfrac{3}{2}$ are reciprocals.

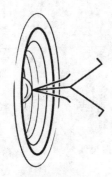

## PORTAL

If you multiply a fraction by its reciprocal, it will always equal one.

Negative reciprocals show up later when we talk about lines with **perpendicular slopes** on page 464.

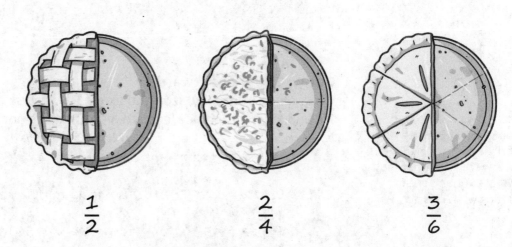

$$\frac{1}{2} \qquad \frac{2}{4} \qquad \frac{3}{6}$$

*The same quantity displayed with different denominators*

# Use the LCM to find the LCD!

You can't add or subtract fractions until they have the *same denominator*. Usually, this requires finding the **least common denominator** (LCD). To find the LCD of a set of fractions, all you have to do is find the least common multiple of their denominators.

---

## EXAMPLE 1

What is the least common denominator of the fractions $\frac{1}{12}$, $\frac{2}{15}$, and $\frac{4}{27}$?

A)  3
B)  150
C)  540
D)  1,620

**Option 1: Solve head-on with factor trees**
The least common denominator will be the LCM of 12, 15, and 27. We could list out the multiples of each looking for a match, but it's faster to find the prime factorization:

| 12 | 15 | 27 |
|---|---|---|
| ③   4 | ③ ⑤ | ③   9 |
| ② ② | | ③ ③ |
| $12 = 2^2 \times 3$ | $15 = 3 \times 5$ | $27 = 3^3$ |

So our LCM needs to have at least two 2's, three 3's, and one 5.

$$\text{LCM} = 2^2 \times 3^3 \times 5 = \boxed{540}$$

**Option 2: Work backwards!**
We can **use our calculator** to divide each answer choice by 12, 15, and 27. If any choice leads to a decimal, it's not a multiple!

A. 3 – This is a factor, not a multiple!

B. 150 ÷ 12 = 12.5. ✗ 150 is not a multiple of 12.

Ⓒ. 540 ÷ 12 = 45 ✓   540 ÷ 15 = 36 ✓   540 ÷ 27 = 20 ✓

# NOTE

Usually, we want to start from the middle when we work backwards. In this case, we're looking for the **SMALLEST** number, so starting with A is safer.

## Use common denominators to add fractions

When we add fractions with the same denominator, we just add the numerators. Pretty simple:

$$\frac{1}{3} + \frac{1}{3} = \frac{2}{3}$$

But let's look at what we're doing when we add the fractions $\frac{2}{3}$ and $\frac{1}{2}$.

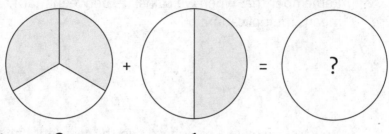

Pieces left → $\frac{2}{3}$ + $\frac{1}{2}$ = ?
Total pieces →

Exactly how much total pie do we have in the picture above? In order to figure this out, we need to find a **common denominator** for our fractions. Or, in tastier terms, cut the pies into **pieces of equal size**. The smallest common multiple of 2 and 3 is 6, so cut each pie into sixths:

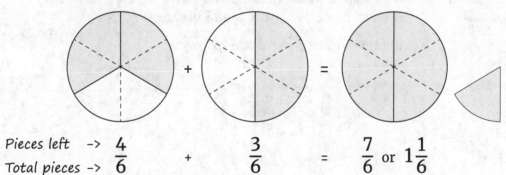

Pieces left → $\frac{4}{6}$ + $\frac{3}{6}$ = $\frac{7}{6}$ or $1\frac{1}{6}$
Total pieces →

Notice that for each pie we changed both the **total number of pieces** (denominator) and the **number of pieces remaining** (numerator). This is why we multiply the top and bottom of a fraction by the same number when changing denominators.

## TO ADD FRACTIONS:

(1) *Find a common denominator*

(2) *Rewrite each fraction as an equivalent fraction with that denominator.*

(3) *Add the numerators.*

## Subtraction works just like addition

We can always think of subtracting as **adding a negative value**. The process for subtracting fractions is the same as for adding them except, in the last step, you **subtract** numerators instead of add!

## Multiply across the numerator and denominator

Let's start by thinking about what it means when we multiply fractions. Remember that when we translate between math and English, " *of* " means multiplication:

$$\frac{2}{4} \times \frac{2}{3} = ?$$

$$\frac{2}{4} \text{ of } \frac{2}{3} = ?$$

Now say we have <u>a pie where two-thirds is left</u>. If we eat two-fourths of the *remaining* two-thirds, we need to divide up the pie into smaller pieces. A logical approach would be to take **two-fourths of each big piece.**

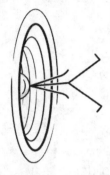

## PORTAL

The processes for combining fractions continue to work even when variables get involved. To see this in action, check out the Advanced Algebra chapter on page 528.

When we cut each big slice into 4 parts, we end up with **12 total pieces**.

If we take 2 small slices from the two 2 original pieces, we eat **4 small pieces**.

In other words, we did the following:

$$\frac{2}{4} \times \frac{2}{3} = \frac{2 \cdot 2}{4 \cdot 3} = \frac{4}{12}$$

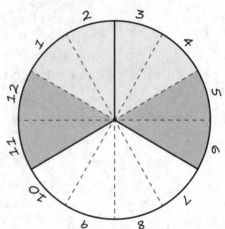

## TO MULTIPLY FRACTIONS:

①  *Multiply across the numerators*

②  *Multiply across the denominators*

③  *Simplify*

## TIP

A number doesn't change if you divide by 1, so you can always write integers as fractions with 1 as a denominator.

e.g., $2 = \frac{2}{1}$

## To divide by a fraction, multiply by the reciprocal

Remember that the reciprocal of a fraction is what you get when you switch (or "flip") the numerator and the denominator. So if you are asked to divide by a fraction, **flip the fraction** and **multiply** as usual:

$$\frac{2}{3} \div \frac{3}{4} = \frac{2}{3} \times \frac{4}{3}$$

*flip and multiply*

$$2 \div \frac{1}{5} = \frac{2}{1} \times \frac{5}{1}$$

*flip and multiply*

## Fractions within fractions (aka fractionception)

When the numerator and/or denominator of a fraction contains another fraction, just treat it as a division problem:

$$\frac{\frac{7}{8}}{\frac{3}{4}} = \frac{7}{8} \div \frac{3}{4} = \frac{7}{8} \times \frac{4}{3}$$

**Use your fraction skills** to rewrite each expression as a single fraction.

1. $\frac{3}{4} + \frac{2}{3} =$ 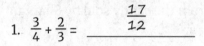 $\frac{17}{12}$

2. $\frac{1}{2} + \frac{3}{7} =$ _____

3. $\frac{5}{8} - \frac{1}{4} =$ _____

4. $\frac{1}{3} + \frac{4}{3} - \frac{1}{6} =$ _____

5. $3 + \frac{3}{8} =$ _____

6. $5 - \frac{12}{7} =$ _____

7. $\frac{2}{5} + \frac{1}{3} + \frac{3}{4} =$ _____

8. $(\frac{3}{5})(\frac{2}{7}) =$ _____

9. $(\frac{4}{3})(\frac{1}{8}) =$ _____

10. $\frac{4}{3} \div \frac{1}{2} =$ _____

11. $\frac{15}{7} \div \frac{3}{2} =$ _____

12. $\dfrac{\frac{2}{3} + \frac{1}{4}}{\frac{5}{7} - \frac{1}{3}} =$ _____

13. $\dfrac{\frac{1}{2}(\frac{5}{8} - \frac{1}{4})}{3} =$ _____

**Answers:** *Bottom of next page.*

## Translating with Fractions

Let's revisit our Art of Translation phrasebook to check two new fraction-specific terms:

- "A number **per** a number" translates into a **fraction**. The first number is the numerator, per is the fraction bar, and the second number is the denominator.

Example:

| Harriet walked | 13 miles | per | 2 hours |
|---|---|---|---|
| H = | 13 mi | / | 2 hr |

- The word **of** still means **multiply**.

Example:

| x | is | one-half | of | y |
|---|---|---|---|---|
| x = | | $\frac{1}{2}$ | × | y |

## EXAMPLE 2

The school band is selling packs of candy for $2 each as a fundraiser. The band earns $3 profit per $10 of candy sold. If a case of candy has 75 packs in it and Shania sells two-thirds of a case, how much profit did the band earn from the candy sold by Shania?

A)  $  0.30
B)  $ 22.50
C)  $ 30.00
D)  $ 45.00

**Last Page:** 1. *given*  2. $\frac{13}{14}$  3. $\frac{3}{8}$  4. $\frac{3}{2}$  5. $\frac{27}{8}$  6. $\frac{23}{7}$  7. $\frac{89}{60}$

8. $\frac{6}{35}$  9. $\frac{1}{6}$  10. $\frac{8}{3}$  11. $\frac{10}{7}$  12. $\frac{77}{32}$  13. $\frac{1}{16}$

SOLUTION

First, establish our goal: We want to know the **profit** based on the amount of candy sold by Shania.

The school band is selling packs of candy for $2 each as a fundraiser. The band earns $3 profit per $10 of candy sold. If a case of candy has 75 packs in it and Shania sells two-thirds of a case, <u>how much profit</u> did the band earn from the <u>candy sold by Shania</u>?

So we want to first find the amount sold by Shania, *then* the profit. From here, let's write what we know and use that to translate toward our goal.

① *write what you know*

$$1 \text{ pack} = \$2$$

$$1 \text{ case} = 75 \text{ packs}$$

② *translate Shania's sales*

$$\text{Sold} = \frac{2}{3} \text{ of a case}$$

$$\text{Packs sold} = \frac{2}{3}(75) = 50 \text{ packs}$$

$$\text{Amount sold} = 50(\$2) = \$100$$

Now that we know Shania sold **50 packs** for **$100**, let's figure out how much profit that earned for the band. The band's earned profit is $3 **per** $10 of candy sold. We can write that as a fraction.

③ *translate profit to fraction*

$$\text{profit} = \frac{3}{10} \times (\text{sold})$$

So if we multiply $100 by $\frac{3}{10}$, we find the band's profit:

④ *apply to Shania's sales*

$$\text{profit} = \frac{3}{10} \times (\$100)$$

$$\text{profit} = \boxed{\$30}$$

C

## Decimals, powers of 10, and scientific notation

Our number system is based around **powers of 10**. Look at the three-digit number **324**. Each digit represents a multiple of a power of 10.

$$324 \;=\; 300 \;+\; 20 \;+\; 4$$
$$324 \;=\; (3 \times 100) \;+\; (2 \times 10) \;+\; (4 \times 1)$$
$$324 \;=\; (3 \times 10^2) \;+\; (2 \times 10^1) \;+\; (4 \times 10^0)$$

Now let's expand the decimal number **324.56** in the same way:

$$324.56 = (3 \times 10^2) + (2 \times 10^1) + (4 \times 10^0) + (5 \times 10^{-1}) + (6 \times 10^{-2})$$

**TIP**

Some questions will ask you to **round** your answers. Pay close attention to whether you're being asked to round to the nearest **hundred** or **hundredth**!

The position to the left or right of the decimal point tells you which power of 10 that digit is multiplied by. This is how we get our place value names:

$$
\begin{array}{ccccccccccc}
1 & , & 3 & 4 & 6 & , & 2 & 0 & 5 & . & 7 & 2 & 8 \\
\hline
10^6 & & 10^5 & 10^4 & 10^3 & & 10^2 & 10^1 & 10^0 & & 10^{-1} & 10^{-2} & 10^{-3}
\end{array}
$$

millions, hundred thousands, ten thousands, thousands, hundreds, tens, ones, tenths, hundredths, thousandths

## Scientific notation is a useful shorthand

Notice we can write 200 as $2 \times 10^2$ and we can write 0.02 as $2 \times 10^{-2}$. This shorthand is called **scientific notation**, and it helps shorten some numbers with an annoying amount of zeroes:

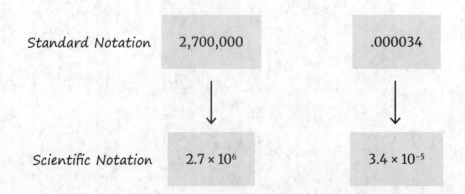

| | | |
|---|---|---|
| Standard Notation | 2,700,000 | .000034 |
| Scientific Notation | $2.7 \times 10^6$ | $3.4 \times 10^{-5}$ |

Scientific notation consists of a decimal number between 1 and 10 multiplied by a power of 10. The power of 10 tells you **how far to move the decimal**, and **which direction** to move it.

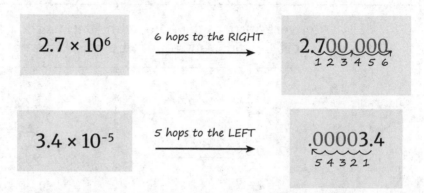

**Convert the numbers** into scientific notation (and vice versa).

| | Number | Scientific Notation |
|---|---|---|
| 1 | | $2.53 \times 10^5$ |
| 2 | 57,400,000,000 | |
| 3 | .000103 | |
| 4 | | $7.203 \times 10^{-8}$ |
| 5 | 1,000,000,000,000,000 | |

## Converting decimals to fractions

Converting a decimal to a fraction is as simple as putting any numbers to the right of the decimal in the numerator. In the denominator, put a 1 followed by as many zeroes as there are digits in the decimal.

.755 has three digits so it converts to $\frac{755}{1000}$.

If the resulting numerator and denominator have any factors in common then you can **simplify** the fraction:

In $\frac{755}{1000}$, 5 is a common factor. This simplifies to $\frac{151}{200}$.

Answers:  1. 253,000   2. $5.74 \times 10^{10}$   3. $1.03 \times 10^{-4}$   4. .00000007203   5. $1.0 \times 10^{15}$

## Converting fractions to decimals

An easy way to convert a fraction to a decimal is to treat the fraction bar as a **division** symbol. When you can, just plug it into your calculator!

**Convert** fractions to decimals and decimals to fractions. Once converted, simplify fractions and round decimals to the nearest hundredth.

1. $\frac{3}{4}$ = _____.75_____

2. 0.8 = _____

3. $\frac{5}{3}$ = _____

4. $\frac{3}{7}$ = _____

5. 0.34 = _____

6. 4.62 =

7. $\frac{2}{9}$ = _____

8. $2\frac{7}{8}$ = _____

9. .125 = _____

10. .501 = _____

## Comparing Fractions/Decimals

There are several ways you can approach situations when you need to determine which of two decimals or fractions is larger.

1. **Convert both of the numbers to decimals.** When you are comparing two decimal numbers, find the first digit from the left where the two numbers differ. The larger number will have the larger digit.

   Example:  3 4 2 . 1 6
   3 4 2 . 6 1
   ↑
   6 is bigger

2. **Convert to fractions with common denominators.** Once the fractions have a common denominator, the larger number will have the larger numerator.

3. **Subtract with your calculator (when able).** If you are comparing A and B, try plugging in "A − B". If the result is positive, A is bigger. If it is negative, B is bigger.

**Answers:**  1. *given*   2. $\frac{4}{5}$   3. 1.67   4. 0.43   5. $\frac{17}{50}$

6. $4\frac{31}{50}$   7. 0.22   8. 2.88   9. $\frac{1}{8}$   10. $\frac{501}{1000}$

**Fill in the blanks** by following the instructions below.

1. Place the following numbers in **ascending order**:

$$\frac{1}{3}, 0.3, \frac{2}{5}, 0.33, \frac{1}{4}$$

— — — — —

2. Place the following numbers in **descending order**:

$$-\frac{2}{3}, -\frac{3}{2}, 2.783, 15.4, \frac{26}{4}, \frac{7}{8}$$

— — — — — —

Scratch Work

**Answers:** 1. $\frac{1}{4}$, 0.3, 0.33, $\frac{1}{3}$, $\frac{2}{5}$  2. 15.4, $\frac{26}{4}$, 2.783, $\frac{7}{8}$, $-\frac{2}{3}$, $-\frac{3}{2}$

449

# Practice Problems

*Select the best answer choice for each equation.*

**1**

Which of the following numbers has the greatest value?

A) 0.125

B) 0.12$\overline{5}$

C) 0.1$\overline{25}$

D) 0.$\overline{125}$

**2**

Which of the following is the least common denominator of the fractions $\frac{5}{33}$, $\frac{7}{18}$, and $\frac{7}{24}$ ?

A) 3

B) 66

C) 198

D) 792

**3**

If the sum of $2\frac{1}{3}$ and $3\frac{1}{2}$ is written as an improper fraction in lowest terms, what is the sum of the numerator and denominator?

A) 12

B) 19

C) 25

D) 41

**4**

Which of the following expressions is equal to 16.3 billion?

A) $1.63 \times 10^{12}$

B) $1.63 \times 10^{11}$

C) $1.63 \times 10^{10}$

D) $1.63 \times 10^{9}$

**5**

Lucy has a craft kit with 1,200 beads. If $\frac{1}{3}$ of the beads are made of glass and 2 out of every 5 beads made of glass are blue, how many blue glass beads are in the kit?

A) 80
B) 160
C) 240
D) 400

**6**

In which of the following are $\frac{2}{3}$, $\frac{4}{9}$, and $\frac{1}{2}$ arranged in descending order?

A) $\frac{2}{3} > \frac{1}{2} > \frac{4}{9}$

B) $\frac{2}{3} > \frac{4}{9} > \frac{1}{2}$

C) $\frac{4}{9} > \frac{2}{3} > \frac{1}{2}$

D) $\frac{4}{9} > \frac{1}{2} > \frac{2}{3}$

**7**

Which of the following expresses the answer to .000094 − .000017 in scientific notation?

A) $77 \times 10^{-4}$
B) $77 \times 10^{-5}$
C) $7.7 \times 10^{-4}$
D) $7.7 \times 10^{-5}$

**8**

On a number line, which of the following numbers is exactly halfway between $\frac{1}{3}$ and 0.8 ?

A) 0.23
B) $.5\overline{6}$
C) .56
D) .73

$$\frac{2}{15} \underline{\quad\quad} \frac{3}{7}$$

Which of the following operations will produce the smallest result when placed in the blank in the expression above?

A) plus
B) minus
C) multiplied by
D) divided by

Suppose $a$ is a positive integer, $b$ is 2 times $a$, and $c$ is 3 times $a$. What is the least common denominator, in terms of $a$, of the fractions $\frac{1}{a}$, $\frac{1}{b}$, and $\frac{1}{c}$?

A) $2a$

B) $\frac{1}{6}a$

C) $6a$

D) $6a^3$

Which of the following is the decimal equivalent of $\frac{7}{22}$?

A) 0.3181818
B) $0.31\overline{8}$
C) $0.3\overline{18}$
D) $0.\overline{318}$

**12**

Let $p$, $q$, and $r$ be distinct prime numbers and suppose $a = pq^2$, $b = p^2q^3$, and $c = pq^2r^2$. If $\frac{1}{a} + \frac{1}{b} + \frac{1}{c} = \frac{n}{abc}$, what is the greatest common factor of $n$ and $abc$?

A) $pq^2$

B) $p^2q^4$

C) $pqr$

D) $p^2q^3r^2$

**13**

When $-2 \leq a \leq 3$ and $4 \leq b \leq 10$, the largest possible value for $\frac{3}{2b - a}$ is:

A) $\frac{1}{2}$

B) $\frac{3}{5}$

C) $\frac{3}{10}$

D) $\frac{3}{17}$

# UNIT | Lines & Functions

## Chapters

## Overview

In this unit, we'll learn about the connection between basic algebra, linear equations, and their illustrations: *graphs*. We'll also practice thinking of equations and graphs as *functions* built on inputs and outputs.

## No Calculator!

These questions often show up on the non-calculator section of the test. Unless otherwise marked, do not use your calculator.

# Equation of a Line

*In this chapter we learn the definition of slope, how to recognize the equation of a line, and what it means when lines are perpendicular and parallel.*

## Graphs are Illustrations

Every line on a graph is attached to a certain mathematical equation that tells you how to find points on that line. You can think of the graph of a line as simply an **illustration** of all the possible solutions to an equation. We can illustrate "$y = 2x + 1$" or "$y = -2x + 1$" just like we can illustrate "Marian Rejewski" or "Tobi the dog."

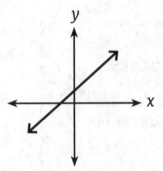

Marian Rejewski

$y = 2x + 1$

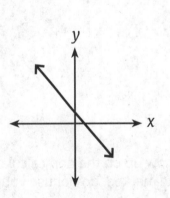

$y = -2x + 1$

Tobi the Dog

## Slope-Intercept Form

Before we can illustrate a linear equation, however, it helps to put the equation into the **slope-intercept form**.

$$y = mx + b$$

We call it the slope-intercept form because that's exactly what it tells us about the line. Just by looking at an equation in this form, we can see the line's **slope ($m$)** and its **$y$-intercept ($b$)**. And if you know these two things, you know exactly how to draw the line!

### $b$  y-intercept

Every line drawing's gotta start somewhere, and there's no better place than the point where the line crosses the y-axis, a.k.a. the **y-intercept**. This is the point where $x$ is zero.

### $m$  slope

The slope of a line is the relationship between two of its points. It tells us whether the line goes uphill or downhill, and just how steep of a hill we're talking. A **positive** slope runs uphill from left to right, while a **negative** slope runs downhill from left to right.

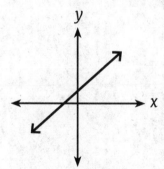

**Positive Slope**

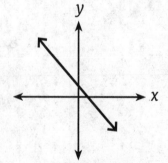

**Negative Slope**

**NOTE**

Sometimes, instead of a slope, you have a flat ground or a sheer cliff. When a line is a flat, horizontal line, it has a **slope of zero**. When a line is a straight, vertical line, its slope is **undefined**.

---

**TIP**

Remember, $x$ comes before $y$ in the alphabet, and $x$ comes before $y$ in the ordered pair!

## Key things to know about the coordinate plane

- Horizontal and vertical gridlines are **perpendicular**.

- The center point at (0, 0) is called the **origin**.

- Up/right from the origin is **positive**; down/left is **negative.**

- Every point is named by its **ordered pair**; first, write the $x$-coordinate for the point, then write the $y$-coordinate.

# TIP

Equations will not always be in slope-intercept form.

Whenever a line's equation is not in the form **y = mx +b**, rearrange it!

## Reading Slope-Intercept Form

Before we try some test problems, let's get used to reading the slope-intercept form. The table below contains a number of linear equations. For problems 1–5, make sure the equation is in the $y = mx + b$ form and determine the slope ($m$) and $y$-intercept ($b$). For problems 6–8, you are told the slope and $y$-intercept of a line and must write its equation in slope-intercept form.

**Fill in the empty entries** in the table below.

| Equation | $m$ | $b$ |
|---|---|---|
| 1. $y = -5x + 4$ | $-5$ | |
| 2. $y = \frac{2}{7}x - 3$ | | |
| 3. $6 = 3x - y$ | | |
| 4. $-32 = -8x + 4y$ | | |
| 5. $8x + y = 0$ | | |
| 6. | $\frac{1}{3}$ | $7$ |
| 7. | $-4$ | $2$ |
| 8. | $\frac{5}{13}$ | $-4$ |

**Answers:** **1)** $m = -5$, $b = 4$  **2)** $m = 2/7$, $b = -3$  **3)** $m = 3$, $b = -6$  **4)** $m = 2$, $b = -8$  **5)** $m = -8$, $b = 0$
**6)** $y = (1/3)x + 7$  **7)** $y = -4x + 2$  **8)** $y = (5/13)x - 4$

# TIP

On the test you might not be given the two points in coordinate form. Sometimes you will have to pull them from a graph, table, or word problem.

## Calculating Slope

We calculate slope as **rise over run**, or change in $y$ over change in $x$:

$$\text{Slope } (m) = \frac{rise}{run} = \frac{y_2 - y_1}{x_2 - x_1}$$

If you're given two points on a line—$(x_1, y_1)$ and $(x_2, y_2)$—you can find the slope just by plugging them into the slope formula above.

**Find the slope** of the lines containing the following pairs of points.

| Points | | Slope |
|---|---|---|
| 1.  $(2, 7)\ (9, 3)$ | $\dfrac{y_2 - y_1}{x_2 - x_1} = \dfrac{3 - 7}{9 - 2} =$ | $-\dfrac{4}{7}$ |
| 2.  $(10, -8)\ (6, 7)$ | | |
| 3.  $(2, 4)\ (1, 9)$ | | |
| 4.  $(-7, 0)\ (-9, -10)$ | | |
| 5.  $(-45, 2)\ (31, -21)$ | | |
| 6.  $(3, a)\ (4, 7)$ | | |
| 7.  $(s, t)(0, 5)$ | | |
| 8.  $(-2, 15)(x, 6)$ | | |

**Answers:**  1) $-\dfrac{4}{7}$   2) $-\dfrac{15}{4}$   3) $-5$   4) $5$   5) $-\dfrac{23}{76}$

6) $7 - a$   7) $-\dfrac{5 - t}{s}$   8) $\dfrac{-9}{x + 2}$

## EXAMPLE 1

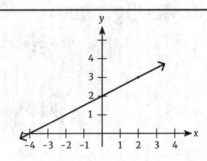

Which of the following represents the relationship between *x* and *y* ?

A)  $x = 2y$

B)  $y = 2x + 2$

C)  $y = 2x + \frac{1}{2}$

D)  $y = \frac{1}{2}x + 2$

**SOLUTION**

Asking for the relationship between *x* and *y* is another way of asking for the equation of the line. Imagine that you wanted to text information about this line to your friend so they could recreate it. You could accomplish that in just three questions:

| *Where does the line cross the y-axis?* | ( 0 , **2** ) |
| *Is the line going uphill or downhill?* | uphill |
| *How much does the line go up for every unit it goes over?* | 1/2 |

### Finding Slope

We can find the slope by looking at the graph or by plugging two points on the graph, **(–4, 0)** and **(0, 2)**, into the slope formula:

$$m = \frac{2 - 0}{0 - (-4)} = \frac{2}{4} = \frac{1}{2}$$

So our *y*-intercept (***b***) is **2**, and our slope (***m***) is **positive** $\frac{1}{2}$. We can plug that into the slope-intercept equation to find our answer:

(1)  *write line equation*      $y = mx + b$

(2)  *plug-in*      $y = \frac{1}{2}x + 2$

**D**

## EXAMPLE 2

A line in the $xy$-plane passes through the origin and has a slope of $\frac{2}{3}$. Which of the following points lies on the line?

A) $(2, 3)$
B) $(3, 2)$
C) $(4, 6)$
D) $(-2, 3)$

### SOLUTION

In this problem, they give us a slope of $m = \frac{2}{3}$. They don't come right out and say "the y-intercept is...", but they do tell us that the line **passes through the origin**, or point (0, 0). That's a y-intercept! So $b = 0$. Now, we can write the equation of this line:

(1) *write line equation*  $\qquad y = mx + b$

(2) *plug-in*  $\qquad y = \frac{2}{3}x$

**Now** we can find a point on this line in many ways.

**Option 1: Working Backwards**
First, let's try a trick that works in multiple situations: **test points with our equation**. Since we have the equation of the line, we can plug each point from the answer choices into our equation. If plugging in the given *x*-value gives the given *y*-value, then that point is on the line!

(A) *Try* (2, 3)  $\qquad y = \frac{2}{3}(2) = \frac{4}{3} \neq 3$  ✗

(B) *Try* (3, 2)  $\qquad y = \frac{2}{3}(3) = 2$  ✓

Bingo! By testing points, we can see that point (3, 2) is on the line.

**Option 2: Draw and Plot**
There's another way to find a point on this line. Since we have a point (0, 0) and we know that the slope goes **up 2** and **right 3**, we can **draw the line** and find our own points one-by-one.

Continued on next page →

**TIP**

Once you know the equation of a line, you can do **almost** anything! Find that equation!

**TIP**

There are two things you need to know to draw a line:

**1)** one point
**2)** the slope

Any time you know these two things, you can start at the point and use the slope to find more points.

So let's use what we know about slope to **find our own points**:

① *start at y-intercept*

② *move up 2, right 3*

$m = \frac{2}{3}$

And voila! The first point we find in this way happens to be our answer: (3, 2).

**Option 3: Adding with Slope**
We could do this same general idea without even drawing a graph. By applying "rise 2, run 3", you can generate as many points as you fancy:

① *first point*                              (0, 0)

                                            +3, +2

② *second point*                     **(3, 2)**

                                            +3, +2

③ *third point*                           (6, 4)

                                            +3, +2

④ *fourth point...*                     (9, 6)

We could keep going forever! But we won't. We can just add points until we see one that is an answer choice, so we can stop at **(3, 2).**

**B**

## EXAMPLE 3

The graph of the linear function $f$ has intercepts at $(a, 0)$ and $(0, b)$ in the $xy$-plane. If $ab < 0$, which of the following must be true about the slope of the graph of $f$?

A) It is positive
B) It is negative
C) It equals zero
D) It is undefined

SOLUTION

This problem is a little abstract, but don't let that scare you. Let's pick out what we have to work with:

- The function is "linear", so it's **a line**.

- The graph has both an $x$-intercept $(a, 0)$ and a $y$-intercept $(0, b)$. The fact that the question gives us points on the $xy$-plane suggests that **drawing a sketch** might be helpful.

- **$ab < 0$**

This last bit tells us that either $a$ or $b$ (but not both!) is negative. Which means, if we're **sketching a line**, there are two different ways we could draw our points:

① *if a were positive...*
   *then b would be negative.*

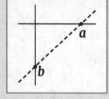

② *if a were negative...*
   *then b would be positive.*

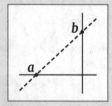

If you imagine "sliding" any of these points toward or away from zero, the steepness of the slope changes, but the fact that it's *positive* never does. Therefore, the answer is **A**— and we just **proved** that if only one of the intercepts is positive, the **slope** must be positive! That's pretty cool.

**A**

## NOTE

Neither $a$ nor $b$ could be 0, because then $ab$ wouldn't be less than zero... it'd just be zero.

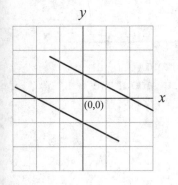

# Parallel lines have identical slopes

Any two lines that are **parallel** have the same exact slope. Which, of course, also means that any two lines with the same slope are parallel! On the test, if you see two equations with the same "m", then you know they must be parallel lines.

Same slopes?
Parallel lines! → $y = 3x + 1,000,000$
→ $y = 3x - 5,000,000$

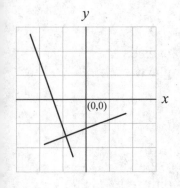

# Perpendicular lines have opposite slopes

Two lines that are perpendicular (meet at a 90° angle) have slopes that are **negative reciprocals** of one another. To find the negative reciprocal of a fraction, flip the fraction and then flip the sign:

$+\dfrac{1}{2}$ ➡ $-\dfrac{2}{1}$     $-\dfrac{3}{4}$ ➡ $+\dfrac{4}{3}$     $+\dfrac{5}{12}$ ➡ $-\dfrac{12}{5}$

So if a line has a slope of $\frac{1}{2}$, then a perpendicular line has a slope of **−2**.

**TIP**

Don't forget to flip the sign when flipping the fraction! There will often be a wrong answer choice that will look perfect if you make this mistake.

opposite slopes?
perpendicular lines! → $y = \dfrac{1}{2}x + 1,000,000$
→ $y = -2x - 5,000,000$

## EXAMPLE 4

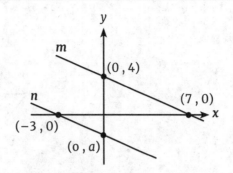

In the $xy$-plane above, line $m$ is parallel to line $n$. What is the value of $a$ ?

SOLUTION

Here's a tip: if you see parallel lines in a coordinate plane, there is a good chance you are going to be working with **slope**—especially if there are two points marked on each line. So let's find the slope of each line:

**TIP**

Whenever you use the slope formula, make sure your negatives are straight:

$$-\frac{4}{7} \neq \frac{-4}{-7}$$

(1) *find **slope** of **line m*** $\qquad slope_m = \dfrac{0-4}{7-0} = -\dfrac{4}{7}$

(2) *find **slope** of **line n*** $\qquad slope_n = \dfrac{a-0}{0-(-3)} = \dfrac{a}{3}$

And since our lines are **parallel**, we know that these slopes must really be the **exact same**. So...

(3) *set slopes equal to each other* $\qquad slope_m = slope_n$

$$-\frac{4}{7} = \frac{a}{3}$$

(4) *cross multiply* $\qquad -12 = 7a$

(5) *solve for a* $\qquad \boxed{-\dfrac{12}{7}} = a$

**D**

## EXAMPLE 5

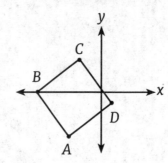

In the *xy*-plane above, *ABCD* is a square. The coordinates of points *A* and *B* are (−3, −4) and (−6, 0), respectively. Which of the following is the equation of the line that passes through points *A* and *D* ?

A)  $y = -\frac{4}{3}x - \frac{7}{4}$

B)  $y = \frac{3}{4}x - \frac{7}{4}$

C)  $y = -\frac{3}{4}x - \frac{7}{4}$

D)  $y = \frac{3}{4}x + \frac{4}{7}$

---

SOLUTION

Let's start by **going over what we know**. We know that *ABCD* is a square, which means each side is *perpendicular* to its adjoining sides. That may help later, so let's keep it in mind.

We also know we are looking for the **equation of a line** that passes through points *A* and *D*. So before we do anything else, let's just jot down the slope-intercept form to start us off:

(1)  *write slope–intercept form*          $y = mx + b$

Okay! To fill out this equation, we'll need to find the **slope (m)** of line $\overline{AD}$. To do that, we need two points on the line. We don't have that... but we *do* have two points on line $\overline{BA}$: **(−3, −4)** and **(−6, 0)**. Since we can, let's go ahead and find the slope of $\overline{BA}$.

(2)  *find slope of* $\overline{BA}$          $m_{BA} = \frac{y_2 - y_1}{x_2 - x_1} = \frac{-4 - 0}{-3 - (-6)} = -\frac{4}{3}$

Continued on next page →

Aha! And remember how we know that line $\overline{AD}$ is *perpendicular* to line $\overline{BA}$? That means their slopes are **negative reciprocals** of each other! If the slope of line $\overline{BA}$ is $-\frac{4}{3}$, then the slope of our line is $\frac{3}{4}$. Let's update our equation:

③ *update equation* $\qquad\qquad\qquad y = \frac{3}{4}x + b$

Now we just need to find **b**. We can do that with our old trick: plugging in a point we know to be on the line. Let's use point **A** **(−3, −4)** to help us find **b**:

④ *plug in (−3, −4)* $\qquad\qquad\qquad y = \frac{3}{4}x + b$

$$-4 = \frac{3}{4}(-3) + b$$

$$-4 = -\frac{9}{4} + b$$

⑤ *solve for b* $\qquad\qquad -\frac{16}{4} + \frac{9}{4} = b$

$$-\frac{7}{4} = b$$

At last, we have the last piece of the line equation! Let's plug **m** and **b** back into the equation for our answer:

⑥ *finalize equation* $\qquad\qquad\qquad y = mx + b$

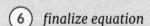 $$y = \frac{3}{4}x - \frac{7}{4}$$

**B**

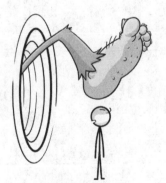

## PORTAL

To see how rates of change can show up in word problems, check out the Basic Modeling chapter on page 763.

## Slope shows up in word problems all the time!

Any time you have a word problem where something is **changing at a fixed rate**—such as the cost of buying more and more items, or the distance you travel each hour—you have a situation that can be modeled with linear growth. The equation you get from this kind of word problem will be an equation of a line, where the **rate of change is the slope**.

# NOTE

The *b* in standard form is **not** the same as the *b* in slope-intercept form.

It'd be nice if standard form used different letters to make that clear, but that's just not the world we live in.

## Standard form provides another shortcut

So far we have been focusing on equations in the **slope-intercept** form of the equation of a line ($y = mx + b$). Sometimes, the test will give you equations for lines in **standard form** ($ax + by = c$). You can always use your basic algebra skills to rewrite the equations in slope-intercept form:

$$ax + by = c \longrightarrow by = -ax + c \longrightarrow y = -\frac{a}{b}x + \frac{c}{b}$$

But notice that when you convert to the standard form, the slope of the line is represented by **−*a/b*** and the *y*-intercept by ***c/b***. That will be true no matter what values are in place for *a*, *b*, and *c*! That can be a helpful shortcut on the test, so let's get some practice with it.

Fill in the empty entries in the table below.

| | Equation | Slope | y-intercept |
|---|---|---|---|
| 1. | $ax + by = c$ | $-\dfrac{a}{b}$ | $\dfrac{c}{b}$ |
| 2. | $2x + 4y = 8$ | | |
| 3. | $x - 12y = 3$ | | |
| 4. | $7x + \frac{1}{2}y = 35$ | | |
| 5. | $\frac{2}{3}x - \frac{4}{3}y = 12$ | | |

Answers    1. *given*    2. $-\frac{1}{2}, 2$    3. $\frac{1}{12}, -\frac{1}{4}$    4. $-14, 70$    5. $\frac{1}{2}, -9$

# EXAMPLE 6

$$y = \frac{2}{3}x + 5$$

Which of the following lines is parallel to the line represented by the equation above?

A) $2x + 3y = 6$
B) $4x - 6y = 10$
C) $9x + 6y = 4$
D) $-6x + 4y = 5$

SOLUTION

We want to find a line that is parallel to $y = \frac{2}{3}x + 5$, which means we need a line with the same slope ($\frac{2}{3}$) but a different $y$-intercept. The equations in the answer choices are all in **standard form**. We *could* rewrite each choice in slope-intercept form, but that would be pretty time-consuming. Let's try to use our shortcut.

Remember that a line in standard form looks like $ax + by = c$ and has slope $-a/b$. Let's use that to pull the slope from each choice:

A) $2x + 3y = 6 \longrightarrow a = 2, b = 3, c = 6 \longrightarrow -a/b = -\frac{2}{3}$

B) $4x - 6y = 10 \longrightarrow a = 4, b = -6, c = 10 \longrightarrow -a/b = \frac{4}{6} = \frac{2}{3}$

Choice B matches! Just to make sure it's not the same exact line, we should check the $y$-intercept. That would be $c/b$, which simplifies to $-5/3$. This means that we have a line with the same slope and a different $y$-intercept—also known as a parallel line!

**B**

# Practice Problems

*Use your new skills to answer each question.*

## 1

A line in the $xy$-plane passes through the origin and the point $(2, 3)$. Which of the following is the slope of the line?

A) $\frac{2}{3}$

B) $\frac{3}{2}$

C) $2$

D) $3$

## 2

The line $y = mx - 7$, where $m$ is a constant, is graphed in the $xy$-plane. If the line contains the point $(6, -3)$, what is the value of $m$?

**3**

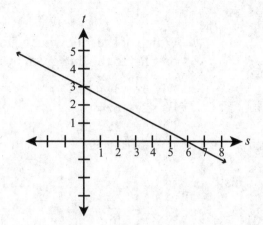

Which of the following represents the relationship between $s$ and $t$?

A) $t = 3s - \dfrac{1}{2}$

B) $t = -\dfrac{1}{2}s + 3$

C) $s = 2t + 3$

D) $s = -\dfrac{1}{2}t + 3$

**4**

The graph of a particular line contains the points $(-1, -3)$ and $(1, 3)$. What is the equation of the line?

A) $y = x + 3$

B) $y = \dfrac{1}{3}x$

C) $y = 3x$

D) $y = 3x + 1$

**5**

$$y = \frac{5}{3}x - 2$$

Which of the following equations represents a line that is parallel to the line given by the equation above?

A) $5x - 3y = 12$
B) $2y - 6x = 5$
C) $5y - 3x = 12$
D) $3x - 5y = 6$

**6**

$$ax + 6y = 3$$
$$bx + 5y = 2$$

If the system of equations above is parallel, which of the following must be a true statement?

A) $5b = 6a$
B) $5a = 6b$
C) $a + b = 11$
D) $ab = 30$

**7**

$$7x + 3y = 4$$
$$-14x + ny = 10$$

The equations above are parallel and $n$ is a constant. If $(1, c)$ is a solution to the second equation, what is the value of $c$ ?

A) $-4$

B) $-\frac{2}{3}$

C) $0$

D) $4$

**8**

The graph of the linear function $f$ passes through the quadrants I, II, and IV. Which of the following is true about the slope of the function $f$?

A) The slope is undefined.
B) The slope is positive.
C) The slope is negative.
D) There is not enough information provided.

**9**

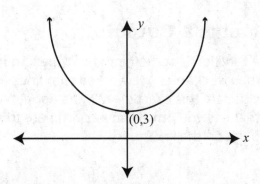

The graph of the parabola $f(x)$ is shown above. If $g(x)$ is a non-vertical linear function which intersects $f(x)$ at exactly one point, which of the following must be true?

A) The slope of $g(x)$ is 0.
B) The slope of $g(x)$ is undefined.
C) $g(x) = 3$
D) The $y$ intercept of $g(x)$ is less than or equal to 3.

**10**

The line $2ax - by = 2$, where $a$ and $b$ are constants, is graphed in the $xy$-plane. If the line contains the point $(2, -4)$, what is the slope of the line in terms of $b$?

A) $-b$

B) $2b$

C) $b + \dfrac{2}{b}$

D) $\dfrac{1 - 2b}{b}$

# Function Machines

*In this chapter, we become familiar with function notation in all of its forms and get used to working with the MACHINE.*

## Inputs & Outputs

A function is something that **takes an input** and **returns an output**. In the last chapter, we worked with lines and their equations, which actually illustrate this exact idea. A line equation can be thought of as a function that lets you **put IN** an *x*-coordinate to **get OUT** the *y*-coordinate at that point on the line.

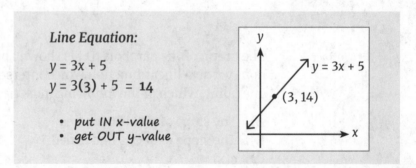

*Line Equation:*

$y = 3x + 5$

$y = 3(3) + 5 = 14$

- *put IN x-value*
- *get OUT y-value*

$y = 3x + 5$

$(3, 14)$

So we can think of the line equation as a perfectly built **function** for finding points on a line. As we dive deeper, however, we sometimes want to graph multiple lines at once, or work with equations where the graph isn't particularly relevant. For those reasons, it helps to use a different notation that emphasizes the connection between inputs and outputs. And *that's* where **function notation** comes in!

## Reading $f(x)$

We read $f(x) = 3x + 5$ as:

"$f$ of $x$ is three times $x$ plus five."

$f$ on its own is NOT a variable, and those parentheses do NOT mean multiplication.

The equals sign here means something like "is defined to be."

## Function Notation & The Machine

Instead of writing an equation in terms of $y$, we can write in terms of $f(x)$:

line equation $\qquad y = 3x + 5$

function notation $\qquad f(x) = 3x + 5$

Function notation makes it clear that the left side of the equation **changes** based on what you plug in for $x$ on the right side. You can think of the $f(\ )$ on the left as the input chute for the **function machine**. Anything you plug into the chute for $x$ replaces the $x$'s on the right. If you plug in a different input, you'll get a different output:

*Function Machine:*

$f(2) = 3(2) + 5 = 11$

$f(-4) = 3(-4) + 5 = -7$

$f(90) = 3(90) + 5 = 275$

- put IN value for x
- get OUT a value for f(x)

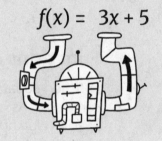

$f(x) = 3x + 5$

## EXAMPLE 1

If $f(x) = -4x + 3$, what is $f(-2a)$ equal to?

A)  $8a + 3$
B)  $-8a + 3$
C)  $-2a - 1$
D)  $8ax + 3$

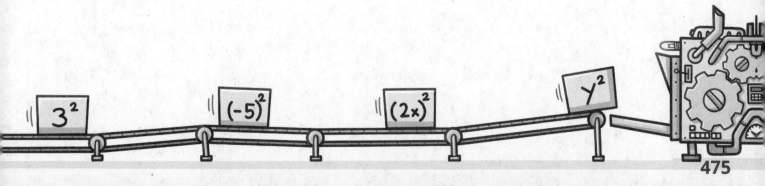

## TIP

It's a good, nay, a GREAT idea to keep the parentheses whenever you make a substitution.

**SOLUTION**

Any time you see an equation whose left side is a letter followed by another letter in parentheses, such as **$f(x)$**, you should assume you are working with a function. In this problem we have a function $f(x)$ to evaluate when $x = -2a$. This means we need to replace each $x$ on the right hand side with **$(-2a)$**:

① *Copy equation* $\qquad f(x) = -4x + 3$

② *Plug in $(-2a)$ for $x$* $\qquad f(-2a) = -4(-2a) + 3$

③ *Simplify* $\qquad f(-2a) = \boxed{8a + 3}$

A

## Functions and Graphs

Function equations and graphs of those equations are two sides of the same coin. As we saw earlier, we can think of the equation of a line as a specific type of function machine that gives us a $y$-coordinate when we plug in an $x$-coordinate. As we plug more and more $x$-coordinates into that function machine, we collect points on that line. We can talk about those points in terms of $xy$-coordinates or in terms of function notation:

> If point $(2, 3)$ is on the graph of $f(x)$, then $f(2) = 3$.
>
> If point $(0, 4)$ is on the graph of $g(x)$, then $g(0) = 4$.

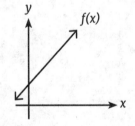

## NOTE

When we plot all of the input-output pairs of function $f(x)$ in a graph, we call that line (or parabola) simply "$f(x)$".

In the next few examples, we'll see how we can be flexible with our understanding of functions as both machines and graphs to solve a number of different types of problems.

## EXAMPLE 2

| z | 1 | 2 | 3 | 4 |
|---|---|---|---|---|
| g(z) | 3 | 1 | −1 | −3 |

The table above shows some values of the linear function $g$. Which of the following defines $g$ ?

A)  $g(z) = z + 2$

B)  $g(z) = 3z − 2$

C)  $g(z) = −2z + 5$

D)  $g(z) = −\frac{1}{2}z + 5$

### SOLUTION

We can solve this problem in two ways. We can think of the function graphically and use our equation of a line skills... or we can think of the function like a machine, and plug-&-chug.

**Option 1: Thinking with Graphs**
We are told that $g(z)$ is a **linear** function. This is just a fancy way of telling us that the graph of $g(z)$ is a **line**. Each column in the table tells us the coordinates of *points* on that line:

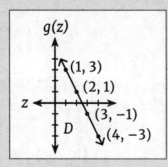

To find the equation of this line, we'll need a slope. We can find that by using any two points on this graph, such as (1, 3) and (2, 1):

(1) *find slope of g(z)* $= \frac{1-3}{2-1} = -\frac{2}{1}$

So the **slope** of the line equation is **−2.** If we look at our answer choices, we see that only **choice C** has the correct slope!

Continued on next page →

## NOTE

Look at the table again. Notice how the values for *g* are going *down* as the values for z go *up*?

If you think about it, this tells you that the slope of the line must be negative. With that clue, you can eliminate choices that do not have a negative slope, making it even easier to work backwards.

**Option 2: Thinking with Functions**

Alternatively, we could work backwards to solve this problem. Each column in the table tells us what we should get OUT of the correct equation for different inputs. In the correct equation, g(1) = 3, g(2) = 1, g(3) = –1, and g(4) = –3. Just like we can "test" line equations by plugging in points, we can also test each answer choice by plugging in z values from the table. The only choice that works with **every value in the table** is choice C:

C) $g(z) = -2z + 5$

$g(1) = -2(1) + 5 = 3$ ✓

$g(2) = -2(2) + 5 = 1$ ✓

$g(3) = -2(3) + 5 = -1$ ✓

$g(4) = -2(4) + 5 = -3$ ✓

C

## EXAMPLE 3

$$h(x) = \frac{5}{2}x + k$$

In the function defined above, *k* is a constant. If $h(-4) = 3$, what is the value of $h(2)$ ?

A)  −2

B)  $-\frac{13}{2}$

C)  13

D)  18

Our goal is to find $h(2)$. To do that, we'll first need to figure out what $k$ is. Luckily, we're given that $h(-4) = 3$. We can plug in this solution in order to **find $k$**.

| | | |
|---|---|---|
| (1) | *Copy equation* | $h(x) = \frac{5}{2}x + k$ |
| (2) | *Plug-in $h(-4) = 3$* | $3 = \frac{5}{2}(-4) + k$ |
| (3) | *Solve for $k$* | $3 = -10 + k$ |
| | | $13 = k$ |

So now that we know what k is, we can **find $h(2)$**:

| | | |
|---|---|---|
| (4) | *Update equation* | $h(x) = \frac{5}{2}x + 13$ |
| (5) | *Plug-in $h(2)$* | $h(2) = \frac{5}{2}(2) + 13$ |
| (6) | *Simplify* | $h(2) = 5 + 13$ |
| | | $h(2) = \boxed{18}$    **D** |

## TIP

Sometimes the SAT will ask you to identify the graph of a function. Figuring out a few key points, such as the $x$ and $y$ intercepts, can help you narrow down the answer choices.

## Every function can be graphed

When you graph a function, say $f(x) = x^2 + 2$, every input value is the $x$-coordinate of a point and the corresponding output is the $y$-value of that point. By plugging in a handful of inputs, you get a handful of points. Connect them to get a sketch of the function's graph.

| $f(x) = x^2 + 2$ | | |
|---|---|---|
| input $(x)$ | output $f(x)$ | point |
| $-2$ | $(-2)^2 + 2 = 6$ | $(-2, 6)$ |
| $-1$ | $3$ | $(-1, 3)$ |
| $0$ | $2$ | $(0, 2)$ |
| $1$ | $3$ | $(1, 3)$ |
| $2$ | $6$ | $(2, 6)$ |

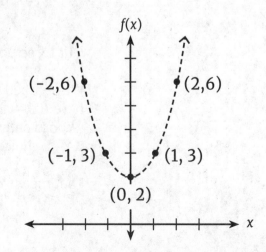

## EXAMPLE 4

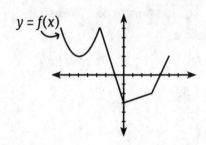

The complete graph of the function $f$ is shown in the $xy$-plane above. For which of the following values of $x$ is $f(x) > x$?

    I.   $x = -5$
    II.  $x = -1$
    III. $x = 5$

A) I only
B) II only
C) I and II only
D) I, II, and III

**SOLUTION**

This problem might look complicated at first, but it's really just asking us to **find the points on the line** at $x = -5$, $x = -1$, and $x = 5$. So let's find the y-value for each one:

    Ⓘ  $(-5, 2)$

    ⒾⒾ  $(-1, 0)$

    ⒾⒾⒾ  $(5, 2)$

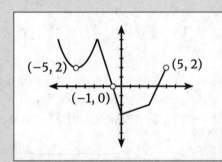

Our three points are **(–5, 2)**, **(–1, 0)**, and **(5, 2)**.

We're asked for which of these points is $f(x) > x$. We know that here $f(x) = y$, so we just need to find the choices where the $y$-coordinate is greater than the $x$-coordinate. Since **2 > –5** and **0 > –1**, choices I and II are correct. III doesn't work because **2 < 5**.

That means **choice C is the answer**!

**C**

## Compound Functions

Sometimes you'll come across functions-within-functions. These are simply **multistep function problems** where you need to *focus on the inside function first* and work your way out.

## EXAMPLE 5

A function $f$ satisfies $f(2) = 4$ and $f(5) = 7$. A function $g$ satisfies $g(5) = 2$ and $g(7) = 3$. What is $f(g(5))$ ?

A)  2
B)  3
C)  4
D)  7

We want to evaluate f(g(5)), so let's **start with the inside function**, g(5). We are told that g(5) = 2, so we can substitute 2 in:

(1)  *substitute*                                    $f(g(5)) = ?$

                                                     $f(2) = ?$

Once we resolve the inside function, we see that what's left is just f(2), which the problem tells us is **equal to 4**!

C

**Use the table** to answer the questions below.

| $x$ | ♥ | 💣 | ◖ | ✳ | ☆ |
|---|---|---|---|---|---|
| $f(x)$ | ☺ | ⚡ | 💬 | ☹ | ♥ |

1. What is $f($💣$)$? _____

2. What is $f($✳$)$? _____

3. If $f(a) = $💬, what is $a$? _____

4. If $f(k) = $☹, what is $k$? _____

5. What is $f(f($☆$))$? _____

**Use the graphs** to find or estimate information about each function.

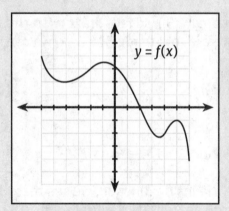

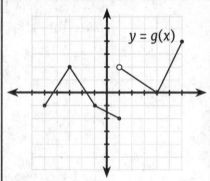

**NOTE**

Whenever you see two points for the same $x$-value, a hollow circle (O) is NOT considered a point on the line, while a solid point (●) is.

6. What is $f(-4)$? _____

7. What is $g(-1)$? _____

8. What is $f(4)$? _____

9. What is $g(1)$? _____

10. What is $g(4)$? _____

11. If $f(a) = 3$ and $-3 < a < 0$, what is $a$? _____

Answers:  1. ⚡   2. ☹   3. ◖   4. ✳   5. ☺

**482**   6. 2   7. -1   8. -2   9. -2   10. 0   11. -2

**Use the functions** to complete the problems below. The first one has already been completed for you because we are generous!

| $f(x) = 3x - 4$ $\qquad$ $g(x) = x^2 - 2x + 7$ $\qquad$ $h(x) = -x + 5$ |
|---|
| 1. $f(100) =$ $3(100) - 4 = 296$ |
| 2. $g(-3) =$ |
| 3. $h(17) =$ |
| 4. $f(x + 5) =$ |
| 5. $h(2x - 3) =$ |
| 6. $g(-7a) =$ |
| 7. $f(2) + f(4) =$ |
| 8. $h(f(4)) =$ |

# Practice Problems

*Use your new skills to answer each question.*

---

**1**

$$f(x) = 3x^2 + bx$$

For the function $f$ defined above, $b$ is a constant and $f(2) = 18$. What is the value of $f(-2)$ ?

A)   -6
B)   0
C)   6
D)   3

**2**

A function satisfies $g(1) = -2$ and $g(3) = 4$. If the function is linear, which of the following defines $g$?

A)   $g(x) = x - 3$
B)   $g(x) = 2x - 4$
C)   $g(x) = 3x - 5$
D)   $g(x) = 4x - 6$

**3**

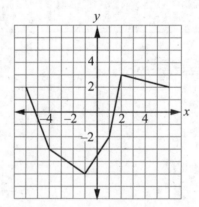

The complete graph of the function $g$ is shown in the $xy$-plane above. If $g(a)$ gives the maximum value of the graph, what is the value of $a$ ?

A)   3
B)   2
C)   -1
D)   -5

**4**

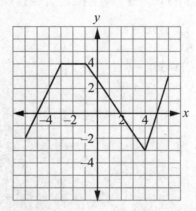

The complete graph of the function f is shown in the *xy*-plane above. Which of the following is equal to 4?

      I. $f(-2.5)$
      II. $f(-1)$
      III. $f(4)$

A)  I only
B)  II and III only
C)  I and II only
D)  I, II and III

**5**

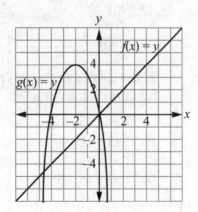

Graphs of functions *f* and *g* are shown in the *xy*-plane above. For which of the following values of *x* does $f(x) + g(x) = 0$ ?

A)  −5
B)  −3
C)  −2
D)  1

**6**

If $f(x) = -7x - 4$, what is $f(-5x)$ equal to?

A) $35x^2 - 4$
B) $-35x - 4$
C) $35x - 4$
D) $35x^2 + 20x$

**7**

A function $f$ satisfies $f(2) = 3$ and $f(4) = 5$. A function $g$ satisfies $g(3) = 4$ and $g(6) = 2$. What is the value of $f(g(3))$ ?

A) 2
B) 3
C) 4
D) 5

**8**

| $x$ | 2 | 3 | 4 |
|-----|---|---|---|
| $f(x)$ | 3 | 7 | 11 |

The table above shows values for the function $f$. If the function is linear, which of the following defines $f$ ?

A) $f(x) = -2x + 7$
B) $f(x) = 3x - 3$
C) $f(x) = 4x$
D) $f(x) = 4x - 5$

**9**

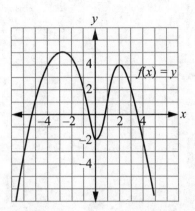

The graph above is a representation of the function $f(x)$. If $f(3) = f(b)$, which of the following could be $b$?

A)  –2
B)  –1
C)  1
D)  2

**10**

If $f(x - 2) = 3x^2 - 5x + 4$, what does $f(-3)$ equal?

A)  46
B)  12
C)  2
D)  –3

**487**

# UNIT | Polynomials

## Chapters

## Overview

In this unit, we'll learn how we can use the distributive property and factoring to work with non-linear functions (a.k.a., equations with $x^2$ and larger exponents).

Just as basic algebra helped us work with the equation of a line, the skills we learn in this chapter will help us to understand the graphs of parabolic equations.

## No Calculator!

These questions often show up on the non-calculator section of the test. Unless otherwise marked, do not use your calculator.

# Factoring Basics

*We're now moving beyond basic algebra into the slightly more complicated, but extremely predictable, world of factoring polynomials. Before we dive in, let's review some factoring basics.*

................................................................................

### Distributive Property

One of our tools for working with algebraic expressions is the distributive property. When we use parentheses as a shorthand for multiplication, this property tells us what to do.

*The outside term gets multiplied (distributed) to **every term** inside.*

### Factors & Factoring

**factoring (v.)**

Rewriting an expression as the product of its components, or "factors".

Now, since we multiplied **3** and **(2x – 5)** to get $6x - 15$, we say 3 and (2x – 5) are each *factors* of $6x - 15$, in the same way that **3** and **5** are *factors* of 15. When we "factor" an expression, like $6x - 15$, or a number, like 15, we are just working in the opposite direction from before:

$$6x - 15$$
$$\swarrow \quad \searrow$$
$$3 \quad (2x - 5)$$

$$15$$
$$\swarrow \searrow$$
$$5 \quad 3$$

*Factors work the same whether they are **expressions** or **integers**.*

# NOTE

In the exponents chapter, we learned that we can call $2x - 5$ a **binomial** factor since it has **two terms**.

When we look for a factor that **all** of the terms have in common, like the 3 in this problem, it's called a **monomial** factor.

A monomial factor can include a variable (e.g., "$3x$").

# Factoring Polynomials

In this chapter, we'll be distributing and factoring with *polynomials*. We'll start off simple, then try tougher and tougher problems. If you understand how we can go from an expression, like $6x - 15$, to its factors, then you already understand the core concept behind even the toughest problems. So before we dive in, let's review the steps:

① *look at the expression*     $6x - 15$

② *see that 3 is a factor of both 6x <u>and</u> −15*     $6x - 15$   $(3)(2x) - (3)(5)$

③ *"factor out" a 3*     $3(2x - 5)$

---

**Fill in the blanks** to complete the solutions below.

| | | |
|---|---|---|
| 1. | *distribute* | $2x(3x^2 + 4x + 5) \ =$ |
| 2. | *think...* | The common term in $12x^2 + 15x + 3$ is _____. |
| 3. | *factor* | $12x^2 + 15x + 3 \ =$ |
| 4. | *distribute* | $7(2a + 3b + c) \ =$ |
| 5. | *factor* | $20ab + 28a^2 + 8a \ =$ |

**Answers:** **(1)** $6x^3 + 8x^2 + 10x$   **(2)** 3   **(3)** $3(4x^2 + 5x + 1)$   **(4)** $14a + 21b + 7c$   **(5)** $4a(5b + 7a + 2)$

## Multiplying Expressions

Sometimes we need to multiply two **expressions** together, such as:

$$(x + 3)(x - 2) = ?$$

The Distributive Property still applies! We need to multiply *every term* in the first expression with *every term* in the second expression. While this might look new and complicated when you first see it, it's actually as simple as doing **two** distributions and adding them together:

$$(x + 3)(x - 2) = x(x - 2) + 3(x - 2)$$

## NOTE

If the first term had been **(x – 3)** instead of (x + 3), then we would be **subtracting** the two distributions:

$$x(x - 2) - 3(x - 2)$$

And *then* we'd have to remember to **distribute the negative** along with the 3.

If we rewrite the multiplication this way, we can see how plain ol' distribution gives us the answer:

$$x(x - 2) + 3(x - 2)$$

$$x^2 - 2x + 3x - 6$$

$$\boxed{x^2 + x - 6}$$

## Pencil Skills

And that's it! So what's the main difference between multiplying two expressions and standard, one-term distribution? Simply the number of steps involved. But we need to be careful! When we're working so many steps at once, the chances of making an error (such as forgetting to distribute a negative) increases.

To help us avoid such errors, we will need to carefully write out each step. Luckily, we have one or two tricks to help us cleanly multiply two expressions together: the **FOIL Method** and the **Box Method**.

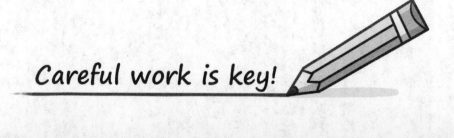

*Careful work is key!*

## FOIL Method

In school you likely learned the FOIL method for multiplying two expressions. FOIL stands for First-Outer-Inner-Last, and it simply gives us an order in which to carry out these four multiplications:

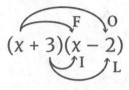

$(x + 3)(x - 2)$

$F$ $O$
$I$ $L$

| | | |
|---|---|---|
| ① | First terms | $(x + 3)(x - 2) = x^2$ |
| ② | Outer terms | $(x + 3)(x - 2) = x^2 - 2x$ |
| ③ | Inner terms | $(x + 3)(x - 2) = x^2 - 2x + 3x$ |
| ④ | Last terms | $(x + 3)(x - 2) = x^2 - 2x + 3x - 6$ |

$$(x + 3)(x - 2) = \boxed{x^2 + x - 6}$$

## Visualizing with the Box Method

We can also visualize this multiplication using the **box method**. To use the box method with two binomials, we draw a two-by-two box, labeling the columns with the terms from one factor and the rows with the terms from the other. Then, for each cell, multiply the row label by the column label. Once you're done, add up each result:

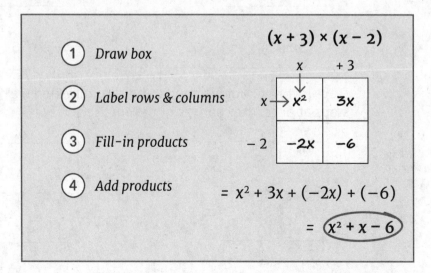

$(x + 3) \times (x - 2)$

| | $x$ | $+ 3$ |
|---|---|---|
| $x$ | $x^2$ | $3x$ |
| $-2$ | $-2x$ | $-6$ |

① Draw box

② Label rows & columns

③ Fill-in products

④ Add products

$= x^2 + 3x + (-2x) + (-6)$

$= \boxed{x^2 + x - 6}$

**FOIL the given factors** to complete the table below.

| Factors | F | O | I | L |
|---|---|---|---|---|
| 1. $(2x + 1)(x + 5)$ = | $2x^2$ + | $10x$ + | $x$ + | $5$ |
| 2. $(x + 3)(x - 7)$ = | + | + | + | |
| 3. $(a + 2)(2a + 3)$ = | + | + | + | |
| 4. $(t - 1)(t - 8)$ = | + | + | + | |

**Use the BOX method** to combine the factors below.

5. $(x + y)(x - y)$

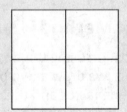

= _____

6. $(2a + 2)(3a - 1)$

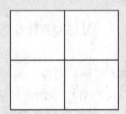

= _____

7. $(3x + 2)(x - 5)$

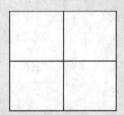

= _____

8. $(3x^2 - 5x + 1)(2x + 4)$

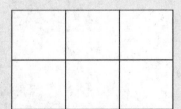

= _____

**TIP**

The box method extends nicely if you need to multiply more complicated polynomials. Just make sure you have a row/column for each term!

**Answers:**
1. *given*
2. $x^2 - 7x + 3x - 21$
3. $2a^2 + 3a + 4a + 6$
4. $t^2 - 8t - t + 8$
5. $x^2 - xy + xy - y^2$
6. $6a^2 - 2a + 6a - 2$
7. $3x^2 - 15x + 2x - 10$
8. $6x^3 - 10x^2 + 12x^2 + 2x - 20x + 4$

# EXAMPLE 1

$$5(3s + 1)(2s - 1)$$

Which of the following is equivalent to the above expression?

A) $20s$
B) $30s^2 - 5$
C) $30s^2 - 5s - 5$
D) $150s^2 - 25s + 25$

## SOLUTION

In this problem we have 3 expressions multiplied together. When we multiply 3 numbers, say 2, 3, and 4, we know that it doesn't matter what order they are multiplied in. For example:

$$2(3 \times 4) = 4(3 \times 2)$$

The same is true when we multiply expressions. That means we can work this problem in whichever way is easiest for us. Let's start by multiplying the two binomials together:

**(1)** *FOIL the binomials*     $(3s + 1)(2s - 1) = 6s^2 + 2s - 3s - 1$

$$= 6s^2 - s - 1$$

*Now* we can multiply the result by 5, remembering to distribute:

**(2)** *multiply by 5*     $5(6s^2 - s - 1) = 30s^2 - 5s - 5$

C

# TIP

The SAT can ask you to factor in a number of ways. Often, you will be asked to **solve** a quadratic equation. Alternatively, you may be asked for a value that **satisfies** the equation or **makes it true**.

## FOIL in reverse to factor polynomials

We can use what we know about FOIL to go the other direction: start with a polynomial, and then **figure out its factors**. The trick is to write out empty factors and think backwards from the quadratic.

$$(\quad)(\quad) = x^2 + 2x - 8$$

Let's start by focusing on the **first term**. What two "first" terms would multiply to equal $x^2$? Two $x$'s would work!

$$(?\quad)(?\quad) = x^2 + 2x - 8$$

$$(x\quad)(x\quad) = x^2 + 2x - 8$$

*What multiplies to $x^2$?*

Next, we need think of both the middle and last term of the quadratic. What two numbers will **add to equal +2** and **multiply to equal −8**?

$$(x\,\underline{?}\,)(x\,\underline{?}\,) = x^2 + 2x - 8$$

*What adds to +2 and multiplies to −8?*

The best way to do that is to **list the factors** of −8, keeping an eye out for two that add to equal positive 2.

| Factors of −8 | | |
|:---:|:---:|:---:|
| +1 | × | −8 |
| +2 | × | −4 |
| +4 | × | −2 |

Once we find a match, we drop them into our factors, and we've done it:

$$(x + 4)(x - 2) = x^2 + 2x - 8$$

## INTERACTIVE EXAMPLE

*Factor:* $x^2 + 3x - 18 = ($ $)($ $)$

**Q1)** What are the **first** terms of the factors?

SOLUTION

To end up with an $x^2$, the first terms must simply be *x*:

$$x^2 + 3x - 18 = (x \quad )(x \quad )$$

**Q2)** To end up with **negative** 18 as a constant, what must the **signs** be in the two factors?

    A)  both are positives
    B)  both are negatives
    C)  one is positive, one is negative

SOLUTION

If the "Last" terms in our factors multiply to be a negative, like –18, then one must be negative and the other positive:

    A̶)̶  (positive #)(positive #) = positive number
    B̶)̶  (negative #)(negative #) = positive number
    (C)  (positive #)(negative #) = **negative** number

# TIP

Studies show that looking at a drawing of a dragon can increase cognitive ability.

This is a pretty dry chapter, so here, have a dragon!

## INTERACTIVE EXAMPLE (continued)

*Factor:* $x^2 + 3x - 18 = (x + \phantom{})(x - \phantom{})$

**Q3)** What are the **factors of −18**?

SOLUTION

Let's write out the different factors of −18:

| Factors of −18 | | | | | |
|---|---|---|---|---|---|
| + 1 | + 2 | + 3 | + 6 | + 9 | + 18 |
| × | × | × | × | × | × |
| − 18 | − 9 | − 6 | − 3 | − 2 | − 1 |

**Q4)** Which pair of factors of −18 will give us a +3x as a middle term?

## Think

If the original polynomial had "−3x" as its middle term instead of "+3x", what would the factors be?

SOLUTION

We need factors of −18 that add up to positive 3. Looking at our table of factors, it looks like +6 and −3 are our best bet:

| Factors of −18 | | | | | |
|---|---|---|---|---|---|
| + 1 | + 2 | + 3 | **+ 6** | + 9 | + 18 |
| × | × | × | × | × | × |
| − 18 | − 9 | − 6 | **− 3** | − 2 | − 1 |

Which means our finished factors are:

$$x^2 + 3x - 18 = (x + 6)(x - 3)$$

# TIP

Any time you come across a quadratic, factoring is a good option to consider! In this problem, a glance at the answer choices tells us that we should **definitely** try factoring!

## EXAMPLE 2

$$3n^2 - 6n - 45$$

Which of the following is equivalent to the above expression?

A) $(n - 3)(n + 5)$
B) $3(n + 3)(n - 5)$
C) $3(n - 3)(n + 5)$
D) $3(n - 15)(n + 3)$

← 

# Try working backwards!

This problem is a great candidate for **working backwards**! Instead of factoring, simply multiply out each answer choice and see which one lands you back at the given expression.

SOLUTION

The answer choices hint to us that we need to factor the original expression. A good place to start is to **look for a common factor**:

(1) *identify any common factor*

$$3n^2 - 6n - 45$$

*multiples of 3!*

(2) *factor out* **(3)**

$$3(n^2 - 2n - 15)$$

Now to **factor the quadratic** in the parentheses. Since the coefficient of $n^2$ is **1**, the first term in each factor will just be $n$:

(3) *set up the first term*

$$3(n^2 - 2n - 15) = 3(n \quad)(n \quad)$$

Next, we need to **factor the –15** at the end. To end up with a negative, we know that one factor *must* be negative:

(4) *place signs*

$$3(n^2 - 2n - 15) = 3(n - \quad)(n + \quad)$$

Next, we need two numbers that **multiply to 15**. Our options are:

(5) *factor* **15**

$$3(n^2 - 2n - 15) \begin{cases} 3(n - 15)(n + 1) \\ or \\ 3(n + 3)(n - 5) \end{cases}$$

Of these two options, only **–5** and **+3** also **add to –2**. So...

(6) *bring it home!*

$$3n^2 - 6n - 45 = 3(n + 3)(n - 5)$$

B

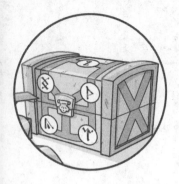

## Factoring with the Box Method

The **box method** can be particularly useful when dealing with problems, like Example 2 on the previous page, where the coefficient of one of your first terms is not simply 1. Let's look at how the box method can help us solve for $x$ by factoring the equation below:

$$6x^2 - 11x - 10 = 0$$

## TIP

There are no common terms in this example, but it never hurts to check!

① *Factor out any common terms.*

② *Draw a box and identify your terms.*

$$\underset{\text{First}}{6x^2} \quad \underset{\text{Middle}}{-11x} \quad \underset{\text{Last}}{-10}$$

③ *Put the first and last terms in opposite corners...*

④ *then find the product of these terms.*

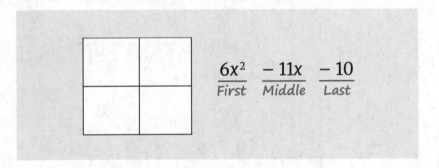

| $-60x^2$ factors | | |
|---|---|---|
| $x$ | × | $-60x$ |
| $+2$ | × | $-30$ |
| $+3$ | × | $-20$ |
| $+4$ | × | $-15$ |

*Bingo!*

This is the only tricky step. A foolproof method is to **list the factors** until you find a pair that adds to the middle term.

⑤ *Find factors of this product that **add to the middle term.***

If we list the factors of $-60x^2$, we find ⟨4x and -15x.⟩

$$(4x)(-15x) = -60x^2$$

$$(4x) + (-15x) = -11x \quad \text{✓} \quad Checks\ out!$$

⑥ Put the factors you found in the **empty corners**.

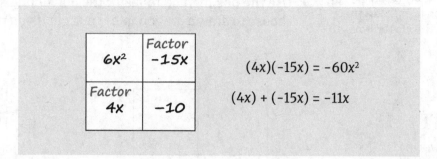

$$(4x)(-15x) = -60x^2$$

$$(4x) + (-15x) = -11x$$

⑦ **Factor out common terms** *from each row and each column*

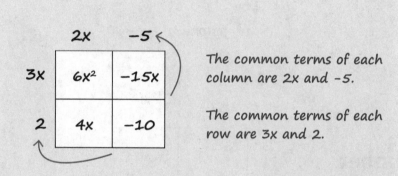

The common terms of each column are 2x and -5.

The common terms of each row are 3x and 2.

## TIP

When factoring out a common term, **take the sign of the closer box.**

Here, for example, the "-5" takes the sign of "-15x" and the "2" takes the sign of "4x".

## PORTAL

The techniques we have been working on will work for most factoring problems on the SAT, but don't despair if they do not! There are additional techniques in Advanced Factoring (on page 602), and you can circumvent factoring altogether with the tools in The Unfactorables (on page 613).

⑧ *Find the sum of the common factors for the columns and the sum of the common factors for the rows.*

*Those are the factors of the polynomial!*

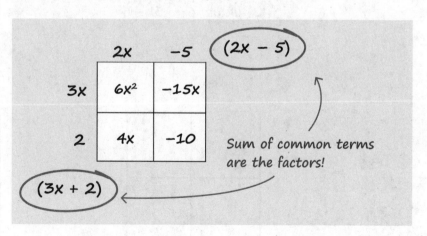

Sum of common terms are the factors!

$$6x^2 - 11x - 10 = (2x - 5)(3x + 2)$$

*Thanks box method!*

## Remember

When factoring out a common term, **take the sign of the closer box**.

## HINT

If there are no common terms, factor out a **1** or **–1**.

## Remember

Before you start filling in the box, make sure there are no common terms to factor out!

### TRY IT OUT

Use the box method to factor the polynomials below. You can also choose to draw a dragon in the margin if you need a little boost.

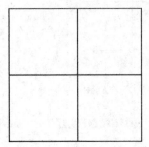

**1.** *factor:* $3x^2 - x - 30$

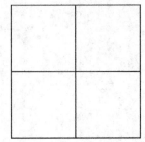

**2.** *factor:* $6x^2 - 7x + 2$

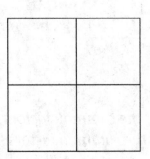

**3.** *factor:* $6x^2 + 5x - 6$

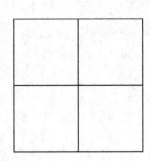

**4.** *factor:* $8x^2 - 32x + 30$

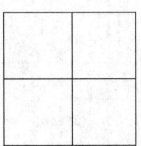

**5.** *factor:* $5x^2 + 34x + 24$

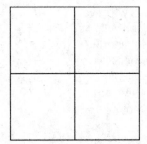

**6.** *factor:* $3x^3 + 10x^2 + 3x$

**Answers:** *See next page.*

# Practice Problems

*Use your new skills to answer each question.*

---

**1**

$$4(3x^2 + 6)(5x^2 + 1)$$

Which of the following is equivalent to the expression above?

A) $60x^4 + 24$
B) $32x^4 + 28$
C) $60x^4 + 132x^2 + 24$
D) $216x^4$

---

**2**

Which of the following is a simplified version of the equation $(x + 3a)(x - 4b) = 0$ ?

A) $x^2 - 12ab = 0$
B) $x^2 - x(3a - 4b) - 12ab = 0$
C) $x^2 - x(3a + 4b) + 12ab = 0$
D) $x^2 + x(3a - 4b) - 12ab = 0$

---

**3**

$$12x^2 + 2x - 24$$

Which of the following is equivalent to the expression above ?

A) $2(3x - 4)(2x + 3)$
B) $(4x - 3)(3x + 8)$
C) $12(x - 2)(x + 1)$
D) $12(x - 1)(x + 2)$

---

**4**

If $(x + 4)(x - 2) = (x + 1)^2 + b$, what is the value of $b$ ?

A) 8
B) -7
C) -8
D) -9

---

**Last Page:** 1. $(3x - 10)(x + 3)$   2. $(3x - 2)(2x - 1)$   3. $(2x + 3)(3x - 2)$

4. $2(2x - 3)(2x - 5)$   5. $(5x + 4)(x + 6)$   6. $x(3x + 1)(x + 3)$

$$\frac{1}{x+b} + \frac{1}{x-b} = \frac{2x}{x^2 - 9}$$

Given the equation above, where $b < 0$ and $|x| \neq b$, what is the value of $b$?

A) $-1$
B) $-3$
C) $-6$
D) $-9$

If $t > 0$ and $t^2 - 25 = 0$, what is the value of $t$?

$$(x - 6)(x + 1) + 10$$

Which of the following is equivalent to the expression above?

A) $x^2 + 5x + 16$
B) $(x + 5)^2 + 10$
C) $(x + 4)(x + 1)$
D) $(x - 4)(x - 1)$

The polynomial $18x^2 + 27x - 56$ has $(6x - 7)$ as a binomial factor. Which of the following is another binomial factor of the polynomial?

A) $(3x + 8)$
B) $(3x - 8)$
C) $(3x + 6)$
D) $(12x + 8)$

**9**

If $u = x + y$ and $v = x + 5y$, which of the following is equivalent to $uv + \left(\frac{v - u}{2}\right)^2$ ?

A) $(x + y)(x + 5y)$
B) $(x + 3y)^2$
C) $(x - 3y)^2$
D) $(x - 3y)(x + 3y)$

**10**

$$x^2 + 12x + 25$$

Which of the following is equivalent to the expression above?

A) $(x + 5)^2$
B) $(x + 6)^2 + 11$
C) $(x + 6)^2 - 11$
D) $(x - 6)^2 + 11$

**11**

Which of the expressions below is a factor of the polynomial $6x^3 + 24x^2 + 30x$ ?

I) $x$
II) $3x - 5$
III) $x + 3$

A) I only
B) II and III only
C) I and II only
D) I, II, and III

**505**

**12**

If $20x^2 - 23x - 21$ factors as $(ax + b)(cx - d)$ where $a$, $b$, $c$, and $d$ are all positive numbers, what is $c$?

# Solving for Zero

*If you can set a polynomial equal to zero, you can solve it!*

If you multiply two (or more) numbers together and the result is **zero**, then one or both of those numbers must have been zero! We can use this fact to solve polynomials. Say you are given the equation below:

$$x^2 + 5x + 6 = 0$$

We can use our reverse FOIL-ing skills to **factor** the left side:

$$(x + 2)(x + 3) = 0$$

**TIP**

If you have a polynomial set equal to zero, **factor and solve**. If it's not equal to zero, make balanced changes until it is!

Now, the above equation is true if either factor equals zero. To solve for the possible values of $x$, we just **set each factor equal to zero**:

$$x + 2 = 0$$
$$x = -2$$

$$x + 3 = 0$$
$$x = -3$$

If you go back and plug in $-2$ or $-3$ for $x$, the original equation will be true! Behold, the true power of factoring!

507

## EXAMPLE 1

If $a^2 + 4a = 32$ and $a > 0$, then $a = ?$

SOLUTION

In order to use the true power of factoring, we need the polynomial to be equal to 0. This means that the first step is to **move everything to one side** of the equation.

| | | |
|---|---|---|
| ① | rewrite equation | $a^2 + 4a = 32$ |

| | | |
|---|---|---|
| ② | gather to one side | $a^2 + 4a - 32 = 0$ |

If we factor the polynomial on the left, we will end up with the product of two things that equal zero. We can then use reverse FOIL to find what those factors are.

| | | |
|---|---|---|
| ③ | prepare to factor! | $(\ ?\ )(\ ?\ ) = 0$ |

| | | |
|---|---|---|
| ④ | what times what is $a^2$? | $(a\ \ )(a\ \ ) = 0$ |

| | | |
|---|---|---|
| ⑤ | what multiplies to $-32$ and adds to $+4$? | $(a + 8)(a - 4) = 0$ |

If **either** of these factors equaled zero, then the equation would be true. That means $a$ is **either** $-8$ or $+4$. But.... look at the original problem. We're given an additional constraint that $a > 0$.

| | | |
|---|---|---|
| ⑥ | solve for a | $a = ④$ or $\cancel{-8}$ |

# TIP

The maximum number of potential solutions for an equation is equal to the highest power of the variable.

This means a quadratic equation ($x^2$) can have up to 2 solutions and a cubic equation ($x^3$) can have up to 3.

## EXAMPLE 2

$$3t^2 - 13t = 10$$

What is a value of $t$ that satisfies the above equation?

### SOLUTION

This problem starts the same exact way as the previous one.

(1) *rewrite equation* $\qquad 3t^2 - 13t = 10$

(2) *gather to one side* $\qquad 3t^2 - 13t - 10 = 0$

Since we have a coefficient in front of the quadratic, our best bet is to use the **box method** for factoring.

(3) *Draw a box*

(4) *Fill in first and last terms*

| $3t^2$ | |
|---|---|
| | $-10$ |

(5) *multiply $3t^2$ and $-10$* $\qquad (3t^2)(-10) = -30t^2$

Next, we need to find factors of $-30t^2$ that **add up to -13**.

(4) *find factors with coefficients that add up to -13.*

*-15 and 2 works!*

| Factors of $-30t^2$ | | |
|---|---|---|
| $-30t$ | $\times$ | $t$ |
| $-15t$ | $\times$ | $2t$ |
| $-10t$ | $\times$ | $3t$ |

**Continued on next page** →

|  | $3t$ | $+ 2$ |
|---|---|---|
| $t$ | $3t^2$ | $2t$ |
| $- 5$ | $-15t$ | $-10$ |

(5) add factors to open boxes.

(6) factor out common terms, keep sign from closer box

(7) write your factors out          $(3t + 2)(t - 5) = 0$

(8) solve for t          $t = \left(-\dfrac{2}{3}, 5\right)$

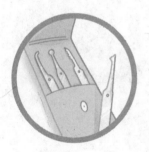

## If given a choice of factors, work backwards

Sometimes the test will give you a polynomial and ask something like "Which of the following is a factor?" For these problems you could just factor, but you can also **test each answer choice** by setting it equal to zero and solving for x. If you plug a value back into the original equation and it also equals zero, that's your answer!

### TRY IT OUT

Which of the following is a factor of $2x^3 - 10x^2 - 4x + 48$ ?

A) $(x - 3)$
B) $(x - 1)$
C) $(x + 1)$
D) $(x + 3)$

SOLUTION

If we set each answer choice equal to zero, we get the possible values 3, 1, -1, or -3. When we plug each one back into the equation, only choice A (3) comes out to zero.

A)  $(x - 3)$    $x = 3$        $2(3)^3 - 10(3)^2 - 4(3) + 48 = 0$

B)  $(x - 1)$    $x = 1$        $2(1)^3 - 10(1)^2 - 4(1) + 48 = 36$

C)  $(x + 1)$    $x = -1$       $2(-1)^3 - 10(-1)^2 - 4(-1) + 48 = 40$

D)  $(x + 3)$    $x = -3$       $2(-3)^3 - 10(-3)^2 - 4(-3) + 48 = -84$

Sure enough, if you factor out the polynomial, you get:

$$2x^3 - 10x^2 - 4x + 48 = 2(x + 2)\underline{(x - 3)}(x - 4)$$

A

## PORTAL

We will look into this idea in more detail in the Advanced Algebra chapter on page 528

## Use factoring skills to simplify fractions

A **rational function** is when you find a polynomial in the denominator of a fraction. Questions involving rational functions are often factoring and polynomial multiplication questions in disguise. Sometimes you can **factor the numerator** (or denominator) and cancel expressions. Other times you have to **find a common denominator**.

## EXAMPLE 4

$$\frac{x^2 + 5x + 6}{x + 2} + \frac{x - 4}{x + 1}$$

Which of the following expressions is equivalent to the above sum when $x \ne -1$ and $x \ne -2$?

A)  $\dfrac{x^2 + 6x + 2}{2x + 3}$

B)  $\dfrac{x^2 + 6x + 2}{x^2 + 3x + 2}$

C)  $\dfrac{x^3 + x^2 - 14x - 24}{x^2 + 3x + 2}$

D)  $\dfrac{x^2 + 5x - 1}{x + 1}$

**511**

SOLUTION

This question is asking us to add two rational functions (fractions with polynomials in the denominator). Eventually, we'll need to find some common denominators... but first let's simplify. The second fraction is as simple as it'll get, but if we **factor** the first fraction, the **denominator will cancel** out:

**(1)** *rewrite the equation* $\qquad\qquad \dfrac{x^2 + 5x + 6}{x + 2} + \dfrac{x - 4}{x + 1} = ?$

**(2)** *factor the numerator* $\qquad\qquad \dfrac{(x + 3)(x + 2)}{x + 2} + \dfrac{x - 4}{x + 1} = ?$

**(3)** *cancel the denominator* $\qquad\qquad \dfrac{(x + 3)}{1} + \dfrac{x - 4}{x + 1} = ?$

Now that we've simplified, let's **find a common denominator**. We can do this by converting the first fraction's denominator to $x + 1$:

**(4)** *convert first fraction* $\qquad\qquad \dfrac{(x + 3)}{1} \cdot \dfrac{(x + 1)}{(x + 1)} + \dfrac{x - 4}{x + 1} = ?$

$$\dfrac{(x + 3)(x + 1)}{x + 1} + \dfrac{x - 4}{x + 1} = ?$$

**(5)** *add the fractions* $\qquad\qquad \dfrac{(x + 3)(x + 1) + (x - 4)}{x + 1} = ?$

This doesn't look like any of our answer choices yet, so let's **simplify the numerator**.

**(5)** *simplify the numerator* $\qquad\qquad \dfrac{(x^2 + 4x + 3) + (x - 4)}{x + 1} = ?$

$$\dfrac{(x^2 + 5x - 1)}{x + 1} = ?$$

At long last, we have a match! Using our factoring and fraction skills, we've discovered the answer is **choice D**.

D

## TIP

Now that we've solved it the head-on way, let's try a workaround. Notice that all the answer choices have the same variable in them...

**Try picking numbers!** Plug zero in for *x* in the problem and the answer choices and look for a match.

# Practice Problems

*Use your new skills to answer each question.*

---

**1**

If $s > 0$ and $s^2 + 3s - 28 = 0$, what is the value of $s$ ?

A) $-7$
B) $3$
C) $4$
D) $7$

**2**

Which of the following polynomial equations has 8 and -2 as solutions?

A) $(x - 8)(x - 2) = 0$
B) $(x + 8)(x + 2) = 0$
C) $(x - 8)(x + 2) = 0$
D) $(x + 8)(x - 2) = 0$

**3**

What values of $x$ are solutions for $x^2 - x = 12$ ?

A) 4 and $-3$
B) $-4$ and 0
C) $-4$ and 3
D) 0 and 4

**4**

$$x^2 - 6x - 27 = 0$$

What is the sum of the two solutions of the equation above?

A) 9
B) 6
C) 0
D) $-3$

**5**

What are the solutions of the equation $3x^2 + 6x - 24 = 0$ ?

A) $x = 2$ and $x = 4$
B) $x = -2$ and $x = 4$
C) $x = 2$ and $x = -4$
D) $x = -2$ and $x = -4$

**6**

The equation $ax^2 + bx + c = 0$, has two solutions of $x = \frac{3}{4}$ and $x = \frac{1}{2}$. Which of the following could be factors of $ax^2 + bx + c$ ?

A) $(4x - 3)$ and $(2x - 1)$
B) $(4x - 1)$ and $(2x - 3)$
C) $(4x + 1)$ and $(2x + 3)$
D) $(4x + 3)$ and $(2x + 1)$

**7**

$$x^2 - x - 30 = 0$$

If $r$ is a solution of the equation above and $r > 0$, what is the value of $r$ ?

**8**

What is the value of $a$ if $x + 1$ is a factor of $2x^3 + x^2 - ax + 4$ ?

A) $-4$
B) $-3$
C) $0$
D) $2$

**9**

What is the product of all values of $k$ that satisfy $4k^2 - 3k = 7$?

A)  $-7$

B)  $-\dfrac{7}{4}$

C)  $-\dfrac{4}{7}$

D)  $\dfrac{7}{4}$

**10**

$$2x^3 + x^2 - 3x = 0$$

Which of the following is the solution set of the equation above?

A)  $\left\{-\dfrac{3}{2}, 0, 1\right\}$

B)  $\left\{-\dfrac{3}{2}, 1\right\}$

C)  $\left\{0, -1, \dfrac{3}{2}\right\}$

D)  $\{0\}$

# Pattern Matching

*In this chapter, we'll practice manipulating equations until they match a given pattern. We'll then use that pattern to determine unknown values.*

## Pattern Matching

Occasionally, you are asked to find multiple unknowns using a single equation. The trick to discovering their values is **pattern matching**. For example, say we are asked find $a$, $b$, and $c$, in the following equation:

$$5x^2 + 3x + 7 = ax^2 + bx + c$$

It would actually be impossible for us to "solve" for each of these unknown variables... but we don't need to! Notice how each side follows the exact same **pattern**:

same pattern! $\longrightarrow$
$$ax^2 + bx + c$$
$$5x^2 + 3x + 7$$

There's an $x^2$ with a coefficient (5 or $a$), an $x$ with a coefficient (3 or $b$), and a constant at the end (7 or $c$). Since they are in the same form, we can simply match $a$, $b$, and $c$ with the numbers on the left!

$$a = 5, \quad b = 3, \quad c = 7$$

Before we look at some test questions, let's get some practice using pattern matching to figure stuff out!

**Use pattern matching** to complete the table below. You may need to rearrange the equation first! Use the bottom of the page for work.

| Equation | $a$ | $b$ | $c$ |
|---|---|---|---|
| 1. $8x^2 + 2x - 15 = ax^2 + bx + c$ | **8** | 2 | -15 |
| 2. $5x^2 - 7x + 12 = ax^2 + bx + c$ | 5 | -7 | 12 |
| 3. $99x^2 - \frac{1}{99}x + 5 = ax^2 + bx - c$ | 99 | $-\frac{1}{99}$ | 5 |
| 4. $-x^2 - x = ax^2 + bx + c$ | -1 | -1 | 0 |
| 5. $7x^2 + \frac{1}{3}x + 4 = ax^2 + \frac{1}{b}x + c$ | 7 | 3 | 4 |
| 6. $x^2 + 2x - bx + 2 = ax^2 + c$ | 1 | 2 | 2 |
| 7. $3x^2 + 6 = ax^2 + bx + 3x + c$ | 3 | -3 | 6 |
| 8. $3x^2 - 17x - 5 = ax^2 + bx + 3x + c$ | 3 | -20 | -5 |

Answers:  1. 8, 2, −15   2. 5, −7, 12   3. 99, $-\frac{1}{99}$, −5   4. −1, −1, 0   5. 7, 3, 4

6. 1, 2, 2   7. 3, −3, 6   8. 3, −20, −5

## EXAMPLE 1

$$3x(2x - 3) + 2(4x + 5) = ax^2 + bx + c$$

In the equation above, $a$, $b$, and $c$ are constants. If the equation is true for all values of $x$, what is the value of $b$ ?

$$b = -1$$

## TIP

Anytime you see "**true for all values of $x$**...", it's likely you are dealing with a simple pattern matching problem.

**SOLUTION**

Our goal is to **simplify the left side** of the equation until it matches the pattern on the right side. So let's start by distributing:

| | | |
|---|---|---|
| **1** | *copy the left side* | $3x(2x - 3) + 2(4x + 5)$ |
| **2** | *distribute* | $6x^2 - 9x + 8x + 10$ |
| **3** | *simplify* | $6x^2 - x + 10$ |

Now we have both sides of the equation in a matching pattern. We want the value of $b$, which is the coefficient of $x$ on the right side. That means our answer is the **coefficient of $x$** on the left:

| | | |
|---|---|---|
| **4** | *match pattern* | $6x^2 - x + 10 = ax^2 + bx + c$ |
| | | $6x^2 - (1)x + 10 = ax^2 + bx + c$ |

So $b$ must equal **-1.**

## EXAMPLE 2

$$\frac{30x^2 - 52x - 12}{kx + 7} = -6x + 2 - \frac{26}{kx + 7}$$

The above equation is true for all values of $x \neq -\frac{7}{k}$, where $k$ is a constant. What is the value of $k$?

$30x^2 - 52x - 38 + 26$

A)  $-6$

B)  $-5$

C)  $5$

D)  $\frac{52}{6}$

SOLUTION

Since we see "for all values of $x$" (except the one that makes the fraction undefined), we are likely dealing with a pattern matching problem. The two sides look nothing alike, though, so we'll need to do some simplifying. Since they make things tricky, let's start by **moving the fractions to one side** and combining:

$$\frac{30x^2 - 52x - 12}{kx + 7} = -6x + 2 - \frac{26}{kx + 7}$$

$$\frac{30x^2 - 52x - 12}{kx + 7} + \frac{26}{kx + 7} = -6x + 2$$

$$\frac{30x^2 - 52x + 14}{kx + 7} = -6x + 2$$

Now we can multiply both sides by the denominator, **$kx + 7$**, in order to **clear those pesky fractions**:

$$(kx + 7)\frac{30x^2 - 52x + 14}{kx + 7} = (-6x + 2)(kx + 7)$$

$$30x^2 - 52x + 14 = -6kx^2 - 42x + 2kx + 14$$

Now we *almost* have an exact pattern match. The only problem is we have **two** $x$ terms on the right... but we can fix that!

Continued on next page →

Let's **move −42x to the left side**. It'll be happier there anyway

$$30x^2 - 52x + 14 \;=\; -6kx^2 - 42x + 2kx + 14$$

$$30x^2 - 10x + 14 \;=\; -6kx^2 + 2kx + 14$$

—*match!*—

Now we're talking! Both sides of the equation now follow the same $ax^2 + bx + c$ pattern. To solve for $k$, we can either match the $x^2$ coefficients or the $x$ coefficients. Either way gives us the answer:

$$
\begin{aligned}
30x^2 &= -6kx^2 \\
30 &= -6k \\
\boxed{-5} &= k
\end{aligned}
\qquad\qquad
\begin{aligned}
-10x &= 2kx \\
-10 &= 2k \\
\boxed{-5} &= k
\end{aligned}
$$

**Bonus Solution: Picking Numbers**

We're told that the equation is true "for all values of $x$." This is often a big sign that we could make things easier for ourselves by **picking numbers**. If it's true for all values of $x$, then it should be true for $x = 1$. Try plugging 1 in for $x$ right from the start, and simplify until you find $k$. This technique is not always useable, but when it is, it can save you a lot of time and heartache.

B

## EXAMPLE 3

If $(mx + 3)(nx - 5) = -6x^2 + rx - 15$ is true for all values of $x$ and $m + n = 1$, what are the two possible values of $r$?

A) −15 and −6
B) −2 and 3
C) −10 and 9
D) −21 and 19

SOLUTION

We're told that the equation is "true for all values of x", and we have way too many unknowns: these are signs that we need to use pattern matching! To do that, we'll need to FOIL the left side:

**(1)** *rewrite the left side* $(mx + 3)(nx - 5)$

**(2)** *FOIL* $mnx^2 - 5mx + 3nx - 15$

Let's pause here and look for a pattern that can help us:

$$\boxed{mnx^2} - 5mx + 3nx - 15 = \boxed{-6x^2} + rx - 15$$

If we focus on the $x^2$ **coefficients**, we can see that $mn = -6$. Let's combine that with what we already know about $m$ and $n$:

$$mn = -6$$
$$m + n = 1$$

Later, we'll talk formally about how to solve "systems of equations" like this, but for now we can just look at it. We need **two numbers** that **multiply to –6** and **add to 1**.

If we play around with it, we find that **m = 3** and **n = –2** would work. Let's try plugging that into our equation and do some pattern matching:

$$(3)(-2)x^2 - 5(3)x + 3(-2)x - 15 = -6x^2 + rx - 15$$
$$-6x^2 - 15x - 6x - 15 = -6x^2 + rx - 15$$
$$-6x^2 - 21x - 15 = -6x^2 + rx - 15$$

*match!*

Bingo! Now that we have a **pattern match**, we see that **r = – 21**. If we check the answer choices, we see that we don't even need to find a second possible value: only **choice D** has –21 in it!

D

## PORTAL

To see how to solve systems of equations, turn to the Solving Systems chapter on page 568.

## EXAMPLE 4

What is the sum of all values of $x$ that satisfy $3x^2 - 18x + 21 = 0$ ?

(A) 6

B) −6

C) $3\sqrt{6}$

D) $6\sqrt{3}$

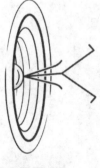

### PORTAL

Forget the quadratic formula? Flip to page 613 for a reminder.

**SOLUTION**

This looks like it's asking us to solve a quadratic. The first thing to try when solving a quadratic is always **factoring.** All of the coefficients are multiples of 3, so we can **pull 3 out**:

**①** *copy equation*        $3x^2 - 18x + 21$

**②** *factor out 3*        $3(x^2 - 6x + 7)$

Now, ordinarily, we would just factor the quadratic and get two answers. But there's a problem. We would need to find two numbers that multiply to 7 and add to −6. But our only choices are 1 and 7 (which add to 8) or −1 and −7 (which add to −8). So neither option works! This doesn't mean there are no solutions... just no solutions that are **whole numbers**.

We can solve *this* problem in two different ways: the "hard work" way or the "hard thinking" way.

**Option A: "Hard Work" Way**
Since we can't factor this quadratic, we'll have to turn to our old, bulky friend: **the quadratic formula**.

**③** *quadratic formula*
$(x^2 - 6x + 7)$      $x = \dfrac{-b \pm \sqrt{b^2 - 4ac}}{2a}$

$a = 1,\ b = -6,\ c = 7$      $x = \dfrac{6 \pm \sqrt{(-6)^2 - 4(7)}}{2(1)}$

                $x = \dfrac{6 \pm \sqrt{8}}{2}$

                $x = \dfrac{6 \pm 2\sqrt{2}}{2}$

                $x = 3 \pm \sqrt{2}$

**Continued on next page** →

Now we have two solutions: $(3 + \sqrt{2})$ and $(3 - \sqrt{2})$. Since the question asks for the sum of all solutions, we just add these:

(4) *add solutions*          $3 + \sqrt{2} \ + 3 - \sqrt{2} = $ ⑥

## Option B: "Hard Thinking" Way

Let's think about this a little bit abstractly. We wish we could factor $x^2 - 6x + 7$ to find the solutions. Let's pretend we can do that and use variables to stand in for the factors. Say our solutions to the quadratic were **r** and **s**. What would that look like?

$$\textit{pretend to factor} \qquad x^2 - 6x + 7 \ = (x - r)(x - s)$$
$$x^2 - 6x + 7 \ = x^2 - rx - sx + rs$$
$$x^2 - 6x + 7 \ = x^2 - (r + s)x + rs$$

Now we can do some pattern matching! For this factoring to work out, it must be true that those last two terms, **r** and **s**, multiply to equal 7... and **add to equal 6**. Otherwise, FOILing wouldn't produce the right quadratic! So:

$$r + s = 6$$

And look! This is exactly what the question asked for. If "**r**" and "**s**" are the solutions to this quadratic, then we've shown just from how factoring works that the solutions must add to equal 6!

**A**

# Practice Problems

*Use your new skills to answer each question.*

---

**1**

$$4x(7x + 2) + 5(x - 4) = ax^2 + bx + c$$

In the equation above, $a$, $b$, and $c$ are constants. If the equation is true for all values of $x$, what is the value of $b$ ?

A)  -20
B)  5
C)  8
D)  13

---

**2**

$$\frac{2y^2 + 11y + 12}{y + 4} = ay + b \quad 3$$

In the equation above, $a$ and $b$ are constants. If the equation is true for all values of $y$, what is the value of $a$ ?

A)  $-\dfrac{3}{2}$

B)  2

C)  3

D)  11

---

**3**

If $(ax - 3)(2x + b) = -2(5x^2 + 8x + 3)$ for all values of $x$, what is the value of $ab$ ?

A)  −16
B)  −10
C)  10
D)  15

**4**

What is the sum of all values of $x$ that satisfy
$3x^2 + 17x - 2 = 0$?

A) $-2$

B) $-\dfrac{2}{3}$

C) $-\dfrac{17}{3}$

D) $17$

**5**

The equation $\dfrac{15x^2 + 21x - 32}{ax - 3} = 3x + 6 - \dfrac{14}{ax - 3}$ is true for all

values of $x \neq \dfrac{3}{a}$, where $a$ is a constant. What is the value of $a$?

A) 3
B) 5
C) 14
D) 15

**6**

The equation $\dfrac{x^2 + 8x - 9}{x - b} = x + 3 - \dfrac{24}{x - b}$ is true for all values of

$x \neq b$, where $b$ is a constant. What is the value of $b$?

A) $-5$

B) $\dfrac{11}{3}$

C) $5$

D) $8$

$$(x - 3)(x - 2)(x + 4) = ax^3 + bx^2 + cx + 24$$

The above expression is true for all values of $x$. What is the value of $c$?

A)  –1

B)  –14

C)  14

D)  24

The expression $6ax + b(x + a) = 14x + 4$ is true for all values of $x$. If $a \neq b$, what is the value of $a$?

A)  $\dfrac{1}{3}$

B)  3

C)  $\dfrac{7}{3}$

D)  12

The expression $(3x + 2y)(x - 4y) = ax^2 + bxy + cy^2$ is true for all values of $x$ and $y$. What is the value of $b$?

A)  –10

B)  –8

C)  –2

D)  14

# UNIT | Applied Factoring

## Chapters

## Overview

In this unit, we'll see the many ways you'll use your factoring skills on the test.

First, we'll learn to use our polynomial skills to combine fractions. Next, we'll see how we can use factoring to transform the quadratic equations of parabolas into three special forms. Finally, we'll dive deeper into the connection between graphs, intercepts, and solutions to equations.

## No Calculator!

These questions often show up on the non-calculator section of the test. Unless otherwise marked, do not use your calculator.

# Advanced Algebra

*The test can devise clever ways to test your comfort with algebraic principles.*

## Working with variables in the denominator

If you know how to work with fractions and how to work with variables, you can deal with both at the same time! Recall that if you want to add or subtract fractions, you need to find a **common denominator**. This is still true when there are variables in the denominator.

| | No Variables | Variables |
|---|---|---|
| Uncommon denominators | $\frac{2}{5} + \frac{3}{4}$ | $\frac{2}{x+3} + \frac{3}{x+4}$ |
| Multiply by 1 to convert | $\frac{2}{5} \cdot \frac{4}{4} + \frac{3}{4} \cdot \frac{5}{5}$ | $\frac{2}{x+3} \cdot \frac{x+4}{x+4} + \frac{3}{x+4} \cdot \frac{x+3}{x+3}$ |
| Common denominators | $\frac{8}{20} + \frac{15}{20}$ | $\frac{2x+8}{(x+3)(x+4)} + \frac{3x+9}{(x+3)(x+4)}$ |
| | $\downarrow$ | $\downarrow$ |
| Combine | $\frac{23}{20}$ | $\frac{5x+17}{(x+3)(x+4)}$ |

## TIP

Try to get the left side of the equation into the same form as the right side, *then* see what you can learn about $a$ and $b$.

### EXAMPLE 1

$$\frac{4}{(x+2)} - \frac{6}{(x+3)} = \frac{(ax+b)}{(x+2)(x+3)}$$

The equation above is true for all $x > 0$ where $a$ and $b$ are constants. What is the value of $a + b$?

A)    0
B)   −2
C)   22
D)   26

## PORTAL

For instruction on Pattern Matching, turn to page 516.

**SOLUTION**

We are told the equation is true for all $x > 0$, and there are two additional two variables ($a$ and $b$). This tips us off that we can use the same skills used in the **Pattern Matching** chapter. To use pattern matching, we first need to put the left and right sides of the equation into the same form. This means we need to combine the fractions on the left by finding a **common denominator**.

(1) *Multiply each fraction by 1*
$$\frac{4}{x+2} \cdot \frac{x+3}{x+3} - \frac{6}{x+3} \cdot \frac{x+2}{x+2}$$

(2) *Distribute*
$$\frac{4x+12}{(x+2)(x+3)} - \frac{6x+12}{(x+2)(x+3)}$$

(3) *Combine*
$$\frac{-2x}{(x+2)(x+3)}$$

(4) *Compare to right side*
$$\frac{-2x}{(x+2)(x+3)} = \frac{(ax+b)}{(x+2)(x+3)}$$

Now that both sides of the equation are a single fraction with the same denominator, we can focus on the numerators.

(5) *Compare numerators*
$$-2x = ax + b$$

(6) *Put into the same form*
$$-2x + 0 = ax + b$$

Pattern matching tells us that $a = -2$ and $b = 0$, so $a + b = \boxed{-2}$.

Yup, looks like you've got a bunch of variables down here! No sweat, we'll clear em out for ya.

## Watch Out for Domain Trickery

Many SAT math problems contain traps for students who are trying to go too quickly through the section. One such trap is an algebra problem that features an equation or expression with a **restricted domain** (i.e., there are *restrictions* on what x can be).

If you see <u>variables in the denominator</u> or <u>variables in square roots</u>, it's always a good idea to go back and **doublecheck** that your answer actually works... especially if you found two possible answers.

### EXAMPLE 2

$$\frac{(3x-1)}{(x+2)} - \frac{(2x+4)}{(x+5)} = \frac{(13x+5)}{(x+2)(x+5)}$$

What is the solution to the equation above?

## Vocabulary: Unknowns, Variables, & Constants

In algebra, we spend a lot of time solving for "unknowns." Sometimes, these unknowns are called *variables* and sometimes they are called *constants*. In many cases the words are interchangeable.

In the generic model for a linear equation, $y = mx + b$, the input ($x$) and output ($y$), are considered **variables** because they can be multiple values. The symbols $m$ and $b$ are **constants**; We might have to solve for them, but for any given model, there is one fixed value for $m$ and one for $b$.

If we are looking at a specific model, say, $y = -3x + 5$, we say that $-3$ and $5$ are the constant values and y and x are the variables.

SOLUTION

Let's start by finding a **common denominator** for the left side:

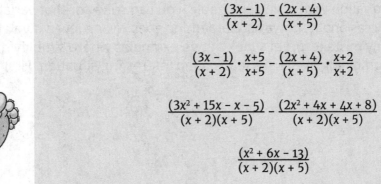

$$\frac{(3x-1)}{(x+2)} - \frac{(2x+4)}{(x+5)}$$

$$\frac{(3x-1)}{(x+2)} \cdot \frac{x+5}{x+5} - \frac{(2x+4)}{(x+5)} \cdot \frac{x+2}{x+2}$$

$$\frac{(3x^2 + 15x - x - 5)}{(x+2)(x+5)} - \frac{(2x^2 + 4x + 4x + 8)}{(x+2)(x+5)}$$

$$\frac{(x^2 + 6x - 13)}{(x+2)(x+5)}$$

Now let's plug that back into the left side of the equation:

$$\frac{(x^2 + 6x - 13)}{(x+2)(x+5)} = \frac{(13x+5)}{(x+2)(x+5)}$$

Now that we have the same denominator on each side of the equation, we can **focus on the numerators**.

$$x^2 + 6x - 13 = 13x + 5$$

$$x^2 - 7x - 18 = 0$$

$$(x + 2)(x - 9) = 0$$

From here, we can see that **$x = -2$ or 9.**

**But we aren't done!** If we look back at the original problem, we see that **$(x + 2)$** is a factor in the denominator in the very first fraction. If we plug −2 in for $x$, we'd get a **zero in the denominator**:

$$\frac{(3x-1)}{(x+2)} = \frac{(3(-2)-1)}{((-2)+2)} = \frac{-7}{0}$$

It's impossible to divide by zero. That means that **$x = -2$** is NOT a valid answer. The answer is **9**.

## PORTAL

Later in this unit, we'll dive deeper into understanding the full meaning of the "solutions" to a quadratic equation. If you're too curious to wait, turn to "Zeros & Solutions" on page 555.

## A problem can have zero or infinite solutions

One of the main premises of algebra is that if you are given a single equation with a single variable, you can solve for that variable. Occasionally, however, something goes wrong (even if you don't make any mistakes!). Let's look at two examples where simplifying and combining like terms leads to an interesting situation. First up:

$$4(x + 3) - 2(x - 2) = 6$$
$$4x + 12 - 4x - 4 = 6$$
$$8 = 6 \; ?!$$

In this case, simplifying the equation led to a **false** statement ($8 = 6$). That means that no matter what we plug in for x it is <u>always</u> going to result in a false statement. There are **zero** valid solutions! Now look at *this* situation:

$$3(2y + 5) = 6(y + 4) - 9$$
$$6y + 15 = 6y + 24 - 9$$
$$6y + 15 = 6y + 15$$
$$0 = 0$$

In the second case, simplifying leaves us with a patently **true** statement. This means that no matter what we plug in for y it is <u>always</u> going to be true. This equation has **infinitely many** valid solutions.

## TIP

This is secretly another type of **pattern matching** problem!

## EXAMPLE 3

$$a(x + 5) - 3 = 4x + 7$$

In the above equation, *a* is a constant. If the equation has no solution, what is the value of *a* ?

SOLUTION

Since we are told that the equation has no solution, we need to find the value of $a$ that makes the $x$'s all cancel when we solve. Start by simplifying the expression:

$$a(x + 5) - 3 = 4x + 7$$

$$ax + 5a - 3 = 4x + 7$$

We need a value of $a$ that makes $ax = 4x$ (so they cancel). Well that's straightforward: $a = 4$ should work! Let's plug that in to make sure we end up with a false statement:

$$(4)x + 5(4) - 3 = 4x + 7$$

$$4x + 17 \neq 4x + 7$$

## EXAMPLE 4

$$y(k - 7) + 2 = k - 5$$

If $k$ is a constant and the equation above has infinitely many solutions, what is the value of $k$?

SOLUTION

When the question says there are infinitely many solutions, it means there are infinitely many values of $y$ that make it true. If we simplify the expression, we need the $y$'s to all cancel out into a true statement.

Right now there is only one $y$ and it's being multiplied by the expression $(k - 7)$. For the $y$ to go away, it must be the case that $k - 7 = 0$, or $k = 7$. Let's confirm that:

$$y(k - 7) + 2 = k - 5$$

$$y((7) - 7) + 2 = (7) - 5$$

$$y(0) + 2 = 2$$

$$2 = 2$$

It worked! Plugging in 7 for $k$ makes all the $y$'s disappear, leaving us with a true statement. For this equation to have infinitely many solutions, $k$ must be 7.

Infinity... what a concept.

# Practice Problems

*Use your new skills to answer each question.*

---

**1**

$$\frac{4x - 24}{x - 6} = x$$

What is the solution to the equation above?

**2**

$$\frac{3x + 10}{x^2 - 4} + \frac{1}{x + 2} = \frac{2}{x + 2}$$

What value of x satisfies the equation above?

A)  −6
B)  −2
C)  2
D)  6

**3**

$$\frac{x}{12} = \frac{3}{x}$$

If x > 0, what is the solution to the equation above?

**4**

$$\frac{1}{2x + 3} - \frac{1}{x - 2} = 1$$

Which of the following gives the solution set of the equation above?

A) $\{-\frac{3}{2}, 2\}$

B) $\{2, \frac{\sqrt{2}}{2}\}$

C) $\{-\frac{\sqrt{2}}{2}, \frac{\sqrt{2}}{2}\}$

D) $\{\frac{\sqrt{2}}{2}\}$

$$\frac{x-2 -2x-3}{(2x+3)(x-2)} = 1$$

$$\frac{-x-5}{(2x+3)(x-2)} = 1 \qquad 0 = 2x^2 - 1$$

$$-x-5 = 2x^2 - x - 6$$

**5**

$$\frac{32}{x^2 - 16} = \frac{4}{x - 4} + \frac{x + 3}{x + 4}$$

What are all of the values of $x$ that satisfy the equation above?

A) 4
B) −7
C) −7 and 4
D) −4 and 4

**6**

$$a(x + 4) - 7 = 3x + 6$$

In the equation above $a$ is a constant. If the equation has no solutions, what is the value of $a$ ?

**7**

$$5x - 3 = k(x + m)$$

In the equation above, $k$ and $m$ are constants. If the equation has infinitely many solutions, what is the value of $m$ ?

A) −3

B) $\frac{5}{3}$

C) $-\frac{3}{5}$

D) $\frac{3}{5}$

**8**

$$\frac{6x + b}{2} = 3x + 4$$

In the equation above, $b$ is a constant. If the equation has infinitely many solutions, what is the value of $b$ ?

**9**

$$5(2x - 1) - 4(3x + 2) = -2x - 13$$

How many solutions does the equation above have?

A)  0
B)  1
C)  2
D)  Infinitely many solutions

**10**

$$7(8x + 3) + 2(3x - 4) = 98x + 49$$

How many values of $x$ satisfy the equation above?

A)  −1
B)  1
C)  0
D)  Infinitely many

**11**

If $x > 3$, which of the following is equivalent to $\dfrac{1}{\dfrac{1}{x + 3} - \dfrac{1}{x + 4}}$ ?

A)  $x^2 + 7x + 12$

B)  $\dfrac{1}{x^2 - 7x - 12}$

C)  $\dfrac{2x + 7}{x^2 - 7x - 12}$

D)  $\dfrac{x^2 - 7x - 12}{2x + 1}$

# Transformers

*In this chapter, we'll look at the graphs of parabolic functions.*

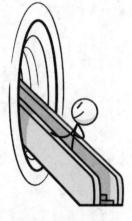

## PORTAL

To see how we can apply this knowledge to real situations, check out Quadratic Modeling, on page 654.

In the *Basic Algebra* chapter, we learned that we can rearrange an algebraic equation as long as we make **balanced changes** to each side. Then, in the *Equation of a Line* chapter, we used that skill to rearrange a linear equation to get it into the slope-intercept form. This lets us see key things about the line's graph.

In this chapter, we'll learn how we can use what we know about *factoring* to rearrange a quadratic equation to get it into one of three specific forms: the **standard** form, the **vertex** form, and the **x-intercept** form. Each form helps us in different ways. Let's look at each form and see what good stuff each one tells us about the parabola.

## The Three Forms

Before we dive into the specifics of each form, let's make a handy-dandy cheat sheet that shows the three forms and what manipulations we make to turn one form into another:

## TIP

No need to worry if you don't know what "complete the square" means; it's an advanced trick that we'll learn later in this very chapter.

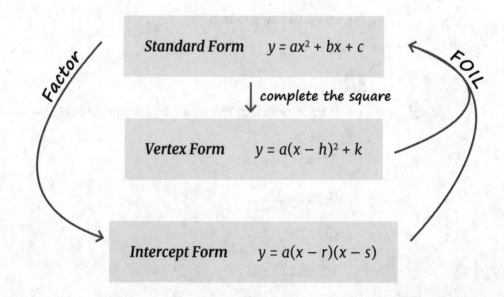

**Standard Form**    $y = ax^2 + bx + c$

*Factor*      *complete the square*      *FOIL*

**Vertex Form**    $y = a(x - h)^2 + k$

*Intercept Form*    $y = a(x - r)(x - s)$

# Direction

When *a*, the coefficient of $x^2$, is positive, the parabola opens upward. When *a* is negative, it opens downard.

# Spread

The larger *a* gets, the skinnier the parabola gets. This is because the **rate of change** of *y* is greater for each increase in *x*.

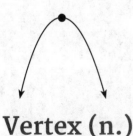

# Vertex (n.)

The lowest point in an upward-facing parabola, or the highest point in a downward-facing parabola.

## Standard Form

In the last chapter, we talked about the quadratic formula and how it can be used to find the solutions of any equation of the form $ax^2 + bx + c = 0$. If we set this equal to y rather than 0, we get the **standard form** of the general parabola:

> **Standard Form**  $y = ax^2 + bx + c$

What cool stuff does the standard form give us? As we've seen, it lets us use the quadratic formula (or our factoring skills) to find the equation's solutions. In addition, *a*, the coefficient of *x*, tells us the **direction** and **spread** of the parabola (see sidebar), while *c* tells us the *y*-intercept of the graph. This is also our "home base." We can manipulate this form to get either the vertex form or the intercept form.

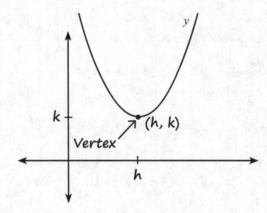

## Vertex Form

A pretty important thing about a parabola is the location of its **vertex**. Any parabola can be manipulated into a form where we can read this straight from the equation. Fittingly, this form is called the **vertex form**:

> **Vertex Form**  $y = a(x - h)^2 + k$

When you have the equation in this form, the coordinates of the vertex are at (*h*, *k*). So, for example, a parabola with the equation $y = (x - 2)^2 + 3$ would have a vertex at point **(2, 3)**.

## PORTAL

To get from the standard form to the intercept form, we use **factoring**.

For a refresher on factoring basics, turn back to page 490.

## Intercept Form

Any parabola that intersects the *x*-axis (not all do!) can be written in a form that easily lets us see **where** those intersections occur:

| Intercept Form | $y = a(x - r)(x - s)$ |
|---|---|

In this form, the x-intercepts happen at **(*r*, 0)** and **(*s*, 0)**. So, for example, a parabola with the equation $y = 2(x - 4)(x + 5)$ would have x-intercepts at **(4, 0)** and **(–5, 0)**. To transform the standard form to the intercept form, we simply **factor** the polynomial.

## BONUS

For any equation in vertex form, write down the coordinates of its vertex. For any in the intercept form, write down its x-intercepts.

We won't have any way of knowing that you did it, but we're working hard on that technology. Promise.

Check the **column** that correctly identifies each equation's form.

| | Equation | Standard | Vertex | Intercept |
|---|---|---|---|---|
| 1. | $y = (x + 3)(x - 4)$ | | | ✓ |
| 2. | $y = x^2 + 2x - 15$ | | | |
| 3. | $y = 3(x + 3)^2 - 10$ | | | |
| 4. | $y = 3x^2 + 12$ | | | |
| 5. | $y = \frac{1}{2}(x - 1)(x - 2)$ | | | |
| 6. | $y = (x - 5)^2 - 99$ | | | |

**Answers:** 1. Intercept $(-3, 0), (4, 0)$   2. Standard   3. Vertex $(-3, -10)$
4. Standard   5. Intercept $(1, 0), (2, 0)$   6. Vertex $(5, -99)$

## EXAMPLE 1

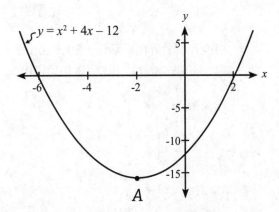

$A$

Which of the following is an equivalent form of the equation of the graph shown in the $xy$-plane above from which the coordinates of vertex A can be identified as constants in the equation?

A) $y = (x + 6)(x - 2)$

B) $y = (x - 6)(x + 2)$

C) $y = (x + 2)^2 - 16$

D) $y = x(x + 4) - 12$

SOLUTION

We know we are looking for a version of the equation that directly tells us the vertex. This means we are looking for the vertex form:

$$\textbf{Vertex Form} \qquad y = a(x - h)^2 + k$$

The *only* answer choice that fits this form is **choice C**.

$$\textbf{Choice C} \qquad y = 1(x + 2)^2 - 16$$

If this is indeed the correct vertex form, then we'd expect the vertex to be at $(h, k)$, which here is $(-2, -16)$. Looking at the graph, that looks about right!

We could also double check by multiplying choice C out and seeing if we end up with the equation given in the graph:

$$(x + 2)^2 - 16 = x^2 + 4x + 4 - 16$$

$$= x^2 + 4x - 12 \checkmark$$

C

## EXAMPLE 2

$$f(x) = (x - 5)(x + 1)$$

Which of the following functions has the same graph as the above function and includes its minimum value as a constant or coefficient?

A) $f(x) = (x - 2)^2 - 9$

B) $f(x) = (x + 2)^2 - 11$

C) $f(x) = x^2 - 4x - 5$

D) $f(x) = x^2 - 5$

If a parabola has a "minimum value," it means the **lowest y-value** that is on the parabola. We must, then, be talking about the **vertex** of an upward-facing parabola. In other words, the question just came up with another weird way to ask:

*"Which of these functions is in the correct vertex form?"*

Choices C and D are in the *standard form*, and D doesn't even represent the same parabola! So we can cross those out. All we need to do now is figure out whether choice A or B is correct.

**Option 1: Plug in the Vertices**

If choice A is correct, then the vertex of $f(x)$ would be at **(2, –9)**. If choice B is correct, then the vertex would be at **(–2, –11)**. Let's test each choice by plugging their x-values into the original function and seeing if the machine spits out the correct y-value:

(1)  *test choice A with (2, –9)*

$$f(x) = (x - 5)(x + 1)$$
$$f(2) = (2 - 5)(2 + 1)$$
$$f(2) = (-3)(3)$$
$$f(2) = \boxed{-9} \checkmark$$

(2)  *test choice B with (–2, –11)*

$$f(x) = (x - 5)(x + 1)$$
$$f(-2) = (-2 - 5)(-2 + 1)$$
$$f(-2) = (-7)(-1)$$
$$f(-2) = 7 \times$$

continue →

**Option 2: Eyeball the Vertex**

We can use our quick-n-dirty eyeballing trick to figure out the correct vertex of this function. We were given the parabola in **intercept form**, so we know from looking at the function that the parabola crosses the x-axis at –1 and 5.

Since parabolas are symmetric, the x-coordinate of the vertex must be exactly halfway between those two points, at **x = 2.** This means that in vertex form, the equation must look like:

$$y = a(x - 2)^2 + k$$

..and the only choice where this is true is **choice A**.

A

# Completing the Square

Ever since the Basic Algebra chapter, we've been doing quite a bit of **balancing equations**. We know that we are free to experiment by adding, subtracting, multiplying, or dividing as long as we keep the equation balanced. So, for example, we know that if we're given the equation below, we are free to add 4 to both sides if we want to:

*totally fine*
$$y = x^2 + 4x - 5$$
$$y + 4 = x^2 + 4x + 4 - 5$$

If we wanted to, instead of adding 4 to both sides, we could also just **add and subtract 4** from one side, which still keeps the equation unchanged:

*perfectly okay*
$$y = x^2 + 4x + 4 - 4 - 5$$

Before worrying about *why* you'd want to do that, make peace in your heart that it's *totally fine to do that if you want to*. Made peace? Good. As it turns out, what we just did was the first step in an extremely helpful trick called **completing the square**, which lets us factor otherwise unfactorable things and force equations *into* vertex form!

Occasionally, the SAT will insert an extra step into the problems we've worked so far. They might ask for the vertex but give you the intercept form, or vice versa. This is where your factoring skills come in! The first step is **always to get to standard form**. From there, you can factor to get intercept form, or complete the square to get vertex form.

## Creating Vertex Form

Say you are given the following standard equation, and are asked to find the vertex. We'll need to transform it into vertex form:

> *Standard Form*    $y = x^2 + 8x - 2$
>
> *Vertex Form*    $y = a(x - h)^2 + k$

To get into vertex form, we will **complete the square**. To do this, we'll:

① *Identify the middle term*    $y = x^2 + 8x - 2$
  $\downarrow$

② *Halve its coefficient...*    $8 \div 2 = 4$

③ *Square that...*    $4^2 = 16$

④ *Add and subtract the result*    $y = x^2 + 8x + 16 - 16 - 2$

**TIP**

Remember, it's crucial to add AND subtract the same number when completing the square. If we don't, we throw off the balance of the whole equation.

By doing this, we create a group ($x^2 + 8x + 16$) that is a **perfect square**:

$$y = (x^2 + 8x + 16) - 18$$
$$\downarrow$$
$$y = (x + 4)^2 - 18$$

And, lo and behold, we have created an equation in **vertex form**! Thanks to our skillful and imaginative use of balanced manipulations and factoring, we can see that the vertex of this parabola is at **(−4, −18)**.

## EXAMPLE 3

$$y = (x - 2)(x - 10)$$

*(handwritten: $x^2 - 12x + 20$)*

The graph of the above equation in the *xy*-plane is a parabola with vertex $(u, v)$. Which of the following is equal to $v$ ?

A)  2
B)  16
C)  −2
D)  −16

*(handwritten: $(x-6)^2 - 16$)*

SOLUTION

One way to solve this problem is to put the equation in vertex form. To get from intercept form to vertex form, we need to multiply it out to standard form and then **complete the square**.

**①** *rewrite equation*        $(x - 2)(x - 10) = ?$

**②** *FOIL to standard form*     $(x - 2)(x - 10) = x^2 - 12x + 20$

Now we can complete the square by **adding and subtracting 36**.

**③** *complete the square*        $y = x^2 - 12x + 20$

$$y = (x^2 - 12x + 36) - 36 + 20$$

$$y = (x - 6)^2 - 16$$

Completing the square has given us an equation in **vertex form**! Looking at the new form of the equation, we can see that our $(u, v)$ vertex must be at **(6, −16)**. That means **$v$ = −16**, making our answer **choice D**!

### Backup Solution: Eyeball the Vertex

We can use the "Eyeball the Vertex" method here as well, though it takes an extra step. We're given the equation in **intercept form**. The equation $y = (x - 2)(x - 10)$ has solutions (*x*-intercepts) at $x = 2$ and $x = 10$. That means the vertex will be halfway between those points, at $x = 6$.

That gives us the x-value, but we need the y-value. But hey, we were given an equation to FIND the y-value. Just plug 6 in for x in the original equation, and the function machine will spit out −16!

$y = x^2 - 12x...$

halve this...
...then square it.

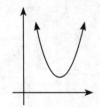

## TIP

This eyeballing trick is great, but only if we know the *x*-intercepts. Some parabolas never cross the *x*-axis at all!

D

## EXAMPLE 4

$$y = -x^2 - 6x - 11$$

The graph of the above equation is a parabola in the $xy$-plane with vertex $(m, n)$. Which of the following is the value of $m + n$?

A) $-2$
B) $-3$
C) $-5$
D) $-17$

$-(x+3)^2 -2$

---

**SOLUTION**

**TIP**

Remember that any variable by itself, like "$x$" or "$w$", has a hidden coefficient of 1.

Similarly, "$-x$" or "$-w$" has a hidden coefficent of $-1$.

We can find the vertex by putting the equation in **vertex form**. The first step is to **factor out the coefficient** of the $x^2$ term to help us do what we gotta do:

**①** *rewrite equation* $\qquad y = -x^2 - 6x - 11$

**②** *factor out $x^2$ coefficient* $\qquad y = -1(x^2 + 6x + 11)$

Now we can complete the square by **adding & subtracting 9**.

**③** *complete the square* $\qquad y = -1(x^2 + 6x + 9 - 9 + 11)$

$$y = -1((x + 3)^2 + 2)$$

**④** *simplify to vertex form* $\qquad y = -(x + 3)^2 - 2$

Now we can see that vertex $(m, n)$ of the parabola is at **(–3, –2)**. Just plug those values in for $m$ and $n$ to find our answer:

**⑤** *plug-in and solve* $\qquad m + n = ?$

$$(-3) + (-2) = \boxed{-5}$$

continue →

**Bonus Shortcut**

Here's a fun shortcut we can use on this problem. Notice that we're given the equation of the parabola in standard form:

$$\text{Standard Form} \qquad y = ax^2 + bx + c$$

$$\text{Equation} \qquad y = -x^2 - 6x - 11$$

Any time you have a parabola equation in the standard form, the **x-coordinate of the vertex** will always equal:

$$x\text{-coordinate of vertex} = \frac{-b}{2a}$$

Which means we can just plug in our $a$ and $b$ values:

$$x\text{-coordinate of vertex} = \frac{-(-6)}{2(-1)} = \frac{6}{-2} = -3$$

We can plug in **-3** for $x$ to find the $y$-coordinate of the vertex:

$$y = -(-3)^2 - 6(-3) - 11$$

$$y = -9 + 18 - 11 = -2$$

Now that we have our $m$ and $n$, we just add them to get $\boxed{-5.}$

C

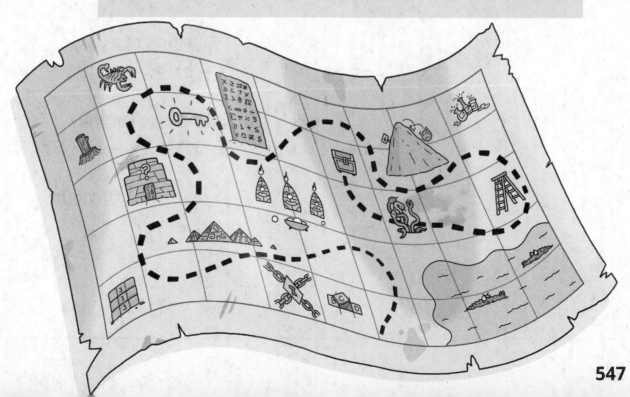

## Equation of a Circle

Occasionally, you'll be asked about the equation of a circle. For these problems, you'll need to memorize one more formula:

The standard equation of a circle centered at $(h, k)$ and with radius $r$ is:

### Equation of a Circle

$$(x - h)^2 + (y - k)^2 = r^2$$

Center: $(h, k)$     Radius: $r$

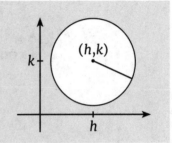

## Digger Deeper

Ever wonder why the equation of a circle is what it is? No? Well, we'll tell you anyways. A circle is the set of points that are a fixed distance (the radius) from a single point (the center). A circle's equation is actually the same exact thing as using the **Pythagorean theorem** or the **distance formula** to find any point on that circle. We can see this if we draw it out.

Pick a point $(x, y)$ on the circle and draw the radius connecting it to the center $(h, k)$. Now draw a right triangle with that radius as the hypotenuse. With this picture, we can see how the equations are related:

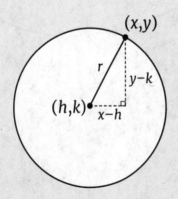

### Equation of a Circle

$$(x - h)^2 + (y - k)^2 = r^2$$

### Distance Formula

$$(x_1 - x_2)^2 + (y_1 - y_2)^2 = d^2$$

### Pythagorean Theorem

$$a^2 + b^2 = c^2$$

## EXAMPLE 5

Which of the following is the equation of a circle in the xy-plane with center $(5, -4)$ and a radius with endpoint $(2, 0)$ ?

A)  $(x - 5)^2 + (y + 4)^2 = 25$
B)  $(x + 5)^2 + (y - 4)^2 = 25$
C)  $(x - 5)^2 + (y + 4)^2 = 5$
D)  $(x + 5)^2 + (y - 4)^2 = 5$

SOLUTION

The first step is to plug what we know about our circle into the standard equation of a circle.

(1)  *rewrite circle equation*  $\qquad (x - h)^2 + (y - k)^2 = r^2$

(2)  *plug in center* $(5, -4)$  $\qquad (x - 5)^2 + (y - (-4))^2 = r^2$

$\qquad\qquad\qquad\qquad\qquad\qquad (x - 5)^2 + (y + 4)^2 = r^2$

After plugging our given center into the equation of a circle, we can see immediately that choices B and D are out. Cross 'em off!

Now we just need to determine the radius of the circle. We aren't told how long the radius is, but we can **solve** for it! We know that point **(2, 0)** is on the circle. Let's plug that into our equation:

(3)  *plug in point* $(2, 0)$  $\qquad (2 - 5)^2 + (0 + 4)^2 = r^2$

(4)  *solve for* $r^2$  $\qquad\qquad\qquad (-3)^2 + (4)^2 = r^2$

$\qquad\qquad\qquad\qquad\qquad\qquad\qquad 9 + 16 = r^2$

$\qquad\qquad\qquad\qquad\qquad\qquad\qquad 25 = r^2$

Now be careful! It's tempting here to solve for the radius, but the equation of a circle is set equal to $r^2$, **not r**. Just to be safe, let's rewrite the standard equation one last time:

(5)  *rewrite circle equation*  $\qquad (x - h)^2 + (y - k)^2 = r^2$

(6)  *plug in what we know*  $\qquad (x - 5)^2 + (y + 4)^2 = 25$   A

## EXAMPLE 6

$$x^2 + y^2 - 4x + 6y = 23$$

The above equation represents a circle in the $xy$-plane. What is the radius of the circle?

A)  2
B)  3
C)  6
D)  36

---

**SOLUTION**

Yowza! This is a tough problem, but all we need to know is **(1)** the equation of a circle, and **(2)** how to complete the square.

To figure out the radius of the circle, we'll need to **rearrange** this equation until it's in the standard equation of a circle form. To do this, we're going to need to **complete the square** *twice!* Once for $x$, and once for $y$. First, let's focus on the $x$'s.

**(1)** *rewrite equation*  $\qquad x^2 + y^2 - 4x + 6y = 23$

**(2)** *gather the variables*  $\qquad \underbrace{x^2 - 4x}_{1} + \underbrace{y^2 + 6y}_{2} = 23$

**(3)** *complete the square (x)*  $\qquad x^2 - 4x + 4 - 4 + y^2 + 6y = 23$

$$(x - 2)^2 - 4 + y^2 + 6y = 23$$

$$(x - 2)^2 + y^2 + 6y = 27$$

**(4)** *complete the square (y)*  $\qquad (x - 2)^2 + y^2 + 6y + 9 - 9 = 27$

$$(x - 2)^2 + (y + 3)^2 - 9 = 27$$

$$(x - 2)^2 + (y + 3)^2 = 36$$

Aha! Now that the equation is in the proper form, we can read the radius. If $r^2 = 36$, then **$r = 6$**. Choice C is the right answer!

C

# Practice Problems

*Use your new skills to answer each question.*

**1**

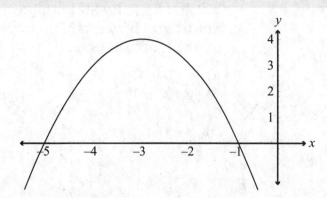

Which of the following equations could be represented by the graph above and has the coordinates of the vertex of the parabola as constants or coefficients?

A) $y = -(x + 3)^2 + 4$
B) $y = -x^2 - 6x - 5$
C) $y = (x - 1)(x - 5)$
D) $y = (x + 1)(x + 5)$

**2**

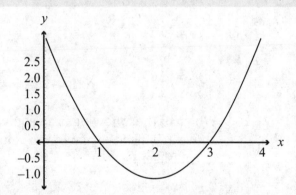

Which of the following equations could be represented by the graph above and has the $x$-intercepts of the graph as constants or coefficients?

A) $y = (x - 2)^2 + 15$
B) $y = x(x + 4) + 3$
C) $y = (x - 1)(x + 3)$
D) $y = (x - 1)(x - 3)$

$$y = x^2 - 2x - 8$$

The equation above represents a parabola in the $xy$-plane. Which of the following is a form of the same equation in which the $x$-intercepts of the parabola are displayed as constants or coefficients?

A) $y = (x + 4)(x - 2)$
B) $y = (x - 4)(x + 2)$
C) $y = x(x - 2) - 8$
D) $y + 9 = (x - 1)^2$

$$y = x^2 + 6x + 5$$

The equation above represents a parabola in the $xy$-plane. Which of the following equivalent forms of the equation displays the coordinates of the vertex of the equation as constants or coefficients?

A) $y = (x + 5)(x + 1)$
B) $y = x(x + 6) + 5$
C) $y = (x + 3)^2 - 4$
D) $y - 5 = x^2 + 6x$

$$f(x) = -2(x + 4)(x - 2)$$

Which of the following is an equivalent form of the function $f$ above in which the maximum value of $f$ appears as a constant or coefficient?

A) $f(x) = -2(x - 1)^2 + 18$
B) $f(x) = -2(x + 1)^2 + 18$
C) $f(x) = -2x^2 + 16$
D) $f(x) = -2x^2 - 4x + 16$

**6**

$$y = c(x^2 - 6x - 1)$$

In the quadratic equation above, $c$ is a constant greater than zero. Which of the following is equal to the minimum value of $y$?

A)  $-10c$
B)  $-9c$
C)  $8c$
D)  $-c$

**7**

The graph of an equation in the $xy$-plane is a parabola with vertex $(3,-2)$, if the equation of the parabola can be written as $x^2 + bx + c$ where $b$ and $c$ are constants, what is the value of $c$?

A)  $-6$
B)  $-2$
C)  $6$
D)  $7$

**8**

$$y = c(x - 3)(x + 5)$$

In the quadratic equation above, $c$ is a non-zero constant. The graph of the equation in the $xy$-plane is a parabola with vertex $(u, v)$. Which of the following is equal to $v$?

A)  $1$
B)  $c$
C)  $-16$
D)  $-16c$

**9**

Which of the following is an equation of a circle in the $xy$-plane with center $(1,2)$ and a radius with endpoint $(-5,-6)$?

A)  $(x - 1)^2 + (y - 2)^2 = 10$
B)  $(x - 1)^2 + (y - 2)^2 = 100$
C)  $(x - 1)^2 + (y + 2)^2 = 100$
D)  $(x - 1)^2 + (y + 2)^2 = 64$

**10**

$$x^2 + 4x + y^2 - 6y = 12$$

The equation above represents a circle in the $xy$-plane. What is the radius of the circle?

A) $2\sqrt{3}$
B) 5
C) 12
D) 25

**11**

$$x + y = \sqrt{8x + 2xy - 7}$$

Which of the following is equivalent to the equation above?

A) $(x - 4)^2 + y^2 = 9$
B) $x(x - 8) + y(y - 2x) = -7$
C) $\sqrt{x + y} = 8x + 2xy - 7$
D) $-7x - 2xy + y = -7$

# Zeros & Solutions

*In this chapter, we take a step back and look at the connections between solutions, zeroes, and x-intercepts.*

## PORTAL

For a refresher on finding the solutions to a quadratic, turn to page 490.

### Different Names for the Same Thing

The key to mastering the SAT Math section is to not just practice different question types, but to learn the connections between similar concepts. In the Solving for Zero chapter, we learned how we can find the **solutions** of a polynomial function by setting it equal to **zero** and factoring:

$$f(x) = x^2 + 7x + 10$$

$$x^2 + 7x + 10 = 0$$
$$(x + 2)(x + 5) = 0$$

*Solutions*  $x = -2, -5$

When we do this, we are finding the *x*-inputs that make a function machine spit out a zero. But let's think *graphically*. If we know that plugging in –2 and –5 for *x* makes f(x) equal *zero*, then that must mean that *y* is zero at those two points. In other words, the **x-intercepts** are:

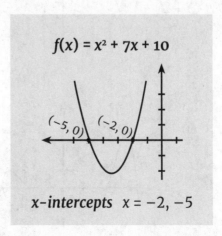

$$f(x) = x^2 + 7x + 10$$

*x-intercepts*  $x = -2, -5$

This means that, if you know the **x-intercepts** of a graph, you also know the **solutions** when you set that function equal to zero. The SAT wants you to be completely comfortable switching between these concepts, so let's get some practice!

## EXAMPLE 1

If the function $g$ has six distinct zeros, which of the following could represent the graph of $g$ in the $xy$-plane?

A)

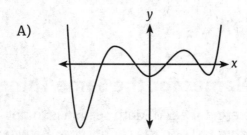

B)

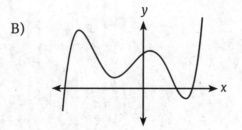

C)

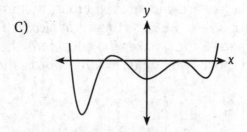

D)

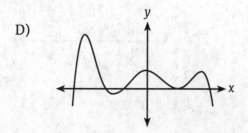

SOLUTION

Since the function has six distinct zeros, that means it **crosses the x-axis six times**. All we have to do is count how many times the graph in each answer choice crosses the *x*-axis.

 *count x-intercepts*

**Choice A:**
6 *x*-intercepts

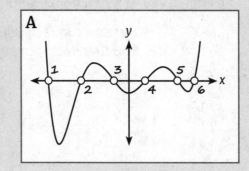

**Choice B:**
3 *x*-intercepts

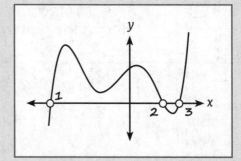

**Choice C:**
5 *x*-intercepts

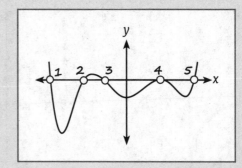

**Choice D:**
5 *x*-intercepts

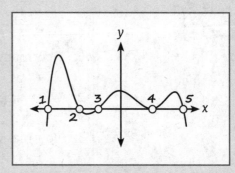

Only **choice A** has a graph that crosses the *x*-axis 6 times, so it could be the graph of a function with 6 solutions.

A

## PORTAL

Need a refresher on factoring polynomials? Turn to the Factoring Basics chapter on page 490.

## Intercepts show you the factors of the polynomial

The $y$-intercept of a function is the point where the function crosses the $y$-axis, which is the point where the input $x$ is 0. Similarly, the $x$-intercepts of a function are the points where the function crosses the $x$-axis.

Here's a fun fact. Before you factor a polynomial, you set it equal to zero. You then factor to get something like:

$$(x - 4)(x + 2) = 0$$
$$x = 4 \text{ or } -2$$

Each factor shows you an $x$-value that, when plugged in, gives an output ($y$-value) of zero. In other words, when you factor a polynomial, you are **finding the $x$-intercepts** of its graph!

---

**Use the graph** to answer the questions below.

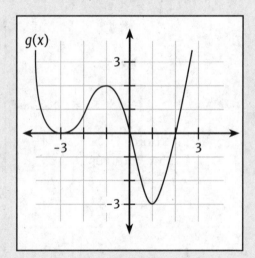

| Question | Answer |
|---|---|
| 1. How many $y$-intercepts are there? | |
| 2. What is/are the $y$-intercept(s)? | |
| 3. How many $x$-intercepts are there? | |
| 4. What is/are the $x$-intercepts? | |
| 5. If the polynomial $g$ were factored, what factors must it have? | |

Answers:  *On the next page*

## EXAMPLE 2

In the $xy$-plane, the graph of function $f$ has $x$-intercepts at $-5$, $0$, and $3$. Which of the following could be the function?

A) $f(x) = (x - 5)(x + 3)$
B) $f(x) = x(x - 5)(x - 3)$
C) $f(x) = (x + 5)(x - 3)$
D) $f(x) = x(x + 5)(x - 3)$

SOLUTION

We know that $x$-intercepts of a function have a $y$-coordinate of 0. That means if we plug $-5$, $0$, and $3$ into the function **equation**, it will spit out a result of **zero**. The simplest way to solve this problem is to do just that: test each answer choice by plugging in the given $x$-values. If the function doesn't spit out a zero for every single one, then it's not the right equation. It turns out that only choice D works for every single value:

plug-in to test choice D

$$x(x + 5)(x - 3) = ?$$
$$0(0 + 5)(0 - 3) = 0 \quad \checkmark$$
$$-5(-5 + 5)(-5 - 3) = 0$$
$$3(3 + 5)(3 - 3) = 0$$

### SHORTCUT: Thinking with Factors

We don't *have* to trial-and-error this problem. When a function is factored out, you can **see** the solutions clearly. If the graph has an $x$-intercept of $k$, then one factor would be:

$$f(x) = (x - k)...$$

That means that just knowing the $x$-intercepts, we can write the factors out and then compare our equation to the answer choices. If there are intercepts at 0, $-5$, and 3, then the factors are:

$$f(x) = (x - 0)(x - (-5))(x - 3)$$
$$f(x) = x(x + 5)(x - 3)$$

And that matches choice D! This is a great example of how we can **save time** if we understand the connection between solutions, factors, and graphs.

D

## EXAMPLE 3

| x | -5 | -2 | 0 | 3 | 6 |
|------|-----|-----|-----|-----|-----|
| f(x) | 10 | 6 | 4 | 0 | 2 |

The function *f* is defined by a polynomial. Some values of *x* with the corresponding values of *f*(*x*) are shown in the table above. Which of the following must be a factor of *f*(*x*) ?

A)  x + 3
B)  x – 3
C)  x – 4
D)  x + 4

In this problem, we're not told what the equation is for f(x), but we are still asked for one of its factors. The table must be important. It gives us a series of inputs & outputs, or (x, y) pairs if you're feeling graphy. How can a point tell us a factor of the equation?

Well, every **x-intercept** of a polynomial's graph tells us one of its factors. An *x*-intercept is **any x input that spits out a zero** for *f*(*x*). Do we see one in the table? Yes! In the fourth column:

| x | -5 | -2 | 0 | **3** | 6 |
|------|-----|-----|-----|-----|-----|
| f(x) | 10 | 6 | 4 | **0** | 2 |

This tells us that when x = 3, the polynomial f(x) = 0. Which means if we factored whatever that polynomial is, one of its factors must be **(x – 3)**. So the answer is B!

B

## EXAMPLE 4

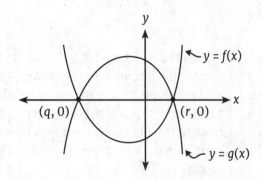

Functions $f$ and $g$, defined by $f(x) = 4x^2 + 4x - 3$ and $g(x) = -4x^2 - 4x + 3$, are graphed in the $xy$-plane above. The graphs of $f$ and $g$ intersect at the points $(q, 0)$ and $(r, 0)$. What is the value of $r$?

A) $-\dfrac{3}{2}$

B) $-3$

C) $\dfrac{1}{2}$

D) $1$

## PORTAL

This equation is a great candidate for factoring with the **box method**! For a review, turn to page 500.

### SOLUTION

We know we want to find r, and we are told that (r, 0) is one of the intersections of f(x) and g(x). We could solve this by setting f(x) and g(x) equal to one another to find the points where they intersect. But let's **use the connection between x-intercepts and factors**. If we factor one of the equations, say f(x), then we'll be able to see the x-intercepts. That will look something like:

$$f(x) = 4x^2 + 4x - 3 = (\ x + \ \ )(\ \ x - \ \ )$$

We know the **coefficients** of the x's must multiply to 4, so they're either 1 and 4 or 2 and 2. The **constants** must multiply to –3, so must be –1 and 3 or 1 and –3. Playing with these combinations a bit, we find one that works:

$$f(x) = 4x^2 + 4x - 3 = (2x + 3)(2x - 1)$$

This means the two x-intercepts are at **x = 1/2** and **x = –3/2**. So which one is r? Looking at the graph, we see that r is positive, so r must equal **1/2**. Our answer is C!

C

## EXAMPLE 5

$$h = -4.9t^2 + 80t$$

Michael is setting up for a fireworks show and needs to determine how far from his launch site the spent fireworks can safely land. He knows that $t$ seconds after launch, the height of a particular firework is given by the above equation. He also knows that, while it is in the air, the firework travels at a rate of 13.6 m/s horizontally from the launch site. About how many meters away from the launch site will the firework remains land?

A)   13.6
B)   16.3
C)   222
D)   327

## PORTAL

This problem gives a good example of a classic **quadratic model**. For more, turn to the Quadratic Modeling chapter on page 654.

For more, turn to the Quadratic Modeling chapter on page 654.

 **SOLUTION**

We're asked to find the **distance** between where the firework was launched and where it will land. Let's draw a picture to help us:

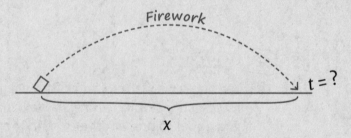

We know it travels left to right at a rate of 13.6 m/s. For this to be helpful, we need to know how long it is in the air. That's where the equation comes in! The equation has two variables: time and height. If we know one, we can find the other.

So... what is the height of the firework when it lands? That would be zero! That means if we find the zeroes of the equation we can figure out how long it was in the air:

①  *set equal to zero*                    $-4.9t^2 + 80t = 0$

②  *factor*                    $t(-4.9t + 80) = 0$

Now to find the values of $t$ that would make this equation true.

continue →

③ *find values of t*

$$t(-4.9t + 80) = 0$$

$$t_1 = 0$$

$$t_2 = \frac{80}{4.9} \approx 16.3$$

So there are two values of $t$ that would make the height zero. That makes sense! The height is zero at two times: when it launches and when it lands. The launch happens at $t = 0$, so the landing must happen at $t \approx 16.3$ seconds.

To find the distance the firework traveled during that time, we multiply 16.3 seconds by the rate it travels:

④ *multiply by the rate*

$$distance = (rate)(time)$$

$$distance = (13.6 \text{ m/s})(16.3 \text{ s})$$

$$distance = \boxed{221.68 \text{ meters}}$$

Boom, problem solved!     C

## TIP

Remember, distance is equal to rate times time. The total distance you drive (100 miles) is your speed (50 mph) times how long you drove (2 hours).

# Practice Problems

*Use your new skills to answer each question.*

---

**1**

The function $g$ has roots at $x = -4$, 1, and 5. Which of the following could be the definition of $g$ ?

A) $g(x) = (x - 4)(x - 1)(x - 5)$
B) $g(x) = (x + 4)(x + 1)(x + 5)$
C) $g(x) = (x + 4)(x - 1)(x - 5)$
D) $g(x) = (x - 4)(x + 1)(x + 5)$

---

**2**

$$f(t) = -4.9t^2 + 5t + 3$$

Maureen dives into a pool from a springboard mounted 3 meters above the water. The function $f(t)$ gives her height above the water $t$ seconds from when she jumps. After about how many seconds does she hit the water?

A) 1.4
B) 3
C) 4.9
D) 5

---

**3**

Particular values of the function $g$ are given in the following table:

| $x$ | $g(x)$ |
|-----|--------|
| -3 | 5 |
| -1 | 0 |
| 0 | 1 |
| 2 | 8 |

Which of the following is a factor of $g$ ?

A) $(x - 1)$
B) $(x + 1)$
C) $(x - 2)$
D) $(x + 3)$

4

The graph of the function $f(x)$ has 3 distinct zeros. Which of the following could be the graph of $f(x)$ ?

A)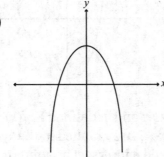

B)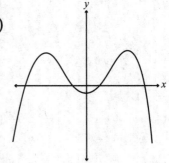

C)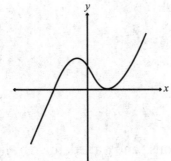

D)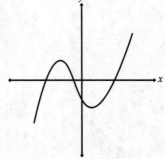

5

$$y = -16t^2 + 48t + 64$$

The equation above represents the height $y$, in feet, of an arrow $t$ seconds after it was launched from the ground at a 30° angle with an initial velocity of 96 feet per second. After approximately how many seconds will the arrow hit the ground?

A)  −1
B)  0
C)  1
D)  4

**6**

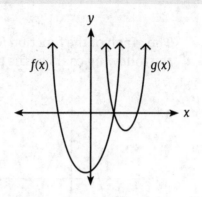

The functions $f$ and $g$, defined by $f(x) = x^2 + x - 6$ and $g(x) = x^2 - 6x + 8$ are graphed in the $xy$-plane above. The graphs of $f$ and $g$ intersect at point $(a, 0)$. What is the value of $a$?

A)  –3
B)  –2
C)  2
D)  4

**7**

The functions $f$ and $g$ are defined by $f(x) = 6x^2 + x + 5$ and $g(x) = 2x^2 - 15x - 2$. For what set of $x$ values does $f(x) + g(x) = 0$?

A)  $\frac{1}{4}$ and $\frac{3}{2}$

B)  $\frac{2}{3}$ and 4

C)  $-\frac{1}{4}$ and $-\frac{3}{2}$

D)  2 and 3

**8**

Functions $f$ and $g$ intersect at the points $(-3, 5)$, $(2, 8)$, and $(11, -17)$. Which of the following could define the function $h(x) = f(x) - g(x)$?

A)  $h(x) = (x + 3)(x - 2)(x - 11)$
B)  $h(x) = (x - 5)(x - 8)(x + 17)$
C)  $h(x) = (x + 2)(x - 6)(x + 6)$
D)  $h(x) = (x - 3)(x + 2)(x + 11)$

# UNIT | Systems of Equations

## Chapters

## Overview

In this chapter, we'll learn how to work with systems of equations. We will use strategies like **stack n' smash** and **substitution** to solve for variables, and study the connection between equations, their solutions, and their graphs.

## No Calculator!

These chapters build skills that you will use throughout both sections of the test. However, we recommend you make computations without your calculator in these chapters.

# Solving Systems

*a.k.a. "Finding a point we can all agree upon."*

## Systems of Equations

### Intersections

The solutions for a system of equations are also the *points* where the graphs of the equations **intersect**.

A **system of equations** has multiple equations with multiple variables. These equations are often (but not always) given to you stacked:

$$x + y = 12$$
$$2x + 10y = 40$$

Systems of equations show up all the time on the test. To "solve" a system of equations, we need to find the values for each variable that make both equations true *at the same time*. For example, the solutions to the system above are **x = 10** and **y = 2**, because plugging those values in makes both equations true.

$$(10) + (2) = 12$$
$$2(10) + 10(2) = 40$$

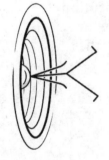

## PORTAL

In this chapter, we learn the tools for solving systems. Many SAT problems ask you to first *create* the system from a word problem. Check out the Advanced Modeling chapter on page 646.

## How to solve a system of equations

To solve a system of equations, we will need to **combine** the equations into a single equation in a way that makes one of the variables disappear. There are two main techniques that we can use to combine equations: *stack-and-smash* and *substitute-and-solve*.

# TIP

Whenever you see one variable that has the **same coefficient in each equation** (like $y$ in this system), try the *stack-and-smash* approach.

## Try solving systems by "stacking and smashing"

Sometimes, the systems of equations are set up so that we can combine them by adding or subtracting like terms. For example, say we were told **$2x - 2y = 5$** and **$4x + 2y = 13$**. We can "stack" these equations and "smash" them by adding corresponding terms:

Add

$$2x - 2y = 5$$
$$+\ 4x + 2y = 13$$
$$\overline{6x + 0y = 18}$$

Notice that this cancelled out the $y$'s, making it easy to solve for $x$. Once we have $x$, we can plug that value into of the original equations to find $y$.

## You may need to change one equation first

In more advanced problems, the systems are good candidates for stacking & smashing but need a little work first. You'll need to make **balanced changes** to one equation to make smashing as effective as possible. For example, neither $a$ nor $b$ will cancel if we "smash" the system below. But what if we multiply the whole first equation by 2?

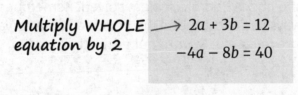

Multiply WHOLE equation by 2 →

$$2a + 3b = 12$$
$$-4a - 8b = 40$$

Notice that if we **multiply** the top equation by 2 (or **divide** the bottom equation by 2) we'll be set up for a smashing good time!

## Balance

Remember, you are free to experiment with the equation. Just remember to **keep it balanced!**

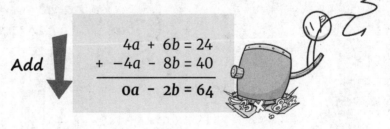

Add

$$4a + 6b = 24$$
$$+\ -4a - 8b = 40$$
$$\overline{0a - 2b = 64}$$

# TIP

The *substitute-and-solve* approach works great if you can easily isolate one variable.

However, notice that you *could* multiply the top equation in this system by 2 and smash away!

## Substitute and solve

Other times, a more subtle approach is best. When you have one equation with an easily-isolated variable, it can be best to solve using **substitution**. Just look for $x$ or $y$ with a coefficient of 1. For example:

$$x - y = 2$$
$$3x + 2y = 26$$

Notice how easy it is to get $x$ or $y$ alone in the top equation? Let's try using that to our advantage. If we add $y$ to both sides of the top equation, we get "$x = y + 2$". We can **substitute** that for $x$ in the bottom equation:

Plug in new "name" for x →

$$3(y + 2) + 2y = 26$$
$$3y + 6 + 2y = 26$$
$$5y = 20$$

From here, we can solve for $y$, and plug that value back into either equation to find $x$. Boom! Problem solved. Remember, you can pretty much always use substitution if it helps you solve an algebra problem; just be sure to carefullly write out each step.

# PORTAL

To see the FIRST time we used this joke, turn to the Basic Algebra chapter on page 414!

The name's x, but YOU can call me (y + 2)!

## EXAMPLE 1

$$x - 2y = -31$$
$$x + 3y = 59$$

What is the value of $x$ in the solution of the system of equations given above?

**Option 1: Stack & Smash**
Looking at these two equations, we see that $x$ has the same coefficient, 1, in both equations. This means that if we **subtract** the equations, the **$x$'s will disappear**.

| | | |
|---|---|---|
| ① stack equations | | $\begin{aligned} x - 2y &= -31 \\ -\quad x + 3y &= \phantom{-}59 \end{aligned}$ |
| ② subtract | | $0 - 5y = -90$ |
| ③ simplify | | $-5y = -90$ |
| ④ solve for $y$ | | $y = \boxed{18}$ |

We're not done yet! We were asked to **solve for $x$**, not $y$. But we can simply **plug-in 18 for $y$** in either equation to find $x$:

| | | |
|---|---|---|
| ⑤ plug-in 18 for $y$ | | $x - 2y = -31$ |
| | | $x - 2(18) = -31$ |
| ⑥ solve for $x$ | | $x - 36 = -31$ |
| | | $x = \boxed{5}$ |

*Smash!*

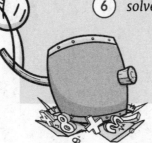

Continued on next page →

**Option 2: Solve & Substitute**

Let's pick an equation to solve for one of the variables. We can easily **solve the first equation for x** by adding 2y to each side:

(1) *solve for x in first equation*    $x - 2y = -31$

$x = -31 + 2y$

Now we can **substitute** (−31 + 2y) for x in the second equation:

(2) *substitute*    $x + 3y = 59$

$(-31 + 2y) + 3y = 59$

$-31 + 5y = 59$

(3) *solve for y*    $5y = 90$

$y = \boxed{18}$

*Substitute!*

Once again, once we find that **y = 18**, we're almost done. We just need to **substitute** that into one of the equations and solve for x. This time, for the heck of it, let's use the second equation:

(4) *plug-in 18 for y*    $x + 3y = 59$

$x + 3(18) = 59$

(5) *solve for x*    $x + 54 = 59$

$x = \boxed{5}$

## EXAMPLE 2

$$3x - 2y = -54$$
$$5x + 4y = -68$$

If $(x, y)$ is the solution to the system of equations above, what is the value of $y$?

SOLUTION

The first thing to notice is that we are solving a system of equations. The coefficients of $x$ are 3 and 5... it will be difficult making these add or subtract in a way that clears the $x$'s, so let's look at $y$.

The coefficients of y in the two equations are –2 and 4. That has potential! Do you see why? If we **multiply the top equation by 2**, then we set up the equations for a clean **stack & add** maneuver:

(1) *multiply first equation by 2*

$$2(3x - 2y = -54)$$
$$5x + 4y = -68$$

$$6x - 4y = -108$$
$$5x + 4y = -68$$

(2) *add equations*

$$6x - 4y = -108$$
$$5x + 4y = -68$$

$$11x = -176$$

(3) *solve for x*

$$x = \boxed{-16}$$

(4) *substitute –16 for x*

$$5(-16) + 4y = -68$$

$$-80 + 4y = -68$$

(5) *solve for y*

$$4y = 12$$

$$y = \boxed{3}$$

## EXAMPLE 3

$$x + 2y = -11$$
$$5x + y = 8$$

If $(x, y)$ is a solution to the system of equations above, what is the value of $2x + y$?

SOLUTION

This question asks for $2x + y$ rather than just $x$ or $y$ alone. Usually, when the SAT asks you for an expression like this (rather than just $x$ or $y$), there is some tricky or clever way to find the answer without fully solving for all the variables.

Let's keep "$2x + y$" in mind and try **adding** the two equations:

(1) *keep "2x + y" in mind*

(2) *add equations*

$$x + 2y = -11$$
$$5x + y = 8$$

$$6x + 3y = -3$$

Notice anything familiar about the result? Hidden inside it is the very same expression we were asked to find:

(3) *simplify*          $3(2x + y) = -3$

(4) *solve for 2x + y*          $2x + y = \boxed{-1}$

Of course, you don't have to see this shortcut. You can **always** solve systems of equations the old-fashioned way by Solving & Substituting. Remember: algebra is just a tool you use to reach your goal!. As long as you **keep things balanced**, you're free to manipulate as you see fit!

## EXAMPLE 4

$$\frac{x+1}{y-1} = 1$$

$$3(y+2) = x$$

If $(x, y)$ is a solution to the system of equations above, what is the value of $y$ ?

SOLUTION

Since we see two equations with the same two variables, we know we're in systems of equations land. First things first: let's clean up that fraction in the first equation:

(1) *clear fraction*

$$\frac{x+1}{y-1} = 1$$

$$x + 1 = y - 1$$

(2) *simplify*

$$x = y - 2$$

That's better! Let's look at our newly cleaned system.

$$x = y - 2$$
$$3(y + 2) = x$$

*Well whaddya know!* Now we have two equations that are solved for x. That means we can just set them equal to each other and solve for *y*.

(3) *set equal*

$$3(y + 2) = y - 2$$

(4) *solve for y*

$$3y + 6 = y - 2$$

$$2y = -8$$

$$y = \boxed{-4}$$

# Practice Problems

*Use your new skills to answer each question.*

---

**1**

$$4x + 5y = -19$$
$$y - 2x = -15$$

What is the solution $(x, y)$ to the system of equations above?

A) $(-6, 1)$
B) $(4, -7)$
C) $(3, -7)$
D) $(5, -2)$

---

**2**

$$x + 3y = 27$$
$$3x + 2y = 11$$

What is the solution $(x, y)$ to the system of equations above?

A) $(0, 9)$
B) $(-1, 7)$
C) $(-3, 10)$
D) $(1, 18)$

---

**3**

$$5x + 7y = 2$$
$$2x + 3y = 0$$

In the system of equations above, what is the value of $x + y$?

A) $-1$
B) $0$
C) $1$
D) $2$

---

**4**

$$4x + 8y = -32$$
$$7x - 3y = 29$$

In the system of equations above, what is the solution $(x, y)$?

A) $(2, -5)$
B) $(-2, -3)$
C) $(-2, 5)$
D) $(-13, 2)$

**5**

$$3x - 5y = 11$$
$$-2x + 4y = -13$$

In the system of equations above, what is the value of $x - y$?

A) $-4$
B) $-2$
C) $2$
D) $4$

**6**

$$ax - by = -2$$
$$6x - 4y = 4$$

In the system of equations above, $a$ and $b$ are constants and $x$ and $y$ are variables. If the system of equations has exactly one solution, what can $\frac{a}{b}$ NOT equal?

A) $-\frac{3}{2}$

B) $-\frac{2}{3}$

C) $\frac{2}{3}$

D) $\frac{3}{2}$

**7**

$$f(x) = -x + 4$$
$$g(x) = 3(x + 2)^2 - 4$$

How many solutions does the system above have?

A) $0$
B) $1$
C) $2$
D) $3$

$$3x - 7y = 35$$
$$x - y = 9$$

What is *x* when the system given above is satisfied?

If the product of *a* and *b* is 50% more than the sum of *a* and *b*, what is the value of $\frac{1}{a} + \frac{1}{b}$ ?

A) $\frac{2}{3}$

B) $\frac{3}{2}$

C) $\frac{1}{5}$

D) $\frac{1}{2}$

$$a = 4800 - 6t$$
$$b = 5400 - 8t$$

In the system of equations above, *a* and *b* represent the distance, in meters, two marathon runners are from the finish line after running for four hours and *t* seconds. How far will runner *a* be from the finish line when runner *b* passes her?

A) 200 meters
B) 300 meters
C) 1000 meters
D) 3000 meters

# Spotting Solutions

*In the previous chapter, we looked at how we can use algebra to discover the solutions to a system of equations. In this section, we will learn about how you can SEE solutions by looking at the graph of a function.*

## NOTE

When we talk about the **graph of a function** we are talking specifically about the line, parabola, or curve itself, not the entire coordinate system around it.

## Solutions to an Equation

You can think of the graph of an equation as simply a **helpful picture** showing every $(x,y)$ pair that makes an equation true. If we see that point $(2, 5)$ is on the graph of $y = 2x + 1$, then we can be sure that plugging 2 in for $x$ in the equation will spit out a y-value of 5. And that will be true for every point we know is on the line. In other words, **points on the line *are* the solutions**.

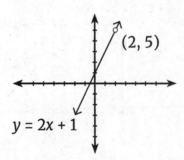

## Solutions to a System of Equations

When we talk about the solutions to a **system** of equations, we are looking for an $(x, y)$ pair that makes *both* equations true. In other words, we're looking for **the point where the graphs intersect**.

In this graph, we can see that the solution to the system of equations is $x = 0$ and $y = 1$. Try it, it works! Don't you wish *all* systems came with graphs?

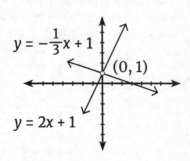

579

## INTERACTIVE EXAMPLE

The function $f(x) = x^5 - 3x^4 - 5x^3 + 15x^2 + 4x - 17$ is graphed in the $xy$-plane below. Now we're going to ask a bunch of questions about it!

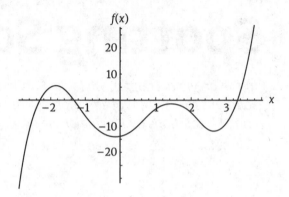

**Q1)** How many solutions are there to the equation $f(x) = 0$ ?

**S1)** The solutions to $f(x) = 0$ are the values of $x$ where the $y$-value is **zero**. In other words, we're looking for the $x$-intercepts. That means the *number* of solutions is the *number* of $x$-intercepts. Simply counting them tells us that there are **3 solutions** to $f(x) = 0$.

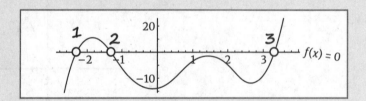

**Q2)** How many solutions are there to the equation $f(x) = -10$ ?

**S2)** This problem is *very* similar to the previous problem. When we were looking for solutions to $f(x) = 0$, we were looking for where the graph crossed the horizontal line at $y = 0$. That means that, here, we want to know how many times the graph crosses a horizontal line at **$y = -10$**. If we draw that line, we see there are **5 solutions** to $f(x) = -10$.

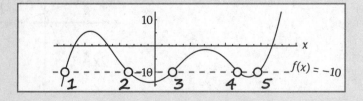

**Q3)** If $k$ is a constant such that the equation $f(x) = k$ has 3 real solutions, which of the following could be the value of $k$?

A)  20
B)  5
C)  −20
D)  −40

**S3)** In the previous question, we wanted to know how many solutions there are for $f(x) = -5$. So, we drew the line y = −5 and counted. This question is essentially asking the same thing, only backwards: where can we draw a horizontal line that crosses the graph of $f(x)$ exactly 3 times? They give us four possible options, so we just need to graph and check each one. You can take it from here:

**Use the graph** to find where $f(x)$ has 3 solutions:

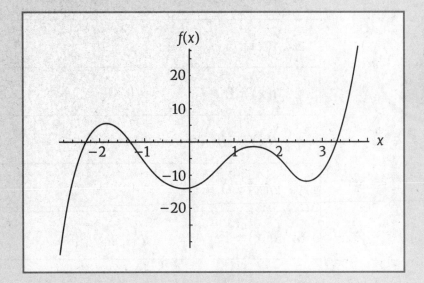

**Use the below graphs** to count the number of solutions.

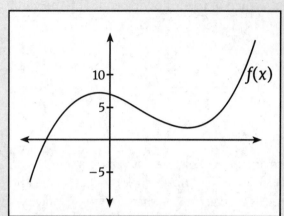

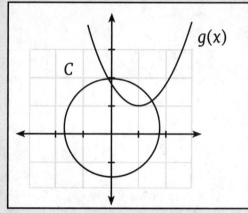

| How many solutions are there to... | # of Solutions |
|---|---|
| 1. $f(x) = -3$ | *1* |
| 2. $f(x) = 5$ | |
| 3. $f(x) = 0$ | |
| 4. $f(x) = 10$ | |
| 5. $g(x) = 0$ | |
| 6. $g(x) = 1$ | |
| 7. $g(x) = 3$ | |
| 8. The system with circle $C$ and line $y = 0$ | |
| 9. The system with circle $C$ and line $y = 2$ | |
| 10. The system with circle $C$ and $g(x)$ | |

Answers: 1. *given*  2. 3  3. 1  4. 1  5. 0
6. 1  7. 2  8. 2  9. 1  10. 2

## PORTAL

For more on determining the number of solutions for an equation, see Advanced Algebra on page 528.

## Numbers of Solutions

As we've seen, the number of solutions can be determined simply by **counting intersection points** on the graph. Occasionally, however, the SAT will give you a system of equations and not the graphs, and ask you to determine how many solutions the system has. So let's think about the different possibilities.

## One, None, or a Ton

With a pair of lines, it turns out there are **three possibilities**, and it all depends on the the *slopes* of the lines.

**One solution**: When two lines have *different slopes*, they have one point of intersection and the system has one solution.

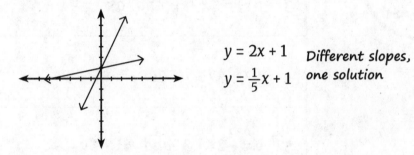

$$y = 2x + 1$$
$$y = \frac{1}{5}x + 1$$

*Different slopes, one solution*

**No solutions**: When two lines have the *same slope* and different $y$-intercepts, they are **parallel** and never intersect. Thus, the system has no solutions.

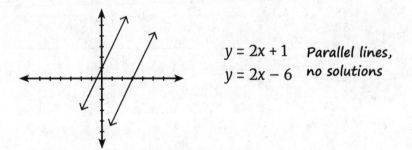

$$y = 2x + 1$$
$$y = 2x - 6$$

*Parallel lines, no solutions*

**Infinite solutions**: When two lines are actually the **same exact line**, then the system has infinitely many solutions. In this situation, you're given a system that appears to be two separate equations. But when you put the equations into slope-intercept form, you end up with identical equations.

## NOTE

The "∞" symbol means "infinite".

**Identify the # of solutions** to each system by writing "1", "0", or "∞".

| System of Equations | # of Solutions |
|---|---|
| 1. $f(x) = \frac{3}{4}x + 7$ and $g(x) = -\frac{3}{4}x + 7$ | |
| 2. $f(x) = 2x + 3$ and $g(x) = 2x + 7$ | |
| 3. $f(x) = \frac{2}{3}x + 3$ and $g(x) = \frac{4}{6}x - 4$ | |
| 4. $3x + 4y = 16$ and $-6x + 8y = 2$ | |
| 5. $y = -2x + 3$ and $6x + 3y = 9$ | |
| 6. $5x + 7y = 2$ and $3x - 4y = -13$ | |

**Answers: 1)** 1 **2)** 0 **3)** 0 **4)** 1 **5)** ∞ **6)** 1

# EXAMPLE 1

$$ax + by = 15$$
$$4x + 3y = 75$$

In the system of equations above, a and b are constants. If the system has infinitely many solutions, what is the value of $\frac{a}{b}$ ?

SOLUTION

**Option 1: Stack & Solve**

If the system has infinitely many solutions, then these equations must be **exactly the same**, other than some balanced changes that don't alter the graph of the line. Our job, then, is to reverse engineer those balanced changes. Since these equations look pretty similar to one another, we might try a hand at **stacking.**

Notice that $75 = 15 \times 5$. This gives us a good idea of where to start:

(1) *multiply top equation by 5*

$$5(ax + by = 15)$$
$$4x + 3y = 75$$

$$5ax + 5by = 75$$
$$4x + 3y = 75$$

Now we can use **pattern matching** to determine that **$5a = 4$** and **$5b = 3$**. Then we can solve for our answer:

(2) *pattern matching*

$$5a = 4$$
$$5b = 3$$

(3) *solve for $\frac{a}{b}$*

$$\frac{a}{b} = \frac{5a}{5b} = \boxed{\frac{4}{3}}$$

continue →

**585**

**Option 2: Thinking with Slope**

If there are infinitely many solutions, then these "overlapping" lines must have the **exact same slope**. We can use that! Let's put the equations in slope-intercept form, and **match their slopes**.

① *rewrite equations*

$$ax + by = 15$$
$$4x + 3y = 75$$

② *slope-intercept form*

$$by = -ax + 15$$
$$3y = -4x + 75$$

$$y = -\frac{a}{b}x + \frac{15}{b}$$

$$y = -\frac{4}{3}x + 25$$

Behold, the power of thinking with slope! By putting both equations in **y = mx + b** form, and knowing that their slopes must be identical, we can easily see our answer.

③ *pattern match*

$$\frac{a}{b} = \left(\frac{4}{3}\right)$$

## All is one

This is yet **another** opportunity to stop and reflect on the connectivity of all things algebra.

Slope, solutions, factors, functions, graphs, ... they're all connected!

## EXAMPLE 2

$$7x - ry = -17$$
$$-3x - 2y = 13$$

In the system of equations above, $r$ is a constant and $x$ and $y$ are variables. For what value of $r$ will the system have no solutions?

A) $-\frac{7}{3}$

B) $-\frac{14}{3}$

C) $\frac{14}{3}$

D) $\frac{3}{14}$

The question asks us to find a value of r so that the system has no solutions. If a system of lines has no solutions, then we must be dealing with parallel lines. And what do we know about parallel lines? They have the **exact same slope**. So let's start by getting these lines into the slope-intercept form.

① *rewrite equations*

$$7x - ry = -17$$
$$-3x - 2y = 13$$

② *change to y = mx + b form*

$$-ry = -7x - 17$$
$$-2y = \phantom{-}3x + 13$$

$$y = \frac{7}{r}x + \frac{17}{r}$$

$$y = -\frac{3}{2}x - \frac{13}{2}$$

③ *set slopes equal to each other*

$$\frac{7}{r} = -\frac{3}{2}$$

④ *cross multiply*

$$3r = -14$$

⑤ *solve for r*

$$r = \boxed{-\frac{14}{3}}$$

## PORTAL

If you need a refresher on parallel lines and slope, turn to page 464.

## Digging Deeper: Number of Solutions

Occasionally, a question will ask you to find the **number of solutions** for a quadratic equation. For example:

How many real solutions $(a, b)$ are there to the system of equations $y = (x - 2)^2$ and $y = -x + 3$?

As we've seen in this chapter, graphing the equations and counting their points of intersection will give you the number of solutions. But what if the equations are not easily graphed, or if you're given a quadratic that does not easily factor? In that case, you can use the quadratic formula and a special formula called the **discriminant**, which will tell you at a glance how many solutions there are for a given equation. For more on this helpful shortcut, check out page 572.

# Practice Problems

*Use your new skills to answer each question.*

---

**1**

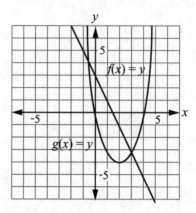

The graphs of $f(x)$ and $g(x)$ are shown above. If the point $(u, v)$ is a solution of the system, which of the following could be $u$?

A) –3
B) 0
C) 1.5
D) 3

---

**2**

$$2x + 3y = 5$$
$$3x + 2y = 0$$

How many solutions does the system above have?

A) 0
B) 1
C) Infinitely many
D) There is not enough information

**3**

$$y = 5x + 4$$
$$6x - y = -1$$

Which of the following is a solution to the system given above?

A) (−3, −11)
B) (1,9)
C) (3,19)
D) (4,24)

**4**

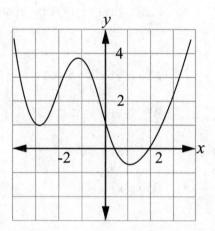

The graph of $f(x)$ is shown above. How many solutions does the equation $f(x) = 3$ have?

$$y = -\frac{2}{5}x + 7$$

$$5y + 2x = 35$$

How many solutions are there to the system of equations given above?

A)  0

B)  1

C)  Infinitely many

D)  There is not enough information given.

If $f(x) = 3x - 4$ and there is no solution to the system consisting of $f(x)$ and $g(x)$, which of the following could be $g(x)$?

A)  $g(x) = -\frac{1}{3}x + 4$

B)  $g(x) = x - 12$

C)  $g(x) = 3x^2 - 4$

D)  $g(x) = x^2$

$$y = u$$

$$y = 2x^2 + v$$

In the system of equations above, $u$ and $v$ are constants. For which of the following values of $u$ and $v$ does the system of equations have exactly two real solutions?

A)  $u = 2, v = 3$

B)  $u = -2, v = -2$

C)  $u = 4, v = 1$

D)  $u = 0, v = 2$

**8**

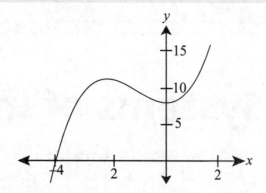

The function $f(x) = x^3 + 3x^2 - x + 7$ is graphed above. If $k$ is a constant and $f(x) = k$ has 3 real solutions, which of the following could be $k$?

A) 0
B) 6
C) 10
D) 15

**9**

$$y = (x - 3)^2 + 2$$
$$y = x - 3$$

How many ordered pairs satisfy the system of equations shown above?

A) 0
B) 1
C) 2
D) Infinitely many

**10**

$$y = x^2 + 3x - 4$$
$$y = 2x + 4$$

How many ordered pairs satisfy the system of equations shown above?

A) 0
B) 1
C) 2
D) Infinitely many

# Systems of Inequalities

*a.k.a. "Just shade above or below the line, depending on the inequality sign."*

........................................................................................................

## Graphing Inequalities

In this chapter, we are going to talk about linear inequalities – which are basically just line equations with an inequality sign instead of an equals sign. The graphs, however, look a bit different.

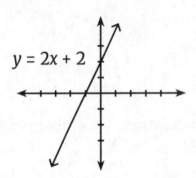 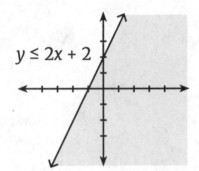

We saw last chapter that when we talk about a linear equation, such as $y = 2x + 2$, the **solutions** of the equation are *xy*-pairs that make the equation true. When we collect and plot every point that makes $y = 2x + 2$ true, we get a line.

But what happens when we swap the "=" sign for a "≤" sign? How is the graph of $y ≤ 2x + 2$ different? First, since the sign means less than *or equal to*, every point that made the equation true before *still* makes this inequality true. So we can start by drawing in the line $y = 2x + 2$. However, for each x-coordinate, we also need to count **every single y-value** that is less than (below) the line. To show this graphically, we just shade the part of the *xy*-plane that contains the solutions.

**NOTE**

If we were graphing

$y < 2x + 2$

...we would draw the line as **dashed** as if to say "Hey, please don't count the points on the line."

## Solving Systems of Inequalities

When we are looking to **solve** a system of inequalities, we are still looking for the points where the solutions intersect. So far, this has just been individual points. But when we are working with inequalities, we are looking for the regions where the shading (a.k.a., *solutions*) overlap.

### INTERACTIVE EXAMPLE

Use the graph below to answer the following questions.

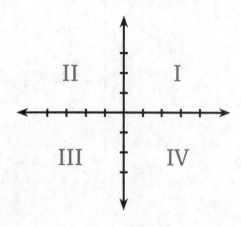

**Q1)** Graph the inequality $y \geq -2x + 3$.

**S1)** Start by graphing the line $y \geq -2x + 3$, which we know must have a y-intercept at (0, 3) and a slope of –2. Then it's time to shade. Since it is **greater than** or equal to, we want to **shade above the line**.

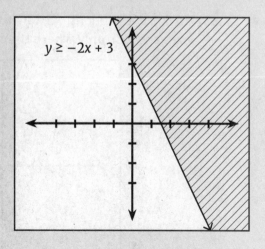

$y \geq -2x + 3$

**TIP**

The SAT expects you to know the standard names for each quadrant. Starting in the top right and moving counter-clockwise, they go: I, II, III, and IV.

**TIP**

You can always double check your thinking by picking any point in the shaded region and plugging it into the inequality.

For example, **(0, 4)** is in the shaded area, and it checks out:

$y \geq -2x + 3$
$4 \geq -2(0) + 3$
$4 \geq 3$

**Q2)** Graph the inequality $y < \frac{1}{2}x + 1$.

**S2)** Start by graphing the line $y < \frac{1}{2}x + 1$, which we know must have a $y$-intercept at (0, 1) and a slope of $\frac{1}{2}$. However, since the sign does not include "or equal to", we should draw a *dotted line*. Since it is **less than**, we want to **shade *below* this line**.

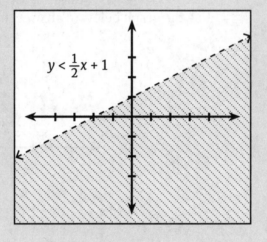

**Q3)** Which quadrants contain solutions of the system below?

$$y \geq -2x + 3$$
$$y < \frac{1}{2}x + 1$$

**S3)** To find the solutions, we want to graph both inequalities on the same axes and look **only where the shaded regions overlap**.

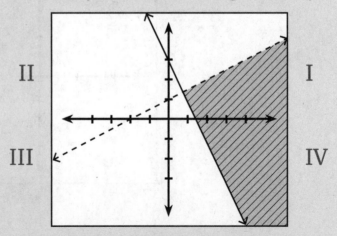

The overlap region contains all the solutions that work for *both* inequalities in the system. The region is in **quadrants I and IV.**

## EXAMPLE 2

$$y \geq x + 1$$
$$y \geq -x + 3$$

In the $xy$-plane, if a point with coordinates $(a, b)$ is a solution to the system of inequalities above, what is the minimum possible value of $b$ ?

SOLUTION

We are looking for a solution to a pair of inequalities, so let's **graph** each one.

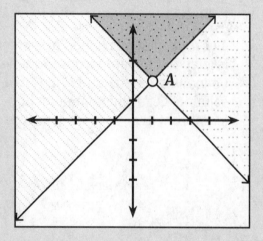

We are asked to find the **minimum possible value** for $b$, which we're told is our $y$-coordinate. That means we need the y-value at the lowest shared point in the overlap region, which we've marked as point $A$ in our graph.

Notice that point A is just the point where the two lines **intersect**. As always, we can find an intersection point by setting the two equations equal to one another:

| | | |
|---|---|---|
| (1) *set equal to each other* | | $x + 1 = -x + 3$ |
| (2) *solve for x* | | $2x = 2$ |
| | | $x = 1$ |
| (3) *plug in 1 for x* | | $y = x + 1$ |
| | | $y \geq 1 + 1 = ②$ |

## EXAMPLE 3

$$y < ax + 1$$
$$y > x + b$$

In the $xy$-plane, if (1,1) is a solution to the system of inequalities above, which of the following relationships between $a$ and $b$ must be true?

A)  $b = a$
B)  $|a| > |b|$
C)  $b > a$
D)  $a > b$

**TIP**

NEVER FORGET:
If you are given a **point**, you can plug that $x$ and $y$ value into the equation to solve for unknown variables.

It's a classic trick.

SOLUTION

Our *usual* first step when presented with a system of inequalities (sketch out a graph) won't work here; there are too many unknowns. On the other hand, we are told that point (1,1) is a solution. Let's plug that point into the equations and see what we learn from it:

(1) *rewrite equations*

$$y < ax + 1$$
$$y > x + b$$

(2) *plug in (1, 1)*

$$1 < a + 1$$
$$1 > 1 + b$$

(3) *simplify*

$$0 < a$$
$$0 > b$$

(4) *combine inequalities*

$$b < 0 < a$$

So $a$ (which is positive) *must* be greater than $b$ (which is negative). That means **our answer is D.**

# Practice Problems

*Use your new skills to answer each question!*

**1**

$$2y - m > 3x$$
$$3y + n > 2x$$

The origin in the $xy$-plane is a solution to the system of inequalities above. Which of the following must be true?

A) $m$ is greater than zero.
B) $n$ is greater than $m$.
C) $m$ is greater than $n$.
D) $m$ is equal to $-n$.

**2**

If Gertie wants to get promoted to the role of project manager at her company, she must work a total of at least 4,000 hours between the two projects she has been assigned, and she must bring in a total of at least $500,000 between the two projects. Gertie predicts she will bring in $100 in revenue for each hour she spends on project $a$ and $150 in revenue for each hour she spends on project $b$. Which set of inequalities represents the work Gertie would have to complete in order to receive her promotion? Let $x$ represent the number of hours spent on project $a$ and $y$ represent the number of hours spent on project $b$.

A) $100x + 150y \geq 500,000$

$x + y \geq 4,000$

B) $\frac{x}{100} + \frac{x}{150} \geq 500,000$

$x + y \geq 4,000$

C) $100x + 150y \geq 4,000$

$x + y \geq 500,000$

D) $x + y \geq 500,000$

$100x + 150y \geq 500,000$

**597**

$$y < -x^2 + c$$
$$y > x + b$$

If $(0, 0)$ is a solution to the system of inequalities above, which of the following describes the relationship between $b$ and $c$?

A) $b > c$
B) $b < c$
C) $|b| < |c|$
D) $|b| > |c|$

$$y \le -x(x + 6)$$
$$y \ge x$$

In the system of inequalities above, what is the $y$-coordinate for the solution that has the smallest value for $x$?

**5**

$$y < -\frac{1}{2}x + a$$
$$y > 2x - a$$

If the value of $a$ is 7, which of the following is a possible solution to the system of inequalities above?

A) $(2, 6)$
B) $(4, 5)$
C) $(5, 4)$
D) $(5, 3)$

**6**

If $y > -\frac{1}{4}x + a$ and $y > 3x + b$ are graphed in the $xy$–plane above and $a$ and $b$ are both positive integers, which of the following quadrants has no solutions to the system?

A) Quadrants I and II
B) Quadrants II and III
C) Quadrants III and IV
D) There are solutions in all four quadrants.

Estella has received either a 90 or a 100 on every spelling quiz she has taken this semester. She has also scored a 90 on at least one spelling quiz and a 100 on more than 4 spelling quizzes. Let $x$ represent the number of spelling quizzes on which Estella has received a 90, and let $y$ represent the number of spelling quizzes on which she has received a 100. Which of the following systems represents all the constraints that $x$ and $y$ must satisfy if Estella's quiz average is above a 95?

A)   $x \geq 1$

    $y > 4$

    $\dfrac{90x + 100y}{x + y} > 95$

B)   $x \geq 1$

    $y > 4$

    $x + y = 5$

    $\dfrac{90x + 100y}{x + y} > 95$

C)   $1 \leq x \leq 4$

    $0 < y < 4$

    $90x + 100y < 95(x + y)$

D)   $x \geq 1$

    $x > 4$

    $x + y \geq 5$

    $\dfrac{90x + 100y}{x + y} > 95$

# UNIT | Spicing It Up

## Chapters

## Overview

In this unit, we learn some **advanced techniques** for finding the solutions for quadratics that do not easily factor.

## No Calculator!

These questions often show up on the non-calculator section of the test. Unless otherwise marked, do not use your calculator.

# Advanced Factoring

*a.k.a. "Jumping through hoops before we can factor like normal."*

We have seen that when we want to find **solutions** to a quadratic equation, it's useful to move everything to one side and factor. Occasionally, you'll run into situations that make this more difficult – for example, when there's an $x^3$ in the equation. These situations look impossible at first, but there's an important thing to remember:

## PORTAL

Need a refresher on factoring polynomials? Turn to the Factoring Basics chapter on page 490 and the Solving for Zero chapter on page 507.

> Nothing is impossible!

We **can** and **will** get around these obstacles! We just need to use a clever trick or two to make factoring easier.

## Factoring by Grouping

Let's look at a technique that is particularly useful for handling cubics. Say we were asked to find a **real solution** to the following equation:

$$x^3 - 3x^2 + 5x - 15 = 0$$

As usual, when we see a polynomial equal to zero, our instinct should be to **factor the polynomial**. Unfortunately, our usual method for factoring quadratics doesn't work when there's an $x^3$ involved...

The first step is to **be confident**: if it's a cubic on the SAT, there *must* be some way to simplify it so that we can factor like normal... we just need to jump through a hoop or two first.

Usually, the first step to factoring is to **factor out a common term**. Is there a term common to every single term in this equation? No! But... what if we **break this equation into two groups:**

$$x^3 - 3x^2 + 5x - 15 = 0$$

$$(x^3 - 3x^2) + (5x - 15) = 0$$

group 1      group 2

Now, are there common terms *within each group*? Yes! We can factor out an $x^2$ from the first group and a 5 from the second group:

factor

$$x^2(x - 3) + 5(x - 3) = 0$$

Do you notice anything about the equation now? We have a new "common term" **(x − 3)** that we can factor out:

factor

$$(x - 3)(x^2 + 5) = 0$$

Now, magically, we have factored our original equation! From these factors, we can see that one real solution for the equation is **x = 3**. Remember: nothing is impossible on the test. If it looks like you can't factor because of a large exponent, try grouping!

## Factoring by Grouping Recap

When you are asked to solve a cubic polynomial, try this:

(1) *copy equation*      $x^3 + 10x^2 + 5x + 50 = 0$

(2) *create groups*      $(x^3 + 10x^2) + (5x + 50) = 0$

(3) *factor out like terms*      $x^2(x + 10) + 5(x + 10) = 0$

(4) *factor out expression*      $(x + 10)(x^2 + 5) = 0$

**Separate each equation into** two groups and factor out common terms.

| | Equation | Group 1 | Group 2 |
|---|---|---|---|
| 1. | $x^3 - 3x^2 + 5x - 15$ | $x^2(x - 3)$ | $5(x - 3)$ |
| 2. | $a^3 + 7a^2 + 5a + 35$ | | |
| 3. | $2x^3 - 9x^2 + 6x - 27$ | | |
| 4. | $21x^3 - 3x^2 - 28x + 4$ | | |
| 5. | $x^3 + 4x^2 - 9x - 36$ | | |
| 6. | $ap + al + np + nl$ | | |

Now **factor the equations** into two factors.

| | Equation | Factors |
|---|---|---|
| 7. | $x^3 - 3x^2 + 5x - 15$ | $(x - 3)(x^2 + 5)$ |
| 8. | $a^3 + 7a^2 + 5a + 35$ | |
| 9. | $2x^3 - 9x^2 + 6x - 27$ | |
| 10. | $21x^3 - 3x^2 - 28x + 4$ | |
| 11. | $x^3 + 4x^2 - 9x - 36$ | |
| 12. | $ap + al + np + nl$ | |

## Factoring with Even Exponents

Let's look at another situation that may look too hard to factor at first:

$$x^6 + 2x^3 + 1 = 0$$

The $x^6$ term might look scary, but this is actually a polynomial you know how to solve! Notice that $x^6 = x^3 \cdot x^3$, which makes your middle ("base") term in the polynomial $x^3$ instead of just $x$. The most common thing to watch for is a polynomial with 3 terms where the larger exponent is **double the smaller**:

$$x^6 + 2x^3 + 1 = (x^3 + 1)(x^3 + 1)$$
$$x^4 - 8x^2 + 6 = (x^2 - 3)(x^2 - 2)$$
$$x^{12} + 8x^6 - 48 = (x^6 + 12)(x^6 - 4)$$

# TIP

If looking at dragons really does increase your cognitive abilities like we said it did in the Factoring Basics chapter, then we're gonna need a bigger dragon for *this* chapter!

Without further ado...

## EXAMPLE 1

$$2u^4 + 7u^2v^2 + 3v^4$$

Which of the following is equivalent to the expression shown above?

A) $(2u^3 + 3v^2)(u^2 + 3v^2)$
B) $(2u + v^3)(u^3 + 3v)$
C) $(2u + v)(u^3 + 3v^3)$
D) $(2u^2 + v^2)(u^2 + 3v^2)$

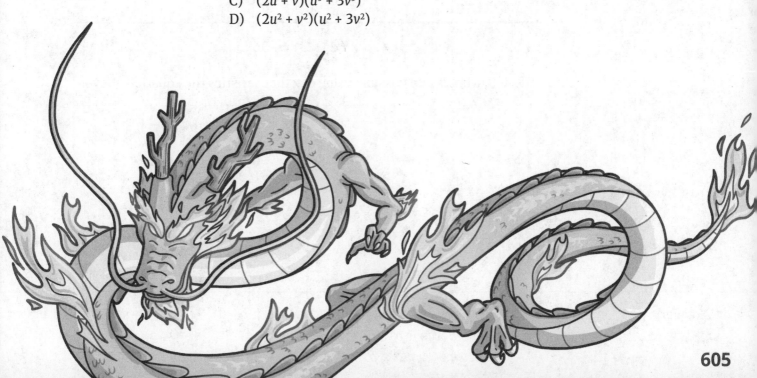

SOLUTION

Looking at the answer choices, they clearly want us to **factor the expression.** Notice that we have terms with $u^4$, $v^4$, and $u^2v^2$.

Since $(u^2)^2 = u^4$ and $(v^2)^2 = v^4$, we want to think about $u^2$ and $v^2$ as our base variables.

$$2u^4 + 7u^2v^2 + 3v^4 = (\_u^2 + \_v^2)(\_u^2 + \_v^2)$$

This is the only setup that would give us the correct variables after FOILing. So all we need to do now is **find the coefficients.** The only factors of 2 are 2 and 1, so let's put that in:

$$2u^4 + 7u^2v^2 + 3v^4 = (2u^2 + \_v^2)(u^2 + \_v^2)$$

Now we just need to find the final coefficients. We want to end up with a 3, so the only possible factors are **3** and **1**. We can't just put them in any order, however. Since we want to end up with a 7 as our middle term, we need to place these coefficients so that the 3 gets multiplied by the 2 when we FOIL:

$$2u^4 + 7u^2v^2 + 3v^4 = (2u^2 + v^2)(u^2 + 3v^2)$$

And that's it! **Our answer is D!**

D

## Workin' Backwards

If this tricky factoring gives you trouble, you can **work backwards** by FOILing out each answer choice. The correct choice will work out to be the given equation!

You could also use the **box method** to factor here!

---

EXAMPLE 2

$$x^3(x^2 - 13) = -36x$$

If $x > 0$, what is one possible value of $x$ that satisfies the equation above?

SOLUTION

Looking for a "value of x that satisfies the equation" just means that we need to solve the polynomial. Which means our first step is to **move everything to one side**.

## TIP

When we factor out an **x** from the whole expression, it tells us that one possible solution to the equation is **x = 0**.

However, since the question tells us that **x > 0**, we can ignore that factor here.

(1) *copy equation*  $\qquad$ $x^3(x^2 - 13) = -36x$

(2) *move to one side*  $\qquad$ $x^3(x^2 - 13) + 36x = 0$

(3) *simplify*  $\qquad$ $x^5 - 13x^3 + 36x = 0$

Next, as always, we want to **pull out any common factors**:

(4) *pull out common term*  $\qquad$ $x(x^4 - 13x^2 + 36) = 0$

Now we just need to **factor $(x^4 - 13x^2 + 36)$**. Since $x^4 = (x^2)^2$, we can factor like normal, using $x^2$ as our base variable:

## TIP

We can factor each factor one more time if we recognize they are each **difference of squares**.

$(x^2 - y^2) = (x + y)(x - y)$

$(x^2 - 9) = (x + 3)(x - 3)$

$(x^2 - 4) = (x + 2)(x - 2)$

Since we know $x > 0$, we can throw out the –3 and –2 solutions.

(5) *factor*  $\qquad$ $x^4 - 13x^2 + 36 = 0$

$\qquad$ $(x^2 - 9)(x^2 - 4) = 0$

(6) *solve*  $\qquad$ $x^2 = 9$
$\qquad$ $x^2 = 4$

$\qquad$ $x = 3$
$\qquad$ $x = 2$

## Use z-substitution to simplify scary problems

Sometimes, it may be tough to wrap your mind around the exponents in a given polynomial. You can always use substitution to simplify things:

(1) *take given equation*  $\qquad$ $x^6 + 2x^3 + 1 = 0$

(2) *substitute $z = x^3$*  $\qquad$ $z^2 + 2z + 1 = 0$

(3) *factor as usual*  $\qquad$ $(z + 1)(z + 1) = 0$

(4) *substitute back in $x^3$*  $\qquad$ $(x^3 + 1)(x^3 + 1) = 0$

## TIP

# EXAMPLE 6

What value of $x$ satisfies the equation $x - \sqrt{x} - 12 = 0$ ?

SOLUTION

There are two approaches we could take to solving this one.

**Option 1: Factoring with $z$**

When you see this equation, you might notice that it almost looks like a factoring problem: an expression with three terms set equal to zero, and the first term ($x$) is the square of the second ($\sqrt{x}$):

$$x - \sqrt{x} - 12 = 0 \leftarrow$$ *Maybe we can factor this?*

It can be tough to wrap your brain around factoring with square roots, so let's rename things to give our brains a break. Let's substitute $z$ for $\sqrt{x}$, and $z^2$ for $x$.

① *Substitute $z$ for $\sqrt{x}$*

$$x - \sqrt{x} - 12 = 0$$
$$z^2 - z - 12 = 0$$

② *Factor new equation*

$$(z - 4)(z + 3) = 0$$

③ *Solve for $z$*

$$z = 4, -3$$

④ *Substitute $\sqrt{x}$ for $z$*

$$\sqrt{x} = 4, -3$$

Hold up! We found two numbers for $\sqrt{x}$, but on the test a square root must equal a **positive** number. Let's throw out $-3$, leaving us with $\sqrt{x} = 4$, or $x = 16$.

**Option 2: Isolate and clear the square root**
If you don't notice that this is secretly a factoring problem, all is not lost! We can get rid of the square isolating the square root by itself so that we can square both sides and make it go away:

(1) *Isolate $\sqrt{x}$*

$$x - \sqrt{x} - 12 = 0$$
$$x - 12 = \sqrt{x}$$

(2) *Square both sides*

$$(x - 12)^2 = (\sqrt{x})^2$$
$$x^2 - 24x + 144 = x$$

(3) *Simplify & factor*

$$x^2 - 25x + 144 = 0$$
$$(x - 9)(x - 16) = 0$$

This tells us the options are 9 and 16. But whenever we work with square roots, we **always** need to check our answers for one that doesn't work. If we plug both back into the original equation, we see that only 16 makes the equation equal to zero:

Test $x = 9$  $\quad x - \sqrt{x} - 12 \rightarrow 9 - 3 - 12 \rightarrow -24 \neq 0$  ✗

Test $x = 16$  $\quad x - \sqrt{x} - 12 \rightarrow 16 - 4 - 12 \rightarrow 0 = 0$  ✓

The correct answer is 16!

# TIP

Substitution is a basic skill in algebra that continues to be useful even in very complex problems.

Remember, you have the freedom to tinker with equations as you see fit, so long as you keep them balanced!

ORIGINAL   $x + \sqrt{x} - 12 = 0$

RESULT   $z^2 + z - 12 = 0$

# Practice Problems

*Use your new skills to answer each question.*

**1**

$$x^3 + 5x^2 - 4x - 20 = 0$$

For what positive real value of $x$ is the equation above true?

**2**

$$x^5 = 7x^3 + 18x$$

If $x > 0$, what is the integer solution to the equation above?

**3**

$$f(x) = x^3 - 7x^2 + 3x - 21$$

The function $f(x)$ is defined above. What is the $x$-coordinate where it crosses the $x$-axis?

**4**

$$x^2(x^2 + 4) = 21$$

For what negative real value of $x$ is the equation above true?

A)  $-21$
B)  $-7$
C)  $-3$
D)  $-\sqrt{3}$

**5**

$$x^5 + 7x^3 - 8x^2 - 56 = 0$$

For what real value of $x$ is the equation above true?

A) $-3$
B) $-2$
C) $2$
D) $3$

**6**

$$4x^3 + 4x^2 - 9x = 9$$

For what positive value of $x$ is the equation above true?

A) $4$

B) $\dfrac{9}{4}$

C) $\dfrac{3}{2}$

D) $1$

**7**

$$4x^4 + 12x^2y^2 + 9y^4$$

Which of the following expressions is equivalent to the expression shown above?

A) $(2x^2 + 3y^2)^2$
B) $(2x + 3y)^4$
C) $(4x^2 + 9y^2)^2$
D) $(4x + 9y)^4$

**HINT**

Before diving into some complicated factoring, look for a **relationship** between $f(x)$ and $g(x)$. The answer choices provide a clue.

**8**

$$f(x) = 3x^3 - 12x^2 + 9x$$
$$g(x) = x^2 - 4x + 3$$

The polynomials $f(x)$ and $g(x)$ are defined above. Which of the following polynomials is divisible by $3x - 2$ ?

A)  $p(x) = f(x) + g(x)$
B)  $q(x) = 3f(x) - 2g(x)$
C)  $r(x) = f(x) - 2g(x)$
D)  $s(x) = -2f(x) + 3g(x)$

**9**

$$g(x) = 2x^3 + 10x^2 + 12x$$
$$h(x) = x^2 + 5x + 6$$

For the polynomials $g(x)$ and $h(x)$ defined above, which of the following polynomials is divisible by $6x + 4$ ?

A)  $k(x) = g(x) + h(x)$
B)  $m(x) = 6g(x) + 4h(x)$
C)  $n(x) = 3g(x) + 4h(x)$
D)  $p(x) = 4g(x) + 6h(x)$

# The Unfactorables

*Let's look at what you can do when factoring just isn't helping.*

## TIP

It's a good idea to fully write out the formula whenever you use it.

## Quadratic Formula

If the test asks you to **solve** a quadratic equation and you see that there are **square roots in the answer choices**, don't bother trying to factor. The question is practically *begging* you to use the quadratic formula.

$$\text{If } ax^2 + bx + c = 0 \text{, then } x = \frac{-b \pm \sqrt{b^2 - 4ac}}{2a}$$

If you have an equation in the form $ax^2 + bx + c = 0$, simply plug your a, b, and c values into the formula and simplify. For example:

$$\text{If } 6x^2 + 7x + 8 = 0 \text{, then } x = \frac{-7 \pm \sqrt{7^2 - 4(6)(8)}}{2(6)}$$

## TIP

This equation is already written in the proper $ax^2 + bx + c = 0$ form. Sometimes, you'll need to do some work to the equation to figure out a, b, and c.

### TRY IT OUT

If $x^2 + 6x + 2 = 0$, then what are two possible values for $x$ ?

SOLUTION

If we were to try and factor this equation with the box method, we'd hit a road block. Luckily, we can use the quadratic formula. Line up the equation with the *a,b,c* form to find our values:

(1) *copy equation* $\qquad x^2 + 6x + 2 = 0$

(2) *compare to a,b,c form* $\qquad ax^2 + bx + c = 0$

(3) *write a, b, c values* $\qquad a = 1,\ \ b = 6,\ \ c = 2$

Now it's just a matter of carefully **plugging in our values**. Always start by writing down the quadratic formula.

(2) *write quadratic formula* $\qquad x = \dfrac{-b \pm \sqrt{b^2 - 4ac}}{2a}$

(3) *substitute* $a = 1,\ b = 6,\ c = 2$ $\qquad x = \dfrac{-6 \pm \sqrt{(6)^2 - 4(1)(2)}}{2(1)}$

(4) *simplify* $\qquad x = \dfrac{-6 \pm \sqrt{28}}{2}$

$\qquad x = \dfrac{-6 \pm 2\sqrt{7}}{2}$

(5) *voila!* $\qquad x = \boxed{-3 \pm \sqrt{7}}$

## NOTE

Notice that solutions $(-3+\sqrt{7})$ and $(-3-\sqrt{7})$ are both **irrational**. That's why we needed to use the quadratic formula to begin with.

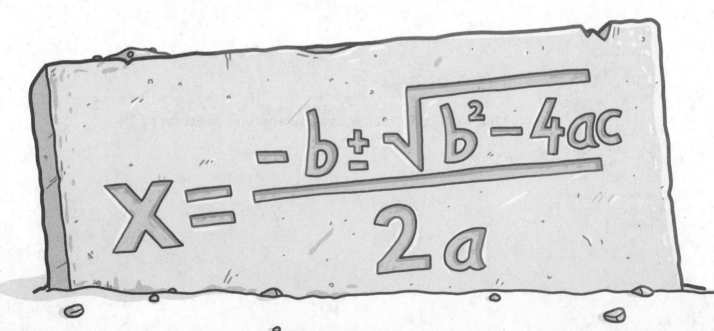

## EXAMPLE 1

$$x^2 - \frac{2m}{3}x = \frac{n}{3}$$

In the quadratic equation above, $m$ and $n$ are constants. What are the solutions for $x$ ?

A) $\quad -\frac{2m}{3} \pm \dfrac{\sqrt{(\frac{2}{3})m^2 + (\frac{4}{3})n}}{2}$

B) $\quad \frac{m}{3} \pm \sqrt{\frac{1}{9}m^2 + \frac{n}{3}}$

C) $\quad 1, -\frac{1}{3}$

D) $\quad \frac{2m}{3} \pm \dfrac{\sqrt{m^2 + (\frac{1}{3})n}}{3}$

The answer choices on this one are a huge sign that we need to use the quadratic formula. Let's start by writing out the formula:

1. *copy quadratic formula* $\qquad x = \dfrac{-b \pm \sqrt{b^2 - 4ac}}{2a}$

Now, we need our original equation to be in form $ax^2 + bx + c = 0$

2. *set equation equal to zero* $\qquad x^2 - \dfrac{2m}{3}x - \dfrac{n}{3} = 0$

So it looks like $a = 1$, $b = -\dfrac{2m}{3}$, and $c = -\dfrac{n}{3}$. Let's plug those in:

3. *plug into QF* $\qquad x = \dfrac{-b \pm \sqrt{b^2 - 4ac}}{2a}$

$$x = \dfrac{\frac{2}{3}m \pm \sqrt{(-\frac{2}{3}m)^2 - 4(1)(-\frac{n}{3})}}{2(1)}$$

4. *simplify* $\qquad x = \dfrac{\frac{2}{3}m \pm \sqrt{\frac{4}{9}m^2 + 4(\frac{n}{3})}}{2}$

**Continued on next page** $\rightarrow$

This doesn't quite look like any of the answer choices, which means we need to do some tricky simplifying:

⑤ *keep simplifying*

$$x = \frac{\frac{2}{3}m \pm \sqrt{\frac{4}{9}m^2 + 4\left(\frac{n}{3}\right)}}{2}$$

*factor out a 4 under the root*

$$x = \frac{\frac{2}{3}m \pm \sqrt{4\left(\frac{1}{9}m^2 + \frac{n}{3}\right)}}{2}$$

*take square root of 4*

$$x = \frac{\frac{2}{3}m \pm 2\sqrt{\frac{1}{9}m^2 + \frac{n}{3}}}{2}$$

*divide both terms by 2*

$$x = \frac{1}{3}m \pm \sqrt{\frac{1}{9}m^2 + \frac{n}{3}}$$

**B**

## THINK

Can you figure out WHY the discriminant tells us the number of real solutions?

Here's a hint: it has to do with that plus or minus symbol, and the fact that you can't talk about the square root of negative numbers without using imaginary numbers ($i$).

## The Discriminant

In the quadratic formula, the stuff beneath the square root ($b^2 - 4ac$) is called the **discriminant**. It has its own fancy name because it can tell us something special about the quadratic as a whole: the total number of possible real solutions to the equation. Once you plug in your $a$, $b$, and $c$ values, look under the square root.

| Discriminant | # of real solutions |
|---|---|
| Positive | Two |
| Equal to Zero | One |
| Negative | None |

When do you need to know this? Rarely, and only in one specific case. If the question asks you **how many real solutions** a problem has, then simply plug-in and read the discriminant.

## EXAMPLE 2

$$6x^2 + 18x - 13$$

How many real solutions does the above equation have?

A) 0
B) 1
C) 2
D) Infinitely many

**SOLUTION**

We want to know about the solutions of a quadratic equation. Our usual first step is to **try factoring**, but that doesn't work well here. Looking at the question, we see that we only care about how many solutions there are – we don't actually need to FIND those solutions. To do this, we need to read the discriminant. We don't even need to write out the whole formula! We can just focus on the $b^2 - 4ac$:

1. *rewrite equation*                     $6x^2 + 18x - 13$

2. *determine a, b, and c*        $a = 6, b = 18, c = -13$

3. *write discriminant*              $b^2 - 4ac$

4. *plug-in values*                 $(18)^2 - 4(6)(-13)$

Now, we COULD multiply this all out, but all we really care about is whether it's going to be positive, negative, or equal to zero, which we can figure out by focusing on the signs. We can see that we have a big, positive number ($18^2$) minus a negative number ($-13$). Since the minus sign and the negative sign will cancel, we'll end up with a big, **positive** number.

$$18^2 + 4(6)(13) > 0$$

When the discriminant is positive, we know there are TWO real solutions. So our answer is C!

C

## Remainder Theorem

One last thing the SAT expects you to memorize is a little something called the **remainder theorem**. This topic, at most, will get tested only once. Here's how it works:

> ### Remainder Theorem
> *If k is the result when a is plugged into a polynomial, then dividing the polynomial by (x − a) gives a remainder of k.*

What does it mean? Let's look at an example. Consider the polynomial:

$$x^2 - 5x + 6$$

Let's try plugging 1 in for $x$ to this polynomial and see what we get:

$$(1)^2 - 5(1) + 6 \ = \ ?$$
$$1 - 5 + 6 \ = \ ?$$
$$-4 + 6 \ = \ 2$$

Plugging in 1 for $x$ gives us a result of 2. The remainder theorem tells us then that if we divide the polynomial by $(x - 1)$, we'll get a remainder of 2. That's it! You don't need to know WHY this is the case, just that it IS the case. Let's look at an example to see how obvious the SAT is when they want to test this theorem:

## EXAMPLE 3

For a polynomial $q(x)$, the value of $q(7)$ is 12. Which of the following must be true about $q(x)$?

A) $x - 19$ is a factor of $q(x)$.
B) $x - 12$ is a factor of $q(x)$.
C) The remainder when $q(x)$ is divided by $x - 7$ is 12.
D) The remainder when $q(x)$ is divided by $x - 12$ is 7.

Not very subtle, are they? We see "remainder" in the answer choices, so it's a pretty good bet that this problem wants us to apply the remainder theorem.

When it says that $q(7) = 12$, it means that if you plug 7 in for x in the polynomial (whatever it is), you get a result of 12. The remainder theorem tells us then that if we divide the polynomial by $(x - 7)$, we'll have a **remainder of 12**.

C

## Recapping The Unfactorables

On tougher polynomial problems, the given quadratic may not easily factor. In these situations, it helps to have a few concepts memorized:

- The **quadratic formula** gives you the solutions for a polynomial without having to factor.

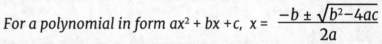

$$\text{For a polynomial in form } ax^2 + bx + c, \quad x = \frac{-b \pm \sqrt{b^2 - 4ac}}{2a}$$

- The **discriminant** ($b^2 - 4ac$) tells you how many real solutions a quadratic has, based on whether it resolves to be positive (two solutions), zero (one solution), or negative (no real solutions).

- The **remainder theorem** tells us that "if $k$ is the result when $a$ is plugged into a polynomial, then dividing the polynomial by $(x - a)$ gives a remainder of $k$.

# Practice Problems

*Use your new skills to answer each question.*

---

**1**

Which of the following is a solution to the equation
$x^2 + 3x - 2 = 0$?

A)  17

B)  $3 + \sqrt{17}$

C)  $-3 + \dfrac{\sqrt{17}}{2}$

D)  $-\dfrac{3}{2} + \dfrac{\sqrt{17}}{2}$

---

**2**

How many real solutions does the equation $x^2 + 4x + 4 = 0$
have?

A)  0
B)  1
C)  2
D)  There is not enough information given.

---

**3**

How many real solutions does the equation $3x^3 + 5x^2 + x = 0$
have?

A)  1
B)  2
C)  3
D)  There is not enough information given.

---

**4**

What is the remainder when the polynomial $x^4 + 3x^2 - 5x + 7$ is
divided by $(x + 2)$?

A)  1
B)  –2
C)  25
D)  45

**5**

What are the real solutions to $-3x^2 + 9x + 7 = 0$ ?

A) $\dfrac{-9 \pm \sqrt{165}}{6}$

B) $-\dfrac{3}{2} \pm \dfrac{\sqrt{165}}{6}$

C) $\dfrac{3}{2} \pm \dfrac{\sqrt{165}}{6}$

D) There are no real solutions.

**6**

For a polynomial $q(x)$, the value of $q(-3)$ is 4. Which of the following must be true about $q(x)$ ?

A) $x - 7$ is a factor of $q(x)$
B) $x - 4$ is a factor of $q(x)$
C) The remainder when $q(x)$ is divided by $x - 3$ is 4.
D) The remainder when $q(x)$ is divided by $x + 3$ is 4.

$$x^2 + 2sx = t + 2$$

In the quadratic equation above, $s$ and $t$ are constants. What are the solutions for $x$ ?

A)  $s \pm \sqrt{s^2 + t + 2}$

B)  $-s \pm \sqrt{s^2 + t + 2}$

C)  $-s \pm \dfrac{\sqrt{4s^2 + t + 2}}{2}$

D)  $-s \pm \sqrt{4s^2 + 4t + 8}$

# Complex Numbers

*Clap your hands if you believe in imaginary numbers.*

### New Problems, New Tools

When you first learned to use math, you worked with only the **natural** set of integers: 1, 2, 3, 4, and so on. In that number set, there's no such thing as "half of 3" or "less than zero," but it was good enough for adding apples together or counting kids on the playground. Eventually, to solve tougher math problems, you needed a new number set (called the **real** numbers) that includes new ideas like *fractions*, *negative numbers*, and *square roots*.

In the real number set, there is no such thing as "the square root of a negative," but it was good enough for most high school math. For some problems, however, you need a number set (called the **complex** numbers) that does include the idea of *the square root of negative one*, which we simply call *i*.

$$i = \sqrt{-1}$$

$$i^2 = -1$$

### Imaginary & Complex Numbers

Now for some quick vocabulary. **Imaginary numbers** are multiples of *i*, such as $6i$, $-15i$, or $2i\sqrt{-3}$. **Complex numbers** are pairs of real and imaginary numbers that are written in the form: $a + bi$. For example:

Real (a) →
$a + bi$
$12 + 6i$
$9 - 2i$
← imaginary (bi)

## Working with *i*

When solving problems involving imaginary numbers, you can treat *i* like you would *x*, *y*, or any other variable. Combine like terms when adding, subtracting, and mutiplying, and FOIL as usual when working with expressions:

$$3i + 2i = 5i$$

$$2i \cdot 2i = 4i^2$$

$$(i + 1)(i - 1) = i^2 - 1$$

Once you've combined like terms, you can **simplify any $i^2$ into -1**. In fact, we can use what we know to simplify *any* power of *i*. After $i^4$, the same pattern just repeats over and over again:

| $i$ | $i^2$ | $i^3$ | $i^4$ | $i^5$ | $i^6$ | $i^7$ | $i^8$ |
|---|---|---|---|---|---|---|---|
| $\sqrt{-1}$ | $-1$ | $-\sqrt{-1}$ | $1$ | $\sqrt{-1}$ | $-1$ | $-\sqrt{-1}$ | $1$ |

*pattern*         *pattern*

**Use the properties of *i*** to simplify each expression below:

| Simplify: | Answer: |
|---|---|
| 1.   $(3 + 2i) + (7i - 4) = ?$ | |
| 2.   $-12 + (6i + 9) = ?$ | |
| 3.   $6i - (2 - 3i) = ?$ | |
| 4.   $(3 + i)(1 - i) = ?$ | |
| 5.   $(-2 - 3i)(-2 + 3i) = ?$ | |
| 6.   $i^{14} = ?$ | |

Answers:    *Bottom of next page.*

## FOILing with "$a + bi$"

Now that we know how to simplify powers of $i$, we can look at how complex numbers show up on the test. To solve these problems, there are three things we need to know:

1. How to **work with $i$**

2. How to **FOIL**

3. What a **complex conjugate** is

The **complex conjugate** of a complex number ($a + bi$) is the same expression, only with the opposite sign in the middle:

| Complex Number | Complex Conjugate |
|:---:|:---:|
| $a + bi$ | $a - bi$ |
| $4 + 2i$ | $4 - 2i$ |
| $8 - 6i$ | $8 + 6i$ |

**TIP**

Multiplying by the complex conjugate creates a **difference of squares**.

$$(x^2 - y^2) = (x + y)(x - y)$$

Why is this useful? The answer lies in what happens when you multiply a number by its conjugate:

$$(4 + 2i)(4 - 2i) = 16 - 4i^2$$

Notice anything about that result? We can simplify it even further! Let's see this idea in action.

## EXAMPLE 1

**TIP**

Notice that all the answer choices are complex numbers in the $a + bi$ form. On test day, that would be your tip off to remember the content from this chapter!

Which of the following is equivalent to $\frac{25}{4 - 3i}$?

A) $4 - 3i$

B) $4 + 3i$

C) $100 + 75i$

D) $\frac{25}{4} - \frac{25}{3}i$

Previous Page:    1. $-1 + 9i$    2. $-3 + 6i$    3. $-2 + 9i$    4. $4 - 2i$    5. $13$    6. $-1$

SOLUTION

We're asked to simplify the given fraction, and we're going to end up with an answer in the **a + bi** form. So—how do we simplify the fraction below?

(1) *vow to one day simplify the fraction* $\dfrac{25}{4 - 3i}$

If we were working with an *x* instead of an *i*, we'd try to get *x* out of the denominator. So let's do that! We can take the numerator and denominator and **multiply by the conjugate** of the complex number on the bottom.

(2) *multiply by conjugate* $\dfrac{25}{4 - 3i} \times \dfrac{(4 + 3i)}{(4 + 3i)}$

*just swap the signs*

Now we can **apply FOIL** to multiply these fractions:

(3) FOIL $\dfrac{25}{4 - 3i} \times \dfrac{(4 + 3i)}{(4 + 3i)} = \dfrac{100 + 75i}{16 - 9i^2}$

Finally, apply what we know about **$i^2$** to simplify what's left:

(4) *simplify $i^2$* $\dfrac{100 + 75i}{16 - 9i^2} = \dfrac{100 + 75i}{16 - 9(-1)}$

$= \dfrac{100 + 75i}{25}$

$= 4 + 3i$

B

## NOTE

Multiplying the top and bottom by the same thing is the same as multiplying by 1. This is always safe to do when simplifying, since it doesn't **change** the value at all.

## PORTAL

We discuss the discriminant on pages 587 and 616.

# Rethinking the Discriminant

For the vast majority of problems, we are only interested in the **real solutions** to an equation. However, in some situations there might also be non-real **complex** solutions.

Remember how we use the **discriminant** in the quadratic formula to determine the number of solutions to a quadratic? We said that there are no solutions if $b^2 - 4ac$ is negative since we can't take the square root of a negative number. As we have seen in this chapter, that isn't true if we allow complex solutions. If we allow complex solutions, we can update our discriminant table:

| Discriminant | # of solutions |
| --- | --- |
| Positive | 2 real solutions |
| Equal to Zero | 1 real solution |
| Negative | 2 non-real complex solutions<br>0 real solutions |

If a polynomial with **real coefficients** has complex roots/solutions, the key thing to remember is that they always come in **conjugate pairs**! You can never have an odd number of complex solutions.

# Practice Problems

*Use your new skills to answer each question.*

**1**

What is the sum of $2 + 3i$ and $4 - 7i$ ?

A) $6 + 10i$
B) $6 + 4i$
C) $6 - 4i$
D) $8 - 4i$

**2**

If $a = -5 + 7i$ and $b = 8 + 4i$, what is $a + b$ ?

A) $3 + 11i$
B) $3 + 3i$
C) $13 + 11i$
D) $13 + 3i$

**3**

What is the product of the complex numbers $(1 + i)$ and $(2 - 3i)$ ?

A) $-1 - i$
B) $2 - 3i$
C) $2 + 2i$
D) $5 - i$

**4**

Simplify the expression $(-5 - 2i)(4 + i) + 17$.

A) $-1 + 13i$
B) $-1 - 13i$
C) $-5 - 13i$
D) $-5 - i$

**5**

Which of the following is equivalent to
$2(i + 4)(2 + 3i) - 5i$ ?

A) $5 + 9i$
B) $5 + 14i$
C) $10 + 14i$
D) $10 + 23i$

**6**

Evaluate the expression $3i^{101}$.

A) $0$
B) $3$
C) $3i$
D) $-3i$

**7**

What is the value of the expression $i^{205} + i^{207}$ ?

A) $0$
B) $2i$
C) $-2i$
D) $2$

**8**

Which of the following is equivalent to $\frac{3 + i}{3 - i}$ ?

A) $\frac{4}{5}$

B) $\frac{4}{5} + \frac{3}{5}i$

C) $\frac{9}{10} + \frac{3}{5}i$

D) $1 + \frac{1}{3}i$

If the expression $\dfrac{2(4 + i) + 5}{(i + 1)(i - 1)}$ is rewritten in

$a + bi$ form, what is the value of $a + b$ ?

A) $-75$

B) $-7.5$

C) $5.6$

D) $15$

Which of the following expressions is equivalent to $9x^2 + 4$ ?

A) $(3x + 2)(3x - 2)$

B) $(3x + 2i)(3x - 2i)$

C) $(3x + 2)^2$

D) $(3x + 2i)^2$

Which of the following could be the full set of complex roots of a cubic polynomial with real coefficients?

A) $\{0, 1, i\}$

B) $\{1, i, 2i\}$

C) $\{2, i\}$

D) $\{3, 2 + i, 2 - i\}$

# UNIT | Modeling

## Chapters

## Overview

In this unit, we practice the **art of translation**: using math equations to model real-world contexts. This skill will not only net you a lot of points on both math sections of the test, it will also improve your understanding of many problem types throughout this book!

## Calculator + Non-Calculator

Modeling questions show up on both math sections. It is generally safe to use your calculator on these practice questions, since modeling questions on the non-calculator section either do not require computations or they use relatively simple numbers.

# Basic Modeling

*The SAT loves testing your ability to model real-world situations with algebra.*

Sometimes, it's easy to forget that there is actually a POINT to all of this math. People use algebra **all the time** to learn things they didn't already know about their daily lives.

A new hire could use algebra to determine whether he'll make enough at his position to move to a better apartment; a car factory owner might use algebra to figure out how many tons of steel she needs to order for a busy month; or a college student might use algebra to tackle a major, existential question, like:

> "Wait... how many cookies did we eat last night?!"

The trick to answering such important questions is to **create an equation** using variables and constants that accurately *models* the specific situation. If you can master this skill, not only will you be a better worker, business-owner, and baker, but you'll also be able to gain a *lot* of easy points on the SAT. So let's use that last question about cookies to practice the fundamentals of **basic modeling**.

## The Chocolate Chip Conundrum

Last night, you and your college roommates went on something of a cookie bender. Excited by finally having a kitchen all to yourselves, the four of you spent the evening baking and consuming chocolate chip cookies from a giant tub of cookie dough that somebody bought as a "joke" the week before. The specifics of the night are a blur when you each awaken the next morning from your respective sugar comas. A panicked disagreement breaks out over exactly how many cookies were eaten during that wild night. You decide to put an end to the debate the only way you know how: by using some good, old-fashioned algebra.

## What is our Target Variable?

The first step is easy: pick a letter to represent what we're looking to find! We want to know how many cookies we ate... We could pick anything, but let's be honest, C is for Cookie (and that's good enough for me).

$$C = ?$$

*"The number of cookies eaten, C, is equal to what?"*

## What Does it Depend On?

Now, how are we going to figure out how many cookies we ate? The key is to identify some other variable that the number of cookies depends on. We bake cookies in groups – one **tray** at a time. If we knew the number of cookies that fit on a tray AND how many trays we baked, we could figure out the number of cookies we made!

Since we don't yet know how many trays we made, let's make it a **variable**, like $t$. We know that our cookie tray comfortably fits 12 cookies at a time. If we made one tray, we'd have 12 cookies. If we made two trays, we'd have 24 cookies. In other words, the number of cookies is equal to twelve times the number of trays we baked. Let's write that in math terms:

$$C = 12t$$

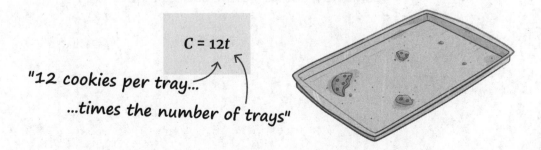

*"12 cookies per tray...*
*...times the number of trays"*

**633**

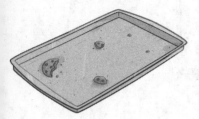

## Tray Size: Coefficients & Slope

Let's think about this 12 in front of the *t* in our equation. It tells us the *rate* at which we are making cookies. What if we used a smaller sheet (or made bigger cookies) so that **only 4 fit on the tray**? To show that, we can just change the coefficient in front of *t*:

$$C = 12t$$

12 cookies per tray

$$C = 4t$$

4 cookies per tray

So this coefficient tells us the **rate** at which the number of cookies changes when the number of trays changes. Sound famililar? This is our rate of change, *a.k.a.* rise over run, *a.k.a.* slope, *a.k.a.* "*m*" in the equation of a line! If we graphed the two equations above, the lines would have different slopes:

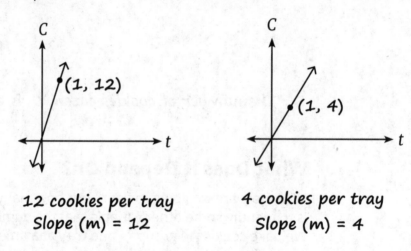

12 cookies per tray
Slope (m) = 12

4 cookies per tray
Slope (m) = 4

## Labeling Points

Notice how, when we are working with a word problem, a point on the line graphs above has a real-world meaning. The horizontal axis in the graph is the number of trays, and the vertical axis is the number of cookies. That means point (1, 12) can be read (1 tray, 12 cookies), and point (1, 4) can be read (1 tray, 4 cookies). We can read equations in the same way, but we'll come back to that.

## Leftovers: Constants & Intercepts

Let's get back to building our equation. Eventually, everyone agrees that you did, in fact, make regular-sized cookies such that 12 cookies fit on each tray. BUT you realize that there are **8 cookies left over** (shocking!). How can we add that information to our equation? Well, no matter how many trays of cookies were baked, we know we'll need to **subtract 8** from that total number to show how many were eaten.

$$C = 12t - 8$$

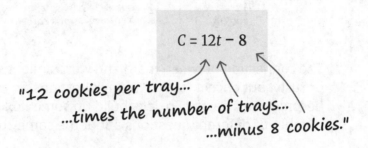

"12 cookies per tray...
...times the number of trays...
...minus 8 cookies."

Now we've got a pretty great-looking equation of a line in the slope-intercept form. Notice that the constant we just added to model the leftovers, **– 8**, matches the "+ $b$" (intercept) part of the equation of a line. Sure enough, when we graph this cookie equation, we see that – 8 is the $y$-intercept.

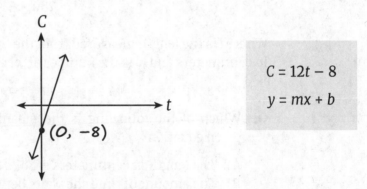

$$C = 12t - 8$$
$$y = mx + b$$

## Conundrum Modeled, Cookie Crumbled

And just like that, we have modeled our cookie conundrum into a linear equation, and (bonus!) even shown how we can graph it. Now all we would have to do to determine the number of cookies eaten is figure out the number of trays baked and plug that number in for $t$.

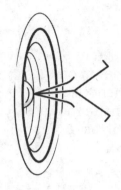

# The Art of Translation

So far, we've seen how we can go from a real-world situation to an algebraic equation. In the process, we saw how we can actually **read** that equation using the real-world context, translating the math into words:

| $C$ | $=$ | 12 | $t$ | $-$ | 8 |
|---|---|---|---|---|---|
| The # of cookies | is | 12 cookies per tray | times the # of trays | | minus 8 cookies. |

The connection between math and words might start out feeling sluggish or rusty, but once it "clicks," many questions on the SAT will instantly become *much* easier! So, let's build up some flexibility by working a number of different questions about the same context.

## PORTAL

If you haven't completed the Art of Translation chapter, turn to page 396.

## INTERACTIVE EXAMPLE 1

Ali always gets her hair cut to the same length. She has found that the current length of her hair can be modeled by the equation

$$l = .25w + 33$$

Where $l$ is the length measured from the top of her head down her back in centimeters and $w$ is the number of weeks since her latest haircut.

**Q1)** Which of the following is the meaning of the number .25 in the given equation?

A) The length in centimeters of Ali's hair after a haircut.
B) The amount of time she waits between haircuts.
C) The length in centimeters her hair reaches before each haircut.
D) The number of centimeters her hair grows each week.

**S1)** Let's start by noticing that the equation is in the slope-intercept form $y = mx + b$. The coefficient **.25** is the **slope** of the line ($m$). Slope (a.k.a, rise over run) shows us a rate of change. So our answer should tell us the *rate* something is *changing*. From just that information, choice D is looking good. Since $l$ stands for the length of her hair, that's what is changing. .25 is the amount, in centimeters, that her hair is changing. And $w$, the number of weeks, tells us what causes $l$ to change.

$$l = .25w + 33$$

Length of hair is .25cm per week plus 33cm.

D

**Q2)** Which of the following is the meaning of the number 33 in the given equation?

   A)  The length in centimeters of Ali's hair after a haircut.
   B)  The amount of time she waits between haircuts.
   C)  The length in centimeters her hair reaches before each haircut.
   D)  The number of centimeters her hair grows each week.

**S2)** Since $w$ is the number of weeks since her haircut, $w = 0$ tells us how long Ali's hair is immediately after getting her hair cut. We can see this if we compare the equation $l = .25w + 33$ to the slope-intercept form $y = mx + b$. We see that the number 33 tells us the **y-intercept** of the line. That means the line crosses the y-axis at (0 weeks, 33 centimeters). In other words, when it's been 0 weeks since her hair cut, Ali's hair is 33 centimeters long.

          **A**

## Creative Exercises

The same equation could model a number of different situations. One of the best ways to get used to this idea is to try to come up with multiple contexts for the same equation. For example, for the equation below, we've come up with three plausible (if slightly odd) contexts that it could represent. We're sure that you could come up with some better ones, so on the next page you'll have an opportunity to do just that!

$$r = 4t + 5$$

"The cost of entering a raffle (r) is equal to 4 dollars per ticket (t) plus a 5 dollar bribe to the officials."

"Richard (r) drinks 5 cups of coffee a day, plus 4 cups per hour of overtime (t)."

"The length of rope (r) to pack is 5 meters plus another 4 meters for each expected snake trap (t)."

**Complete the tables** by coming up with contexts that might be modeled by the each equation. This is a creative exercise, so let your imagination run wild. We've come up with one of our own to get you started.

| $c = 1.5d + 7$ | |
|---|---|
| Context 1 | The total weight, in pounds, of my Calico cat named Cali (c) is at least 7 pounds plus an additional 1.5 pounds per day off her diet (d).<br><br>c = weight of cat      1.5 = pounds per day<br>d = days off diet      +7 = starting weight |
| Context 2 | c =      1.5 =<br>d =      +7 = |
| Context 3 | c =      1.5 =<br>d =      +7 = |

| $f = 1,000 - 13p$ | |
|---|---|
| Context 1 | f =      −13 =<br>p =      1,000 = |
| Context 2 | f =      −13 =<br>p =      1,000 = |
| Context 3 | f =      −13 =<br>p =      1,000 = |

**Complete the table** by matching each context with the equation that best models it. We have completed the first one for you.

| Match | Context | Equation |
|---|---|---|
| **E** | The profit Martha earns from a bake-sale is $5 per brownie sold, minus the $45 she spent on supplies. | A) $a = -3b + 60$ |
| | The perceived temperature on a –6°C day drops 3°C for every additional mile per hour of wind. | B) $a = 6b + 3$ |
| | In a psychology study, the average time it takes to finish a particular task alone is 60 minutes. Every added team member cuts that time down by 3 minutes. | C) $a = -3b - 6$ |
| | The amount of hard drive space taken up by Ty's work project is 3mb for a single instructions file, plus 6mb per video she creates. | D) $a = 3b + 60$ |
| | A scientist is studying the effects of a particular "diet" on a 60cm tall plant. She discovers that the plant grows 3cm every week that it is on the diet. | ~~E)~~ $a = 5b - 45$ |

**Answers:** E, C, A, B, D

## INTERACTIVE EXAMPLE 2

Morgan is following a strength training exercise plan that claims anyone following it can increase the number of consecutive pushups they can do by 13 pushups per week. Morgan can do 12 consecutive pushups before starting the plan.

**Q1)** Which of the following expressions gives the number of pushups Morgan should be able to do after following the plan for *t* weeks?

    A)  12t + 13

    B)  13t + 12

    C)  13t − 12

    D)  (12)(13)t

**S1)** The number of pushups is supposed to change by a constant amount each week, so the model should be linear and look like $y = mx + b$.

- **y** stands for the thing we are interested in – the total number of pushups Morgan can do.

- **m** stands for the slope, so it's the rate at which the number of pushups Morgan can do changes each week (13 per week).

- **b** stands for the y-intercept, so the number of pushups Morgan starts out being able to do (12 pushups).

If we bring that information in, we get:

$$y = 13t + 12$$

*The # of pushups Morgan can do (y) equals 13 pushups per week (t) plus 12 pushups.*

**B**

# PORTAL

For information about place values and rounding, turn to page 446.

**Q2)** After how many weeks will Morgan be able to do 50 consecutive pushups, rounded to the nearest tenth of a week?

    A)  2

    B)  2.7

    C)  2.9

    D)  3

**S2)** We want to know **when** Morgan will be able to do 50 pushups. To figure that out, we can use the formula we built in the previous questions! Since $t$ is our time variable and $y$ is the number of push-ups, we can set the equation equal to 50 pushups and solve for $t$:

$$50 \text{ pushups} = 13t + 12$$
$$38 = 13t$$
$$2.9 \text{ weeks} \approx t$$

We can check this in another way. If we start at 12 pushups and increase by 13 each week, then we can just add 13 each week and look for when we hit 50 pushups.

| Week | 0 | 1 | 2 | 3 |
|------|-----|-----|-----|-----|
| Pushups | 12 | 25 | 38 | 51 |

C

**Write an equation** to model each scenario in the blank provided.

| Context | Model |
|---------|-------|
| Lucy can use a total of 1024 MB of data. Streaming a video uses 1.6 MB every minute. Model data left ($d$) in terms of minutes streamed ($t$). | $d = 1024 - 1.6t$ |
| A taxi charges a base fare of $10.50 and an additional $.45 per mile. Model taxi fare ($f$) in terms of miles driven ($m$). | $f =$ |
| Jose runs 2 miles to a race track, runs 6 miles per hour while he races on the track, then runs the 2 miles home. Model total miles run ($m$) in terms of race length in hours ($h$). | $m =$ |
| Tobi the corgi has a rope that was originally comprised of 350 strings twisted together. He rips out 4 strings a day. Model strings left ($s$) in terms of days ($d$). | $s =$ |
| Proper clown shoe length starts at 15 inches, with a half-inch added for every year the clown has been a part of the clown union. Model shoe length ($c$) in terms of years in the union ($y$). | $c =$ |

Answers:  1. *given*  2. $f = .45m + 10.50$  3. $m = 6h + 4$
4. $s = 350 - 4d$  5. $c = 15 + .5y$

## INTERACTIVE EXAMPLE 3

Luis works as a caterer. He charges a setup fee plus an additional amount for each guest expected at the event. The equation $c = 12g + 55$ gives the total amount Luis charges in dollars ($c$) in terms of the expected number of guests ($g$).

**Q1)** A client calls and informs Luis that there are going to be 8 more guests for an event than originally expected. How much will Luis increase the amount he charges for the event?

    A)  $8

    B)  $96

    C)  $151

    D)  $440

**S1)** Since $c$ is the total cost and $g$ is the number of guests, the number 12 in the equation (our rate of change coefficient) tells us that it costs **$12 per guest**. This means that he will charge $12 for each of the 8 additional guests. So if we simply multiply, we can find the cost:

$$12(8) = 96 \text{ dollars}$$

So it will cost $96 to fund an additional 8 guests.

                                                       **B**

**Q2)** Luis discovers that people are frequently underestimating the number of guests for events that he caters, so he decides to adjust his pricing model. In the updated model, he assumes there will be 4 more guests than the number $g$ that the client gives him. Which of the following equations could be Luis's new model?

    A)  $c = 16g + 55$

    B)  $c = 12g + 59$

    C)  $c = 12(g + 4) + 55$

    D)  $c = 12(g - 4) + 55$

# NOTE

Another possible correct answer would **distribute the 12**.

$c = 12g + 48 + 55$

$c = 12g + 103$

**S2)** We are told that Luis is assuming there will be **4 more guests than the number $g$** that is provided. Translating this into math means that we want to replace "$g$" with "**$(g + 4)$**". This gives us:

$$\text{old} \quad c = 12g + 55$$
$$\text{new} \quad c = 12(g + 4) + 55$$

So the answer is **choice C**.

                                                       **C**

# Practice Problems

*Use your new skills to answer each question.*

**1**

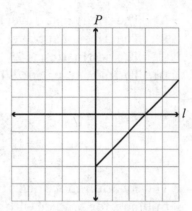

The graph above displays the total profit $P$, in dollars, after selling $l$ cups of lemonade. What does the $l$-intercept represent in the graph?

A) The initial cost of starting a lemonade stand
B) The total cups of lemonade sold
C) The total profit the lemonade stand makes in a day
D) The cups of lemonade sold to break even

**2**

The total price, in dollars, that a jet-ski rental company charges a group of over five people can be calculated by the equation $10px - 24$, where $p > 5$ is the number of people in the group and $x$ is the number of hours the group will be using the jet-skis. Which of the following is the best interpretation of the number 10 in the expression?

A) The company charges $10 per hour for each individual.
B) A maximum of 10 people can be in each group.
C) The price each member in the group will pay is $10.
D) Each member of the group will spend a maximum of 10 hours renting the jet-skis.

$$M = 250 - 20d$$

The equation above gives the number of miles $M$ a tribe still has to travel before reaching its destination, where $d$ is the number of days it has been since the tribe first left. What is the meaning of 250 in the equation?

A) The tribe must travel for 250 days.
B) The tribe must travel 250 miles every day.
C) The destination is 250 miles from the initial location.
D) The tribe traveled 250 miles the first day.

$$T = 45 + 15r$$

The equation above gives the number of tickets $T$ sold, in millions, for a movie with an average movie critic rating of $r$, where $r$ must be between 0 and 10. If movie theaters sold a total of 105 million tickets for a certain movie, what was the average movie critic rating of that movie?

A) 10
B) 8
C) 7
D) 4

$$P = 264.50 + 20m$$

Last year, Fabio bought a piggy bank to hold all of his savings. Ever since then, Fabio has been putting a fixed amount of money into his piggy bank every month. The equation above gives the amount of money $P$, in dollars, Fabio now has in his piggy bank after $m$ months. If the equation was graphed in the $xy$-plane, with $P$ on the $y$-axis and $m$ on the $x$-axis, what would be the meaning of the $y$-intercept?

A) Fabio deposits $264.50 every month.
B) Fabio now has $264.50 in his piggy bank.
C) Fabio put $264.50 in his piggy bank the day he bought it.
D) Fabio can only put a maximum of $264.50 in his piggy bank.

**6**

The equation $S = 14 + 3.5t$ gives the speed $S$ of a ball, in feet per second, $t$ seconds after it was kicked down a hill. After how many seconds will the ball be rolling down the hill at 42 feet per second?

A) 16
B) 12
C) 8
D) 4

**7**

Elmer works at a call center, and the number of people Elmer still needs to call on a given day can be modeled by $C = 150 - 20h$, where $h$ is the number of hours Elmer has worked that day. What is the meaning of 20 in the equation?

A) Elmer must call 20 people every day.
B) Elmer still has 20 more people to call that day.
C) Elmer will work 20 hours this week.
D) Elmer calls 20 people every hour.

**8**

At a fast food restaurant, the price of a value meal, consisting of 30 chicken nuggets, is three times the price of a kid's meal, consisting of 8 chicken nuggets. If the price of a kid's meal is 4 dollars and the price of a value meal is $n$ dollars, which of the following is true?

A) $\frac{n}{3} = 4$

B) $4n = 3$

C) $3n = 4$

D) $n + 4 = 3$

**9**

Avery and Patrick work in the telesales department of a company. Last Friday, Avery made $x$ phone calls each hour for 6 hours and Patrick made $y$ phone calls each hour for 8 hours. Which of the following represents the total number of phone calls Avery and Patrick made last Friday?

A) $6x + 8y$
B) $6y + 8x$
C) $48xy$
D) $14xy$

# Advanced Modeling

*Often, the SAT tests your modeling skills alongside other concepts.*

## Modeling with Graphs

In the previous chapter, we saw that we could think of a "rate of change" as both the **coefficient** in an equation and as the **slope** of the line in the graph of the equation. Occasionally, the SAT will test your ability to model with a graph rather than with an equation. Let's look at an example.

## INTERACTIVE EXAMPLE

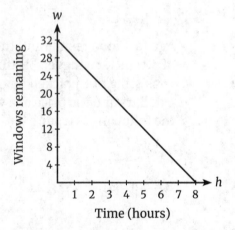

Seana has a job as a window cleaner for a particular office building. The above graph models her work on a typical day. $W$ is the number of windows she has left to clean that day and $h$ is the number of hours she has worked so far that day (not counting breaks).

**Q1)** What does the *w*-intercept in the graph represent?

    A) The total number of windows she washes in a typical day.

    B) The exact number of windows she washes every day.

    C) The number of windows she can typically wash per hour.

    D) The time it typically takes her to wash one window.

**SOLUTION**

To understand the *w*-intercept, we first need to understand what each axis tells us. The axis labels and the description below the graph help us out. The vertical (*w*) axis tells us the **number of windows remaining**, and the horizontal (*h*) axis tells us the **number of hours worked**. That means we could read the point (0, 32) as (0 hours, 32 windows remaining).

Since the *w*-intercept occurs where $h = 0$, we know that it must tell us the **total number of windows remaining** at the beginning of the work day. That narrows it down to A or B. The problem tells us that the graph models a *typical* day, so A is the better answer

.

        **A**

**Q2)** Which of the following is the best interpretation of the slope of the line?

    A) The total number of windows she washes in a typical day.

    B) The exact number of windows she washes every day.

    C) The number of windows she can typically wash per hour.

    D) The time it typically takes her to wash one window.

**SOLUTION**

The slope of a line is always the rate of change, so our answer needs to be a **rate**. This means we can immediately eliminate A and B. Recall that:

$$slope = \frac{change\ in\ y}{change\ in\ x}, \text{ or } \frac{change\ in\ w}{change\ in\ h}$$

This means that our answer should be in terms of windows (*w*) per hour (*h*). This corresponds with answer choice C.

        **C**

**Q3)** What does the $h$-intercept in the graph represent?

A)  The number of windows she washes by the end of the day.
B)  The number of windows she washes each hour.
C)  The earliest she can finish her work.
D)  The number of hours she typically needs to finish her work.

SOLUTION

The $h$-intercept is the point on the line where $w$, the number of windows remaining to be washed, is zero. This means it is the point where she finishes her work. Since $h$ is the number of hours she has worked, that means the $h$-intercept tells us the amount of hours she works before her work is finished on a typical day.

D

## Modeling with Systems of Equations

So far, the models we have looked at have all had one equation. Sometimes, situations are more complicated and it takes two (or more) equations to fully describe them. When this happens, the SAT asks you to create a **system of equations** to model the situation, and then solve the system to find the answer to a question.

## PORTAL

If you need to learn or review how to solve systems of equations, turn to page 568.

## EXAMPLE 1

Mary is designing a quilt that uses two different sizes of squares. The smaller squares have 5 inch sides and the larger squares have 10 inch sides. If Mary wants the finished quilt to be 60 inches by 80 inches and contain 120 total squares, how many of the smaller squares will she use?

A)  24
B)  48
C)  96
D)  100

**648**

 SOLUTION

Let *s* be the number of smaller squares and *l* be the number of larger squares. Before we do anything else, let's establish our goal. We're asked to find the number of small squares, so:

 *establish your goal*   $s = ?$

We know we need a total of **120 squares**, so let's model that:

(1) *write first equation*    #small + #large = #total

$$s + l = 120$$

From the side lengths, we can figure out that the small squares are 25 square inches and the larger ones are 100 square inches. We also know the finished quilt will be 60 inches by 80 inches, or **4800 square inches**. So we can show how each type of square contributes to the total area in a second equation:

(2) *write second equation*    (area)s + (area)l = total area

$$25s + 100l = 4800$$

And now we have a system we can use to solve for *s*!

(3) *write system*    $s + l = 120$

$$25s + 100l = 4800$$

It looks like **substitution** will serve us well here. If we use the first equation to get something we can plug in for *l* in the second equation, we'll be able to solve for *s*.

(4) *solve for l in 1st equation*    $l = 120 - s$

(5) *substitute into 2nd*    $25s + 100(120 - s) = 4800$

(6) *simplify*    $25s + 12{,}000 - 100s = 4800$

$$-75s = -7200$$

$$s = 96$$

C

## EXAMPLE 2

A mad scientist has designed two kinds of robots that both utilize a certain kind of widget. The hopping robots, $h$, require 2 widgets each and the flying robots, $f$, require 3 widgets each. The scientist wants to produce no less than 5 of each type of robot, and at least 20 robots total. If she has a stash of 100 widgets, which of the following systems models the possible numbers of robots she can create?

A) $h = 5$
   $f = 5$
   $h + f < 20$
   $2h + 3f = 100$

B) $h \geq 5$
   $f \geq 5$
   $h + f \geq 20$
   $3h + 2f < 100$

C) $h > 5$
   $f > 5$
   $h + f = 20$
   $2h + 3f = 100$

D) $h \geq 5$
   $f \geq 5$
   $h + f \geq 20$
   $2h + 3f \leq 100$

## TIP

**Eliminate choices as you go!** Notice that we can narrow our choices down to either B or D by step 2. The only difference between the two are the coefficients of $h$ and $f$ in the last inequality, which saves us from having to write the equation from scratch.

At this point, we only have to check the problem for how many widgets each robot type gets.

SOLUTION

This problem asks us to *model* four different **inequalities**. Looking at the choices, we can see that getting the less than, greater than, equal to distinction will be important, so let's take it slow:

(1) *"No less than 5 of each type of robot"*    $h \geq 5$    $f \geq 5$

(2) *"at least 20 robots total"*    $h + f \geq 20$

(3) *"No more than 100 widgets, using 2 per hopping and 3 per flying"*    $2h + 3f \leq 100$

D

# Practice Problems

*Use your new skills to answer each question.*

**Questions 1-2 refer to the following information:**

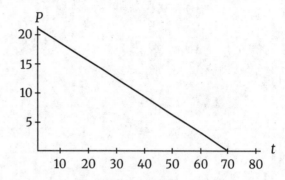

Lorraine is doing her math homework and the above graph shows the number of homework problems $P$ she has left after working on her homework for $t$ minutes.

**1**

What does the $P$-intercept represent?

A) The time it takes her to do one question
B) The amount of time it will take her to finish the assignment
C) The total number of homework problems she needs to complete
D) The number of problems in the section her class is currently working on

**2**

After how many minutes will she have finished half of her assignment?

35 minutes

The sum of four numbers is 765. The sum of the first two numbers is 25% more than the sum of the other two numbers. What is the sum of the first two numbers?

A) 170
B) 340
C) 425
D) 530

$1.25x + x = 765$

$2.25x = 765$

$$a = 1.5x + 1.50$$
$$b = 1.25x + 4.50$$

In the system of equations above, $a$ and $b$ represent the cost, in dollars, of buying $x$ buffalo wings at two different restaurants. What amount of money will get you the same number of buffalo wings at both restaurants?

A) 12
B) 19.5
C) 20
D) 29.5

$1.5x + 1.5 = 1.25x + 4.5$

$0.25x = 3$

$x = 12$

A semi-trailer truck is carrying exactly 20,000 kg of cargo consisting of 300-kg crates and 400-kg crates. If the truck is carrying eight 300-kg crates, how many 400-kg crates is the truck carrying?

$20000 - 8(300) = 17600$

$400 \overline{)17600}$

$44$

If Julian's height $h$ is within 4 inches of the average height, $a$, of an 18-year-old male, which of the following inequalities MUST be true?

I. $h + a < 4$
II. $-4 < h - a < 4$
III. $|h - a| < 4$

A) III only
B) II and III only
C) I and III only
D) I, II, and III

**Questions 7–8 refer to the following information:**

$$P(t) = 2t + 10$$
$$A(t) = 40 - t$$

Function $A(t)$ models the speed, in meters per second, of Aaron's car $t$ seconds after passing a police car. Since Aaron was driving over the speed limit, the police officer sped up to Aaron's car to pull him over. Function $P(t)$ models the speed, in meters per second, of the police officer's car $t$ seconds after Aaron passed it.

**7**

At 8 seconds after the police officer caught Aaron speeding, by how much had the speed of the police car changed?

A)  The speed of the police car increased by 4 meters per second.
B)  The speed of the police car decreased by 16 meters per second.
C)  The speed of the police car decreased by 26 meters per second.
D)  The speed of the police car increased by 16 meters per second.

**8**

After how many seconds will Aaron's car and the police car be going the same speed?

A)  10 seconds
B)  20 seconds
C)  30 seconds
D)  70 seconds

$2t + 10 = 40 - t$

$3t = 30$

$t = 10$

# Quadratic Modeling

*The curveball of mathematical models*

.......................................................................................................

## Modeling a ball tossed up into the air

The SAT loves to give you models—mathematical equations that you can use to compute real world information. Most of these equations are **linear** models, meaning they have the form $y = mx + b$. Now let's look at what it means when the test describes a **quadratic** model. The most common scenario modeled by a quadratic equation is projectile motion (e.g., throwing a ball up in the air and watching it fall back down).

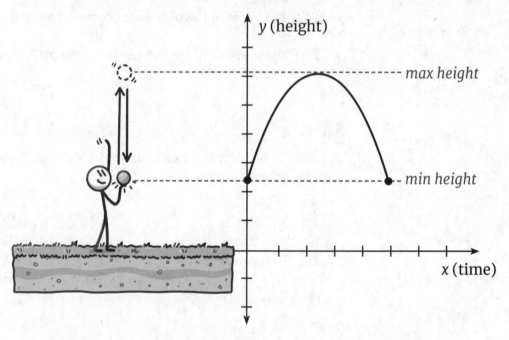

The graph above models the illustrated scenario: the ball is thrown up into the air, reaches a maximum height, falls back down, and is caught. To help understand the model, consider the questions below:

1.  Why doesn't the curve start at the origin?

2.  Why does the curve stop before crossing the x-axis?

3.  If the ball is thrown straight up into the air, why does the curve travel along the x-axis?

## Throwing a ball and letting it drop off a cliff

Now let's look at the same model in a slightly different scenario. In this situation, you're standing on a cliff side and you throw the ball straight up into the air. Rather than catch the ball, you let it drop far below you. How will the model change? How will the graph change?

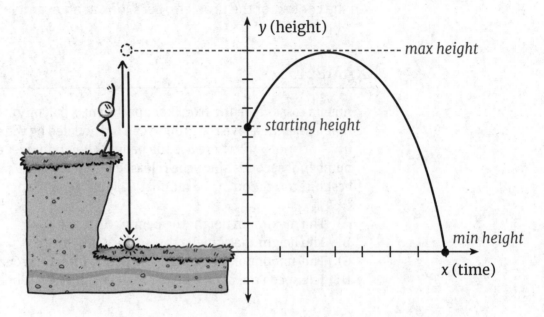

## You can use models to find interesting info

There are a few *particularly* interesting things about a quadratic model that the test is likely to focus on. Let's consider each in the context of the models shown.

- **The y-intercept:** If we set x to zero, in the examples above, we find the *starting height* of the ball when thrown. When in doubt, try plugging zero in for your input variable and see what you learn!

- **The x-intercepts:** If we set y to zero, the model will tell us when the ball hits the ground (where the height is zero). With a quadratic curve, this will give you <u>two</u> answers—use common sense to determine which answer makes the most sense in context.

- **Maximums and minimums:** The highest and lowest points on a curve. Pay careful attention to whether they are asking for the input or the output on this kind of question.

- **A particular point on the curve:** You may be asked to find a specific piece of information by plugging in an input and finding the corresponding output. In this case, you simply treat the model like a function with inputs and outputs.

# Interpreting and using a quadratic model

Some quadratic modeling problems will ask you to *interpret* a model that you are given. To do this you have to combine what you know about the different forms of the quadratic equation from the Transformers chapter with the context of the problem. Let's look at an example:

## EXAMPLE 1

Amelia tosses a penny from her apartment's balcony and determines that its height above the ground can be modeled by the equation $h = -16t^2 + 6t + 42$ where $h$ is the penny's height in feet and $t$ is the number of seconds since she released it. Which of the following is the best interpretation of the number 42 in this equation?

A)  The maximum height the penny will reach
B)  The height that Amelia tosses the penny from
C)  The amount of time before the penny hits the ground
D)  The speed the penny will be traveling at when it hits the ground

## PORTAL

For a review of the standard form, turn to "Transformers" on page 538.

SOLUTION

The equation we are given is in the standard form:

$$y = ax^2 + bx + c$$
$$h = -16t^2 + 6t + 42$$

We can see the 42 matches up with $c$. If you remember your standard form, you know that $c$ tells you the **y-intercept** of the graph. You can check this by plugging in 0 for $t$; when no time has passed ($t = 0$), the height ($h$) is equal to 42.

In other words, the **initial height** of the penny is 42 feet.

B

Some modeling questions assume you understand how to interpret the equation and ask you to compute a specific piece of information.

## TIP

If you have a graphing calculator, the easiest way to solve this problem would be to graph it and use the calculator's tools to find the maximum.

## EXAMPLE 2

Liam kicks a soccer ball and determines that the height of its path can be modeled by the quadratic equation $y = -4.9x^2 + 17.6x$, where $x$ is the number of seconds after he kicks the ball and $y$ is the height of the ball in meters. What is the maximum height the ball reaches, to the nearest tenth of a meter?

SOLUTION

We are given a quadratic model, $y = -4.9x^2 + 17.6x$, and asked to find the **maximum height**. Height is the *output* of the model, which means we are looking for the $y$-coordinate of the highest point (the vertex) of the parabola. We could put this equation into **vertex form** to more easily see the vertex coordinates. But, there's a shortcut: remember that the vertex is always <u>halfway between the $x$-intercepts</u>. Let's find those by plugging in zero for $y$:

(1) *plug-in $y = 0$*  $\qquad\qquad\qquad$  $0 = -4.9x^2 + 17.6x$

(2) *factor out an $x$*  $\qquad\qquad\qquad$  $0 = x(-4.9x + 17.6)$

(3) *solve for $x$*  $\qquad\qquad\qquad$  $x = 0, \frac{17.6}{4.9} \approx 3.59$

## NOTE

On this particular problem, you get the same answer even if you round to the nearest 10th at every step. This is not always going to be true. You should always keep an extra digit or two to avoid rounding errors.

Now we know that the ball hits the ground at 0 and 3.59 seconds. Because this model is a parabola, the maximum height will occur halfway between these $x$-intercepts, around **1.80 seconds**. To get the height at this time, plug in this time for $x$ into the model and use your calculator to find the answer:

(4) *plug-in $x = 1.80$*  $\qquad\qquad$  $y = -4.9(1.80)^2 + 17.6(1.80)$

$\qquad\qquad\qquad\qquad\qquad\qquad\qquad$  $y \approx \boxed{15.8 \text{ meters}}$

## Picking the best model for the occasion

Some questions will give you a scenario and data and ask you to pick an equation or graph that best models the situation. For these problems you can work out the equation yourself and then match it to the answer choices if you want to, but most of the time it is going to be much faster to **work backwards**. Check the proposed models against the information/data you are given and see which one makes sense. This is notably easier than the toughest type of modeling question...

## Creating your own model

The hardest quadratic modeling problems will give you a situation, tell you that you need a quadratic model, and then expect you to both create *and* apply the model. For these problems you will be given one or more points, and your job is to use the different forms of quadratic equations:

> Use **standard** form, $y = ax^2 + bx + c$, if given coordinate points.
>
> Use **vertex** form, $y = a(x - h)^2 + k$, if given the vertex.
>
> Use **intercept** form, $y = a(x - u)(x - v)$ if given the $x$-intercepts.

## EXAMPLE 3

| Velocity (m/s) | Kinetic Energy (J) |
|:---:|:---:|
| 0 | 0 |
| 5 | 145 |
| 10 | 580 |

The kinetic energy, in Joules, of an object is related to its velocity, in meters per second, by a quadratic model. The kinetic energy of a particular object at three different velocities is given in the table above. What would the kinetic energy be in Joules when the velocity of this object is 20 m/s?

**SOLUTION**

Our eventual goal is to find the kinetic energy given a particular value for the velocity. This means we need an equation. The question tells us that we want a **quadratic** model, and we are given three coordinates in the table.

Let's **try to make an equation** in the form of $y = ax^2 + bx + c$, where our input ($x$) is velocity and our output ($y$) is kinetic energy. Let's then plug in the first point and see what we learn.

①    *write the equation form*      $y = ax^2 + bx + c$

②    *plug in first point* $(0,0)$      $0 = a(0)^2 + b(0) + c$

                                                   $0 = c$

Great! We've got one of the constants figured out. Now let's plug in the other two points:

③    *plug in second point* $(5, 145)$      $y = ax^2 + bx$

                                                   $145 = a(5)^2 + b(5)$

                                                   $145 = 25a + 5b$ ✓

④    *plug in third point* $(10, 580)$      $580 = a(10)^2 + b(10)$

                                                   $580 = 100a + 10b$ ✓

Now we have a **system of equations** with two unknowns, so you can use your favorite method for solving systems. We'll try multiplying the first equation by two, then subtracting:

⑤    *multiply 1st equation by 2*      $2(145) = 2(25a + 5b)$

                                                   $290 = 50a + 10b$

⑤    *stack n' smash (subtract)*      $290 = 50a + 10b$

                     $-$           $580 = 100a + 10b$

                             $-290 = -50a$

                               $5.8 = a$

Whew! Finding $a$ was some work, but now we can easily find $b$ by plugging in 5.8 for $a$ in either equation...

---

**TIP**

If you are given a point where $x = 0$, that's always going to be the best place to start plugging in: it will simplify the equation and reveal helpful information.

**PORTAL**

If you got stuck on solving this system of equations, review "Solving Systems" on page 568.

Continued on next page →

⑥ *plug in 5.8 for a to find b*     $580 = 100a + 10b$

$580 = 100(5.8) + 10b$

$580 = 580 + 10b$

$0 = b$

Aha! Now we know that $a = 5.8$, $b = 0$, and $c = 0$. Let's plug that into our model. Then, to find the kinetic energy ($y$) where the velocity ($x$) is 20, we simply plug in 20 for $x$:

⑦ *write the final model*     $y = 5.8x^2$

⑧ *plug in 20 for x and solve*     $y = 5.8(20)^2$

$y = 5.8(400)$

$y = \; 2,320 \, \text{J}$

## TIP

In this case, the vertex of the parabola was at the origin. Had we known that for sure, we could have skipped a number of steps; however, this will not always be the case!

# Practice Problems

*Use your new skills to answer each question.*

**1**

$$f(x) = -0.5(x - 1.9)^2 + 1.805$$

A particular garden has an arched bridge that spans a small stream. The bridge's elevation, in meters, above the rest of the path can be modeled by the function above, where $x$ is the horizontal distance, in meters, from the bridge entrance. The graph of $y = f(x)$ is shown in the $xy$-plane below.

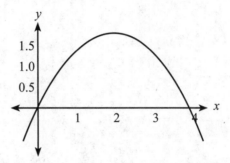

The gardener is considering replacing this arched bridge with a flat bridge. How long would the flat bridge need to be?

A) 1.805 meters
B) 1.9 meters
C) 3.61 meters
D) 3.8 meters

**2**

$$t(x) = -0.16x^2 + 3.84x + 56$$

A scientist uses a quadratic model to model the temperature changes over the course of a particular spring day. The equation above gives the temperature, in degrees Fahrenheit, $x$ hours after sunrise. What is the meaning of $(8, t(8))$ in this context?

A) The temperature is 8 degrees $t(8)$ hours after sunrise.
B) The temperature is $t(8)$ degrees at 8 am.
C) The temperature is $t(8)$ degrees 8 hours after sunrise.
D) The temperature increases by $t(8)$ degrees every 8 hours.

**3**

$$h(x) = -4.9x^2 + 223.3$$

When a model rocket is launched, its height in meters above the ground can be modeled by the function $h(x)$ above, where $x$ is the number of seconds after the launch. The graph $y = h(x)$ crosses the $x$-axis at the points 0 and $a$. What does $a$ represent?

A) The horizontal distance traveled by the rocket before it hits the ground.
B) The time when the rocket is at its highest point above the ground.
C) The time when the rocket hits the ground.
D) The maximum height attained by the rocket.

**4**

$$p(d) = -50d^2 + 1250d - 6000$$

A company has discovered that its profit can be modeled by the above equation where $d$ is the price, in dollars, at which it sells its devices. Based on this model, what is the company's expected profit in dollars if it sells its devices for $10 each?

**5**

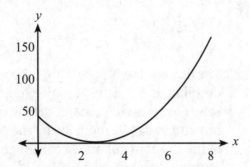

A toy car initially traveling East experiences constant acceleration as it slows down and then continues back to the West. The graph shows the quadratic function $K$ that models the kinetic energy, in joules, of the car as a function of the time $t$ in seconds since the car began accelerating. Which of the following equations could define $K$?

A) $K(t) = 5.76(t - 2.7)^2$
B) $K(t) = 5.76(t - 2.7)^2 + 42.3$
C) $K(t) = 5.76(t + 2.7)^2 + 42.3$
D) $K(t) = 5.67(t - 42.3)^2 + 2.7$

**6**

$$h(x) = -16t^2 + 48t + 160$$

A stick is thrown from a bridge into the river below. The equation above models the height, in feet, of the stick above the water $t$ seconds after the stick was released. After how many seconds does the stick hit the water?

T=5

**7**

$$r(x) = 516d - 43d^2$$

The drama club is preparing for the upcoming school musical and deciding how much it should charge per ticket. By looking at ticket sales from previous years, they estimate that the amount of revenue brought in can be modeled by the equation above, where $d$ is the price of the ticket in dollars. According to this model, what is the maximum revenue they can earn?

A) $6
B) $12
C) $516
D) $1,548

**8**

The distance in meters an object in free fall remains from the ground can be modeled by a quadratic function that is defined in terms of $t$, where $t$ is the time in seconds since the object was released. An object is dropped from 4,250 meters above the ground. After 10 seconds, it is 3,750 meters above the ground; after 20 seconds, it is 2,250 meters above the ground. How many meters above the ground will it be after 25 seconds?

1125

**Questions 9 and 10 refer to the following information**

A toy rocket is launched at an angle so that it travels down a field as it arcs through the air. The height, in feet, of the rocket $t$ seconds after being launched is given by the equation $h(t)$; the horizontal distance, in feet, that the rocket has traveled $t$ seconds after being launched is given by the equation $d(t)$.

$$h(t) = -16.1t^2 + 96.5t$$

$$d(t) = 55.5t$$

**9**

What is the maximum height, in feet, achieved by the rocket on its flight? Round your answer to the nearest foot.

**10**

How far, in feet, from the launch point does the rocket land? Round your answer to the nearest foot.

# Exponential Models

*The most advanced modeling problems deal with exponential growth.*

When we need to model a situation where one variable grows or shrinks by a *constant amount* for every unit change in a second variable, we use a **linear model**. For example, every ticket sold adds exactly $3 to the total amount raised. The *hundredth* ticket sold earns just as much as did the *first* ticket sold: three dollars.

In this chapter, we will look at a different kind of growth. For example, a population of rabbits that is *doubling* each year or a savings account that gains interest based on a *percentage* of the current balance. In these situations where something is being multiplied (or divided) by a constant factor, we need a model that shows **exponential** growth.

**Identify** whether each situation is linear or exponential.

| | Situation | Linear or Exponential? |
|---|---|---|
| **1.** | The population of mosquitos at a lake doubles every week. | |
| **2.** | Jace earns $8 per hour for babysitting. | |
| **3.** | A savings account earns .05% interest. | |
| **4.** | A swimming pool is being filled by a hose at a rate of 6 gallons per minute. | |
| **5.** | A treatment wipes out one-third of the remaining bacteria with every dose. | |
| **6.** | The population of a town has been increasing by factor of 4 every 5 years. | |

**Answers:** *See next page.*

## INTERACTIVE EXAMPLE

A mad scientist has figured out how to program his robots so that they can build and program *more* robots. It takes each robot one day to make and program a new robot. The mad scientist builds three robots before turning them loose to construct an army. Since each robot makes a new robot each day, the number of robots will double each day. The following table summarizes the number of robots he has at the end of each day:

| Time (days) | # of Robots | Written with Multiples | Written with Exponents |
|:---:|:---:|:---:|:---:|
| 0 | 3 | 3 | 3 |
| 1 | 6 | 3 × 2 | $3 \times 2^1$ |
| 2 | 12 | 3 × 2 × 2 | $3 \times 2^2$ |
| 3 | 24 | 3 × 2 × 2 × 2 | $3 \times 2^3$ |
| 4 | 48 | 3 × 2 × 2 × 2 × 2 | $3 \times 2^4$ |

**Q1)** Write an equation to model the number of robots after t days.

SOLUTION

We were told that the number of robots **doubles** each day. So we can see from the table that we get the next day's number of robots by **multiplying** by 2. This means we are dealing with *exponential growth*.

Exponents are just a shorthand for repeated multiplication. In the table, we can see how to write the number of robots using exponents. If, for example, we wanted to know how many robots he would have after **1 day**, it would be **3 × 2¹ = 6** robots. To see how many robots he'd have after 2 days, it would be **3 × 2² = 12,** and so on. So to model this growth, the number of robots after *t* days would be:

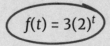

$$f(t) = 3(2)^t$$

**Answers: 1)** Exponential  **2)** Linear  **3)** Exponential  **4)** Linear  **5)** Exponential  **6)** Exponential

In the previous example, our model follows the standard equation for exponential growth:

$$\textit{Exponential Growth:} \quad f(t) = P(r)^t$$

Where P is the **starting amount**, r is the **rate** at which it is growing (or decaying), and t is the length of time it's been growing.

## When it's Tougher

The vast majority of the time all you need to know for SAT exponent problems is the standard equation above. Occasionally, on the hardest problems, you will work with time intervals that require careful calculations. Suppose our mad scientist wanted to know how many robots he has in terms of *hours* instead of days. Then, the number doesn't double when $t = 1$, it doubles when $t = 24$ (robots don't need sleep). So how could we rewrite the equation to show this?

$$f(t) = 3(2)^{\frac{t}{24}} \qquad \text{\# of robots doubles at } t = 24$$

This way, the exponent doesn't become 1 until $t = 24$. Now, suppose he optimizes the programming so that the robots can make a new robot every **8 hours**. This means that the first doubling occurs at $t = 8$, so the exponent needs to be 1 when $t = 8$.

$$f(t) = 3(2)^{\frac{t}{8}} \qquad \text{\# of robots doubles at } t = 8$$

## PORTAL

You can think of exponential growth as **repeated percent change**. To see more on this topic, flip to page 707.

**668**

## INTERACTIVE EXAMPLE 2

Kaja opened a new savings account. She determines that if she doesn't deposit or withdraw any money, the amount of money (in dollars) in the account after $t$ years will be modeled by the equation:

$$f(t) = 8,000(1.03)^t$$

**Q1)** What was Kaja's initial deposit?

**SOLUTION**

The variable, $t$, is in the exponent, so we know we are dealing with an exponential model. The standard form of an exponential model is:

$$f(t) = P(r)^t$$

In the standard form, the starting amount is **P**. If we compare Kaja's model to the standard model, we can see that **P = $8,000**.

$$f(t) = P(r)^t$$

$$f(t) = 8,000(1.03)^t$$

**TIP**

In the financial world, the starting amount is often refered to as the *principal*. This is why we use the letter $P$ in the general model for exponential growth.

**TIP**

In general, for interest problems, you can think of the rate as

$$r = 1 + \frac{I}{100}$$

where $I$ is the interest rate.

**Q2)** What is the **interest rate** on the account?

A) 1.03%
B) 0.03%
C) 3.00%
D) 8,000%

**SOLUTION**

This one's a bit trickier! We want to know about the *interest* **rate**, so we want to look at **r = 1.03**. This tells us that the amount in the account at the end of one year, or $f(1)$, will be **1.03 times** the amount at the beginning of the year.

But we have to be careful. The interest is the **new money** added each year. If we were just multiplying by 1, then the money would never change. If we multiplied by 2, then the amount would double every year. So what does mutiplying by 1.03 mean? It means we're **increasing** the current balance by **3%** year.

C

**669**

**Q3)** Which of the following graphs shows the growth of the money in Kaja's account?

A)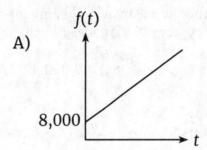

B)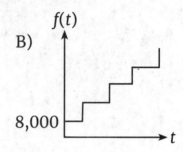

C)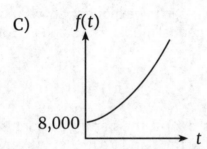

D)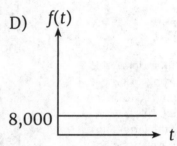

SOLUTION

Let's look at each answer choice:

**Choice A** shows **linear** growth, where the growth rate (slope) is constant. We are dealing with **exponential** growth, where the amount earned increases each year. This one's out.

**Choice B** shows a step function. This is what the graph might look like if Kaja were regularly depositing money into her account in chunks. That isn't the situation though, so we can eliminate B.

**Choice C** looks good - it starts at 8,000 and then grows at an increasing rate, earning more and more each year. This kind of curve looks like exponential growth. C is probably the right answer.

**Choice D** shows Kaja's money remaining constant – she never has more than $8,000. This is what the graph might look like if Kaja just put the money under her mattress and forgot about it.

Thus, the answer is C!

C

# INTERACTIVE EXAMPLE 3

Arturo is a chemist and discovers that the rate of a particular chemical reaction is dependent on the concentration of one of the reactants. The integrated rate law states that the concentration of this reactant decreases exponentially. Arturo runs experiments and finds that 10% of the remaining reactant is converted to products each minute. He starts an experiment with 350 grams of the reactant.

**Q1)** Which of the following equations could Arturo use to determine the amount of reactant remaining after t minutes?

A)  $f(t) = .9(350)^t$
B)  $f(t) = 350(.1)^t$
C)  $f(t) = 350(1.1)^t$
D)  $f(t) = 350(.9)^t$

SOLUTION

The general form of an exponential equation, as we know, is

$$f(t) = P(r)^t$$

*P* is the starting amount, which here is **350**. This means we can immediately eliminate choice A.

r is the rate, the fraction of the initial amount that will be present when *t* = 1. Here, we know that it is **decreasing by 10%**. This means that r will be 1 – .10 = **.9**. Alternately, you know that if it is decreasing by 10% there will be 90% left, so **r = .9**. So our formula would be:

$$f(t) = 350(.9)^t$$

This matches answer choice D.

D

**Q2)** Rounding to the nearest gram, how much of the reactant has been converted after 10 minutes?

A) 0

B) 122

C) 228

D) 350

## TRAP

Always double-check what the question is asking for before you decide you are done!

---

SOLUTION

In the previous problem, we found the formula for the amount of reactant remaining after $t$ minutes. Let's plug in 10 for $t$:

$$f(t) = 350(.9)^t$$

$$f(t) = 350(.9)^{10} = 122$$

But be careful! Rereading the question, we notice that it doesn't ask how much is **left**, it asks how much has been *converted*. Since we started with 350 and have 122 left, we can subtract to find that 350 – 122 = **228 grams** have been converted. Tricky!

So the answer is **C**.

C

# Practice Problems

*Use your new skills to answer each question.*

---

**Questions 1 and 2 refer to the following information:**

Compounded annually: $x(1 + \frac{r}{100})^t$

Compounded quarterly: $x(1 + \frac{r}{400})^{4t}$

Compounded monthly: $x(1 + \frac{r}{1,200})^{12t}$

The equations above describe the value of three types of bank accounts $t$ years after an initial deposit of $x$ dollars was made with an annual interest rate of $r$%. Christina opened a bank account with an interest rate of 6% that is compounded annually, and she initially deposited $100 into her account.

**1**

What is the value, in dollars, of Christina's account after one year?

$106

**2**

Christina's friend Amy opened an account that earns 6 percent interest compounded monthly. Amy also made an initial deposit of $100 into her account on the same day Christina made a deposit of $100 into her account. After 20 years, how much more money will Amy's initial deposit have earned than Christina's initial deposit? (Round your answer to the nearest cent.)

$100(1.005)^{12(20)}$     $100(1.06)^{(20)}$

331.02              320.71

$10.31

**3**

A 525-gram sample of an unknown substance is observed in a laboratory. Once the substance is put in a graduated cylinder filled with salt water, the substance starts to dissolve at an hourly rate of 4 percent. Which of the following functions $f$ models the amount of dissolved substance, in grams, $x$ hours later?

A) $f(x) = 525(0.96)^x$
B) $f(x) = 525(0.04)^x$
C) $f(x) = 525 - 525(0.96)^x$
D) $f(x) = 525 - 525(0.04)^x$

**4**

The population of birds in a state forest is estimated over the course of twelve years, as shown in the table below.

| Year | Population |
|------|------------|
| 1994 | 200 |
| 1997 | 400 |
| 2000 | 800 |
| 2003 | 1,600 |
| 2006 | 3,200 |

Which of the following best describes the relationship between the year and the estimated bird population over the 12 year time period?

A) The estimated population of birds has increased linearly.
B) The estimated population of birds has decreased linearly.
C) The estimated population of birds has experienced exponential growth.
D) The estimated population of birds has experienced exponential decay.

**5**

Company XYZ had a poor earnings report, which resulted in its stock price of $142 dropping by 3% each day for five days after the report was released. Which of the following functions $f$ models the company's stock price, in dollars, $x$ days after the earnings report, where $x \leq 5$ ?

A)  $f(x) = 142(0.97)^x$

B)  $f(x) = 142(0.03)^x$

C)  $f(x) = 0.97(142)^x$

D)  $f(x) = 0.03(142)^x$

**6**

Which of the following scatterplots shows a relationship that is appropriately modeled by the equation $y = ax^b$, where both $a$ and $b$ are positive and $b > 1$ ?

A)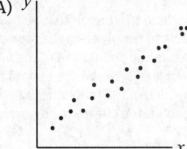

B)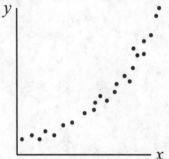

C)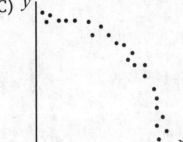

D)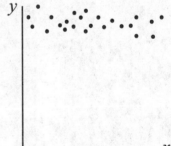

The population of lizards in a particular forest has increased by 8% every year due to a new wildfire preservation initiative. If there were 2,000 lizards living in the forest when the initiative was first put into place, which of the following functions $f$ represents the number of lizards living in the forest $t$ years after the initiative was implemented?

A) $f(t) = 2,000(.08)^t$

B) $f(t) = 2,000(1.08)^t$

C) $f(t) = 1.08(2,000)^t$

D) $f(t) = 2,000(8)^t$

A village located in a region that is in a severe drought has not been able to supply enough crops to its citizens. This has resulted in the population of the village decreasing by 6% every 2 years. If the current population of the village is 15,000, which of the following expressions shows the village's population $t$ years from now?

A) $f(t) = 15,000(0.94)^{\frac{t}{2}}$

B) $f(t) = 15,000(0.94)^{2t}$

C) $f(t) = 15,000(0.06)^{\frac{t}{2}}$

D) $f(t) = 15,000(0.06)^{2t}$

**9**

The people in a town in Paraguay are currently trying to control the piranha population of a lake. The plan they will implement is predicted to decrease the number of piranhas by 22% every 3 years. If the current population of piranhas is 2,000, which of the following expressions shows the predicted number of piranhas in the lake $t$ years from now?

A)  $f(t) = 2,000(0.22)^{3t}$

B)  $f(t) = 2,000(0.22)^{\frac{t}{3}}$

C)  $f(t) = 2,000(0.78)^{\frac{t}{3}}$

D)  $f(t) = 2,000(0.78)^{3t}$

**10**

The mayor of a city in Kansas decided to increase the city's population by giving anyone who moved to the city a free t-shirt. This initiative caused a population boom where the number of residents increased by 8% every four months. If the initial population of the city was 5,000, which of the following expressions shows the city's population $y$ years from now?

A)  $f(y) = 5,000(1.08)^{4y}$

B)  $f(y) = 5,000(1.08)^{3y}$

C)  $f(y) = 5,000(0.92)^{4y}$

D)  $f(y) = 5,000(0.92)^{3y}$

# Applied Algebra

*The non-calculator section tests the very same basic algebra skills we've practiced so far in the form of scientific word problems. Your job is to look past the science jargon and focus on making balanced manipulations.*

## TIP

The modeling problems in the last couple of chapters ask you to read or create a model, then use it to solve a problem. This chapter looks at problems that give you complicated looking models for involved situations.

Luckily, you don't really need to understand what these models mean. Instead, your main task on these problems is to rearrange the complicated formula for a specific variable.

## Alphabet Soup

Algebra word problems can look a bit like alphabet soup at first glance. You will be given a scientific context and presented with an equation involving a (potentially) large number of variables. After all that setup, you will simply rearrange the equation and solve for a different variable than the one that's given. The only thing you need the paragraph for is to know what the different variables stand for.

As a warm-up, let's practice solving for different variables. The algebra rules you have practiced work just as well with a bunch of variables as they did when there were just one or two!

**Fill in the blanks** to complete the solution below.

| If $s = 654 + 5.7t$, then $t = ?$ | |
|---|---|
| 1. Rewrite equation | |
| 2. Subtract to isolate $t$ | $s - ($ $) = 654 - ($ $) + 5.7t$ |
| 3. Write the result | $= 5.7t$ |
| 4. Divide | $=$ |
| 5. Write the result | $= t$ |

Answers: **(1)** $s = 654 + 5.7t$ **(2)** 654, 654 **(3)** $s - 654$ **(4)** $(s - 654) \div 5.7 = 5.7t \div 5.7$ **(5)** $(s - 654) \div 5.7 = t$

### EXAMPLE 1

$$PV = nRT$$

# Chemiwhat?

This equation comes from Chemistry, but (mercifully) you don't need to know a *thing* about Chemistry to solve these problems. They are just basic algebra problems in disguise.

**DISCLAIMER:**
We are in no way knocking Chemistry – it's actually pretty awesome when you get into it.

For an ideal gas, the pressure $P$, volume $V$, number of moles $n$, and temperature $T$ are related by the above equation through the proportionality constant $R$. Which of the following equations lets you solve for the temperature if you know the other variables?

A)    $T = \dfrac{nR}{PV}$

B)    $T = PVnR$

C)    $T = \dfrac{1}{PVnR}$

D)    $T = \dfrac{PV}{nR}$

# TIP

Variables won't always be the first letter of the word they represent, so it's always smart to check the paragraph!

Checking the answer choices is an easy way to see what variable you are solving for.

First, **identify what you're solving for**: temperature.

Next, scan the paragraph (or just glance at the answer choices) to **find the variable** that represents temperature: $T$. So really, the problem is as simple as "solve the equation for $T$." We might not fully comprehend what happens to gassy moles under pressure, but we can *definitely* solve for $T$:

①   *rewrite the equation*      $PV = nR\mathbf{T}$   ← *our focus!*

②   *isolate* $T$      $(\frac{1}{nR})PV = nRT(\frac{1}{nR})$

③   *celebrate. ya done.*      $\boxed{\dfrac{PV}{nR} = T}$

                                         **D**

*(Gassy mole)*

## EXAMPLE 2

$$P = \frac{S-E}{S}$$

A company uses the above equation to determine what profit ratio $P$ they get when they make $S$ dollars worth of sales and have $E$ dollars in expenses. Which of the following equations would allow the company to determine how much it needs to make in sales to reach a target profit ratio if expenses are fixed?

A) $\ S = \frac{E}{1-P}$

B) $\ S = \frac{P-1}{E}$

C) $\ S = \frac{1-P}{E}$

D) $\ S = \frac{P-E}{P}$

SOLUTION

The first step is always to **determine what you are solving for**. In this case, we are asked for **sales**, which is represented by $S$.

 GOAL: solve for S $\qquad P = \frac{S-E}{S}$

Unfortunately, our target variable ($S$) is in both the top *and bottom* of the fraction. That's trouble. So let's multiply both sides by $S$ to **get rid of that fraction** and go from there:

1. *clear denominator* $\qquad (S)\,P = \frac{S-E}{S}(S)$

$$SP = S - E$$

2. *gather the S's* $\qquad SP - (S) = S - (S) - E$

$$SP - S = -E$$

3. *factor out an S* $\qquad S(P-1) = -E$

4. *solve for S* $\qquad S = \frac{-E}{P-1}$ or $\boxed{\frac{E}{1-P}}$ **A**

## EXAMPLE 3

$$E = \tfrac{1}{2}mv^2 + mgh$$

Conservation of energy tells us that the total energy $E$ of a pendulum of mass $m$ is constant at every point in its swing. The above equation shows how that energy is split between kinetic and potential energy at any given point, in terms of the pendulum's velocity $v$, its height $h$ above the lowest point in its swing, and the gravitational constant $g$. Which of the following equations gives the height of the pendulum in terms of the other variables ?

A)  $h = \dfrac{E - \tfrac{1}{2}v^2}{g}$

B)  $h = E - \tfrac{1}{2}mv^2 - mg$

C)  $h = \dfrac{E}{mg} - \dfrac{v^2}{2g}$

D)  $h = \dfrac{E - v^2}{mg}$

SOLUTION

The first thing we need to do is **formulate the first law of thermodynamics** for a compressible, closed system:

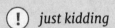 (!) *just kidding* $\qquad we = jk$

We defintely don't have to do that. While that *is* an impressive paragraph of physics goodness up there, we're just here to rearrange some formulas and go home. Our goal is to make balanced changes until height, **h**, is alone on one side:

(1) *rewrite equation* $\qquad E = \tfrac{1}{2}mv^2 + mgh$

(2) *subtract* $\qquad E - \tfrac{1}{2}mv^2 = mgh$

(3) *divide* $\qquad \dfrac{E - \tfrac{1}{2}mv^2}{mg} = h$

*Hmm...* we got **h** alone on one side but the equation doesn't match any of the answer choices! Our work is good so far, though, so there **must** be a way to simplify our equation...

## Work with confidence!

If you carefully write out each step of your work, you can quickly check to see that you're on the right track when you hit a slight roadblock. That way, you can focus on finding a way **forward**.

Continued on next page → **681**

**TIP**

You can split a fraction when there are things being added or subtracted in the **numerator**.

If the addition was in the denominator we would have to find something else to try.

So, now we have a new goal:

 **GOAL:** *simplify* $\qquad h = \dfrac{E - \frac{1}{2}mv^2}{mg}$

What could we do to simplify? Well, one idea is to try **splitting the fraction**... so why not, let's try it:

④ *split the fraction* $\qquad h = \dfrac{E}{mg} - \dfrac{\frac{1}{2}mv^2}{mg}$

⑤ *cancel the m's* $\qquad h = \dfrac{E}{mg} - \dfrac{\frac{1}{2}\cancel{m}v^2}{\cancel{m}g}$

$\qquad\qquad\qquad\qquad\quad h = \dfrac{E}{mg} - \dfrac{\frac{1}{2}v^2}{g}$

This looks familiar! Our equation is looking a lot like choice C:

**C)** $\quad h = \dfrac{E}{mg} - \dfrac{v^2}{2g} \qquad \longleftrightarrow \qquad h = \dfrac{E}{mg} - \dfrac{\frac{1}{2}v^2}{g}$

The only difference is a **2** in the denominator instead of a **1/2** in the numerator... and that's the same thing!

Think about it: we could write **1/2** as **2⁻¹**... and then drop the 2 to the denominator. Which means... *C is the correct answer!*

C

## EXAMPLE 4

$$G = -RT \ln K$$

The standard change of Gibbs free energy for a system at equilibrium is described by the above equation in terms of the temperature $T$, the equilibrium constant $K$, and a proportionality constant $R$. Which of the following expresses the temperature in terms of the other quantities?

A) $\quad T = \dfrac{G - \ln K}{-R}$

B) $\quad T = \dfrac{\ln K - G}{-R}$

C) $\quad T = \dfrac{G}{-R \ln K}$

D) $\quad T = G + R - \ln K$

**SOLUTION**

The first step is to **determine what we're asked to solve for**. In this case, we are looking for **temperature**, again denoted by $T$. In our equation, $G = -RT \ln K$, we notice that $T$ is being multiplied by "$\ln K$". This is the "natural log" function, but that doesn't matter and we don't need to know what that is to solve this problem! We can treat the whole expression ($\ln K$) as a single chunk. Since that chunk is being multiplied to T, we can just divide both sides by **(–R)** and by **($\ln K$)** to isolate T:

*our focus!*

(1) *rewrite equation* $\qquad G = -RT\ln K$

(2) *divide by (–R)* $\qquad \dfrac{G}{-R} = T\ln K$

(3) *divide by ($\ln K$)* $\qquad \dfrac{G}{-R\ln K} = T$

C

# Practice Problems

*Select the best answer choice for each question.*

---

**1**

$$\frac{1}{T} = \frac{1}{R} + \frac{1}{S}$$

When two resistors are in parallel in a circuit, their combined resistance $T$ is the reciprocal of the sum of the reciprocals of the resistance of the two individual resistors $R$ and $S$ as shown in the equation above. Which of the following equations gives the resistance $S$ needs to have if we know the resistance of $R$ and the desired combined resistance?

A)  $S = \frac{T(R)}{R - T}$

B)  $S = \frac{T(R)}{T - R}$

C)  $S = R + T$

D)  $S = \frac{T - R}{R(T)}$

---

**2**

$$V = IR$$
$$P = IV$$

When we are looking at an ideal circuit, the above equation explains the relationship between the voltage $V$, current $I$, resistance $R$, and power $P$. Which of the following equations gives an expression for the resistance of the circuit in terms of the voltage and power?

A)  $R = \frac{V}{P}$

B)  $R = \frac{V^2}{P}$

C)  $R = \frac{P}{V^2}$

D)  $R = \frac{P}{V}$

**3**

$$F = \frac{G(m_1 \cdot m_2)}{r^2}$$

The gravitational force $F$ between two objects a distance $r$ apart with masses $m_1$ and $m_2$ respectively is shown in the equation above. $G$ is a gravitational constant. Which of the following expressions gives the mass of the first object in terms of the other values?

A)  $m_1 = \frac{FGm_2}{r^2}$

B)  $m_1 = -\frac{FGm_2}{r^2}$

C)  $m_1 = \frac{Fr^2}{G} - m_2$

D)  $m_1 = \frac{Fr^2}{Gm_2}$

**4**

$$\delta = \frac{1}{\sqrt{1 - (\frac{v}{c})^2}}$$

The Lorentz factor $\delta$ is important for a number of calculations in relativistic mechanics. In the above equation, $v$ is the relative velocity of the object and $c$ is the speed of light. Which of the following equations would let us find the relative velocity of the object if we knew the Lorentz factor?

A)  $v = c\sqrt{1 - \frac{1}{\delta^2}}$

B)  $v = c - \frac{c}{\delta}$

C)  $v = c^2 - \frac{c^2}{\delta^2}$

D)  $v = c\sqrt{\delta^2 - 1}$

$$n_1\sin(\Theta_1) = n_2\sin(\Theta_2)$$

When a ray of light passes between materials, it refracts. Snell's law, given above, describes the relationship between the angle of incidence $\Theta_1$ in a material with index of refraction $n_1$ and the angle of refraction $\Theta_2$ in a material with index of refraction $n_2$. A scientist knows the angle of incidence and index of refraction of the first material. If they want to find the necessary index of refraction to attain a specific angle of refraction in the second material, which of the following equations should they use?

A) $n_2 = n_1\sin(\Theta_1) - \sin(\Theta_2)$

B) $n_2 = \dfrac{\sin(\Theta_1)}{n_1\sin(\Theta_2)}$

C) $n_2 = \dfrac{n_1\sin(\Theta_1)}{\sin(\Theta_2)}$

D) $n_2 = \dfrac{n_1\Theta_1}{\Theta_2}$

$$v^2 = v_0^2 + 2a(x - k)$$

The above equation gives the square of the velocity $v$ of a car given its initial velocity $v_0$, constant acceleration $a$, current position $x$ and starting position $k$. Which of the following equations would allow you to solve for the starting position of the car if you knew its current position, acceleration, and current velocity?

A) $k = \dfrac{v_0^2 - v^2 - x}{2a}$

B) $k = v^2 - v_0^2 - 2ax$

C) $k = \dfrac{v^2 - v_0^2}{2ax}$

D) $k = x - \dfrac{v^2 - v_0^2}{2a}$

**Questions 7-8 refer to the following information:**

The real cash flow, $R$, in dollars, from a bank deposit after one year is given by $R = \frac{N}{1+I}$, where $R$ is the real cash flow in dollars, $N$ is the nominal cash flow in dollars, and $I$ is the rate of inflation.

**7**

Which of the following equations gives the rate of inflation in terms of real and nominal cash flow?

A)  $I = \frac{N}{R} - 1$

B)  $I = \frac{R-1}{N}$

C)  $I = \frac{N}{R+1}$

D)  $I = \frac{R}{N} + 1$

**8**

If the nominal cash flow of a bank deposit was $35, but the real cash flow for that deposit was $34, what was the inflation rate for that year, rounded to the nearest percent?

A)  1%
B)  2%
C)  3%
D)  4%

$$t = \sqrt{\frac{2h}{9.81}}$$

The time $t$ it takes, in seconds, for an object to hit the ground after getting dropped from rest at a height $h$, in meters, is given by the equation above.

**9**

Which of the following equations gives the height from which the object was dropped in terms of the time it took for the object to hit the ground?

A) $h = \sqrt{\frac{9.81t}{2}}$

B) $h = \frac{2t^2}{9.81}$

C) $h = \frac{9.81t^2}{2}$

D) $h = (9.81)(2)t^2$

**10**

Francesca dropped a pebble into a river while standing on a bridge 20 meters above the river. Approximately how long will it take for the pebble to leave Francesca's hand and land in the river?

A) 2 seconds
B) 4 seconds
C) 8 seconds
D) 16 seconds

**Questions 11–13 refer to the following information:**

$$\$2,750 + \$37E = B$$

The total operating budget for a certain manager each year is given by the equation above, where $E$ represents the number of employees the manager oversees and $B$ represents the total operating budget in dollars.

**11**

Which of the following expressions gives the number of employees in terms of the total operating budget?

A) $E = \dfrac{2750 - B}{37}$

B) $E = \dfrac{2750 + B}{37}$

C) $E = \dfrac{B - 2750}{37}$

D) $E = \dfrac{B + 2750}{37}$

**12**

If the manager has an operating budget of \$17,550, how many employees does the manager have?

A) 300
B) 350
C) 400
D) 450

**13**

What is the meaning of \$2,750 in the equation?

A) The manager has an operating budget of \$2,750.
B) The manager can spend \$2,750 per employee.
C) The manager must spend \$2,750 each year.
D) The manager has at least \$2,750 for the operating budget.

# UNIT

# Data Analysis: Part 1

## Chapters

## Overview

In this unit, we dive into the Data Analysis questions that make up a large chunk of the Calculator section. We'll be looking at tables of data, finding proportions, and converting feet to inches and back again.

## Calculator!

Data Analysis questions only show up on the Calculator section, accounting for 35% to 50% of all questions on the section! Use your calculator when completing these chapters.

# Piece over Whole

*Percentages and proportions are all about piece over whole.*

## Percentages

The word percent tells us that we are looking at how many we get for every (**per–**) one hundred (**–cent**). This gives us the following equation for finding a percentage:

$$\frac{\%}{100} = \frac{piece}{whole}$$

Percentage questions focus on three components: the size of a piece, the size of the whole, and the percentage that represents that relationship. You'll be given two of these components and asked to find the third.

## EXAMPLE 1

What is 15% of 60?

A) 4
B) 9
C) 15
D) 90

Our first step with a word problem is to **translate into math**.

 *Translate*

| ~~What~~ | ~~is~~ | ~~15%~~ | ~~of~~ | ~~60?~~ |
|---|---|---|---|---|
| ? | = | .15 | × | 60 |

 *Calculate*

$$(.15)(60) = ?$$

$$(.15)(60) = \boxed{9}$$

**TIP**

Data Analysis questions come in many forms. You may be given data about some piece of a population and asked to calculate a percentage, or you'll be given a proportion and a population, and asked to calculate how many total individuals fall into that particular group. Either way, it's all about pieces and wholes.

**Continued on next page** →

# TIP

Focus on which numbers are attached to "is" and "of".

(4 IS) WHAT PERCENT (OF 5)?

You can set up your work using the formula below:

$$\frac{is}{of} = \frac{\%}{100}$$

$$\frac{4}{5} = \frac{x}{100}$$

Then cross-multiply and solve for x!

Let's set up the same problem using a piece-over-whole fraction:

① write percent formula    $\frac{\%}{100} = \frac{piece}{whole}$

② fill in what we know    $\frac{15}{100} = \frac{x}{60}$

③ solve for **x**    $60(\frac{15}{100}) = x$

$$\frac{90}{10} = x$$

⑨ $= x$

**Translate and solve** the word problems below.

| Problem | Solution |
|---|---|
| 1.  What is 60% of 15? | |
| 2.  32 is 20% of what number? | |
| 3.  What percent of 70 is 14? | |
| 4.  5% of 200 is two-fifths of what number? | |
| 5.  What is ⅓% of 170? | |

Scratch Work

**Answers:**   1. $x = .60(15)$   2. $32 = .20x$   3. $(\frac{x}{100})70 = 14$   4. $.05(200) = \frac{2}{5}x$   5. $x = \frac{1/3}{100}(170)$

$x = 9$      $x = 160$      $x = 20$      $x = 25$      $x = \frac{17}{30}$

## EXAMPLE 2

Pooja just returned from a backpacking trip and is going through the pictures she took. Of the 375 pictures, she finds that 28% contain at least one animal. How many of her pictures do not contain an animal?

A) 18
B) 72
C) 105
D) 270

We know that **28%** of the pictures contain an animal, and there are a total of **375 pictures**. We can use the percentage to find out exactly how many of the 375 pictures contain an animal. If **$a$** is the number of pictures **with** animals, then:

① *write percent formula*  $\dfrac{\%}{100} = \dfrac{piece}{whole}$

② *fill in what we know*  $.28 = \dfrac{a}{375}$

③ *solve for $a$*  $.28(375) = a$

$105 = a$

Careful – we're not done yet! We are asked for the number of pictures **without** animals, which means we need to subtract 105 from our total:

④ *subtract 105 from total*  $375 - 105 = \boxed{270}$

**Bonus Solution**
We could have easily skipped a step here. They told us that 28% of the pictures DO contain an animal, but asked for the number that do NOT contain an animal... which means that 28% isn't *really* our percentage. 100% – 28% = **72%**. *That's* the percentage of the whole without animals in them. This makes it simple:

⑤ *multiply whole by percent*  $(.72)(375) = \boxed{270}$  C

## TIP

When working with percentages, we usually use a decimal. So instead of writing "28% of 375 pictures", we can just write:

**.28(375)**

## It's a Trap!

Beware the traps the SAT lays in the wrong answers! If you aren't reading carefully, it would be easy to take 28% of 375 and think you are done. This gives 105, which is choice B!

## Proportions

What's the difference between proportions and percentages? Not a whole lot, actually. To find the percentage, we just divide the piece over the whole fraction to get a decimal. The proportion is just that piece over whole fraction... no dividing required! In other words, percentages are decimals and proportions are fractions. That's it!

## INTERACTIVE EXAMPLE

Ice Cream Sales

| Mix-ins | Ice Cream Flavors | | | | |
|---|---|---|---|---|---|
| | Vanilla | Chocolate | Strawberry | Mocha | Total |
| Sprinkles | 3 | 6 | 8 | 10 | 27 |
| Nuts | 4 | 5 | 4 | 4 | 17 |
| Cookie dough | 6 | 5 | 4 | 1 | 16 |
| Pretzels | 9 | 8 | 2 | 11 | 30 |
| Total | 22 | 24 | 18 | 26 | 90 |

The *What's the Scoop?* ice cream shop ran a recent special where customers got to pick one of its four base ice cream flavors and one mix-in. The table above represents their sales during the special.

**Q1)** What proportion of the customers ordered strawberry with nuts?

**TIP**

Be sure to simplify proportions whenever possible. When we see fractions in an algebra problem, we usually "clear" them by multiplying both sides by the denominator. If we MUST put up with them, we simplify those suckers as much as humanly possible.

**SOLUTION**

To build our proportion, we just need to put the **piece** (# who ordered strawberry with nuts) over the **whole** (total # of customers).

The number who ordered strawberry with nuts can be found in the second row of the strawberry column: **4 people**. The **total overall number** of customers can be found in the very bottom right of the table: **90 people**. So our proportion is:

$$\frac{piece}{whole} = \frac{4}{90} = \boxed{\frac{2}{45}}$$

**Q2)** What proportion of the customers who ordered pretzels as their mix-in also ordered chocolate ice cream?

## Percentage

If we wanted to know what **percentage** of the customers who ordered pretzels also ordered chocolate, we would just divide:

$$\frac{8}{30} \approx .27 = \textbf{27\%}$$

Because, honestly, nobody likes fractions.

SOLUTION

We have to be careful here because our "whole" is no longer ALL customers. They ask for the proportion of the number of customers that ordered pretzels **(whole)** who *also* got chocolate ice cream **(piece)**.

The total number of customers who ordered pretzels is found in the *fourth row* of the *"Total"* column: **30 people.** The number of customers who ordered both pretzels and chocolate ice cream can be found in the *fourth row* of the *"Chocolate"* column: **8 people.** Now that we've carefully determined our piece and whole, we know our proportion:

$$\frac{piece}{whole} = \frac{8}{30} = \boxed{\frac{4}{15}}$$

## EXAMPLE 3

A mad scientist has automated the process of building his robot army. He randomly selects 3 robots to test from every 50 he produces. At this rate, how many robots will he test if he creates an army of 1000 robots?

## Percentage

If you were told what **percent** of robots he tests, you could use the same process to solve the problem. 3 out of 50 is the same as 6%.

$$\frac{3}{50} = \frac{6}{100} = \frac{x}{1,000}$$

## Rates of Change

Whether you use percent or proportion, you end up doing the same thing: take a rate from one population (3/50 or 6%) and multiply it by a different population.

## TIP

Probability questions on the SAT are simply proportion questions asked with slightly different language.

You'll still be working with tables or paragraphs of data, and your job is **still** to compare the size of a "piece" with the size of the "whole" population.

---

**SOLUTION**

The phrase "at this rate" is often a good sign we're dealing with a proportions problem. In particular, we are given one proportion for a small group (3 robots tested out of every 50) and asked to apply it to a larger population (1000 robots). To solve, we can just set up two equal proportions – one for the small population and one for the large population. Then we can fill in what we know:

1. *set up proportions*

$$\frac{piece_s}{whole_s} = \frac{piece_L}{whole_L}$$

2. *fill in what you know*

$$\frac{3 \ tested}{50 \ robots} = \frac{?? \ tested}{1,000 \ robots}$$

Now we can see what we're solving for. Let $x$ be the number that would be tested out of 1,000 robots.

3. *solve for x*

$$\frac{3}{50} = \frac{x}{1,000}$$

$$\frac{3,000}{50} = x$$

$$\boxed{60} = x$$

---

## Probability

Probability is a tool for measuring the likelihood that something will happen on a scale of 0 (not gonna happen) to 1 (definitely happening).

| 0 | .5 | 1 |
| --- | --- | --- |
| *not gonna happen* | *a coin flip* | *definitely happening* |

The probability of an event happening is still all about piece over whole! The number of outcomes that satisfy the event is the piece. The total number of outcomes is the whole.

$$\text{Probability } (x) = \frac{piece}{whole} = \frac{\text{\# of outcomes that satisfy } x}{\text{\# of total possible outcomes}}$$

**697**

## EXAMPLE 4

|  | Shady Grove | Johnson Park |
|---|---|---|
| Swallowtails | 12 | 6 |
| Monarchs | 18 | 10 |
| Other | 7 | 5 |

Kai is studying butterfly populations at two local parks. He spent an afternoon at each park catching, classifying, and releasing butterflies. The table above shows a record of all butterflies caught during the afternoon. Assuming that Kai's sample is representative of the butterfly populations in each park, what is the probability that a random butterfly caught in Shady Grove will be a swallowtail?

A) $\dfrac{3}{17}$

B) $\dfrac{7}{17}$

C) $\dfrac{12}{37}$

D) $\dfrac{28}{37}$

## PORTAL

For this question, you don't need to worry about what a "representative sample" is.

However, if you're curious, check out the **Study Design** chapter on page 763 to see how the SAT will test this idea directly.

---

SOLUTION

We are asked for the probability that a butterfly caught in Shady Grove will be a swallowtail. That means our proportion will be:

$$probability = \frac{piece}{whole} = \frac{\#\ of\ swallowtails\ in\ Shady\ Grove}{total\ \#\ of\ butterflies\ in\ Shady\ Grove}$$

Our job then is to find the values for the numerator and the denominator using the table. First, let's grab the numerator. The # of swallowtails in Shady Grove can be found in the first row of the Shady Grove column: **12 swallowtails.** Let's fill that in:

$$probability = \frac{piece}{whole} = \frac{12\ swallowtails}{total\ \#\ of\ butterflies\ in\ Shady\ Grove}$$

Now to find our denominator. The table doesn't tell us any totals, so we'll need to add up the Shady Grove column ourselves...

 Continued on next page →

SHADY GROVE TOTAL = 12 + 18 + 7 = 37

Adding up the Shady Grove column, we get **37** for our "whole" population. That's our denominator, and it gives us an answer!

$$probability = \frac{12\ swallowtails}{37\ butterflies\ in\ Shady\ Grove} = \left(\frac{12}{37}\right)$$

There we have it! The probability of catching a swallowtail butterfly in Shady Grove is 12 over 37. Our answer is **C**!

C

## EXAMPLE 5

|            | < 70% | 70-90% | 91-100% | Total |
|------------|-------|--------|---------|-------|
| Teacher A  | 3     | 15     | 7       | 25    |
| Teacher B  | 5     | 10     | 12      | 27    |
| Total      | 8     | 25     | 19      | 52    |

The data in the table summarize the results of a Calculus test. There are two sections of the class, each taught by a different teacher. The number of students in each class whose score fell within a given range is recorded above. If a student is chosen at random from among those who scored a 70 or above, what is the probability that student is from Teacher A's section?

A) .25
B) .48
C) .50
D) .52

We need to determine the total **population** we are choosing the student from, and the **trait** that we're interested in.

The question says "If student is chosen at random from among those who scored a 70% or above..." so our population is **all students who scored 70 or above**. This means we need to add up all students in the "70-90%" and "91-100%" columns. Luckily, we have a "total" row that we can use.

|  | < 70% | 70-90% | 91-100% | Total |
|---|---|---|---|---|
| Teacher A | 3 | 15 | 7 | 25 |
| Teacher B | 5 | 10 | 12 | 27 |
| Total | 8 | 25 | 19 | 52 |

$$25 + 19 = 44$$

So our population of students who scored 70% or above is **44**.

We want to find the probability that a student in this population is in Teacher A's section. To do that, we should focus on just the first row for those same two columns:

|  | < 70% | 70-90% | 91-100% | Total |
|---|---|---|---|---|
| Teacher A | 3 | **15** | 7 | 25 |
| Teacher B | 5 | 10 | 12 | 27 |
| Total | 8 | 0 | 19 | 52 |

$$15 + 7 = 22$$

There are 22 students who scored a 70% or above in Teacher A's section. That's the "piece" with the trait we want! Now we can set up our proportion. Looking at the answer choices, we can see that we need to divide our fraction to get a decimal:

$$probability = \frac{\#\ with\ trait}{population} = \frac{22}{44} = \frac{1}{2} = \boxed{.50}$$

C

The table below shows the number of Bachelor's degrees granted in the United States between the years 2008 and 2012 in several STEM fields. **Use the table** to answer the questions that follow.

Number of STEM Bachelor's Degrees Conferred in U.S.

| Major | 2008 | 2009 | 2010 | 2011 | 2012 | Total |
|---|---|---|---|---|---|---|
| Engineering | 68,431 | 68,911 | 72,654 | 76,376 | 81,382 | 367,754 |
| Math | 15,192 | 15,496 | 16,030 | 17,182 | 18,842 | 82,742 |
| Physical Sciences | 22,179 | 22,688 | 23,379 | 24,712 | 26,663 | 119,621 |
| Biological Sciences | 79,829 | 82,825 | 86,400 | 90,003 | 95,849 | 434,906 |
| Computer Science | 38,476 | 37,994 | 39,589 | 43,072 | 47,384 | 206,515 |
| Total | 224,107 | 227,914 | 238,052 | 251,345 | 270,120 | 1,211,538 |

| Question | Answer |
|---|---|
| 1. What is the probability that a randomly chosen graduate in 2009 majored in mathematics? | |
| 2. What is the probability that a randomly chosen engineer who graduated between 2008 and 2011 graduated in 2010? | |
| 3. What is the probability that a randomly chosen computer scientist who graduated during these five years graduated in 2010? | |
| 4. What is the probability that a randomly chosen STEM graduate from these five years graduated in 2012? | |
| 5. If a randomly chosen 2011 graduate did not major in Engineering, what is the probability that they majored in computer science? | |
| 6. What is the probability that a randomly chosen student who graduated in 2010, 2011, or 2012 majored in either Physical or Biological Sciences? | |

# Pieces & Wholes

The trick to these questions is keeping track of your pieces and wholes for each problem.

Don't try to keep it all in your head! Use your pencil to take notes while you plug values into your calculator

**Answers:** *See next page.*

# Practice Problems

*Use your new skills to answer each question.*

## 1

36% of the seniors at Washington High School take AP Calculus. If there are 575 seniors, how many are taking AP Calculus?

A) 16
B) 36
C) 207
D) 517

## 2

| | robins | cardinals | chickadees | blue jays |
|---|---|---|---|---|
| Saturday | 3 | 7 | 5 | 7 |
| Sunday | 4 | 9 | 7 | 8 |

Loretta went bird watching one weekend and recorded the number of the four most common birds she saw in the table above. If 24% of the birds she saw were her favorite type of bird, which bird is her favorite?

A) robin
B) cardinal
C) chickadee
D) blue jay

**Answers for previous page: 1)** .07 **2)** .25 **3)** .19 **4)** .22 **5)** .25 **6)** .46

**3**

$\frac{3}{4}$ of a particular library's collection is fiction and $\frac{3}{8}$ of the fiction collection is fantasy. What proportion of the library's book collection is fantasy?

A) $\frac{9}{32}$

B) $\frac{1}{2}$

C) $\frac{8}{9}$

D) $\frac{9}{8}$

**4**

| Apples Eaten in a Week | | | | |
|---|---|---|---|---|
| 0 | 0 | 0 | 1 | 1 |
| 1 | 2 | 3 | 3 | 3 |
| 3 | 4 | 6 | 6 | 7 |
| 8 | 8 | 10 | 12 | 14 |

The table above lists the number of apples a random sample of 20 students ate in one week during their lunch period. If 2,000 students go to the school, which of the following is the best estimate for the expected number of apples that will be consumed by students at the school every week?

A) 4.6
B) 9.2
C) 920
D) 9,200

| Results of a Math Test | | | | | |
|---|---|---|---|---|---|
| | 100-90 | 89-80 | 79-70 | 69-60 | ≤ 59 |
| Attended review sessions | 15 | 10 | 2 | 1 | 0 |
| Did NOT attend review sessions | 8 | 8 | 6 | 6 | 4 |

The table above summarizes the results of 60 high school students who took the same math test. If one of the high school students who made an 80 or higher was chosen at random, what is the probability that the student attended the review sessions?

A) $\frac{15}{26}$

B) $\frac{7}{18}$

C) $\frac{15}{41}$

D) $\frac{25}{41}$

| | Math | Reading | Writing | TOTAL |
|---|---|---|---|---|
| Baseball | 15 | 39 | 50 | 104 |
| Basketball | 7 | 32 | 11 | 50 |
| Soccer | 20 | 19 | 7 | 46 |
| Total | 42 | 90 | 68 | 200 |

The graph above shows the distribution of preferred subject in school and preferred sport to play for 200 people at a local high school. If a student is chosen at random, what is the probability that the student will be a soccer player whose favorite subject in school is writing?

A) 0.035
B) 0.103
C) 0.152
D) 0.255

7

|  | Likes Spam | Does NOT Like Spam |
|---|---|---|
| Male | 92 | 158 |
| Female | 8 | 242 |
| Total | 100 | 400 |

The owner of a local deli is considering the idea of selling spam. In order to decide if this is a good idea or not, the owner takes a survey of 500 of his customers. The results of his survey are shown in the table above. What percentage of his female customers like spam?

A) 16%
B) 8%
C) 3.2%
D) 1.6%

8

| Sleeping Positions | | | | |
|---|---|---|---|---|
|  | Back | Stomach | Side | Total |
| Male | 17 | 16 | 7 | 40 |
| Female | 3 | 12 | 25 | 40 |
| Total | 20 | 28 | 32 | 80 |

The table above summarizes the results of 80 participants in a sleep study to see what sleeping positions were most common among males and females. Participants were categorized by the sleeping positions: sleeping on the back, sleeping on the stomach, or sleeping on one side. If a female participant is chosen at random, what is the probability that she sleeps on her side?

A) $\frac{5}{8}$

B) $\frac{25}{33}$

C) $\frac{33}{40}$

D) $\frac{7}{26}$

Jackson does a survey and learns that $\frac{2}{5}$ of his classmates are only children, $\frac{1}{3}$ have exactly one sibling, and the rest have two or more siblings. If 8 of his classmates have 2 or more siblings, how many are only children?

Aja is sorting through her beads while designing a necklace and finds that the ratio of yellow beads to green beads is 2 to 5. If she has 35 green beads, how many yellow beads does she have?

A) 10
B) 14
C) 15
D) 21

# Percent Change

*In this chapter, we get practice working with percentages that grow or shrink over time. There is a very specific way to reflect this in your work, and many students make errors in the process. So let's practice!*

## Working with Decimals

Say you learn that the price of a pair of pants ($x$) has **increased by 20%**. Let's write that in words and then translate to math:

| "the new price | is equal to | the price | plus | 20% of the price." |
|---|---|---|---|---|
| *new price* | $=$ | $(100\%)x$ | $+$ | $(20\%)x$ |

$$\text{*new price*} = (120\%)x \text{ or } \boxed{1.2x}$$

Notice that, to show a 20% increase, we end up just **multiplying by 1.2**. This is an extremely helpful shortcut, and it works for decreases too. If you see a "20% decrease", you can write that as:

$$100\%x - 20\%x = 80\%x$$
$$1.0x - 0.2x = 0.8x$$

## TIP

This principle applies when comparing two separate quantities. "20% more" is the same thing as "20% increase."

So... if the price of *my* pants was **30% more** than the price of your pants, then my pants cost **1.3 times** the price of your pants!

Write each percent increase or decrease **as a decimal.**

| % Change | ↑ 20% | ↑ 18% | ↓ 92% | ↑ 8% | ↓ 2.3% | ↑ 120% |
|---|---|---|---|---|---|---|
| Decimal | 1.2 | | | | | |

**Answers:** *bottom of next page*

## EXAMPLE 1

Kendrick challenged his friend Sherane to a sit-ups competition. They each took 1 minute to complete as many sit-ups as possible. Kendrick told Sherane how many he did and she responded that she did 15% more. If Sherane did 46 situps, how many did Kendrick do?

A) 7
B) 39
C) 40
D) 54

## TIP

We could work backwards here! Since we know that Kendrick did fewer sit-ups than Sherane, we know that choice D can't be right.

We can then calculate 115% of A, B, and C to see which one works out to 46.

### SOLUTION

We should always start off word problems like this by translating into math. We know that Sherane did **15% more** than Kendrick. Fifteen percent MORE means 100% of Kendrick's amount **plus** another 15% of Kendrick's amount. Let's translate that:

1  *Translate:*  $S = 100\%K + 15\%K$

"S did 15% more than K"  $S = 1K + .15K$

$S = 1.15K$

We're also told that Sherane did 46 situps. Let's plug that in for *S*:

2  *substitute 46 for S*  $46 = 1.15K$

3  *solve for K*  $\dfrac{46}{1.15} = K$

$\boxed{40} = K$

C

**Previous Page:**  1. *given*  2. 1.18  3. .08  4. 1.08  5. .977  6. 2.2

# EXAMPLE 2

Jerome is an astronomer and has been studying a table of the distances of various celestial objects from Earth. He notices that the distance to the star *Pollux* is about 48.3% less than the distance to the star *Aldebaran*. If it is about 65.3 light years to *Aldebaran*, about how far, in light years, is it to *Pollux*?

A) 31.5
B) 33.8
C) 126.3
D) 135.2

Per usual, we should start by practicing some **art of translation**. We are told that the distance to Pollux is about **48.3% less** than the distance to Aldebaran.

| | | |
|---|---|---|
| ① *Translate:* | | $P = 100\%A - 48.3\%A$ |
| *"P is 48.3% less than A"* | | $P = 1A - .483A$ |
| | | $P = .517A$ |

And since the distance to Aldebaran is **65.3 light years**, we know:

② *Substitute 65.3 for A* $\qquad$ $P = .517(65.3)$

$$P = \boxed{33.76}$$

B

## Compound Percentages

Imagine that you're out shopping and see a pair of pants on a mannequin marked "$100." Next to the mannequin is a sign that says **"50% off!"**, and, upon further inspection, you discover *another* sign that says *"take an additional 50% off!"* Now, odds are you wouldn't think:

*"Sweet! Free pants!"*

...and skip out of the store with the stolen goods. You'd understand intuitively that the first sign marked the pants down to about $50, and the second knocked it down to something like 20 or 30 bucks. In the "real world", this seems obvious. However, this is a common mistake students make when working with percentages on the test. Remember, you have to take each percent change one at a time:

$$50\% \text{ off } x = .5x$$

$$50\% \text{ off the } 50\% \text{ sale price} = .5(.5x) = .25x$$

## PORTAL

*How do you get to the top of Mount Everest?*

*One step at a time.*

Word problems might sound complicated when you first read them, but each individual step is one you already know how to do! Turn to page 632 for practice with modeling word problems.

### EXAMPLE 3

Eloise bought dinner at her favorite restaurant. She brought a coupon for 15% off the total cost of the meal. A 7% sales tax was added to the discounted price and Eloise added a 20% tip on the original price of the meal. In terms of the original price $p$, how much did Eloise pay?

A) $1.12p$

B) $(1.07)(.85)(1.2)p$

C) $(1.07)(.85) + (1.2)p$

D) $(1.07)(.85)p + (.20)p$

# TIP

If you don't immediately see your answer in the choices, don't panic! See if you can simplify or rearrange your answer to get one of the choices. For example, here, a correct choice could even have looked like:

**[(1.07)(.85) + .2]*p***

**SOLUTION**

There's a lot going on here, so let's work through one bit at a time. First, we're told she has a 15% coupon. This means **15% less**, which we can represent as **.85*p***.

$$\text{Discount price after coupon} = (1 - .15)p = .85p$$

Next, there is a **7%** sales tax **added** to this discounted price. To increase by 7%, we can **multiply the discount price by 1.07**.

$$\text{Discount Price} + \text{Sales Tax} = 1(.85p) + .07(.85p) = (1.07)(.85p)$$

Then we just need to **add** the tip. We have to be careful here: it says the tip is **20% of the *original* price**, which we can represent as (.20)*p*.

$$\text{Taxed Discount} + \text{Tip} = \boxed{(1.07)(.85p) + (.20)p}$$

D

# Calculating Percent Change

Occasionally, you'll be asked to calculate a percent change by comparing a new and old value. For example, in keeping with our stolen pants example, you might be told that the pants were originally $52 and were marked down to $13. That's a great deal! But *how* great is it? To find the **percent change** between those prices, you can use this simple formula:

$$\% \text{ Change} = \frac{|new - old|}{old} \times 100$$

$$\% \text{ Change} = \frac{|13 - 52|}{52} \times 100 = \frac{39}{52}(100) = \boxed{75\% \text{ change}}$$

One thing to watch out for when working with percent change: this does NOT mean that the new price is 75% of the original price. Since we **decreased** by 75%, that means the new price is 100% – 75% = **25%** of the original price. Remember your piece-over-whole relationships and work out each step carefully!

**Use the percent change formula** to complete the table below.

| # | Old Price | New Price | % Change |
|---|-----------|-----------|----------|
| 1 | $200 | $80 | |
| 2 | $65 | $39 | |
| 3 | $1,000 | $1,120 | |
| 4 | $16 | $1 | |
| 5 | $11,235 | $6,516.30 | |
| 6 | $81,321 | $47,166.18 | |

**Answers:** 1. 60%   2. 40%   3. 12%   4. 93.75%   5. 42%   6. 42%

# Practice Problems

*Use your new skills to answer each question.*

**1**

Terry went shopping and bought 5 T-shirts and 2 sweaters. The price of a sweater is 30 percent more expensive than that of a T-shirt, and Terry paid a total of $121.60. What was the price of a sweater?

A)  $16.00
B)  $19.00
C)  $20.80
D)  $24.70

**2**

Five friends buy concert tickets together because the band is having a promotion where, for every four tickets purchased, the fifth ticket will be discounted by $10. The group of friends splits the cost of the 5 tickets equally such that each paid $38. What percent discount did each friend receive?

A)  5%
B)  10%
C)  15%
D)  25%

**3**

Kyle, Claire, and Fabio all went to the same bakery together and bought pumpkin spice pastries. Kyle paid the full price for his pastry, Claire used a coupon for $1 off her pastry, and Fabio used a coupon for 20 percent off his pastry. If Kyle, Claire, and Fabio paid a total of $10.20 for the three pastries, how much did Kyle pay for his pastry?

A)  $3.00
B)  $3.20
C)  $3.30
D)  $4.00

**4**

Eliza is doing a chemistry experiment and finds that the actual weight of the product is 15% less than the predicted weight. If she expected to get 150 grams of product, how much did she actually get?

**5**

Bryant is looking at his power bill. He sees that in May when the weather was mild it was $48 and in July when he ran the AC a lot it was $178. What was the percent increase in his bill from May to July?

A) 2.7%
B) 3.7%
C) 270%
D) 370%

**6**

A triangle's base was increased by 15%. If its area is increased by 38%, what percent was the height of the triangle increased by?

$$0.69bh = \frac{1}{2}(1.15b)(xh)$$

$$0.69 = 0.575x$$

20%

**7**

If a circle's circumference is decreased by 12%, what percent is the diameter decreased by?

A) $2\sqrt{3}$ %
B) 6%
C) 12%
D) 24%

# Unit Conversions

*In this chapter, we learn to use proportions to convert one unit into another.*

.................................................................................

## Focus on Units

Word problems, by their nature, tend to be filled with units. Whether we're talking about pounds of hamburgers or how many miles someone ran after eating hamburgers, units are usually just labels for the variables in our math equations. Occasionally, however, the test-writers will **tell** you values in one unit (like miles) but then **ask** for an answer in a different unit (like feet).

The good news is that every time the test-writers do this, they <u>underline</u> the changed units! Plus, you'll always be given a **proportion** that you can use to convert your answer into the new units. Let's see that in action.

## EXAMPLE 1

A 1.5 pound batch of fudge is poured into a 6 inch × 8 inch pan and allowed to cool. It is then cut into one-inch squares. What is the weight, in <u>ounces</u>, of each square? (1 pound = 16 ounces)

A) $\frac{1}{2}$

B) $\frac{1}{3}$

C) 1

D) 6

## TIP

Convert your units at the very beginning of the problem whenever possible.

We are asked for the weight in ounces, but we're given a weight in pounds. Let's start by converting the units so we don't forget later. Since we currently have pounds and want ounces, we need to divide by the number of pounds and multiply by the number of ounces:

**(1)** *convert units*  $(1.5 \text{ pounds}) \times \dfrac{16 \text{ ounces}}{1 \text{ pound}} = \textbf{24 ounces}$

This means we have a **total of 24 ounces** of fudge. We're asked to determine how many ounces a 1-inch square weighs, so let's think about how many squares there are:

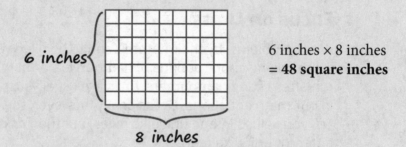

6 inches × 8 inches
= **48 square inches**

So our **24 ounces** of fudge get cut up into **48 squares**. To find out how much each square weighs, we just do the math equivalent of chopping up fudge: dividing!

**(2)** *divide*  $\dfrac{24 \text{ ounces}}{48 \text{ squares}} = \boxed{\dfrac{1}{2}}$

A

## EXAMPLE 2

The average flight speed of a particular gryphon is 78 km/hr. At this rate, which of the following is closest to the distance, in kilometers, the gryphon can travel in 13 <u>minutes</u>?

A) 6
B) 17
C) 360
D) 1,014

You might see this problem and recall that:

$$distance = rate \times time$$

The only problem is that the time unit in the given rate (km/hr) is not the same as the unit we are asked about (minutes)! Since the rate is already in hours, let's just convert 13 minutes into hours. There are 60 minutes in an hour, so:

$$13 \ \cancel{minutes} \times \frac{1 \ hour}{60 \ \cancel{minutes}} = \frac{13}{60} \ hr$$

So we know that the gryphon flies 78km per hour, and we want to know how far it would get in $\frac{13}{60}$ of an hour:

$$\frac{13}{60} \ \cancel{hr} \times \frac{78km}{1 \ \cancel{hr}} = \boxed{16.9 \ km}$$

## TIP

You could also convert speed into km/min, and then multiply by 13.

**BONUS: Estimation**

In the midst of all this hardcore math genius that we've got going on, it can be easy to forget that sometimes "just sorta estimating" can often work wonders. Take this problem for example...

**13 minutes is a little under a quarter of an hour**. Which means the gryphon will fly *about* a quarter of the distance it would fly in an hour. We know it flies 78km in an hour, so...

$$78 \div 4 = 19.5$$

The only answer that's close to that number is **Choice B**, 17 km. Behold, the power of estimating!

B

## EXAMPLE 3

| | |
|---|---|
| Number of tablespoons per ounce of butter | 2 |
| Number of teaspoons per tablespoons | 3 |
| Number of ounces per pound | 16 |
| Number of tablespoons per cup | 16 |
| Number of tablespoons per pound of butter | 32 |
| Number of grams per ounce | 28.3 |
| Number of grams of flour per cup | 120 |

Latisha is planning to make a batch of cookies. The recipe calls for 1 and a half cups of butter. She has a 1 pound block of butter and a scale that can give weight in either ounces or grams. To the nearest gram, how many <u>grams</u> of butter should she weigh out for her cookies?

A)    12
B)    180
C)    340
D)  1,440

SOLUTION

This problem gives us a whole table full of conversion factors, so we are going to have to pick out which ones we need. Let's start by identifying what we know and what we want.

**1.5 cups** butter = **?? grams** butter

We need to use some information from the table to connect cups with grams. "Cups" only shows up in two rows, and the last one is about flour, not butter. We can convert cups to tablespoons, so let's go ahead and set that up:

(1)  *convert cups to tbsp*        $(1.5 \text{ cups}) \times \dfrac{16 \text{ tbsp}}{1 \text{ cup}} = \textbf{24 tbsp}$

Progress! Now, it'd be great to know how many grams are in a tablespoon, but we don't have that. But we CAN get to grams in two steps... do you see how?

**TIP**

You can think of unit conversions in terms of proportions:

$$\frac{16 \text{ tbsp}}{1 \text{ cup}} = \frac{x \text{ tbsp}}{1.5 \text{ cups}}$$

Continued on next page →

We DO have ounces per tablespoon and grams per ounces in the table. If we convert tablespoons to ounces and then ounces to grams, we're golden!

② convert tbsp to ounces $\qquad$ $(24 \ tbsp) \times \dfrac{1 \ ounce}{2 \ tbsp} = 12 \ ounces$

③ convert ounces to grams $\qquad$ $(12 \ ounces) \times \dfrac{28.3 \ grams}{1 \ ounce} = 340 \ grams$

There we go! Apparently, there are 340 grams in a cup and a half of butter. Good to know!

Just to recap, let's see the whole conversion written out:

$$1.5 \ \text{cups} \cdot \dfrac{16 \ tbsp}{1 \ cup} \cdot \dfrac{1 \ ounce}{2 \ tbsp} \cdot \dfrac{28.3 \ grams}{1 \ ounce} = \boxed{340 \ grams}$$

C

## EXAMPLE 4

The *shaku*, a Japanese unit of length, is approximately equal to 30.3 cm. The *koku* is a Japanese unit of volume equal to 10 cubic *shaku*. Approximately how many <u>cubic meters</u> is one *koku* ? (100 cm = 1 meter)

A)  0.278
B)  3.03
C)  3.58
D)  278.00

SOLUTION

There are two interesting things about this problem. First, it has units you probably aren't used to seeing. No problem, we can just use unit conversion! Second, it works with both lengths *and* volumes. We'll deal with that shortly.

We know we want to get from *koku* to **cubic meters**. The only thing we know about *koku* is that there are 1 *koku* for every 10 cubic *shaku*, so let's start there:

$$1 \; koku \cdot \frac{10 \; shaku^3}{1 \; koku} \; ... \; ? \; meters^3$$

Now, how can we get from cubic *shaku* to cubic meters? We know that 1 *shaku* = 30.3 cm, which means that 1 cubic *shaku* is $(30.3)^3$ cubic centimeters. Let's add that to our unit conversion train:

$$1 \; koku \cdot \frac{10 \; shaku^3}{1 \; koku} \cdot \frac{(30.3)^3 \; cm^3}{1 \; shaku^3} \; ... \; ? \; meters^3$$

So far we've converted koku to cubic shaku to cubic centimeters. Now we need to convert cubic centimeters to cubic meters. We know that 1m = 100cm, which means that 1 cubic meter = $(100)^3$ cubic centimeters. If we add that, we finish the link!

$$1 \; koku \cdot \frac{10 \; shaku^3}{1 \; koku} \cdot \frac{(30.3)^3 \; cm^3}{1 \; shaku^3} \cdot \frac{1 \; meter^3}{(100)^3 \; cm^3} = \; ? \; meters^3$$

To put this into our calculator, we can type:

$$(1 \cdot 10 \cdot (30.3)^3) \div 100^3 = .278 \; meters^3$$

A

# Practice Problems

*Use your new skills to answer each question.*

**1**

Virginia is laying out a path using 10 inch square paving tiles. If the path is 15 feet long, how many tiles will she need to complete it? (12 inches = 1 foot)

A)  $\dfrac{3}{2}$

B)  8

C)  18

D)  180

**2**

A Martian year is about equal to 1 year, 320 days, and 18 hours in Earth terms. About how many Earth hours is one Martian year? (1 Earth year = 365 days)

A)  7,698
B)  12,330
C)  16,440
D)  16,458

**3**

As lava flows and cools, the radius of a particular volcanic island is growing at an average rate of 0.75 inches per hour. Given that there are 12 inches per foot, how many days will it take for the island's radius to grow by 3.5 feet?

A)  2.33
B)  4.67
C)  31.75
D)  42

**4**

If $w$ weeks and 3 days is equal to 66 days, what is the value of $w$ ?

**5**

An apple pie recipe calls for six apples. If each apple weighs about $\frac{1}{2}$ pound and the pie is cut into 7 slices, about how many <u>ounces</u> of apple are in each slice? (1 pound = 16 ounces)

A)  0.29
B)  1.7
C)  4.6
D)  6.8

**6**

Jaron's favorite yarn comes in 50 gram balls. He uses two balls and knits a scarf that is 18 cm by 150 cm. If he uses 3 balls of yarn and knits a scarf that is 25 cm wide, how long will it be (in centimeters)?

A)  54
B)  108
C)  162
D)  2,700

**7**

The UK Weights and Measures Act of 1835 defined a stone as 14 lbs and a hundredweight as 4 stone. If someone weighs two hundredweight, 1 stone, and 6 pounds, what is their weight in <u>pounds</u>?

# UNIT

# Data Analysis: Part 2

## Chapters

## Overview

In this unit, we get to become scientists ourselves. We'll be discussing "good" and "bad" study design, as well as how to make conclusions based on data using basic statistics like mean, median, and range.

## Calculator!

Data Analysis questions only show up on the Calculator section, accounting for 35% to 50% of all questions on the section! Use your calculator when completing these chapters.

# Basic Statistics

*Let's look at commonly used statistics, what they tell us, and how they differ.*

## The average is the sum divided by the count

The most straightforward statistics problems ask for the average (or mean) of a list of numbers. To find the average, find the **sum** of the numbers and divide by the **count**. If you wanted to find the average of the *first five integers*, you'd calculate:

$$Average = \frac{SUM}{COUNT} = \frac{1 + 2 + 3 + 4 + 5}{5} = \frac{15}{5} = \boxed{3}$$

**VOCAB**

The sum of a data set is what you get if you add each item.

The count is the number of items in a data set.

### EXAMPLE 1

**NOTE**

Some problems, like this one, will give you the individual values. Other problems may just give you a sum, average, or count.

Morgan went out to lunch for 5 consecutive days and spent the following amounts: $6.50, $11.78, $15.32, $9.21, and $9.17. To the nearest cent, what was the average cost of Morgan's lunches?

A) $5.52
B) $8.67
C) $10.00
D) $10.40

Just some average Count.

To find the average, we need the sum and count. To find the sum, we just add up the prices we're given. Since we have 5 prices, the count is 5. Let's roll:

$$Average = \frac{SUM}{COUNT} = \frac{6.5 + 11.78 + 15.32 + 9.21 + 9.17}{5} = \frac{51.98}{5} = \boxed{10.396}$$

If we round that average to the nearest cent, we get **$10.40**.

D

## Use what you're given to find what you need

The average formula is made of the three components: average, sum, and count. Often, the SAT will give you two of these and ask you for the third. Just **plug in what you know** and **solve for what you need**.

**TIP**

Tackle multistep problems one bit at a time. If you can't see the path to the answer right away, follow this strategy:

1. Write what you know

2. Find out what you can

When you find new information, ask "how can I use this?" This will lead you through the problem.

## EXAMPLE 2

The mean of Jerome's scores on his first 3 calculus tests is 87. There are two tests remaining and he wants his final test average to be at least 90. What is the minimum mean he can get on his final two tests to achieve his goal?

A) 90
B) 91.5
C) 93
D) 94.5

### SOLUTION

This is a multistep problem, but each step is just using the average formula to solve for a missing piece. Even if you can't see the path to the answer, just **find what you can** with what you're given.

(1) *write what you know*     $87 = \dfrac{sum\ of\ first\ 3\ tests}{3}$

(2) *find what you can*     $261 = sum\ of\ first\ 3\ tests$

This is a good start! We used the average formula, plugged in what we were given, and found new information. Let's keep going.

Continued on next page →

# TIP

This problem is a great opportunity to try working backwards!

Let's write out Jerome's goal, using this new information. Over 5 tests, Jerome wants an average of 90. The only piece we don't know is the sum of the last 2 tests:

③ *write Jerome's goal*  $$90 = \frac{261 + sum\ of\ last\ 2\ tests}{5}$$

④ *find what you can*  $$450 = 261 + sum\ of\ last\ 2\ tests$$

$$189 = sum\ of\ last\ 2\ tests$$

Now we know the sum and count for the last 2 tests. We're set up to find the average:

⑤ *find average of last 2 tests*  $$x = \frac{sum}{count}$$

$$x = \frac{189}{2}$$

$$x = \boxed{94.5}$$

D

# TIP

If we had an even number of students, then nobody would be standing directly in the middle. In that case, the median is the **average of the two students in the middle.**

## The median is the middle number

Average is only one way to describe a data set. The SAT will also ask about the **median** of a data set. For example, let's look at the heights of a college basketball starting lineup:

| Height (in inches) | | | | |
|---|---|---|---|---|
| 77 | 75 | 73 | 77 | 79 |

When the data is arranged *in numerical order*, the **median** is the number smack-dab in the center. Since the heights above are not in numerical order, we need to rearrange to find the median:

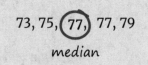

73, 75, ⑦77, 77, 79
*median*

## EXAMPLE 3

69, 65, 22, 20, 31, 24, 28, 24, 21, 21, 21, 7

The values listed above show the number of points scored by the Green Valley high school football team in the first 12 games of the season. What was the median number of points?

A) 21
B) 22
C) 23
D) 24

SOLUTION

Any time you are looking for the median, the first step is to rewrite the numbers in numerical order:

7, 20, 21, 21, 21, 22, 24, 24, 28, 31, 65, 69

Now we need to find the middle number. One way to do this is to cross of pairs of of highest/lowest numbers until only 1 or 2 numbers remain.

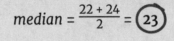

7, 20, 21, 21, 21, 22, 24, 24, 28, 31, 65, 69

We have 2 numbers left, so our median will be their *average*:

$$median = \frac{22 + 24}{2} = \boxed{23}$$

C

# mode (n.)

The word *mode* can mean "a fashion or style in clothes, art, literature, etc."

In fact, "mode" is the French word for "fashion."

When something is in fashion, you tend to see it everywhere—just like the mode in a data set!

## The mode is the number that occurs most often

In our data set, the number 77 occurs *twice*, while every other number occurs only once. That means our **mode** is 77.

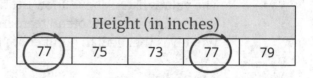

| Height (in inches) | | | | |
|---|---|---|---|---|
| 77 | 75 | 73 | 77 | 79 |

## The range is a measure of data's spread

Measures of spread describe how similar or varied the set of observed values are. The **range** of a set of data is the difference between the largest and smallest values. A large range suggests that the data set is spread out, while a small range suggests that it is highly concentrated. In our data set, the shortest person has a height of 73 inches and the tallest has a height of 79 inches, so the range is:

$$Range = 79 - 73 = \boxed{6\ inches}$$

**Fill in the statistics** for each data set below.

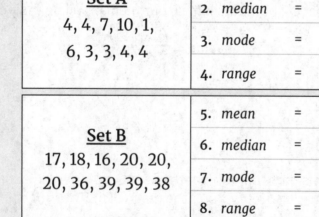

**Set A**
4, 4, 7, 10, 1, 6, 3, 3, 4, 4

1. mean   =
2. median  =
3. mode   =
4. range  =

**Set B**
17, 18, 16, 20, 20, 20, 36, 39, 39, 38

5. mean   =
6. median  =
7. mode   =
8. range  =

**Set C**
12, 12, 12, 11, 12, 13, 14, 12, 11

9. mean   =
10. median  =
11. mode   =
12. range  =

Answers:  1. 4.6   2. 4   3. 4   4. 9   5. 26.3   6. 20
7. 20   8. 23   9. 12.11   10. 12   11. 12   12. 3

## deviate (v.)

The verb "to deviate" means to stray or swerve from a primary path.

So it makes sense that small "deviations" mean the data is tightly clustered, while large deviations mean it's all over the place.

# Standard Deviation

The **standard deviation** is a measure of the average distance between any given data point and the mean. In our data set, it would tell us whether there were a lot of different heights in the lineup, or if players were mostly similar in height. Luckily, the SAT doesn't require you to compute the standard deviation. Instead, you may need to estimate which of 2 sets likely has the larger or smaller standard deviations.

Tools for estimating standard deviation:

- The minimum possible standard deviation is 0 and occurs when every number in a set is identical.

- Larger range tends to lead to larger standard deviations.

- Data points far from the mean increase standard deviation.

### TRY IT OUT

Order Sets A, B, and C from the exercise on the previous page from smallest standard deviation to largest.

In Set C, the numbers are tightly clustered around the mean (12). Its range (3) is the smallest of the sets. This set probably has the smallest standard deviation.

Set A is more spread out than Set C, but there are still many points clustered around the mean (4.6). The range (9) is larger than Set C's, but not as large as Set B's.

Set B has the largest range (23). Notice that the mean is 26.3 but the closest point to the mean (20) is a whole 6.3 away! These two factors mean Set B likely has the largest standard deviation.

*Standard Deviations: Set C < Set A < Set B*

## Boxplots

A boxplot is a way to visualize five different statistics in a given data set, including: ① the minimum value, ② the 25th percentile, ③ the median, ④ the 75th percentile, and ⑤ the maximum value.

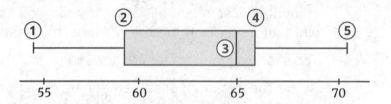

This boxplot tells us that the minimum value is just below 55, the 25th percentile is just below 60, the median is right at 65, the 75th percentile is about 66, and the maximum value is just above 70.

## INTERACTIVE EXAMPLE

| Number of cars washed | | | | | | | | |
|---|---|---|---|---|---|---|---|---|
| Time | 9–10 | 10–11 | 11–12 | 12–1 | 1–2 | 2–3 | 3–4 | 4–5 |
| Saturday | 3 | 5 | 7 | 8 | 6 | 4 | 6 | 5 |
| Sunday | 2 | 3 | 2 | 10 | 5 | 5 | 3 | 5 |

To raise funds for their high school e-sports team, a number of students held a weekend carwash. They washed cars each day, starting at 9 a.m. and going until 5 p.m. The above table lists the number of cars that were washed during each hour. Use the data in the table to answer the questions below.

**Q1)** Finish the following histogram to accurately represent the data.

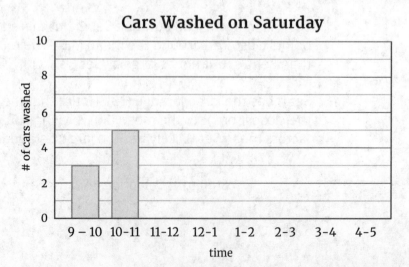

### Cars Washed on Saturday

# TIP

The *x*-axis on this dot plot lists the possible # of cars washed each hour. The number of dots above each possibility is just a count of the number of times that # shows up in the table.

Here, we see no 0's or 1's in the table for Sunday, so there are **no dots** above them. We see "2" twice, so there are **two dots**, etc.

**Q2)** Finish the following dot plot to accurately represent the data:

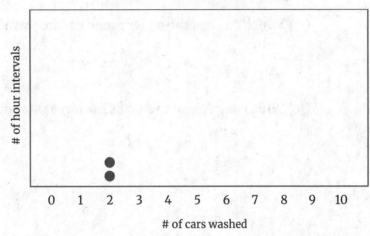

**Cars Washed on Sunday**

*Stack dots to show the # of times each number shows up in the "Sunday" row*

**Q3)** What was the median number of cars washed per hour on Saturday?

**S3)** Since we are looking for the **median**, we need to put the data for Saturday in numerical order. Fill in the blanks below, starting with the smallest number and ending with the largest:

_____ , _____ , _____ , _____ , _____ , _____ , _____ , _____

How many data points are there? _____

Since there are an **even** number of data points, we need to average the two middle terms to find our median. In other words, we need a number that is directly between the two numbers in the middle of the list. If they are the same number, then it's just that number!

**Median:** _____

**Answers:** 3. List = 3, 4, 5, 5, 6, 6, 7, 8   Data points = 8   Median = 5.5

**Q4)** What was the **mean** number of cars washed per hour on Sunday?

**Q5)** Which day had the wider **range** of cars washed per hour?

**Q6)** Which day do you think has the larger **standard deviation**?

SOLUTION

To find the **mean** number of cars washed on **Sunday**, we take the data from the appropriate row of the table (or from the dot plot we made earlier), find the sum, and then divide by the total number of data points. **Fill in the blanks** below to find the mean:

$$Mean = \frac{sum\ of\ terms}{\#\ of\ terms} = \underline{\hspace{3cm}} = \underline{\hspace{3cm}}$$

The **range** is the largest value minus the smallest value. Fill in the blanks below to find the range for each day:

$$Range = Largest - Smallest$$

$$Saturday = \underline{\hspace{1.5cm}} - \underline{\hspace{1.5cm}} = \underline{\hspace{1.5cm}}$$

$$Sunday = \underline{\hspace{1.5cm}} - \underline{\hspace{1.5cm}} = \underline{\hspace{1.5cm}}$$

So the wider range is on which day? _____

The **standard deviation** is a measure of the spread of the data set. So we need to determine which day's data are **more spread out**. On both days, the data is fairly clustered EXCEPT for the hour where they washed **10 cars on Sunday**. This data point will significantly increase the standard deviation on Sunday.

Answers:

4. Mean = $\frac{35}{8}$ = 4.375

5. Saturday = 8 − 3 = 5    Sunday = 10 − 2 = 8    Wider range = Sunday

6. The largest standard deviation is probably Sunday.

# Some questions test your ability to think logically

Some questions ask for statistics without giving you the raw data set. In these cases, you can use logic or picking numbers to find the answer.

## TIP

"Consecutive" numbers follow each other in order, without any gaps. So "consecutive even" numbers would be numbers you get by counting by 2.

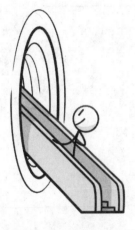

## PORTAL

We can also pick numbers to solve this problem, though that can be more time-consuming. For practice with picking numbers, turn to page 404.

### EXAMPLE 4

A data set contains 10 consecutive even numbers. What is the difference between the mean and the median for this set?

**SOLUTION**

One way to think about the mean of a data set is what you get if you evened out the distribution: borrowing from the bigger numbers and giving to the smaller ones. To help see this, imagine a row of **baskets of apples**, each with 2 more apples in than the one before. We have an even number of baskets (10), so the **median** falls between the two middle baskets. One basket has 1 fewer apples than the median, and the next has 1 more than the median. Imagine you move 1 apple from the larger basket to the smaller one; now, you've *averaged* the two middle baskets, leaving the median number of apples for the row in each basket.

Next, picture the baskets on either side of the middle two: the smaller one has 3 fewer apples than the median, while the larger has 3 more. Again, we can average these two to the median amount by moving 3 apples from the larger basket to the smaller.

We can repeat this process for each subsequent pair of baskets, and they'd always average out to the same number of apples as the median baskets. That shows us that if you have 10 consecutive, even numbers, the difference between their mean and median would always be <u>zero</u>.

Continued on next page →

**Alternative Solution: Picking Numbers**

The question tells you that the data set has 10 consecutive even numbers, so you're free to just make your own data set fitting that description. Let's make it as small as possible:

$$\{2, 4, 6, 8, 10, 12, 14, 16, 18, 20\}$$

Using this set, we can compute the **median**: $\frac{10 + 12}{2} = 11$

And the **mean**: $\frac{2 + 4 + 6 + 8 + 10 + 12 + 14 + 16 + 18 + 20}{10} = 11$

Since they're the same, the difference is $11 - 11 = 0$.

## EXAMPLE 6

Data set B is formed from data set A by adding 5 to every element of set A. Which of the following statements must be true?

I.   The mean of set A is 5 more than the mean of set B.
II.  Set A and Set B have the same range.
III. The median of set B is 5 more than the median of set A.

A) I only
B) II only
C) II and III only
D) I, II and III

# TIP

To pick numbers, just create set A then add 5 to each number for set B:

**A:** {4, 5, 16, 29, 40}

**B:** {9, 10, 21, 34, 45}

From here, you can calculate the mean, median, and range for each set and check the given statements.

We could pick numbers to create our own data set, but it is safer and faster if we can think through each statement logically.

**I.  The mean of set A is 5 more than the mean of set B.**

If each number in the set is larger, the average will be larger. Set B was formed by adding 5 to each term in set A. This means that the mean of set B should be *bigger* than the mean of set A, not the other way around, so this statement is FALSE.

**Continued on next page** →

**II. Set A and Set B have the same range.**

The range is the difference between the biggest and smallest numbers in the set, or how far apart they are on the number line. Since we added the same number (5) to each number, we simply shifted the biggest and smallest numbers the same distance up the number line, keeping the range the same. This statement must be TRUE.

**III. The median of set B is 5 more than the median of set A.**

If we add 5 to every number in set A, we do not change the order of the elements: we just shift them up the number line. This means that the median is also just shifted up by the same amount, so this statement is TRUE.

Since II and III are true and I is false, the answer is **C**.

C

## EXAMPLE 7

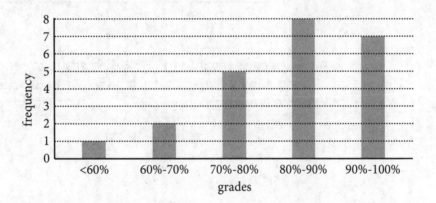

Mr. Evans created the histogram above to summarize the scores his students got on a recent test. Which of the following could be the median score for the class on this test?

A)  65 %
B)  72 %
C)  83 %
D)  96 %

SOLUTION

Note that we don't actually have all of the data we would need to calculate the median. However, this question doesn't ask us to determine what the median definitely <u>is</u>, it just asks us to use the information we are given to determine whether the numbers we are given *could* be the median.

While we can't determine the median exactly, we can determine **which of the histogram bars contains the median**. By counting up the number of students represented by each bar, we can determine that there are 1 + 2 + 5 + 8 + 7 = **23 students** in the class. That means there should be 12 students below the student with the median score and 12 students above the student with the median score. If we start counting up 12 students from the left...

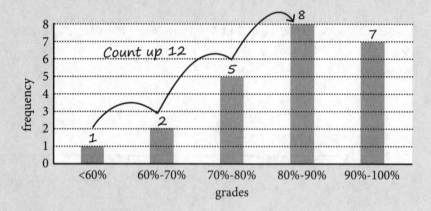

...we need to dip into the 80%-90% group to reach 12 students. That means the median *must* be between 80% and 90%, making **choice C** the only answer.

C

# Practice Problems

*Use your new skills to answer each question.*

**1**

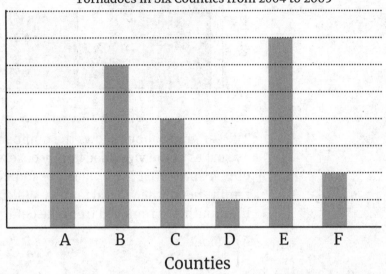

Tornadoes in Six Counties from 2004 to 2005

Counties

The number of tornadoes in 6 counties from 2004 to 2005 is shown in the graph above. If the total number of tornadoes from 2004 to 2005 is 2,300, how many tornadoes did County E have in that time period?

A) 7
B) 70
C) 700
D) 7,000

**2**

Set A contains 10 integers and has a mean of 23. Set B contains 20 integers and has a mean of 32. Suppose Set C is formed by combining sets A and B. What is the mean of Set C?

A) 15.8
B) 27.5
C) 29
D) 30

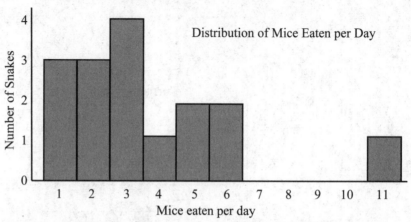

Distribution of Mice Eaten per Day

The bar graph above shows the number of mice eaten per day by snakes of the viperidae family observed in the jungle. The outlier snake that ate 11 mice was found to be of the colubris family, not of the viperid family. Which will change the most if the outlier is removed from the data?

A)  Mode
B)  Mean
C)  Median
D)  They will all change by the same amount.

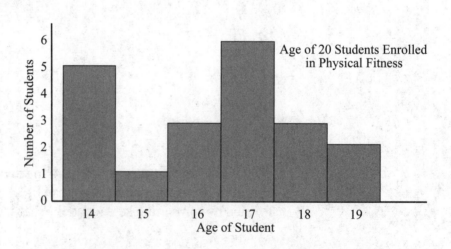

Age of 20 Students Enrolled in Physical Fitness

Based on the histogram above, of the following, what is the closest to the average (arithmetic mean) age of the students in the Physical Fitness class?

A)  14
B)  15
C)  16
D)  17

**5**

An accountant of a Fortune 500 company found that the mean salary of an employee in the company was $84,302 and the median salary of an employee in the company was $55,000. Which of the following situations could explain the difference between the mean and the median salaries of employees in the company?

A)   The salaries of employees are all very similar.
B)   Most salaries of employees in the company are between $55,000 and $84,302.
C)   There are a few employee salaries that are much higher than the rest.
D)   There are a few employee salaries that are much lower than the rest.

**6**

$$12, 5, 17, 21, 9$$

What is the absolute value of the difference between the mean and median of the list of numbers above?

**7**

The median of a set of consecutive integers is $s$ and the range of the same set is $r$. In terms of $r$ and $s$, what is the minimum number in the set?

A)   $s - \dfrac{r}{2}$

B)   $\dfrac{s - r}{2}$

C)   $r - s$

D)   $s - r$

| Team A | | Team B | | Team C | | Team D | |
|---|---|---|---|---|---|---|---|
| Player 1 | 20 | Player 1 | 5 | Player 1 | 25 | Player 1 | 5 |
| Player 2 | 20 | Player 2 | 10 | Player 2 | 30 | Player 2 | 5 |
| Player 3 | 25 | Player 3 | 15 | Player 3 | 35 | Player 3 | 25 |
| Player 4 | 30 | Player 4 | 20 | Player 4 | 35 | Player 4 | 35 |
| Player 5 | 30 | Player 5 | 25 | Player 5 | 45 | Player 5 | 45 |

The table above shows the average number of points scored per game by the players of four teams. Based on this data, which team has the largest standard deviation in number of points per player per game?

A) Team A
B) Team B
C) Team C
D) Team D

| Top 10 Home Run Hitters of All Time | | | |
|---|---|---|---|
| Baseball Player | Number of Home Runs | Baseball Players | Number of Home Runs |
| 1. Barry Bonds | 762 | 6. Ken Griffey | 630 |
| 2. Hank Aaron | 755 | 7. Jim Thome | 612 |
| 3. Babe Ruth | 714 | 8. Sammy Sosa | 609 |
| 4. Alex Rodriguez | 687 | 9. Frank Robinson | 586 |
| 5. Willie Mays | 660 | 10. Mark McGwire | 583 |

The table above lists the number of home runs of the top ten home run hitters of all time. According to the table, what was the mean number of home runs of the baseball players listed above? (Round your answer to the nearest home run.)

660

# Trend-spotting

*It's time to learn yet another way to think about **slope**. In this chapter, we are going to look at how we use slope to interpret trends in data.*

................................................................................................................

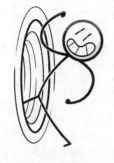

## PORTAL

For a refresher on the basics of slope, turn to the Equation of a Line chapter on page 456.

In this section, we will be talking a lot about slope. This time, our focus isn't on calculating slope, but rather interpreting slope. We'll ask questions like: where does the graph increase? Where does it stay constant? Where is the graph decreasing most quickly?

## Generally vs. Strictly

We say that a graph (or data set) is **strictly** increasing if every data point is larger than the previous with no exceptions. In other words, straight uphill with no breaks in between! If the graph (or data) has an overall upward trend but also has a few plateaus or small dips, we can say it is **generally** increasing.

**Strictly Increasing**

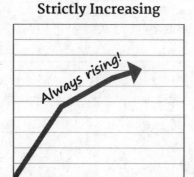

Always rising!

**Generally Increasing**

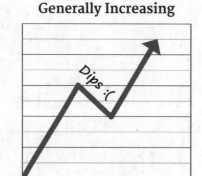

Dips :(

## INTERACTIVE EXAMPLE

The graph below shows the elevation of a loop trail, with trail distances measured clockwise from the trail head.

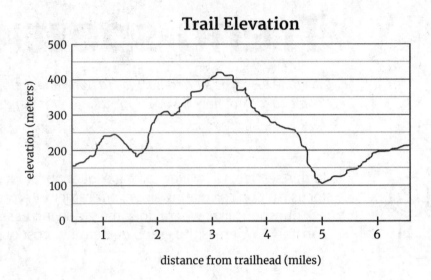

**Trail Elevation**

**Q1)** Over which of the following intervals is the trail generally increasing in elevation?

A) .5 miles to 1.5 miles
B) 1.5 miles to 3 miles
C) 3 miles to 4 miles
D) 4 miles to 5 miles

**S1)** Let's look at what happens for each of the listed intervals:

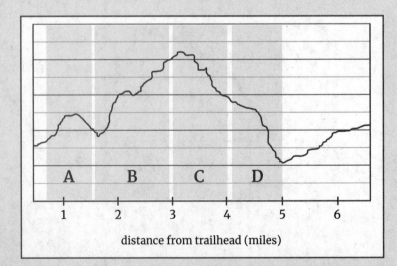

Choice A is up and down, and choices C and D are *decreasing*. Only **choice B** is generally increasing.

**B**

**Q2)** Over which of the following intervals is the trail strictly decreasing?

A) .5 miles to 1.5 miles
B) 1.5 miles to 3 miles
C) 3 miles to 4 miles
D) 4 miles to 5 miles

**S2)** We are looking at the same intervals as before. Since we are looking for decrease this time, let's focus on choices C and D:

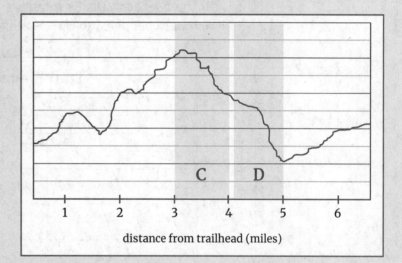

distance from trailhead (miles)

Let's look at choice C. From 3 to 4 miles, the trail is mostly going down in elevation, but it starts by going up a bit, and plateaus briefly midway down. That's generally decreasing, but not strictly.

Choice D, on the other hand, shows a **strictly decreasing** trend. It doesn't go down at a constant rate, but there are no moments of plateau or increase.

**D**

**Q3)** How many miles along the trail does a hiker reach the maximum elevation?

A) 1.2
B) 3.1
C) 5
D) 430

**S3)** Since the *y*-axis is elevation, we need to find the tallest point on the
graph. The question asks us to report "how many miles along the
trail" this peak happens, so we need to find the *x*-coordinate.

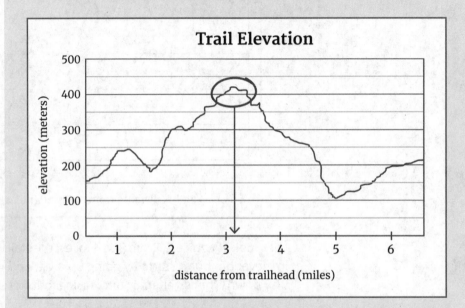

The peak happens a little past **3 miles**, so the answer is B!       **B**

**Q4)** What is the significance of the *y*-intercept in this graph?

    A)  The trail starts at an elevation of 0 meters.
    B)  The trail never crosses the *x*-axis, so it never gets to sea level.
    C)  The trail's lowest point has an elevation of about 155 meters.
    D)  The trailhead has an elevation of about 155 meters.

**S4)** Let's look at the *y*-intercept and see what we learn:

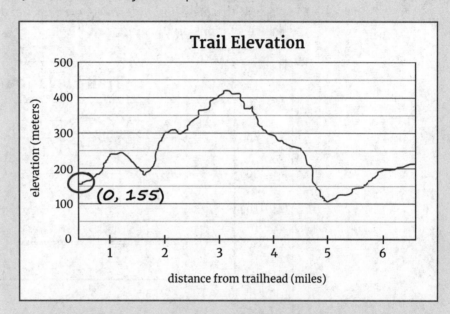

The coordinates of the point are somewhere around:

$$y\text{-}intercept = (0, 155)$$

Now we just need to interpret this in context using the axis labels. Let's **write in the labels** for the *x* and *y* coordinate:

$$y\text{-}intercept = (0 \text{ miles from trailhead}, 155 \text{ meters elevation})$$

Aha! Just labeling *x* and *y* does most of the interpretation for us! The *y*-intercept tells us that if you're standing at the trailhead, you are at 155 meters elevation. That's exactly what **choice D** says!

D

**Q5)** What is the elevation difference between the highest and lowest points on the trail?

A) 110

B) 280

C) 330

D) 430

**S5)** To find the elevation difference, we first need to find the min and max elevations on the graph.

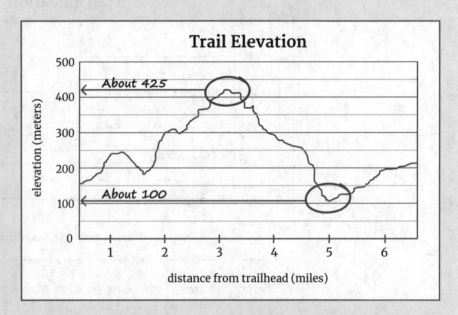

So the max elevation is around 425 meters, and the min elevation is around 100 meters. Now we just need to find the difference:

$$425 - 100 = 325 \text{ meters}$$

The choice that is closest to our estimate is **choice C**.

C

## EXAMPLE 2

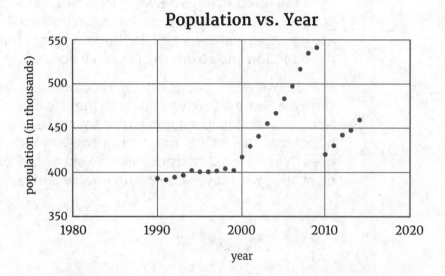

**Population vs. Year**

The graph above shows the population of Atlanta, GA each year from 1990 to 2014. Based on the graph, which of the following best describes the general trend of the population over this time period?

A) The population generally increased each year since 1990.
B) The population was relatively steady until 2000, after which it steadily increased.
C) The population changed unpredictably, so there is no general trend.
D) The population stayed fairly steady between 1990 and 2000, when it started growing quickly. It fell sharply in 2010 before starting to grow again.

SOLUTION

Let's test each answer choice with the graph. Only the correct choice will accurately describe the trends we see.

A) There was a a huge drop in 2010, so it's not true that the population generally increased.

B) The statement here is only true up until 2010, not 1990-2014.

C) There were two points where the behavior changed, but there are clear trends in each decade.

D) **Yes!** This answer identifies the three different regions of the graph and appropriately describes each of them.

D

## Slope & Relationships

The great thing about graphs and other visualizations is that they allow us to see **relationships** between variables. In the previous example, the graph showed us the relationship between time and the population of Atlanta. When we described the trends in that graph, we were describing the **direction** and **strength** of that relationship.

Let's say we were curious whether adding a new "miracle" fertilizer will correlate ('have a relationship') with the size of a plant. If adding more fertilizer made the plant grow, we'd say there was a **positive** relationship. If adding more fertilizer made the plant shrink, then we'd say there was a **negative** relationship. If adding more and more fertilizer did zilch for the plant, then we'd say there was **no relationship**.

Positive          Negative          None

Finally, we use the words **strong** and **weak** to describe how tight the connection is between the two variables. If every application of the fertilizer caused a proportional growth spurt (or shrinkage), we'd say there was a strong relationship. If instead the growth spurts were less predictable, we'd say there was a weak relationship.

## Digging Deeper

Notice that we use the exact same words (*positive* & *negative*) to describe **relationships** as we do to describe **slope**. That's because slope, relationships, and rates are all getting at the same idea: how much does changing *one* variable (*x*) affect a different variable (*y*) ?

When you have an equation with a large, positive slope, like:

$$y = 50x + 2$$

..then changing *x* even from 1 to 2 has a **positive** impact on *y*. Another way to phrase that is to say "*x* and *y* have a **positive** relationship."

Now that we know the connection between slope and relationships, let's look at examples of what different correlations look like **graphically**.

## PORTAL

To see how slope comes up algebraically, check out the Equation of a Line chapter on page 456.

## Positive Relationships

When variables have a **positive** relationship, they increase together.

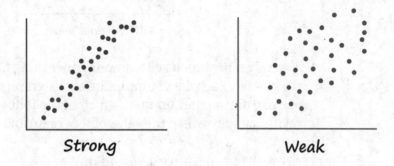

Strong          Weak

## Negative Relationships

In a **negative** relationship, one variable decreases when the other increases.

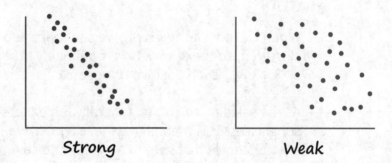

Strong          Weak

## No Relationship

When there is no relationship between the variables, you'll see a straight horizontal or vertical line, or a seemingly random spread of data points.

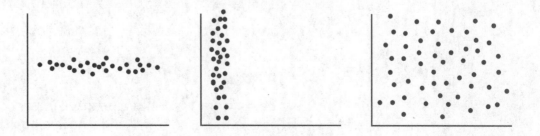

## EXAMPLE 3

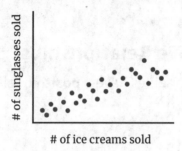

A stand on the beach sells, among other things, both ice cream and sunglasses. Each data point in the above graph represents the sales for one day during the summer. Which of the following best describes the relationship between the sales of ice cream and sunglasses?

A) A strong, negative association
B) A strong, positive association
C) A weak, positive association
D) No association

SOLUTION

When we look at the graph, we see that the data is tightly clustered, so the association is definitely **strong**. That points to A or B. Now... is it a positive or negative association?

As the sales of ice cream generally increase, so do the sales of sunglasses. This means they have a **positive** relationship. The answer choice that gets this right is choice B.

B

# Practice Problems

*Use your new skills to answer each question.*

1

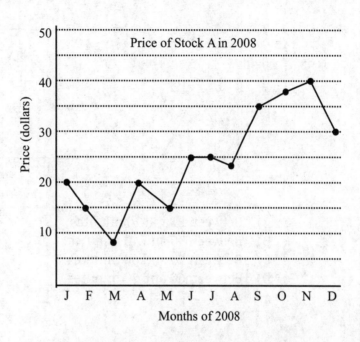

The price of a stock was recorded on the first day of every month of 2008. Based on the graph, which of the following gives a two month interval in which the price of the stock increased and then decreased?

A) February to April
B) June to August
C) September to November
D) October to December

Phoebe is a professional photographer who hiked to a waterfall in order to take some pictures for her next art show. The graph below shows the speed at which she hiked during her trip to and from the waterfall. During which interval did Phoebe stop to take pictures of the waterfall?

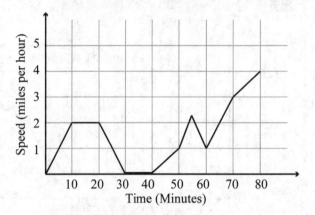

A) Between 10 and 20 minutes
B) Between 30 and 40 minutes
C) Between 50 and 60 minutes
D) Between 60 and 70 minutes

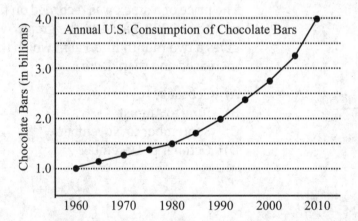

The graph above shows the total number of chocolate bars consumed each year in the United States. Based on the graph, which of the following best describes the relationship between the chocolate bar consumption growth from 1960 to 1980 and the growth from 1990 to 2010?

A) From 1960 to 1980, consumption growth was linear, whereas from 1990 to 2010, the growth was exponential.
B) From 1960 to 1980, consumption growth was exponential, whereas from 1990 to 2010, the growth was linear.
C) Consumption growth was exponential for both time periods.
D) Consumption growth was linear for both time periods.

**4**

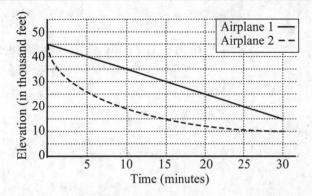

The graph above shows the elevation of two airplanes. Which of the following statements correctly compares the average rate at which the elevation of the two airplanes changed?

A) From 0 to 15 minutes, the rate of change in elevation of Airplane 1 is greater than that of Airplane 2, whereas from 20 to 30 minutes, the rate of change in elevation of Airplane 2 is greater than that of Airplane 1.

B) From 0 to 15 minutes, the rate of change in elevation of Airplane 1 is less than that of Airplane 2, whereas from 20 to 30 minutes, the rate of change in elevation of Airplane 2 is less than that of Airplane 1.

C) In every 5-minute interval, the rate of change in elevation of Airplane 1 is greater than that of Airplane 2.

D) In every 5-minute interval, the rate of change in elevation of Airplane 1 is less than that of Airplane 2.

**5**

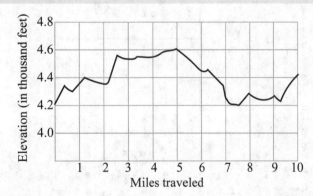

Kari went on a hiking trip, and the graph above shows Kari's elevation while hiking on the trail. Over which interval did Kari experience the largest change in elevation?

A) From mile 1 to mile 3

B) From mile 2 to mile 4

C) From mile 5 to mile 7

D) From mile 7 to mile 10

**6**

Which of the following graphs best shows a strong positive association between $x$ and $y$ ?

A)

B)

C)

D)

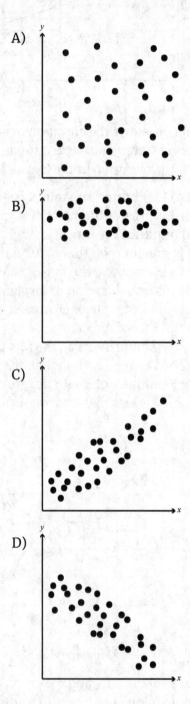

# Line of Best Fit

*In this chapter, we'll learn how we can use the equation of a line to describe the relationship between two variables.*

.................................................................................................

At the end of the last chapter, we described the relationship between two variables by looking at some scatterplots. Notice that when you look at a scatterplot with a strong relationship, your brain automatically notices a line-like pattern in the data:

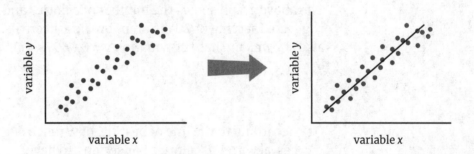

The data points **look** like they are clustered around a line. We call this invisible (but super important) line the **line of best fit** for the data. And like all lines, the line of best fit has an equation and a slope that we can use to find out interesting stuff! You won't ever need to *calculate* the line of best fit yourself, but you will be asked to use your knowledge of slope and the equation of a line to make **estimates** about the data.

## Estimation Tool

A line of best fit is an extremely useful estimation tool. If we plug an *x* into the equation of the line of best fit, it will spit out a *y*-value that is **most likely** to correspond with that input. People use this statistical tool all the time. A business might use it to predict future sales based on past years' sales, or an airport might use it to predict how many travelers to expect during the summer.

The math behind all of this is simple equation-of-a-line stuff. As we've done before, we'll be working with $y = mx + b$, plugging in points, and focusing on slopes. Let's get some practice!

## INTERACTIVE EXAMPLE

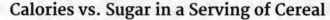

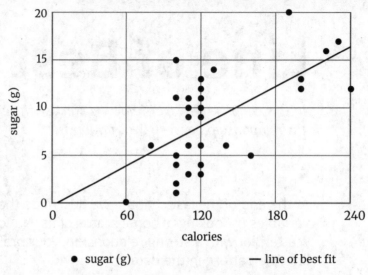

The above graph shows the number of calories and grams of sugar in a suggested serving of 30 different breakfast cereals. The line of best fit is also shown, and has the equation $y = 0.0697x - 0.335$.

**Q1)** According to the line of best fit, how much sugar would you expect a cereal with 180 calories per serving to have?

A) about 5 grams
B) about 8 grams
C) about 10 grams
D) about 12 grams

**NOTE**

Notice that even though we don't have a data point at 180 calories, we can **estimate** it using the line of best fit!

**S1)** This question asks us to use the line of best fit to estimate the amount of sugar per serving for a cereal with 180 calories per serving. Sugar is on the $y$-axis, so we want the $y$-value on the line of best fit at 180 calories. If we slide our finger up from 180 on the $x$-axis until we hit the line of best fit, we see that the line crosses somewhere between 10 and 15 on the $y$-axis. Only **choice D** falls in that range, so it must be our answer!

D

**Q2)** One cereal in the study had 0 grams of sugar per serving, as shown on the graph. For that cereal, about how much less sugar does it have than the line of best fit would predict?

A) 0

B) 2

C) 4

D) 6

**S2)** Step 1 is to find the data point that represents the cereal with 0 grams of sugar. Since sugar is on the *y*-axis, we are looking for a data point on the x-axis, where the *y*-coordinate is zero. That data point is at 60 calories:

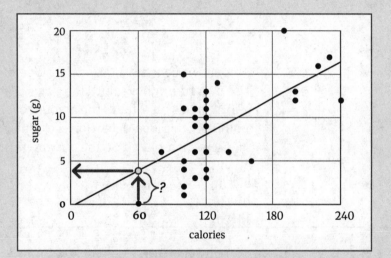

Next we need to know how much sugar the **line of best fit** predicts at **x = 60**. If we slide up to the line and check the *y*-value at that point, we see that it predicts about **4 grams** of sugar for 60 calories. To find how much less it has than was predicted, we need to subtract:

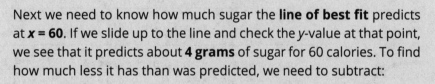

$$predicted - actual = 4 - 0 = \boxed{4}$$

**Choice C** is the best answer.

C

## Plug in!

Remember, we can always find a point on a line if we're given the equation and a coordinate.

$0.0697x - .335 = y$
$0.0697(60) - .335 = 3.8$

Which is about 4!

**Q3)** Which of the following best explains how the number 0.0697 in the equation of the line of best fit relates to the scatterplot?

A) Every cereal will have at least 0.0697 grams of sugar per serving.

B) On average, we estimate that the amount of sugar per serving will increase by 0.0697 grams for every additional calorie per serving.

C) A gram of sugar has 0.0697 calories.

D) There are exactly 0.0697 grams of sugar per calorie of cereal.

**S3)** Let's compare the equation of the line of best fit to the standard equation of a line:

$$y = mx + b$$

$$y = 0.0697x - .335$$

This shows us that 0.0697 is the slope of the line of best fit. Slope is rise over run, or how much the *y*-axis changes for each change in the *x*-axis. In this case, that's the amount of **sugar per calorie**. Choices B and D get this idea right. However, line of best fit gives us *estimates*, NOT exact absolutes. So the answer must be choice B.

**B**

---

**Use the previous graph** to answer each question.

| Question | Prediction |
|---|---|
| One serving of *Sweet Cuppin' Cakes* cereal has 15 grams of sugar. About how many calories does the line of best fit predict it will have? | |
| If *Chunky Tree Bark* cereal contains 140 calories per serving, about how many grams of sugar does the line of best fit predict it will have? | |
| If a single serving of *Chocolate Frosted Sugar Bombs* has 300 calories, how many grams of sugar does the line of best fit predict it to have? | |

---

**Answers:** 　Sweet Cuppin' Cakes: ~220 calories

Chunky Tree Bark: ~9g sugar

Chocolate Frosted Sugar Bombs: ~20g sugar

# Practice Problems

*Use your new skills to answer each question.*

**1**

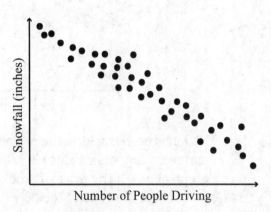

The graph above gives the number of people in Telluride, Colorado who drove each day it snowed in the city in relation to the number of inches of snowfall on that respective day. Which of the following correctly describes the correlation of the graph above?

A)  Strong positive correlation
B)  Strong negative correlation
C)  Weak positive correlation
D)  Weak negative correlation

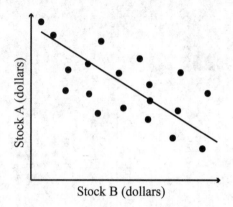

Nick has been tracking the prices, in dollars, of two stocks and recording their values in relation to one another in the graph above. If the price of Stock A drops, what will Nick's line of best fit predict Stock B will do?

A) Stock B will decrease in value.
B) Stock B will increase in value.
C) Stock B will remain at the same price.
D) A prediction cannot be determined.

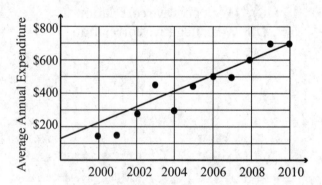

According to the line of best fit in the scatterplot above, which of the following best approximates the year in which the average annual expenditure on cellular phone services was estimated to be $300?

A) 2002
B) 2003
C) 2004
D) 2005

**4**

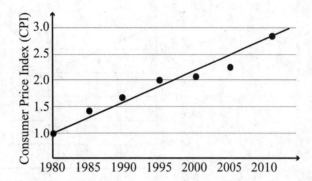

The Consumer Price Index (CPI) of the U.S. in the graph above is defined to be the ratio of the current average price of goods to the average price of goods in 1980. Which of the following conclusions is supported by the graph?

A) The initial CPI of 1980 was 1.
B) The initial CPI of 1980 was $1.
C) The CPI in 1981 was 100 percent greater than the CPI in 1980.
D) The CPI has grown by about 100% since 1980.

**5**

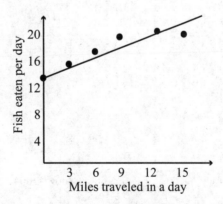

The scatterplot above gives the number of fish a grizzly bear eats in one day in relation to the number of miles the grizzly bear traveled that day. The line of best fit is also shown and has the equation $y = 0.5x + 13$. Using the line of best fit, what would be the best approximation for how many fish a bear would eat in one day if it traveled 22 miles that day?

A) 11 fish
B) 22 fish
C) 24 fish
D) 35 fish

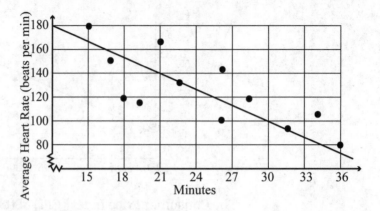

The runners of a 5K race all wore heart rate monitors. The data from each runner's heart rate monitor was then plotted against the number of minutes it took them to finish the 5K. The runner with an average heart rate of 80 beats per minute ran the 5K in how many more minutes than the time predicted by the line of best fit?

A)   1.5 minutes
B)   8.0 minutes
C)   10.0 minutes
D)   36.0 minutes

# Study Design

*Occasionally, the SAT will directly test your understanding of basic study design vocabulary, as well as how different factors affect the conclusions you can draw from data.*

......................................................................................................

### Study Vocabulary

Let's start with a review of some basic vocabulary. All studies begin with a basic question that the scientists are seeking to answer. For example, let's say we want to design a study to answer the question:

> **Question:** Do 10th graders feel prepared for the SAT?

## Why sample?

Most of the time, it isn't practical (or possible) to survey every single member of a population (things cost money).

Luckily, we don't need to! If we are smart about it, we can study a small piece of that bigger population and still answer our question. That small piece is called a **sample**.

A **population** is the *entire* group we want to learn something about. Depending on what we're interested in, this could be "all girls in third period calculus" or "all teenagers in the United States." In our case, the population would be "all 10th graders."

A **sample** is a smaller piece of the larger population. The difference between a good sample and a bad sample rests on whether the sample is *representative* of the population. Scientists have to be very careful about how they choose their sample – if they mess this part up, then they can't really claim that their findings answer the question at hand!

population

sample

## What is a bad sample?

A bad sample is one that is *not* representative of the larger population. In our study, if we only surveyed 10th graders who have a copy of *Applerouth's Guide to the SAT*, then we would have picked a *bad* (not representative) sample. Can you see why?

Because... those students probably feel **more** prepared than students who do NOT have a study guide. That would cause us to overestimate how prepared ALL 10th graders feel for the SAT.

## What is a good sample?

# Proportions

If 5% of all 10th graders own this book, then 5% of our sample should too. Similarly, if only 15% of 10th graders in the country go to private school, then we should make sure only 15% of our sample goes to private school.

A good sample is one that *is* representative of the larger population. When it comes down to it, it's really all about **proportions**. It's okay if SOME proportion of the students we survey own a copy of *Applerouth's Guide to the SAT*, so long as it's the same proportion as in the population of all 10th graders.

If a sample is chosen **randomly** from the entire population, we usually assume it is representative. That's because, when a sample is chosen from the population at random, every individual has an equal chance of being chosen. Let's look at a couple of examples of good and bad sampling. For each example, ask yourself "Why might the bad sample affect our conclusion?"

**Question:** Do students at Emory University like coffee?

**Population:** all students at Emory University
**Good Sample:** random selection of all Emory students
**Bad sample:** all students in an 8:00 am History class.

**Question:** Are female students at your high school interested in adding a competitive math team?

**Population:** female students at your high school
**Good Sample:** random selection of girls in your high school
**Bad sample:** random selection of all U.S. high school students

# EXAMPLE 1

When applying for funding, zoologists want to discuss the public interest in their research. They take a random sample of 500 people in their nation to contact with a survey. They fail to reach 17 of the people but receive responses from the other 483. One of the questions on their survey asks "In your opinion, how important is it to you to have access to a zoo ?" Options include "Not important," "Somewhat important," "Very important," and "No opinion." When zoologists analyze the data, they find that 73% of all respondents either said "Somewhat important" or "Very important."

For which of the following regions is it reasonable to assume that the survey is a representative sample?

I.   The city in which the scientists live

II.  The nation in which the scientists conducted the study

III. Countries neighboring the nation in which the scientists conducted the study

    A) II only
    B) I and II only
    C) II and III only
    D) None

**SOLUTION**

Any time you get a problem that asks you to determine which of three statements is valid, you need to go through each statement and determine whether it is correct.

**Statement I:** The random sample was taken from the nation as a whole. It's very possible that different cities within the country have different opinions about zoos; maybe the city where the scientists live is particularly Pro-Zoo! We can't assume data for the whole country applies to one city, so we can eliminate I.

**Statement II:** The survey was given to a random sample chosen from the whole nation, so it is indeed reasonable to assume that it is a representative sample! This one's good.

**Statement III:** The passage indicates that only the one nation was included in the sample. Neighboring countries are a separate population, so we can't use this sample to talk about them.

Since only statement II checks out, our answer is A.

A

# TIP

Even perfectly selected samples will provide *estimates*—not certainties.

When working with questions about studies and margins of error, look for answer choices that use words like **plausible** or **likely**, as these communicate the appropriate level of uncertainty.

## Let's think about margin of error (then candy)

Taking a smart sample lets us estimate properties of the entire population, **but it is still an estimate**. A sample's *margin of error* is the measure of how far above or below an estimate based on that sample is likely to be, just due to the random nature of sampling.

The basic math of margin of error works like this: if you are told that a random sample of a population shows 15% with a specific trait, but are told there is a **margin of error** of 10%, that means that the actual fraction of the total population with that trait is most likely between 5% and 25%. If that's still a little unclear, then let's think about candy.

## Okay NOW let's think about candy

Imagine you have a **bucket of 1000 assorted candy pieces** and you want to know what percent of the candies are Sour Tarts (your fave).

our favorite

You *could* carefully sort and count all 1000 of the candies, but most people don't consider that a fun use of time. Instead we can estimate by taking out smaller **samples**. Let's grab a handful of candy and see how many are our favorite:

# NOTE

On the test, you will not be asked to calculate margin of error—statisticians have complex formulas to figure this out. Like we do here, the test will often just tell you the margin of error.

**Sample size:** 10
**# of favorite:** 4 (40%)
**Margin of Error:** 30%

In this handful, 4 out of 10 (40%) of the candies are your favorite type. Not bad! But, does that mean we can say for sure that 40% of the *entire* bucket is your favorite? Nope! Do you see why not?

# What if we pulled out different samples?

Maybe you got lucky and happened to grab a good handful, or maybe there's actually a lot more of your favorite hiding in there. We could **repeat this test** and see different results:

*2 out of 10 (20%)*      *4 out of 10 (40%)*      *5 out of 10 (50%)*

Each of the new piles is a random sample of the candies in the bowl, so it is reasonable to use <u>any</u> of them to estimate the percent of the candies that are your favorite. However, random chance means that the exact make up of the samples vary. The **margin of error** is a reminder that even though sampling is useful, it is not exact.

So far, drawing 10 pieces at a time, we're seeing a 30% margin of error. That is pretty large - knowing that the percentage is somewhere between 10% and 70% isn't very useful. If you want a more precise estimate, you could take a **larger sample** of 50 candies:

**Sample size:** 50
**# of favorite:** 17 (34%)
**Margin of Error:** 13%

Counting a pile of 50 is still a lot less work than counting 1000, and by taking a larger sample we **decrease the margin of error**. Instead of 30%, the margin of error here is about 13%. Since 34% of this sample were your favorite, this tells us that the true percentage of the candies in the bowl that are your favorite is likely somewhere between 21% and 47%:

34 – 13 = 21%
34 + 13 = 47%

## EXAMPLE 2

A high school with 3000 students is considering making a change to the dress code. A member of the student council randomly surveys 300 students to see whether they support the change. After analyzing the survey she reports back to the student council that the 68% of the students approved of the change, with a margin of error of 3%. Which of the following statements is a plausible conclusion based on her results?

A) Exactly 68% of the students in the school approve of the proposed new dress code.
B) There are 2040 students in the school who approve of the proposed new dress code.
C) About 3% of the students were not surveyed.
D) It is likely that somewhere between 65% and 71% of the students in the school approve of the proposed new dress code.

This is a straightforward test of your understanding of margins of error. The survey gives 68% as an estimate of the proportion of the students who approve of the dress code, but it doesn't tell us that exactly 68% actually do…

There could be some error due to the nature of randomness in sampling, so choice A is wrong.

Choice B computes 68% of 3000 and asserts that this is the <u>exact</u> number of students who support the dress code. Again, we don't know that it is exactly this value, so it is wrong.

Choice C gives a misconception of the meaning of margin of error. The Margin of Error measures how far off our estimate is based just on randomness - it doesn't take potential problems with the survey method into account.

Choice D is correct. It gives a range for the population percentage by taking the estimate and adding and subtracting the given margin of error: 68 − 3 = 65% and 68 + 3 = 71%.

D

## Study Types

There are three main types of studies that the SAT looks at. In an **observational study**, scientists simply observe how a sample acts in its natural environment, recording what they see. In a **sample survey**, scientists recruit a sample, ask questions, and record the responses. In a **controlled experiment**, scientists carefully create a controlled environment, recruit a sample, divide it into two groups, then compare the outcomes for the two groups.

The benefit of controlled experiments over other types of studies is they allow scientists to show a *causal relationship* between variables. If you're just observing that happier people go on more walks, for example, you can't say whether being happy causes people to walk more, or vice-versa, or whether some third factor is causing both!

## Must, Likely, Could, Can't

Throughout the SAT, the test will sometimes ask you to evaluate the **validity** of statements by using qualifiers like "must be true" or "could be true." This is particularly common on statistics questions. When these come up, it is important to pay careful attention to how they qualify what they are asking. Think about what it means when you say the following things about a statement:

- **Must be true**: Given the information you have, you *know* that the statement *absolutely* has to be true in <u>all</u> cases, not just one. If they've given you the data for a sample and you can calculate the sample mean, you know the mean exactly.

- **Likely true**: The evidence you have supports the statement you've been asked to evaluate, but you don't have enough evidence to say that it is 100% definitely true. A statement that is likely to be true is a reasonable (or plausible) conclusion to draw.

- **Could be true**: The statement you've been asked to evaluate and the other information you are given in the problem are *compatible*. You don't know for sure if the statement is true, but you also don't know for sure that it is false.

- **Can't be true**: The statement you've been asked to evaluate <u>contradicts</u> information you were given in the problem. For example, you are given incomplete data and can tell that the median *must* be somewhere between 5 and 10. It **can't** be 4.

**TIP**

Be extra careful with "must be true" statements, especially if you solved a problem by picking numbers. It's possible to get an outcome with one set of data that is not true for ALL possible sets.

**TIP**

Note that anything that is likely to be true could be true, but not the other way around. There are some unlikely scenarios that might not directly contradict the information you've been given.

769

**Use the survey results below** to evaluate the 10 statements that follow by checking the column for each to indicate whether it must, could, or can't be true.

A researcher wants to study how much time local high school students are spending on homework each day. They give a survey to a random sample of 300 students at the local high school. The results of the survey are shown in the table below. The researcher reports that 37% of the local students are spending between 2 and 4 hours on homework per day (margin of error: 5%)

|  | < 2hrs / day | 2-4hrs / day | 4+hrs / day |
|---|---|---|---|
| # of Students | 145 | 111 | 44 |

| # | Statement | Must be true | Likely true | Could be true | Can't be true |
|---|---|---|---|---|---|
| 1 | 37% of the students in the sample spend 2-4 hours per day on homework. | X | | | |
| 2 | 37% of the students at the high school spend 2-4 hours per day on homework. | | X | | |
| 3 | 40% of the students in the high school spend between 2 and 4 hours a day on homework. | | X | | |
| 4 | 45% of the students in the high school spend between 2 and 4 hours a day on homework. | | | X | |
| 5 | If the researcher took another sample, exactly 37% of the students in that sample would spend 2-4 hours per day on homework. | | | X | |
| 6 | All students spend at least 1 hour a day on homework. | | | X | |
| 7 | Between 32 and 42% of the students at the high school spend between 2 and 4 hours per day on homework. | | X | | |
| 8 | 37% of the students in the sample spend at least two hours a day on homework | | | | X |
| 9 | More than half of the students in the sample spent at least 2 hours a day on homework. | X | | | |
| 10 | The median number of hours per day that students in the sample spend on homework is less than 2. | | | | X |

**Answers:** Bottom of the next page.

# Practice Problems

*Use your new skills to answer each question.*

**1**

In order to determine if Migraine Medication A is more effective than Migraine Medication B, a research study was conducted. From a large population of people who have recurring migraines, 600 participants were selected at random. 200 of those participating were given a placebo, 200 of those participating were given Migraine Medication A, and the last 200 participants were given Migraine Medication B. The resulting data show that participants who received Medication A experienced more relief than those who received Medication B, and both Medications A and B worked substantially better than the placebo. Based on the results of the study, which of the following is an appropriate conclusion?

A) Migraine Medication A is the most effective migraine medication on the market.
B) People with acute migraines need only take the placebo.
C) Migraine Medication A will work for anyone who takes it.
D) Migraine Medication A is likely to give more migraine relief than Migraine Medication B.

**2**

Samuel owns a chain of restaurants called Sam's Salads that offer a strictly vegetarian cuisine. Samuel wants to open up a Sam's Salads in a new city, so he decides to survey 250 people who entered a local burger place in the city. Of the 250 people surveyed, 7 were vegetarians, 8 did not answer the survey, and the rest were not vegetarians. Which of the following makes it least likely that a reliable conclusion can be drawn about the percentage of vegetarians in the city?

A) The number of people who refused to respond
B) Where the survey was conducted
C) The sample size
D) The population size

**Exercise Answers:**

| 1. Must | 2. Likely | 3. Likely | 4. Could | 5. Could |
|---------|-----------|-----------|----------|----------|
| 6. Could | 7. Likely | 8. Can't | 9. Must | 10. Can't |

**771**

**3**

A mad scientist is doing quality control on the automated production of his robot army. He inspects a random sample and determines that 87% of the robots are error free with a margin of error of 4% at the 95% confidence level. Which of the following is most likely to be the true percentage of robots that are error free?

A)  4%
B)  85%
C)  92%
D)  99%

**4**

Teresa wants to gauge interest among the senior class in having a class t-shirt, but it isn't practical for her to poll all of the seniors. Which of the following sampling methods would be best?

A)  Hand out a survey in her math class
B)  Set up a table in the cafeteria where students can choose to stop and fill out a survey
C)  Have the counselor give her a random list of seniors to contact
D)  Ask everyone on the bus she rides home

**5**

Cuifu is a biologist studying the panda population of China. His team has been monitoring and tagging the pandas in the Minshan Mountains in Sichuan. When he tells his family about his work, his aunt wants to know how many pandas there are in all of China. She takes the population density he has found and multiplies it by the land area of China. Will this method accurately predict the total panda population?

A)  Yes, because you can use a sample to estimate the population.
B)  Yes, because Cuifu's team has been studying the entire population in the Minshan Mountains.
C)  No, because the sample was not taken randomly.
D)  No, because we can't assume that the population in the Minshan Mountains is representative of the population across all of China.

**6**

A marine biologist selected a random sample of 40 Pacific herring from a school and found that the mean length of the herring in the sample was 25.0 centimeters (cm) with an associated margin of error of 6.1 cm. Which of the following is the best interpretation of the marine biologist's findings?

A) All herring in the sample have a length between 18.9 cm and 31.1 cm.

B) Most herring in the school have a length between 18.9 cm and 31.1 cm.

C) Any length between 18.9 cm and 31.1 cm is a plausible value for the mean length of the herring in the school.

D) Any length between 18.9 cm and 31.1 cm is a plausible value for the mean length of the herring in the sample.

**7**

As part of a health initiative, a large company provided all of its employees with wearable step-counting devices. After 6 months, they surveyed a random sample of their employees to find out whether the employees felt that having the step tracker encouraged them to be more active. Using that sample data, the company estimated that 56% of their employees felt that the device encourages them to be more active. The margin of error for this estimation is 4%. Which of the following is the most appropriate conclusion about the employees at the company, based on the given estimate and margin of error?

A) It is likely that at least 56% of the employees feel the device encourages them to be more active.

B) It is plausible that the percentage of employees who feel that the device encourages them to be more active is between 52% and 60%.

C) The percentage of employees who feel that the device encourages them to be more active is between 54% and 58%.

D) The company is between 52% and 60% sure that their employees feel the device encourages them to be more active.

The quality control team in a factory selected a random sample of widgets and measured the weight of each widget. After analyzing the results, the report estimated that the widgets produced in the factory have a mean weight of 2.58 grams, with a reported margin of error of .16 grams. Which of the following is the best conclusion based on this analysis?

A) It is likely that most widgets produced by this factory weigh exactly 2.58 grams.

B) All widgets produced by this factory weigh at least 2.42 grams.

C) It is likely that all widgets produced by this factory weigh between 2.42 grams and 2.74 grams.

D) The mean weight of all widgets produced in this factory is probably between 2.42 and 2.74 grams

# UNIT | Geometry & Trigonometry

## Chapters

## Overview

The SAT puts much less emphasis on geometry & trigonometry than the ACT. There are only a few points to be earned from these questions, though they may pull from a wide range of different topics. In this unit, we review the basic geometry & trigonometry rules that may show up.

## Calculator + Non-Calculator

Geometry and Trigonometry questions show up on both math sections, but those that require heavy computations show up in the calculator section. Make computations without your calculator, unless otherwise noted.

# Geometry

*The number of points you can earn from Geometry questions is low compared to the amount you need to know to answer any question that might come up. If you're comfortable with Geometry already, use this chapter as a refresher. If not, don't fret about learning every single rule!*

The SAT math tests rarely have more than 2 or 3 Geometry questions. However, they can pull from a wide range of different topics. In this chapter, we'll do a quick review of the concepts that might show up and look at a few examples of how they are tested. You should not expect to see everything in this chapter on each test.

## Hey, Thanks for the Box!

The first thing to know is that the information box they give you at the start of the math sections is *all* geometry. It doesn't have **everything** you could possibly need, but it if you are stuck - especially on a problem involving **area or volume** - remember to check back for a hint!

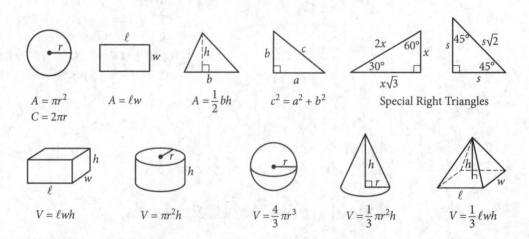

If you have this information memorized, that's great! But if you don't, you shouldn't spend time trying to shove it in your brain – after all, you'll have this on the test, and there are only a few geometry questions anyway.

# Angles

First, angles can be measured in either **radians** or **degrees**.

$$180° = \pi \text{ radians}$$

Angles in a **triangle** add up to **180°**. As do angles in a **straight line**.

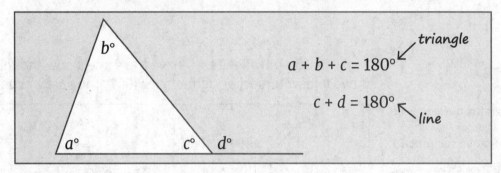

$a + b + c = 180°$ — triangle

$c + d = 180°$ — line

This is true for ANY straight line, no matter how many angles comprise it.

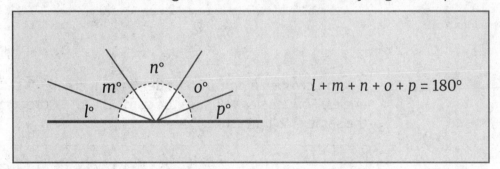

$l + m + n + o + p = 180°$

Angles in a **quadrilateral** (any 4 sided shape) add up to **360°**.

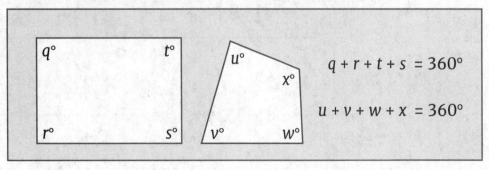

$q + r + t + s = 360°$

$u + v + w + x = 360°$

If two lines intersect, we call the angles that are opposite each other **vertical** angles. Vertical angles always have the **same angle measure**.

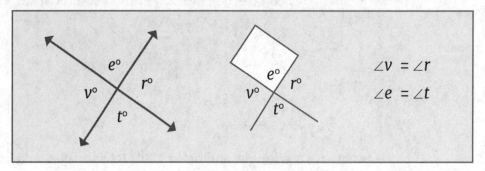

# TIP

On a graph, the slopes of two perpendicular lines are **negative reciprocals**.

$$y = 3x + 4$$
$$y = -\frac{1}{3}x + 7$$

The slopes of parallel lines are **identical**.

$$y = 2x + 13$$
$$y = 2x - 89$$

Two lines are **parallel** if they have the same slope and thus never intersect. If two lines intersect at right angles (90°), they are **perpendicular**.

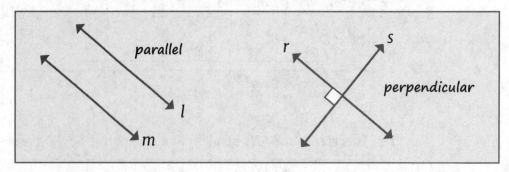

If a **line crosses a pair of parallel lines**, it creates a set of matching angles. Four angles will have the same BIG measure and four will have the same small measure.

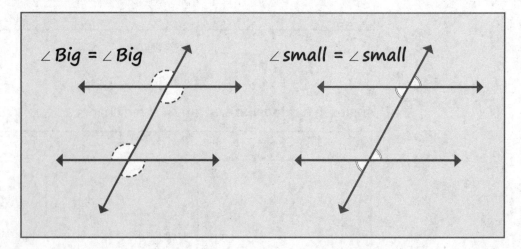

## EXAMPLE 1

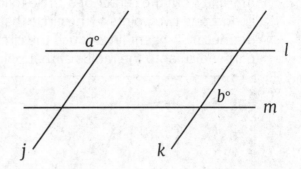

In the figure above, lines *j* and *k* are parallel, and lines *l* and *m* are parallel. If $a = 12k - 1$ and $b = 13k + 31$, then what is the value of *k*?

A) 3.6
B) 6.0
C) 8.4
D) 9.0

## TIP

If you don't see how two angles on a geometry problem should be related, just start filling in anything you *can* figure out. As you get more things labeled, it gets easier to see relationships.

SOLUTION

The first rule to help us out is:

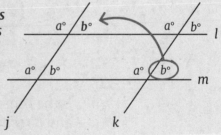

(1) *a line crossing **parallel lines** forms 2 sets of equal angles*

$$\angle \text{Big} = \angle \text{Big}$$
$$\angle \text{small} = \angle \text{small}$$

And since there are **180° in a line**, we know that **a + b = 180**. If we substitute in what we're told in the prompt, we can solve for k:

(2) *substitute*

$$a + b = 180$$
$$(12k - 1) + (13k + 31) = 180$$
$$25k + 30 = 180$$
$$25k = 150$$
$$\boxed{k = 6}$$

B

## TIP

If there's a circle involved **find the radius**. Almost everything is related to the radius, so if you find the radius you can usually find whatever is being asked for.

If you get a question about a circle in the **coordinate plane**, find the center, look for radii, and watch out for right triangles hidden in the coordinate grid.

## Circles

Any line from the center of a circle to its edge is a **radius**. Any line connecting two points of the circle that goes through the center is a **diameter**. Tangent lines touch the circle at only one point and are perpendicular to the radius at that point.

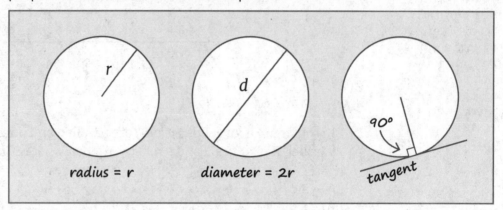

The **circumference** of a circle is equal to $2\pi r$. The **area** is equal to $\pi r^2$.

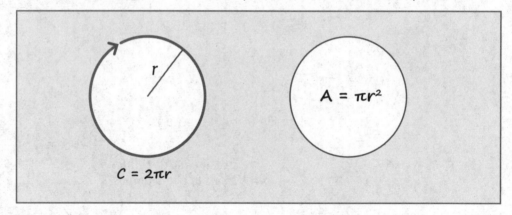

If $C$ is the center of the circle and lines $AE$ and $BE$ are tangent to the circle at $A$ and $B$ respectively, then the measure of $\angle ACB$ is twice the measure of $\angle ADB$ and the sum of the measures of $\angle ACB$ and $\angle AEB$ is 180°.

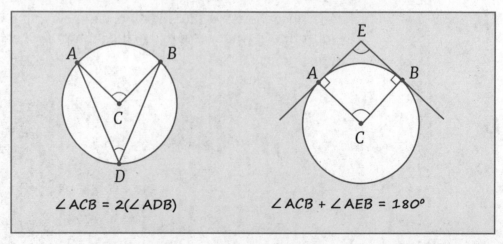

# Area, Perimeter, Volume

Whenever you are given a complex shape, you can **break it up** into triangles and quadrilaterals to find its area, perimeter, or angles.

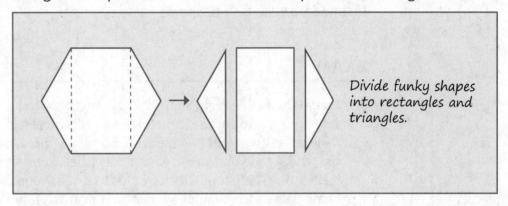

Divide funky shapes into rectangles and triangles.

**Equilateral** triangles have **three equal sides** and three 60 degree angles. **Isosceles** triangles have two equal sides and the angles opposite those sides are also equal.

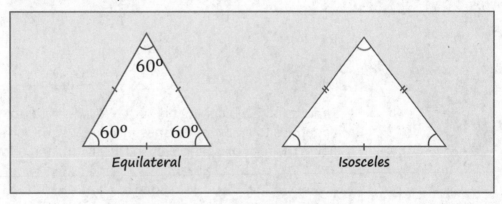

Equilateral          Isosceles

If you have a **right triangle** you can use the **pythagorean theorem**:

## TIP

There are very few integer triples small enough to come up in a right triangle. The common ratios are:

  3 : 4 : 5
  5 : 12 : 13

Look for any multiple of these to quickly identify right triangle lengths (e.g., **6:8:10** or **10:24:26**).

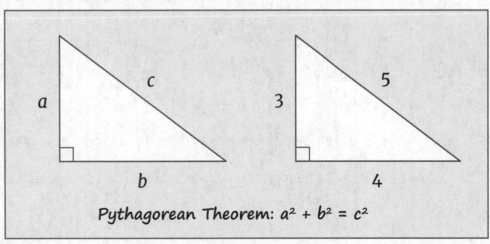

Pythagorean Theorem: $a^2 + b^2 = c^2$

# Volume

Often, the SAT will ask you to work with multiple area or volume formulas at once. Let's look at an example where remembering to **check the formula box** can be a big help.

## EXAMPLE 2

Larry is at an ice cream shop and debating between two options. The first option is to get the ice cream in a cylindrical cup with a diameter of 6 inches and a height of 4 inches, completely filled and leveled off at the top. The second option is a completely filled cone with a diameter of 4 inches and a height of 6 inches, plus half of a scoop on top shaped like a hemisphere with diameter 4 inches. How many more cubic inches of ice cream would he get with the cup than with the cone?

A) $1\frac{1}{3}\pi$

B) $17\frac{1}{3}\pi$

C) $22\frac{2}{3}\pi$

D) $24\pi$

### SOLUTION

There's quite a bit going on here. We'll need to use three volume equations to answer this question, so let's check the box, copy down the formulas, and plug in the given $r$ and $h$ for each shape:

| Cup ($r = 3$, $h = 4$) | Cone ($r = 2$, $h = 6$) | Top ($r = 2$) |
|---|---|---|
| $V_{cup} = \pi r^2 h$ | $V_{cone} = \frac{1}{3}\pi r^2 h$ | $V_{top} = \frac{1}{2}(\frac{4}{3})\pi r^3$ |
| $V_{cup} = \pi(3)^2(4)$ | $V_{cone} = \frac{1}{3}\pi(2)^2(6)$ | $V_{top} = \frac{1}{2}(\frac{4}{3})\pi(2)^3$ |
| $V_{cup} = 36\pi$ | $V_{cone} = \frac{1}{3}\pi(24)$ | $V_{top} = \frac{16}{3}\pi$ |
| | $V_{cone} = 8\pi$ | |

So our options are a cup of $36\pi$ in³ or a cone of $(8\pi + \frac{16}{3}\pi) = 13\frac{1}{3}\pi$.

To figure out how much more a cup is, we can subtract:

$$36\pi - 13\frac{1}{3}\pi = 22\frac{2}{3}\pi$$

C

# Geometry and Proportions

The SAT often focuses on proportional ratios in circles and triangles.

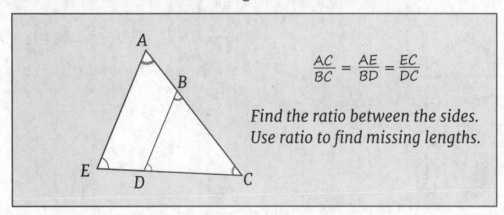

$$\frac{\text{Piece}}{\text{Whole}} = \frac{\text{Angle measure}}{360°} = \frac{\text{Arc length}}{\text{Circumference}} = \frac{\text{Wedge area}}{\text{Circle area}}$$

If two triangles have **equal angle measurements**, the triangles are **similar**. That means their sides lengths follow the same ratio.

$$\frac{AC}{BC} = \frac{AE}{BD} = \frac{EC}{DC}$$

*Find the ratio between the sides.*
*Use ratio to find missing lengths.*

# EXAMPLE 3

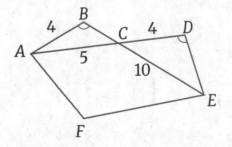

In the figure above, the measure of $\angle ABC$ is equal to the measure of $\angle CDE$. Segments $\overline{BE}$, $\overline{FE}$, and $\overline{AF}$ all have the same length. Segments $\overline{AB}$ and $\overline{CD}$ each have length 4 and segments $\overline{AC}$ and $\overline{CE}$ have lengths 5 and 10, respectively. What is the perimeter of polygon $ABCDEF$?

# TIP

In the original figure, the similar triangles are reflected across point *C*. This makes it a little tricky to keep straight which sides correspond with one another.

Make it easy on yourself: **redraw the triangles**, lining up corresponding angles and sides.

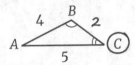

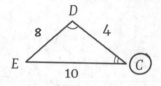

**The first thing to notice is that** $\triangle ABC$ **and** $\triangle CDE$ **must be similar triangles** since they have at least 2 angles in common: we're *told* $\angle ABC$ and $\angle CDE$ are equal, and $\angle ACB$ and $\angle ECD$ are *vertical* angles. Let's compare corresponding sides to find a locked ratio:

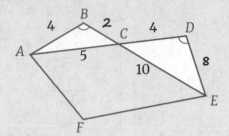

$$\frac{\triangle ABC}{\triangle CDE} = \frac{AC}{EC} = \frac{AB}{ED} = \frac{BC}{DC}$$

$$\frac{\triangle ABC}{\triangle CDE} = \frac{5}{10} = \frac{4}{ED} = \frac{BC}{4}$$

It looks like the sides of $\triangle CDE$ are **twice the length** of the sides of $\triangle ABC$. That means that $DE = 8$ and $BC = 2$. Since we now know that $BE = 12$, we know the $AF = 12$ and $FE = 12$. If we add all of the sides on the perimeter, we get:

$$perimeter = AB + BC + CD + DE + EF + AF$$

$$perimeter = 4 + 2 + 4 + 8 + 12 + 12 = \boxed{42}$$

# Practice Problems

*Use your new skills to answer each question.*

---

**1**

A slushy stand uses dome-shaped lids that resemble a hemisphere, and the volume of a lid is $\frac{16}{3}\pi$ cubic inches. What is the diameter of the cups used for these lids?

**2**

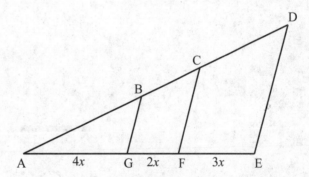

In the figure above, lines $\overline{BG}$, $\overline{FC}$, and $\overline{DE}$ are all parallel. If the length of $\overline{AD}$ is 108 inches, what is the length, in inches, of $\overline{BC}$?

A) 12
B) 24
C) 36
D) 48

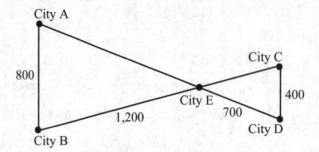

Carol took a 700-mile plane trip from City D to City E to visit Jessica, who flew 1,200 miles from City B to City E. Carol and Jessica then parted ways and traveled to Cities A and C, respectively. If the distance between City C and City D is 400 miles and the distance between City A and City B is 800 miles, how long, in miles, will Carol's plane trip be from City E to City A? (Note: ∠*ABE* is equal to ∠*ECD* and City E is on both line $\overline{AD}$ and line $\overline{BC}$)

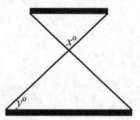

The drawing of an hourglass above consists of two similar isosceles triangles. What is the value of *x* in terms of *y* ?

A)  $x = y$

B)  $x = 180 - y$

C)  $x = 180 - 2y$

D)  $x = \dfrac{180 - y}{2}$

**5**

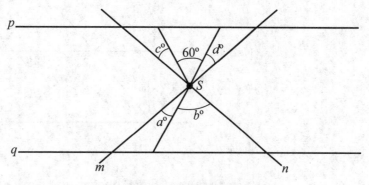

(figure not drawn to scale)

In the figure above, lines *m* and *n* intersect at point *S*, and lines *p* and *q* are parallel. If *c* + *d* = 2*a* and *b* = 80, what is the sum of *a*, *b*, *c*, and *d*?

A) 120
B) 140
C) 180
D) 200

**6**

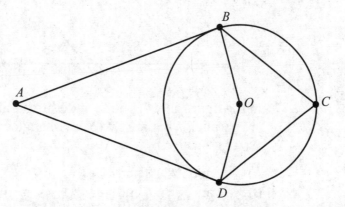

In the figure above, point *0* is the center of the circle, and line segments $\overline{AB}$ and $\overline{AD}$ are tangent to the circle at points *D* and *B* respectively. If the area of the sector formed by arc *BOD* is $\frac{5}{12}$ the area of the circle, what is the value of the measure of ∠*BAD* added to the measure of ∠*BCD*?

A) 30°
B) 75°
C) 105°
D) 180°

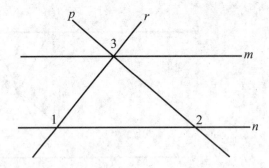

In the figure above, lines *m* and *n* are parallel. If ∠1 is 120° and ∠2 is 140°, what is the measure of ∠3 ?

A)   20°
B)   40°
C)   60°
D)   80°

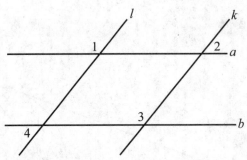

In the figure above, lines *a* and *b* are parallel, and lines *l* and *k* are parallel. What are two pairs of angles that each add up to 180° ?

A)   ∠2 and ∠4, ∠1 and ∠3
B)   ∠2 and ∠1, ∠4 and ∠3
C)   ∠1 and ∠2, ∠4 and ∠2
D)   Cannot be determined.

**9**

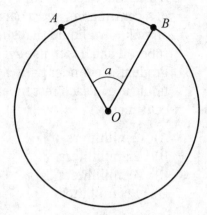

In the figure above, the circle has an area between 120 and 124 square inches, and the area of the sector formed by ∠AOB has an area between 20 and 21 square inches. What is one possible integer value of *a* ?

**10**

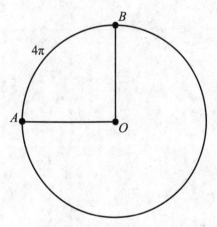

In the circle above, ∠AOB is a right angle and the length of minor arc AB is 4π inches. What is the area of the circle, in square inches?

A)  16
B)  16π
C)  64π
D)  128π

**789**

**11**

A scientist needs to fill a graduated cylinder with a diameter of 4 centimeters and a height of 6 centimeters halfway with an unknown liquid that she has stored in 6 identical test tubes. If she has to use every test tube in order to fill the graduated cylinder halfway, how many milliliters of the liquid are in each test tube? (1 milliliter is equal to 1 cubic centimeter.)

A)  2 milliliters
B)  $2\pi$ milliliters
C)  $4\pi$ milliliters
D)  $12\pi$ milliliters

# Trigonometry

*Let's review the trigonometry concepts that might show up on the test.*

................................................................................................

### SohCahToa

There are three key functions from trig that you need to know: sine, cosine, and tangent. On the SAT, you'll see them labelled as **sin**θ, **cos**θ, and **tan**θ, where θ is the angle of a right triangle. These functions tell us how an *angle* of a right triangle relates to the *sides* of the right triangle. To help us review what we mean by sin, cos, and tan, let's first draw and label a right triangle, focusing on one angle:

## Important

If we were focusing on angle B instead of angle A, the sides would have different labels!

Side AC would be "opposite" angle B, and side BC would be "adjacent." The hypotenuse is always the hypotenuse.

① *Draw a right triangle*

② *Focus on angle A*

③ *Label the hypotenuse*

④ *Label legs "adjacent" to A and "opposite" from A*

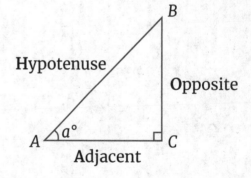

Sine, cosine, and tangent are functions, complete with inputs and outputs. They take an **angle** of a triangle (such as angle *A* above) as an input and spit out a **fraction** which is a ratio of the different sides:

$$\text{Sin } A = \frac{Opposite}{Hypotenuse} \qquad \text{Cos } A = \frac{Adjacent}{Hypotenuse} \qquad \text{Tan } A = \frac{Opposite}{Adjacent}$$

To answer basic trig questions, you'll need to memorize these ratios. Luckily, we have "SohCahToa" to make this a simpler task. "**Soh**" reminds you that <u>S</u>ine is <u>O</u>pposite over <u>H</u>ypotenuse. "**Cah**" reminds you that <u>C</u>osine is <u>A</u>djacent over <u>H</u>ypotenuse. And "**Toa**", well, you get the picture!

791

**Use SohCahToa** to complete the trig function identities below.

| Triangle | SohCahToa |
|---|---|
|  | 1.  $\text{Sin } A = \dfrac{\text{Opposite}}{\text{Hypotenuse}} = \dfrac{4}{5}$ |
| | 2.  $\text{Cos } A = \dfrac{\text{Adjacent}}{\text{Hypotenuse}} = \underline{\qquad}$ |
| | 3.  $\text{Tan } A = \dfrac{\text{Opposite}}{\text{Adjacent}} = \underline{\qquad}$ |

Now do the same thing, but **focus on angle B.**

| Triangle | SohCahToa |
|---|---|
| | 4.  $\text{Sin } B = \dfrac{\text{Opposite}}{\text{Hypotenuse}} = \dfrac{9}{15}$ |
| | 5.  $\text{Cos } B = \dfrac{\text{Adjacent}}{\text{Hypotenuse}} = \underline{\qquad}$ |
| | 6.  $\text{Tan } B = \dfrac{\text{Opposite}}{\text{Adjacent}} = \underline{\qquad}$ |

## Remember

When we change the angle we're focusing on, the side labels change too!

Now work backwards! Use SohCahToa to **label the sides of the triangle**.

## Familiar

Do these side ratios look familiar? This is one of the "special" right triangles.

| Triangle | SohCahToa |
|---|---|
| | $\text{Sin } B = \dfrac{\text{Opposite}}{\text{Hypotenuse}} = \dfrac{13}{26}$ |
| | $\text{Cos } B = \dfrac{\text{Adjacent}}{\text{Hypotenuse}} = \dfrac{13\sqrt{3}}{26}$ |
| | $\text{Tan } B = \dfrac{\text{Opposite}}{\text{Adjacent}} = \dfrac{13}{13\sqrt{3}}$ |

**Answers:  1)** 4/5  **2)** 3/5  **3)** 4/3  **4)** 9/15  **5)** 12/15  **6)** 9/12

Side $\overline{AB}$ = 26    Side $\overline{BC}$ = 13√3    Side $\overline{AC}$ = 13

# Even More Drills!

There's no better way to solidify SohCahToa in ya' brain than to use it over and over. Complete the drill below to check your understanding.

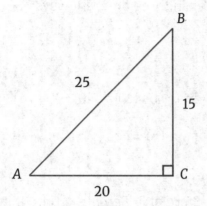

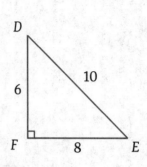

## Notice

Many of the trig ratios for triangles *ABC* and *DEF* simplify to the same fraction. Why is that?

It's because these triangles are **similar.** Though their side lengths are different, their proportions are the same.

**Bonus Notice**: they are both special 3-4-5 right triangles!

**Use SohCahToa** and the above triangles to complete the table.

| SohCahToa | |
|---|---|
| 1.  $\sin(B) =$ | 7.  $\tan(A) =$ |
| 2.  $\sin(E) =$ | 8.  $\tan(D) =$ |
| 3.  $\cos(A) =$ | 9.  $\sin(A) =$ |
| 4.  $\cos(D) =$ | 10. $\sin(D) =$ |
| 5.  $\tan(B) =$ | 11. $\cos(B) =$ |
| 6.  $\tan(E) =$ | 12. $\cos(E) =$ |

**Answers:** **1)** 20/25  **2)** 6/10  **3)** 20/25  **4)** 6/10  **5)** 20/15  **6)** 6/8
**7)** 15/20  **8)** 8/6  **9)** 15/25  **10)** 8/10  **11)** 15/25  **12)** 8/10

## MEMORIZE: Special Trig Identity

There is a special identity that shows up pretty regularly on the SAT, so it's worth memorizing. You don't really need to know WHY it's true, but we'll cover that in a second to help you remember it. Here is essentially the same idea written in three different ways:

$$\sin(\theta) = \cos(90 - \theta)$$
$$\cos(\alpha) = \sin(90 - \alpha)$$

$$\text{if } \sin(x) = \cos(y), \text{ then } x + y = 90$$

### One More

Similarly, it can be helpful to remember this handy identity:

$$\sin^2(x) + \cos^2(x) = 1$$

Just memorize that. Stare at it. *Become* it. Burn it into your brain.... Done?

Okay, now let's chat about why this is a thing. Notice that, because what's "adjacent" and what's "opposite" switch depending on which angle you focus on, **sin (A)** is equal to **cos (B)**:

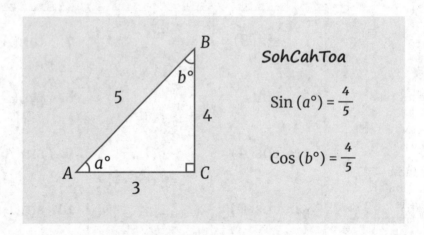

Now, if all angles add up to 180°, and one angle is 90°, then the other two *must* add up to 90°. That means we could write angles A and B in a different way, solving the mystery behind that bulky thing we memorized:

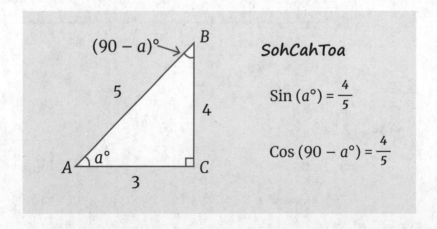

## EXAMPLE 1

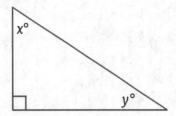

In the triangle above, sine of $x°$ = 0.6. What is cosine of $x°$ ?

A)  0.36
B)  0.6
C)  0.8
D)  1.66

SOLUTION

At first this problem might seem tough, but we shouldn't worry about that just yet! We see "sine" and "cosine," so we should immediately write SohCahToa:

   ①  *write SohCahToa!*       **SohCahToa**

Step one done! Now, the only weirdness is that the problem uses decimals when we're used to dealing in fractions. But that's no problem, we can change 0.6 to a fraction:

   ②  *write 0.6 as a fraction*       $\sin(x) = 0.6 = \frac{6}{10}$

Now we're getting somewhere. We know that sine is O/H. So we can use this information to label our triangle.

   ③  *label triangle*

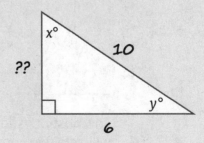

**Continued on next page →**

Now to find cos(x), we just need that third side. Luckily, we can use the **pythagorean theorem** to find that third side.

④ *use pythag's theorem*

$$A^2 + B^2 = C^2$$

$$6^2 + B^2 = 10^2$$

$$36 + B^2 = 100$$

$$B^2 = 64$$

$$B = 8$$

Bingo! Using the information given to us, SohCahToa, and pythagorean's theorem, we know the third side length is 8. Now to find cos(x), we just apply SohCahToa again:

⑤ *find cos(x) with "Cah"*

$$\cos(x) = \frac{8}{10} = \boxed{0.8}$$

C

## Radians

Instead of degrees, we can also measure angles in **radians**. The measure of an angle in radians is the *length of the arc* it would span if it were at the center of a circle with radius 1 (often called the "unit circle"):

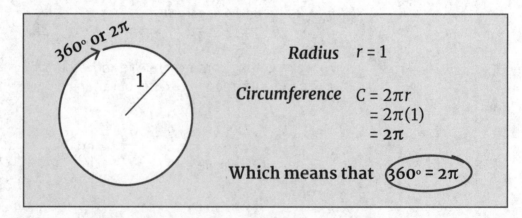

Radius    $r = 1$

Circumference    $C = 2\pi r$
$\qquad\qquad\qquad = 2\pi(1)$
$\qquad\qquad\qquad = 2\pi$

**Which means that    360° = 2π**

For most questions involving radians, just remembering that **360° = 2π** will help you convert degrees to radians and vice versa.

## Unit Circle

You may remember learning a good bit about the unit circle in school. It looks something like this:

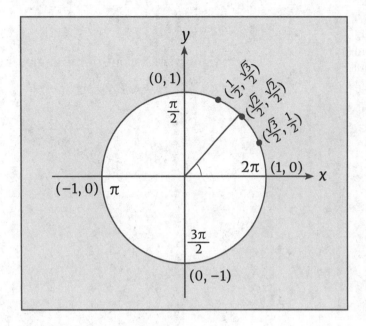

## Use Special Right Triangles

Here's some good news: you don't have to memorize this unit circle for the SAT! We can find any point or angle on the unit circle if we draw a right triangle using the information we're given. As we'll see in the practice problems, there are really only two types of special triangles that come up in unit circle problems:

# Drawing Triangles

If you're given a radians measurement, you can figure out the right triangle by **converting it to degrees**.

If you're given a point, then the x and y coordinates tell you the **length of the legs** of the triangle.

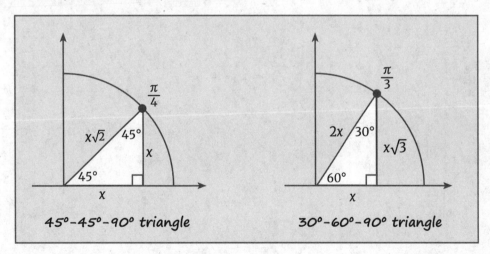

You can use these **special right triangles**, coupled with the knowledge that **360° = 2π**, to answer unit circle questions on the test. And remember, these special right triangles are given to you in the instructions box! So when in doubt, **check the box**.

# Practice Problems

*Use your new skills to answer each question.*

---

**1**

In a right triangle, one of the angles measures $x°$ where $\sin(90° - x°) = \frac{3}{5}$. What is $\cos(x°)$ ?

**2**

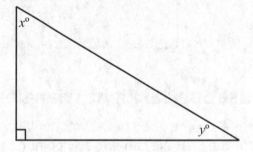

If $\cos(x°) = \frac{1}{2}$, what is the value of $\sin(y°)$ ?

A)  $\frac{1}{2}$

B)  $\frac{\sqrt{3}}{2}$

C)  $\frac{\sqrt{2}}{2}$

D)  $\frac{\sqrt{3}}{3}$

**3**

In a circle with center $O$, the central $\angle AOB$ has a measure of $\frac{\pi}{x}$ radians. If the area of the sector formed by angle $\angle AOB$ is one sixth the area of the circle, what is the value of $x$ ?

**4**

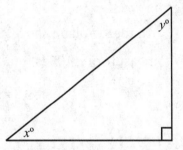

For the right triangle above, which of the following must be true?

I. $\sin(x) = \cos(x)$
II. $\sin(y) = \cos(x)$
III. $\cos(y) = \sin(x)$

A) I
B) I and II
C) II and III
D) I, II, and III

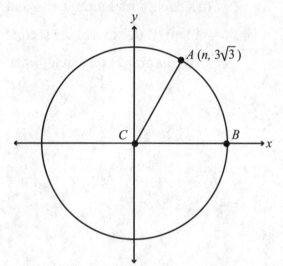

In the xy-plane above, $C$ is the center of the circle, and the measure of $\angle ACB$ is $\frac{\pi}{3}$ radians. What is the value of $n$?

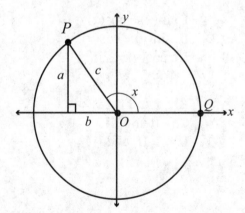

In the xy-plane above, $O$ is the center of the circle, and the measure of $\angle POQ$ is $x°$. What is the value of $\sin(x)$?

A) $\frac{b}{c}$

B) $\frac{a}{c}$

C) $-\frac{b}{c}$

D) $-\frac{a}{c}$

# UNIT | Math Review

## Practice Time

The following pages contain a PSAT-length math test. Section 3 should be taken **without** use of your calculator. On Section 4 you can go hog-wild with that calculator. Time yourself to get a feel for the pacing of a PSAT or SAT test. When you're ready for the real deal, take the mock test in the back of the book.

# Math Review (No Calculator)
## 25 MINUTES, 17 QUESTIONS

This is a PSAT-length math section for practicing your new skills! Answers are in the back of the book.

## DIRECTIONS

**For questions 1-13**, solve each problem, choose the best answer from the choices provided.
**For questions 14-17**, solve the problem and write your answer in the space provided.

## NOTES

1. The use of a calculator **is not permitted.**

2. All variables and expressions used represent real numbers unless otherwise indicated.

3. Figures provided in this test are drawn to scale unless otherwise indicated.

4. All figures lie in a plane unless otherwise indicated.

5. Unless otherwise indicated, the domain of a given function $f$ is the set of all real numbers $x$ for which $f(x)$ is a real number.

## REFERENCE

$A = \pi r^2$
$C = 2\pi r$

$A = \ell w$

$A = \frac{1}{2}bh$

$c^2 = a^2 + b^2$

Special Right Triangles

$V = \ell wh$

$V = \pi r^2 h$

$V = \frac{4}{3}\pi r^3$

$V = \frac{1}{3}\pi r^2 h$

$V = \frac{1}{3}\ell wh$

The number of degrees of arc in a circle is 360.
The number of radians of arc in a circle is $2\pi$
The sum of the measures in degrees of the angles of a triangle is 180.

**1**

If $4x + 7 = 10$, what is the value of $8x + 2$ ?

A)  3

B)  7

C)  8

D)  20

**2**

On Saturday, Car A drove $m$ miles per hour for 7 hours and Car B drove $n$ miles per hour for 8 hours. In terms of $m$ and $n$, what was the total number of miles that Cars A and B drove on Saturday?

A)  $8m + 7n$

B)  $56mn$

C)  $7m + 8n$

D)  $15mn$

**3**

Phil earns $9 an hour for washing his parents' 3 cars. His parents also give him an extra $4 if he remembers to close the garage door afterwards. Which of the following expressions could be used to show how much Phil earns if he washes each car and remembers to close the garage door?

A)  $9x + 4$, where $x$ is the number of hours

B)  $4x + 9$, where $x$ is the number of hours

C)  $x(9 + 3) + 4$, where $x$ is the number of cars

D)  $(4x + 9) + 3$, where $x$ is the number of cars

CONTINUE

**4**

$$x + y = 0$$
$$4x - 3y = 21$$

Which ordered pair $(x, y)$ satisfies the system of equations above?

A) $(4, -3)$

B) $(-3, -3)$

C) $(-3, 3)$

D) $(3, -3)$

**5**

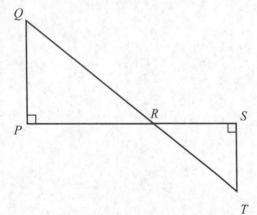

In the figure above, $PQ$ and $TS$ are each perpendicular to $PS$. If $QT = 64$ and the ratio of $ST$ to $QP$ is 3:5, what is the length of $\overline{RT}$?

A) 8

B) 16

C) 24

D) 40

**6**

Lauren is in charge of dispatching tour buses for an historic city. There are large tour buses that seat 60 people and smaller tour buses that seat 40 people. If Lauren dispatches 50 tour buses one week to pick up 2,300 people, and every bus was filled to capacity, how many large tour buses did Lauren dispatch?

A) 10

B) 15

C) 25

D) 35

**7**

If $\dfrac{x^2}{y} = 2$, what is the value of $\dfrac{4y}{x^2}$ ?

A)  2

B)  4

C)  6

D)  8

**8**

$$2x^2 + 11x - 21 = 0$$

If $m$ and $n$ are two solutions of the equation above and $m > n$, which of the following expressions is the largest?

A)  $m - n$

B)  $n - m$

C)  $2m$

D)  $-n$

**9**

A publishing company uses a large, industrial printer to produce copies of its current best-selling book. The printer can only print a certain number of pages before it needs to be cleaned. The number of pages that remain to be printed before the next cleaning can be modeled with the equation $P = 1500 - 7h$, where $P$ is the number of pages remaining to be printed and $h$ is the number of hours that the printer has been printing. What is the meaning of the value 1500 in this equation?

A)  The printer will print the pages in 1500 hours

B)  The printer prints at a rate of 1500 pages per day

C)  The printer prints at a rate of 1500 pages per hour

D)  The printer prints a total of 1500 pages each cycle

**10**

$$f(x) = a(x - 2)^2 + 1$$

The function $f$ above has constant $a$. If $f(6) = 9$, what is the value of $f(-2)$?

A)  33

B)  16

C)  9

D)  –1

CONTINUE

**11**

When line $n$ is graphed in the standard $(x, y)$ coordinate plane, it passes through the origin and has a slope of $\frac{2}{5}$. Which of the following is a point that lies on line $n$?

A)  $(0, 5)$

B)  $(2, 5)$

C)  $(5, 5)$

D)  $(10, 4)$

**12**

$$g(x) = 4(x^2 + 7x + 8) - 8(x + j)$$

If $g(x)$ is divisible by $x$, and $j$ is a constant, what is the value of $j$ ?

A)  4

B)  0

C)  -3

D)  -4

**13**

A parabola with equation $y = ax^2 + bx + c$ passes through the point $(-2, -3)$. If $a = \frac{1}{2} b$, then $c = ?$

A)  6

B)  3

C)  −1

D)  −3

**14**

If $\frac{a}{4} = b$, and $2b - 3 = 1$, what is the value of $a$?

**16**

If $a > 1$, what is the value of $\frac{2a(3a)^2}{3a^3}$?

**15**

When $k = 2\sqrt{3}$, $4k = \sqrt{3x}$. What is the value of $x$?

**17**

If $x - 4$ is a factor of $x^2 - 3kx + 4k$ and $k$ is a constant, what is the value of $k$?

# STOP

# Math Review (Calculator)
## 45 MINUTES, 31 QUESTIONS

This is a PSAT-length math section for practicing your new skills! Answers are in the back of the book.

---

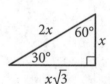

---

**1**

Carissa joins a book club that charges a yearly fee of $10, as well as $0.75 per book she borrows through the club. Which of the following functions gives Carissa's cost, in dollars, for a year in which she borrows $x$ books?

A)  $C(x) = 10.75x$

B)  $C(x) = 10x + 0.75$

C)  $C(x) = 10 + 0.75x$

D)  $C(x) = 5 + 25x$

**2**

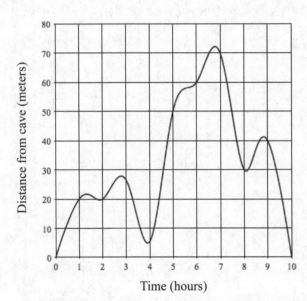

Time (hours)

A bear's distance from its cave varies as it forages its environment throughout the day. The graph above shows the bear's distance from the cave over a 10-hour period. During which period is the bear's distance from its cave strictly increasing then strictly decreasing?

A)  Between 0 and 3 hours

B)  Between 3 and 5 hours

C)  Between 5 and 8 hours

D)  Between 7 and 10 hours

**3**

For every 700 office chairs sold at an office furniture store, 4 are returned for minor defects. At this rate, out of the 42,000 office chairs sold per year, how many should the store expect to be returned for minor defects?

A)  200

B)  240

C)  280

D)  320

**4**

If $16 + 2x$ is 7 more than 15, what is the value of $4x$ ?

A)  3

B)  6

C)  12

D)  28

CONTINUE

**Questions 5-6 refer to the following information.**

The number of millimeters a sunflower grows in one month is directly proportional to the number of gallons of water the sunflower receives in that month. A sunflower will grow 90 millimeters in one month if its receives 6 gallons of water.

**5**

How many millimeters will a sunflower grow in one month if it receives 15 gallons of water?

A)  540

B)  270

C)  225

D)  180

**6**

A gardener plants her sunflower seeds in nutrient-deficient soil, which causes a 34% decrease in the growth of the sunflowers. How many millimeters do her sunflowers grow in one month if she gives the sunflowers 6 gallons of water?

A)  30.6

B)  59.4

C)  66

D)  77

**7**

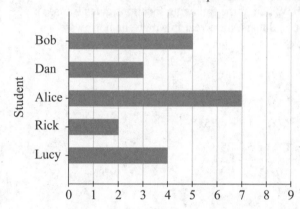

Total Points Won by Students in Competition

A competition awarded points to 5 students who participated, as shown in the graph above. If the combined total of points earned by the 5 students is equal to 2,100, what is an appropriate label for the horizontal axis of the graph?

A)  Number of points (in tens)

B)  Number of points (in hundreds)

C)  Number of points (in thousands)

D)  Number of points (in tens of thousands)

**8**

Samantha answered exactly 85 percent of the questions on her Biology test correctly. Which of the following could be the total number of questions on Samantha's Biology test?

A)  22

B)  20

C)  18

D)  14

CONTINUE

**9**

What is the slope of the line in the xy-plane that passes through the points $(-\frac{9}{2}, 2)$ and $(-\frac{1}{2}, 7)$?

A)  −1

B)  $-\frac{4}{5}$

C)  1

D)  $\frac{5}{4}$

**10**

Which of the following values for x is NOT a solution of the inequality $2x + 3 \le 5x + 9$?

A)  −3

B)  −2

C)  −1

D)  0

**11**

In a certain board game, each player starts out with 90 tokens and can only gain more by rolling "doubles", which earns the player m additional tokens. Abigail avoids losing any tokens, and rolls doubles 12 times during the game. If she finishes with 162 tokens, what is the value of m?

A)  2

B)  5

C)  6

D)  10

**12**

|  | Juniors | Seniors | Total |
|---|---|---|---|
| Basketball | 23 | 8 | 31 |
| Lacrosse | 26 | 29 | 55 |
| Soccer | 17 | 22 | 39 |
| None | 20 | 45 | 65 |
| Total | 86 | 104 | 190 |

The junior and senior class at a high school was given a survey asking what sport they planned on playing that year. The survey data was collected and compiled into the table above. Which of the following categories accounts for approximately 9 percent of the entire population surveyed?

A)  Juniors planning to play lacrosse

B)  Juniors planning to play soccer

C)  Seniors planning to play lacrosse

D)  Seniors planning to play basketball

**13**

$$231 - 11x = y$$

A new grocery store is giving a free T-shirt to a certain number of lucky customers each day, while supplies last. The equation above can be used to model the number of T-shirts, y, left to be given away x days after the promotion began. What does it mean that (21,0) is a solution to this equation?

A)  The store gives away 21 T-shirts each day.

B)  The store has a total of 21 T-shirts to give away.

C)  After 11 days, the store will have 21 T-shirts left to give away.

D)  It will take 21 days to give away the store's supply of T-shirts.

CONTINUE

14

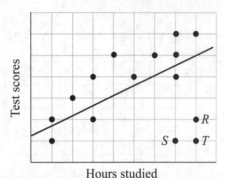

Hours studied

A teacher wants to show her students the relationship between the number of hours spent studying and test scores. She plots the results of 15 students' most recent test scores in the graph above. She then discovers that students R, S, and T studied for the wrong test and, as a result, should not have been considered in the data. If she removes these three scores and redraws the graph, how will the graph's line of best fit change?

A)  Its slope will decrease.

B)  Its slope will increase.

C)  Its slope will stay the same.

D)  The line will be unaffected by the change.

15

Kiki and Thomas ran a two-day fundraiser where they sold pies and cookies. On the first day, they sold 80 pies and 120 cookies. On the second day, however, they sold 30 percent fewer pies and 40 percent fewer cookies. By what percentage did the total volume of baked goods sold decline from the first day to the second?

A)  10

B)  35

C)  36

D)  70

16

$$y > x + s$$
$$y < -x + t$$

In the xy-plane, (0, 0) is a solution to the system of inequalities above. Which of the following relationships between s and t must be true?

A)  $s > t$

B)  $s < t$

C)  $|s| > |t|$

D)  $s = -t$

17

A concession stand sells hot dogs for $3.75 each and soda for $1.50 each. In one day, the stand sells a combined total of 123 hot dogs and sodas, earning $378 from the sales. How many hot dogs were sold that day?

A)  83

B)  86

C)  93

D)  102

**18**

|        | Group A | Group B | Total |
|--------|---------|---------|-------|
| None   | 42      | 57      | 99    |
| 1 to 3 | 93      | 82      | 175   |
| 4 or more | 65   | 61      | 126   |
| Total  | 200     | 200     | 400   |

A nutritionist recruited two distinct populations to participate in a survey. One group (Group A) consisted of 200 people who regularly eat breakfast; the other (Group B) consisted of 200 people who usually skip breakfast. Each person was asked to report their daily intake of servings of fruits and vegetables, and the results were recorded in the table above. If a person is chosen at random from among those who eat at least 1 serving of fruits and vegetables, what is the probability that the person belonged to Group B?

A) $\dfrac{61}{200}$

B) $\dfrac{143}{200}$

C) $\dfrac{143}{301}$

D) $\dfrac{301}{400}$

**19**

Shakir is a manager who is evaluating the productivity of two employees. Based on his study, he concludes that Employee A, on average, completes 25% more assignments than Employee B does. If Employee A completes 85 assignments, about how many assignments will Employee B complete?

A) 63

B) 68

C) 106

D) 110

**20**

Researchers conducted a survey of the salaries for graphic designers with similar amounts of experience and education. They found that the mean salary was $45,000 and the median salary was $60,000. Which of the following situations could explain the difference between the mean and median salaries?

A) The designers all earn the same salary.

B) Many designers earn salaries between $45,00 and $60,000.

C) A few designers earn much more than the rest.

D) A few designers earn much less than the rest.

**21**

Susan estimates that she will have to study $x$ hours for her finals next week, where $x > 40$. The goal is for the estimate to be within 4 hours of the time it will actually take her to study. If Susan meets her goal and it takes her $y$ hours to complete all of her studying, which of the following inequalities represents the relationship between the estimated time and the actual studying time?

A) $x + y < 4$

B) $y > x + 4$

C) $y < x - 4$

D) $-4 < x - y < 4$

CONTINUE

**Questions 22-24 refer to the following table.**

Estimated Annual Budget for Sectors of the U.S. Federal Budget from 2016 to 2019

| Sector | Year | | | |
|---|---|---|---|---|
| | 2016 | 2017 | 2018 | 2019 |
| Pensions | 1,012 | 1,062 | 1,118 | 1,188 |
| Health Care | 1,107 | 1,134 | 1,175 | 1,273 |
| Education | 119 | 130 | 139 | 147 |
| Defense | 852 | 840 | 823 | 835 |
| Welfare | 393 | 402 | 402 | 414 |
| Transportation | 99 | 104 | 107 | 108 |

The table above lists the estimated annual budget, in millions of dollars, for each of six different sectors of the U.S. Federal Budget from 2016 to 2019.

**22**

Which of the following best approximates the average rate of change in the estimated annual budget for pensions from 2017 to 2019?

A) $50 million per year

B) $63 million per year

C) $126 million per year

D) $176 million per year

**23**

Of the following, which program's ratio of its 2016 to its 2019 estimated budget is closest to the health care sector's ratio of its 2016 budget to its 2019 budget?

A) Pensions

B) Education

C) Defense

D) Welfare

**24**

Which of the following graphs could represent the estimated change in the welfare budget over the years 2016 to 2019, inclusive ?

A)

B)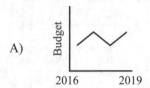

C)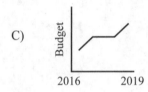

D)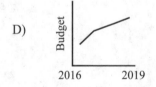

**25**

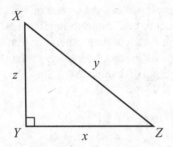

In right triangle *XYZ* above, sin *Z* is equal to which of the following?

A) $\dfrac{x}{y}$

B) $\dfrac{z}{y}$

C) $\dfrac{z}{x}$

D) $\dfrac{y}{z}$

**26**

A painter is making a rectangular canvas for a large-scale painting. The canvas has a length that is 8 feet less than twice its width. What is the perimeter, in feet, of the canvas if the area is 570 square feet?

A) 74

B) 80

C) 98

D) 104

**27**

$$h = -4.9t^2 + 16t$$

For a science project, Mark built a slingshot contraption that launches a sphere straight up into the air. He then built the equation above to show the approximate height, *h*, in meters, of the sphere *t* seconds after it is launched from the slingshot with an initial velocity of 16 meters per second. After approximately how many seconds will the sphere hit the ground?

A) 2.0

B) 2.7

C) 3.3

D) 4.0

CONTINUE

**28**

Earl can string at least 8 guitars per hour and at most 16 guitars per hour. Based on this information, what is a possible amount of time, in hours, that it could take Earl to string 56 guitars?

**29**

A local magnet school wishes to obtain a 5:2 student-to-teacher ratio. The school currently has 50 teachers on staff for a population of 180 students. The school expects the total student population to increase by 40 next year. How many additional teachers must the school add next year to reach its target ratio?

**30**

A college professor assigns a class of 105 students a group project to be completed in groups of 3 or 4. If each group of students has either 3 or 4 students and there will be 31 groups, how many of the students will work in a group of 3 students?

**31**

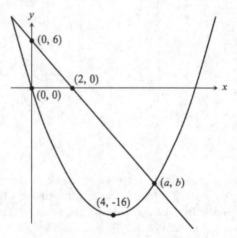

In the xy-plane above, (a, b) are the coordinates of one of the points of intersection of the graphs of a linear function and a quadratic function. If the graph of the quadratic function has its vertex at (4, -16), what is the value of a?

**STOP**

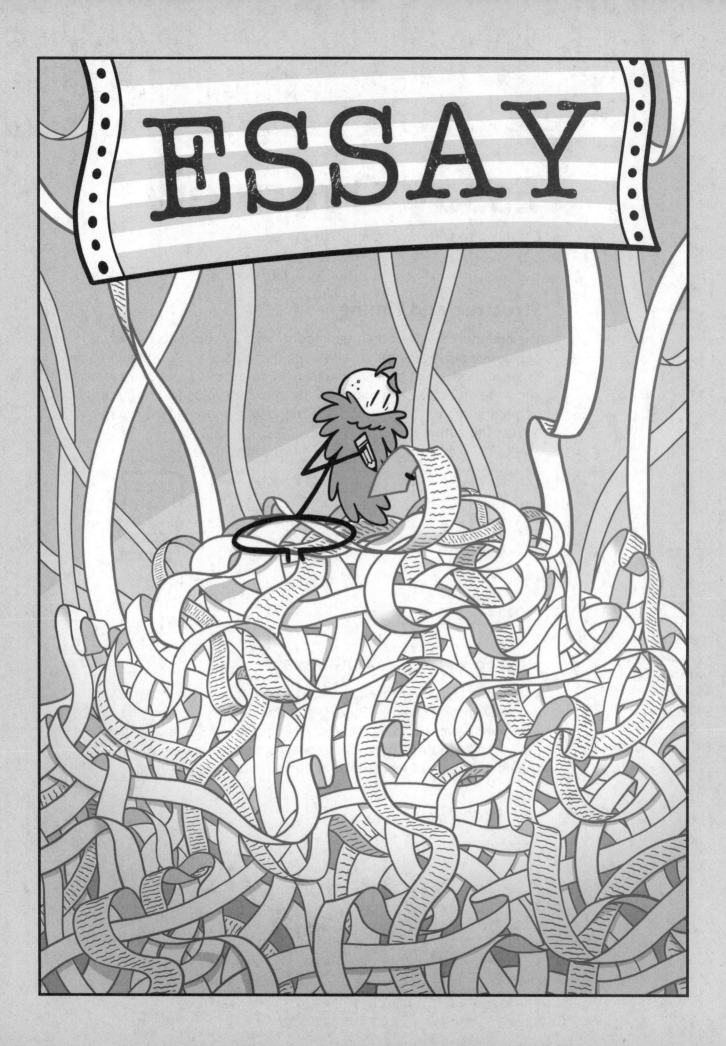

# Essay Overview

*Get your nitty gritty details about the SAT essay here!*

## Structure and Timing

The optional Essay section presents you with a short (600-700 words) persuasive passage—that is, a passage that tries to persuade the reader of the author's point of view. You have **50 minutes** to read the passage and write an essay explaining how the author develops and supports his or her argument. You should not respond with your opinion, but only discuss the author's opinion.

**Passage**

**minutes**

**Essay**

**TIP**

If you're taking the SAT more than once, you don't need to register for the essay every time! Once you're satisfied with your score, you can take the regular 4 sections and then skip out early!

## How to sign up for the essay

To take the test with the essay, you *must* choose the "SAT with essay" option when you register. There is an additional fee to cover the cost of processing and grading the essays. Some colleges do not require the essay section, but many do. Each college's website or admissions office should let you know whether or not they require the SAT essay.

## Each essay is given three subscores

The SAT essay has three subscores: Reading, Analysis, and Writing, each on a scale from 2 to 8. We'll dive into each score in more detail later, but here's the basic idea of each score:

- **Reading score:** this reflects how accurately and fully your essay characterizes <u>what</u> the argument in the passage actually *was*.

- **Analysis score:** this reflects how well your essay explains <u>how</u> the author develops his or her argument, as well as <u>why</u> the author chose to use specific rhetorical devices.

- **Writing score:** this reflects how well written your essay is, considering factors like organization, vocabulary, and sentence structure.

## Each essay is scored by two graders

Two graders, working independently from each other, grade your essay. Each grader assigns a score between 1 and 4 for each of the three subscores. Your final score for each category is between 2 and 8, reflecting the sum of the scores given by each grader (as shown in the diagram below).

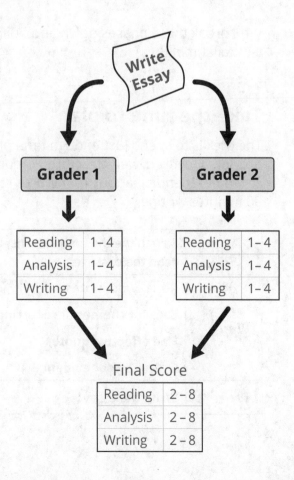

# Essay Strategy

*Let's learn how to build a solid essay one step at a time.*

## Core strategy

Our core strategy has three phases: first read, then plan, and then write. Pay attention to those first two steps! Failure to read leads to an offtopic essay, while lack of planning leads to a rambling, unfocused one.

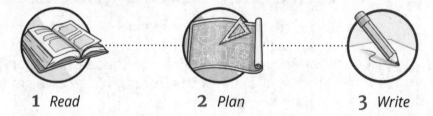

**1** *Read*        **2** *Plan*        **3** *Write*

We'll break these phases down and build an essay step-by-step... but first, let's talk timing.

## Take the time to plan

The trick is to spend just enough time planning your essay so that you provide a focused, well-structured argument. We suggest the following schedule, spending about 10 minutes reading, 10 minutes planning, and 30 minutes writing.

# TIP

Keep in mind that longer essays tend to get higher scores. If you are a slower writer, you may want to allot more time to writing the essay. However, don't skip planning entirely!

| | | |
|---|---|---|
| **Read** | Skip to the the **instructions**, then **actively read** the passage. | 10 minutes |
| **Plan** | Review your **notes** | 1 minute |
| | Look for **themes** or **recurring examples** | 4 minutes |
| | Find **effective quotes** | 4 minutes |
| | Organize your **evidence** | 1 minute |
| **Write** | **Write** the essay | 30 minutes |

# Foundations of a good essay

Without a proper foundation, the Eiffel Tower would look a lot more like the Leaning Tower of Pisa, and your essay scores will lean a lot closer to a 2 than to a 8. Here are the 8 elements of a solid foundation for your essay. The icons tell you which step helps you achieve each element.

① **Actively read the passage** the essay section is also a reading test and you'll need to focus your argument around the content given in the passage. Reading is the crucial first step!

② **Use quotes effectively** to show that you understand the argument. But don't pad your essay with overly long quotes!

③ **Be well-organized.** Make sure you have a clear introduction, a few strong body paragraphs, and a tight conclusion.

④ **Be focused on your topic.** Stick to the passage and don't get side-tracked expressing your own opinions.

⑤ **Transition smoothly between paragraphs:** the flow of your essay is important; use good segues and transitions that lead from one paragraph or example to the next.

⑥ **Demonstrate skillful use of vocabulary:** instead of writing "this shows that..." break out a more advanced synonym: "the author's quote demonstrates/clarifies/exemplifies..."

⑦ **Use a variety of sentence structures:** simple sentences lead to bored graders, so spice things up with complex sentences.

⑧ **More is better:** the test booklet give you 4 pages, so be sure to use as much as you can. Longer essays show more effort.

# Persuasive Argument

*A persuasive essay tries to—you guessed it—**persuade** the reader to come around to the author's point of view.*

.................................................................................

Before we jump into how to write the essay, it's important to think about what makes a good persuasive argument. Let's look at persuasive essays discussing one of the most pressing questions of our time: **who is the best superhero?** We'll start with one that is less-than-effective.

## A PASSIONATE, YET UNPERSUASIVE ARGUMENT

Space Laser Man is the best superhero ever created! He can fly and his kicks shoot out lasers. Space Laser Man is way better than Robo Tiger, who is just a robot dressed up as a tiger. Who would design a robotic tiger and not give it the ability to fly and shoot lasers? A fool who knows nothing about the real world, that's who! Laser kicks will always beat metal claws, especially when he shoots them while flying.

I polled a couple of my friends and they all agree that Space Laser Man is the best ever. My friend, Aaron, who has every issue of *United Justice Friendship Co-op*, thinks Space Laser Man should leave the Co-op, because he could defeat more villains by himself. Instead, Space Laser Man gets distracted having to save Nautical Nate when he gets trapped in a uranium powered fishing net or getting in an argument with Mr. Minutia over who left their dishes in the sink at the Co-op.

In conclusion, Space Laser Man will always be the greatest superhero ever and he should probably leave the *United Justice Friendship Co-op* and just concentrate on firing laser kicks at villains.

**Q1**  **Why did the author think Space Laser Man was best?**

**Q2**  **Why is this argument unpersuasive?**

## Where's the evidence?

This essay doesn't contain many facts to support the author's theory that Space Laser Man is the best superhero. It focuses a lot on the **what**, but not a lot on the **why**. Why is shooting lasers so much better than being a robot? Why are laser kicks better than metal claws?

Without **evidence**, I don't think I can trust the author's argument. The author's "friend Aaron" may be an expert on superheroes, but he may be just a random guy! Why should I take his word on this topic? This essay is full of opinions, but very short on persuasion. Next let's look at another essay that addresses the same topic.

## A MORE PERSUASIVE ARGUMENT

Who is the greatest superhero of all time? It's an intriguing question for fans of superheroes and has led to a diversity of opinions. Unfortunately, analyzing fans' opinions in mass often feels like looking for subtlety in the chattering howls of hungry hyenas. Rather than attempting to determine subjective "greatness," analyzing a superhero's popularity can lead to quantifiable metrics. Dr. Cadenhead, a professor at the Lilburn College of Fantasy Arts, has determined a method to track superhero preferences over time by analyzing the frequency of something he calls "hashtags" in social media.

Cadenhead's findings revealed an unexpected trend: Space Laser Man has skyrocketed in popularity over the last three years. In 1997, Space Laser Man ranked 316th in superhero popularity according to Cadenhead's findings. By 2014, Space Laser Man had broken into the top 20! While Space Laser Man trails behind many legendary superheroes—Robo Tiger, The Indestructible Thud, and Goose Kid— there has been a tangible rise in Space Laser Man's popularity.

What could account for Space Laser Man's rise in appeal? The best way to understand the trend is to investigate his fans. By and large, Space Laser Man appeals to adolescent males, especially those with limited social experience. His primary superpowers, laser-kicks and flying, represent a fight-or-flight binary that makes it easy to process potential danger. His lack of romantic subplot means that his fans can enjoy his adventures without having to navigate stories with complex interpersonal narratives.

According to researchers at the Comic Book Institute of North America, 40% of superhero fans are males between the ages of 13 and 22. These fans are the primary consumers of Space Laser Man's stories of good and evil, and the the number of sales—$39 million in the last fiscal quarter alone—prove that Space Laser Man is undisputably popular. However, if his popularity will continue or if his die-hard base will grow up and move to more mature narratives remains to be seen.

**Q1** Why did the author think Space Laser Man was best?

**Q2** Why is this argument more persuasive?

## Oh, *there's* the evidence!

This is a great argument! The author isn't trying to argue that Space Laser Man is *subjectively* better than other superheroes; instead, she's arguing that Space Laser Man is a very popular superhero.

It all comes down to **evidence**. The author backs up her claims with facts, numbers, research, data... the works! This essay still tells us what Space Laser Man does (laser kicks and flying), but also explains **why** that is important to the argument (the fight-or-flight binary is appealing, making him very popular). The author **cites reputable sources**: Dr. Cadenhead is an expert with evidence to back up his claims, and the Comic Book Institute of North America sounds very prestigious. After reading this essay, I am persuaded that Space Laser Man is a very popular superhero.

## Good News

The good news is the SAT essay will only use quality pieces of writing, so you will not have to pick apart a bad argument. However, by analyzing a weak argument and a strong argument, you can start to notice what makes an essay persuasive, and therefore, effective.

# Reading Score

*Did you understand the passage? Can you summarize the author's argument?*

................................................................

## Skip to the Instructions!

Every SAT essay has the same structure: reading instructions (these are always the same), then the essay, then the writing instructions. Your first step is to **skip to the writing instructions**.

> As you read the passage below, consider how Brianna Schemanke witz uses
>
> - evidence, such as facts
> - reasoning to
> - stylistic or p
>   to emotion,

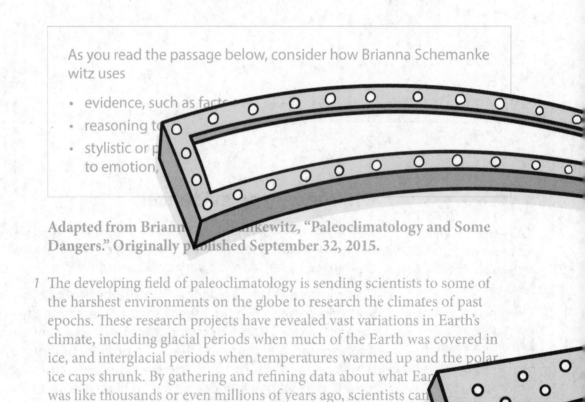

Adapted from Brianna ~~Schemanke~~witz, "Paleoclimatology and Some Dangers." Originally published September 32, 2015.

1 The developing field of paleoclimatology is sending scientists to some of the harshest environments on the globe to research the climates of past epochs. These research projects have revealed vast variations in Earth's climate, including glacial periods when much of the Earth was covered in ice, and interglacial periods when temperatures warmed up and the polar ice caps shrunk. By gathering and refining data about what Ear~~th~~ was like thousands or even millions of years ago, scientists can ~~make~~ better calculations about what Earth's climate will be like in the ~~future.~~ They can also better understand the complex mechanisms that ~~drove~~ climate changes in the past, and build better ~~models~~ ~~to~~ understan~~d~~ climate trends. Right now, the~~y~~ ~~have~~ ~~a~~ ~~cruc~~ial quest~~ion:~~ what is the exact relationship b~~etween~~ increased temperatures?

2 The evidence is encoded in many ways:
microscopic dust and soot, even the var~~iations~~ ~~in~~ ~~tree~~ ~~ri~~ngs.
(These striations show the changes thr~~ough~~ ~~light~~ ~~and~~ ~~da~~rk bands

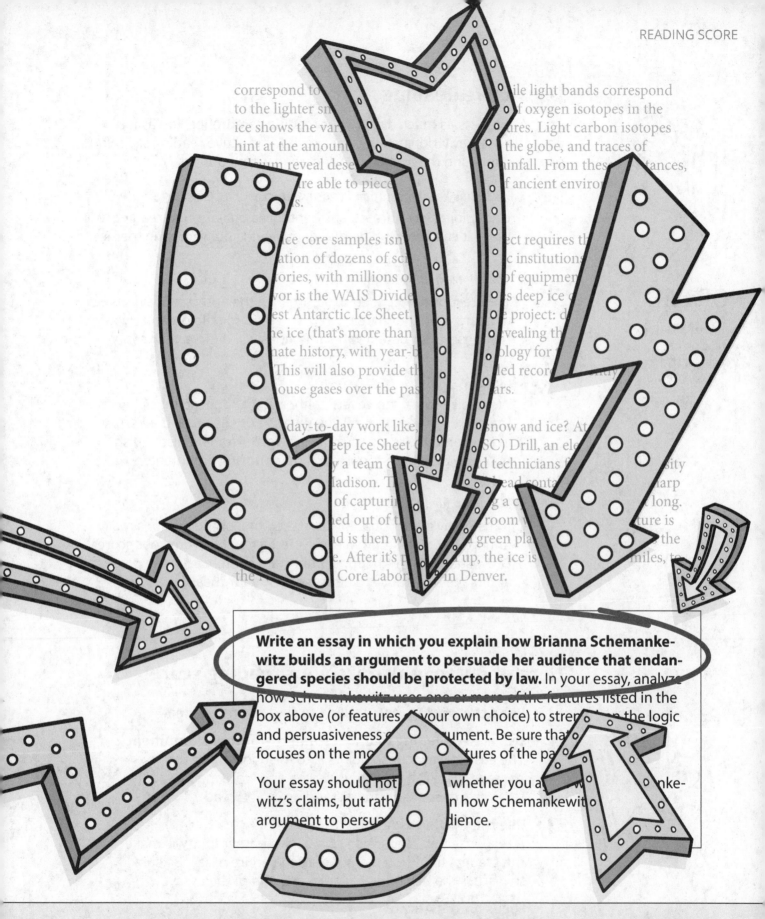

correspond to ... ...ile light bands correspond
to the lighter sn... ...f oxygen isotopes in the
ice shows the var... ...res. Light carbon isotopes
hint at the amount... ...the globe, and traces of
...ium reveal dese... ...ainfall. From the... ...tances,
...re able to piece... ...f ancient enviro...
...s.

...ce core samples isn... ...ect requires th...
...ation of dozens of sc... ...c institutions...
...ories, with millions o... ...of equipmen...
...vor is the WAIS Divide... ...s deep ice c...
...est Antarctic Ice Sheet... ...core project: d...
...ne ice (that's more than... ...vealing th...
...ate history, with year-b... ...ology for...
...This will also provide th... ...ed recor... ...tly...
...ouse gases over the pas... ...ars.

...day-to-day work like, ... ...snow and ice? At...
...eep Ice Sheet (...SC) Drill, an ele...
...y a team o... ...d technicians f... ...sity
...Madison. T... ...ead conta... ...arp
...of capturi... ...g a c... ...long.
...ed out of t... ...room... ...ture is
...d is then w... ...n green pla... ...the
...e. After it's p... ...up, the ice is... ...miles, t...
...the ... ...Core Labor... ...in Denver.

**Write an essay in which you explain how Brianna Schemanke-witz builds an argument to persuade her audience that endan-gered species should be protected by law.** In your essay, analyze how Schemankewitz uses one or more of the features listed in the box above (or features of your own choice) to strengthen the logic and persuasiveness of... ...rgument. Be sure that... focuses on the mo... ...tures of the pa...

Your essay should not... ...whether you a... ...nke-witz's claims, but rath... ...n how Schemankewit... argument to persua... ...dience.

---

Here the test writers tell you the author's argument! **This is super useful to know in the beginning**, so be sure to read this first. This will help you to identify main ideas and key examples from the very start.

## PORTAL

For more Active Reading practice, go to page page 34 in the Reading section.

## Use Active Reading

The SAT Essay is as much about your reading comprehension as it is about your essay writing ability. Let's review the active reading skills you'll use to understand the author's position and write your essay.

(1) *Underline key information in each sentence*

Underlining key phrases and sentences on your first reading will make it easier to find helpful quotes and spot recurring themes.

(2) *Take Notes in the Margin*

Your response will need to summarize the author's positions, so write notes in the margin while you read to help organize your response. Your paragraph summaries will outline your essay!

(3) *Circle Logic Words*

Words like "but," "however," "although," and "despite" signal that the author is about to tell you what he or she *really* thinks. Get in the habit of circling these "logic words" to help distinguish between the author's position and opposing arguments.

(4) *Star Main Ideas*

If the essay graders think you missed one of the author's really important points, they will likely deduct points from your score. Draw stars next to the most important sentences in the passage and make sure they are addressed by your thesis.

## Here's how to maximize your reading score!

- **Read the writing instructions to find the main idea**

- **Use active reading to understand the author's argument**
  The easiest way to lose points is to misunderstand the passage. Take the time to underline and write margin notes to quickly check your understanding as you read.

- **Use the whole essay**
  A response that focuses on one or two paragraphs will make the graders think you did not read the entire essay. Be sure to discuss the beginning, middle, *and* end of the essay.

- **Focus on the Author**
  Sadly, the SAT graders are not interested in your opinion! Make sure that you express the author's position and do not filter that position through your own feelings.

# Analysis Score

*How did the author persuade you of his or her argument? What persuasive elements were used, and what was the effect on the reader?*

The analysis score reflects your ability to explain how the author develops his or her ideas. The majority of your essay will be dedicated to this analysis, so this score is extremely important! To ace the analysis, your job is to:

## TIP

No author will use everything (or even most things) on this list! When you're writing your essay, focus on the 3-4 elements the author uses most frequently and most persuasively.

① *Show how the author builds an argument*

What stylistic and persuasive elements did the author utilize? Hard data? Quotes from experts? Fancy metaphors? All these and more can help build an argument.

② *Explain how each element affects and persuades the reader*

The SAT wants you to discuss the **why** and **how** of the essay, not just summarize what the author said. *Why* does the author quote an expert? *How* does using the chosen examples help persuade the reader?

## Stylistic and Persuasive Elements

Below, you'll find a list of stylistic and persuasive elements authors use to make a point. On the next few pages, we define each element, look at examples, and discuss how to spot them each one in an essay.

**Facts and Rhetoric**

- empirical evidence
- quotes from an expert
- anecdotes
- rhetorical question
- counter-argument
- hypothetical example
- juxtaposition
- satire

**Emotional/Figurative Language**

- pathos
- sensory detail
- personification
- metaphor
- simile
- allusion
- metonymy
- synecdoche

# Persuasive Elements: Facts and Rhetoric

Using these elements helps ground an argument in the real world by appealing to the analytical/thinking side of the reader.

| Empirical Evidence | |
|---|---|
| **How to spot it** | Empirical evidence is just a fancy word for using statistics and studies. When you see data and percentages, that's empirical evidence. |
| **Example** | *Southern Delaware has gradually become the oral hygiene capital of the nation. A 2013 study by Truex and Findlay found that 38% of Southern Delaware middle-schoolers plan to pursue a career in dentistry.* |
| **Why it's used** | Showing that scientific studies agree with the author's beliefs can be very persuasive evidence. |
| **Quote from an Expert** | |
| **How to spot it** | This is when an author cites another expert. Look for quotes from folks with fancy titles. |
| **Example** | *"Despite the availability of downloadable and streamable music, vinyl records have surged in popularity," says Artie Newhouse, owner of The Vinyl Countdown in Locust Grove, GA.* |
| **Why it's used** | These quotes show that other smart people agree with the author. |
| **Personal Experience and Anecdotes** | |
| **How to spot it** | An anecdote is whenever the author starts talking about a personal experience and how that experience affected him or her. |
| **Example** | *I came to understand the environmental importance of Northwest Minnesota during a college geology field trip to the region.* |
| **Why it's used** | They show that their opinion is not purely theoretical, but based in real-life experiences. |
| **Rhetorical Question** | |
| **How to spot it** | A rhetorical question is a question that the author intends to answer. |
| **Example** | *Why would anyone study the life cycles of lobsters? My interest developed through a summer internship on a Portland, Maine fishing boat.* |
| **Why it's used** | Rhetorical questions allow the author to introduce a topic in a way that allows for greater exploration. |

## Counter Argument/Antithesis

| | |
|---|---|
| **How to spot it** | This is when the author acknowledges an opposing viewpoint. Look for logic words like "however" and "but" after a counter argument to find the author's position. |
| **Example** | *Many self-proclaimed "experts" believe that it is only a matter of time before someone captures a living Sasquatch.* |
| **Why it's used** | Counter arguments can strengthen the author's own argument because the author can now directly dispute the other side's claims. |

## Hypothetical Example

| | |
|---|---|
| **How to spot it** | The author will use words like "suppose," "imagine," or "if" to indicate the example is what could happen. |
| **Example** | *Suppose that the wooly mammoth had survived the last Ice Age. Its effect on the contemporary North American ecosystem would be dramatic.* |
| **Why it's used** | Hypothetical examples allow an author to explore future consequences of current actions. |

## Juxtaposition

| | |
|---|---|
| **How to spot it** | Just look for two examples that the author compares and contrasts. |
| **Example** | *While Chihuahuas and Golden Retrievers are both popular dog breeds in America, their differences allow them to excel in different living environments.* |
| **Why it's used** | A juxtaposition allows for the author to analyze two sides of an argument and possibly reach a consensus. |

## Satire

| | |
|---|---|
| **How to spot it** | Look for the author saying the opposite of his or her point. Often times the author will place a word or phrase in quotation marks to emphasize its sarcastic use. |
| **Example** | *With multiple ethics violations and a string of shady land deals under his belt, the Governor exemplifies the "career" politician.* |
| **Why it's used** | Satire allows the author to express contempt for something but also use humor to keep the reader engaged. |

# Persuasive Elements: Emotional/Figurative Language

Using these elements helps persuade the reader by appealing to his or her imagination and emotions.

| Pathos/Appeal to Emotion | |
|---|---|
| **How to spot it** | Look for language meant to make the reader experience an emotion. |
| **Example** | *Children in underfunded orphanages subsist off of paltry meals of barely nutritious food wishing everyday for some kind of comfort and salvation.* |
| **Why it's used** | If the author can affect our emotions, then we are more likely to be persuaded. |
| Sensory Detail | |
| **How to spot it** | The author will describe an experience by referring to senses like sight, hearing, or touch. |
| **Example** | *A walk on the beach always calms me; the sand massages in between my toes, the salty sea air envelopes my nostrils, and the ocean itself keeps a steady rhythm as each wave cascades on the shoreline.* |
| **Why it's used** | Sensory details help a reader to imagine a situation and place him or herself in the example. |
| Personification | |
| **How to spot it** | If an author starts giving non-humans human emotions, then you know it is personification. |
| **Example** | *My car loves ethanol-based fuel as ethanol makes it hum a happy tune as it cruises down the road.* |
| **Why it's used** | Personification helps readers to identify with non-humans. |
| Metaphor | |
| **How to spot it** | Look for figurative language that describes something with the qualities of another thing. |
| **Example** | *The cruel Arctic wind slapped me across the face.* |
| **Why it's used** | A metaphor helps the reader to make a connection or understand a situation in a new way. |

## Simile

| | |
|---|---|
| **How to spot it** | If you see figurative language that uses "like" or "as" to create a comparison, you have found a simile. |
| **Example** | *During an Olympic decathlon, athletes must run like gazelles, leap like kangaroos, and throw like chimpanzees.* |
| **Why it's used** | A simile, like a metaphor, can help the reader to see a topic or situation in a new way. |

## Allusion

| | |
|---|---|
| **How to spot it** | When the author indirectly references a famous story or historical event. |
| **Example** | *Standing against a Goliath, the small town's residents knew they needed to consolidate their efforts in order to preserve their historic downtown from outside developers.* |
| **Why it's used** | Allusions relate a topic to a well-known cultural reference and in doing so, help the topic feel more significant to the reader. |

## Metonymy

| | |
|---|---|
| **How to spot it** | If the author uses an associated object to represent the actual subject, then you are looking at metonymy. |
| **Example** | *The Oval Office made a statement today that reflects an important shift in the allocation of international aid.* |
| **Why it's used** | Metonymy allows authors to vary their word choice rather than using the proper name all the time. |

## Synecdoche

| | |
|---|---|
| **How to spot it** | When the name of a part represents the whole thing, you have a synecdoche. |
| **Example** | *The hands of labor reached an accord with the suits in management.* |
| **Why it's used** | A synecdoche can draw emphasis to a particular quality of a subject. |

Let's review the second superhero essay from earlier in this chapter. **Circle and label any persuasive and/or stylistic elements you see**.

Who is the greatest superhero of all time? It's an intriguing question for fans of superheroes and has led to a diversity of opinions. Unfortunately, analyzing fans' opinions in mass often feels like looking for subtlety in the chattering howls of hungry hyenas. Rather than attempting to determine subjective "greatness," analyzing a superhero's popularity can lead to quantifiable metrics. Dr. Cadenhead, a professor at the Lilburn College of Fantasy Arts, has determined a method to track superhero preferences over time by analyzing the frequency of something he calls "hashtags" in social media.

Cadenhead's findings revealed an unexpected trend: Space Laser Man has skyrocketed in popularity over the last three years. In 1997, Space Laser Man ranked 316th in superhero popularity according to Cadenhead's findings. By 2014, Space Laser Man had broken into the top 20! While Space Laser Man trails behind many legendary superheroes—Robo Tiger, The Indestructible Thud, and Goose Kid—there has been a tangible rise in Space Laser Man's popularity.

What could account for Space Laser Man's rise in appeal? The best way to understand the trend is to investigate his fans. By and far, Space Laser Man appeals to adolescent males, especially those with limited social experience. His primary superpowers, laser-kicks and flying, represent a fight-or-flight binary that makes it easy to process potential danger. His lack of romantic subplot means that his fans can enjoy his adventures without having to navigate stories with complex interpersonal narratives.

According to researchers at the Comic Book Institute of North America, 40% of superhero fans are males between the ages of 13 and 22. These fans are the primary consumers of Space Laser Man's stories of good and evil, and the the number of sales—$39 million is the last fiscal quarter alone—prove that Space Laser Man is undisputably popular. However, if his popularity will continue or if his die-hard base will grow up and move to more mature narratives remains to be seen.

Answers:

*rhetorical question*

Who is the greatest superhero of all time? It's an intriguing question for fans of superheroes and has led to a diversity of opinions. Unfortunately, analyzing fan *metaphor* n mass often feels like look *antithesis* ety in the chattering howls of hungry hyenas. Rather than attempting to determine subjective "greatness," analyzing a su *expert opinion* rity can lead to quantifiable metrics. Dr. Cadenhead, a professor at the Lilburn College of Fantasy Arts, has determined a method to track superhero preferences over time by analyzing the frequency of something he calls "hashtags" in social media.

Cadenhead's findings revealed an unexpected trend *empirical evidence* s skyrocketed in popularity over the last three years. In 1997, Space Laser Man ranked 316th in superhero popularity according to Cadenhead's findings. By 2014, Space Laser Man had broken into the top 20! While Space Laser Man trails behind many legendary superheroes—Robo Tiger, The Indestructible Thud, and Goose Kid—there ha *rhetorical question* in Space Laser Man's popularity.

What could account for Space Laser Man's rise in appeal? The best way to understand the trend is to investigate his fans. By and far, Space Laser Man appeals to adolescent males, especially those with limited social experience. His primary superpowers, laser-kicks and flying, represent a fight-or-flight binary that makes it easy to process potential danger. His lack of romantic subplot means that his fans can enjoy his adventures without having to navigate stories with complex interpe *citing experts* es. *empirical evidence*

According to researchers at the Comic Book Institute of North America, 40% of superhero fans are males between the ages of 13 and 22. These fans are the primary consumers of Space *empirical evidence* of good and evil, and the the number of sales—$39 million is the last fiscal quarter alone—prove that Space Laser Man is undisputably popular. However, if his popularity will continue or if his die-hard base will grow up and move to more mature narratives remains to be seen.

## Author's Tone

A great way to increase your analysis score is to address the author's tone. You can focus on a specific example or paragraph, and/or address the overall tone. A discussion of the author's tone allows you to analyze specific word choices and contextualize the persuasive elements used.

Let's look at some examples:

## EXAMPLE 1

When evaluating the long-term impact of hydraulic fracturing, commonly referred to as "fracking," we should not blend knee-jerk anxieties with a smattering of facts. Neither banning a process outright nor allowing unrestricted resource extraction is a sensible plan. We cannot allow the conflicting desires of economy and ecology to wage war against the realities of statistics and specific data.

Circle all the words that describe the tone of the passage:

| | | | |
|---|---|---|---|
| Objective | Impassioned | Empathetic | Analytical |
| Measured | Confrontational | Decisive | Emotional |

The author wants to evaluate both sides and reach a consensus between "economy and ecology," which would be best described as **Analytical** and **Measured**. The author also makes definitive statements about what cannot be done, and uses strong language like "knee-jerk anxieties" and "wage war." These words create an **Impassioned** and **Decisive** tone.

## EXAMPLE 2

Imagine the majesty of the Northern California redwood forests. Visualize the sunlight peeking in between the towering sequoias. Inhale the crisp scent of pine needles. This is a timeless experience that needs to be treasured and curated. Now, think about your own time on this earth, and then imagine how much time a sequoia has experienced. To think that humans can happily chop down a thousand year old tree for some lumber is the most tragic manifestation of shortsightedness.

Circle all the words that describe the tone of the passage:

| | | | |
|---|---|---|---|
| Objective | Impassioned | Empathetic | Analytical |
| Measured | Confrontational | Decisive | Emotional |

This author wants you to feel the same way she does, asking you to imagine and feel the scenery. This pull on emotions creates an **Impassioned**, **Empathetic**, and **Emotional** tone.

## Using Quotes Effectively: Keep 'em short!

The graders know you can pad out a paper with lengthy quotes, so an effective response will use quotes to further and support the analysis. They expect you to back up quotes from the essay with some sweet interpretations. **You must always offer your analysis of any quote you use!**

For example, instead of writing this:

In the essay, the author states "that 80% of deciduous trees in Northwestern Idaho have a parasitic infection," which is true.

You could offer this analysis:

When the author states "that 80% of deciduous trees in Northwestern Idaho have a parasitic infection," she backs up her previous concerns with a statistic that helps the reader to envision the scope of the epidemic.

839

## TIP

Never quote entire sentences! Instead, combine short quotes with your own paraphrases. You can usually narrow down the meat of the quote to a few words.

Instead of this:

> When the author says, "that humans can happily chop down a thousand year old tree for some lumber is the most tragic manifestation of shortsightedness," it shows that the author dislikes cutting down trees.

You could write:

> The author uses the sense of time to persuade the reader; for example, when he states that cutting down a redwood tree, "is the most tragic manifestation of shortsightedness." The author needs for the reader to ponder the long term consequences of logging, so using the word "shortsightedness" frames the discussion in a larger, and longer, conversation.

Anyone can string together a series of quotes, so make sure that you give appropriate context and analysis for your quotes.

## Here's how to maximize your analysis score!

- **Specifically describe the author's devices and tone**
  A great way to show mastery of the essay is to label the devices that the author uses. This shows a deep understanding of the rhetoric of writing and will help frame your analysis.

- **Explain every quote used in your paper**
  Any quote you use needs to explained. Quotes from the passage must be integral to your analysis.

- **Explain rather than rephrase**
  The graders are on the lookout for the student who just rewrites the given essay. Make sure the grader knows that you not only comprehend the author's argument, but also understand how the author persuades the reader.

# Writing Score

*Is your essay organized, with interesting vocab and varied sentence structures?*

## Organization

The easiest way to improve your writing score is to organize your essay. You need a **clear introduction** that presents both the topic and the author's opinion. Each **body paragraph** should be focused on a specific part of the passage, which could be a specific quote, paragraph, or persuasive device. Finally, you will need a **conclusion** that will tie all your paragraphs together.

## Introduction

The graders like the first paragraph in your response to address the author's topic before digging into the thesis. A strong introduction will not jump right into this thesis, but rather will **start with the broad picture**, **then focus in on the author's point**. Let's look at an author's thesis and a possible introduction:

### EXAMPLE 1

The government needs to enact stronger restrictions on logging in the Pacific Northwest in order to protect a variety of endangered bird species.

*There is great disagreement about how the United States uses its natural resources. Society needs raw materials to sustain and grow, yet we all acknowledge that irreversible damage to ecosystems should be avoided. The author takes a clear stance on the side of ecology, but limits his scope to the timber-rich forests of the Pacific Northwest. Through the use of metaphors, personal narrative, and governmental agency provided statistics, the author argues that logging restrictions are necessary to maintain avian diversity in the Pacific Northwest.*

**Q1** **What makes this an effective introduction?**

## Breaking down an effective introduction

Let's look at what this response does that sets it up for success. The first two sentences **address the big picture**: industry versus environment.

> *There is great disagreement about how the United States uses its natural resources. Society needs raw materials to sustain and grow, yet we all acknowledge that irreversible damage to ecosystems should be avoided.*

Next, it **shifts** from a broad concern to the narrow focus of the author.

> *The author takes a clear stance on the side of ecology, but limits his scope to the timber-rich forests of the Pacific Northwest.*

The final sentence addresses the author's thesis and also lists the devices the author uses.

> *Through the use of metaphors, personal narrative, and governmental agency provided statistics, the author argues that logging restrictions are necessary to maintain avian diversity in the Pacific Northwest.*

After reading this introduction, the graders know what the student response will analyze in the body paragraphs: metaphors, personal narrative, and statistics. This makes it *much* easier for the graders to see they have a well-organized essay on their hands!

**TIP**

Your English teacher may call this a **three-prong thesis**, as it include three specific examples. This format will work great for the SAT Essay.

## Body Paragraphs

The body paragraphs will need to be specific to your passage, so there is not one template that will work every time. If the author has a different focus in each paragraph, then you could analyze one topic at a time. If the author uses several persuasive devices again and again, then you could write one paragraph per device.

Whichever organization you choose, each paragraph should:

- Use short quotes and rephrasing to highlight a persuasive element

- Explain how the element supports the author's main argument

- Explain the effect of the element on the reader

Let's look at a sample body paragraph one sentence at a time:

> Your first sentence **transitions** smoothly from the previous paragraph and **establishes the topic** of the new paragraph. Each body sentence **gives evidence** for your analysis. You may **quote** a point made by the author or describe a specific device used. The **concluding sentence** should relate evidence back to your **thesis**.

## Conclusion

Your conclusion must be a separate paragraph that sums up your essay. Any essay without a conclusion will automatically lose points for being incomplete. Your conclusion should **restate your thesis** and **summarize the main points** of your body paragraphs.

### Here's how to maximize your writing score!

- **Organize your essay!**
  Make sure that you have an introduction, body paragraphs, and a conclusion.

- **Address the topic first, then the author's opinion.**
  Your introduction should state the overarching topic and then use that discussion to frame the author's argument.

- **Use effective language.**
  Avoid first person sentence and vague pronouns. Use specific vocabulary and complex sentences to express your analysis.

# Tips for effective writing

Here are some tips that to help you pick the right words for your paper.

- **Avoid first person.** The reason you should avoid a first person perspective (sentences with I as the subject) is that your focus should be on the author's point of view, not your perception of the issue. Remember that the graders do not want to read your opinion on the topic; you need to stick to what the author does in his or her essay. The easiest way to stay on task in your response is to avoid first person sentences.

- **Use precise language**. It's easy to fall into a trap of using vague words and familiar phrases. Instead of writing "he is worried about its impact," try writing "Dr. Acula expresses concern about the spread of garlic in American cuisine, as exposure to garlic can negatively affect citizens that share his background."

- **Use a variety of sentences.** Reading short, choppy sentences becomes tiring. Try to diversify your writing style by creating complex sentences that develop and distinguish your ideas. Here are some ways to vary your sentences beyond the same old "Subject predicate object" song-and-dance.

# Practice varying your sentence structure

A **semicolon** can spice up your writing by changing its rhythm; just remember that a semicolon must connect two independent clauses.

In the front of a sentence, a **prepositional phrase** can add context before the reader discovers the subject of the sentence

The **appositive**—a description of the subject offset by commas or hyphens—can allow the writer to add valuable detail within a sentence.

**Write a sentence** that uses a **semicolon**:

**Write a sentence** that starts with a **prepositional phrase**:

**Write a sentence** that uses an **appositive**:

# Essay Walkthrough

*In this chapter, you'll practice actively reading an argument and then test your understanding by grading some sample essays.*

........................................................................

## Let's see our essay strategy in action

On the next page, we'll get a chance to read a passage and work through our straegy step-by-step. Remember: our core strategy has three phases: read, plan, and write.

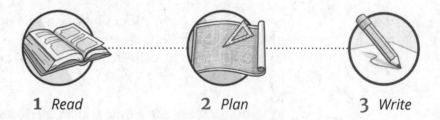

**1** *Read*  **2** *Plan*  **3** *Write*

We'll walk through each step together, keeping in mind the ways we can maximize our reading, analysis, and writing score.

## Remember timing

We will have a chance to practice our timing on some practice essays later, but here's a quick review of our strategy and timing:

| Read | Skip to the the **instructions**, then **actively read** the passage. | 10 minutes |
|------|------|------|
| **Plan** | Review your **notes** | 1 minute |
| | Look for **themes** or **recurring examples** | 4 minutes |
| | Find **effective quotes** | 4 minutes |
| | Organize your **evidence** | 1 minute |
| **Write** | **Write** the essay | 30 minutes |

## *Actively read (~10 minutes on the test)*

Be sure to **skip to the instructions** at the end of the passage. Once you know your mission, go back and **actively read** the passage.

---

As you read the passage below, consider how Nigel Winterbottom uses

- evidence, such as facts or examples, to support claims.
- reasoning to develop ideas and to connect claims and evidence.
- stylistic or persuasive elements, such as word choice or appeals to emotion, to add power to the ideas expressed.

---

**Adapted from Dr. Nigel Winterbottom, "Writing through the ages."**
**© 2015 by Ermahgerd College.**

1   In many ways, we live in an astounding age where our ability to communicate seems endless. With a few taps and swipes, we can send our thoughts across the world, delivered to millions, if not billions, of people in the blink of the eye.

2   It would seem that we live in a time that has perfected communication, but perhaps we have traded ease for quality. Are our "tweets," "e-mails," "texts," and "posts" better than the writings from earlier generations? To answer that question, we should look at the differences in how we write. In the past, letters from family and friends would be cherished; hours would be spent organizing ideas and selecting words. Writers placed emphasis on the quality of calligraphy and saw their handwriting as a means of artistic expression. Depending on the physical distance, a letter could take months to arrive, so a writer had to focus on what was important, not just an immediate reaction to the current situation. Writing letters also had a tangible cost in terms of postage and materials, especially before the advent of mass-produced paper and refillable pens. The end result was a body of writing significantly more impactful than a misspelled, acronym-heavy text message.

3   Beyond informal writings between individuals, there was also a shift in published work. Around 1500, book publishing in Europe took a great leap forward with the advent of the printing press. Previously, books were transcribed by hand; with the printing press, another key role in the publishing world, the editor, came into prominence. Before a page could be published, someone would need to overlook the writer's work and check for possible errors. The editor would eventually serve an essential role of revision before the author's ideas could reach the public. The relationship between the writer and editor can be paramount to the success of the book. John Green, author of many popular young-adult novels including *The Fault*

*in Our Stars*, readily acknowledges the impact his editor, Julie Strauss-Gabel, has on his writing, going as far as to say, "I've never written a book without Julie. I wouldn't know how to do it." Now, thanks to the immediacy of blogs and print-on-demand publishers, many authors can circumvent the keen eye of the editor and inflict their half-baked creations on the world. Writing should not be a transcript of our thoughts, but rather a perfection of our ideas, and oftentimes, the sage wisdom of a seasoned editor is needed to help trim the gristle.

4 Some may say that we are in the golden age of literacy. Indeed, a study of nationwide literacy rates conducted by the National Assessment of Education Sciences shows a marked increase in literacy over the last 100 years with only 0.06% of the adult population categorized as "functionally illiterate." While I applaud the progress, I am often appalled at the execution. According to Pew Research Center, 28% of American adults do not read a single book in a year, and it shows in their writing. Today's society demands literacy for gainful, sustained employment, but the same society undervalues literary depth. A "bookworm" continues to be a derisive term and the "Internet," which once mandated literacy for its use has gradually chipped away at the need for literacy. As the Internet has evolved, it has pushed away from writing to other modes of communication. Blogs and forums have made way for photo and video sharing services. Perhaps most telling is the rise in popularity of "emojis," icons used to represent concepts. These are more similar to hieroglyphics than English composition and reflect a complete break from the mechanics of sentences. While emojis can capture a simple emotion and events, they cannot express complex ideas. Is there an emoji capable of expressing ambivalence?

5 Certainly we cannot collectively shelve our computers and phones to take up the quill and inkpot of our forefathers, because at best it would merely be a defiant act of nostalgia. A better approach is to embrace the writing acumen of our ancestors and continue to write works of quality and insight regardless of the medium. Then, we can use our current interconnectivity to its maximum effect.

---

Write an essay in which you explain how Nigel Winterbottom builds an argument to persuade his audience that we should be concerned about the contemporary quality of writing. In your essay, analyze how Winterbottom uses one or more of the features listed in the box above (or features of your own choice) to strengthen the logic and persuasiveness of his argument. Be sure that your analysis focuses on the most relevant features of the passage.

Your essay should not explain whether you agree with Winterbottom's claims, but rather explain how Winterbottom builds an argument to persuade his audience.

# Active Reading Example

> Write an essay in which you explain how Nigel Winterbottom builds an argument to persuade his audience that **we should be concerned about the contemporary quality of writing.** In your essay, analyze how Winterbottom uses one or more of the features listed in the box above (or features of your own choice) to strengthen the logic and persuasiveness of his argument. Be sure that your analysis focuses on the most relevant features of the passage.
>
> Your essay should not explain whether you agree with Winterbottom's claims, but rather explain how Winterbottom builds an argument to persuade his audience.

*counter argument*

1   In many ways, we live in an <u>astounding age</u> where <u>our ability to communicate seems endless.</u> With a few taps and swipes, <u>we can send our thoughts across the world</u>, delivered to millions, if not billions, of people in the blink of the eye.

*rhetorical question*

  2   It would seem that we live in a time that has perfected communication, (but) perhaps <u>we have traded ease for quality.</u> Are our "tweets," "e-mails," "texts," and "posts" better than the writings from earlier generations? To answer that question, <u>we should look at the differences in how we write.</u> In the past, <u>letters from family and friends would be cherished</u>; hours would be spent organizing ideas and selecting words. <u>Writers placed emphasis on the quality of calligraphy</u> and saw their handwriting as a means of artistic expression. Depending on the physical distance, a letter could take months to arrive, so a writer had to focus on what was important, not just an immediate reaction to the current situation. <u>Writing letters also had a tangible cost</u> in terms of postage and materials, especially before the advent of mass-produced paper and refillable pens. The end result was a <u>body of writing significantly more impactful</u> than a misspelled, acronym-heavy text message.

*juxtaposition between then and now*

*transition to new topic*

3   Beyond informal writings between individuals, <u>there was also a shift in published work.</u> Around 1500, book publishing in Europe took a great leap forward with the advent of the printing press. Previously, <u>books were transcribed by hand</u>; with the printing press, another key role in the publishing world, <u>the editor, came into prominence.</u> Before a page could be published, someone would need to overlook the writer's work and check

*historical reference*

848

for possible errors. The editor would eventually serve an essential role of revision before the author's ideas could reach the public. The relationship between the writer and editor can be paramount to the success of the book.

*juxtaposition* — John Green, author of many popular young-adult novels including *The Fault in Our Stars*, readily acknowledges the impact his editor, Julie Strauss-Gabel, has on his writing, going as far as to say, "I've never written a book

*quote from an expert* — without Julie. I wouldn't know how to do it." Now, thanks to the immediacy of blogs and print-on-demand publishers, many authors can circumvent the

*synecdoche* — keen eye of the editor and inflict their half-baked creations on the world. *metaphor* Writing should not be a transcript of our thoughts, but rather a perfection of our ideas, and oftentimes, the sage wisdom of a seasoned editor is needed to help trim the gristle. *metaphor*

*counter argument*

4  Some may say that we are in the golden age of literacy. Indeed, a study of nationwide literacy rates conducted by the National Assessment of Education Sciences shows a marked increase in literacy over the last 100 years with only 0.06% of the adult population categorized as

*empirical counter-evidence* — "functionally illiterate." While I applaud the progress, I am often appalled at the execution. According to Pew Research Center, 28% of American

*empirical evidence* — adults do not read a single book in a year, and it shows in their writing. Today's society demands literacy for gainful, sustained employment, but the same society undervalues literary depth. A "bookworm" continues to be a derisive term and the "Internet," which once mandated literacy for its use has gradually chipped away at the need for literacy. As the Internet has evolved, it has pushed away from writing to other modes of communication. Blogs and forums have made way for photo and video sharing services. Perhaps most telling is the rise in popularity of "emojis," icons used to represent concepts. These are more similar to hieroglyphics

*juxtaposition* — than English composition and reflect a complete break from the mechanics of sentences. While emojis can capture a simple emotion and events, they cannot express complex ideas. Is there an emoji capable of expressing ambivalence?

5  Certainly we cannot collectively shelve our computers and phones to take up the quill and inkpot of our forefathers, because at best it would merely be a defiant act of nostalgia. A better approach is to embrace the writing acumen of our ancestors and continue to write works of quality and insight

regardless of the medium. Then, we can use our current interconnectivity to its maximum effect.

## Plan (~10 minutes on the test)

After **reviewing your notes,** looking for **recurring themes,** finding effective **quotes,** and **organizing your evidence,** write down an outline for your intro, body, and concluding paragraphs.

---

### Introduction

- The **topic**: how writing has changed because of technology
- The author's **position**: writing has gotten easier to create and publish, but not necessarily better
- How the author **persuades** the reader: juxtaposition, counter argument, word choice, and historical evidence

### Body Paragraphs

- Paragraph 1: (topic for paragraph + helpful quote)
- Paragraph 2: (topic for paragraph + helpful quote)
- Paragraph 3: (topic for paragraph + helpful quote)

### Conclusion – *State your second example in a sentence*

- Restate thesis and connect back to cited evidence

---

## Write (~30 minutes on the test)

Let's take some time to evaluate some responses to Dr. Winterbottom's essay. On the next few pages, you'll find 4 students' responses to the passage. Give the responses scores in all 3 categories:

**READING:** Does the essay explain the author's argument?

**ANALYSIS:** Does the essay analyze the author's persuasiveness?

**WRITING:** Is the essay well-organized and well-written?

## EXAMPLE 1

I think the author does not like most writing. He says "It would seem that we live in a time that has perfected communication, but perhaps we have traded ease for quality." Writing is pretty easy write now as I can just have my phone write up what I say. I think the author likes old books, because he used printting presses and John Green, I haven't read John Green book, so I don't know if they are any good.

The author picks on emojis, which is kinda funny. I like to use emojis in texts but some times I confuse my mom. I guess the author and my mom are kinda the same. He says that emojis are "similar to hieroglyphics" which I sorta guess is true.

The passage ends with saying "A better approach is to embrace the writing acumen of our ancestors and continue to write works of quality and insight regardless of the medium. Then, we can use our current interconnectivity to its maximum effect." I thought that this was a good ending and persuaded the audience.

How would you score this essay?

Reading (from 1 to 4) _____

Analysis (from 1 to 4) _____

Writing (from 1 to 4) _____

This response misses the main point of the author's argument: the quality of writing today is in trouble. It almost gets close at one point ("Writing is pretty easy right now", "the author likes old books") but then veers away again. The response also misses the point of the supporting examples dealing with John Green and emojis. We'd give it a **reading score** of 1 out of 4.

The essay includes quotes but doesn't connect them to a main thesis. We'd give it an **analysis score** of 1 out of 4.

No thesis, no body paragraphs, no organization! There are several run-on sentences and the language is too casual. The passage has common spelling and grammatical mistakes that confuse the meaning. We' give it a **writing score** of 1 out of 4.

# Compare the next two essays

Read examples 2 and 3 below, then assign scores to each one before reading how we'd score them on the next page.

## EXAMPLE 2

Dr. Winterbottom is concerned with the current quality of writing. He feels that writing has gotten easier but not better. To persuade his audience, Dr. Winterbottom uses a lot of different examples to show how writing has changed, but not necessarily for the better.

The essay begins by Winterbottom discussing the progress made in creating and publishing writing, which some call "an astounding age." However, the second paragraph reveals that Winterbottom disagrees, saying that "we have traded ease for quality." He then uses some historical examples to show how much care was placed on writing earlier. He emphasizes the quality, craftsmanship, and expense that went into writing a letter long ago.

The next paragraph discusses published writing and brings up the idea that an editor is useful to make better writing. Here, Winterbottom uses a quote to show how a successful writer relies on an editor.

In the next paragraph, Winterbottom thinks about whether we are more or less literate. He uses some data to show that literacy rates are high but responds by saying "while I applaud the progress, I am often appalled at the execution," mentioning that 28% of American adults didn't read a book last year. He is concerned that we are writing simpler and simpler and using emojis the same way the Egyptians used hieroglyphics. While this works for simple ideas, like happiness, emojis cannot show complex emotions. The essay ends by not suggesting that we abandon technology, but use it to "write works of quality and insight regardless of the medium."

How would you score this essay?

Reading (from 1 to 4) _____

Analysis (from 1 to 4) _____

Writing (from 1 to 4) _____

## EXAMPLE 3

Throughout the passage, we can see that author, Nigel Winterbottom, has a concern with the quality of contemporary writing. Winterbottom uses historical juxtaposition, contemporary evidence, and word choice to persuade the audience to agree with him that writing used to mean more, that we ignore the importance of editing, and we are moving away from written communication.

Winterbottom first starts with the counter-argument before offering his own opinion that "we have traded ease for quality." He then juxtaposes older forms of writing that required more skill and effort. Winterbottom clearly prefers these writings, opposed to current emails and texts. He emphasizes this slide in quality by referring to them as "misspelled, acronym-heavy text message" as opposed to a letter from long ago written in calligraphy.

Winterbottom's next key point is how important the editor is towards creating quality writing. Again, he starts with a historical juxtaposition, but this time he refers to the early era of the printing press. He shows how important editing is now by including a quote by John Green, who attributes much of his literary success to his editor Julie Strauss-Gabel. Unfortunately for Winterbottom, most writers now do not use an editor, thanks to the ease of online publishing. Winterbottom concludes this paragraph by offering his insight that "writing should not be a transcript of our thoughts, but rather a perfection of our ideas," which nicely sums up his belief that the quality of writing is important.

Winterbottom's third point relates directly to literacy and its perceived decline. He uses contemporary evidence, in terms of overall literacy rates, but then finds fault in this study by cleverly stating " while I applaud the progress, I am often appalled at the execution," as 28% of Americans didn't read a book last year. This line nicely shows how Winterbottom is concerned with the quality of writing, rather than a simple definition of literate versus illiterate. He argues that we are experiencing a lapse in quality as emojis take over written communication. Winterbottom specifically uses the word "ambivalence," the state of mixed emotions, to show how limiting emojis can be.

Winterbottom's persuasive passage used enough juxtaposition, evidence, and careful word choice to not only make readers to evaluate the current state of writing, but also provoke readers to take action to make sure that their own writing works to counteract this trend.

How would you score this essay?

Reading (from 1 to 4) _____

Analysis (from 1 to 4) _____

Writing (from 1 to 4) _____

**Example 2 Scores**

The essay focuses on the author's main argument and identifies supporting details, but either misinterprets the significance of those details (emoji/hieroglyphic link) or fails to connect them to the larger point (yes, letters were expensive, but what did that lead to?). It includes a few brief quotes, but they are not integrated very effectively. We'd give it a **reading** score of 2.

The response does not address the main task of the assignment: analyzing the argument. It spends most of the time restating the author's argument rather than analyzing literary and rhetorical elements used in the essay. We'd give it an **analysis** score of 1.

The essay states a thesis in a brief and effective introduction and few grammar/syntax errors. However, it lacks a conclusion and uses mainly basic sentence structures. We'd give it a **writing** score of 2.

**Example 3 Scores**

The response effectively summarizes both the author's main point and the ways it is supported throughout the essay. It effectively uses quotes and direct references to support interpretation of the author's opinions. We'd give it a **reading** score of 4.

The response lists several literary elements used by the author and begins to describe how they are used, but strays somewhere in the middle and begins recapping the argument rather than analyzing it. The third point in the thesis (word choice) is never addressed in the body paragraphs. We'd give it an **analysis** score of 3.

There are a few grammatical errors, but the essay does use some complex sentence structures. The thesis is clear and the paragraphs are fairly well-organized. The writing is straightforward and easy to understand. We'd give it a **writing** score of 3.

## EXAMPLE 4

Writing will continually evolve from generation to generation as words and grammatical conventions fall out of favor. Dr. Nigel Winterbottom understands this, but he shows great concern towards the direction current writing has gone. Winterbottom not only persuades his audience that writing is heading towards decline, but he also valiantly fights against this trend with skillful refutation of counter arguments, expert language choices, and historical juxtapositions.

Winterbottom uses a counter argument to introduce the essay, offering a positive account of our "astounding age" and our ability to create and share information. Yet, Winterbottom then asks if our fast-paced " 'tweets,' 'e-mails,' 'texts,' and 'posts' " are better than the laborious writing process of history. He juxtaposes the present writing style of "misspelled, acronym-heavy texts" with the past's "emphasis on the quality" of writing. This stark contrast forces the reader to consider whether this contemporary writing style has lost that emphasis on quality in the pursuit of convenience. This juxtaposition is essential to Winterbottom's argument, since he wants to prescribe a course of action, "to embrace the writing acumen of our ancestors and continue to write works of quality and insight," without coming across as stodgy and off-puttingly retro.

In the third paragraph, Winterbottom extends his use of historical juxtaposition, this time comparing the editors of early printed materials to the editor-less blogs and forums of today. Winterbottom then chooses to quote an expert, the author John Green, to support the assertion that the editor offers "an essential role of revision" that is missing in much of today's writing. By using a popular author that many in his audience would know, Winterbottom builds the reader's confidence in his assertions. Had he chosen a more pretentious writer, the quote would be less effective and would reinforce the fallacy that Winterbottom wishes for writers to return to the "quill and the inkpot."

Winterbottom continues to use counter argument to persuade the audience that the current state of writing is troubling. In the fourth paragraph, Winterbottom references the fact that 0.06% of adults are "functionally illiterate." He then quickly reframes the argument, pointing out the empirical evidence that annually, 28% of American adults "do not read a single book." This counter argument shows that the illiteracy rate may be low, but that data point cannot express the depth of literacy that Winterbottom feels is becoming lost. Winterbottom then returns to a historical juxtaposition, but delves deeper into the past, alluding to ancient Egyptian hieroglyphics as a precursor to today's emojis. Winterbottom chooses one word, "ambivalence," to describe an emotion that cannot be expressed with a cartoon-faced emoji. His word choice is excellent, because ambivalence expresses his feelings about the current state of writing. He solidifies this opinion in the final paragraph by arguing we should not "shelve our computers," but instead "write works of quality and insight regardless of the medium." Despite all of the dire proclamations, Winterbottom believes we are still capable of great writing; the conclusion leaves the reader feeling hopeful and inspired, rather than wallowing in negativity.

As a whole, Winterbottom's essay accomplishes an impressive feat: it addresses the current lackluster quality of writing while also being an example of clever and precise writing. Winterbottom leads us through centuries of writing, yet never lets us get lost along the way so that by the end, the audience is inspired to continue the tradition of excellent writing.

How would you score this essay?

Reading (from 1 to 4) _____

Analysis (from 1 to 4) _____

Writing (from 1 to 4) _____

**SOLUTION**

The response grasps not only the author's main point, but also the more subtle elements of it. All quotes and examples are given with correct interpretation of the author's intentions and are directly connected to the structure of the larger argument.

The response gives not only concrete elements of rhetorical technique, but also more abstract and subtextual dynamics used by the author to persuade readers. It also addresses the effect of those elements on the reader.

There are very few errors and the essay presents everything in a fluent style, with a complexity of structure at both the sentence and paragraph levels. The response has a clear and logical organization supporting a strong thesis.

We'd give it a perfect score: 4's across the board.

# Practice Essays

*Now it's your turn! Practice writing your own essays with the given prompts.*

## Practice Makes Perfect

Over the next several pages, you will have the opportunity to write 4 practice essays. Each essay will be based on a passage modeled after those on the official test.

If possible, space out your practice; put at least a day or two between essays. This will give you time to reread your own essay with a critical eye and make plans for improvement. If you can, get feedback from others on your essay.

## Focus on Improvement

As you work your way through this section, make sure you're practicing the key skills that we've covered so far. Time yourself, using the table below to make sure you're moving through each step at the right pace.

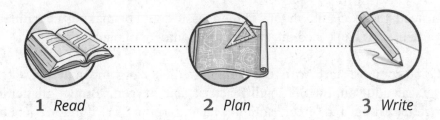

**1** *Read*　　　**2** *Plan*　　　**3** *Write*

| Read | Skip to the the **instructions**, then **actively read** the passage**.** | 10 minutes |
|---|---|---|
| **Plan** | Review your **notes** | 1 minute |
| | Look for **themes** or **recurring examples** | 4 minutes |
| | Find **effective quotes** | 4 minutes |
| | Organize your **evidence** | 1 minute |
| **Write** | **Write** the essay | 30 minutes |

As you read the passage below, consider how Mercedes Breckenridge uses

- evidence, such as facts or examples, to support claims.

- reasoning to develop ideas and to connect claims and evidence.

- stylistic or persuasive elements, such as word choice or appeals to emotion, to add power to the ideas expressed.

**Adapted from Mercedes Breckenridge, "Composting: Turning Garbage into Gold."**

1   As every gardener knows, nothing compares to a loamy shovelful of rich, dark soil, loaded with nutrients and teeming with fat, happy earthworms. And the best way to achieve this sublime soil? A heaping layer of decaying organic matter, also known as compost. While dumping fertilizers might offer fast short-term results, in the long term there's no substitute for compost.

2   To many, the art of composting seems counterintuitive, and perhaps even a bit off-putting. Why would someone want to collect a lot of smelly garbage? (A healthy compost pile thrives on organic matter as eclectic as used coffee grounds and broken egg shells, rotting banana peels and old scraps of lettuce, and grass clippings from the freshly mowed lawn.) It's certainly *easier* to just throw all that away.

3   But turning too quickly to the trash service has negative effects. The Environmental Protection Agency reports that food scraps represent 20 to 30 percent of Americans' trash. in 2012, that equaled approximately 35 million tons of food waste—the majority of it headed straight to a landfill. And landfills may be the single largest emitters of toxic methane gas, a major culprit behind harmful climate change.

4   Instead, those 35 million tons of food waste could be making a big difference to your garden, your bank account, and the environment of planet Earth.

5   Good compost starts with four main ingredients: organic material, water (rain will do, or you can add your own), friendly bacteria, and oxygen. "Brown" matter like dead leaves is rich in carbon, and "green" stuff like lawn clippings is rich in nitrogen; both are essential elements in healthy soil, and should be balanced one to one. Meanwhile, the bacteria and oxygen work together to process and decompose the material into compost.

6   Along with carbon and nitrogen, the finished compost is filled with recycled nutrients— the essential minerals like phosphorous and potassium that all help green stuff thrive. Plants grown in nutrient-rich soil don't just grow faster and healthier; they also produce more nutritious fruit and vegetables, bringing a better meal to your plate.

7   Adding compost to the soil also enhances its texture, turning it into a dense, crumbly soil called loam, well-aerated with oxygen pockets and moisture channels. This high-quality soil is called humus, and it's more resistant to soil erosion and better able to retain oxygen, water, and nutrients. In fact, a five percent increase in organic material in the soil

quadruples water retention, which means less watering… a *lot* less watering. That much less watering means a lower water bill, for sure, and is also a big help in areas with water shortages due to dry seasons and droughts. With drought increasing in communities all over the world, this is a big deal.

8   Along with money saved on your water bill, there are other cost benefits too. You won't have to buy commercial fertilizers, and if you pay by volume for trash pick-up, you can also save a lot on your garbage service. Plus, the healthy bacteria and microbes in compost will increase your garden's resistance to disease and pests, increasing crop yield and saving money that might otherwise be spent on pesticides.

9   With all of composting's obvious benefits, a number of beloved celebrities and famous figures are jumping on the bandwagon and spreading the word. Their numbers include Kristen Bell, Julia Roberts (she spoke eloquently on the topic to Oprah, who also composts!), and Jason Mraz, who composts on his own farm. Even the White House has three compost bins!

10   In 2013, the *Washington Post* reported on composting's growing popularity across the nation, writing, "Increasingly, local governments, entrepreneurs, and community activists are experimenting with composting." They cited an impressive 170 composting programs throughout the country, up from twenty just eight years previously. Cutting-edge metropolises like San Francisco and New York City, along with small but forward-thinking towns, are expanding their composting programs and making it easier than ever for residents to turn their old, smelly food scraps into "black gold": valuable compost.

11   Ready to try your own hand at composting? It's shockingly easy. All you need to begin is a large bucket with a tightly closing lid, or better yet, a bin positioned in a sunny spot in the yard. Add leftover food scraps (vegetarian preferred) and yard clippings like grass and leaves. When the stuff is well-decomposed, spread on a garden plot, add to landscaping, or scoop into indoor plants like flowers and herbs. Voila: you're a smart gardener—and a steward of planet Earth.

---

Write an essay in which you explain how Mercedes Breckenridge builds an argument to persuade her audience that they should start composting. In your essay, analyze how Breckenridge uses one or more of the features listed in the box above (or features of your own choice) to strengthen the logic and persuasiveness of her argument. Be sure that your analysis focuses on the most relevant features of the passage.

Your essay should not explain whether you agree with Breckenridge's claims, but rather explain how Breckenridge builds an argument to persuade her audience.

**IMPORTANT:** **DON'T WRITE OUTSIDE THE BORDER.**

**PLANNING PAGE** You may plan your essay in the unlined planning space below, but use only the lined pages following this one to write your essay. Any work on this planning page will not be scored.

Use next 4 pages for your ESSAY ⟶

**DO NOT WRITE OUTSIDE OF THE BOX.**

You may continue on the next page.

**DO NOT WRITE OUTSIDE OF THE BOX.**

You may continue on the next page.

**DO NOT WRITE OUTSIDE OF THE BOX.**

**DO NOT WRITE OUTSIDE OF THE BOX.**

**STOP**

As you read the passage below, consider how Stewart Topor uses

- evidence, such as facts or examples, to support claims.
- reasoning to develop ideas and to connect claims and evidence.
- stylistic or persuasive elements, such as word choice or appeals to emotion, to add power to the ideas expressed.

**Adapted from Stewart Topor, "Stop buying into the 'busyness' narrative, and start using the time you have."**

1 We've all heard the news: Americans are busier than ever, perhaps the busiest people in human history. We're over-scheduled, over-booked and overworked, spending every waking hour rushing from appointment to appointment, rarely getting a moment's peace or a full night's sleep. Ask a friend how they're doing lately, and the typical answer is: "Busy." Or occasionally, "Slammed." Sometimes, "Everything's crazy over here."

2 The narrative that Americans are overwhelmingly busy has taken hold as unassailable fact. But is it actually true? The answer may surprise you.

3 Since 1961, the University of Oxford's Centre for Time Use Research has been conducting extensive, detailed research into how people spend their time. This research is collected via time-use diaries—which are exactly what they sound like. Participants log their activities from day to day, hour to hour. These time-use diaries have been gathered in nearly 40 countries over the course of 50 years, and represent around 850,000 days logged.

4 Sociologist and time-use scholar John Robinson has worked extensively with these diaries. Robinson says that, while people report extreme busyness, the numbers don't really add up. Despite the widely accepted narrative that we're busier than ever before, the average number of work hours per week has not actually gone up significantly since the 1980s.

5 This conclusion is supported by the US Bureau of Labor Statistics, which gathers data on how Americans spend their time. According to the 2014 American Time Use Survey numbers, employed people logged an average of 7.8 hours per workday—a manageable 39 hours per work week, nothing like the excessive fifty-, sixty-, or eighty-hour workweeks so often claimed. On an average day, 96 percent of people found time for leisure activities like watching TV, playing a sport, or hanging with friends. In fact, the average leisure time was a generous 5.3 hours a day. And participants slept an average of 8.8 hours a night, a perfectly healthy amount.

6 The unavoidable conclusion is that people are prone to exaggerating the number of hours they work, and underestimating the amount of sleep they get or time they have to relax. Perhaps this is due to a negative cognitive bias: people are more likely to remember the bad days over the good, emphasizing the sleepless night rather than the restful one, and

the long, harried day at the office rather than the Friday they left early. They're more likely to think of an overworked Wednesday than a lazy Sunday as "a typical day," even though both days happen only once a week. Another factor is the desire people have to *seem* busy, with its connotations of being hard-working, ambitious, high-impact, and perhaps irreplaceable. In today's tough economy, that impulse makes sense; the best way to secure your spot in your workplace is to give the impression that you're doing the work of two individuals, perhaps three. On the other hand, someone who never seems overworked might be the first to get a pink slip if layoffs arrive.

7   Whatever the cause, time-use diaries show that the hyperbole around work hours is quantifiable. The average person overstates their working hours by five to ten percent. And the people who claim to work the most exaggerate the most; instead of being the hardest workers, they're the biggest fibbers. People who thought they worked 75 hours a week overestimated by as much as 50 percent. "One study tracking people's estimated and actual workweeks found that those claiming to work 70, 80 or more hours were logging less than 60," writes time-use expert Laura Vanderkam in the *Wall Street Journal*.

8   A successful author, Vanderkam has published several books exploring the discrepancy between the hours we have and the hours we *think* we have. She argues that we have a lot more time than we think; we just need to take advantage of it. Her conviction grew out of her own experience. In that same 2012 *Wall Street Journal* article, she writes, "What I thought was a 60-hour workweek wasn't even close." After keeping a time diary, she began to understand where her time really went — and put it to much better use.

9   These findings suggest that as much as anything else, "busyness" is a state of mind. We have more time than we think we do, and acknowledging that fact can enable us to lead more enjoyable lives, with less stress and greater focus. So next time you're tempted to lament how busy you are, take a step back. Instead, focus on all the time you do have — and figure out how you can better use those hours in a way that's productive and fulfilling.

---

Write an essay in which you explain how Stewart Topor builds an argument to persuade his audience that people are less busy than they realize. In your essay, analyze how Topor uses one or more of the features listed in the box above (or features of your own choice) to strengthen the logic and persuasiveness of his argument. Be sure that your analysis focuses on the most relevant features of the passage.

Your essay should not explain whether you agree with Topor's claims, but rather explain how Topor builds an argument to persuade his audience.

**IMPORTANT:** **DON'T WRITE OUTSIDE THE BORDER.**

**PLANNING PAGE** You may plan your essay in the unlined planning space below, but use only the lined pages following this one to write your essay. Any work on this planning page will not be scored.

**Use next 4 pages for your ESSAY** ⟶

**BEGIN YOUR ESSAY HERE.**

You may continue on the next page.

**DO NOT WRITE OUTSIDE OF THE BOX.**

You may continue on the next page.

**DO NOT WRITE OUTSIDE OF THE BOX.**

You may continue on the next page.

**DO NOT WRITE OUTSIDE OF THE BOX.**

**STOP**

**Adapted from P. W. Curtstein, "Don't Fear Nanotech. Embrace It… and Fund It."**

1  Nanotechnology may represent doomsday in fear-mongering sci-fi thrillers or clickbait-style news headlines. Perhaps it's not surprising; history has shown that humanity often irrationally fears what it doesn't understand, and nanotech is one of the most mind-bending new technologies around. But despite its esoteric nature, nanotech is something that humans will master, not the other way around. And B-rate movies aside, "nanotech gone wild" is no more realistic a threat to human civilization than dinosaur outbreaks or robots from the future. In fact, nanotech offers amazing benefits. Instead of fearing this fascinating technology, we should embrace it.

2  The U.S. government understood this early, and in 2000, began pouring funding into nanotech research and development. Thanks to this support, nanotech has made amazing leaps and bounds in the past fifteen years; according to the federal National Nanotechnology Initiative, 800 products relying on nanoscale elements are already on the market. A few examples: computer chip elements that have helped shrink computers from room-sized giants to pocket-sized smart phones; "hydrophobic" coating on textiles that repels liquids to stop stains; and carbon nanotubes used to add durability to items ranging from tennis rackets to space rockets.

3  Why does nanotech hold such promise?

4  To understand the answer to this question, you must grasp how mind-bogglingly small the nanoscale truly is. There's the microscale, which covers things we call "microscopic": bacteria, viruses, cells. Then, smaller than that, there's the nanoscale. A strand of hair is about 100 thousand nanometers wide. Nanotech elements are typically less than 100 nanometers. So when we talk about nanotech, we're talking about elements about 1/1000 the width of a human hair.

5  When matter is reduced to this scale, it expresses different properties, and undergoes different processes. It can become stronger, lighter, more durable, and better at conducting electrical signals. Things that seem like magic at the human scale become totally feasible at the nanoscale.

6  As a result, nanotechnology represents a new world—with astonishing possibilities on the horizon. For example, a high-speed nanomotor recently designed at the University of Texas at Austin. This motor is 500 times smaller than a grain of salt, and could travel inside the human body to administer insulin or destroy cancer cells.

7   Nanotechnology is already transforming medicine. Doctors can inject nanoparticles into the human body to detect bacteria, viruses, tumors, or the presence of Alzheimer's disease. Nanoparticles can be programmed to deliver a drug payload directly to a single cell, enabling extremely targeted pharmaceutical treatments. Medical advances like these could one day save the life of someone you love... even your own.

8   Another horizon is manufacturing. One recent example is graphene: a material made from a single layer of carbon atoms assembled hexagonally. At one atom wide, it's so thin it's essentially two-dimensional. Graphene is flexible, transparent, and light, but thanks to the unbreakable bonds between carbon atoms, it's also very strong—207 times stronger than steel. A "magic" material like this can revolutionize technological devices from cellphones to solar cells. And it's already under development in next-generation water filtration systems, which will turn salty ocean water into potable fresh water, or remove toxins to make contaminated water safe to drink.

9   Finally, nanotechnology will change computing forever. According to renowned computer scientist Ralph Merkle, "Nanotechnology will let us build computers that are incredibly powerful. We'll have more power in the volume of a sugar cube than exists in the entire world today." Imagine a computer smaller than an ant, and you get the idea. The next step is turning single molecules into processing units.

10  Nanotechnology can work marvels that seem like miracles: curing diseases from inside the body... turning brackish and polluted water into life-giving sustenance on the spot... creating artificial blood cells, bionic implants, and replacement limbs... crafting body armor that's light as cotton but bullet-proof...the list goes on. Jay West, senior director for Chemical Products and Technology at the American Chemistry Council, calls nanotechnology "an enabling science," saying "innovations in nanotechnology are already improving our society in areas such as healthcare, energy efficiency, environmental remediation, and even national security."

11  The naysayers on nanotechnology may not be *completely* wrong: every new technology undoubtedly comes with risks. But new technologies have also improved the world in countless tangible ways. People live longer, healthier lives; many diseases have been eradicated; across the globe, we're better educated, better connected, and better fed than ever been before.

12  Nanotechnology will allow us to continue that trend from the twentieth century into the twenty-first. Support funding for nanotechnology research and development—and support the making of a better world.

---

Write an essay in you explain how P. W. Curtstein builds an argument to persuade her audience that we need to embrace the potential of nanotechnology. In your essay, analyze how Curtstein uses one or more of the features listed in the box above (or features of your own choice) to strengthen the logic and persuasiveness of his argument. Be sure that your analysis focuses on the most relevant features of the passage.

Your essay should not explain whether you agree with Curtstein's claims, but rather explain how Curtstein builds an argument to persuade his audience.

**IMPORTANT:** **DON'T WRITE OUTSIDE THE BORDER.**

**PLANNING PAGE** You may plan your essay in the unlined planning space below, but use only the lined pages following this one to write your essay. Any work on this planning page will not be scored.

Use next 4 pages for your ESSAY ⟶

**BEGIN YOUR ESSAY HERE.**

**DO NOT WRITE OUTSIDE OF THE BOX.**

**DO NOT WRITE OUTSIDE OF THE BOX.**

**DO NOT WRITE OUTSIDE OF THE BOX.**

**STOP**

As you read the passage below, consider how Kurt Stolid uses

- evidence, such as facts or examples, to support claims.
- reasoning to develop ideas and to connect claims and evidence.
- stylistic or persuasive elements, such as word choice or appeals to emotion, to add power to the ideas expressed.

**Adapted from Kurt Stolid, "Brainstorming is Bad for Business. Do This Instead.**

1   Imagine this: you're a team leader, and you've been tasked with generating creative ideas, whether for an innovative product, an inventive marketing campaign, or a resourceful solution to an industry problem. Chances are, your first thought will be to call all your team members to the table for a brainstorming session. But according to innovation experts, you might want to think again.

2   The concept of brainstorming was first advanced in the 1950s by advertising agency executive Alex Osborn. He defined his technique with four key rules: First, generate as many ideas as possible. Second, focus particularly on ideas that are original and off-the-wall. Third, mash-up ideas to combine and refine. Fourth, no criticizing! There are no stupid ideas at the brainstorming table.

3   As the old saying goes, "Two heads are better than one," and Osborn was convinced that his creative employees would perform better as a team.

4   On the surface, it makes sense. "Brainstorming seems like an ideal technique, a feel-good way to boost productivity," Jonah Lehrer wrote in a 2012 *New Yorker* titled "Groupthink." "But there is a problem with brainstorming. It doesn't work."

5   In 2015, Tomas Chamorro-Premuzic advanced a similar view in the *Harvard Business Review*. "After six decades of independent scientific research, there is very little evidence for the idea that brainstorming produces more or better ideas than the same number of individuals would produce working independently. In fact, a great deal of evidence indicates that brainstorming actually harms creative performance."

6   But why? To understand the downsides of brainstorming, let's go back to that hypothetical meeting you've called with your team. You've got a team member—we'll call him Bob—who's popular with the group (he always brings the best donuts). Bob is confident and outgoing, so when the team meets around the table, it's natural for Bob to supply the first idea. It's also natural for everyone else to respond positively… and that can influence the rest of the discussion. But unfortunately, Bob isn't the best creative thinker on the team—he's just the best at arguing for his own ideas.

7   Conversely, your team member Lucy is an extremely creative person. She's a careful, methodical thinker who's great at coming up with state-of-the-art solutions, but she's also shy and introverted, and it takes her a while to formulate her idea to the point where she feels comfortable sharing it with the group. By that point, everyone else around the table is already feeling comfortable with Bob's plan… and Lucy isn't the type to argue passionately for her own position.

8   The problem is clear: Bob isn't actually the best at coming up with ideas, he's merely the best at expressing them.

9   There are a number of group dynamics like this one that hamper the productivity of group brainstorming session. For one thing, the first ideas often predict the rest of the conversation—even though first ideas are typically the least original and most clichéd. For another, discussing ideas in front of a group often creates a "herd mentality"—people feel pressured to go with the flow and conform to the team, so instead of really quirky thoughts getting a chance to thrive, people tend to stick with what's safe and familiar. A third problem: freeloaders. Not everyone wants to do the hard work of generating creative ideas, so some people will inevitably piggyback onto others' contributions. Sometimes, that's not even conscious: hearing someone's idea before you get a chance to formulate your own can curtail your own creative process, and push your thought process in an already-trod direction.

10  So, next time you find yourself working with a group, consider some alternatives to the traditional brainstorming process. Ask the quieter folks in your group to weigh in; don't make them fight to communicate their ideas (which may be stellar!). Rather than outlawing criticism, encourage constructive criticism, which helps get everyone engaged and pushes people beyond the familiarity of the first idea.

11  Or, if you want to shake things up even more, get together to establish your shared goal, and then stage a "break-out session" where each individual comes up with three to five ideas on their own. Then, when you return to the table, each person can take a turn sharing their best idea with the group. An approach like this actually elicits the best creative thinking that each person has to offer—while still taking advantage of the power of collective problem-solving.shortages due to dry seasons and droughts. With drought increasing in communities all over the world, this is a big deal.

---

Write an essay in which you explain how Kurt Stolid builds an argument to persuade his audience that brainstorming does not produce effective results. In your essay, analyze how Stolid uses one or more of the features listed in the box above (or features of your own choice) to strengthen the logic and persuasiveness of his argument. Be sure that your analysis focuses on the most relevant features of the passage.

Your essay should not explain whether you agree with Stolid's claims, but rather explain how Stolid builds an argument to persuade his audience.

**IMPORTANT:** **DON'T WRITE OUTSIDE THE BORDER.**

**PLANNING PAGE** You may plan your essay in the unlined planning space below, but use only the lined pages following this one to write your essay. Any work on this planning page will not be scored.

**Use next 4 pages for your ESSAY** ⟶

**BEGIN YOUR ESSAY HERE.**

You may continue on the next page.

**DO NOT WRITE OUTSIDE OF THE BOX.**

You may continue on the next page.

**DO NOT WRITE OUTSIDE OF THE BOX.**

**STOP**

# BEYOND

## THE

# CONTENT

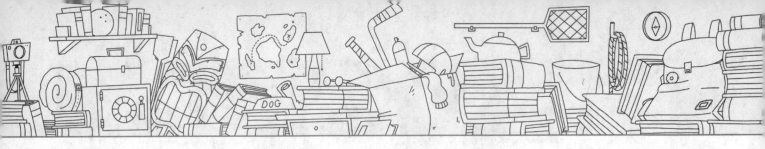

# Believe in Yourself

*Studies show that your level of self-confidence can affect your score.*

## Taking a test is its own skill

To fully prepare for the SAT, you need to accomplish 3 goals:

(1) *Understand the **structure and format** of the SAT*

(2) *Master the **content** assessed on all sections of the test*

(3) *Master **test–taking skills** to thrive in a timed, pressured environment*

The final component, test-taking skills, is the most neglected aspect of test preparation. However, for many students, improving this skill is what will give you the most points. So what are test-taking skills? The first, most important aspect deals with **confidence and beliefs**.

## Beliefs about yourself affect your score

Whether you believe that you are a good test-taker or a bad test-taker, that **belief** will impact your score on the SAT. In fact, self-appraisal of your ability is a better predictor of how you will do on the SAT than your *actual* level of ability! If you repeatedly tell yourself that you are not going to do well on this test, you can override your actual abilities and sabotage your performance. And conversely, if you believe you will succeed on the SAT, this belief will improve your performance. Thoughts are powerful!

You've got this!

## Natural Test-Takers vs. Everybody Else

Some of you may fall under the category of **natural test-takers**. You might even enjoy standardized tests, treating them like a game where you set challenges and work to overcome them. You've likely developed some conscious or subconscious behaviors that help you succeed.

Most people are *not* natural test-takers. Some students get nervous or a little stressed when sit for an SAT. Other students feel **eternally cursed** when it comes to tests. They believe that no matter how much they prepare, they will never do well. If that sounds like you, read on.

# TIP

Think of a single success in your testing past, no matter how small, and hold on to it. We're going to replicate that success through specific behavior.

## Negative Beliefs about Testing

If you feel karmically challenged by the SAT, it's important that you examine the *origins* of your negative beliefs. Ask yourself:

1. When did you start to believe that you were "bad at testing?"
2. Are you focusing on a few isolated instances of poor performance?
3. Are you **ignoring instances of strong performance?**
4. Are you really **always** bad at testing in every possible context?

The truth is doing well or freezing up on a test is all about behavior—and behavior can be changed. The very first behavior to change is how you speak about yourself.

## Watch your words: your mind is listening!

When it comes to making global statements about your testing abilities, be careful not to sell yourself short. Rather than saying, "I am miserable at testing," shift and rephrase the statement.

> "I used to struggle with testing, but now I'm open to the **possibility** of doing better."

Your mind likes to be consistent, and it tends to back up your words with actions. Optimists score higher; don't close the door on what's possible!

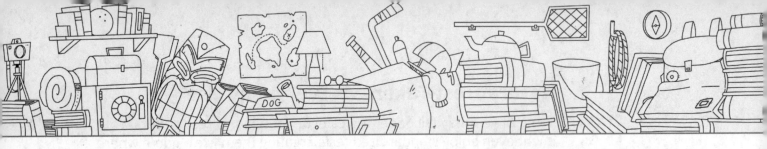

# Overcome Anxiety

*Test anxiety stems from a potentially useful thought: "Hey, this test counts. I need to do well." When this thought becomes invested with too much energy, however, it starts to hurt your score.*

### The fight-or-flight reflex can kick in on test day

When you are stressed about an upcoming test, your body reacts in the same way it would to an actual physical threat. These two thoughts cause the *same exact chemicals* to surge through your body:

> *"Ahh! A test!"*    and    *"Ahh! A lion!"*

When those stress hormones hit your bloodstream, your muscles begin to tense, your heart rate and respiratory rate change, and your breathing may become increasingly shallow. With less oxygen going to your brain, **you start to lose focus.** Distracted, you no longer think or process information as clearly, and your working memory becomes impaired. This increases your chances of escaping a lion... but significantly lowers your chances of acing the SAT!

## Some anxiety helps. Too much anxiety hurts.

A **low** level of anxiety is actually **useful** because it drives you to prepare and stay focused during the SAT. There is a tipping point where things shift from good to bad.

The simple graph below illustrates the continuum of anxiety and its impact on performance. What it tells us is that **some** anxiety is good; too much is harmful. We want to reach the optimal point, so we have just the right amount of anxiety.

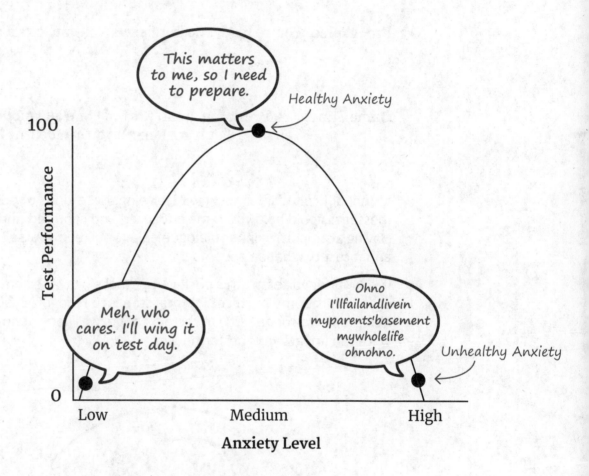

## So what can you do about anxiety?

There are several strategies to address heightened anxiety. We each have a number of voices inside our heads (some of us have more voices than others) that provide a running commentary on life. Some of these voices are negative, but others are positive and encouraging. Learning to manage your own inner-dialogue and focus on the positive voices is one of the keys to succeeding on the SAT.

## Listen to your inner coach

When it comes to inner dialogue, most good test-takers have a major resource on their side: their inner coach. For most students, their inner coach is actually a composite figure, created from pieces of their favorite coaches, teachers, or mentors rooting for them to succeed.

Your inner coach can help you relax or get focused before and during the test by sending you supportive messages.

**Pre-game:** "You're ready. Go in relaxed. You can knock this out."

**Game Time:** "You're doing great. It's only one question, don't worry about it. Let it go. Relax... you can do this."

It's not difficult to imagine how receiveing these kinds of positive messages could help you remain focused and centered during the SAT. Having a supportive inner dialogue helps you keep yourself paced, calm, and focused. What an advantage!

If your inner voice isn't this positive yet, that's okay! It's something we can change with some practice. The first step is to recognize your anxiety. The next step is to conquer it! On the next page, we'll look at how a negative voice can impact your performance.

**TIP**

For most students, their inner coach is actually a composite figure, created from pieces of their favorite coaches, teachers, or mentors from life experience, books, or movies.

**TIP**

Having a supportive inner dialogue helps you keep yourself paced, calm, and focused. What an advantage!

## Do not listen to your inner anxiety monster

For other students who have not yet tapped into their inner coach, another creature may appear instead: **the anxiety monster**. The monster feeds on fear and is continually scanning the environment for potential catastrophes. He causes negative statements that cause more negative statements, raising anxiety and dropping performance.

## How to conquer the anxiety monster

If you don't deal with the monster directly and **confront** these negative statements, you run the risk of being influenced by them. If you allow yourself to focus your energy on thoughts of failure, your mind may subconsciously begin to turn these thoughts into reality.

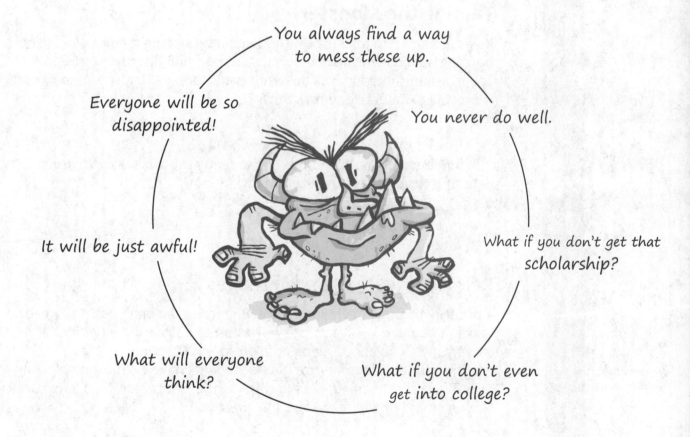

You always find a way to mess these up.

You never do well.

Everyone will be so disappointed!

It will be just awful!

What if you don't get that scholarship?

What will everyone think?

What if you don't even get into college?

## Naming the Monster

If you can give your monster a name, you can deal with him more easily and address him directly. Though you will know the right name for your monster, for now, we'll call him Rupert.

It's important to remember that Rupert actually works *for* you (though he's not the world's best employee), and he is taking up space in your head. If you stop feeding Rupert energy and attention, he will disappear.

## Taming the Monster

If you are about to take the SAT and Rupert is stoking the fire of anxiety, bringing up those negative thoughts, address him directly. At this point you may banish Rupert to a deserted island, and let him entertain himself while you go in there and rock the SAT.

"Listen, buddy. I've had enough. I'm ready for this test. I'm **done** listening to your negative statements."

## Reinforcing Positive Messages

A positive message might not banish Rupert on the first pass. You need to hear it about 20 times before you'll start to believe it. So reinforce! Leave yourself an encouraging note on your refrigerator. Put up a sticky note on your bathroom mirror. Some students have even been helped by recording a short 5 minute audio track on their voicemail, iPod, or smart phone reminding themselves to stay positive.

"You're ready for this.  You've worked hard.  You can rock this test."

Mix this message in with your favorite songs and positively rock out on the way to the test. In the right frame of mind, you'll get your best score.

# Focus on your breath

Just as you can address anxiety by shifting your thoughts and your inner dialogue, you can also address anxiety by making subtle physical adjustments.

The quickest way to shift from anxiety to relaxation is through **breathing**. It is physically impossible to breathe in a deep and relaxed manner and simultaneously feel intense anxiety.

## 1 Take deep breaths

Deep breaths should come from your diaphragm, not your chest. When you breathe deeply, your stomach should go out (think of the Buddha). If your shoulders rise while you are inhaling, you are breathing from your chest rather than your diaphragm. **Think Buddha.**

## 2 Slow things down

Count to 3 during the inhalation, pause at the peak of the breath and then count to 3 during the exhalation: this will begin to automatically relax your entire body.

## 3 Practice breathing while counting backwards

Count backwards from 10 to 1, silently in your head, breathing slowly and deeply from your diaphragm with every count. 10....9....8....7.... With each breath, imagine yourself becoming more and more relaxed.

## 4 Sigh deeply or make yourself yawn

Yawning is like pressing a reset button in your brain. Yawning has many beneficial effects and can actually help you increase your level of focus and energy.

## Use a physical trigger to relax

You can use a physical cue or trigger to bring yourself to a more relaxed state. Create a link between a simple movement and a state of relaxation. Make the  movement— start to relax!

## 1 Choose a cue

You can associate a specific cue with starting to relax. Pick one that works for you, or simply make up your own. Here are a few examples:

- squeezing three fingers together three times
- tapping your knee slowly three times
- putting one hand on top of the other

## 2 Get relaxed

Once you've officially started to relax with your cue, it's time for calm:

- Close your eyes
- Take 3 deep breaths
- Feel your body become more relaxed
- Tense your muscles, hold for a full breath, and then release
- Take 3 more deep breaths using the 3 count:

> Breathe in. Hold. Breathe Out.
> 1       2       3

## 3 Link 'em up

Perform your chosen trigger in this relaxed state, and create a mental association between the physical motion and a state of deep relaxation. You will need to do this a few times to create a stronger association.

## 4 Cue the relaxation during the test

During the test, whenever you feel anxiety coming on, perform your cue to activate your relaxed state. Take deep breaths, and begin to relax.

# Test Day Anxiety

*Sitting down and taking the test can trigger anxiety in a lot of students. Let's think about good practices at specific moments during the test.*

.................................................................................................

### When the Test Begins

Some students become nervous the moment the test begins. They hear the proctor say, "You have 55 minutes... open your test booklet and begin." They hear the sound of turning pages fill the room, and they start to sweat. When the proctor says "begin," **pause** and **take a moment for yourself.** Once you're centered and calm, turn the page and begin.

### At the Five-Minute Warning

Some students lose their cool at the 5-minute warning. They panic and start to rush, even when they are on track to finish in time. In their rush, they are frequently more careless.

When you hear the 5-minute warning, **pause** and **take a moment for yourself.** Once you're centered and calm, make any necessary adjustments, prioritize the remaining questions, and get back to the test.

## A missed problem can feel like a disaster...

Some students start to feel stressed when they just **know** they missed that last problem. They worry so much about that missed point that they have trouble concentrating on the next several questions. They get hung up on one little point and make that missed question feel like a disaster. That anxiety monster starts to drown out the inner coach, kicking that fight-or-flight response into high gear. This just makes it all the more likely they'll miss the **next problem**, starting a negative cycle.

## ...but it's just a speedbump on the way to success

Here's the thing: you don't need to get every single question right. Not even close! One point is just that—one single point. Think of a missed problem as just a **speedbump** on the way to your best score yet. Remember this if you start to feel worried after a tough problem.

Keep cool, keep perspective, and **keep your eyes on the finish line!**

# Picture Success

*Using your imagination, you can rewire your brain to feel more confident.*

### Rewiring your brain

To learn the power of imagination, talk to any professional athlete. These folks walk into something very much like a testing environment each time they calmly walk out onto the court or field (in front of millions of people, no less). To get centered, they tap into the power of **creative visualization**. At home, in the locker room, before taking a shot, they picture themselves performing and succeeding.

They do this because it works. The brain has a hard time distinguishing between **imagined** reality and **actual** reality. When you *imagine* lifting your hand, the same parts of the brain are triggered as when you *actually* lift your hand. Similarly, when you vividly imagine yourself calmly taking a test, your brain will *remember* the experience and start to associate confidence with testing.

Later, when you walk into a testing room, your brain will scan the environment to relate the current situation to past experiences and determine how to respond. If you can only remember bad experiences full of anxiety and disappointment, walking into that room will cause anxiety. But by using creative visualization, you can **break that cycle.** You actually have the power to create a new "script" for your brain to follow when you confront new testing situations.

## TIP

If you can vividly imagine an event, engage your senses and emotions, and reinforce it through repetition, your brain will begin to treat the event like it is real rather than imagined.

## Create a new script with creative visualization

Let's walk through an example of how simply imagining the many details of success on the SAT can increase your confidence and reduce anxiety. To establish a new, positive "memory," we'll need to be detailed so your brain will buy it. Let's walk through a script.

### You wake up confident & refreshed

Imagine yourself waking up the morning of the SAT. You turn off your alarm and get out of bed. You do your morning routine and have a **healthy breakfast**. You begin to feel awake and alert, ready for the task ahead of you. You grab your backpack with your admission ticket, ID, pencils, calculator, water, and snacks and head to the test center.

Before you enter, you take a deep breath. "I've worked hard. I'm ready for this test; I'm going to go in there and knock this out," you tell yourself. You walk to the registration line. You show your ID and ticket, and make your way to your testing room where other students are getting situated. Some are fidgety; others are barely awake. You spot an empty seat.

### You take a seat and get ready

You find your seat, put away your things and settle in. Visualize yourself **feeling ready and relaxed**. The proctor asks you to clear your desk and passes out materials. You bubble-in all the info: name, date of birth, testing site, etc. Imagine the feel of the pencil in your hand, marking the bubbles on the answer sheet. The proctor announces the beginning of the first section. "Open your test booklets to Page 1. You have 65 minutes to complete the Reading section. Begin." You take a deep breath and begin.

Continued on next page →

## You begin taking the test

The Reading passages are new, but you tackle each one **using strategies you practiced**, like active reading, throwaways, and evidence. You move quickly, eye on the clock, and moving on if you get stuck on a tough question.

During your ten minute break, you walk, stretch, and snack. You're soon moving through the Writing section, where you see the same sort of questions you've practiced in this book. You move through the section, using context clues and reading full sentences. You have time left over, which you use to review your answer choices.

Next are the math sections. The first dozen problems are pretty easy, but you make sure there are no careless errors. The problems get more difficult, but you are able to remember the formulas that you've been studying. You feel like this is your best performance yet!

## You confidently put your pencil down

The proctor calls an end to the final section. While you wait for the booklets to be picked up, you push away thoughts of tough questions. Instead, you take a few moments to visualize the score you want to achieve on the SAT. Imagine that number.

Move forward in time. Imagine yourself going online the morning of score release day. See your score report, and visualize the goal you set for yourself directly next to your name. Really see it. You've accomplished your goal. All your hard work paid off! Feel the emotions that come with that.

## Rehearse to build up confidence

Once you have created this vision and filled it with details that work for you, repeat it every few days. Students who have used this technique and tapped into the power of their imaginations have made massive score gains on the SAT! Try this out for yourself, and see how it works for you.

# Practical Tips

*Let's get practical! What small details will help you succeed?*

### During the week before the SAT

In the last week before the SAT, continue to review your materials. Take a practice test to work on timing. You cannot cram for the SAT, but you want to keep the momentum going in the days leading up to the test.

### Two days before the SAT

The Thursday night before the SAT is a very important night. A good night's sleep **Thursday** will have an enormous impact on your level of energy and ability to focus on **Saturday**. The effects of a poor night's sleep generally hit you the hardest **two days later**. So get to bed early Thursday, and give yourself a full 7 to 8 hours of sleep.

### On the day before the SAT

- **Lightly review** a completed practice test and go over your notes.

- **Take a walk** and **picture a successful test day**, reinforcing what you want to happen in the morning.

- **Keep your thoughts positive**. You're ready. You've worked hard. Tomorrow you are going to do your absolute best.

- **Go to bed on time.** Be sure you get 7-8 hours of sleep.

- **Set your alarm clock!** Use the alarm on your cell phone as a backup.

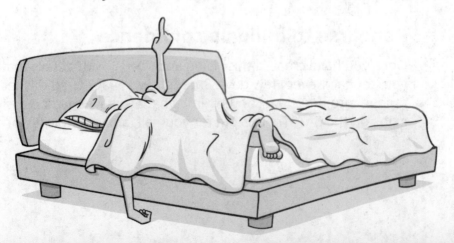

## Prepare your bag for test day

Pack the following materials in a bag that you can grab in the morning before you go to the test.

1. Your SAT Admission **Ticket**

2. An acceptable (not expired) **photo ID**

3. Printed directions to the test center

4. 3-4 sharpened No. 2 **pencils** (pens and mechanical pencils are not allowed)

5. A graphing **calculator** (make sure it's charged or bring extra batteries)

6. A digital **watch** or one with a second hand—not a smart watch

7. Bottle of **water**

8. **Snacks**: fruit and snack bars are great for the short breaks

**TIP**

In some testing centers, the clock may be behind you (or the room may not have a clock at all). Your proctor also may not give you 5-minute warnings, so having a watch can be very helpful!

## On the morning of the test

- Wake up early

- Eat a healthy **breakfast**

- Dress in comfortable clothes and in layers. Test rooms may be cold or hot; layers give you options.

- **Leave early** for the testing site. Give yourself plenty of time for traffic or other potential delays, especially if you've never been to the testing location before.

## Before the test, prime your brain for success

You really do have a 1-track mind. The 24 hours before your test, saturate your brain with thoughts and images of success. Get that mental pathway "primed," or turned on.

Think about Einstein. Think about smart people. Research shows that if you think about great problem solvers and people you admire, you awaken potential within yourself. By thinking about Einstein before the test, you act more like Einstein when it counts!

## During the test administration

- Don't be thrown off by the energy of others. Stay in your zone. You've worked hard; you're prepared. Stay focused on your optimal performance.

- Bubble-in your Scantron sheet carefully. Some students transfer answers one test-page at a time rather than question-by-question. This can save a few minutes, eliminating much of the time spent going back and forth between the test booklet and the answer sheet.

- Pace yourself. Use your watch to regulate your timing.

- Use your break. Drink some water and eat a snack. You will need fluids and some extra fuel to keep you going between 8:00 am and 12:00 pm. Take this time to refocus: "You're doing great...only two more sections left."

- Be your own cheerleader. Be your own coach. Use self-talk to keep yourself engaged and focused. It's a long test. It helps to have some encouragement.

## After the test

Congratulations! Now go out and play! You deserve it!

# Practice Test

*There's nothing like timed practice to help you prepare for the SAT.*

## It's a Matter of Time

The practice test to follow will allow you to practice your pacing, flex your new skills, and get more comfortable taking a complete SAT. The test simulates the difficulty, language, and timing of the official test. Take this opportunity to time yourself, taking short, 10-minute breaks between sections. To take the full test, you should reserve **3.5 hours**.

After the test, you'll find instructions on how to obtain an estimated score. Use this score to identify the best areas on which to focus your studies in the coming weeks.

| TEST BREAKDOWN | | |
|---|---|---|
| Section | Time Limit | Questions |
| Reading | 65 minutes | 52 questions |
| Writing | 35 minutes | 44 questions |
| Math – No Calculator | 25 minutes | 20 questions |
| Math – Calculator | 55 minutes | 38 questions |

# Mock SAT
## Answer Sheet

A pencil must be used to fill out this form. Each mark needs to be dark and to completely fill in the intended circle. Do not write anywhere outside of the boxes provided to you. Completely erase any errors or stray marks. Filling out this answer sheet properly will ensure accurate score reporting.

**Last Name**

**First Name**

**Today's Date**

- Jan
- Feb
- Mar
- Apr
- May
- Jun
- Jul
- Aug
- Sep
- Oct
- Nov
- Dec

**Test Form**

- Practice Test #1
- Practice Test #2
- Practice Test #3
- Practice Test #4

**HS Grad Year**

I agree to refrain from any activity that may be considered cheating as described to me by the proctor. I confirm that the information I provide on this page and the next is accurate (to the best of my understanding). I will take this mock exam as seriously as an official exam.

_____        _____
Your Signature                          Today's Date

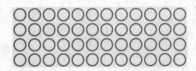

906

## Student Account Information:

Fill out your Applerouth ID or
enter a four-digit PIN that you can use to receive
your graded score report online.

Then fill out the Event Code.

See your confirmation email for details,
or ask your proctor for assistance.

**Applerouth ID**

or

**PIN**

**Event Code**

## Parent Contact Information:

Please provide us with contact information for your (primary) parent or guardian so that we can
return your scores to you after this mock has been graded.

**Parent/Guardian Last Name**

**Parent/Guardian First Name**

**Parent/Guardian Phone**

## Parent/Guardian Email

## SECTION 1

| | | | | | | | |
|---|---|---|---|---|---|---|---|
| 1 (A)(B)(C)(D) | | 14 (A)(B)(C)(D) | | 27 (A)(B)(C)(D) | | 40 (A)(B)(C)(D) | |
| 2 (A)(B)(C)(D) | | 15 (A)(B)(C)(D) | | 28 (A)(B)(C)(D) | | 41 (A)(B)(C)(D) | |
| 3 (A)(B)(C)(D) | | 16 (A)(B)(C)(D) | | 29 (A)(B)(C)(D) | | 42 (A)(B)(C)(D) | |
| 4 (A)(B)(C)(D) | | 17 (A)(B)(C)(D) | | 30 (A)(B)(C)(D) | | 43 (A)(B)(C)(D) | |
| 5 (A)(B)(C)(D) | | 18 (A)(B)(C)(D) | | 31 (A)(B)(C)(D) | | 44 (A)(B)(C)(D) | |
| 6 (A)(B)(C)(D) | | 19 (A)(B)(C)(D) | | 32 (A)(B)(C)(D) | | 45 (A)(B)(C)(D) | |
| 7 (A)(B)(C)(D) | | 20 (A)(B)(C)(D) | | 33 (A)(B)(C)(D) | | 46 (A)(B)(C)(D) | |
| 8 (A)(B)(C)(D) | | 21 (A)(B)(C)(D) | | 34 (A)(B)(C)(D) | | 47 (A)(B)(C)(D) | |
| 9 (A)(B)(C)(D) | | 22 (A)(B)(C)(D) | | 35 (A)(B)(C)(D) | | 48 (A)(B)(C)(D) | |
| 10 (A)(B)(C)(D) | | 23 (A)(B)(C)(D) | | 36 (A)(B)(C)(D) | | 49 (A)(B)(C)(D) | |
| 11 (A)(B)(C)(D) | | 24 (A)(B)(C)(D) | | 37 (A)(B)(C)(D) | | 50 (A)(B)(C)(D) | |
| 12 (A)(B)(C)(D) | | 25 (A)(B)(C)(D) | | 38 (A)(B)(C)(D) | | 51 (A)(B)(C)(D) | |
| 13 (A)(B)(C)(D) | | 26 (A)(B)(C)(D) | | 39 (A)(B)(C)(D) | | 52 (A)(B)(C)(D) | |

## SECTION 2

| | | | | | | | |
|---|---|---|---|---|---|---|---|
| 1 (A)(B)(C)(D) | | 12 (A)(B)(C)(D) | | 23 (A)(B)(C)(D) | | 34 (A)(B)(C)(D) | |
| 2 (A)(B)(C)(D) | | 13 (A)(B)(C)(D) | | 24 (A)(B)(C)(D) | | 35 (A)(B)(C)(D) | |
| 3 (A)(B)(C)(D) | | 14 (A)(B)(C)(D) | | 25 (A)(B)(C)(D) | | 36 (A)(B)(C)(D) | |
| 4 (A)(B)(C)(D) | | 15 (A)(B)(C)(D) | | 26 (A)(B)(C)(D) | | 37 (A)(B)(C)(D) | |
| 5 (A)(B)(C)(D) | | 16 (A)(B)(C)(D) | | 27 (A)(B)(C)(D) | | 38 (A)(B)(C)(D) | |
| 6 (A)(B)(C)(D) | | 17 (A)(B)(C)(D) | | 28 (A)(B)(C)(D) | | 39 (A)(B)(C)(D) | |
| 7 (A)(B)(C)(D) | | 18 (A)(B)(C)(D) | | 29 (A)(B)(C)(D) | | 40 (A)(B)(C)(D) | |
| 8 (A)(B)(C)(D) | | 19 (A)(B)(C)(D) | | 30 (A)(B)(C)(D) | | 41 (A)(B)(C)(D) | |
| 9 (A)(B)(C)(D) | | 20 (A)(B)(C)(D) | | 31 (A)(B)(C)(D) | | 42 (A)(B)(C)(D) | |
| 10 (A)(B)(C)(D) | | 21 (A)(B)(C)(D) | | 32 (A)(B)(C)(D) | | 43 (A)(B)(C)(D) | |
| 11 (A)(B)(C)(D) | | 22 (A)(B)(C)(D) | | 33 (A)(B)(C)(D) | | 44 (A)(B)(C)(D) | |

## SECTION 3

| | | | | | |
|---|---|---|---|---|---|
| 1 (A)(B)(C)(D) | | 6 (A)(B)(C)(D) | | 11 (A)(B)(C)(D) | |
| 2 (A)(B)(C)(D) | | 7 (A)(B)(C)(D) | | 12 (A)(B)(C)(D) | |
| 3 (A)(B)(C)(D) | | 8 (A)(B)(C)(D) | | 13 (A)(B)(C)(D) | |
| 4 (A)(B)(C)(D) | | 9 (A)(B)(C)(D) | | 14 (A)(B)(C)(D) | |
| 5 (A)(B)(C)(D) | | 10 (A)(B)(C)(D) | | 15 (A)(B)(C)(D) | |

Grid in this section as directed in SECTION 3 of your exam booklet.

Only answers that are bubbled-in will be scored.

| 16 | 17 | 18 | 19 | 20 |
|---|---|---|---|---|

909

1. A B C D
2. A B C D
3. A B C D
4. A B C D
5. A B C D
6. A B C D
7. A B C D
8. A B C D

9. A B C D
10. A B C D
11. A B C D
12. A B C D
13. A B C D
14. A B C D
15. A B C D
16. A B C D

17. A B C D
18. A B C D
19. A B C D
20. A B C D
21. A B C D
22. A B C D
23. A B C D
24. A B C D

25. A B C D
26. A B C D
27. A B C D
28. A B C D
29. A B C D
30. A B C D

Grid in this section as directed in SECTION 4 of your exam booklet.

Only answers that are bubbled-in will be scored.

31

32

33

34

35

36

37

38

_____
_____
_____
_____
_____
_____
_____
_____
_____
_____
_____
_____
_____
_____
_____
_____
_____
_____
_____
_____
_____
_____
_____
_____
_____
_____
_____

# Reading Test

## 65 MINUTES, 52 QUESTIONS

**Turn to Section 1 of your answer sheet to answer the questions in this section.**

## Questions 1-10 are based on the following pasage.

This passage is adapted from Louisa May Alcott, *Work: A Story of Experience*. Originally published in 1873. In the story, Christie has just told her Aunt Betsey her plans to leave home.

Having kissed the old lady, Christie swept her work away, and sat down to write the letter which was the first step toward freedom. When it was done, she drew
Line nearer, to her friendly confidante the fire, and till late into
5 the night sat thinking tenderly of the past, bravely of the present, hopefully of the future. Twenty-one to-morrow, and her inheritance a head, a heart, a pair of hands; also the dower of most New England girls, intelligence, courage, and common sense, many practical gifts, and,
10 hidden under the reserve that soon melts in a genial atmosphere, much romance and enthusiasm, and the spirit which can rise to heroism when the great moment comes. Christie was one of that large class of women who, moderately endowed with talents, earnest and
15 true-hearted, are driven by necessity, temperament, or principle out into the world to find support, happiness, and homes for themselves. Many turn back discouraged; more accept shadow for substance, and discover their mistake too late; the weakest lose their purpose and
20 themselves; but the strongest struggle on, and, after danger and defeat, earn at last the best success this world can give us, the possession of a brave and cheerful spirit, rich in self-knowledge, self-control, self-help. This was the real desire of Christie's heart; this was to be her lesson
25 and reward, and to this happy end she was slowly yet surely brought by the long discipline of life and labor. Sitting alone there in the night, she tried to strengthen herself with all the good and helpful memories she could recall, before she went away to find her place in the
30 great unknown world. She thought of her mother, so like

herself, who had borne the commonplace life of home till she could bear it no longer. Then had gone away to teach, as most country girls are forced to do. Had met, loved, and married a poor gentleman, and, after a few
35 years of genuine happiness, untroubled even by much care and poverty, had followed him out of the world, leaving her little child to the protection of her brother.
Christie looked back over the long, lonely years she had spent in the old farm-house, plodding to
40 school and church, and doing her tasks with kind Aunt Betsey while a child; and slowly growing into girlhood, with a world of romance locked up in a heart hungry for love and a larger, nobler life.
She had tried to appease this hunger in many ways,
45 but found little help. Her father's old books were all she could command, and these she wore out with much reading. Inheriting his refined tastes, she found nothing to attract her in the society of the commonplace and often coarse people about her. She tried to like the
50 buxom girls whose one ambition was to "get married," and whose only subjects of conversation were "smart bonnets" and "nice dresses." She tried to believe that the admiration and regard of the bluff young farmers was worth striving for; but when one well-to-do neighbor
55 laid his acres at her feet, she found it impossible to accept for her life's companion a man whose soul was wrapped up in prize cattle and big turnips.

**1**

Which choice best describes what happens in the passage?

A) A character flees from her home to get away from a childhood of disappointment.

B) A character reminisces about her upbringing the night before embarking on her own.

C) A character gradually admits that she has made a hasty decision.

D) A character reconsiders her choices after learning about the stories of other young women.

**2**

Which of the following statements about Christie is most strongly suggested by the passage?

A) She has unique physical gifts that she inherited from her parents.

B) She was unduly neglected by her uncle and aunt.

C) She must be dependent on herself to create her own success.

D) Her background left her ill-equipped for life on her own.

**3**

The second paragraph serves to

A) show that Christie is one of many young women yearning for independence.

B) chastise Christie's decision to leave her Uncle and Aunt's home.

C) analyze how often young women are unable to find a successful career.

D) show how different Christie is from her Aunt.

**4**

Christie indicates that she considers success to be

A) independence and a home of her own.

B) a self-reliant and courageous character

C) a place in genteel society.

D) recognition of her intelligence and independence.

**5**

Which choice provides the best evidence for the answer to the previous question?

A) Lines 7-12 ("also … comes")

B) Lines 13-17 ("Christie … themselves")

C) Lines 20-23 ("but the … self-help")

D) Lines 47-49 ("Inheriting … about her")

**6**

As used on line 39, "plodding" suggests that Christie

A) had no interest in learning how to read or write.

B) has been tired of the monotony of her routine for most of her life.

C) had planned to leave the farm house for a long time.

D) lacked good judgement from ignoring the moral lessons taught to her.

**7**

As used on line 46 "command" most nearly means

A) possess.

B) require.

C) organize.

D) recite.

**8**

The passage indicates that Christie views her local marriage prospects as

A) having priorities and interests different than her own.

B) showing little interest in her as the men do not appreciate her love of literature.

C) being obsessed with rural concerns and fearful of city life.

D) more wealthy and indifferent to her struggles.

**9**

The passage implies that Christie's mother

A) abandoned Christie to focus on becoming a teacher.

B) met an early death.

C) no longer bothers to write to Christie.

D) made the same mistakes that Christie will make.

**10**

Which choice provides the best evidence that Christie sees herself as more worldly than the people she grew up around?

A) Lines 30-32 ("She thought … longer")

B) Lines 32-33 ("Then … do")

C) Lines 36-37 ("had followed … brother")

D) Lines 47-49 ("Inheriting … about her")

**Questions 11-20 are based on the following passage.**

The passage is adapted from "Keepin' it Real: Linguistic Models of Authenticity Judgments for Artificially Generated Rap Lyrics" by Folgert Karsdorp, Enrique Manjavacas, Mike Kestemont. Copyright 2019 Karsdorp et al. The passage discusses Natural Language Generation, a software process that transforms structured data into natural language.

Due to recent advances in computer technology, communication—be it verbal or not—is no longer a privileged kind of interaction that can only take
Line place between human agents. Increasingly, people
5 interact with a variety of artificial agents, sometimes even without being fully aware of whether or not their conversation partners are in fact human. Chatbot interfaces for customers at company websites are but one example of a popular application of natural
10 language generation (NLG). Through advances in neural language modeling, it has become possible to generate synthetic texts in a variety of genres and styles.
In spite of the impressive advances in the field of NLG, however, the evaluation of such generative models
15 remains a thorny issue—the same goes for generative models in other domains. This is especially true for texts produced in more specific artistic domains, such as literature or lyrics, where evaluative procedures must cover much more than basic criteria, such as grammatical
20 correctness. Our interest is in the issue of authenticity, i.e. a system's ability to conceal its artificial nature.
In this study, we report on a large-scale experiment in which we have crowd-sourced authenticity judgments for synthesized text at a music festival in the Netherlands.
25 As a case study, we have turned to rap lyrics, an established sub-genre of present-day popular music that is known for its typical textual and rhythmical properties. We chose the specific application domain of rap lyrics, not only because this text variety would
30 appeal to festival goers, but also because it is rich enough in constraints related to themes and style to make it a challenging domain for state of the art text generators.
The experiment took the form of an online game, which was played independently by individual
35 participants. The stimuli in the experiment were fragments of original, authentic rap lyrics and synthetic fragments generated by one of the six artificial language models. These fragments were presented to the participants in the form of two types
40 of questions (which were randomly alternated):

A. The participants were simultaneously presented with an authentic fragment and an artificially generated fragment of rap lyrics, in written form on opposite sides of a computer screen. The user had to decide which fragment was the authentic one.

B. The participants were presented with a single fragment of rap lyrics, in written form on a computer screen. The user had to decide whether the fragment was authentic or computer-generated.

The interface would provide visual feedback as to the correctness of an answer immediately after it had been entered and would briefly display the original artist and song title for the authentic lyrics. There are two important differences between both question types. In (A), participants typically had to process relatively more text than in (B), because there were two fragments involved and the allowed time for solving the question was the same in (A) and (B). One might hypothesize that this would render (B) easier than (A) in terms of cognitive processing time. On the other hand, (B) only presented participants with a single fragment, meaning that users were unable to explicitly compare an artificial with an authentic fragment.

How accurate were the participants at detecting authentic rap lyrics? On average, authenticity detection accuracy was above chance level (50%), with participants correctly distinguishing between original and generated text 61.1% of the time. With a 58% median accuracy, participants performed significantly worse on questions of type-B than of type-A (64%), suggesting that the ability to explicitly compare two fragments made the task easier. Furthermore, while more time spent answering type-B questions led to an increasing precision in detecting authentic lyrics, it did not positively affect the accuracy of spotting generated lyrics. This could be due to a gradual change in perception bias: initially, participants showed a bias towards the perception of texts as being generated, perhaps out of an urge to demonstrate that they could not be 'fooled' by a computer. This urge may have been tempered over time through immediate visual feedback.

Natural language generation offers increasingly valuable possibilities for real-world applications in industry and creative arts. As techniques continue to mature in this field, we can expect a further intensification of the contact between human language users and systems for automated text generation. The perceived authenticity of such systems—be it in a conversational setting or not—will be key to these systems' success: in many domains, we can expect a more meaningful engagement with a

system on the user's part if the system features human-like behaviour. While we do not expect new rap songs penned by artificial ghostwriters any time soon, more research effort should be directed to integrate domain-specific data models into (neural) language generation systems to help create "authentic" experiences for users.

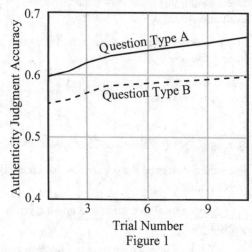

Figure 1

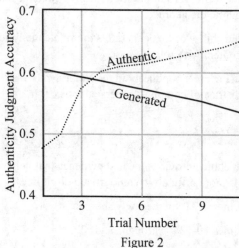

Figure 2

**11**

The passage describes the day-to-day interactions with NLG as

(A) common and often unnoticed by the user.

B) problematic to many writers and artists who desire authentic interactions.

C) growing rapidly due to compatibility with many genres of art.

D) usually off-putting as users expect personalized conversations.

CONTINUE

**12**

The use of the word "thorny" in line 15 conveys the sense that

A) some research into generative models may be dangerous.

B) research into this topic may require specific evaluation criteria.

C) disagreements regarding the research methods may impact funding.

D) results from this type of research may be troubling to many scientists.

**13**

The researchers designed the experiment to center on rap lyrics because of

A) the genre's appeal to participants and its lyrical constraints.

B) the difficulties in programming the rhythms that define the genre.

C) the ability of text generators to imitate the lyrical content with relative ease.

D) the genre's popularity in the Netherlands and a distrust of computer generated music.

**14**

Which choice provides the best evidence that believable NLG is more difficult in some artistic disciplines?

A) Lines 4-7 ("Increasingly...human")

B) Lines 10-12 ("Through...styles")

C) Lines 16-20 ("This...correctness")

D) Lines 81-83 ("Natural...arts. ")

**15**

In the experiment presented in the passage, type A questions, unlike type B questions, always

A) gave the participant the option to not answer.

B) presented a comparison between generated and authentic rap lyrics.

C) offered only one example and participants decided whether it was authentic or not.

D) appeared at the beginning of each game, which later moved to the more difficult questions.

**16**

Which choice best expresses an assumption the researchers made when designing their experiment?

A) Participants would prefer the generated lyrics rather than the authentic ones.

B) Participants would recognize the authentic lyrics from famous rap songs.

C) Participants would find the online game engaging and would therefore want to do well.

D) Participants would be excited to find out that rap lyrics could be written by artificial ghostwriters.

**17**

In line 88, "domains" most nearly means

A) applications.

B) properties.

C) inputs.

D) estates.

**18**

Which choice regarding the accuracy of the participants is supported by Figure 1 and the passage?

A) As the trial number increased, accuracy on Question type A increased, but decreased for Question type B.

B) As the trial number increased, accuracy on Question type B increased, but decreased for Question type A.

C) As the trial number increased, accuracy on both question types increases, but the average stayed below 50% accuracy for all trials.

D) As the trial number increased, accuracy on both question types increases, and then average stayed above 50% accuracy for all trials.

**19**

According to the passage, the decrease in accuracy when evaluating generated lyrics, as depicted in figure 2, is most likely caused by

A) the change in user preference towards the answers as the game went on.

B) fatigue felt after answering questions across multiple trials.

C) the quality and consistency of the generated lyrics.

D) the rhymetical complexity common within the rap genre.

**20**

Which choice provides the best evidence to the previous question?

A) Lines 25-28 ("As...properties")

B) Lines 38-40 ("These...questions")

C) Lines 68-70 ("With...(64%)")

D) Lines 75-80 ("This...feedback")

**Questions 21-31 are based on the following passage.**

Passage 1 is adapted from Liza Gross, "Untapped Bounty: Sampling the Seas to Survey Microbial Biodiversity." ©2007 by Liza Gross. Passage 2 is adapted from Kira O'Day, "Gut Reaction: Pyrosequencing Provides the Poop on Distal Gut Bacteria." ©2008 Kira O'Day. Both passages discuss bacteria, a type of microbe.

**Passage 1**

Being invisible to the naked eye, microbes managed to escape scientific scrutiny until the mid-17th century, when Dutch scientist Antonie van Leeuwenhoek
*Line* invented the microscope. These cryptic organisms
5 continued to thwart scientists' efforts to probe, describe, and classify them until about 40 years ago, owing largely to similar body structures that are hard to visually differentiate and obscure body functions that make them notoriously difficult to grow in a lab.
10    Most of what we know about the biochemical diversity of microbes, however, comes from the tiny fraction that do submit to lab investigations. Not until scientists determined that they could use molecular sequences, or an organism's unique DNA code, to
15 identify species and determine their evolutionary heritage did it begin to become apparent just how diverse microbes are. We now know that microbes are the most widely distributed organisms on earth, having adapted to environments as diverse as boiling sulfur
20 pits and the human gut. Accounting for half of the world's biomass, microbes provide essential ecosystem services by cycling the mineral nutrients that support life on earth. And marine microbes remove so much carbon dioxide from the atmosphere that some scientists
25 see them as a potential solution to global warming.
   Yet even as scientists describe seemingly endless variations on the cosmopolitan microbial lifestyle, the concept of a bacterial species remains elusive. Some bacterial species (such as anthrax) appear
30 to have little genetic variation. In other species (such as *Escherichia coli*), individuals can have completely different sets of genes, challenging scientists to explain the observed diversity.
   The emerging field of environmental genomics
35 aims to capture the full measure of microbial diversity by trading the lens of the microscope for the lens of genomics. By recovering communities of microbial genes where they live (streams, oceans, even the human gut), environmental genomics avoids the need to culture
40 uncooperative organisms in labs. And by analyzing

factors found in the microbes' environments, such as pH, salinity, and water temperature, it sheds light on the biological processes encoded in the genes.

**Passage 2**

The human distal gut hosts a bustling community
45 comprising thousands of different kinds of bacteria. Fortunately, most of these intestinal residents don't cause disease but instead play key roles in nutrition, metabolism, pathogen resistance, and immune response regulation. Unfortunately, these beneficial bacteria
50 are just as susceptible to the antibiotics we take to treat disease-causing bacteria. Antibiotics drastically alter the balance among members of different taxa* of beneficial distal gut bacteria that have coevolved with one another and with their human host.

55     To find out more about the changes taking place in the gut during antibiotic treatment, researchers extracted DNA from stool samples collected from three healthy adults before, during, and after treatment for five days with ciprofloxacin (a broad-spectrum
60 antibiotic that is used to treat a variety of bacterial conditions such as infections of the lower respiratory or urinary tracts). Ciprofloxacin was selected because of its safety profile and the previous belief that it does not harm the most abundant bacteria of the distal gut.

65     Researchers confirmed the presence of over 5,600 bacterial taxa in the human gut—far more taxonomic richness than had been seen in previous investigations of host-associated bacterial communities. They also found that ciprofloxacin had a dramatic effect on
70 microbial communities and that the specific bacterial taxa most strongly affected varied among the human hosts. Ciprofloxacin treatment caused a sizeable decrease in taxonomic richness in two of the participants, while bacterial diversity was somewhat less strongly
75 affected in the third participant. Most members of the bacterial community returned to pretreatment numbers within four weeks following treatment.

Although the effects on their gut inhabitants were profound, none of the participants reported any changes
80 in their gut function either during or after treatment, indicating that the tremendous diversity of the distal gut bacterial community makes it both resilient and functionally redundant. Notably, however, some taxa had not recovered completely even six months later. Because
85 specific bacterial taxa are responsible for different aspects of nutrition, metabolism, and immune response, even seemingly minor changes in the composition of the gut microbial community as the result of antibiotic treatment

might have long-term effects on health that could go
90 undetected in the relatively short length of the study.

\* Plural form of *taxon*, a distinct group or unit.

**21**

As used in line 37, "recovering" most nearly means

A)  healing.

B)  overcoming.

C)  increasing.

D)  retrieving.

**22**

The author of Passage 1 refers to global warming in order to

A)  note a common misconception about an event.

B)  explain a new phenomenon.

C)  highlight an action's unexpected effect.

D)  present a potential solution to a problem.

**23**

As used in line 67, "richness" most nearly means

A)  abundance.

B)  affluence.

C)  intensity.

D)  flavor.

**24**

The author of Passage 1 suggests that until recently, microbes were considered

A) detrimental.

B) mysterious.

C) controversial.

D) innovative.

**25**

Which choices provides the best evidence that bacteria are found in a variety of environments?

A) Lines 4-9 ("These … lab")

B) Lines 17-20 ("We … gut")

C) Lines 20-23 ("Accounting … earth")

D) Lines 34-37 ("The emerging … genomics")

**26**

The primary finding in Passage 2 is that the antibiotic Ciprofloxacin dramatically decreases the diversity of the bacteria found in the distal gut but

A) all original taxa can be located within the host after a few weeks.

B) the functional capabilities of the gut do not change.

C) it may be unsafe for people to consume even for short periods of time.

D) its use increases a person's rate of metabolism.

**27**

Which choice provides the best evidence for the answer to the previous question?

A) Lines 62-64 ("Ciprofloxacin … gut)

B) Lines 78-83 ("Although … redundant)

C) Lines 83-84 ("Notably … later")

D) Lines 84-90 ("Because … study")

**28**

The main purpose of both passages is to

A) question the methods used to cultivate microbes.

B) discuss the prevailing knowledge regarding the diversity of microbial life.

C) describe the evolutionary relationship between microbes and humans.

D) explain the change over time in the classification of microbes.

**29**

Unlike the author of Passage 1, the author of Passage 2 acknowledges the

A) abundance of bacteria on Earth.

B) diversity between different taxa of bacteria.

C) harmful nature of some bacteria.

D) critical role bacteria play within their habitats.

CONTINUE

**30**

Which choice best describes the relationship between the two passages?

A) Passage 2 analyzes the implications of the results that are described in Passage 1.

B) Passage 2 draws alternative conclusions from the evidence presented in Passage 1.

C) Passage 2 describes a study used to investigate a particular aspect of a topic introduced in Passage 1.

D) Passage 2 summarizes the negative reactions to the questions raised in Passage 1.

**31**

The authors of both passages would most likely agree with which of the following statements about the current understanding of bacterial species?

A) The invention of the microscope was the most important scientific advance in discovering the microbial world.

B) Antibiotics alter the abundance and diversity of bacteria in the distal gut of humans.

C) Very few of the existing species of bacteria have been identified.

D) Traditional methods of classifying organisms based on morphology are more useful than molecular sequencing.

**Questions 32-41 are based on the following passage.**

This passage is adapted from James Madison, *Federalist No. 14. Objections to the Proposed Constitution From Extent of Territory Answered*. Originally published in 1787. The Federalist Papers were a series of influential articles offering opinions on creating a new government in the aftermath of the Revolutionary War.

We have seen the necessity of the Union, as our bulwark against foreign danger, as the conservator of peace among ourselves, as the guardian of our commerce
Line and other common interests, as the only substitute for
5 those military establishments which have subverted the liberties of the Old World, and as the proper antidote for the diseases of faction, which have proved fatal to other popular governments, and of which alarming symptoms have been betrayed by our own. All that remains, within
10 this branch of our inquiries, is to take notice of an objection that may be drawn from the great extent of country which the Union embraces. A few observations on this subject will be the more proper, as it is perceived that the adversaries of the new Constitution are availing
15 themselves of the prevailing prejudice with regard to the practicable sphere of republican administration, in order to supply, by imaginary difficulties, the want of those solid objections which they endeavor in vain to find.
    The error which limits republican government to a
20 narrow district has been unfolded and refuted in preceding papers. I remark here only that it seems to owe its rise and prevalence chiefly to the confounding of a republic with a democracy, applying to the former reasonings drawn from the nature of the latter. The true distinction between
25 these forms was also adverted to on a former occasion. It is, that in a democracy, the people meet and exercise the government in person; in a republic, they assemble and administer it by their representatives and agents. A democracy, consequently, will be confined to a small
30 spot. A republic may be extended over a large region.
    To this accidental source of the error may be added the artifice of some celebrated authors, whose writings have had a great share in forming the modern standard of political opinions. Being subjects either of an absolute
35 or limited monarchy, they have endeavored to heighten the advantages, or palliate the evils of those forms, by placing in comparison the vices and defects of the republican, and by citing as specimens of the latter the turbulent democracies of ancient Greece and modern
40 Italy. Under the confusion of names, it has been an easy task to transfer to a republic observations applicable to a democracy only; and among others, the observation that

**CONTINUE** ▶

it can never be established but among a small number
of people, living within a small compass of territory.

45      Such a fallacy may have been the less perceived, as
most of the popular governments of antiquity were of
the democratic species; and even in modern Europe, to
which we owe the great principle of representation, no
example is seen of a government wholly popular, and
50 founded, at the same time, wholly on that principle. If
Europe has the merit of discovering this great mechanical
power in government, by the simple agency of which
the will of the largest political body may be concentered,
and its force directed to any object which the public
55 good requires, America can claim the merit of making
the discovery the basis of unmixed and extensive
republics. It is only to be lamented that any of her citizens
should wish to deprive her of the additional merit of
displaying its full efficacy in the establishment of the
60 comprehensive system now under her consideration.

     As the natural limit of a democracy is that distance
from the central point which will just permit the most
remote citizens to assemble as often as their public
functions demand, and will include no greater number
65 than can join in those functions; so the natural limit of
a republic is that distance from the centre which will
barely allow the representatives to meet as often as may
be necessary for the administration of public affairs. Can
it be said that the limits of the United States exceed this
70 distance? It will not be said by those who recollect that
the Atlantic coast is the longest side of the Union, that
during the term of thirteen years, the representatives of
the States have been almost continually assembled, and
that the members from the most distant States are not
75 chargeable with greater intermissions of attendance than
those from the States in the neighborhood of Congress.

## 32

In the passage, Madison states that a republic can

A) be less stable than Ancient Greek democracies.

B) be less desirable than a democracy because a
republic uses elected officials.

C) function properly over a great area of land.

D) be similar to the monarchies of European nations.

## 33

Which choice provides the best evidence for the answer
to the previous question?

A) Lines 21-24 ("I remark … latter")

B) Line 30 ("A republic … region")

C) Lines 34-40 ("Being … Italy")

D) Lines 50-57 ("If Europe … republics")

## 34

The first sentence of the passage (lines 1-9) primarily
serves to

A) address the danger of attack by other nations.

B) summarize topics previously addressed.

C) express concern over managing a complex
undertaking.

D) dismiss objections that are no longer relevant.

## 35

As used in line 10, "branch" most nearly means

A) support.

B) outreach.

C) topic.

D) bureau.

## 36

In the passage, ancient Greece and modern Italy are
given as examples that

A) show that democratic nations cannot succeed.

B) are used by supporters of a traditional monarchy.

C) inspired the desire for freedom in America.

D) suggest that democracies can compete successfully
against monarchies.

**37**

The passage references a confusion of names in regards to

A) the subtle differences between a democracy and a republic.

B) how different states refer to each other.

C) language differences among nations.

D) debate over geographic regions.

**38**

As used in line 44, "compass" most nearly means

A) direction.

B) path.

C) belief.

D) range.

**39**

Madison critiques democracy by arguing that democracies

A) restrict personal freedom.

B) often evolve into a different system.

C) have limitations of scale.

D) promote an impossible ideal.

**40**

Which choice provides the best evidence for the answer in the previous question?

A) Lines 19-21 ("The error ... papers")

B) Lines 24-25 ("The true ... occasion")

C) Lines 45-50 ("Such ... principle")

D) Lines 61-65 ("As ... functions")

**41**

The last paragraph (lines 61-76) addresses

A) the process for electing representatives.

B) the need for more frequent meetings of elected officials.

C) the practicality of assembly over a large geographic region.

D) the need for more transportation options in the interior of the country.

**Questions 42-52**

This passage is adapted from Mary Hoff, "DNA Amplification and Detection Made Simple (Relatively)." ©2006 Public Library of Science. The passage discusses DNA amplification, the production of multiple copies of a sequence of DNA.

Twenty-three years ago, a man musing about work while driving down a California highway revolutionized molecular biology when he envisioned a technique
Line to make large numbers of copies of a piece of DNA
5 rapidly and accurately. Known as the polymerase chain reaction, or PCR, Kary Mullis' technique involves separating the double strands of a DNA fragment into single-strand templates by heating it, attaching primers that initiate the copying process, using DNA polymerase
10 to make a copy of each strand from free nucleotides floating around in the reaction mixture, detaching the primers, then repeating the cycle using the new and old strands as templates. Since its discovery in 1983, PCR has made possible a number of procedures we
15 now take for granted, such as DNA fingerprinting of crime scenes, paternity testing, and DNA-based diagnosis of hereditary and infectious diseases.

As valuable as conventional PCR is, it has limits. Heat is required to separate the DNA and cooler temperatures
20 are needed to bind the primer to the strands, so the reaction chamber must repeatedly cycle through hot and cold phases. As a result, the technique can only be performed in laboratories using sophisticated equipment.

Now Olaf Piepenburg, Niall Armes, and colleagues
25 have come up with a new approach to DNA amplification that can be carried out at a constant temperature, using only a tiny amount of DNA, without elaborate equipment. Called recombinase polymerase amplification (RPA), the technique opens the door to dramatically extending
30 the application of DNA amplification in fieldwork and in laboratories where PCR machines are not available.

RPA uses five main ingredients: a sample of the DNA to be amplified; a primer–recombinase complex, which initiates the copying process when it attaches to
35 the template; nucleotides from which to form the new strands; a polymerase, which brings them together in the right order; and single-stranded DNA-binding proteins (SSBs), which help keep the original DNA from zipping back together while the new DNA is being made. The
40 primer–recombinase complex is able to attach to the double-stranded DNA, eliminating the need to heat the mixture. After the complex is in place, it disassembles, allowing the DNA polymerase to begin synthesizing a

new strand of DNA complementary to the template, while
45 the SSBs attach to and stabilize the displaced strand. Under the right conditions—a precise milieu of process-regulating chemicals—the process automatically repeats, resulting in an exponential increase in the DNA sample.

The researchers tested the sensitivity, specificity, and
50 speed of RPA by using it to amplify three kinds of human DNA, as well as DNA from *Bacillus subtilis*. They found the technique to be rapid and accurate. However, when using RPA to detect the presence of a specific type of DNA–such as in a test for a suspect's DNA at a crime
55 scene–the primer used to disassemble the DNA strands could produce a false positive result. To counteract this, the researchers developed a detection method that causes the sample to glow in the presence of the DNA being tested for, but not in the presence of primer alone.

60 To demonstrate the usefulness of the new system, the researchers used it to test for the presence of methicillin-resistant *Staphylococcus aureus* (MRSA), a disease-causing bacterium known as a "superbug" because it is unharmed by penicillin antibiotics. They
65 found that RPA could detect a miniscule amount of the superbug: fewer than ten copies of MRSA DNA. It could also determine the presence of three different genotypes of MRSA, and distinguish them from a methicillin-sensitive *S. aureus* strain. How easy would
70 it be to apply such a test in real-life situations? The researchers demonstrated one possible approach by encapsulating the entire process in a dipstick that could be used in the field to detect the presence of a pathogen.*

*organism, such as a bacterium, that causes a disease

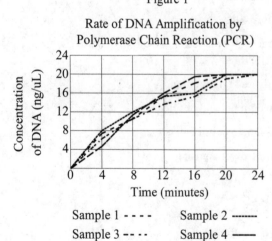

Figure 1

Rate of DNA Amplification by
Polymerase Chain Reaction (PCR)

Concentration of DNA (ng/uL) vs. Time (minutes)

Sample 1 - - - -     Sample 2 --------
Sample 3 -- - ··     Sample 4 ———

**CONTINUE**

Figure 2

Rate of DNA Amplification by
Recombinase Polymerase Amplification (RPA)

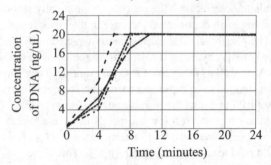

Sample 1 - - - - 　　Sample 2 --------
Sample 3 - - - · 　　Sample 4 ———

**42**

The primary purpose of the passage is to

A) recount the development and application of a technique.

B) evaluate the research that led to a scientific discovery.

C) summarize the findings of a long-term research project.

D) explain the evolution of a branch of scientific study.

**43**

The author views the technique of polymerase chain reaction (PCR) as

A) costly and unimportant.

B) conventional and obsolete.

C) beneficial yet limited.

D) restricted yet amusing.

**44**

Based on the fourth paragraph (lines 32-48), it can be inferred that without the use of SSBs during RPA, DNA would

A) reform its original shape.

B) acquire a new shape.

C) overheat.

D) copy itself.

**45**

As used in line 46, "right" most nearly means

A) reasonable.

B) conservative.

C) correct.

D) pleasing.

**46**

What does the author suggest about the DNA found in Bacillus subtilis?

A) Slow and methodical RPA analysis can be completed on it.

B) It is different from the DNA found in humans.

C) It glows in the presence of primer.

D) It is unharmed by penicillin antibiotics.

**47**

What choice provides the best evidence for the answer to the previous question?

A) Lines 49-51 ("The researchers … subtilis")

B) Lines 51-52 ("They … accurate")

C) Lines 56-59 ("To counteract … alone")

D) Lines 60-64 ("To demonstrate … antibiotics")

CONTINUE

**48**

The author mentions MRSA to

A) provide a real-life example for the application of a scientific tool.

B) describe the spread of an infectious disease.

C) critique a practical technology.

D) criticize Piepenburg's approach.

**49**

The passage implies that, unlike PCR, RPA

A) uses elaborate equipment.

B) is a multi-step process.

C) can be performed at crime scenes.

D) requires extreme temperatures.

**50**

Which choice provides the best evidence that PCR provided important innovations in DNA evidence?

A) Lines 7-12 ("separating … primers")

B) Lines 13-17 ("Since … diseases")

C) Lines 18-22 ("Heat … phases")

D) Lines 70-73 ("The researchers … pathogen")

**51**

According to Figure 2, the DNA from which sample was the first to reach a concentration of 20 ng/$\mu$L?

A) Sample 1

B) Sample 2

C) Sample 3

D) Sample 4

**52**

Taken together, the two figures suggest that

A) PCR amplifies DNA more quickly than does RPA.

B) PCR amplifies DNA more accurately than does RPA.

C) RPA amplifies DNA more quickly than does PCR.

D) RPA amplifies DNA more accurately than does PCR.

# STOP

**If you finish before time is called, you may check your work on this section only.
Do not turn to any other section.**

**No Test Material On This Page**

# Writing and Language Test
## 35 MINUTES, 44 QUESTIONS

**Turn to Section 2 of your answer sheet to answer the questions in this section.**

**Questions 1-11 are based on the following passage.**

**Is chocolate a health food?**

The news media love stories that uncover healthy foods. People love to read about a new "superfood" that will offer a **1** multitude of health benefits. Even better are stories about secretly healthy foods. One food that has garnered a lot of praise lately is **2** chocolate, it has been touted for containing high amounts of flavonol. While its flavanol content is certainly beneficial, chocolate's other ingredients may undermine its potential as a health food.

---

**1**

Which of the following would be the best substitution for the underlined word?

A) cluster

B) variety

C) heap

D) colony

---

**2**

A) NO CHANGE

B) chocolate, which

C) chocolate; which

D) chocolate, but it

---

CONTINUE ▶

Flavonols are types of antioxidants that are used in the human body to repair and rebuild cells. Cocoa powder, a primary ingredient in **3** <u>chocolates, is</u> especially high in flavonols, which have shown in scientific studies to increase blood flow to the brain and improve memory. The news of chocolate's new health benefits was very well-publicized, as a common "guilty pleasure" food became a healthy food overnight. There appeared to be only one catch: the health benefits were most pronounced with dark chocolates, since **4** <u>it contains</u> more cocoa powder than milk chocolates or white chocolates do. **5** Now it seemed health conscious people could have their cake and eat it too, as long as the cake was made with dark chocolate containing lots of flavonols!

**3**

A) NO CHANGE

B) chocolates is

C) chocolates, are

D) chocolates are

**4**

A) NO CHANGE

B) it contained

C) they contain

D) they are containing

**5**

The writer is considering adding the following sentence at this point:

> "Most people do not think of white chocolate as comparable to darker chocolates, but all types come from the same cocoa plant."

Should the author include this sentence?

A) Yes, because it defines a term that would otherwise puzzle readers.

B) Yes, because it shows why white chocolate is not as healthy as dark chocolate.

C) No, because it contradicts statements made later in the passage.

D) No, because it blurs the focus of the paragraph.

CONTINUE ▶

[6] Additionally for chocolate lovers, there are other health factors that must be considered when evaluating chocolate—factors that seriously detract from the health benefits. Flavonols are naturally bitter; anyone who [7] has tasted pure cocoa powder knows that it is far too bitter to be eaten by itself. Chocolate derives much of its deliciousness from its other ingredients, chiefly sugar and cocoa butter. Both contain a high calorie count, and cocoa butter is made of saturated fats that can negatively [8] affect you're cholesterol levels. Another key factor is that much of the flavonol found in cocoa powder is destroyed during the chocolate making process. In order to get a large enough dose of flavonol to make a noticeable impact, a person would have to eat seven chocolate bars a day. [9]

6
A) NO CHANGE
B) Happily
C) Unfortunately
D) Consequently

7
A) NO CHANGE
B) will be tasting
C) taste
D) tasting

8
A) NO CHANGE
B) effect your
C) effect ones
D) affect one's

9
The author wants to add a sentence that concludes the paragraph and refers to the opening of the passage. Which choice accomplishes this goal?

A) There are few people who would describe that amount of chocolate as healthy eating!

B) Anyone living with high cholesterol should search out other sources of flavonols.

C) Even the most devoted chocolate lover would balk at such a large daily consumption.

D) Kilwin's, an independent chocolatier, is currently developing a chocolate-making method to reduce the amount of flavonols lost in the process.

There are many other foods that contain flavonol without chocolate's high sugar and calorie count. Black tea offers the greatest amount of flavonol and has no calories, as long as no sugar is added. Onions, too, are packed with flavonol, but, like cocoa powder, they lose much of their dietary impact when cooked. **10** **11** While the nutrition of black tea has received some favorable press, it is doubtful that there will be many news stories encouraging readers to eat raw onions for their health. Questions 12-22 are based on the following passage.

Top ten foods that contain
the most flavonol per gram.

| Food | Percent of total flavonols consumed (%) |
| --- | --- |
| Tea<br>  Black, brewed<br>  Black, brewed, decaffeinated | <br>32.11<br>5.70 |
| Onion<br>  Boiled, drained<br>  Raw | <br>3.81<br>21.46 |
| Apples<br>  Raw, with skin | <br>7.02 |
| Beer<br>  Regular | <br>6.20 |
| Lettuce<br>  Iceberg, raw | <br>1.93 |
| Coffee<br>  Brewed from grounds | <br>1.74 |
| Tomato<br>  Puree, canned<br>  Red, ripe, raw | <br>1.45<br>1.17 |

**10**

Does the table provided support the statement made in the preceding sentence?

A) Yes, because onions have more flavonol than cocoa powder.

B) Yes, because the percentage of flavonol is higher in raw onions than in cooked onions.

C) No, because black tea has more flavonol than raw onions.

D) No, because cooking onions does not change the percentage of flavonol.

**11**

Which of the following provides a concluding sentence that restates the main argument of the passage?

A) NO CHANGE

B) Those seeking truly healthy foods, not just those celebrated in the media, would do well to look beyond a bar of chocolate.

C) Canned tomatoes, however, have more flavonol than their raw counterparts.

D) Clearly, chocolate does not contain enough flavonol to be labeled a healthy food.

CONTINUE

**Media Archivists**

When you think of a library, you probably imagine a large collection of books, neatly arranged by topic or author. While preserving and cataloging books **12** <u>is</u> still an important venture, more and more libraries are expanding their collections to include other media, including photos, film, and music. Libraries need media archivists to help maintain and **13** <u>resell</u> vintage **14** <u>media, the field</u> has come to prominence in recent decades as libraries embrace a digital world.

**12**

A) NO CHANGE

B) are

C) are becoming

D) have been

**13**

Which choice establishes a topic described later in the passage?

A) NO CHANGE

B) restore

C) discard

D) alphabetize

**14**

A) NO CHANGE

B) media, but the field

C) media; so the field

D) media, and the field

The continued growth of this field may come as a surprise, as it seems we live in a world where any film, song, or TV show is instantly available via online streaming. While there is indeed extensive access to contemporary media, [15] whose looking for older titles can often come up empty handed. The historical value of many older audio-visual productions was not realized at the time, and copies were often thrown out or left to degrade. [16] Despite this, 90% of the films produced before 1929 are now considered lost; film distributors would trash used film prints because the film stock used at the time was highly flammable and prone to spontaneous combustion. From the 1930s to the 1950s, live radio theater was very popular, but few of these performances were ever recorded since the only way to preserve sound involved carving an acetate disc in real time and those fragile discs would quickly wear out and degrade. [17]

**15**

A) NO CHANGE
B) these
C) those
D) which

**16**

A) NO CHANGE
B) However,
C) For instance,
D) Likewise,

**17**

At this point, the writer would like to add an additional example at this point that addresses another type of media that was difficult to preserve. Which choice best accomplishes this goal?

A) Many actors that were once popular on radio and television have now been forgotten.

B) Early television shows were also performed live and would need to be filmed via a telecine device, which added a significant cost to the production and often resulted in a loss of clarity.

C) Cartridge-based video games of the 1980s and 1990s have fared better, as all of the data exists on a relatively stable circuit board.

D) Inner Sanctum Mysteries, which broadcast from 1941 until 1952, had 532 unique episodes, but less than 200 have survived.

[18] Now is a critical time for media conservation as magnetic tape, the primary storage medium from the 1960s through the 1990s, is showing its age and many tapes are becoming unstable. [19] Magnetic tape uses a magnetized coating on a strip of thin plastic to record information. It is found in VHS tapes, audio cassettes, and even large format reels. As tapes age, the magnetic coating can flake off, leading to the loss of the information contained within. This degradation is not fixable. The only way to prevent media stored in this way from disappearing is to transfer the information to a digital platform, which keeps media archivists busy and in high demand.

For someone interested in becoming a media archivist, receiving a master's degree in library science is a prerequisite for many full time jobs. Before entering a masters program, a bachelor's degree is necessary, and many aspiring archivists use that time to develop expertise in one media type, whether it be film studies, musicology, or art history. Classes in chemistry can also be helpful, especially for archivists interested in preserving and restoring film [20] stock: as the chemicals in the emulsion (the part that [21] contains the image can) become unstable. If digitizing older media is more enticing, then classes in digital art or sound recording would be useful skills. Once media is digitized, visual scratches can be removed and audio hiss can be reduced.

**18**

Which choice best establishes that preserving media is an urgent mission?

A) NO CHANGE

B) Many films are quickly forgotten

C) Salaries for media archivists continue to grow

D) Digital recording continues to be popular

**19**

Which choice best combines the underlined sentences?

A) Found in VHS tapes, audio cassettes, and even large format reels, a magnetized coating on a strip of thin plastic is called magnetic tape and is used to record information.

B) Magnetic tape uses a magnetized coating on a strip of thin plastic to record information and it is found in VHS tapes, audio cassettes, and even large format reels.

C) Magnetic tape—which is found in VHS tapes, audio cassettes, and even large format reels—uses a magnetized coating on a strip of thin plastic to record information.

D) VHS tapes, audio cassettes, and even large format reels use a magnetized coating on a strip of thin plastic to record information, and it is called magnetic tape.

**20**

A) NO CHANGE

B) stock, the

C) stock, as, the

D) stock, as the

**21**

A) NO CHANGE

B) contains the image) can become

C) contains the image can become)

D) contains) the image, can become

Many archives and libraries offer internships, giving students the opportunity to get hands on experience with extensive media collections. These internships can help students build important industry connections, **22** which can lead to full time employment. As libraries continue to evolve in the 21st century, media archivists will continue to curate ever-expanding collections.

**22**

Which choice best emphasizes how internships can benefit students?

A) NO CHANGE

B) although many interns are not paid for their work.

C) and may necessitate moving to a new city.

D) but these positions can be very competitive.

CONTINUE ▶

**Questions 23-33 are based on the following passage.**

**Are 42 strings better than 6?**

In 1984, jazz guitarist Pat Metheny contacted Canadian guitar maker Linda Manzer with an unusual request for a stringed [23] instrument: a guitar with "as many strings on it as possible." Manzer kept the standard 6-string guitar neck untouched, and instead added two smaller necks set at diagonals and several harp-like strings across the body of the guitar. The result was the Pikasso guitar, a maze of 42 overlapping strings.

[1] The name of the guitar clearly [24] evades famed Spanish modern artist Pablo Picasso. [2] Picasso was instrumental in developing [25] Cubism a type of painting that attempts to represent objects from simultaneous yet opposing points of view. [3] Early in [26] Picassos Cubist phase, he often would paint still-lifes, frequently including a guitar among the objects. [4] Picasso would often break apart the pattern of strings and frets, depicting the guitar as seen through a kaleidoscope. [5] Manzer's Pikasso guitar was envisioned as a physical recreation of one of Picasso's impossible Cubist guitars. [27]

**23**

A) NO CHANGE
B) instrument. A guitar
C) instrument, it was for a guitar
D) instrument; a guitar

**24**

A) NO CHANGE
B) provokes
C) engages
D) references

**25**

A) NO CHANGE
B) Cubism; a type
C) Cubism, a type
D) Cubism. Being a type

**26**

A) NO CHANGE
B) Picasso's Cubist phase
C) Picasso's Cubist's phase
D) Picasso Cubist's phase

**27**

The author is considering adding the following sentence at this point:

> This effect was created by breaking down the subject into flattened, geometric forms and depicting it from different angles.

This sentence should be placed where in Paragraph 2?

A) After sentence 1
B) After sentence 2
C) After sentence 3
D) After sentence 4

**CONTINUE** ▶

Should we call the Pikasso guitar a success? The answer is a matter of perspective and priority. The construction of the guitar is impeccable, and the very fact that an acoustic guitar made of wood can withstand that amount of string tension is extremely impressive. Manzer is clearly a skilled luthier able to build an instrument **28** that is intricate in its complexity. Whether or not the guitar is aesthetically pleasing depends on a personal preference for excess or minimalism. Should a guitar have embellishments or stick to practical essentials?

Perhaps the most important area to judge the Pikasso **29** guitar, its usability as a musical instrument, is where it disappoints the most. Pat Metheny has had over a quarter of a century to master the Pikasso guitar, yet he appears entirely uneasy when playing the 42-stringed behemoth. The guitar's cumbersome girth and width impact the natural grace of a guitar player. **30** At best, he sticks to the traditional guitar neck, ignoring the harp-like strings. At worst, Metheny's hands meander across the instrument, plucking harp strings simply because they are there.

---

**28**

A) NO CHANGE

B) of uncommon complexity.

C) that is exceedingly complicated and convoluted.

D) of shockingly surprising intricacy.

**29**

A) NO CHANGE

B) guitar, it's

C) guitar–it's

D) guitar–its

**30**

The author wants to add the following phrase to the preceding sentence, replacing the period with a comma:

> "which many beginners struggle with, even on a standard acoustic guitar."

Should the writer make this change?

A) Yes, because it adds a detail that clarifies the author's feelings about guitarists.

B) Yes, because it adds a transition between the Pikasso guitar and Methany's overall ability on guitar.

C) No, because it interrupts the flow of the paragraph with an irrelevant digression.

D) No, because it implies that Metheny is a beginner guitarist.

CONTINUE ▶

A sampling of Metheny's songs featuring the Pikasso guitar [31] will be finding most of them sound strikingly similar, and many of his best songs are played on a traditional acoustic guitar. Metheny brings the Pikasso guitar out on stage mostly for its theatricality, [32] or its musicality.

In the world of musical instruments, there will always be a desire for the unique and the exotic. The Pikasso guitar itself has been eclipsed by another Manzer creation, the 52 string Medusa guitar, which features three playable necks. [33]

**31**

A) NO CHANGE

B) would find that

C) will have found that

D) would be revealing

**32**

A) NO CHANGE

B) and

C) rather than

D) because of

**33**

Which of the following concluding sentences would best reflect the tone of the passage?

A) Whether or not the Medusa guitar will be more musically useful than its predecessor remains to be seen.

B) It is truly unfortunate that a talented guitar builder wastes her talents on such pointless guitars.

C) The Medusa cost over $50,000 dollars, so don't expect to see one in a guitar store anytime soon.

D) Hopefully someone soon will build a guitar with 100 strings!

CONTINUE

**Question 34-44 are based on the following passage.**

**Migratory patterns of American young adults**

We tend to think of migration in terms of flocks of birds and herds of animals, moving from one area to another in search of resources and favorable climates. Humans migrate too, although our movements often go unnoticed [34] between the interwoven chaos of contemporary life. Immigration and emigration between countries are the easiest migrations to [35] notice, yet they involve visas and border crossing. Within a single country, migrations are less obvious, but determining who migrates and for what reasons can illuminate important social trends.

[36] Gathering accurate data on migrations is very difficult, and best left to government entities such as the United States Census. The Census takers track migration by asking the participants if they have changed cities within the last year; any person who answers yes is considered a migrant, [37] which means that they moved recently. The group that has moved the most in the last ten years has been young adults, [38] being defined by the U.S. Census as people from the age of 18 to 34.

**34**

A) NO CHANGE
B) out of
C) along
D) among *(circled)*

**35**

A) NO CHANGE
B) notice, since *(circled)*
C) notice. Because
D) notice; as

**36**

Which choice provides the smoothest and most effective transition between the first and second paragraphs?

A) NO CHANGE *(struck through)*
B) The United States Census provides valuable information for researchers in many fields. *(struck through)*
C) Using data from the United States Census, sociologists can track which categories of people move. *(circled)*
D) The United States Constitution mandates a Census be taken every ten years to determine how the population of the country is changing.

**37**

A) NO CHANGE
B) which includes people who move
C) as these are the people who have moved
D) DELETE the phrase *(circled)*

**38**

A) NO CHANGE
B) defined *(circled)*
C) defining
D) be defined

CONTINUE ➡

Between 2010 and 2012, the migration rates for young adults **39** exceeded the average population's rate. Dividing up the **40** young population into three subcategories, uncovers some of the reasons for all this moving. People 18 to 26 years old accounted for nearly half of the movers in the young adult group, representing 20.8 percent of the total population movement within the country.

[1] This explains why small towns with colleges and universities **41** see the largest influx of migration, as students arrive each fall to attend the schools. [2] As University-level education becomes the cultural norm, an increasing number of young adults choose to leave their hometowns to pursue a higher education. [3] Once college is finished, the same young adults may have to relocate again in order to find employment. [4] There are multiple reasons for the young adult migration trend. **42**

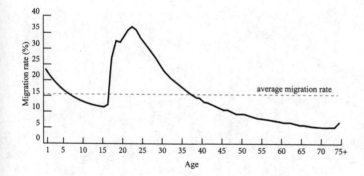

Migration Rates, 2010-2012

Which choice gives an accurate representation of the figure?

(A) NO CHANGE

B) declined as age increased.

C) remained above 30%.

D) remained unchanged as age increased.

A) NO CHANGE

B) young population, into three subcategories, uncovers

C) young population into three, subcategories uncovers

(D) young population into three subcategories uncovers

(A) NO CHANGE

B) view

C) perceive

D) comprehend

Which of the following is the most logical order for the sentences in the third paragraph?

A) NO CHANGE

B) 2, 1, 3, 4

C) 4, 1, 2, 3

(D) 4, 2, 1, 3

CONTINUE

Another reason for so much movement within this section of the population is the change in manufacturing in the United States. A half-century ago, the "factory town" was a common phenomenon. **43** There a family could expect steady employment and benefits, with successive generations following in their parent's footsteps and taking a similar job with the primary employer. As manufacturing shifted from domestic production to imports, the job stability in factory towns disappeared as well, **44** leading younger generations to spread their wings and look for better job opportunities. Those who leave will likely never come back to their hometowns. As this generation migrates across the country, the population redistribution will likely have a long-lasting effect on the demographics of the nation, determining which cities and regions grow and prosper and which recede into history.

**43**

(A) NO CHANGE

B) When

C) If

D) Since

**44**

Which choice provides a detail that best relates to the analogy presented in the first sentence of the passage?

(A) NO CHANGE

B) and census trackers can feel that calculating the exact numbers of these populations is like counting dust in a windstorm.

C) although new "green" technologies may eventually lead to the flowering of environmentally conscious manufacturing jobs.

D) but many towns go through changing tides of growth and shrinkage.

# STOP

**If you finish before time is called, you may check your work on this section only.**
**Do not turn to any other section.**

# Mathematics Test – No Calculator
## 25 MINUTES, 20 QUESTIONS

Turn to Section 3 of your answer sheet to answer the questions in this section.

$A = \pi r^2$
$C = 2\pi r$
$A = \ell w$
$A = \frac{1}{2}bh$
$c^2 = a^2 + b^2$

Special Right Triangles

$V = \ell wh$
$V = \pi r^2 h$
$V = \frac{4}{3}\pi r^3$
$V = \frac{1}{3}\pi r^2 h$
$V = \frac{1}{3}\ell wh$

The number of degrees of arc in a circle is 360.
The number of radians of arc in a circle is $2\pi$
The sum of the measures in degrees of the angles of a triangle is 180.

**CONTINUE**

## 1

Which of the following statements is true about the equation $y = (x - 3)^2$ ?

A) $y$ is always less than 3.

B) $y$ is always greater than 3.

C) $y$ is always greater than –2.

D) $y$ is always greater than x.

## 2

| $n$ | 2 | 3 | 4 |
|---|---|---|---|
| $f(n)$ | 3 | 4 | 5 |
| $g(n)$ | 4 | 2 | 6 |

The table above shows values of the functions $f$ and $g$. What is the value of $f(g(2))$ ?

A) 3

B) 4

C) 5

D) 6

## 3

$$x + y = 9$$
$$5x + y = -19$$

According to the system of equations above, what is the value of $y$ ?

A) –7

B) 4

C) 5

D) 16

## 4

$$g(x) = \frac{3}{a}x - 24$$

In the function above, $a$ is a constant. If $g(9) = 12$, what is the value of $g(3)$ ?

A) 12

B) –3

C) –12

D) –36

**5**

$$4[(x + 6)(x - 1) + 10]$$

Which of the following is equivalent to the expression above?

A)  $4x^2 + 5x + 16$

B)  $4(x + 5)^2 + 10$

C)  $4(x + 4)(x + 1)$

D)  $4(x - 4)(x - 1)$

**6**

For what value of $n$ will 8 equal $\frac{3-n}{3+n}$?

A)  $-\frac{7}{3}$

B)  $-\frac{29}{3}$

C)  $-3$

D)  $\frac{9}{2}$

**7**

In an effort to eat healthier, Cambry is trying to decrease her weekly consumption of candy bars, and she has decided to do this by decreasing the number of candy bars she eats each week by a constant rate. If Cambry's candy bar eating plan allows her to eat 21 candy bars during week 2 and 9 candy bars during week 5, how many candy bars will the candy bar eating plan allow Cambry to eat during week 6 ?

A)  3

B)  4

C)  5

D)  6

**8**

$$x = 2y$$
$$6y - 3x = 4$$

The graph of each equation above in the $xy$-plane is a line. Which of the following statements is true about these two lines?

A)  The slope of both lines is negative.

B)  The lines are the same.

C)  The lines are parallel.

D)  The lines are perpendicular.

CONTINUE

**9**

$$(m - 3)^2 = 5m + p$$

If $p = -1$, what is the solution set of the equation above?

A) $\{10, 1\}$

B) $\{10\}$

C) $\{1\}$

D) $\{-10, -1\}$

**10**

If $\frac{3}{x} = \frac{15}{x+16}$, what is the value of $\frac{24}{x}$?

A) 6

B) 5

C) 4

D) 3

**11**

$$y = x^2 + a$$
$$y = -x^2 + b$$

In the system of equations above, $a$ and $b$ are constants. Which of the following must be true if the system of equations has two solutions?

A) $a$ is less than $b$.

B) $a$ is greater than $b$.

C) $a$ is equal to $b$.

D) $a$ and $b$ are both equal to zero.

**12**

On September 4, 2014, Janet and Esther started a bake sale to raise money for their high school drama department. The drama department's budget is currently $650 and their goal is to raise the budget to $900. If Janet and Esther increase the drama department's budget by $36 every day by selling baked goods, and $d$ represents the number of days since September 4, 2014, which of the following inequalities describes the set of days $d$ in which Janet and Esther have yet to reach their goal?

A) $900 - 36 > d$

B) $650 < 36d$

C) $900 > 36d$

D) $650 + 36d < 900$

**13**

The functions $f$ and $g$ are defined by $f(x) = 2x^2 + x - 2$ and $g(x) = -x^2 - 2x - 4$. For what set of $x$ values does $f(x) + g(x) = 0$ ?

A)  {2, 3}

B)  {−2, 3}

C)  {−1, −3}

D)  {1, 3}

**14**

$$\frac{4-2i}{1+i}$$

If the expression above is rewritten in the form $a + bi$, where $a$ and $b$ are real numbers, what is the value of $a + b$ ?

A)  −3

B)  −2

C)  2

D)  4

**15**

$$x^2 = 2rx + \frac{d}{2}$$

In the quadratic equation above, $r$ and $d$ are constants. What are the solutions for $x$ ?

A)  $x = 2r \pm \dfrac{\sqrt{4r^2 + 2d}}{2}$

B)  $x = 2r \pm \dfrac{\sqrt{4r^2 + 2d}}{4}$

C)  $x = r \pm \dfrac{\sqrt{4r^2 + 2d}}{2}$

D)  $x = r \pm \dfrac{\sqrt{4r^2 + 2d}}{4}$

**CONTINUE**

945

## DIRECTIONS

**For questions 16-20**, solve the problem and enter your answer in the grid, as described below, on the answer sheet.

1. Although not required, it is suggested that you write your answer in the boxes at the top of the columns to help you fill in the circles accurately. You will receive credit only if the circles are filled in correctly.

2. Mark no more than one circle in any column.

3. No question has a negative answer.

4. Some problems may have more than one correct answer. In such cases, grid only one answer.

5. **Mixed numbers** such as 3 ½ must be gridded as 3.5 or 7/2. (If  is entered into the grid, it will be interpreted as $3\frac{1}{2}$, not 3 ½.)

6. **Decimal answers:** If you obtain a decimal answer with more digits than the grid can accommodate, it may be either rounded or truncated, but it must fill the entire grid.

Answer: $\frac{7}{12}$  Answer: 2.5

Write answer in boxes. ← Fraction line

Grid in result. ← Decimal point

Acceptable ways to grid $\frac{2}{3}$ are:

Answer: 201 – either position is correct

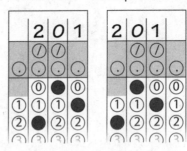

**NOTE:** You may start your answers in any column, space permitting. Columns you don't need to use should be left blank.

## 16

A zoo has 3 different pens, Pen A, Pen B, and Pen C, for holding animals. Pen A has half the area of that of Pen B, and Pen A has one third of the area of Pen C. If Pens A, B, and C have a combined area of 7,200 square feet, what is the area of the biggest pen?

## 17

The sine of one angle of a right triangle is $\frac{12}{13}$. What is the cosine of that angle?

## 18

$$f(x) = x^3 - cx^2 + 4x - 4c$$

In the function $f$ above, $c$ is a constant. How many $x$-intercepts does the function have?

## 19

$$3x + ay = 6$$
$$bx + 4y = 8$$

If the system above represents parallel lines, what is the value of $ab$ ?

## 20

When companies have between 100 and 500 employees, the average annual pay raise decreases at a constant rate as the number of employees in the company increases. Company A has 100 employees and the average employee raise is $1,700. Company B has 450 employees and the average employee raise is $1,200. For every 7 employees hired, how much does the annual raise decrease? Round your answer to the nearest dollar.

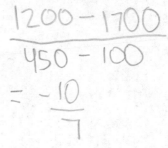

# STOP
**If you finish before time is called, you may check your work on this section only.
Do not turn to any other section.**

**No Test Material On This Page**

# Mathematics Test – Calculator

## 55 MINUTES, 38 QUESTIONS

Turn to Section 4 of your answer sheet to answer the questions in this section.

---

### DIRECTIONS

**For questions 1-30**, solve each problem, choose the best answer from the choices provided, and fill in the corresponding circle on your answer sheet. **For questions 31-38**, solve the problem and enter your answer in the grid on the answer sheet. Please refer to the directions before question 16 on how to enter you answers in the grid. You may use any available space in your test booklet for scratch work.

### NOTES

1. The use of a calculator **is permitted.**
2. All variables and expressions used represent real numbers unless otherwise indicated.
3. Figures provided in this test are drawn to scale unless otherwise indicated.
4. All figures lie in a plane unless otherwise indicated.
5. Unless otherwise indicated, the domain of a given function $f$ is the set of all real numbers $x$ for which $f(x)$ is a real number.

### REFERENCE

$A = \pi r^2$
$C = 2\pi r$

$A = \ell w$

$A = \frac{1}{2} bh$

$c^2 = a^2 + b^2$

Special Right Triangles

$V = \ell wh$

$V = \pi r^2 h$

$V = \frac{4}{3}\pi r^3$

$V = \frac{1}{3}\pi r^2 h$

$V = \frac{1}{3}\ell wh$

The number of degrees of arc in a circle is 360.
The number of radians of arc in a circle is $2\pi$
The sum of the measures in degrees of the angles of a triangle is 180.

---

**CONTINUE**

**1**

At the beginning of each semester, an English teacher assigns each of her students a participation grade of 42. Over the course of the semester, she will award 2.5 points to a student every time the student voluntarily participates in class discussion, but the student does not receive extra points if the teacher calls on him or her to answer a question. At the end of a semester, a particular student has a participation grade of 82. How many times did she participate in class voluntarily?

A) 15

B) 16

C) 17

D) 18

**2**

Felix is saving up money to buy a new laptop that costs $1,400. If Felix has already saved $900, and he saves an additional $50 each week, how much money will Felix have saved $w$ weeks from now?

A) $50 + 900w$

B) $1,400 + 50w$

C) $900 + 50w$

D) $900 - 50w$

**3**

Americans eat an average of 1,500 hamburgers every second. If 45% of all hamburgers are eaten in the Southeast of the United States, which of the following equations represents the total number of hamburgers $x$ Americans in the Southeast eat in $m$ minutes?

A) $x = \dfrac{(0.45)60m}{1,500}$

B) $x = \dfrac{(0.45)1,500m}{60}$

C) $x = (0.45)1,500(60m)$

D) $x = (0.45)1,500m + 60$

**4**

A member of the journalism club gives a poll to a group of high school juniors and seniors asking whether or not they had attended last weekend's varsity basketball game. Of the 25 juniors and seniors polled, 6 juniors and 10 seniors attended the game. Assuming that the results of this poll accurately reflect the decisions of the 450 juniors and seniors at the school to attend or not attend the basketball game, approximately how many juniors and seniors attended the game?

A) 200

B) 225

C) 250

D) 300

**5**

The force, in Newtons, exerted on an object is equal to the mass, in kilograms, of the object multiplied by the acceleration, in meters per second squared. If a force of 2 Newtons accelerates an object by 8 meters per second squared, what is the mass of the object in kilograms?

A) 16

B) 8

C) 4

D) 0.25

**6**

Fiona and Sebastian made a combined total of $1,000 last week waiting tables. If Fiona made 76 more dollars than Sebastian did, what fraction of the $1,000 did Sebastian make?

A) $\dfrac{231}{500}$

B) $\dfrac{49}{100}$

C) $\dfrac{269}{500}$

D) $\dfrac{58}{100}$

**7**

| Voting Preference for Town of Smithfield 2012-2013 | | | | | | | |
|---|---|---|---|---|---|---|---|
| | Age of voting population | | | | | | |
| Candidates | 18-27 | 28-37 | 38-47 | 48-57 | 58-67 | 68+ | Total |
| Candidate A | 43 | 76 | 79 | 82 | 36 | 27 | 343 |
| Candidate B | 36 | 45 | 54 | 51 | 19 | 21 | 226 |
| Candidate C | 8 | 12 | 9 | 15 | 18 | 32 | 94 |
| Undecided | 2 | 6 | 5 | 4 | 9 | 8 | 34 |
| Total | 89 | 139 | 147 | 152 | 82 | 88 | 697 |

The table above shows the voting preferences of a poll given to 697 residents of Smithfield. Polled residents had a choice of three candidates or undecided. Of the polled residents between 48 and 67 years of age, approximately what percentage favored Candidate C ?

A) 5%

B) 10%

C) 14%

D) 22%

**8**

The graph of a linear function f has a positive slope with intercepts $(a, 0)$ and $(0, b)$, where $a$ and $b$ are non-zero integers. Which of the following statements about $a$ and $b$ could be true?

A) $a + b = 0$

B) $a - 2b = 0$

C) $a = b$

D) $0 < a < b$

CONTINUE ➡

**Questions 9-10 refer to the following information.**

| Year | Total population | U.S. supply of seafood | Per capita consumption of imported seafood | Per capita consumption of domestic seafood |
|------|------------------|------------------------|--------------------------------------------|--------------------------------------------|
| 2005 | 297 | 20,529 | 36.7 | 32.4 |
| 2006 | 299 | 20,960 | 38.3 | 31.6 |
| 2007 | 302 | 20,484 | 37.3 | 30.6 |
| 2008 | 305 | 19,252 | 35.9 | 27.3 |
| 2009 | 307 | 18,900 | 35.4 | 26.1 |

The table above shows the total U.S. population in millions of persons, supply of seafood in millions of pounds, and per capita consumption of imported and domestic seafood in pounds, from 2005 to 2009.

**9**

In 2008, the per capita consumption of imported seafood was approximately what percent greater than the per capita consumption of domestic seafood?

A) 20%

B) 25%

C) 30%

D) 45%

**10**

From 2006 to 2009, what was the average annual rate of decrease in the U.S. supply of seafood, in millions of pounds (Round your answer to the nearest pound)?

A) 515

B) 543

C) 687

D) 2,060

**11**

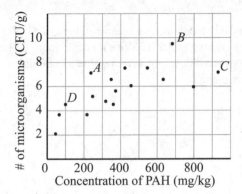

In the graph above, a study examines the number of microorganisms present in soil with varying concentrations of polycyclic aromatic hydrocarbon (PAH), a byproduct of various industrial processes. Four petri dishes listed above were exposed to various concentrations of PAH, and the number of colony-forming units (CFU) were counted after a week of incubation. For what petri dish was ratio of the number of microorganisms to the concentration of PAH the greatest?

A) A

B) B

C) C

D) D

12

| $x$ | $f(x)$ |
|-----|--------|
| –5  | 0      |
| –1  | 36     |
| 0   | 0      |
| 1   | 6      |
| 2   | 0      |

The function $f$ is defined by a polynomial. Some values of $x$ and $f(x)$ are shown in the table above. Which of the following could define $f$?

A)  $(x - 5)(x + 2)$

B)  $(x + 5)^2(x - 2)^3$

C)  $x^2(x + 5)(x - 2)^2$

D)  $x(x + 5)(x - 2)$

13

Since government officials of North Dakota allowed for an increase in the number of drilling sites for oil, the state's population is projected to increase by 19% every three years. If the population of the state is currently 700,000, which of the following expressions shows the state's population x years from now?

A)  $f(x) = 700,000(0.81)^{\frac{x}{3}}$

B)  $f(x) = 700,000(0.81)^{3x}$

C)  $f(x) = 700,000(1.19)^{\frac{x}{3}}$

D)  $f(x) = 700,000(1.19)^{3x}$

CONTINUE

## Questions 14-15 refer to the following information.

A speleologist visits a particular cave on the same day every year and has been recording the lengths of a particular stalactite and the stalagmite growing up directly below it. The lengths in millimeters from several years are recorded in the table below.

| Year | Stalagmite length | Stalactite length |
|------|-------------------|-------------------|
| 2010 | 30.76 | 345.12 |
| 2011 | 30.77 | 345.25 |
| 2012 | 30.78 | 345.38 |
| 2013 | 30.79 | 345.51 |

**15**

The height of the cave where the stalagmite and stalactite are located is one meter. If the growth rates remain constant, in which year will the two meet? (1 meter = 1000 millimeters)?

A)  4458

B)  4940

C)  6468

D)  6949

**16**

| 16 ounces (oz) = 1 pound (lb) |
|---|
| 128 fluid ounces (fl. oz) = 1 gallon (g) |

One gallon of honey weighs approximately 12 pounds. If one gallon of honey is mixed into 5 gallons of water to make tea, how many <u>ounces</u> of honey will be in each 8 fluid ounce cup of the tea?

A)  1

B)  2

C)  3

D)  4

**14**

If the stalactite continues to grow down from the top of the cave at the same rate, how long will it be in 2230 ?

A)  347.72

B)  373.72

C)  375.02

D)  635.02

**17**

Which of the following is NOT a solution of the inequality $4x - 2 \geq 3x - 8$ ?

A) $-7$

B) $-6$

C) $-5$

D) $-4$

**18**

A researcher observes that an incubated bacteria colony with initial population $I$ doubles every hour. Which of the following functions would estimate the population $P$ of a bacteria colony after $h$ hours of incubation?

A) $P(h) = 2Ih$

B) $P(h) = I + 2h$

C) $P(h) = (I)(2^h)$

D) $P(h) = 2$

**19**

Suzie can pay \$7.50 for a softcover comic book and \$12 for a hardcover comic book. If she spends more than \$35 but less than \$40 on comic books and buys at least 2 hardcover books, what is one possible number of softcover comic books that she bought?

A) 1

B) 2

C) 3

D) 4

**20**

A party planner has ordered a certain number of appetizers for a party. If each party attendant gets 3 appetizers, there will be 2 appetizers left over, and if each party attendant gets 4 appetizers, the planner will be short 13 appetizers. How many appetizers did the party planner order?

A) 14

B) 15

C) 45

D) 47

CONTINUE

**Questions 21-22 refer to the following information.**

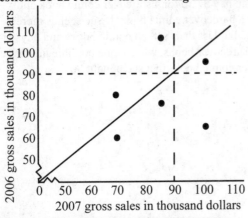

2006 gross sales in thousand dollars

2007 gross sales in thousand dollars

Line of profitability for 2006  - - - - -
Line of profitability for 2007  - - — — -

The scatterplot above shows the gross sales, in thousands of dollars, for six franchise restaurants in 2006 and 2007. The solid line indicates the same gross sales in 2007 as in 2006.

**21**

For how many of the restaurants did the gross sales from 2007 exceed those of 2006 ?

A) 1

B) 2

C) 3

D) 4

**22**

For the restaurant that saw the greatest decrease in gross sales from 2006 to 2007, the manager will set the goal of matching the 2007 revenue of the restaurant that saw the greatest increase in gross sales for that period. How much more will the restaurant need to make in gross sales to reach that goal?

A) $5,000

B) $10,000

C) $15,000

D) $20,000

**23**

A group in Everitt polled two groups of 50 people and asked their ages. In Group A the standard deviation of the ages was 7 years and in Group B the standard deviation of the ages was 13 years. Which of the following statements could be true?

A) The ages of people in Group A are closer to the average age of Group A than the ages of the people in Group B are to the average age of Group B

B) The ages of people in Group B are closer to the average age of Group B than the ages of the people in Group A are to the average age of Group A.

C) The distributions of ages in Groups A and B are about the same.

D) None of the above conclusions are valid.

**24**

The area of an equilateral triangle is $36\sqrt{3}$, what is the height of the triangle?

A)  6

B)  $6\sqrt{3}$

C)  $9\sqrt{3}$

D)  $12\sqrt{3}$

**25**

$$g(x) = \frac{2x - 6}{3x^3 + 15x^2 + 2x + 10}$$

For what value of $x$ is the function $g$ above undefined if $x \leq 0$ ?

A)  −5

B)  −3

C)  −23

D)  $-\dfrac{2}{3}$

**26**

A produce company sells watermelons that are advertised to weigh $m$ pounds. In order to maintain customer satisfaction, each watermelon sold cannot vary by more than 1 pound from the advertised weight. If a watermelon that weighs $n$ pounds meets the weight standards, which of the following inequalities represents the relationship between the advertised weight and the weight $n$ of the watermelon?

A)  $-1 \leq m - n \leq 1$

B)  $m \leq n - 1$

C)  $m \leq 1 \leq n$

D)  $m + n \leq 1$

**27**

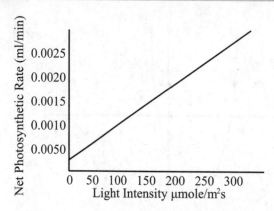

The rate at which a plant absorbs carbon dioxide and emits oxygen, called the net photosynthetic rate in milliliters per minute, is modeled for various light intensities, measured in micromoles (μmole) per square meter per second, using the equation $P = 0.00005I + 0.003$, where $P$ represents the net photosynthetic rate, in milliliters per minute, and $I$ represents the light intensity, in micromoles per square meter per second. Which of the following best explains the $y$-intercept on the graph?

A)  When there is no light, a plant will emit 0.003 ml of oxygen per minute.

B)  When there is no light, a plant will absorb 0.003 ml of oxygen per minute.

C)  At a light intensity of 0.003 μmole, a plant emits 0.00005 ml of oxygen per minute.

D)  At a light intensity of 0.00005 μmole, a plant emits 0.003 ml of oxygen per minute.

CONTINUE

**28**

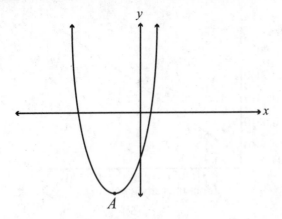

Which of the following is a form of the equation for the graph shown above from which coordinates of vertex A can be identified as constants or coefficients in the equation?

A)  $y = (x + 6)(x - 2)$

B)  $y = (x - 6)(x + 2)$

C)  $y = (x(x + 4)) - 12$

D)  $y = (x + 2)^2 - 16$

**29**

If the average of $a$ and $2b$ also equals the average of $b$ and $2c$, what is the average of $a$ and $b$ in terms of $c$ ?

A)  $c$

B)  $2c$

C)  $\dfrac{2c}{3}$

D)  $\dfrac{1}{c}$

**30**

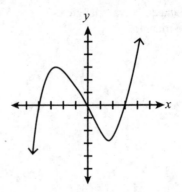

The function above, $f(x)$, has $x$-intercepts at -4, 0, and 3. If $a$ is a positive constant and $f(x) = a$ has two real solutions, what is one possible value of $a$ ?

A)  −1

B)  1

C)  3

D)  4

## DIRECTIONS

**For questions 31-38**, solve the problem and enter your answer in the grid, as described below, on the answer sheet.

1. Although not required, it is suggested that you write your answer in the boxes at the top of the columns to help you fill in the circles accurately. You will receive credit only if the circles are filled in correctly.

2. Mark no more than one circle in any column.

3. No question has a negative answer.

4. Some problems may have more than one correct answer. In such cases, grid only one answer.

5. **Mixed numbers** such as 3 ½ must be gridded as 3.5 or 7/2. (If  is entered into the grid, it will be interpreted as ³½, not 3 ½.)

6. **Decimal answers:** If you obtain a decimal answer with more digits than the grid can accommodate, it may be either rounded or truncated, but it must fill the entire grid.

Answer: $\frac{7}{12}$

Write answer in boxes. → Fraction line ←

Grid in result.

Answer: 2.5

Decimal point ←

Acceptable ways to grid $\frac{2}{3}$ are:

Answer: 201 – either position is correct

**NOTE:** You may start your answers in any column, space permitting. Columns you don't need to use should be left blank.

CONTINUE →

**31**

The mayor of Apelburg started an initiative to increase the number of trees in the city at a constant rate until there will be 80,000 trees by 2030. If the city is projected to have 64,000 trees by 2020, how many trees will be planted every two years?

**32**

Geoffrey can approximate the grade he will receive on a test with the equation $60 + 8h$, where $0 \leq h \leq 5$ is the number of hours Geoffrey spends studying for the test. What is the increase in Geoffrey's score for each additional hour of studying?

**33**

A dram is $\frac{1}{16}$ of an ounce. A dram is also approximately 1.77 grams. If there are 16 ounces to a pound, what fraction of a pound is 90 grams? (Round to the nearest thousandths place.)

**34**

The livestock on Darnell's farm solely consist of cows and chickens. Darnell owned 160 chickens but recently bought $x$ more chickens. If Darnell owns 80 cows, how many chickens did Darnell buy if 20% of his farm animals are cows?

**35**

The period of a simple pendulum with a mass attached to a string is approximated by the equation $T = 2\pi\sqrt{\frac{L}{9.8}}$ where $L$ is the length of the string, in meters, and $T$ is the duration of the period, in seconds. A physicist compares two pendulums with strings of lengths 16 meters and 9 meters. What is the ratio of the period of the longer string pendulum to that of the shorter string pendulum?

**36**

A wedge of a circle has a central angle measure between 70° and 80°. If the area of the circle is 38 square inches, what is one possible value for the area of the wedge?

---

**Questions 37-38 refer to the following information.**

The base sales tax for the state of Georgia is 4%, with an additional local sales tax of 3%. By contrast, the base sales tax for the state of Iowa is 6%, with no additional local sales tax.

If a resident of Georgia and a resident of Iowa spent the same amount of money, including tax, for groceries, the relationship between what they paid can be modeled by the equation $(1 + G)(x) = (1 + I)(y)$, where $x$ represents the cost of the groceries in Georgia before tax is applied, $G$ represents the sales tax for Georgia, $y$ represents the cost of the groceries in Iowa before tax is applied, and $I$ represents the sales tax for Iowa.

**37**

What is the value of $I$ in the equation?

**38**

If a resident of Georgia and a resident of Iowa each purchased $300 in groceries, including tax, how many more groceries would a resident of Iowa have been able to purchase, in dollars, not including the sales tax? Round your answer to the nearest cent.

---

## STOP
**If you finish before time is called, you may check your work on this section only.**
**Do not turn to any other section.**

# Scoring Your Test

**Answers to the test can be found in the answer key on page 970.**

Your raw scores (the number of questions you answered correctly) will help you calibrate how well you mastered the content in this book. Use the table on the next page to translate your raw score into to an estimated scaled score, keeping in mind that the College Board is still in the process of adjusting the scoring tables for the upcoming tests.

## Scoring your Test

To score your test, first obtain your Reading, Writing, and Math raw scores by adding up correct answers in sections as indicated in the table below. Fill in the third column with your raw scores.

| Section | Count # correct to find Raw Scores | My Scaled |
|---------|------------------------------------|-----------|
| Reading | Section 1 = <br> (0-52) | (10-40) |
| Writing | Section 2 = <br> (0-44) | (10-40) |
| Math | Sections 3 + 4 = <br> (0-58) | (200-800) |

) Add & ) x10

Next, obtain your **scaled scores** for each section using your raw scores and the table on the next page. You will find a **Math score** between 200-800, a **Reading score** between 10-40, and a **Writing score** between 10-40. Add your Reading and Writing scores and multiply by 10 to get your **Evidence-Based Reading and Writing Score** between 200-800.

Your total score is found by adding your Math Score (200-800) and your Evidence-Based Reading and Writing Score (200-800).

MATH  +  READING  =  TOTAL
(200-800)  & WRITING  (400-1600)
(200-800)

| Raw Score | Scaled Score | | | Raw Score | Scaled Score | | |
|---|---|---|---|---|---|---|---|
| | Reading + Writing | | Math | | Reading + Writing | | Math |
| 0 | 10 | 10 | 200 | 30 | 27 | 30 | 580 |
| 1 | 10 | 10 | 200 | 31 | 28 | 31 | 590 |
| 2 | 10 | 10 | 210 | 32 | 28 | 31 | 600 |
| 3 | 11 | 11 | 230 | 33 | 28 | 32 | 600 |
| 4 | 12 | 12 | 250 | 34 | 29 | 32 | 610 |
| 5 | 13 | 13 | 270 | 35 | 29 | 33 | 620 |
| 6 | 14 | 14 | 280 | 36 | 30 | 33 | 630 |
| 7 | 15 | 15 | 300 | 37 | 30 | 34 | 640 |
| 8 | 16 | 16 | 320 | 38 | 31 | 35 | 650 |
| 9 | 16 | 16 | 340 | 39 | 31 | 36 | 660 |
| 10 | 17 | 17 | 350 | 40 | 32 | 37 | 670 |
| 11 | 18 | 18 | 360 | 41 | 32 | 37 | 680 |
| 12 | 18 | 18 | 370 | 42 | 33 | 38 | 690 |
| 13 | 19 | 19 | 390 | 43 | 33 | 39 | 700 |
| 14 | 20 | 19 | 410 | 44 | 34 | 40 | 710 |
| 15 | 20 | 20 | 420 | 45 | 35 | | 710 |
| 16 | 21 | 21 | 430 | 46 | 35 | | 720 |
| 17 | 21 | 22 | 450 | 47 | 36 | | 730 |
| 18 | 22 | 23 | 460 | 48 | 37 | | 730 |
| 19 | 22 | 23 | 470 | 49 | 38 | | 740 |
| 20 | 23 | 24 | 480 | 50 | 39 | | 750 |
| 21 | 23 | 24 | 490 | 51 | 39 | | 750 |
| 22 | 23 | 25 | 500 | 52 | 40 | | 760 |
| 23 | 24 | 26 | 510 | 53 | | | 770 |
| 24 | 24 | 26 | 520 | 54 | | | 780 |
| 25 | 25 | 27 | 530 | 55 | | | 790 |
| 26 | 25 | 27 | 540 | 56 | | | 790 |
| 27 | 26 | 28 | 550 | 57 | | | 800 |
| 28 | 26 | 29 | 560 | 58 | | | 800 |
| 29 | 27 | 29 | 570 | | | | |

## Writing

### Comma Basics

1) C
2) D
3) D
4) B
5) A
6) D
7) B
8) C
9) A
10) D

### All About Clauses

1) A
2) B
3) C
4) B
5) C
6) B
7) A
8) B
9) D
10) C
11) A
12) B
13) C

### Practice Passage 1

1) D
2) A
3) C
4) A
5) C
6) D
7) A
8) B
9) A
10) A
11) C

### Tense Switch

1) B
2) D
3) B
4) A
5) B
6) A
7) D
8) B
9) A
10) D

### Subject-Verb Agreement

1) C
2) B
3) B
4) A
5) B
6) D
7) C
8) A

### Pronoun Error

1) D
2) B
3) D
4) B
5) C
6) A
7) D
8) C

### Possession

1) C
2) A
3) D
4) B
5) A
6) D
7) B
8) B
9) A
10) B

### Practice Passage 2

1) B
2) A
3) B
4) D
5) C
6) A
7) C
8) C
9) D
10) B
11) B

### Parallelism

1) D
2) A
3) B
4) D
5) C
6) D
7) D
8) C

## Writing

### Misplaced Modifier

1) C
2) D
3) D
4) A
5) C
6) A
7) D

### Practice Passage 3

1) D
2) B
3) A
4) C
5) C
6) D
7) B
8) C
9) A
10) D
11) C

### Redundancy

1) C
2) D
3) D
4) C
5) D
6) D
7) B
8) D
9) B

### Prepositions

1) B
2) D
3) A
4) C
5) C
6) B
7) C
8) B
9) B

### Vocabulary in Context

1) B
2) D
3) B
4) B
5) D
6) A
7) D
8) A
9) C
10) A

### Practice Passage 4

1) C
2) B
3) C
4) B
5) A
6) A
7) D
8) C
9) B
10) D
11) B

### Logical Connectors

1) D
2) D
3) B
4) C
5) C
6) C
7) A
8) C
9) D
10) B

### Combining Sentences

1) C
2) A
3) B
4) B
5) D
6) C
7) B
8) D

### Order Placement

1) C
2) B
3) C
4) B
5) D
6) A
7) C
8) A

## Writing

### Practice Passage 5

1) C
2) A
3) D
4) B
5) B
6) D
7) C
8) B
9) A
10) D
11) A

### Accomplish a Task

1) D
2) A
3) B
4) B
5) C
6) A
7) C
8) B
9) C
10) D
11) C
12) D
13) B
14) D
15) B
16) D

### Add and Delete

1) C
2) A
3) C
4) B
5) A

### Describing Data

1) D
2) C
3) A
4) B
5) D
6) A

### Practice Passage 6

1) A
2) C
3) B
4) B
5) B
6) B
7) A
8) C
9) B
10) A
11) D

## Math

### Working Backwards

1) D, WB
2) A, PN
3) C, WB
4) B, WB
5) D, PN
6) D, WB
7) C, WB
8) D, PN
9) C, WB
10) C, PN
11) A, PN

### Basic Algebra

1) B
2) 5
3) C
4) C
5) B
6) D
7) C
8) D
9) C
10) A

### Exponents

1) C
2) D
3) A
4) D
5) C
6) D
7) A
8) A
9) B
10) D

## Math

### Fractions

1) B
2) D
3) D
4) C
5) B
6) A
7) D
8) B
9) D
10) C
11) C
12) B
13) B

### Equation of a Line

1) B
2) 2/3
3) B
4) C
5) A
6) B
7) A
8) C
9) D
10) D

### Function Machines

1) C
2) C
3) B
4) C
5) B
6) C
7) D
8) D
9) B
10) B

### Factoring Basics

1) C
2) D
3) A
4) D
5) B
6) 5
7) D
8) A
9) B
10) C
11) A
12) 4

### Solving for Zero

1) C
2) C
3) A
4) B
5) C
6) A
7) 6
8) B
9) B
10) A

### Pattern Matching

1) D
2) B
3) B
4) C
5) B
6) A
7) B
8) A
9) A

### Advanced Algebra

1) 4
2) A
3) 6
4) C
5) B
6) 3
7) C
8) 8
9) D
10) B
11) A

### Transformers

1) A
2) D
3) B
4) C
5) B
6) A
7) D
8) D
9) B
10) B
11) A

### Zeros and Solutions

1) C
2) A
3) B
4) D
5) D
6) C
7) A
8) A

## Math

### Solving Systems

1) B
2) C
3) D
4) A
5) B
6) D
7) C
8) 7
9) A
10) D

### Spotting Solutions

1) D
2) B
3) C
4) 4
5) C
6) D
7) C
8) C
9) A
10) C

### Systems of Inequalities

1) B
2) A
3) B
4) -7
5) C
6) C
7) A

### Advanced Factoring

1) 2
2) 3
3) 7
4) D
5) C
6) C
7) A
8) C
9) C

### The Unfactorables

1) D
2) B
3) C
4) D
5) C
6) D
7) B

### Complex Numbers

1) C
2) A
3) D
4) B
5) D
6) C
7) A
8) B
9) B
10) B
11) D

### Basic Modeling

1) D
2) A
3) C
4) D
5) C
6) C
7) D
8) A
9) A

### Advanced Modeling

1) C
2) 35
3) C
4) B
5) 44
6) B
7) D
8) A

### Quadratic Modeling

1) D
2) C
3) C
4) 1,500
5) A
6) 5
7) D
8) 1,125
9) 145
10) 333

## Math

### Exponential Models

1) 106
2) 10.31
3) C
4) C
5) A
6) B
7) B
8) A
9) C
10) B

### Applied Algebra

1) A
2) B
3) D
4) A
5) C
6) D
7) A
8) C
9) C
10) A
11) C
12) C
13) D

### Piece Over Whole

1) C
2) C
3) A
4) D
5) D
6) A
7) C
8) A
9) 12
10) B

### Percent Change

1) C
2) A
3) D
4) 127.5
5) C
6) 20
7) C

### Unit Conversion

1) C
2) D
3) A
4) 9
5) D
6) C
7) 132

### Basic Statistics

1) C
2) C
3) B
4) C
5) C
6) 0.8
7) A
8) D
9) 660

### Trend-spotting

1) D
2) B
3) A
4) B
5) C
6) C

### Line of Best Fit

1) B
2) B
3) A
4) A
5) C
6) A

### Study Design

1) D
2) B
3) B
4) C
5) D
6) C
7) B
8) D

### Geometry

1) 4
2) B
3) 1400
4) C
5) B
6) C
7) D
8) B
9) $59 \le x \le 63$
10) C
11) B

### Trigonometry

1) 3/5
2) A
3) 3
4) C
5) 3
6) B

## Math

### Math Review (NC)

1) C
2) C
3) A
4) D
5) C
6) B
7) A
8) A
9) D
10) C
11) D
12) A
13) D
14) 8
15) 64
16) 6
17) 2

### Math Review (C)

1) C
2) C
3) B
4) C
5) C
6) B
7) B
8) B
9) D
10) A
11) C
12) B
13) D
14) B
15) C
16) B
17) B

18) C
19) B
20) D
21) D
22) B
23) A
24) C
25) B
26) C
27) C
28) $3.5 \le x \le 7$
29) 38
30) 57
31) 6

## Practice Test

### Reading

1) B
2) C
3) A
4) B
5) C
6) B
7) A
8) B
9) B
10) D
11) A
12) B
13) A
14) C
15) B
16) C
17) A
18) D
19) A
20) D
21) D

22) D
23) A
24) B
25) A
26) B
27) B
28) B
29) C
30) C
31) C
32) C
33) B
34) B
35) C
36) B
37) A
38) D
39) C
40) D
41) C
42) A
43) C
44) A
45) C
46) B
47) A
48) A
49) C
50) D
51) A
52) C

### Writing

1) B
2) B
3) A
4) C
5) D
6) C
7) A

| Practice Test | |
|---|---|
| 8) | D |
| 9) | A |
| 10) | B |
| 11) | B |
| 12) | A |
| 13) | B |
| 14) | D |
| 15) | C |
| 16) | C |
| 17) | B |
| 18) | A |
| 19) | C |
| 20) | D |
| 21) | B |
| 22) | A |
| 23) | A |
| 24) | D |
| 25) | C |
| 26) | B |
| 27) | B |
| 28) | B |
| 29) | A |
| 30) | C |
| 31) | B |
| 32) | C |
| 33) | A |
| 34) | D |
| 35) | B |
| 36) | C |
| 37) | D |
| 38) | B |
| 39) | A |
| 40) | D |
| 41) | A |
| 42) | D |
| 43) | A |
| 44) | A |

**Math (No Calculator)**

| | |
|---|---|
| 1) | C |
| 2) | C |
| 3) | D |
| 4) | C |
| 5) | C |
| 6) | A |
| 7) | C |
| 8) | C |
| 9) | A |
| 10) | A |
| 11) | A |
| 12) | D |
| 13) | B |
| 14) | B |
| 15) | C |
| 16) | 3600 |
| 17) | 5/13 |
| 18) | 1 |
| 19) | 12 |
| 20) | 10 |

**Math (Calculator)**

| | |
|---|---|
| 1) | B |
| 2) | C |
| 3) | C |
| 4) | D |
| 5) | D |
| 6) | A |
| 7) | C |
| 8) | A |
| 9) | C |
| 10) | C |
| 11) | D |
| 12) | C |
| 13) | C |
| 14) | B |

| | |
|---|---|
| 15) | C |
| 16) | B |
| 17) | A |
| 18) | C |
| 19) | B |
| 20) | D |
| 21) | D |
| 22) | C |
| 23) | A |
| 24) | B |
| 25) | A |
| 26) | A |
| 27) | A |
| 28) | D |
| 29) | A |
| 30) | C |
| 31) | 3200 |
| 32) | 8 |
| 33) | 0.199 |
| 34) | 160 |
| 35) | 4/3 or 1.33 |
| 36) | $7.39 \leq x \leq 8.44$ |
| 37) | 0.06 |
| 38) | 2.65 |

# Citations

Passage, p. 37: Louise Walsh. "Play's the thing." University of Cambridge, originally published August 4, 2015. <www.cam.ac.uk/research/features/plays-the-thing

Passage, p. 40: McNeile, H.C. "A Question of Personality." Originally published 1921. <http://www.gutenberg.org/ebooks/49590?msg=welcome_stranger#a-question-of-personality>

Passage, p. 59: Young, Emma. "10 Mysteries of you: Superstition." New Scientist 05 Aug 2009. 09 Sept 2009. <http://www.newscientist.com/article/mg20327201.400-10-mysteries-of-you-superstition.html> Printed with permission of newscientist.com.

Passage, p. 77,80: Harper, Ida Husted. The Life and Work of Susan B. Anthony Vol. 1. The Bowen-Merrill Company, 1899. <https://www.gutenberg.org/files/15220/15220-h/15220-h.htm>

Passage, p. 81: Sarah Collins. "New design points a path to the 'ultimate' battery." University of Cambridge, originally published October 29, 2015. <http://www.cam.ac.uk/research/news/new-design-points-a-path-to-the-ultimate-battery>

Passage, p. 85 University of Cambridge Communications Team. "Stormy cluster weather could unleash black hole power and explain lack of cosmic cooling." University of Cambridge. Originally published October, 21 2019 <https://www.cam.ac.uk/research/news/stormy-cluster-weather-could-unleash-black-hole-power-and-explain-lack-of-cosmic-cooling>

Passage p. 95 Francey, Damien; Bergmüller, Ralph (2012) "Images of Eyes Enhance Investments in a Real-Life Public Good" PLoS ONE 7(5): e3739. doi.org/10.1371/journal.pone.0037397

Passage, p. 98: Hoff M (2007) "What's Behind the Spread of White Syndrome in Great Barrier Reef Corals?" PLoS Biol 5(6): e164. doi:10.1371/journal.pbio.0050164

Figure, p. 99: Xue, Y., Z. Hu, A. Kumar, V. Banzon, T. M. Smith, and N. A. Rayner, 2012: [Global oceans] Sea surface temperatures [in "State of the Climate in 2011"]. Bull. Amer. Meteor. Soc., 93 (7), S58–S62. <https://www.climate.gov/news-features/understanding-climate/state-climate-2011-sea-surface-temperature>

Passage, p. 109 Atherton, Getrude. "The Striding Place" Originally published as "The Twins" 1896 <http://www.gutenberg.org/ebooks/14256>

Passage, p. 129: Stanton, Elizabeth Cady; Anthony, Susan B.; Gage, Matilda Joslyn. HIstory of Woman Suffrage, Vol. 1. Copyright 1881.

Passage, p. 147: (2004) "Natural Biodiversity Breaks Plant Yield Barriers." PLoS Biol 2(10): e331. doi:10.1371/journal.pbio.0020331

Passage, p. 155: Gross L (2006) "Math and Fossils Resolve a Debate on Dinosaur Metabolism." PLoS Biol 4(8): e255. doi:10.1371/journal.pbio.0040255

Passage, p. 175 Seabury, Samuel. "Free Thoughts on the Proceedings of the Continental Congress. Originally published in 1774. <http://anglicanhistory.org/usa/seabury/farmer/01.html>

Passage, p. 176 Hamilton, Alexander. "A Full Vindication of the Measures of the Congress." Originally published in 1774. <https://founders.archives.gov/documents/Hamilton/01-01-02-0054>

Figure, p. 378 "Unemployment rates and earnings by educational attainment, 2018." U.S. Bureau of Labor Statistics. <https://www.bls.gov/emp/chart-unemployment-earnings-education.htm>

Figure p. 380 "Market Penetration of ADAS and Robotic Vehicles" Yole Développement, 2018 <https://www.motortrend.com/uploads/sites/5/2019/12/Market-penetration-ADAS-and-robotic-vehicles.jpg>

Passage 1, p. 912: Alcott, Louisa May. Work: A Story of Experience. Boston, 1901.

Passage p. 914 Karsdorp, Folgert; Manjavacas, Enrique; Kestemont, Mike (2019) "Keepin' it Real: Linguistic Models of Authenticity Judgments for Artificially Generated Rap Lyrics." PloS One oi.org/10.1371/journal.pone.0224152.

Passage 3, p. 917: Gross L (2007) "Untapped Bounty: Sampling the Seas to Survey Microbial Biodiversity." PLoS Biol 5(3): e85. doi:10.1371/journal.pbio.0050085

Passage 4, p. 918: O'Day K (2008) "Gut Reaction: Pyrosequencing Provides the Poop on Distal Gut Bacteria." PLoS Biol 6(11): e295. doi:10.1371/journal.pbio.0060295

Passage 5, p.920, : Hamilton, Alexander; Jay, John; Madison, James. The Federalist Papers. Originally published in 1788. <https://www.gutenberg.org/files/1404/1404-h/1404-h.htm?

Passage 6, p. 923: Hoff M (2006) "DNA Amplification and Detection Made Simple (Relatively)." PLoS Biol 4(7): e222. doi:10.1371/journal.pbio.0040222